Peace
and
Security
in
Northeast
Asia

A Study of The Nautilus Institute

Peace and Security in Northeast Asia

The Nuclear Issue and the Korean Peninsula

Young Whan Kihl
Peter Hayes

Editors

An East Gate Book

M.E. Sharpe
Armonk, New York
London, England

An East Gate Book

Copyright © 1997 by M. E. Sharpe, Inc.

Library of Congress Cataloging-in-Publication Data

Peace and security in Northeast Asia : the nuclear issue and
the Korean Peninsula / Young Whan Kihl and Peter Hayes, editors.
p.   cm.
"An East Gate book."
Includes bibliographical references and index.
ISBN 1-56324-789-5 (hardcover : alk. paper).
ISBN 1-56324-790-9 (pbk. : alk. paper)
1. National security—Korea (North)   2. Nuclear weapons—Korea
(North)   3. Korea (North)—Foreign relations—United States.
4. United States—Foreign relations—Korea (North)
I. Kihl, Young, W., 1932–   .   II. Hayes, Peter, 1953–   .
UA853.K5P34   1996
327.1′74′095193—dc2-   96-6318
CIP
Printed in the United States of America

The paper used in this publication meets the minimum requirements of
American National Standard for Information Sciences—
Permanence of Paper for Printed Library Materials,
ANSI Z 39.48-1984.

BM (c)   10   9   8   7   6   5   4   3   2   1
BM (p)   10   9   8   7   6   5   4   3   2   1

Contents

Foreword

Whatever hazards the future may hold, peace and security in Northeast Asia today depend heavily on developments on the Korean Peninsula. Korea and Taiwan—both legacies of World War II and its aftermath—are the two immediate challenges confronting the Pacific region.

In the absence of any institutional peacemaking or peacekeeping structure in this region, and with effective balance-of-power politics rendered difficult if not impossible due to the fragility of all major power relationships, approaches to problems like divided Korea have relied on the construction of ad hoc coalitions or, more precisely, the development of a series of concentric arcs.

In the case of Korea, the first arc has been that of North Korea (the Democratic People's Republic of Korea, or DPRK) and South Korea (the Republic of Korea, or ROK). Without a constructive relationship between them—or some extreme happening such as collapse or war—no genuine solution can be achieved. Above this arc, however, has been a second, composed of the four major powers having a strong interest in Korea—the United States, China, Japan, and Russia. With the first arc largely negative, the actions and inactions of the second arc in recent years have been of critical importance to developments, and generally, the United States has taken the leadership role. A third arc exists in the form of international organizations—both economic and political-strategic. If greater advances were made in the lower arcs, they could assume a more vigorous role.

The recent interaction of these three arcs constitutes a fascinating picture. Historically, Korea—whether united or divided—has had three options with respect to external relations: isolation, balancing foreign forces, and alliance with one or more outsiders. Since its emergence, North Korea has at one time or another pursued all three approaches, either singly or in combination. It commenced existence as an ally, more accurately, a client—of the Soviet Union. Later, as the Sino-Soviet cleavage unfolded, it sought to play one power off against the other, with a decided tilt toward China at most points; as problems emerged with both big Communist states, the quotient of isolation—never absent—rose, reaching new heights in the 1990s, when the DPRK could count on no trustworthy allies.

The course pursued by South Korea since 1945 has been more consistent. After the disaster of 1950, when the United States misled the Communists as to its commitment to ROK security, the South Korean security alliance with the United States has been firm, although there has been no absence of tension over various issues, especially in recent times when ROK nationalism has risen in company with that of other Asian societies.

Difficulties in North–South relations are not surprising. Although these two societies have a common historical heritage and share certain cultural traits, the developmental gap is huge and still growing. South Korea is the truly revolutionary society, with economic growth having had an enormous impact on politics and culture, including significant generational differences. The North remains a very traditional society in many respects, with only a few modern embellishments such as mass mobilization. Here, worship of the leader, an absence of mobility, and bare subsistence-level livelihood characterize the scene even as the twentieth century comes to a close.

Naturally, the DPRK leadership is reluctant to bring the South too extensively, too intimately into its domain. With per capita income probably one-eighth to one-tenth that of the ROK, and an enormous difference in the amenities of life available, a sudden intrusion of southern life and culture into the North would be dangerous. Thus, united front policies have prevailed over efforts to cement official relations, with an emphasis on recruiting those alienated or sympathetic to appeals for brotherhood.

Periodically, to be sure, the two governments have seemed ready to move forward together, from the dramatic Joint Communiqué of July 4, 1972, to the extensive agreements of December 1991. But to date, hopes for a sustained dialogue and concrete accomplishments have been thwarted.

Thus, activities have been concentrated in the second arc and its interaction with each of the parties in the first arc. In these respects, moreover, the focus has been heavily on the nuclear issue. In this regard, the United States has played the dominant role, although it has frequently been influenced by others and has, in some instances, depended heavily on their support.

When the United States was exploring sanctions in an effort to stop the DPRK nuclear program, it became clear that China would oppose any such action in the United Nations, and there was very limited enthusiasm for the idea elsewhere. The tortuous negotiations between the International Atomic Energy Agency (IAEA) and the DPRK, together with the U.S.-DPRK discussions that eventually led to the October 1994 Geneva Agreed Framework, constituted an alternative route that elicited much greater international support and, at certain points, assistance from other major states, including China.

It is often said that by playing its nuclear card skillfully and bargaining in a tough manner, North Korea not only brought the United States to the bargaining table but exacted major concessions from Washington—and through Washington, from others. Some argue that too much was conceded or that, through nuclear blackmail, a renegade was rewarded, setting a bad precedent.

Those who support the Agreed Framework generally agree that it is not perfect and that the possibility of failure cannot be excluded. They assert, however, that it provides for a strict monitoring of the DPRK nuclear program over an extensive time period, thereby greatly reducing the risk of a weapons program by a notably unreliable state. They further point out that the DPRK has agreed to measures beyond those required by the Nuclear Non-Proliferation Treaty.

They also argue that it is a program that has brought maximum approval from nations differing on many other issues as well as cooperation through the Korean Peninsula Energy Development Organization (KEDO), with South Korea in a key role. No alternative, they insist, was available except at much higher cost and risk.

There can be no doubt that the DPRK objectives are to move first toward official relations with the United States, then Japan. Pyongyang has not been oblivious to the success of Seoul's *nordpolitik* and the degree to which its bargaining strength—as well as its economy—would be enhanced by official relations or even near-official relations with these two countries. It has also been aware of the possibility of a serious cleavage between South Korea and the United States, given the complexities of the present course, including matters of timing, extent of assistance to a North in dire straits, and leadership or initiative. The U.S.-ROK relationship has unquestionably been rendered more delicate in recent times.

At this juncture, one must contemplate a number of possible future scenarios with respect to North Korea, including variations within each major possibility. One scenario that cannot be ruled out is that of collapse or, as a variant, a rising, protracted factional struggle within the DPRK elite. Given the number of serious issues to be faced, the uncertain quality of leadership, and the great hardships now being endured, these possibilities must be considered.

Another scenario is that of North Korea's "hunkering down"—namely, making minimal economic change due to a fear of its political repercussions and maintaining a hard authoritarianism under military primacy. Some other nations have endured poor conditions for decades under such a formula, although few if any have occupied the geopolitical position of North Korea, surrounded as it is by rapidly developing states (the Russian Far East excepted for the present), including a state of its own cultural heritage.

A third scenario is that of a "soft landing"—namely, the peaceful evolution of the DPRK through a gradually expanding economic reform program and increasing interaction with the region and the world. It is this scenario to which current external policies are directed.

The first scenario in its extreme form would impose enormous economic and political costs on the ROK and, quite possibly, on others, especially neighbors. The variant would threaten to regionalize a domestic conflict, with one or more factions turning outward for support. The second scenario would intensify tension on the peninsula and might well lead to various forms of military action. Thus, it is understandable why the third scenario is considered most desirable by the great majority of external actors, despite the fact that no one can guarantee its success.

One of the great advantages of the essays that follow is that they approach the subject from the widest possible range of aspects and perspectives. The scientific analyses presented relating to nuclear programs will bring data previously unknown to most others. The essays dealing with confidence-building measures present a variety of viewpoints on both specific and general issues relating to security in this era. The section on the role of the major powers illustrates the critical importance of the second arc of which I spoke earlier, and the final section deals with some of the challenges that are to be faced in the decades ahead. Thus, this volume illuminates its central subject with a breadth and depth warranting careful examination.

Robert A Scalapino
Berkeley, California

Preface

The controversy over North Korea's "suspected" nuclear weapons program epitomizes the security dilemma of the Korean Peninsula in the post–Cold War era. World attention was focused on Korean security issues once again when Pyongyang announced its withdrawal from the Nuclear Non-Proliferation Treaty (NPT) on March 12, 1993, and then "suspended" the withdrawal on June 11, one day before it was to take effect. Because the realization of North Korea's nuclear ambition would bring new uncertainty and instability to the Northeast Asian region, there was an intensive policy debate and discussion among media and governments in search of a rational solution and workable settlement for the issue.

As a nuclear weapons state, North Korea would pose a threat to the security and interests of the regional and global powers in Northeast Asia, including South Korea, Japan, China, Russia, and the United States. Seoul and Tokyo could be moved to acquire their own nuclear capabilities, thereby unleashing a nuclear arms race in the region. As nuclear weapons states, Beijing, Moscow, and Washington are apprehensive lest these non-nuclear states in the region emerge as new nuclear club members and challenge their hard-earned status as nuclear powers. Given these realities, a nuclear war scenario involving North and South Korea in the post–Cold War era cannot be ruled out unless the powder keg on the Korean Peninsula can be defused.

The authors of this book address the critical question: how best to maintain and promote peace and security in Northeast Asia. The underlying assumption is that North Korea's nuclear controversy is part and parcel of the larger issue of the Korean Peninsula and regional security and that the failure to resolve the nuclear controversy might unleash horizontal nuclear proliferation. The authors present arguments and evidence as to what transpired in active policy debates and discussions during the years 1992–1995. The world was kept in suspense during this period until North Korea's nuclear potential was finally capped—at least temporarily—by the terms of the October 21, 1994, Geneva Agreed Framework between the United States and the Democratic People's Republic of Korea.

The book collects essays and reports written by leading experts and specialists on the nuclear issue and the Korean Peninsula. Most were commissioned by the Nautilus Institute for Security and Sustainable Environment, a policy-related think tank based on the U.S. West Coast. The editors have supplemented this collection with timely and influential essays published in periodicals during the height of the nuclear controversy.

North Korea has been an enigmatic country that is not well known to the outside because of its long-standing policy of seclusion and isolation from the rest of the world. In this post–Cold War era of fallen communism, North Korea continues to adhere to the ideology of *juche* (self-reliance) and socialism; in so doing, it remains the last Leninist state and a hard-line Stalinist regime. North Korea today is commanded by Kim Il Jong Il, son of the founding leader, Kim Il Sung, who died in July 1994 after forty-nine years of dictatorial rule. Kim Il Sung's death was inauspicious because North Korea was in the midst of conducting delicate diplomatic negotiations with the United States on the critical aspects of the nuclear confrontation and preparing for a possible "breakthrough" summit with South Korea's president Kim Young Sam. The latter meeting was a casualty of Kim's death. The former process continues, albeit slowly and perilously. The resultant Agreed Framework has broad implications for North Korea and other post–Cold War regional conflicts elsewhere.

Unfortunately, the post–Kim Il Sung North Korea has not been managed successfully. The country performed worse economically than at any time in its history. Its sinking economy is clearly in dire need of resuscitation and restoration of its key infrastructures. Unlike the days of North Korea's nuclear threat in 1992–1995—the focus of the present book—there is a new threat on the Korean Peninsula centered on North Korea because of the real possibility of the regime's total collapse. North Korea in 1996, as the *New York Times* (February 18, 1996) commented, is an economic basket case of failed and fallen socialism, similar to the now-defunct communist states in Eastern Europe and the former Soviet Union. The United States and its allies South Korea and Japan now seem to have a different kind of worry—that North Korea is in so much trouble economically that it could eventually fall apart. Rather than eliminate a threat, the sudden collapse of North Korea could touch off internal chaos, a flood of refugees, and—if things got truly desperate—war with the South.

Nonetheless, tensions on the Korean Peninsula and military readiness have not abated. North Korea continues to forward-deploy its troops along the demilitarized zone (DMZ) that separates the forces and peninsula into two hostile camps. The security threat that North Korea poses—in terms of either nuclear or conventional weapons—is still real and very much part of the concerns shown by policy makers and in diplomatic circles. For instance, in February 22, 1996, remarks to the U.S. Senate Select Committee on Intelligence, Director of Central Intelligence John Deutch stated that North Korea must be prevented "from obtaining the guidance and control technology that could make its long-range missiles accurate, as well as deadly." He also added that as long as North Korea "remains isolated, xenophobic, militaristic, and resistant to reform and its hostility toward the South is unabated," the downward spiral of the economy "will be difficult to reverse."

The editors have undertaken this project in the belief that we need to generate more information about North Korea and disseminate that knowledge widely to the outside world. North Korea's technology, infrastructure, and institutions, as well as the problems and difficulties that the country is facing in its attempt to bring about alternatives to a nuclear weapons program, are recounted in the present volume. To date, much analysis of North Korea has been produced without firsthand experience of the country and without reference to North Korean sources. Much of the research provided in this book breaks new ground in this respect and reflects North Korea's hesitant but nonetheless discernible moves to open up to the external world.

The editors also believe that constructive and viable alternatives are available to the Korean peninsula nuclear issue in the form of an environmentally sound, ecologically sustainable energy development in Northeast Asia. Workings of the Korean Peninsula Energy Development Organization (KEDO) in this regard will and must receive special attention. Founded in March 1995 as a mechanism for implementing the October 21, 1994, "Agreed Framework" between the United States and the Democratic People's Republic of Korea, the KEDO began work in July and signed the Supply Agreement with the DPRK in December. The KEDO has worked so far to finance the shipment and delivery of heavy oils to North Korea on a regular basis. It has also completed the site survey for the construction of two light-water reactors and is ready to break ground on the project site by dispatching hundreds of technicians to the north. As a new and innovative experiment in international cooperation, the KEDO offers what its executive director, Ambassador Stephen W. Bosworth, calls "a realistic third way where countries can band together in an *ad hoc* fashion to tackle a specific, common task" between the two familiar established channels of either working through the intergovernmental organizations like the United Nations or the multinational corporations and enterprises of private companies. In this respect, the KEDO presents itself as a viable alternative and workable model that could be replicated elsewhere in a different set of circumstances to solve international problems and to further the cause of international institution and peace-building.

Finally, the editors would like to express appreciation to each of the contributing authors of this volume, who gave their invaluable support and cooperation to make this book possible. They wish to thank officials of the foundations that funded the research reported in this volume, including Tom Graham, Karen Harris, Ruth Hennig, Sally Lilienthal, Tara Magna, George Petovich, Beckie Rittgers, and Nancy Stockman; and key intellectual advisers to the overall project, including Dr. Tony Namkung and Scott Snyder, and a number of U.S., South Korean, and North Korean officials who prefer to remain anonymous. We also thank the coordinator of the NAPSNet project, Dana Fisher, for her consistent effort to provide readers with instantaneous, global access via the Internet to the draft versions of the papers collected in this book. Several faculty members and graduate students at Iowa State University assisted in the completion of this project by offering their wise counsel and logistic support: India Grey, Patrick James, Yong S. Lee, Donald Leopard, James McCormick, Aekyung Moon, Hyunglae Park, and Steffen Schmidt. Finally, they wish to thank the editorial staff at M.E. Sharpe, who displayed their professionalism in the completion of the book: Dorothy Lin, Douglas Merwin, Angela Piliouras, and Susan Cohan.

Dr. Bob Scalapino deserves our special thanks for encouraging us to continue the project and for providing the valuable foreword to the book.

The Editors

Peace
and
Security
in
Northeast
Asia

1

Introduction: A Road Map for Korean Security and Peace Building

Young Whan Kihl and Peter Hayes

This book addresses the important policy questions of how to bring about peace and security in Northeast Asia. In a geopolitical sense, the Korean Peninsula occupies a pivotal location—the strategic place where the major powers' interests converge. The initiative for Korean security and peace building must start with an effort to reduce chronic tensions in Korea. There is a pressing need today to turn the heavily armed and fortified Korean Peninsula into a nuclear-free peace zone.

The challenge in post–Cold War Northeast Asia is, indeed, to resolve the dilemma—and the irony—that, in an unresolved Cold War legacy, Korea remains divided. Inter-Korean relations are as frozen as ever. Today, the Korean Peninsula is still one of the world's dangerous tension spots long after the conclusion of the Korean War (1950–53). The 1.1 million–strong heavily armed North Korean army confronts an equally strong well-equipped South Korean army of 650,000 soldiers, together with 38,000 U.S. combat troops.

The security of Korea—a primary topic of this book—was the focus of worldwide attention and headline news in 1993–95 when a crisis was precipitated by North Korea's "suspected" nuclear weapons program. North Korea resisted international pressures by defying the International Atomic Energy Agency (IAEA) safeguard measures and inspection of the nuclear reactor facilities in Yongbyon, 60 miles north of Pyongyang. In May 1994, North Korea went ahead

3

with the removal of 8,000 fuel rods from its 5 megawatt electrical experimental nuclear reactor. This move led the U.S. Clinton administration to issue a warning that North Korea's extracted fuel rods could be processed into purified pluto-nium for manufacturing five to six nuclear bombs.

This standoff, dubbed by some as the first post–Cold War nuclear crisis, was triggered by the United Nations Security Council's move to impose economic sanctions on North Korea. Although the crisis was defused on time by diplomatic means, the nuclear time bomb in Korea continues to tick and remains under close international surveillance. The Agreed Framework, signed on October 21, 1994, in Geneva, by the United States and the Democratic People's Republic of Korea (DPRK), is discussed in several chapters in parts one and three. It stipulates that North Korea will "freeze" and "terminate," in due course, its nuclear program in exchange for U.S. guarantee to provide North Korea with two light-water reac-tors (LWRs) by the year 2003.

Peace, Security, and Conflict Issues: A Comprehensive View

This book examines North Korea's nuclear controversy from the perspective of a variety of policies and alternatives. These include a discussion of nuclear reactor technology and technology transfer (Part One), economic sanctions and incen-tives as well as the environmental (external) challenges posed by the nuclear issues and the nuclear-free zone for Korea (Part Two), strategic calculus and confidence-building measures (Part Three), and international perspectives of the major powers and South Korea (Part Four).

To highlight the centrality of the DPRK's nuclear threat, this book utilizes a broad and all-inclusive analytical perspective that reflects an interdisciplinary orientation. The purpose here is to cast the conceptual net widely so as to capture the sense of urgency regarding the threat of horizontal nuclear proliferation that North Korea's nuclear capability poses to the Northeast Asia region in the post–Cold War era. The following key assumptions underlie the present study of peace and security:

First, *peace and security are inseparable.* Not only are they intertwined as human activities, but they are also interrelated in the global and regional con-texts. What happens in the Northeast Asian corner of the globe, for instance, is not confined to the region but has ramifications for the larger community of East Asia and the Asia-Pacific region. Opposing nuclear arms proliferation in the Korean context will spill over beyond the region to other regions and parts of the world. Hence, strengthening horizontal nuclear nonproliferation in Asia pro-motes both the regional and global security agendas.

Second, *peace is indivisible as a set of ideas but the strategy for peace-build-ing must start from the concrete issues and problem areas that are readily identifiable.* Hence, a "peace by pieces" strategy reflects a more sensible and realistic approach to the problem solving of the peace and security agenda in the region. Peace in the post–Cold War era involves more than the hardware and technology of military security and deterrence, which reflects a conventional and restrictive perspective. Peace is also a matter of promoting cooperation among the people and nations of the world, which reflects a more positive and inclusive perspective.

Third, *peace and security in the nuclear age reflect both high and low political dimensions of national security.* The difference between these dimensions may be exploited to promote ecologically sustainable development. We must address not only the hardware aspect of nuclear weapons deployment by the region's nuclear weapons states—including the United States, China, and Russia—but also the software strategy of how to dissuade the nuclear ambitions of non-weapon states and also to promote the reduction of nuclear weapons stockpiles and their eventual elimination. These challenges of how to promote confidence-building measures involving both nuclear and conventional weapons in the region (high-politics issues), in turn, may be combined with a sense of concrete and practical measures to promote regions economic and ecological developments (low-politics issues).

This is why peace and security in Northeast Asia will not come about *unless and until* the welfare issues of the environment and economic development are settled while the questions of horizontal nuclear nonproliferation and confidence-building measures are worked out as well.

Armed with these analytic tools and approaches to peace, this book provides a road map for Korean security and peace building. Readers will be exposed to a variety of obstacles and rugged terrain, in several steps and stages, before reaching the final destination of establishing a nuclear-free peace zone for the Korean Peninsula.

Two Track Approaches to Development and Security

Track One: Sustainable Energy Development and Security

Nuclear power—often promoted in Japan, the ROK, and the United States—as a cleaner alternative to coal—poses its own environmental and security-related problems. Since demand for energy in Northeast Asia will grow exponentially in the coming decades, the need to develop feasible, least-cost policy and technology alternatives is urgent.

Electricity generation in APEC Asian states is projected to increase from its 1991 level of 235 GWe to 1,000 GWe in 2010—an annual 8 percent increase. This projected increase will require some $297 billion over the 1991–2000 period; and an additional $557 billion from 2000 to 2010. About 62 percent of this demand is projected to be in China. It is highly improbable that China can sustain this rate of rapid investment in electric power plants which amounts to an average of $26 billion/year. Moreover, the investment required to control China's sulfur emissions with the best available technology would amount to $34 billion per year (see Table 1.1 below)

Table 1.1

Estimated Annual Costs to Achieve Best Available SO$_2$ Emission Technology Controls ($/y)

China:	$34.2 billion
Japan:	$6.1 billion
DPRK:	$3.1 billion
ROK:	$3.8 billion
Taiwan:	$3.0 billion

Note: Resolution Level, Projected 2020 Emissions Using Best Available Technology: (BAT): = 50%.
Source: M. Amann, J. Cofalia, "Scenarios of Future Acidification in Asia: Exploratory Calculations," RAINS-ASIA report, May 1995.

The critical missing link in many discussions of the energy–environment dilemma in Northeast Asia is how much it would cost to achieve sulfur emission and greenhouse gas reductions in China using best available energy efficiency technology rather than primarily emission control technology. If acid rain in China can be reduced by energy efficiency, cleaner coal and control technologies, and a combination of fuel switching (natural gas supplemented by renewables), then a substantial fraction of the annual costs referred to above could be avoided. The potential gains may persuade China to accept substantial "green" and efficiency investment by Japan and other donor states. On the other hand, the threat of China's acid rain may induce Japan and South Korea to lead in innovative financing of the energy sector in China (and North Korea) in ways that provide more energy at lesser cost.

Given these voracious capital demands, is nuclear power compatible with the trend toward privatization of energy utilities? Are there proliferation-related issues, and if so, can these be managed? How serious is the risk of energy supply cutoff given diverse supply markets? What is the best technological and economic response to the risks of cutoff? Table 1.1 is an estimation of annual costs of emission control for five countries in the region projected into the year 2020.

A serious discussion about alternatives to both dirty coal and nuclear power in Northeast Asia has barely begun. Early studies suggest that investment in clean coals, fuel switching, and energy efficiency may be optimal on financial, as well as environmental and security grounds. Multilateral collaboration spearheaded by the ROK and supported by the United States and Japan to promote ecologically sound and secure energy development in Northeast Asia would be a crucial step in energy development in the region as a whole. Before the governments make such a commitment and crystallize it in the form of joint initiatives, a consensus must emerge among key thinkers and opinion makers in the two countries. Scholars play an important image framing or "epistemic" role in setting such agendas. Non-governmental organizations can move speedily to formulate and pose such questions to governments in ways that are politically potent.

The recognition of a shared regional and global environment could generate a new stimulus for regional cooperation based on an emerging concept, "environmental security." By building the foundation for institutionalized environmental governance in the region, countries will initiate the habit of dialogue so crucial to confidence building at the geopolitical level.

Track Two: Elimination or Control of Nuclear Weapons

United States security alliances in Asia were built around U.S. nuclear hegemony. Mutual Assured Destruction, for instance, provided a legitimating ideology for forward deployment and various doctrines pertaining to the use—and non-use—of U.S. nuclear weapons. Deep institutional integration developed around nuclear weapons deployed on host nations at U.S. bases, in command posts, in joint targeting, during exercises, and in de facto sharing of nuclear weapons (as in the U.S.-ROK artillery forces to deliver nuclear weapons against the DPRK). American nuclear weapons were a unique capability that underpinned the ideology and institutional integration in each bilateral alliance in Asia.[1]

In the post Cold War period, the rationale for American extended deterrence is obscure. The weapons themselves have been withdrawn from theater forces. Many of theater and battlefield weapons have been dismantled, and the organizational infrastructure decertified or demobilized. In short, the United States unilaterally (and largely unnoticed) virtually abolished extended deterrence.[2] It still asserts rhetorically that it holds a nuclear umbrella over allies such as Japan and the ROK. But does anyone seriously believe that the United States would use any nuclear weapon except to deter direct nuclear threats or as weapons of last resort with which to respond to direct nuclear attacks against the United States itself?

It is incumbent, therefore, to examine not only what will be the post Cold War but also the post-nuclear regional security system in Northeast Asia. The nascent ASEAN Regional Forum cannot serve as a framework for a security system in Northeast Asia built around conventional defenses. The issues which divide and threaten the states of Northeast Asia are too intractable and too specific for the Forum. Rather, the states in the region—and the United States given its long-standing alliances—must fashion a new concept for regional security which does not rest on nuclear weapons.

Outline of Chapters

In Part One, three chapters deal with the basic question of how and why nuclear reactor technology and its transfer to communist North Korea make sense to preserve peace and stability in Northeast Asia. It focuses on an attempt to put to rest North Korea's desire to acquire nuclear weapon–state status by diplomatic means through the signing of an Agreed Framework between the United States and the Democratic People's Republic of Korea.

Chapter 2, by Salomon Levy, discusses the technical details of supplying light-water reactors to North Korea and the implications of replacing the existing (and old) graphite-moderated reactor technology. The chapter surveys several cases in which the United States transferred LWR technology to other countries. It also examines the possibility of the Republic of Korea's (ROK's) supplying LWR technology to the DPRK and discusses potential problems associated with such a transfer to North Korea, such as its "safety culture" being different, and possible solutions to these problems.

Chapter 3, by Peter Hayes, examines the economic costs and benefits of replacing North Korea's existing reactor technology with LWR technology. The chapter raises both the pros and cons of LWR transfer to the DPRK in terms not only of the cost-benefit calculus but also of the relative proliferation intensity between the two reactor systems (LWRs and North Korea's indigenous reactors). The DPRK's electricity needs are also analyzed and estimated from the perspective of energy supply sources, including nuclear power. The implications of LWR technology transfer to the DPRK are then presented in terms of reference cases illustrating whether the DPRK has abided by Non-Proliferation Treaty (NPT) provisions with full-scope IAEA safeguards. Raising such questions led to the next logical step in diplomatic negotiations, thereby presaging a quid pro quo settlement between the United States and the DPRK in the form of the 1994 Geneva Agreed Framework.

Chapter 4, by Leonard S. Spector, provides a balance sheet of the advantages and disadvantages of the historic Agreed Framework. This agreement established a formula for a step-by-step process for settling the nuclear issue between North Korea and the United States. The chapter is a transcript of testimony by one of the leading experts on the nuclear nonproliferation issue before the U.S. House of Representatives Committee on International Relations, Subcommittee on Asia and the Pacific. In commenting on the U.S.–DPRK Agreed Framework, the author gives a balanced overview of not only the risks and flaws but also the benefits that may accrue from the transfer of LWR technology to the DPRK.

In Part Two, five chapters deal with the economics of the North Korean nuclear controversy. It raises the question of how international sanctions were considered but not adopted and why the negative sanctions were deemed counterproductive and unnecessary. Because sanctions might or might not have worked to resolve North Korea's nuclear controversy, the discussion shows how and why positive incentives were better strategies for bringing about a settlement of the nuclear dispute between North Korea and the United States.

Chapter 5, by Mark J. Valencia, advocates engaging North Korea economically in the new Pacific community in the making. The attempt to engage North Korea in the process of community building must begin, according to the author, in relatively innocuous fields such as environmental protection, including control of marine pollution in the Sea of Japan, and economic development, where North Korea will be enticed to cooperate more with the United States, Japan, and South Korea in the evolving regional Pacific community.

Chapter 6, by Peter Hayes and Lyuba Zarsky, raises the question of why regional environmental cooperation is needed in Northeast Asia. The critical environmental issues in the region that may be amenable to regional cooperation include transfrontier air pollution, marine pollution, migratory animals, and economic integration. Some of the ongoing regional initiatives to foster cooperation on environmental issues are also discussed. These include the Northwest Pacific Region Action Plan (NOWPAP), sponsored by the United Nations Environment Program (UNEP); the scientific activity on marine pollution sponsored by the United Nations Educational, Scientific, and Cultural Organization (UNESCO); as well as concerns regarding implementation plans and strategies, such as capacity building, monitoring, verification and enforcement, financing and public education.

Chapter 7, by Kimberly Ann Elliott, presents the argument that economic sanctions against North Korea on the nuclear issue will not work. She briefly surveys the North Korean economy, including overall production and trade patterns in the key sectors of food, energy, technology, and currency. After specifying an analytical framework for economic sanctions, the author applies the framework to North Korea to see whether economic sanctions make sense in achieving the objectives of nuclear nonproliferation. Whether economic sanctions will work against North Korea would depend, according to the author, on what the North Korean leader wants to do in terms of either maintaining the status quo of autarky or moving toward an open-door policy. In light of the Agree Framework, her argument appears to be proven valid with hindsight.

Chapter 8, by Peter Hayes, examines the relationship between environmental problems and economic crisis in North Korea. The author argues convincingly that environmental restoration is central to a successful structural adjustment and economic revival in North Korea. After providing basic environmental data, the chapter discusses the most pressing environmental problems and challenges in four sectors: agriculture, water, mining, and forestry. The environmental ideology, laws, and administrative system of North Korea are also reviewed, as well as some initiatives deemed necessary to improve environmental management in North Korea.

Chapter 9, by Peter Hayes and David F. Von Hippel, zeros in on the challenging task of engaging North Korea on energy efficiency. Energy efficiency improvements in the DPRK may be the key to resuscitating its stagnant economy. After identifying some of the problems faced in the energy sector, such as technological bottlenecks and underutilization of energy facilities, the chapter develops indicative estimates of the potential for implementing energy efficiency and renewable energy in the industrial, residential, transportation, and military end use sectors. It also describes some of the means whereby the DPRK's energy problems can be addressed through international cooperation.

In Part Three, five chapters address how diplomatic and strategic moves were employed in conducting sensitive negotiations between the United States and the DPRK. The eventual result was a compromise settlement of North Korea's nuclear controversy. These chapters include an analysis of North Korea's strategic decision to rely on brinkmanship and high-risk gamesmanship, the level of progress in implementing the Agreed Framework, the founding of the KEDO (Korean Peninsula Energy Development Organization) and the Kuala Lumpur agreement of May 1995, North Korea's internal decision-making process on the nuclear issue, the fallout of the U.S.–DPRK agreement on the future of the U.S.–ROK alliance, and bilateral and multilateral approaches to confidence-building measures.

Chapter 10, by Young Whan Kihl, examines the ways in which confrontation on the nuclear issue was turned into a compromise settlement, thereby avoiding a military showdown in favor of diplomacy in the form of the Geneva Agreed Framework. Some lessons of the 1994 Korean nuclear crisis are drawn from the case study of North Korea as a small, surviving Leninist state in confrontation with the United States as the only remaining superpower. North Korea's negotiating behavior vis-à-vis the United States, coupled with its intransigent behavior toward the IAEA, has provided an occasion for the small state to learn to play the game of nuclear brinkmanship with skill and tact, although the ultimate outcome can be judged only with the passage of time.

Chapter 11, by Scott Snyder, discusses a road map for normalizing relations between the United States and North Korea beyond the Geneva Agreed Framework. It examines the subsequent developments in implementing the terms of the agreement, including the establishment of the KEDO. He analyzes North Korea's policy options of either continuing with the implementation process or discarding the terms of the agreement. The key to success is, of course, the follow-up measures of normalizing U.S.–DPRK relations, which, in turn, depends on the continuity of IAEA safeguard inspections and the willingness of North Korea to abide by the terms of the Geneva agreement.

Chapter 12, by Alexandre Y. Mansourov, analyzes North Korea's decision-making process regarding the nuclear issue on the eve of the 1994 crisis. The chapter examines the country's internal political dynamics, including the rising role of technocrats. Mansourov argues that North Korea's nuclear game plan was orchestrated by the then Great Leader Kim Il Sung with the help of his followers in the Ministry of Atomic Energy Industry and the Ministry of Foreign Affairs.

Chapter 13, by Peter Hayes and Stephen Noerper, examines the future of the U.S.–South Korea alliance in a new era of East Asia's post–Cold War security environment. North Korea's continued forward deployment of immense conventional forces and recent nuclear threat, however, provide the most obvious rationale for maintaining the security alliance. The new concerns about rapid militarization in an economically dynamic People's Republic of China (PRC) and Asian nations' concerns about the development of Japanese capabilities provide further rationale for maintaining a strong U.S. presence. Maintaining U.S. force levels is also defended on the ground that it appears to be cost effective in an era of dramatic cost cutting given the host-nation support (HNS) offered by Japan and South Korea.

Chapter 14, by Janice M. Heppell, discusses the challenge of confidence-building measures in Northeast Asia by transposing the Conference on Security and Cooperation in Europe (CSCE) type of multilateral security framework to the Asia-Pacific region. The chapter examines various factors both promoting and preventing consensus regarding the imposition of sanctions on North Korea, which has been considered by the neighboring countries of China, Japan, Russia, South Korea, and the United States. Whether the multilateral approach will succeed or fail, in terms of the confidence-building measures (CBMs), depends primarily on *bilateral* relations between the pairs of Asian countries, according to the author. Although multilateralism is advocated, the chapter maintains that peace and security in the region will be built on a foundation of bilateralism.

In Part Four, six chapters address the external environment of the major powers and the systemic context of the Korean Peninsula nuclear crisis of 1992–95. Most of the chapters in this part were commissioned by the Nautilus Institute to examine the linkage between the residual nuclear force deployment by several nuclear powers and the danger of horizontal nuclear proliferation in the region. North Korea's nuclear ambition, if realized, would likely mean further horizontal nuclear proliferation in this region where there already exists the problem of excessive nuclear force deployment by the nuclear powers and vertical nuclear proliferation. This residue of the Cold War will complicate relations among the major powers and their policies toward the Korean Peninsula, with their professed goal of realizing a nuclear-free Korean Peninsula.

Chapter 15, by Gerald Segal, discusses the nuclear force deployment in Northeast Asia by three nuclear states—the United States, China, and Russia—with a view to their respective links to the issue of halting nuclear proliferation in Korea and Japan. As the two nuclear superpowers, the United States and Russia, reduce their arsenals, it is evident that midlevel nuclear powers such as China must join in the process of reducing arsenals and restructuring their arsenals to rely less on land-based systems and more on sea-launched ballistic missiles (SLBMs). Arms-control measures and agendas are deemed necessary. Also discussed are the need to strengthen the Non-Proliferation Treaty regime and the continued moratorium on nuclear testing through the eventual signing of a comprehensive test ban treaty (CTBT).

Chapter 16, by Dunbar Lockwood, also discusses the status of the three nuclear powers in the region—the United States, Russia, and China—in terms of their status as nuclear weapons states and the deployment of nuclear and conventional forces. The chapter advocates a moratorium on additional nuclear force deployment by the United States and Russia, by implementing START Treaties provisions, to be followed by similar moves by China.

Chapter 17, by Ralph A. Cossa, continues the discussion of nuclear force deployments by the major powers in the region, particularly with regard to the implications for arms control and nonproliferation of these nuclear weapons. The chapter notes that relations among the three nuclear powers are less competitive and seemingly more cooperative than in the past but that a great deal of uncertainty still remains, especially regarding the extent and locations of nuclear inventories. Hence, greater nuclear transparency on the part of all three nations is deemed necessary to build confidence among themselves and throughout the region. This measure could ensure the continued existence of a credible deterrent to North Korea's nuclear development should the current attempt to dissuade North Korean proliferation fail. This and the subsequent three chapters address the subject of the region's nuclear-free zone ideas.

Chapter 18, by John E. Endicott, examines the impact of the limited nuclear-free zone idea on the deployment of nuclear weapons in the region. The chapter advocates the creation of a multilateral verification agency, to be based in Vladivostok, that would oversee implementation of the agreement. This cooperative regional security arrangement would replace Cold War–era confrontation with a new sense of regional cooperation. The chapter concludes with a recommendation for halting the nuclear force deployment in the region in order to achieve a regionwide nuclear-free zone in Northeast Asia.

Chapter 19, by Seongwhun Cheon, presents a South Korean perspective on regional non-nuclear options. It discusses an earlier North Korean plan for a nuclear weapons–free zone. This plan is compared with South Korea's own proposal for denuclearization of the Korean Peninsula as well as the joint declaration on the denuclearization of the Korean Peninsula that both North and South Korea signed and put into effect in 1992. Factors that inhibit the implementation of the denuclearization plan are analyzed. The chapter ends with a plea for linking bilateral inter-Korean efforts with promoting multilateral confidence-building measures in the region.

Chapter 20, by Dingli Shen, examines the Chinese perspective on the Korean Peninsula nuclear-free zone. It advocates engaging North Korea in a program of verifiable nuclear weapons inspection and monitoring. After reviewing various plans and kinds of nuclear weapons–free zones, the article notes some of the issues critical to establishing the Korean nuclear-free zone and the conditions deemed essential for the success of such a plan. After establishing "an intrusive and symmetrical safeguards institution" that would monitor both North and South Korea, the chapter argues, the Korean Peninsula nuclear-free zone could be integrated into a verifiable regional nuclear weapons–free zone scheme.

Chapter 21, by Peter Hayes and Young Whan Kihl, presents a concluding set of observations on future prospects for maintaining peace and security in Northeast Asia. Two track approaches to development and security in Northeast Asia, as suggested in the preceding discussion, are further articulated in terms of identifying some of the more concrete measures and steps deemed necessary for bringing about peace and security in the region, that is, going beyond the nuclear weapons-free Korea toward regionally sustainable energy development in Northeast Asia.

Finally, peace and security in Northeast Asia in and around the Korean peninsula to be institutionalized in the post-Cold War era may be placed in a broader context of history and economic dynamism. The dramatic end of the Cold War confrontation between the United States and the former Soviet Union in 1991 did not bring about a similar epochal transformation in "the correlation of forces" in the Northeast Asia region surrounding the Korean Peninsula. Some of the chapters in part 4 describe the great powers' military force deployment, both conventional and nuclear, in the region. Maintaining the existing force structure and preparedness is considered prudent because of the regional dynamics associated with robust economic growth and potential political instability that may arise from contingencies such as Korea's approaching reunification.

To the extent that the nuclear conflict with the DPRK is contained with respect to the Geneva Agreed Framework and its implementation through the activities of the KEDO, the prospects for peace and security in the Korean Peninsula have measurably improved. Hopefully, this tenuous Agreed Framework will lead to the next logical step, which is to institutionalize the peacebuilding process in Korea and eventually establish nuclear-free zone in the Korean Peninsula. If this effort is successful, it will help ensure the stability of Northeast Asia as well as the regional power balance and peace of the Asia-Pacific region into the twenty-first century. Greater regional economic integration may be fostered by the nuclear-free security environment around the Korean peninsula. Then Korea will once again become the light in the East pointing toward a more peaceful and prosperous world for tomorrow.

Notes

1. See Peter Hayes, *Pacific Powderkeg, American Nuclear Dilemmas in Korea*. Lexington, MA: Lexington Books, 1990; Peter Hayes et al., *American Lake: The Nuclear Peril in the Pacific*, New York: Viking/Penguin, 1986.

2. See M. D. Millot et al., "The Day After . . ." Study: Nuclear Proliferation in the Post-Cold War World, Santa Monica, CA: RAND, 1993, p. 68.

Part One

Technology: Nuclear Reactor and Technology Transfer

2

Supply of Light-Water Reactor(s) to Pyongyang: Technological Issues and Possible Solutions

Salomon Levy

The transfer of light-water reactor (LWR) technology to North Korea (the Democratic People's Republic of Korea, or DPRK) has been negotiated during high-level talks between North Korea and the United States. The pros and cons of such a transfer were covered by Peter Hayes,[1] and the purpose of this chapter is to provide details about the practical issues that might be raised by such a transfer and to suggest possible ways to resolve them.[2]

This chapter first reviews past LWR technology transfers from the United States to other countries and identifies the preferred method of transfer to the DPRK. Next, the countries capable of carrying out the transfer are considered and the appropriate choice(s) identified. Finally, key technical problems associated with the transfer of LWR technology are summarized and suggestions for their solution provided.

History of LWR Technology Transfer

Light-water reactor technology was developed in the United States, where it was first applied successfully to commercial power production.[3] Two principal varieties of LWR were utilized in the United States: the boiling-water reactor (BWR), in which the steam entering the electrical turbine generator is generated in the reactor, and the pressurized-water reactor (PWR), which employs steam generators to separate the light-water coolant in the reactor from the steam flowing to the turbine. The BWR was developed exclusively for power generation, and the American designer of BWRs (General Electric) was the first to commercialize that design. The PWR was designed originally for submarine propulsion and was later adapted to electrical power production. The original U.S. designer of PWRs (Westinghouse) was the first to commercialize it. These two reactor types have gone on to become the dominant suppliers of nuclear-generated electrical power all around the world, with about twice as many PWRs operating today as BWRs.

The initial transfer of LWR technology outside the United States was carried out by General Electric and Westinghouse, and it took three different forms, depending on the recipient country's plans for nuclear power generation, its fiscal resources, and its engineering, manufacturing, and construction capabilities. The three forms of technology transfer can be categorized in terms of the degree of LWR technology transfer.

Case 1: Full Technology Transfer. In this case, the U.S. vendors of LWR power plants provided the full LWR technology to equivalent companies in other countries (for example, France, Germany, Japan). That transfer of technology included design information about a power station operating in the United States; the engineering, construction, and manufacturing methodology employed in the plant; as well as training of the licensee personnel. Consulting services were available whenever requested. Improvements in design and developmental results continued to flow to the licensee after those improvements had been applied operationally in the United States. There was a requirement for a backflow of information to the licenser regarding changes and improvements made by the licensee. Such licenses involved significant initial fees and royalties when the licenser sold its own version of LWR power plants. In many cases, the licenser or a licensee–licenser joint venture supplied the first power station and subsequent significant evolutions of that design. With time, most licensees formulated their own design to fit their country's needs, and several (i.e., Siemens and Framatome) became capable of competing against the original licenser. Also, with time, other U.S. vendors (Combustion Engineering, subsequently bought out by ASEA Brown Boveri, and Babcock & Wilcox) became capable of supplying LWRs and licensing their technology.

Case 2: Supply of a Prototype Plant and Stepwise Evolution into a Comprehensive Transfer of Technology. This case applies to countries that had an immediate need for power and decided for economic or other reasons (for example, independence of fuel supply) to use nuclear power. However, they lacked the resources or capability to use most of the elements of a full license. Subsequently, as they developed that capability, they would acquire the technology stepwise, primarily from the original vendor and in a few cases partly from its competitors. There are many reasons for the stepwise approach, including the time required to develop nuclear-engineering curricula in local universities; put in place the necessary regulations, codes, and standards; and upgrade quality assurance and manufacturing technology. Another consideration was the realization that the transfer of some elements of LWR technology would not be economical until the number of reactors in a given country, and their manufacturing volume, was large enough. Several countries have followed this pattern (for example, South Korea and Taiwan).

Case 3. Supply of an Initial Prototype and Subsequent Prototype Plants with Very Limited Transfer of Technology. This case applies to countries whose primary interest was in economic nuclear power production. Generally, their demand for nuclear electrical power was small enough not to justify cases 1 and 2. Currently, this is true, for example, of the Krsko plant operating in Slovenia or the Koeberg plants in South Africa. It should be noted that in the United States, over the years, knowledge about the construction and design of some elements of nuclear plants was taken over by architect–engineers (for example, Bechtel, Sargent & Lundy). Such architect–engineers have become responsible for overall project management and design and construction of the non-nuclear systems, or so-called balance of plant (BOP). Also, it should be realized that some countries (for example, Russia and China) have developed LWR technology on their own; however, they have tended to find themselves in a continuous catch-up mode with respect to evolving western LWR technology.

Based on the preceding brief history, the best strategy for North Korea would be to select case 3 and possibly evolve later into case 2 when it could be justified. Case 1 is not viable as the requisite funds, resources, and capability are not available in the DPRK, nor will they become available for a rather long period of time. It would be premature to go to case 2 until the first nuclear plant had been completed satisfactorily in the DPRK and until the projected growth in nuclear power in North Korea was established firmly and justified economically.

Also, a premature selection of case 2 could have a significant negative economic impact. For example, Brazil acquired considerable LWR technology from Germany early, and it built large, costly manufacturing facilities that were never utilized. If LWR technology is to be transferred to North Korea, only case 3 makes sense at the present time. That was the strategy used in Taiwan and South Korea before it was subsequently evolved into case 2. That strategy has been effective in those two countries and it should be in North Korea.

Sourcing of LWR Technology

Between 1991 and 1993, it became evident that North Korea desired LWR technology and that its transfer must go directly or indirectly through the United States. France, Germany, and mainland China were not interested in working as supplier through the United States. Japan has the necessary capabilities and might have been willing to work through the United States, but has shown no interest to date in exporting nuclear power plants anywhere in the world.[4] Russia might have been much more acceptable to North Korea, but it was not clear why the United States would need to be involved in such a transfer unless it would have provided funding for the project—an absurd proposition. Furthermore, Russia's VVER LWR does not meet all U.S. safety standards in such areas as fire prevention, earthquake protection, and severe accident mitigation, which would make it even more difficult for the United States to sponsor the transfer of Russian LWR technology.

Since Taiwan is not yet ready for LWR technology transfer, this left the U.S. vendors and South Korea as the only two possible sources to furnish LWR technology to the DPRK through the United States. From the outset, the United States made it clear to the DPRK that the only acceptable supplier of the LWR technology was the Republic of Korea (ROK). Eventually, the DPRK accepted this reality.

The ROK as a Source of LWR Technology

The ROK has achieved LWR technology transfer with the purchase of two PWRs from Combustion Engineering. These units have an electrical output of 950 megawatts electrical and are expected to go into operation in 1998–99. The ROK has developed a South Korean LWR standard based on that technology. It is patterned after the CE-80+ ALWR version about to be approved by the NRC in the United States.

There are many advantages to the ROK involvement as envisaged in the Agreed Framework:

• The South Koreans speak the same language as the North Koreans and understand the culture prevalent in that part of the world.

• The ROK was willing to finance a significant portion of the project, supplemented by Japan and the other partners in KEDO. One way to reduce the costs to the ROK of the project would be to transmit a good portion of the power produced by the plant back to the ROK initially. The ROK might also be much more willing to accept repayment in kind (such as raw materials and food) from the DPRK. U.S. suppliers have shown little interest in such an approach.

• The ROK could be a source of spare parts and other support during plant construction and operations in the DPRK. For example, if the plant installed in the DPRK were identical to plants existing in the ROK, operator and maintenance training could be obtained in the ROK for the first project without having to build a plant simulator and a training center in the DPRK. Such a strategy would not only reduce costs but also encourage continued cooperation between the two Koreas.

• The ROK's capability in managing large projects is well established. Most

South Korean nuclear projects have been completed relatively on schedule and close to the projected costs. The ROK has manufacturing facilities capable of producing most of the components and satisfying the required nuclear quality level. Its universities have strong nuclear-engineering schools, which North Koreans could attend until similar capability was developed in the DPRK.

On the other hand, there are several obstacles to successfully implementing the ROK's dominant role in the transfer of LWR technology to the DPRK:

• The project cannot succeed unless the ROK and the DPRK work together. The project will require a back-and-forth flow of information and personnel over the territorial boundaries. Mistrust between the two countries is very great, and it will take many years to overcome past years of dislike and conflict. Also, mistrust is likely to resurface several times during this project. Consequently U.S. participation as envisaged in the Agreed Framework as the project's architect-engineering coordinator is necessary, to start the project and bring it to a successful conclusion. Duke Engineering was appointed in 1996.

• The ROK lacks the capability to supply all the components and services for an LWR. For example, key safety-related valves and pumps are not yet fabricated in the ROK. The same is true of instruments and particularly of digital control systems and their software. Independent quality assurance (QA) coverage is still being obtained from U.S. architect engineers. ROK simulators for training operators are probably behind comparable versions in the United States. However, the missing components, services, and software can be obtained from the United States.

Potential Transfer Problems and Possible Solutions

Key areas of concern regarding the transfer of LWR technology to the DPRK include determining the characteristics of North Korea's first power plant; developing a strong DPRK compliance group, together with a safety culture; establishing a strong project management and scheduling team; and avoiding certain pitfalls that have beset other such technology-transfer efforts.

Establishing the Characteristics of the First DPRK Power Plant

The precise type of LWR, its size, and its location have to be defined early before contractual agreement is reached on the transfer of technology. There are different types of LWRs and different versions among the available PWRs and BWRs. If the ROK involvement and component supply approach is to be pursued, the LWR had to be a PWR. As the latest LWR design in the ROK is to be adopted, it was inevitable that the LWR be the Combustion Engineering CE-80+ standard type adopted in the ROK. This approach will be the least costly and has the greatest chance of helping to normalize relations between the ROK and the DPRK.

The location of the plant and its features are important. There would be an advantage to a site not far from the ROK to allow easy access and eventual connection of power transmission grids. Also, nuclear power plants need a strong electrical grid to provide power for the removal of decay heat during nuclear plant shutdowns. The present DPRK grid would not satisfy this important safety requirement.

The size of the plant is usually determined by economic considerations and the overall capacity and stability of the grid system. Nuclear power plant costs decrease with plant size, and the largest possible size is usually selected. North Korea's current available electrical capacity is estimated at between 10,000 and 12,000 megawatts electrical,[5] which suggests an optimal nuclear plant size of at most 600–800 megawatts electrical, allowing for the grid weakness and future growth, not the gigawatt size plant to be transferred. However, most LWRs built in recent years have been at or above 1,000 megawatts electrical, and there is a significant cost advantage to using a plant that is already designed and under construction. Furthermore, the ROK standard plant is 1,000 megawatts electrical. That size plant can be introduced safely in the DPRK only with a tieback to the ROK electrical grid. With no tieback to the ROK, a 1,000–megawatt electrical plant might still be the best choice if it could be operated below its rated capacity during the first few years of operation until the DPRK electrical grid grew and became more stable.

The proposed site at Sinpo needs to be studied in terms of population, seismic, flooding, and geological conditions. Access to the site and transportation of large components to it as well as availability of construction materials are other important considerations. It would take at least one year to eighteen months to verify that a site is suitable for nuclear construction. Site visits commenced in 1995, but the detailed surveys remain in the future.

Developing a Strong Compliance Group and a Safety Culture

In a nuclear power plant, safety must always be the dominant objective because the risks associated with the release of fission products from such plants can be enormous. Although the power plant owner has many inherent reasons to operate a plant safely, a regulatory or compliance group has been found necessary to ensure that the plant is kept on safe grounds at all stages of design, construction, and operation. The DPRK must now develop and maintain such a group. It must define the applicable DPRK regulations and how to implement them. An exchange agreement with the NRC would be appropriate, and training of DPRK regulators through assignments in the United States would be desirable. Because this program takes several years to implement, most countries have required that the first nuclear plant they acquire be a duplicate of a plant being constructed or operated in the supplying country and that the plant satisfy all the safety regulations prevailing there. This is a good approach, but the DPRK would still need regulators able to pass judgment on the safety of the plant once it became operational and started to undergo changes. These regulators should be placed in a different agency, independent from the one responsible for operation of the plant. Finally, the regulators would have to have the authority to stop work and shut down the plant if necessary.

A safety culture must be instilled in all personnel associated with a DPRK nuclear plant. This imperative requires understanding and analysis of plant performance and intensive training of plant operators and maintenance personnel. The magnitude of this job should not be underestimated. Between 500 and 700 people are needed to operate and support a 1,000–megawatt electrical plant. The DPRK could acquire a core of this capability by assigning a limited number of its personnel at the suppliers, at the architect engineers' facilities, and at similar operating plants. With time, this capability would have to be developed within the DPRK. Also, the DPRK should eventually consider joining the World Association of Nuclear Operators (WANO). This would allow DPRK personnel to participate in the peer review of other LWRs and enable foreign LWR personnel to visit the DPRK plant. These visits are only advisory in nature, but they still provide a chance to keep up with how operational excellence is achieved at other plants worldwide.

Establishing a Strong Project Management and Scheduling Team

A significant portion of the costs associated with a nuclear power plant depend on its construction schedule. A construction schedule of sixty to seventy-two months can be attained only with a strong project management and scheduling team. This requires an organization with clearly established responsibilities and accountabilities. The scope of supply of the various participants needs to be defined before the start of the project. This means that a visit to the DPRK will be necessary to establish and agree on its supply capability. For example, most concrete construction materials and some balance-of-plant components could be obtained from the DPRK. Also, it will be desirable to recruit a majority of the field workers from the DPRK and even to train them to perform such difficult tasks as nuclear-related welding. However, the project and scheduling team should be controlled by the supplier of LWR technology. Parallel positions could be assigned to DPRK personnel to assure the transfer of project and scheduling techniques to the DPRK. The same strategy should be used for the plant startup.

The schedule and budget would be satisfied only if changes and interferences were kept to a minimum during the project. In particular, politics could have no role in the process or the costs would rise sharply and the schedule would be extended by several years. All these issues are potentially contentions and remain to be negotiated as of early 1996.

Avoiding Previous Pitfalls

The "previous pitfalls" category includes the following:

- Utilizing more than one type of LWR. This would only increase both personnel-training needs and the quantity of technology and manufacturing knowledge to be absorbed.
- Premature use of local components. Inferior components would have a negative impact on plant power generation.
- Weak compliance group. The power plant personnel would emphasize power production at the expense of safety and good maintenance.
- Inadequate fuel cycle planning. In some cases, there was a failure to recognize the generation of low- to medium-activity wastes and the need to provide for their storage. In others, there was a premature rush to install fuel fabrication and other fuel treatment facilities. All such facilities are strongly volume-dependent and should not be considered until the volume justifies them (for example, six nuclear power plants). For those concerned about cutoff of supplies, limited inventory buildup of nuclear fuel could provide protection. Long-term planning for the disposal of spent fuel would need to be considered because the suppliers of LWR technology will not agree to dispose of the fuel they have fabricated or to store the high-activity wastes it may generate.

Notes

1. See Peter Hayes, "Supply of Light-Water Reactors to the DPRK," this volume.
2. It is worth mentioning that my expertise lies in the area of nuclear reactor technology and construction, especially in the ROK. My knowledge of the DPRK's industrial and electrical capabilities, however, is very limited, and the observations in this chapter rely heavily upon information provided in Chapter 3 of this volume by Peter Hayes: "Supply Light-Water Reactors to the DPRK." Also, political and legal issues are excluded from this evaluation.
3. Ibid.
4. Ibid.
5. Ibid.

Supply of Light-Water Reactors to the DPRK

Peter Hayes

In this chapter, I examine the transfer of light-water reactor (LWR) technology to North Korea (the Democratic People's Republic of Korea, or DPRK), which emerged as an important issue at the third round of high-level talks between North Korea and the United States held in Geneva in July 1993.

Emergence of the LWR Issue

The DPRK has developed its nuclear fuel cycle capability for many years and has obtained substantial assistance from the international community—via the International Atomic Energy Agency (IAEA) and the United Nations Development Program (UNDP)—to this end, especially for uranium prospecting. The specific issue of DPRK cooperation with South Korea (the Republic of Korea, or ROK) on nuclear research and development was also raised in the Korean bilateral commissions pursuant to the 1991 nonaggression declaration, albeit with little progress.

The North Koreans denounced a South Korean proposal to build a nuclear power plant on or near the demilitarized zone to be run jointly. But in June 1992, they revealed an interest in light-water reactors in discussions with the director general of the International Atomic Energy Agency, Hans Blix. Blix had told the North Koreans that their reactors were outmoded and uneconomic. In response, North Korean officials recognized the economic advantage of shifting to light-water reactors.[1]

After the DPRK announced its intention to withdraw from the Nuclear Non-

25

Proliferation Treaty (NPT) in March 1993, interest in this possibility intensified. In my discussions with senior North Korean officials in May 1993, I asked three questions:

1. Would North Korea cooperate with South Korea on joint development of peaceful nuclear power technology?
2. Would North Korea agree to putting its plutonium (along with that of South Korea) under *joint* North–South Korean control?
3. Would North Korea change to light-water reactors if South Korea or the international community provided the technology?

Senior party foreign policy maker Kim Yong Sun prefaced his response by stating that science and technology traverse political boundaries and ideology. He continued as follows:

> About the possibility of nuclear cooperation, whatever the form and size of such cooperation for peaceful purposes, it should be studied and researched. Science surpasses ideology and borders. There are several additional documents on exchanges and cooperation in which cooperation is scientific, not only political and cultural. If we seek broad scientific exchanges, why not nuclear cooperation?; but not only nuclear, we should cooperate in all fields. In the 10 point program [for reunification, announced in April 1993], we also mention this issue where it refers to everyone making their own contribution with power, knowledge and money. When we say knowledge, this contains fields such as scientific cooperation including nuclear cooperation for peaceful purposes and not only between North and South Korea, but also with the international community.[2]

Thus, it was no surprise that the North Koreans raised the issue of shifting to light-water reactor technology at the second round of high-level talks in New York in June 1993. In response, the American negotiators indicated that the United States would support such a move as LWR technology is inherently less proliferation-prone than the graphite reactors under construction in North Korea. But they suggested that the issue was moot until the DPRK complied fully with its full-scope safeguards commitment under the NPT. Moreover, they informed the North Koreans that the appropriate way to pursue this possibility was to discuss it with South Korea and with Russia, which asserted at that time that it would supply four such reactors when the North complied with its NPT obligations and finds a way to pay for the transfer. There the matter rested until Geneva.

In Geneva, the North Koreans raised the reactor technology transfer issue on July 16, 1993, after an initial round of discussions had already been completed. The North Koreans stated that the real source of the problem regarding the nuclear issue is their inferior graphite nuclear reactors, which they were forced to adopt because no one would help them with anything else. They suggested that the only way to solve the nuclear problem would be for the DPRK to adopt and to obtain light-water reactor technology.

The Americans promptly agreed. They also stated, however, that only after the immediate problem was solved in relation to implementing the safeguards agreement would the United States explore ways for North Korea to obtain light-water reactors. They cautioned the North Koreans to keep in mind that the U.S. government does not sell power reactors. Moreover, they stated, North Korea would have to arrange financing with private corporate suppliers.

Although the North Koreans sought (and did not obtain) an American commitment that the DPRK should be supplied with light-water reactors at that time, they also referred to the Russian deal to supply them with four reactors. They appeared at the Geneva meeting to be satisfied with Russian LWR technology so long as the United States (or someone else) financed the transfer. In one aside, the Americans suggested that as South Korea has light-water reactors, the North Koreans should raise the issue of financing with Seoul.

The North Koreans also stated that the best way to proceed would be to implement their safeguards obligations step by step with progress in achieving light-water reactor technology transfer, culminating in access to sites (they did not refer to special inspections specifically, although referring to "sites" implies this). The American side promptly disabused them of this notion, insisting that substantive discussions and measures to transfer light-water reactor technology could come only after the DPRK was in full compliance with the safeguards accord.

The text of the joint U.S.–DPRK statement issued on July 19, 1993, in Geneva referred obliquely to all of these issues (see appendix 3.1). One phrase included the words: "on the premise that a solution related to the provision of light water moderated reactors (LWRs) is achievable." This phrase referred to the variety of obstacles that had to be overcome in order for the United States or any other supplier to transfer LWR technology to the DPRK including then COCOM (NATO's Co-ordinating Committee) controls, and U.S. legislation on terrorism and trading with enemy states.

For all these reasons, the statement that "the USA is prepared to support the introduction of LWRs" and "to explore with the DPRK ways in which LWRs could be obtained" was qualified with the phrase "including technical questions related to the introduction of LWRs." This phrase referred, in turn, to these difficult legal and practical questions outlined above, which had to be resolved in subsequent talks.

Thus, the DPRK's line in Geneva in July 1993 was new and potentially significant. The DPRK shifted blame from U.S. policy to the fact that North Korea has inferior nuclear technology, which, it suggested, inadvertently implied that it is interested in nuclear weapons. The shift signified that the leadership in Pyongyang had tilted away from its anti-NPT hard line. In short, the approach taken in Geneva appeared designed to keep open a face-saving way out of the nuclear impasse created by Pyongyang while sustaining the DPRK's nuclear weapons option for the moment. The LWR issue gave the DPRK a tactical advantage in ongoing negotiations as it maintained ambiguity as to its ultimate intentions while giving the appearance of being a confidence-building measure that might increase the transparency of the DPRK's nuclear program.[3] Kang Sok Ju (head of the North Korean delegation at the Geneva talks) said, for example, that his government proposed switching to more modern reactors to "prove the point" that it does not want nuclear weapons.[4]

Undoubtedly, the DPRK also aspired to match South Korea and Japan in terms of perceived technological prowess and prestige associated with nuclear power programs, although (as I will argue later in the chapter) it can ill afford to pursue this objective.

Some American officials at Geneva observed that it was easy for the DPRK to make this move knowing that the many obstacles to transferring light-water reactor technology would not be overcome, at least not in a time frame that would have been meaningful to the nuclear issue. With hindsight, it appears that they were wrong. Others believed that the DPRK was setting its price for compliance with the NPT at a level that required the American side to clear the way for upgrading trade and investment relations between the two countries and, thus, with the rest of the world. In this sense, nuclear technology transfer impelled by the threat of nuclear proliferation was an excellent battering ram to pound against the American closed-door policy toward the DPRK. It resulted directly in the October 1994 Agreed Framework which committed the United States, among other things, to facilitate the transfer of two LWRs to the DPRK.

Proliferation Intensity of LWRs versus Indigenous Reactors

The DPRK has developed the basic infrastructure for a nuclear fuel cycle with a view to constructing and operating a nuclear power plant. In 1991, Kim Chol Ki, director of the Science and Technology Bureau of the DPRK Ministry of Atomic Energy Industry, told me that North Korea had plans to build a 1.76–gigawatt electric nuclear power plant as part of the Third Seven Year Plan for the DPRK. He anticipated that the plant would have four 440–megawatt electric units operating on a two-on, two-off shift to provide backup against outage.[5]

In 1993, the South Korean Atomic Energy Research Institute released a report entitled "The Present Status of Atomic Energy Development in North Korea," according to which the DPRK has operated a 5–megawatt reactor at Yongbyon since 1986 and has a 50–megawatt electric reactor under construction at Yongbyon that is due to become operational in 1995 as well as a 200–megawatt electric power reactor under construction at Taechon that was due to become operational in 1996. The report also stated that the DPRK planned to build a 635–megawatt power reactor at Sinpo on the northeast coast—destined to be-

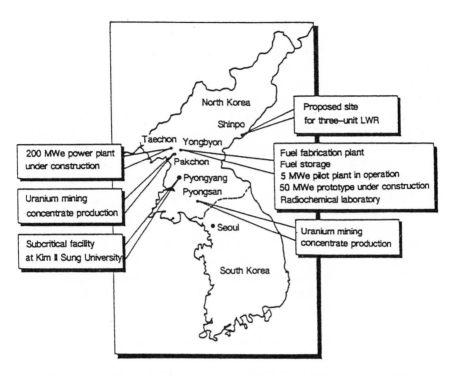

Source: "North Korea's Nuclear Power Programme Revealed," *Nuclear News* (July 1992), 2.

come the site for the LWRs envisaged in the Agreed Framework.[6] An American analyst has reported a different range of reactor sizes and locations in the DPRK than those listed in this South Korean report.[7] I have assumed that the South Korean data are more accurate as they are consistent with the facilities declared to the International Atomic Energy Agency (see Figure 3.1).[8]

In May 1993, I visited the Heavy Industry Sector exhibit in Pyongyang, which features a display of the DPRK's nuclear fuel cycle facilities. It included a scale cutaway model of the 200–megawatt electric reactor, which revealed primary and secondary heat-exchange systems for the gas coolant, and two generators. From the satellite positioning and tracking (SPOT) photographs of Yongbyon released by the Tokai Research Image Center in Tokyo, it is evident that the Yongbyon reactors were not intended for electricity production, as there were no power lines to or from the reactor sites.

From this information, I infer that the DPRK's *power* reactor program commenced with the 200–megawatt gas-cooled reactor, and not with the reactors at Yongbyon.

Scenarios for Comparison

The rationale for proposing to shift the DPRK from its graphite-moderated, gas-cooled reactor program to LWR technology is the latter's relatively lower proliferation proneness. Assuming that the DPRK will have to abandon its indigenous 200–megawatt electric reactor in order to obtain LWR technology—as occurred in the Agreed Framework—the two fuel cycles must be compared with respect to two criteria (see Table 3.1). First, the DPRK could be inside or outside of the NPT, and the IAEA's full-scope safeguards system will or will not be applied to its nuclear facilities. Second, it could have its own or LWR technology. These possibilities produce the following four possible scenarios:

1. The DPRK is in the NPT and has only the 200–megawatt electric reactor—operating in power, not weapons-grade plutonium production mode—under full-scope safeguards.
2. The DPRK is in the NPT, has only an LWR—operating in power, not weapons-grade plutonium production, mode—under full-scope safeguards.
3. The DPRK is not in the NPT and has only the 200–megawatt electric reactor, operating in weapons-grade plutonium production mode without safeguards.
4. The DPRK leaves the NPT after obtaining an LWR and operates it in weapons-grade plutonium production mode without safeguards.

   In this chapter, I will examine the issue of proliferation intensity by comparing only two of these four possible scenarios—namely, the DPRK outside the NPT running a 200–megawatt electric indigenous reactor (scenario B1 in Table 3.1) versus the DPRK inside the NPT running a 1–gigawatt electric LWR under full-scope IAEA safeguards (scenario A2 in Table 3.1).
   To simplify the analysis, therefore, I assume that the United States will hold out for the following "package" before it seriously entertains the idea of transferring LWR technology to the DPRK:

   • The "radiochemical" laboratory or reprocessing facility will be dismantled along with any other plutonium-separation facilities, hot cells, and so forth.
   • The IAEA will be permitted (at least eventually if not immediately) to resolve discrepancies between North Korean operating records and actual plutonium-separation activities as indicated by sampling, inspection of disputed sites, and so forth.
   • The IAEA board of governors will have determined that North Korea is in compliance with its safeguards agreement under the NPT, at least with reference to the existing reactors at Yongbyon, (and eventually, will decommission these plants in return for shifting to LWRs.
   • North Korea will abandon construction of its 200–megawatt electric

Table 3.1

Possible Reference Scenarios

	A	B
	DPRK in NPT with full-scope IAEA safeguards	DPRK out of NPT with no IAEA safeguards
1. DPRK indigenous 200–megawatt electric reactor only	**A1**	**B1**
	DPRK in NPT with full-scope IAEA safeguards	DPRK out of NPT; 200–megawatt electric indigenous reactor
2. Light-water reactor only	**A2**	**B2**
	DPRK in NPT with full-scope IAEA safeguards	DPRK out of NPT; LWR transferred

graphite-moderated, gas-cooled reactor in anticipation of receipt of LWR technology.

• North Korean spent fuel from an LWR will be kept in holding ponds at the reactor site or at a dedicated facility, and plutonium in it will not be separated in offshore reprocessing plants for recycling into LWR mixed oxide (MO) fuel or into an eventual fast reactor program in the DPRK.

• North Korea will rely on external suppliers of enriched uranium LWR fuel.

I assume also that a 1–gigawatt electric LWR reactor would be supplied by South Korea for the purposes of comparison.[9]

Relative Proliferation Propensity

At the end of the Geneva talks, the international media reported that U.S. officials prefer that the DPRK adopt LWR technology because it is inherently less suited for making nuclear weapons.

In reality, determining the relative proliferation propensity of different fuel cycles is a complex matter. John Holdren has suggested the following four factors against which different fuel cycles can be judged for their susceptibility to diversion of fissile materials (see appendix 3.2):

1. *Quality of fissionable materials:* the degree of enrichment of uranium and the ratio of fissionable to nonfissionable plutonium isotopes

2. *Quantity of fissionable material:* the number of critical masses per gigawatt electric–year of operation

3. *Barriers:* the chemical barriers to the diversion and use of fissile materials,

such as form and dilutants of uranium and plutonium, and the radiological barriers associated with spent fuel of low or high burnup

4. *Detectability:* the degree to which the fuel cycle requires new operations or significant modifications and/or entails radiological releases that can be monitored effectively

It is evident that the once-through LWR (in the case presented by Holdren, a pressurized-water reactor, or PWR) and CANDU (Canadian deuterium uranium) fuel cycles are significantly less susceptible to diversion of fissile materials than other power reactor fuel cycles.[10] It is not easy to directly compare the DPRK's 200–megawatt electric reactor (even after scaling down to account for the difference in plant size between the DPRK plant and that assumed by Holdren) because the DPRK has not released detailed design information for that reactor. It is therefore necessary to define a "reference" DPRK power plant to compare with an LWR in terms of their relative proliferation proneness.

Reference DPRK Reactor

In this subsection, I describe the basic physical parameters of the British plutonium production reactors in order to "design" a reference DPRK reactor to compare with LWR technology.

The DPRK reportedly told the International Atomic Energy Agency that its reactors are modeled after the British Calder Hall reactors built to produce plutonium for nuclear weapons.11 They were graphite-moderated, carbon dioxide–gas-cooled reactors fueled with natural uranium metal rods clad in a magnesium alloy ("magnox"). The second generation of four magnox reactors was known as Chapel Cross. Both generations produced plutonium but generated electricity as a by-product. All eight reactors were nominally rated at 50–megawatts electric (net).[12] Another source rates the early Calder Hall reactors at 225 megawatt thermal and 41–megawatts electric (net);[13] I adopt 50–megawatts electric in this study.

When the magnox reactors are used primarily to produce electricity, operators typically set fuel burnup at 3,000–4,000 megawatt-days per metric ton of uranium fuel.[14] The core measured about 14 meters wide by about 8 meters high. Each fuel channel in the reactor contained a stack of six fuel elements, each of which, in turn, consisted of massive, solid rods of natural uranium metal about a meter long and 3 centimeters wide. Each stack of six fuel elements weighed about 77 kilograms. Each core contained about 1,691 fuel channels, for a total of assembly of about 10,146 fuel elements. The total uranium fuel contained in the core was about 112 metric tons of natural uranium (excluding cladding).

The fuel could be replaced in later, civilian magnox reactors while producing electric power by using on-line, continuous refueling techniques, and about three fuel channels were refueled per week.[15] Spent fuel from gas-cooled magnox reactors cannot be stored indefinitely in water because the magnox alloy (magnesium alloy containing 0.8 percent aluminum, 0.002–0.005 percent beryllium, 0.008 percent cadmium, and 0.006 percent iron) corrodes slowly in water. (Dry storage, however, is feasible although difficult.) Each metric ton of magnox fuel irradiated for 1,000 megawatt-days contained about 998 kilograms of unconverted uranium and 0.8 kilogram of plutonium.[16]

When operated to produce weapons-grade plutonium, as they were between 1956 and 1964, the Calder Hall and the four next-generation Chapel Cross reactors were run rather differently. Instead of continuous refueling, the whole core was irradiated and removed about twice a year (allowing for about three months of repair and maintenance work). To produce very pure plutonium without the bothersome isotopes that impede weapons production, the burnup rate was reduced to about 400 megawatt-days-thermal per metric ton of fuel, at which rate, about 79 kilograms of weapons grade plutonium were produced per reactor year.[17]

On this basis, what can be said about the proliferation propensity of a 200–megawatt electric scale-up of the early graphite-moderated, gas-cooled reactors compared with an LWR when measured against the factors listed above (see Table 3.2)?

In terms of *quality*, replacing the DPRK reactor with LWRs would increase the international community's leverage over the front end of the DPRK's fuel cycle by virtue of the latter's resultant dependency on imported uranium enrichment services.

On the back end of the fuel cycle, it would also reduce the quality of the plutonium available from spent fuel by increasing the amount of plutonium isotopes that might prematurely initiate a nuclear chain reaction in a weapon (unless the LWR were removed from the NPT regime and operated to maximize the production of weapons-grade plutonium).

In terms of *quantity*, a 1-gigawatt electric LWR would produce about 250 kilograms of plutonium per year. A DPRK 200–megawatt electric reactor scaled up from Calder Hall technology and operated in plutonium-production mode could produce about 315 kilograms of weapons-grade plutonium.[18] Thus, two LWRs transferred to the DPRK would *increase* the quantity of plutonium to be controlled under safeguards. In the LWR case, the diversion of 1 percent per year would yield a "bomb" quantity of plutonium (5 kilograms for weapons-grade plutonium), but only marginally.

In terms of *chemical barriers*, LWR technology is fairly resistant on the front end in that the fissile material is in oxide form, albeit not mixed with an effective diluent. However, the gas-cooled reactor would use natural uranium fuel, which would be even more difficult to utilize for weapons purposes than low-enriched uranium oxide for LWR fuel. So long as both fuel cycles do not introduce plutonium recycling, they are equivalent in terms of chemical and radiological barriers to diverting spent fuel from storage to weapons activities. Indeed, due to the difficulty of storing spent magnox fuel in water for long periods, North

Table 3.2

Relative Proliferation Intensity of LWR versus DPRK Indigenous Reactor

	PWR once through fuel cycle per GEw-year		DPRK indigenous reactor fuel cycle per 0.2 GWe-year operated to maximize plutonium production	
	enriched uranium	spent fuel storage	natural uranium	spent fuel storage
Quantity of fissile material and main dilutants at this point	855 kg U235 in 28,500 kg Pu U238, 3% enrichment	250 kg of (69% fissile) in 26,000+ kg uranium and zero % fission products	336 kg of U235 in 223,664 kg of U238 enrichment	315 kg of weapons grade plutonium in approx. 223,000 kg of U238 and fission products
Further processing needed from this point to use in nuclear explosives	Extensive further isotopic enrichment required	Chemical separation from uranium and fission products required	Enrichment from scratch required	Chemical separation from uranium and fission products required for use in nuclear explosives storage may require reprocessing of wastes

Proliferation susceptibility indices (5 = worst, 1 = best)

Quality				
As is	1	3	1	4
Enrichment	5	4	5	4
Quantity	4	4	1	4
Barriers				
Chemical	4	2	4	2
Radiological	5	1–2	5	2
Detection	3	1	5	1

Source: J. Holdren, "Civilian Nuclear Technologies and Nuclear Weapons Proliferation," in C. Schaerf et al, *New Technologies and the Arms Race*, St. Martin's Press, New York, 1989, pp. 182–185; text for DPRK reactor.

Note: See Appendix 2 for definitions of numerical weights.

Korea argued that it might be obliged to reprocess the fuel for safety reasons and has already cited precedents to this effect in Britain, France, and Japan.[19] Some experts contend that dry storage is feasible, however.[20]

In terms of *detectability* of diversion, an LWR fuel cycle appears to offer significant advantages. If we assume that the DPRK would operate its reprocessing plant in scenario B1 (go it alone with its own 200–megawatt electric plant outside the NPT system) but would abandon it along with the 200–megawatt electric reactor in scenario A2 (rely on LWR technology), then the LWR would reduce the opportunities for diversion at various points in the reprocessing and recycling portions of the fuel cycle from relatively high to essentially zero. The LWR is inherently easier to safeguard as shutdown is obvious and required for removal of any fuel rods (although the fact that an LWR is relatively easier to control in this respect is not relevant to the comparison with the DPRK indigenous plant because I assume that this reactor would only operate outside the NPT, whereby diversion detectability becomes moot).

Overall, therefore, the major reduction in proliferation intensity associated with switching to LWR technology would be (1) the increased dependency of the DPRK on the international community for enrichment services and (2) the reduced opportunity for and enhanced detectability of diversion of plutonium from LWR spent fuel under safeguards versus an indigenous reactor operating outside the NPT. Finally, inducing the DPRK to abandon the 200–megawatt electric reactor would lay to rest any possible rationale for completing and operating its reprocessing facility in order to store spent fuel safely. Aside from these advantages, the LWR is only marginally less proliferation-prone than the indigenous plant from a technical perspective.

Other Considerations

Six other factors offset or reinforce these marginal technical advantages of an LWR over an indigenous DPRK reactor.

First, LWRs in North Korea could legitimate continued accumulation of weapons-relevant skills that could be mobilized on short notice to produce nuclear weapons from a large stock of accumulated plutonium in spent fuel. Thus, the acquisition of LWRs is consistent with the DPRK's maintaining a posture of studied ambiguity as to its ultimate intentions with respect to nuclear weapons.

Second, the DPRK could reduce the leverage implicit in its reliance on imported enriched uranium fuel by stockpiling this material (assuming that it could afford to do so and that this step passed unnoticed by the international community).

Third, LWR or "reactor-grade" fuel containing excessive amounts of the plutonium isotopes Pu 240 and Pu 242 is still usable for a nuclear weapon, at a cost to expected yield and certainty of yield as compared to weapons using "weapons-grade" material. It is noteworthy that it is *not* appreciably more difficult to design a weapon using reactor- rather than weapons-grade plutonium.[21]

Fourth, the DPRK could operate an LWR (presumably after departing from the NPT) to minimize the production of these inconvenient isotopes by shutting down the reactor more frequently to remove irradiated fuel (but at a cost to electricity production).[22]

A "modernized" DPRK that is rendered capable of running (or even constructing) LWRs could also become a more active and disruptive exporter of nuclear technologies than it would if it only had access to its own relatively primitive nuclear technology. Weighing against this disadvantage of an LWR is the fact that although the DPRK could become a more capable and potentially disruptive supplier of nuclear fuel cycle technologies, materials (such as graphite), and techniques by virtue of having an LWR fuel cycle, it would be less likely to have developed and to transfer nuclear weapons capabilities at all under the political conditions in which an LWR might be transferred to the DPRK. Conversely, it might develop and share nuclear weapons–related expertise with other states in the near term if left to its own devices, whereas it would take many years (up to fifteen years for advanced reactor core components) for the DPRK to develop exportable expertise in LWR manufacture.[23]

One other issue is worth mentioning. North Korean officials have noted that South Korea's nuclear power reactors might be hit during a war. These reactors present tempting radiological targets.[24] By the same token, a large-scale nuclear power plant in North Korea presents the South with a reciprocal targeting option. Having a much larger reactor program (twelve power reactors operating or under construction), the South proffers the North ten to fifteen times as much radiological damage potential as one reactor in the North would proffer the South. But a large reactor in the North would make the implicit threat to attack a radiological target in wartime a risk shared by both sides, which, in principle, provides the South with a qualitatively similar deterrent against such attack.[25] Although an LWR might contain much more fission products and radioactive materials than the DPRK's 200–megawatt electric plant, the switch to LWR technology per se would make little difference to this factor.

In this section, I have shown that an LWR offers some inherent advantages over North Korea's own reactor in terms of the criteria of quantity and quality of fissile materials, chemical and radiological barriers, and detectability. I also noted that six other factors should be considered in relation to the transfer of an LWR to North Korea: continued DPRK ambiguity as to ultimate proliferation intention, fuel stockpiling, the utility of LWR-grade plutonium for nuclear weapons, the possibility that an LWR could be used to make weapons-grade plutonium, North Korea's export behavior, and the issue of radiological targeting in wartime in the Korean Peninsula.

In the next section, I analyze the economic soundness of a nuclear power plant in the North Korean energy economy.

The DPRK's Electricity Needs and Nuclear Power

As of 1991, the DPRK planned to build only one nuclear power plant. When that is completed successfully, North Korean officials asserted that they would develop further plants "in accordance with the needs of national economic growth."[26] Under the Agreed Framework, they have committed their economy to having two LWRs.

There is little doubt that the DPRK is suffering from acute energy shortages,

Table 3.3

DPRK Energy Supply Balance, 1991 Estimate (10^{15} joules)

	Gas	Coal	Electricity	Other[a]	Total
Primary production	—	1,285.4	343.3[b]	37.7	1,666
Imports	—	75.4	—	—	314.0
Exports	—	—	?[c]	—	—
Primary supply	—	1,360.8	343.3[b]	37.7	1,980.5
Net transformation	—	−314.0	−167.5	—	−494.1
Final consumption	—	1,046.8	175.9[d]	37.7	1,485.9

Source: Economist Intelligence Unit, *China, North Korea Country Profile 1992–93* (1993), p. 80, citing Energy Data Associates.

Notes:

[a]No accounting for fuelwood and other bioenergy fuels.

[b]Primary electricity production, imports, and exports are expressed as input equivalents on an assumed efficiency of 33 percent.

[c]No account of small exports of hydroelectricity to China, nor jet bunkers and international shipping.

[d]Output basis.

both of petroleum fuels (especially in the transport sector, probably in industry, and possibly in fertilizer production) and of electricity.

The DPRK's Present Energy System

In this subsection, I analyze the components of North Korea's existing energy system, including the energy and electricity sectors, the generating plant, and the transmission and distribution system.

Energy Sector. As is well known, the DPRK relies heavily on coal, hydro-power, and imported oil for its energy supplies. Table 3.3 shows an approximate energy supply balance for the DPRK. This subsection focuses on the energy sector, which accounts for the bulk of the DPRK's greenhouse gas emissions.

The institutional arrangements in the energy sector are complicated and reflect a high degree of functional fragmentation. The energy sector in the DPRK has no single specialized institutional authority or ministry responsible for energy analysis, integrated planning, and management. These tasks are scattered among the following agencies and ministries:

• Coal exploration, mining, and supply are under the jurisdiction of the Ministry of Coal Mining.

• The electric power sector development, power generation, distribution, and sales are the responsibility of the Electric Power Industry Commission (EPIC; see below for details).

- Energy statistics and energy-planning activities are performed by the State Planning Commission, incorporating the Central Statistics Bureau under its authority. The State Commission for Science and Technology acts as a consulting body in these activities, mainly providing appropriate recommendations and software for energy plan formulation and decision making.
- Supervision of energy flow and reasonable consumption of the fuel in the transport sector is assigned as a function of the State Transport Commission.
- The Ministry of Atomic Energy Industry is in charge of development, construction, and power generation of nuclear power plants as well as nuclear fuel supply.
- The External Economic Affairs Commission is responsible for purchase of crude oil and petroleum fuels, as well as all imported machinery and equipment for the energy sector.
- The Ministry of Machine Building Industry is responsible for the manufacture and supply of domestic power equipment. Most of the research and development work for the energy sector is performed by the institutes affiliated with the Academy of Sciences, although all the above-mentioned ministries and commissions have their own research institutions.
- The nonstanding State Committee for Energy, chaired by the prime minister, discusses and decides on major issues in the energy sector.
- Research and development activities related to the energy sector performed by institutions affiliated with the various ministries are coordinated by the State Commission for Science and Technology.

This functionally differentiated and fragmented institutional framework results in poor policy coordination and program implementation. There is no comprehensive energy policy in the DPRK. There is no apparent economic rationale to the existing price structure for different energy forms. There are not even rudimentary markets to facilitate economically efficient transactions between energy-related supply and demand entities. Planning and fuel allocation are also inhibited by the apparent nonexistence of a basic energy supply/demand balance in the DPRK. Indeed, a UNDP energy-efficiency-improvement project in the DPRK is meant to create just such a balance at the proposed Center for the Rational Use of Energy.

Electricity Sector. North Korea claims to have about 12,000 megawatts electric of installed capacity, with an available capacity of 10,000 megawatts electric. Approximately 50 percent of the generating capacity is hydroelectric, and about 50 percent is thermal, mostly coal-fired. About 84 percent of the electrical energy is fired by coal.

Generating Plant. Although there are more than five hundred generating plants, only sixty-two major power plants are linked to the nationally interconnected transmission system. The latter system, in turn, transports about 85 percent of the generated electrical energy. (The residual 15 percent of the electrical energy is generated by self-reliant industrial facilities and by small, isolated, and mostly hydroelectric units.) Of the plants linked to the transmission system, twenty are thermal (eighteen being coal-fired, two being oil-fired), and forty-two are hydroelectric.[27] The largest thermal unit is at Bukchang, with an installed capacity of 1,600 megawatts electric. The largest hydroelectric plant is at Supung, with an installed capacity of 700 megawatts electric (seven 100–megawatt electric turbines).[28] The output of the latter plant is shared by the DPRK and China.

The North Koreans run the thermal, mostly coal-fired, plants as base-load units and use the hydroelectric plants to meet peak-load demands. When demand exceeds supply, the supply to consumers is suppressed. The DPRK Electric Power Industry Commission estimates that it has to accommodate a generating gap of at least 500 megawatts electric. Blackouts occur and loads are shed regularly, resulting in large production losses. In the winter (November–December), load shedding reaches 1,000 megawatts electric due to the accumulation of snow. In summer—particularly in March through May—shortage of water at hydroelectric reservoirs forces the power system operators to shed as much as 2,000 megawatts electric for up to an hour at a time. Bad weather can worsen the situation as storms, old and low-quality equipment, and incorrect operation of protective devices cause the transmission system to fail.

Consequently, the quality of electric power in the DPRK is also poor in terms of frequency (often found at 57–59 hertz, well below the permissible deviation from the standard 60 hertz) and voltage (which frequently fluctuates). The power factor at load centers is also low and averages 0.8, which can badly damage end-use equipment.

Transmission and Distribution System. The transmission system is isolated from neighboring countries (except for a 60 kilovolt line feeding power to a remote area of China). The DPRK uses 220– and 110–kilovolt lines for bulk transmission; 60, 10, and 3.3 kilovolts for distribution; and 380/220 volts at 60 hertz for distribution to consumers. The government states that 100 percent of households and industry are electrified. As not all consumers are metered, the exact quantity and sectoral distribution of electrical end use are not known.[29] The government states that transmission losses are about 10 percent, and distribution losses are about 6 percent. However, some observers believe that this official estimate (like generation figures) is optimistic, to say the least. It is reported that the transmission and distribution system urgently needs to be refurbished.

Generation Difficulties

The DPRK government claimed that generation in 1989 was about 50–55 terawatt hour electric.[30] Informed observers in Pyongyang estimate that the actual generation in 1992 was about 31–32 terawatt hour electric and that the annual shortfall is between 10 and 12 terawatt hour electric.[31] This difference reflects all the problems of generation, load shedding, and transmission and distribution losses referred to above.

In the DPRK's generating plants, machinery cannot be maintained or repaired adequately due to the shortage of spare parts, testing equipment, and obsolete and incomplete monitoring and control instrumentation in the power plants. The official estimate of thermal power generation of the thermal-to-electricity conversion efficiency of 34 percent is likely a substantial overestimate. At the Pyongyang Thermal Power Station, for example, major equipment is deteriorating due to the limited capabilities to track thermal performance, poor instrumentation and testing equipment, and the lack of a comprehensive maintenance program. All these technical problems are worsened by the shortage of skilled staff able to use what equipment exists. About 211 gigawatt hour electric of electricity generated at the station (or 5 percent of its nominal and 7 percent of its actual rated output at a 100 percent capacity factor) is lost due to acute problems such as boiler outages.

Coal Shortages. The power sector is also afflicted by problems originating in the coal-mining industry. Coal shortages (reportedly due to the classic command-and-control bind of shortage of coal for steel and power production on the one hand and transport constraints on getting coal to end users due to steel shortages on the other) have constrained the power output at thermal power stations. Also, the Institute for Coal Selection lacks equipment to determine the energy content of mined coal. Consequently, power station operators may not know the quality of fuel loaded into steam boilers at generation plants. The DPRK lacks a long-range coal-mining industry development program and master plan for each coalfield and basin to determine the best allocation of investment resources in coal production in relation to projected consumption needs. Moreover, that coal which is produced is not cleaned before it is sent to consumers which imposes operating and pollution problems (from ash) for power plant operators. Perhaps 60 percent of the coal used in power plants is wasted in inefficient combustion.

It has been estimated that the equivalent of at least 6 million metric tons of coal are wasted in the whole country and that simply using high-temperature waste heat rationally would increase electricity-generating capacity by 400 megawatts electric. Most of the industrial furnaces and ovens that vent exhaust gases at temperatures of more than 500 degrees centigrade do not recover the heat for preheating fuel or other uses. Nor are piping or furnace walls insulated due to the lack of insulation materials. Almost no use is made of modern heat exchangers or simple heat pumps.

Expansion Plans. The government emphasizes expansion of the power sector in its plans and allocated 3 billion won for this purpose during the most recent (1987–1993) plan. It aimed to increase power capacity to 19,000 megawatts electric and to generate 100 terawatt hour electric in 1993. These goals were ambitious and highly unrealistic, and were likely not realized.

To this end, the DPRK is building twelve new hydroelectric plants amounting to an additional 2,500 megawatts electric (the largest is 800 megawatts electric).[32] The government also plans to construct 4,000 megawatt electric of thermal power plants, ranging from 200 to 1600 megawatts electric. It now proposes to add two gigawatts of nuclear power plant.[33] Finally, the government intends to upgrade the transmission network by expanding it and introducing 330–kilovolt transmission in the mid-1990s (to increase eventually to 500 kilovolts).

Institutional Weakness. The Electric Power Industry Commission is the key power sector institution that plans and develops power generation, transmission, distribution, and end-use sales and has ministerial status in the government.

Within EPIC, the Electric Power Dispatching Bureau is responsible for the Electric Power Production and Dispatching Control Center (EPPDCC), which, in turn, monitors and coordinates the functions of the power system with its fifty-strong staff. EPPDCC is responsible for planning hydroelectric and thermal power plants; monitoring the status of generating units for efficiency and reliability of supply; monitoring the system flow of electricity at voltage levels at or above 110 kilovolts; planning and implementing repair and maintenance of the system; responding to faults and contingencies in the power system; and collecting and storing data on system operation. It also supervises eleven regional power-dispatching centers. It is supported by the Institute of Electric Power and Telecontrol in the areas of telecommunications and control, computer equipment, and software.

Load Dispatch Difficulties. Given the complexity of the power system, EPPDCC requires instant access to accurate and salient information on sixty-two power plants, fifty-eight substations, and eleven regional transmission and distribution dispatching centers. The system operators at EPPDCC, however, rely on phone or telex messages for status updates on the value of such parameters as voltage, current, active power, and frequency at a load center, or a drop in system frequency due to a fall in generation. Relatedly, if a transmission line is tripped out-of-service due to a fault, then the network configuration must be reconstituted immediately or whole sections of the system become isolated. The slow pace and unreliability of the information systems used by EPPDCC virtually ensure that the system operators cannot restore the system to working order. As of late 1992, EPPDCC operated one old desktop personal computer to collect and analyze system performance data, but it could not handle the processing of planning and logging information. Blackouts continue unabated in the mid-nineties.

Thus, the power system lacks a modern, automated, and computerized supervisory and monitoring capability that can support a load-dispatching function in real time. The pilot project under way with UNDP support to rectify this deficiency covers four critical power plants and substations only and will not resolve this problem at a system level.

Vast End-Use Energy Waste. In addition to the problems noted above, the consumption at point of end use of electricity is also very inefficient in the

DPRK. The government estimates that industries typically waste between 30 percent and 50 percent of energy supplied. In the building sector, many residential buildings are not insulated. Space heating is by hot-water pipes embedded in the floor with a single on/off valve per apartment. The source of heat is centralized and is linked to power plant waste steam output on a district basis. (Cooking is by bottled gas or kerosene, with fuel stored on balconies.)[34] Aside from dramatically increasing comfort levels in North Korean buildings, properly insulating walls and windows would reduce the demand for "waste" steam from power plants, which could be used better on-site at power plants to increase the generating efficiency (or reduce fuel usage) of electricity. The government has recognized that large opportunities exist to reduce energy waste and has established a Center for Rational Energy Use to this end.

In short, the main characteristic of the DPRK's power sector is its extraordinary wastefulness—waste in fuel production, waste in transmission and distribution, waste in end uses of electricity, and waste of scarce skilled labor. The DPRK's power sector is badly organized and managed. It cannot operate efficiently due to obsolete equipment and procedures. It is hard to imagine it effectively operating a modern nuclear power plant, let alone two.

Implications for Nuclear Power in the DPRK

From an economic perspective, the DPRK's priorities for public investment in increasing energy services obtained from its energy sector probably should be as follows (in order of most to least important):

1. Improve energy efficiency in end uses, especially in large and centralized consumers such as industrial plants and buildings.
2. Reduce energy losses in generation, transmission, and distribution in the existing power system.
3. Increase the quality and quantity of domestic energy resources (coal and water storage).
4. Provide new energy service capacity based on integrated, least-cost power planning that puts marginal supply options on an equal footing with marginal end-use efficiency options.
5. Construct new generating capacity as needed after all the above priorities have been achieved.

This analysis suggests that constructing a nuclear power plant in the DPRK is likely to be a high-cost, low-priority way to fulfill energy demands. The demonstration effect of the Japanese and South Korean nuclear power programs makes it difficult to argue this case effectively with North Koreans—but the fact that these two countries have overinvested in a costly energy option should not disguise the fact that the DPRK can ill afford to waste money on a nuclear power plant when many other options exist to supply energy services at far lower cost, faster, and with less risk. Indeed, continuing to divert a large fraction of North

Korea's scientific and technological talent to a nuclear power program may significantly worsen the chronic and pressing problems of the conventional power sector described above.

Technical Problems Associated with the Transfer of LWR Technology

In addition to the opportunity cost of foregone energy services that nuclear power plants would impose on North Korea's economy, such plants would also pose formidable technical challenges, including maintaining system reliability, following load patterns with a base-load plant, safe operation, delay, and timing.

A nuclear power plant might also be technologically ill suited for the DPRK power system. First, it is unclear whether a 1–gigawatt electric plant at Sinpo (or elsewhere) would be small enough not to threaten the power system's stability (crudely, no generating unit should exceed more than about 10–20 percent of the total system capability—or the available system reserve—or the operation of the whole system may be threatened due to unexpected outages).[35] Detailed review of the DPRK transmission system would be necessary to answer this question. Inspection of Table 3.4, however, indicates that the DPRK barely meets the reliability criterion—assuming that its total actual generating capacity of 10,000 megawatts electric feeds into one national, highly interconnected transmission grid. Conversely, by the time that the DPRK might bring an LWR on-line, the grid might have grown enough to accommodate a large LWR.

Second, a nuclear power plant is usually operated as a base-load plant and cannot be quickly powered up and down to follow peak demand cycles. Ascertaining whether a nuclear power plant would be technically appropriate in relation to demand patterns would require access to data either as yet uncollected, or not released, by the DPRK government.

Third, it remains an open question as to whether a nuclear power plant could be operated safely and its output dispatched, given the parlous nature of the current power operating infrastructure described in the previous section. Admittedly, it would take five to seven years (if South Korea were to be the supplier and provide the architect-engineers) before an LWR could be built in the DPRK, which would provide some time to train power system and nuclear plant operators. Nonetheless, the status of the current power system does not inspire confidence that safety and operational objectives would be achieved in a DPRK nuclear power program. Attempting to operate an LWR in the DPRK will pose an environmental threat to domestic populations as well as to neighboring states already sensitive to radioactive fallout issues in the aftermath of Chernobyl and Russian radioactive waste dumping in the Sea of Japan.

Fourth, transferring two LWRs will take years—many years. The tasks of financing, site selection, power system upgrade, fuel cycle infrastructure, fuel supply contract, technology supply and architect-engineering contracts, training of operators and technicians, and actual construction and testing will all have to

Table 3.4

Relationship between Installed Capacity and Size of Plant
(in megawatts electric)

Installed Capacity Must Be at Least		To Accommodate a Single Plant of	
850	MWe	100	MWe
3,300	MWe	300	MWe
9,200	MWe	600	MWe
20,000	MWe	1,000	MWe

Source: R.J. Barber Associates, *LDC Nuclear Power Prospects, 1975–1990: Commercial, Economic and Security Implications,* ERDA-52 US-2, p. 11-8.

be completed before the first LWR will deliver the first kilowatt hour electric into the North Korean power grid.

A *minimum* of six years will be required, including one year to set up the deal and five years to construct an LWR.[36] Given the difficulties of building a nuclear power plant in North Korea, where there exist basic legal and administrative barriers to the operation of foreign firms and in which the economic infrastructure is so poorly developed that an architect-engineering firm will have to import virtually all supplies and much of the requisite skilled labor force, a more reasonable estimate of the time to complete the plant might be eight to ten years.

Critical Issues Regarding the Transfer of LWR Technology

Thus far in this chapter, I have: (1) described the emergence of the LWR transfer issue in the context of the nuclear weapons issue, (2) compared the relative proliferation intensity of LWRs relative to an indigenous North Korean nuclear power reactor, and (3) demonstrated that North Korea probably will incur significant opportunity costs if it pursues a nuclear power program rather than cheaper and less risky ways to meet its energy needs.

In this section, I turn to the concern that lies at the heart of the LWR transfer issue: why did the North Koreans raise this demand, and is it sensible to meet it? In international meetings, North Korean officials often repeat the slogan, "We mean what we say, and we say what we mean." In reality, fathoming the North Koreans' intentions has been the most difficult aspect of the past and ongoing nuclear negotiations, and the LWR transfer issue is no exception.

In sum, the following conclusions can be drawn from the preceding four sections of this chapter:

• *Conclusion 1*: The North Koreans raised the LWR transfer issue to keep their options open by defining a face-saving exit from the NPT impasse that they had created and to create a battering ram with which to break down the U.S. closed-door policy on trade, investment, and aid to the DPRK.

• *Conclusion 2*: An LWR presents marginal advantages over the indigenous North Korean reactor in terms of relative proliferation intensity, but the critical issue is the implementation of full-scope safeguards and compliance with NPT obligations, not the relative technical characteristics of nuclear fuel cycles.

• *Conclusion 3*: An LWR is probably an expensive way to meet North Korea's energy needs and is dubious from an economic perspective.

The North Koreans who make decisions in Pyongyang know these facts and will have drawn their own conclusions. The corollary of these conclusions is that they seek primarily to realize intangible benefits such as prestige, the impression of modernity, and symbols of external recognition of the durability of their rule, as well as possibly more tangible gains in terms of reopening trade and financial relations with the external world (see the last section of the chapter).

The critical issue is whether provision of the two LWRs will induce the North Koreans to dismantle their reprocessing plant and their own reactors as is required by the Agreed Framework, and whether they will allow full-scope safeguards to be implemented. If so, then providing LWRs is a cheap way to preserve the peace and restore the nuclear nonproliferation order in Northeast Asia. If not, then the transfer issue is simply a diversion introduced by North Korea to stall for time while it pursues a nuclear weapons program or seeks other options.

Indeed, it is noteworthy that the DPRK's current rulers have no absolute assurance that they will ever receive an LWR given the long lead times involved. It follows that however *politically* important an LWR transfer agreement might be to ensuring that full-scope safeguards are applied to the DPRK's nuclear fuel cycle, the two LWRs cannot substitute for other benefits sought by the regime that might have an immediate and tangible impact on its survival prospects. These include negative security assurances (that is, assurances that the United States will not launch an attack against it), an end to the joint U.S.–ROK Team Spirit military exercises, and a general upgrading of U.S.–DPRK relations.

By demanding that LWR technology be transferred, North Korea has set a high price for complying with the NPT. But in doing so, it has at least defined a specific way to resolve the standoff that proved acceptable to all parties and against which progress can be measured quite precisely. Striking this deal also symbolizes that the United States—and, by implication, the rest of the world—recognizes the political autonomy of the North Korean state.

It is difficult to be optimistic at this late stage in the endgame. North Korea has barely fulfilled the two conditions to which it agreed in the Agreed Framework. It has done nothing to date to resolve the outstanding issues with the IAEA and continues to hamper the IAEA conduct of routine inspections.

Appendix 3.1   Text of U.S.–DPRK Nuclear Statement

The delegations of the United States of America (USA) and the Democratic People's Republic of Korea (DPRK) met from July 14–19, 1993, in Geneva for a second round of talks on resolving the nuclear issue.

Both sides reaffirmed the principles of the June 11, 1993, joint USA/DPRK statement.

For its part, the USA specifically reaffirmed its commitment to the principles on assurances against the threat and use of force, including nuclear weapons.

Both sides recognize the desirability of the DPRK's intention to replace its graphite-moderated reactors and associated nuclear facilities with light water moderated reactors. As part of a final resolution of the nuclear issue, and on the premise that a solution related to the provision of light water moderated reactors (LWRs) is achievable, the USA is prepared to support the introduction of LWRs and to explore with the DPRK ways in which LWRs could be obtained.

Both sides agreed that full and impartial application of IAEA safeguards is essential to accomplish a strong international nuclear non-proliferation regimes. On this basis, the DPRK is prepared to begin consultations with the IAEA on outstanding safeguards and other issues as soon as possible.

The USA and DPRK also reaffirmed the importance of the implementation of the North–South Joint Declaration on the Denuclearization of the Korean Peninsula. The DPRK reaffirms that it remains prepared to begin the North–South talks, as soon as possible, on bilateral issues, including the nuclear issue.

The USA and DPRK have agreed to meet again in the next two months to discuss outstanding matters related to resolving the nuclear issue, including technical questions related to the introduction of LWRs, and to lay the basis for improving overall relations between the DPRK and the USA.[37]

Appendix 3.2 Relative Proliferation Intensity Rankings

Relative proliferation-susceptibility of fission fuel cycles

Fuel cycle and point of vulnerability	Quantity of fissile material & main dilutant(s) at this point (per 1-GWe reactor/yr)	Further processing required from this point for use in nuclear explosives	Indices of relative susceptibility (5 = worst, 1 = best)					
			Quality			Barriers		
			As is	Enrch	Quantity	Chmcl	Radgl	Detection
PWR/ONCE-THROUGH								
enriched uranium	855 kg U235 in 28500 kg U238 (3% enrch)	extensive further isotopic enrichment	1	5	4	4	5	3
spent-fuel storage	250 kg Pu (69% fiss) in 26000 + kg U, FP	chemical separation from U & FP	3	4	4	2	1–2	1
PWR-PU-RECYCLE								
reprocessed Pu	440 kg Pu (61% fiss), possibly mixed with U	chemical separation from U (if present)	3	4	4	3–4	4	4
CANDU/ONCE-THROUGH								
on-line removal of fuel rods	345 kg fissile Pu in 128000 kg U, FP	chemical separation from U & FP	4	4	4	2	2	2
CANDU/PU RECYCLE								
reprocessed Pu	188 kg fissile PU, possibly mixed with U	chemical separation from U (if present)	4	4	4	3–4	2	4
HTGR/U233 RECYCLE								
enriched uranium	325 kg U235 with 25 kg U 238 (93.5% enrch)	minor chemical processing at most	5	5	3	4	5	5
reprocessed U233	190 kg U233 + 50 kg U235	minor chemical processing at most	4	4	3	4	3	4
HTGR/DENATURED								
fabricated fuel	650 kg U233, 235 in 5500 kg U + 10000 kg Th	chemical separation from Th, further enrichment	1	4	4	3	3	1
LMFBR/NATURAL U FEED								
reprocessed Pu	2350 kg Pu (80% fiss), possible mixed with U	chemical separation from U (if present)	4	4	5	3–4	4	4

Abbreviations: chemcl = chemical, enrch = enriched, fiss = fissile, FP = fission products, GWe = electrical gigawatt, radgl = radiological.
Sources: Report of the American Physical Society Study Group on Nuclear Fuel Cycles, *Reviews of Modern Physics*, vol. 50, no. 1, part II, January, 1978; Office of Technology Assessment, *Nuclear Proliferation and Safeguards* (Washington, D.C., 1977).

(continued)

(Appendix 3.2 continued)

*Definition of ranking in factors**

• *Quality.* The two categories under this heading relate to before and after possible isotopic enrichment beyond the state in which the material occurs ordinarily in the fuel cycle. The rankings are: 5 = uranium with U-235 > 90 percent; 4 = uranium with 60 percent < U-235 < 90 percent or U-233 > 40 percent, or plutonium with over 75 percent fissile isotopes: 3 = plutonium with less than 75 percent fissile isotopes; 2 would be reserved for uranium with 20 percent < U-235 < 60 percent or 12 percent < U-233 < 40 percent; and 1 would relate to material, such as tritium or uranium with lower fissile concentrations than those already listed, which can play useful supporting roles in nuclear weapons but cannot by itself initiate a nuclear explosion.

• *Quantity.* Here the number of critical masses per 1-GWe reactor per year is the key to the rankings: 5 = > 100 critical masses (that is less than 1 percent/yr diversion yields a 'bomb quantity' of material); 4 = 30 to 100 critical masses; 3 = 10 to 30; 2 = 3 to 10; 1 = < 3.

• *Chemical barriers.* 5 = fissile material in metallic form and not mixed with effective dilutant; 4 = fissile material in oxide form and not mixed with effective dilutant; 3 = plutonium mixed with significant non-fissile uranium; 2 = plutonium mixed with fission products and non-fissile uranium; 1 = plutonium or uranium-233 mixed with fission products and thorium.

• *Radiological barriers.* 5 = radiation levels associated with high-enriched U-235, or lower; 4 = those associated with various plutonium mixtures; 3 = those associated with uranium-233 and associated isotopes; 2 = those associated with low-burn-up reactor fuel; 1 = those associated with high-burn-up reactor fuel.

• *Detectability.* While a more refined indexing scheme could certainly be developed, only two factors have been considered here: first (from easiest to hardest to detect), whether diversion requires qualitatively new operations (for example, reprocessing from an otherwise once-through fuel cycle), significant modification of existing operations (for example, use of an enrichment facility to attain a much higher U-235 percentage than for reactor fuel), or simply the redirection of existing process streams (as in plutonium diversion from a fuel cycle that is already recycling it); and, second, whether the radiological signature of the material is unusually helpful for monitoring.

*Source: John Holdren, "Civilian Nuclear Technologies and Nuclear Weapons Proliferation," in C. Schaerf *et al.*, *New Technologies and the Arms Race,* St. Martin's Press, New York, 1989, pp. 182–185; cited by permission of the author.

Notes

1. R. Jeffrey Smith, "North Korea May Consider Reducing Atom Program," *Washington Post* wire service story, June 22, 1992.

2. P. Hayes, "Report on Trip to Pyongyang, May 8–11, 1993," Nautilus Pacific Research, Berkeley, CA, May 1993.

3. North Korea's ambassador to Austria stated on June 11 that North Korea may make its nuclear program more "transparent" in order to show that it is not developing nuclear weapons. He cited the example of Brazil and Argentina, which had remained outside the Nuclear Non-Proliferation Treaty while achieving international legitimacy in their nuclear programs.

"North Korea Studies Ways to Make Nuclear Program 'Transparent,'" Pacific Rim Intelligence Report, Yonhap News Service, June 11, 1993.

4. A. Higgins, "Korea, Reactor," Associated Press wire story, July 19, 1993.

5. Briefing from and interview with Kim Chol Ki, Pyongyang, October 4, 1991.

6. Kim Hong-muk, "Energy Institute Reports Status of DPRK Nuclear Facilities," *Dong-a-Ilbo*, Korean, July 8, 1993, p. 2; cited in FBIS-EAS-93-130, July 9, 1993, pp. 28–29.

7. J. Bermudez, "North Korea's Nuclear Infrastructure," *Asia Pacific Defense Review* 1 (1993), pp. 4–8.

8. "North Korea's Nuclear Power Programme Revealed," *Nuclear News* (July 1992), p. 2.

9. South Korea would require U.S. approval to permit licensed U.S. technology to be transferred, probably in the shape of South Korean standardized LWR reactors. In the current budgetary climate, I presume that the U.S. Export-Import Bank and PEFCO) would neither finance nor guarantee the sale of a reactor to the DPRK by U.S. reactor vendors. Relatedly, I also suppose that secondhand reactors such as the Westinghouse 640–megawatt electric plant at Bataan in the Philippines or for sale by utilities in the United States would not be available for sale to the DPRK due to the lack of financing. Given that Japan and the DPRK both wish to settle fundamental issues (such as reparations) before they deal with each other directly in areas such as nuclear trade, I conclude that Japan would not supply LWR technology to the DPRK.

10. I will ignore here denatured high-temperature gas-cooled reactor fuel cycles as such reactors are not commercially available due to their uncompetitive economics.

See Nuclear Energy Policy Study Group, *Nuclear Power: Issues and Choices* (Cambridge, MA: Ballinger, 1977), p. 404; and American Physical Society, "Report to the APS by the Study Group on Nuclear Fuel Cycles and Waste Management," *Review of Modern Physics* 50, no. 1, part 2 (January 1978), p. S156.

11. "North Korea's Nuclear Power Programme Revealed," p. 2.

12. Nuclear Assurance Corporation, *Nuclear Materials and Fuel Cycle Services, Sources, Inventories and Stockpiles*, report to U.S. Arms Control and Disarmament Agency, volume 1, September 1983, p. 220.

13. John Simpson suggests that these figures should be: for Calder Hall reactors, 270 megawatt thermal, 61 megawatts electric (gross), and 50 megawatts electric (net); and for Chapel Cross reactors, 260 megawatt thermal, 60 megawatts electric (gross), and 48 megawatts electric (net). According to Simpson, the 50–megawatt electric figure adopted in this study may be higher than the figure that applied when the reactors were used for plutonium production, in part because the fuel now used is slightly enriched. Consequently, the suggested plutonium production rate used in this study may be overstated by up to 30 percent to 40 percent. If so, then the DPRK indigenous reactor would produce substantially less plutonium than a 1–gigawatt electric LWR rather than approximately the same amount. Thus, my conclusion as to the relative proliferation proneness of the two fuel cycles is unaf-

fected. Indeed, my conclusion that the LWR does not offer a major advantage in terms of quantities of plutonium produced is strengthened if Simpson is correct.

D. Gurinsky and S. Isserow, "Nuclear Fuels," in *The Technology of Nuclear Reactor Safety, Reactor Materials and Engineering*, volume 2, ed. T. Thompson and J. Beckerley (Cambridge, MA: MIT Press, 1973), p. 74; personal communication from John Simpson, October 13, 1993.

14. A megawatt-day-thermal is a measure of the energy released by a given mass of nuclear fuel due to fission.

15. According to Simpson, the first-generation Calder Hall and Chapel Cross reactors did not have a provision for on-load refueling.

16. Nuclear Assurance Corporation, *Nuclear Materials and Fuel Cycle Services, Sources, Inventories and Stockpiles*, report to U.S. Arms Control and Disarmament Agency, volume 2, September 1979, pp. IV-4, IV-5.

17. The Calder Hall (CH) and follow-on Chapel Cross (CC) reactors were rated at a nominal 50 megawatts electric, equivalent to 250 megawatts electric (at a conversion efficiency of about 22.5 percent). The CH and CC reactors generated 19 terawatt hour electric between 1956 and 1964, equivalent to a thermal output of 3,500 megawatt-days-thermal over that period for all eight reactors. At a burnup of 400 megawatt-days-thermal per metric ton of fuel to optimize the production of weapons-grade plutonium, about 8,750 metric tons of fuel were irradiated to a level of 400 megawatt-days-thermal per metric ton. At 0.36 kilogram of weapons-grade plutonium per metric ton of fuel irradiated to this burnup, total plutonium production between 1956 and 1964 in the eight CH and CC reactors was about 3.15 metric tons. The CH and CC reactors accumulated about 40 reactor-years of operation in plutonium-production mode up to 1964, resulting in an annual weapons-grade plutonium-production rate of about 79 kilograms per reactor-year.

Personal communication, Frans Berkhout, September 14, 1993; D. Albright, F. Berkhout, and W. Walker, *World Inventory of Plutonium and Highly Enriched Uranium, 1992* (New York: Oxford University Press, 1992), pp. 41–42.

18. If the plant were operated to maximize electricity output (as it presumably would be so long as the DPRK stayed in the NPT) with a burnup of about 4,000–5,000 megawatt-days-thermal per metric ton of fuel, then the 200–megawatt electric plant would produce substantially less plutonium (about 50 kilograms, according to expert sources) than the LWR. However, I have precluded this case from consideration in this study to simplify the analysis.

19. Albright, Berkhout, and Walker, *World Inventory*, p. 72; M. Hibbs, "South Korea Renews Quest for Plutonium Separation Ability," *Nucleonics Week*, October 29, 1992, p. 7.

20. Indeed, Wylfa power station utilizes dry storage for magnox fuel in the United Kingdom. Specialists state that the fuel can be dry-stored for at least a decade or longer, but great care must be taken; and dry storage will not handle all aspects of spent-fuel storage (in particular, damaged fuel rods must be treated separately). I am grateful to insights on this topic provided by Frans Berkhout, David Albright, and John Simpson.

21. See J. Karsen Mark, "Explosive Properties of Reactor Grade Plutonium," *Journal of Science and Global Security* 4 (1993), pp. 111–28; and J. Karsen Mark, "Reactor-Grade Plutonium's Explosive Properties," Nuclear Control Institute, Washington DC, August 1990.

22. J. Holdren, "Civilian Nuclear Technologies and Nuclear Weapons Proliferation," in *New Technologies and the Arms Race*, ed. C. Schaerf et al. (New York: St. Martin's Press, 1989), p. 173.

23. S. Droutman, *International Deployment of Commercial Capability in Nuclear Fuel Cycle and Nuclear Power Plant Design, Manufacture and Construction for Developing Countries*, Westinghouse Electric Corporation report to Oak Ridge National Labo-

ratory, ORNL/Sub-7494/4, October 1979, pp. 6–122, 10–9.

24. B. Ramberg, *Destruction of Nuclear Energy Facilities in War: The Problem and the Implications* (Cambridge, MA: Lexington Books, 1980), p. 90.

25. Of course, such targeting would be illegal under international law, but this law might have limited relevance to the behavior of the antagonists in the midst of a hot war in Korea.

26. Briefing from and interview with Kim Chol Ki, op cit.

27. The DPRK imports oil, mostly from China (by pipeline) and Iran (by sea). A trickle was supplied since 1992 from Russia. Before the international situation changed in the early 1990s, the DPRK imported about 4 million metric tons per year. In 1992, the DPRK imported about 40,000 metric tons from Russia (down from its former Soviet Union level of 800,000–900,000 metric tons per month), about 400,000–600,000 metric tons per month from Iran, and about 100,000 metric tons per month from China. The DPRK is to pay for half of the Chinese oil in hard currency (although it reportedly has failed to do so, much to China's chagrin); the rest is financed by soft loans. The bulk of this oil is used in agriculture (for fertilizer production and in agricultural mechanized processing) and in the transport sector. The DPRK's two oil refineries have a capacity of about 4.5 million metric tons per year. Russia also supplies about 245,000 metric tons of coking coal for use in the DPRK steel industry, paid for in part by the barter of raw materials and goods and by the export of North Korean labor in Siberian forestry projects.

28. The seven largest thermal plants are listed in the accompanying table. The former Soviet Union/Russia supplied the technology for the following stations: Bukchang, Pyongyang, East Pyongyang (still under construction), Chanjin (which is being refurbished with Russian assistance), Wunggi, and Sun Bun. A new 170–megawatt electric station to be built with Russian credit is under discussion.

The DPRK's Seven Largest Thermal Plants

Plant	In-Service Date	Number of Units	Installed Capacity (megawatts electric)	Actual Loading (megawatts electric)	Annual Production, 1991 (TWhe)
Bukchang	December 1973	16	1,600	1,056	9.25
Pyongyang	June 1968	9	500	345	3.00
Wunggi (oil)	April 1973	4	200	146	1.30
Choq zin	March 1984	3	150	142	1.20
Sunchon	May 1988	4	200	133	1.20
Chongchongan	March 1979	4	200	116	1.10
East Pyongyang	February 1992	1	50	28	unknown

29. Rural households and agriculture reportedly use about 2.2 billion kilowatt hour electric per year. Otherwise, little is publicly known about sectoral electricity consumption.

30. A terawatt hour electric is 10^{12} watt-hours of electricity.

31. It is possible that the generation figures are more or less correct but that upward of 50 percent of generated electricity is lost in transmission and distribution and that 31–32 terawatt hour electric is the correct figure for end-use consumption.

32. The largest five are Supon, 735 megawatts electric; Hojgonggan, 394 megawatts electric; Unbon, 400 megawatts electric; Saduso, 451 megawatts electric; and Kanggye, 246 megawatts electric.

33. The 1986 contract with the former Soviet Union was for a 1,760-megawatt electric nuclear power plant. The former Soviet Union also provided technical assistance to survey potential sites. This agreement has been taken over by Russia and is on hold until the issue of IAEA safeguards is resolved.

34. W. Fawcett, *Modernization of Construction Design and Calculation Centre, Pyongyang, DPR Korea*, mission report to the U.N. Center on Human Settlements, October 1990, p. 17.

35. See R.J. Barber Associates, *LDC Nuclear Power Prospects, 1975–1990: Commercial, Economic and Security Implications,* ERDA-52 UC-2, p. 11–8.

36. On July 24, 1993, South Korea's unification minister, Han Wan-sang, said that South Korea could provide financial and technological aid for the LWR transfer, conditional upon the DPRK's compliance with the Geneva agreement with the United States. "South Korea May Help North Convert Nuclear Reactors," Reuters wire story, July 24, 1993.

37. Reuter's wire service, July 19, 1993.

U.S.-DPRK Agreed Framework on Nuclear and Related Issues: Congressional Testimony

Testimony of Leonard S. Spector,
Carnegie Endowment for International Peace

I am the Director of the Carnegie Endowment's Nuclear Non-Proliferation Project, which has staff and activities in Washington, D.C., and Moscow.

I greatly appreciate the opportunity to testify before the Committee concerning the October 21, 1994, Agreed Framework understanding on nuclear and related issues between the United States and Democratic People's Republic of Korea.

Despite a number of important flaws, I believe this agreement represents an important step forward for U.S. efforts to eliminate the threat of North Korea's acquiring nuclear arms.

Overview

Restrictions on North Korea. As a first step for assessing the accord, it should be appreciated that the extent to which it will constrain North Korea's nuclear activities is quite extraordinary. Under the agreement:

> North Korea has agreed to freeze operations at, or construction of, every nuclear facility that is of concern to the United States because of its weapon potential, and this freeze is verified by the International Atomic Energy Agency (IAEA). The IAEA has indicated that North Korea is currently complying with this undertaking.

North Korea has also agreed that it will not separate plutonium—enough for four to five nuclear weapons—from the spent fuel it removed last spring from the five-megawatt reactor at Yongbyon. Again, the IAEA has verified the status of the fuel, and discussions between North Korea and the United States indicate that the North is indeed ready to proceed with measures that will make reprocessing the material unnecessary.

Pyongyang has also agreed that it will ship the spent fuel out of North Korea and that it will thereafter dismantle all facilities of proliferation concern to the United States, again under IAEA supervision.

With the exception of the involuntary denuclearization imposed on Iraq after the 1991 Gulf War, there has never been an international agreement that goes so far to eliminate an emergent nuclear weapons capability.

Phasing of implementation. A particular strength of the agreement lies in its phasing of the reciprocal obligations it contains. Stated succinctly, throughout the duration of the agreement the United States (and its friends) will be able to determine before they act whether Pyongyang is operating in good faith and is living up to its obligations under the accord.

Under the agreement, for example, we have just provided an initial 50,000 tons of heavy oil to North Korea to compensate it for its projected energy losses from the shut-down of the five-megawatt reactor at Yongbyon. But before we took this step, we were able to verify that they had, in fact, frozen their nuclear program.

We will shortly provide about $10 million in technical assistance for the long-term storage of the plutonium-bearing spent fuel from that reactor. But before we do so, we will know that the freeze is continuing and that the North is willing to store the material rather than reprocess it.

We must next arrange with South Korea and Japan for the sale to North Korea of the two LWRs [light-water reactors] and arrange with these two countries and other friends for increased shipments of heavy oil. But again, at each step of the way, we will know before whether the North is complying with its undertakings. Similarly, four to six years down the road, before we ship key components for the LWRs, the IAEA will have to be satisfied that all discrepancies are resolved concerning North Korea's initial inventory.

The phasing of the agreement from this point on will be based on the principle of "simultaneity" rather than on the "taking turns" approach, but the effect will be the same: we will not be expected to proceed with or complete an action on our side unless North Korea is proceeding with or completing a reciprocal action on its side.

Thus as we begin transferring key nuclear components, the North will have to begin shipping the spent fuel from the five-megawatt reactor at Yongbyon out of the country, and as we complete the first LWR, they must complete the transfer of all this material abroad. Thereafter, as our side supplies additional fuel for the first LWR and continues construction of the second one, the North must begin to dismantle its most sensitive nuclear facilities (the gas-graphite reactors, reprocessing plant, etc.), and as the second LWR is completed, this dismantling must also be finished. These steps are outlined in Chart 4.1 that I have appended at the end of my testimony, which highlights this phased approach.

At any stage along the way, if the North ceases to comply with its obligations, we will hold back further compliance from our end—halting shipments of oil, transfers of nuclear goods, and construction of the LWRs—while simultaneously using diplomatic and economic pressure to bring the North into conformity with its obligations.

At the worst, should the agreement break down at some point in future years, we and our friends will still have enjoyed a period of reassurance during which we could be confident that the DPRK was not rapidly enlarging its stockpile of separated plutonium, as it undoubtedly would have done in the absence of the Agreed Framework.

At best, we will enjoy such reassurance for many years and will ultimately see the dismantlement of a very dangerous nuclear-weapons program.

Flaws—and Compensating Factors

The agreement is not without its drawbacks, however. The most serious is that it postpones the IAEA's ability to resolve uncertainties about the DPRK's past production of plutonium and, thus permits Pyongyang to retain whatever material it may now have, possibly enough for one or two nuclear devices. The agreement also fails to penalize the North for its bald refusal to permit the special inspections that the agency has sought since the fall of 1992 and for its blatant disregard of agency procedures during the May–June 1994 defueling of the five-megawatt reactor at Yongbyon.

There is no denying that these are unfortunate aspects of the Agreed Framework.

It is important, however, to realize that compliance with IAEA rules is not an end in itself. Rather it is a means to an end, namely that of retarding the spread of nuclear weapons. The Agreed Framework has weaknesses on the IAEA side of the ledger, but other non-proliferation restrictions that it imposes more than compensate for these.

In particular, the Agreed Framework's unusual restrictions on North Korea go so far beyond the normal requirements of the Nuclear Non-Proliferation Treaty (NPT).

> Under the NPT, states are permitted to build and operate any type of nuclear plant, no matter if they are optimized for the production of material for nuclear weapons, as long as they are subject to inspection. But under the Agreed Framework, North Korea is required to freeze and then dismantle facilities that we believe are intended for weapons purposes.

Under the NPT, states are permitted to separate and stockpile plutonium, again, as long as it is kept under IAEA safeguards. But under the Agreed Framework, the North has agreed not to reprocess spent fuel that it now possesses and to dismantle its reprocessing facility at Yongbyon.

As for the IAEA, although it is prevented from implementing special inspections for a number of years, it is given added responsibilities under the Agreed Framework that go well beyond its normal duties. Specifically, it is called upon to verify the freeze and dismantling called for by the agreement, as well as the shipment out of North Korea of existing stocks of spent fuel. Thus while the agreement deals a blow to the agency's prestige in one respect, it bolsters the agency in other ways.

It should also be stressed that the IAEA has played a crucial role in creating the circumstances that led to the unusual restrictions on North Korea embodied in the Agreed Framework. It was the IAEA's identification of discrepancies in North Korea's initial inventory and the agency's dogged pursuit of the matter that brought the issue to the United Nations. This led to the very real threat of economic sanctions that, in turn, ultimately brought Pyongyang to accept the extraordinary restrictions in the Agreed Framework. What we have seen is the agency successfully fulfilling its mission, serving as the trigger for a very powerful international response to a new threat of proliferation. Should similar circumstances arise in another instance, the country at issue—looking back at the agency's behavior in the case of North Korea—would have added reason to fear that the agency would discover any activities violative of the IAEA/NPT system and that it would be able to galvanize a potent reaction from the international community.

Let me now attempt to address three recurrent questions about the Agreed Framework.

1.   Are the LWRs that will be provided to North Korea by South Korea and Japan more "proliferation resistant" than the gas-graphite reactors North Korea will be dismantling;
2.   Is the Agreed Framework a dangerous precedent; and
3.   Can the North Koreans be trusted?

1. Are LWRs more "proliferation resistant" than the gas-graphite reactors?

The answer is, "Yes." The LWRs North Korea will be receiving are considerably less likely to contribute to proliferation than the gas-graphite units it now has or is building because of timing, political, and technical factors.

Timing factors. First, the most important non-proliferation feature of the LWRs is that they do not yet exist. It will be ten years before the first comes on line and even if at that juncture they posed a proliferation risk that were comparable to that presented by North Korea's gas-graphite reactors, we would still be much better off since we would have enjoyed a decade during which the threat of North Korea's obtaining a substantial nuclear arsenal would have been greatly reduced.

Political factors. Second, there will be important political restraints on the LWRs that do not exist in the case of the gas-graphite units, restraints that will substantially reduce the risk that the new reactors will be misused. The reactors will be built, and North Korean operators will be trained, for example, with the assistance of South Korean, Japanese, and possibly, U.S. engineers and technicians. It is inevitable that some of these foreign specialists will continue to work with the North Koreans to help run the plants after they are built, as is traditional in other nuclear electric power plant transfers to developing countries; indeed the presence of such foreign technicians will be essential to the smooth running of the facilities. This will be an important added safeguard against the misuse of the plants.

An additional political restraint stems from the fact that the reactors must be fueled with low-enriched uranium, which North Korea cannot produce. Thus fuel will have to be provided by a foreign supplier, with Japan probably the most likely candidate. Significantly, the fuel supply contract will permit the seller to establish clear rules about the future disposition of that fuel, including a prohibition on reprocessing the material and/or a requirement that it be transferred out of North Korea. The fuel supply contract thus provides a mechanism for enforcing the North's commitment not to build reprocessing or enrichment plants contained in the February 1992 Declaration on the Denuclearization of the Korean Peninsula that it signed with South Korea.

Equally important, the fact that fuel must be supplied from abroad will permit the United States and its friends to freeze fuel supplies at the earliest sign of improper activities involving the LWRs. In contrast, the North's gas-graphite reactors use indigenously produced fuel, providing no leverage for the United States and its friends.

At a broader—and potentially far more important level—it is also to be hoped that in ten years' time, the DPRK will be far more tractable and reliable than it is today, because of the political and economic openings it will have made to the outside world and to South Korea, in particular. This would further reduce the proliferation potential of the LWRs.

Technical factors. Finally, the LWRs are more proliferation resistant on technical grounds. To begin, as the Administration has stressed, fuel from gas-graphite reactors consists of uranium metal pellets that are inserted into tubes of magnesium-oxide alloy. The "magnox" fuel cycle assumes that this fuel is to be reprocessed soon after it is discharged from the reactor in order to extract its plutonium; thus magnox fuel is not designed to remain in long-term storage in reactor cooling ponds and will disintegrate into dangerous radioactive rubble unless extraordinary precautions are taken. (We are currently assisting the North Koreans to take such measures in an effort to maintain the 8,000 fuel rods that were discharged last spring from the five-megawatt reactor at Yongbyon.)

LWR fuel, in contrast, consists of uranium oxide pellets sheathed in zirconium alloy tubes that can remain in storage indefinitely and need never undergo reprocessing. Thus LWRs are more "proliferation resistant" than gas-graphite reactors because they do not envision the separation of weapons-usable nuclear material, while gas-graphite reactors normally lead to technical circumstances that propel the reactor operator towards the acquisition of that material—and provide a convenient, seemingly legitimate rationale for doing so.

An additional factor that makes LWRs more proliferation resistant is that reprocessing LWR spent fuel to obtain plutonium is considerably more complex than reprocessing spent fuel from gas-graphite reactors. Currently the Yongbyon reprocessing plant cannot handle LWR fuel. This means that if the North Koreans were to abrogate the current agreement, say one year after the first LWR came on line but before the Yongbyon reprocessing plant had been dismantled, they would not be able to obtain plutonium for perhaps twelve to eighteen months, providing a critically important opportunity for diplomacy and sanctions to attempt to reverse their abrogation decision. In contrast, if the North were to complete the two gas-graphite reactors now under construction and later abrogated a pledge not to extract plutonium, it could start separating the material immediately at its existing reprocessing facility.

Contingent danger vs. immediate threat. There is one aspect of the LWRs that will, however, make them more dangerous from the standpoint of proliferation than the gas-graphite units, and that is their size. The LWRs will have a combined capacity of 2,000 megawatts (electric) in contrast to the 255 megawatts (electric) of the gas-graphite reactors. This means that the LWRs will inevitably produce far more plutonium in their spent fuel than the gas-graphite reactors would have.

By the time that plutonium will be produced in significant quantities in the LWRs, however, the North will no longer have a facility in which to separate the material, since the existing reprocessing plant at Yongbyon must be dismantled by the time the second LWR comes on line. This will be one or two years after the first LWR begins operating, at which point the North will have accumulated only one or two years' worth of spent LWR fuel from that first unit. If the Yongbyon reprocessing plant has not been dismantled as required under the Agreed Framework, no new fuel will be provided for either of the LWRs. And, should an impasse be reached at this juncture, as noted above, the existing reprocessing plant would not be equipped to handle spent LWR fuel, a factor which would provide the opportunity to resolve the crisis through diplomacy, sanctions, or even military action.

As the years go by, large quantities of plutonium-bearing spent fuel will, of course, accumulate as the LWRs operate. However, unless the North is able to build a major reprocessing plant totally in secret, there should be ample warning before it could begin to extract the plutonium from the spent fuel for bombs. (Construction of such a plant, it may be added, would violate the February 1992 North South Declaration on the Denuclearization of the Korean Peninsula.)

Admittedly, the risk that North Korea might be able to build a clandestine reprocessing facility cannot be completely ruled out, nor can we rule out the possibility that some day it might abrogate all of its agreements and openly build a new plant in which it might then reprocess illicitly seized LWR spent fuel. However, these distant contingencies, against which we will have many safeguards (including continual IAEA monitoring of the LWRs), must be balanced against the far more immediate and certain threat posed by the gas-graphite reactors, the existing accumulations of spent fuel, and the existing reprocessing plant at Yongbyon—the threat that will be eliminated by the Agreed Framework.

On balance, therefore, taking all of the foregoing factors into account, I believe that the LWR versus gas-graphite reactors trade-off in this case is one that significantly enhances the security of the United States and its allies.

2. Is the Agreed Framework a dangerous precedent?

As suggested earlier, there is no question that some aspects of the Agreed Framework are disadvantageous to U.S. non-proliferation goals. The key point to bear in mind, however, is that the North Korean case is unique and the precedent set by the Agreed Framework is very complex and ambiguous. Only if similar circumstances presented themselves once again would the agreement have strong precedential value.

The case of Iran, for example, is very dissimilar from that of North Korea. Tehran argues that if the United States and its Western allies are willing to sell LWRs to North Korea even though that country is not in compliance with its IAEA obligations, then the United States and its friends cannot reasonably refuse to sell such reactors to Iran, which is fully complying with the IAEA's strictures.

To become eligible for the LWRs, however, North Korea will have to comply with IAEA rules; moreover, it will also have to go far beyond them by freezing and dismantling sensitive nuclear plants, foregoing reprocessing, shipping spent fuel out of the country, etc. Iran has not offered to accept comparable restraints, and, in the view of U.S. officials, its continued pursuit of a program to develop nuclear arms should therefore disqualify it from receiving civilian nuclear transfers.

Some opponents of the Agreed Framework argue that it also sets the unfortunate precedent of "paying off" a would-be proliferant to gain its compliance with its international obligations. Again, however, the North is not receiving economic rewards merely for complying with the requirements of the IAEA and the NPT; it is accepting restrictions on its nuclear affairs that go far beyond what these require.

Whether the United States and its friends should ever offer rewards for the acceptance of nuclear restraints, no matter how sweeping, is a larger question. Here, it is by no means clear that the North Korean case is actually setting a precedent or that if it were, it would be a bad one. Indeed, we have used this very approach in another context with considerable success, spending heavily to assist Russia, Belarus, Kazakhstan, and Ukraine to dismantle strategic nuclear systems and providing significant economic assistance in many cases to sweeten the deal. In this context, we consider such expenditures to be a wise investment for U.S. national security. It also appears that we would be prepared to restore hundreds of millions in economic aid to Pakistan if it partially rolled back its nuclear weapons program—accepting restrictions far more limited than those accepted by Pyongyang.

The Agreed Framework also sets a precedent for the IAEA. As argued above, however, while the agency's right to pursue special inspections will not be vindicated for a number of years, the agreement enhances its stature in other respects because the agency is being given added monitoring responsibilities in North Korea and because it has shown itself to be effective in triggering a powerful international response to violations of non-proliferation norms.

3. Can the North Koreans be trusted?

Ultimately, if the benefits of the Agreed Framework are to outweigh its flaws, they must be implemented, and this will depend on North Korea's behavior.

The agreement is not based on trust, however; it is based on performance. As I stressed at the outset of my testimony, each step of the way, the North Koreans will have to meet their obligations before we are required to meet ours. So far, they have done so.

Moreover, if at any point the agreement breaks down, we will still have been better off for having had it in place until that time because of the freeze it imposes on North Korea's most disturbing nuclear activities.

If we are lucky, the dialogue that the agreement fosters between North Korea on the one hand and the United States, South Korea, and Japan on the other will help to open the North to the outside world and create added incentives for it to moderate its behavior not only in the nuclear area but also with respect to missile development and sales. These may prove to be added benefits of the accord.

But even if relations remain tense, as long as North Korea continues to perform, U.S. national security and global efforts to curb the spread of nuclear weapons will be enhanced by our performing our side of the bargain.

Conclusion

In sum, I believe that the Agreed Framework, despite its flaws, is advantageous for the United States and bolsters global efforts to curb the spread of nuclear arms. I therefore believe it deserves support.

Chart 4-1

Overview of Reciprocal Nuclear Obligations under October 21, 1994, U.S.-DPRK "Agreed Framework"

Period	North Korean Obligations	U.S. and Allied Obligations
Step 1a: October 1994– January 1995	FREEZE OPERATION AND CONSTRUCTION of all weapons-oriented nuclear facilities and permit IAEA verification of freeze. Maintain spent fuel from five-megawatt reactor at Yongbyon without reprocessing (plutonium separation. (Retains possible undeclared inventory of plutonium.)	
Step 1b: January 1995		SUPPLY 50,000 TONS HEAVY OIL; initiate discussions with allies on construction of two LWRs in DPRK. SUPPLY TECHNICAL ASSISTANCE to support preservation of fuel.
Step 2a: Four to six years following date of agreement (from early October 1994 to 1999/2001	CONTINUE VERIFIED FREEZE on operations and construction; CONTINUE PRESERVATION OF SPENT FUEL. Retains possible undeclared inventory of plutonium.)	
Step 2b:		Arrange for increasing SUPPLY OF HEAVY OIL UP TO 500,000 TONS/YEAR. Arrange with KEDO for sale of two LWRs to DPRK; BEGIN CONSTRUCTION; no NSG-list components to be provided; negotiate U.S.-DPRK agreement for nuclear cooperation (before start of 3b) Continue supplying up to 500,000 tons of heavy oil annually.
Step 3a: Four to six years from date of agreement (1999–2001)	PERMIT IAEA FULL ACCESS (including special instructions) to resolve all outstanding questions, including discrepancies in initial DPRK inventory. Place any previously undeclared plutonium under IAEA inspection.	
Step 3b:		BEGIN TRANSFER OF NUCLEAR SUPPLIERS GROUP-LIST components. Continue supplying up to 500,000 tons of oil annually.
Step 4a and 4b: 1999–2001 to 2005+ *Simultaneous, reciprocal steps: U.S. action to take place as DPRK action takes place*	BEGIN SHIPMENT OF SPENT FUEL from five-megawatt reactor OUT OF DPRK. Continue verified freeze and full IAEA access	CONTINUE TRANSFER OF NSG-LIST COMPONENTS CONTINUE CONSTRUCTION OF TWO LWR'S Continue supplying up to 500,000 tons of oil annually.
Step 5a and 5b: 2005+ *Simultaneous, reciprocal steps: U.S. action to take place as DPRK action takes place*	COMPLETE REMOVAL OF SPENT FUEL from five-megawatt reactor DPRK BEGIN DISMANTLING of sensitive nuclear plants Continue verified freeze and full IAEA access	COMPLETE START UP LWR #1 (and provide initial fuel) Continue supplying up to 500,000 tons of oil annually

Chart 4-1 *(continued)*

Period	North Korean Obligations	U.S. and Allied Obligations
Step 6a and 6b: 2006+ *Simultaneous, reciprocal steps: U.S. action to take place as DPRK action takes place*	COMPLETE DISMANTLING of sensitive nuclear plants	COMPLETE LWR #2; LWR #2 BEGINS OPERATING PROVIDE INITIAL FUEL FOR LWR #2 PROVIDE ADDITIONAL FUEL FOR LWR #1
Step 7a: 2006+	Continue full IAEA access; begin/continue barter payments for LWRs	
Step 7b:		PROVIDE ADDITIONAL FUEL for both LWRs.

DPRK = Democratic People's Republic of Korea
ROK   = Republic of Korea
NSG = Nuclear Supplier's Group
IAEA = International Atomic Energy Agency
LWR = Light Water Reactor

Part Two

Economics: Sanctions, Incentives, or Development?

5

Engaging the DPRK Economically

Mark J. Valencia

North Korea's angling for foreign investment and diplomatic recognition may be the silver lining in the dark cloud of pessimism surrounding the North Korean nuclear controversy. The nuclear issue remains a significant obstacle to improved relations between North Korea and the United States, as well as the rest of the region. The United States has oscillated between using disincentives such as sanctions and limited cooperative measures as embodied in the Agreed Framework to persuade North Korea to abandon its apparent drive for a nuclear weapon. It is appropriate to examine whether expanded political and economic cooperation should be used to facilitate the implementation of the Agreed Framework. The seemingly reform-minded economists in North Korea's Ministry of External Economic Relations[1] should not be seen as anything other than loyal functionaries doing the bidding of the supreme leadership. However, if an economic incentive portion of U.S. policy pays dividends, the status of the reformers may be strengthened and North Korea will have gained confidence to expand such cooperation with its neighbors. Moreover, such economic cooperation may ease any eventual transformation of the economy. The approach might be one of step-by-step rewards for positive progress in political relations.

It should be remembered that prior to the surfacing of the nuclear issue, the general trend was toward an incipient economic opening of North Korea and an

This chapter is based on a longer manuscript prepared for Nautilus Pacific Research under a grant from the Rockefeller Foundation. I would like to acknowledge the helpful comments of Peter Hayes and Lyuba Zarsky of Nautilus Pacific Research and Chon Soohyun, Charles Morrison and especially Zha Daojiong of the East–West Center.

improved political relationship with the United States, Japan, and—most dramatically—South Korea. Indeed, there is an influential school of thought in South Korea that believes that Pyongyang's fundamental attitude is gradually becoming more positive and that to enhance long-term regional security, North Korea's tentative economic opening should be supported.[2] This is consistent with a common Asian perspective that to change a society one must engage it and influence it through a wide spectrum of multilateral initiatives. And it was only in November 1993, at the Seattle Asia–Pacific Economic Cooperation (APEC) meeting, that President Clinton dreamed of "a Korean Peninsula that no longer braces for war . . . a region where . . . security and stability are assured by mutual strength, respect and cooperation; a region in which diverse cultures and economies show their common wisdom and humanity by joining to preserve the glory of the Pacific environment for future generations." As Clinton concluded, "such goals extend beyond tomorrow's agenda. But they must not be beyond our vision."[3] Solutions to Northeast Asian regional issues may be sought through a series of concentric arcs: the immediate parties, the most intensely interested external nations, and the regional or international organizations that can exercise influence or offer assistance.[4] Present trends provide an unequaled opportunity to think boldly and to be innovative about solutions in general and about regime building in particular.

Northeast Asia and the North Pacific are still almost unique for their lack of regional institutions.[5] This impoverishment reflects the conflicts among the governments in the region, particularly the divided countries—Korea and China—which create enormous problems of membership. There is, however, a gradual development of a thin net of regional institutions covering the region in the economic, the environmental, and to a lesser degree, the political arena, but within a broader Asia–Pacific framework.[6] Indeed, a very "soft" regionalism may be emerging—associations that lack organizational structure but instead are based on the flow of capital, technology, goods, and people across ideological-political boundaries. The region is also affected by several emerging global trends—economic regionalism, the growth of natural economic territories (NETs),[7] and regional cooperation on environmental protection and on implementation of the provisions of the Law of the Sea Convention.

Multilateral organizations in the Asia–Pacific region have increased from nearly nil in the 1940s to more than seventy in the 1980s, including the quasi-governmental Pacific Economic Cooperation Council (PECC) and the Asia–Pacific Economic Cooperation grouping.[8] In earlier years, Asia–Pacific regional organizations largely originated outside the region to assist in the development of nations within the region. Indeed, the region previously obtained and maintained what cohesiveness it had through bilateral arrangements between smaller states and their protectors—especially the United States. More recently, the impetus to establish regional organizations has originated much more often from, and has been directed by, the nations within the region as self-help initiatives. This regional multilateralism is relatively new to Asia, and more regional "self-help" associations can be expected.

If the current impasse can be resolved peacefully, the general dissipation of Cold War tension and the incipient trends toward multilateralism in Northeast Asia present opportunities for involving North Korea in regional regimes. To build confidence and experience in the norms of behavior in international society, efforts to engage North Korea should begin now in relatively innocuous fields such as environmental protection and economic development. Thus, the United States, Japan, and South Korea should be ready to reach beyond symbolism to specifics in the event of progress in the resolution of the nuclear impasse. But what particular initiatives are of interest and immediate relevance to North Korea—and what specifically should the United States, Japan, and South Korea be prepared to do to encourage North Korea's participation?

The sweeping reform in former communist countries has isolated North Korea—both politically and economically.[9] Its GNP decreased by 5.2 percent in 1991 and by 7.6 percent in 1992. Food and energy shortages have spread. Pyongyang has publicly acknowledged that its survival depends on gaining foreign exchange and technology and is thus striving to rebuild its trade relations severed by the breakup of the USSR.

Before the nuclear issue heated up, North Korea was pushing for better relations with South Korea, Japan, and the United States. Indeed, desirous of Japanese yen, North Korea had begun to negotiate colonial reparations of $US 5 billion from Japan. And South and North Korea had agreed on reconciliation, nonaggression, and exchanges and cooperation. For example, discussions with South Korean Daewoo Chairman Kim Woo Choong focused on setting up light industrial plants in Nampo, building a gas pipeline from Yakutia to South Korea, using North Korean labor on Daewoo's overseas projects, and constructing road and rail links between the two.

In December 1992, a major party and cabinet change politically reaffirmed North Korea's policy of a limited accommodation with these countries and a cautious economic opening. The new leaders are more moderate and internationalist than their predecessors.[10] A revised constitution has added clauses encouraging joint ventures, guaranteeing the rights of foreigners, and establishing a basis for expanded ties with capitalist countries. And North Korea has now promulgated laws on foreign investment, joint ventures, and foreign enterprises, allowing 100 percent foreign ownership.

It has also moved forward with plans for a free-trade zone in the Rajin-Sonbong area and a free-trade port in Chongjin, as well as with infrastructure development for its portion of the Tumen River Area Development Program (TRADP). Jilin Province of China has agreed to invest in and jointly use Chongjin Port.[11] North Korea has thus embarked on an ever so tentative program of economic reform. Nevertheless, any economic opening is likely to be gradual and tempered by ideological and social discipline.

Economic Cooperation

The emergence of NETs or proposed NETs in Asia is one consequence of the amelioration of political and ideological tensions. Indeed, the very concept of a NET implies (at least in Northeast Asia) the existence of significant previous political barriers to interaction. This cross-border utilization of economic complementarities for rapid growth in trade, investment, technology transfer, and division of labor can be spontaneous and driven by private enterprise such as the "Greater China" NET—Hong Kong, Taiwan, and southern China. Others are largely the result of governmental or negotiated intergovernmental initiatives designed to combine the distinct labor, capital and natural resource endowments of adjacent subregions. In Northeast Asia, a broad NET may be emerging that includes northern and western Japan, the Russian Far East, Manchuria, North and South Korea, and Mongolia.[12]

North Korea is already involved in two regional economic activities:

1. The Northeast Asia Economic Forum[13]—a nongovernmental organization devoted to facilitation of research, dialogue, and dissemination of information on economic cooperation in Northeast Asia
2. The Tumen River Area Development Project[14]—an international free-trade zone at the trijunction of Russia, North Korea, and China that proposes to combine complementary factor inputs such as Russian and Mongolian resources, Chinese and North Korean labor, and Japanese and South Korean capital, technology, managerial expertise, and markets

Scholars have proposed two other approaches that might include North Korea:

1. An Association of Northeast Asian Economies[15]—a loose association of province-level officials and their relevant staff to discuss the "rules of the game," regional product standards, and cross-border infrastructure development plans and thus help close the information gap constraining regional decision making
2. A Northeast Asia Development Bank[16] (much more of a reach)—a regionally focused institution that would finance or arrange for financing of infrastructure and "start-up" projects, and upgrade financial capabilities while functioning as a clearing union

A long laundry list of sectoral projects has also surfaced: monitoring and management of labor flows,[17] transportation and communication infrastructure projects that would enhance economic cooperation,[18] a mechanism to improve shipping safety,[19] and management of air traffic.[20] In the energy sector, a Northeast Asia Energy Consortium[21] could promote a consensus on energy saving, diversification of supplies, integration of networks, nuclear safety, and environmental protection. It could also enhance security of energy supply and demand, examine the feasibility of large transnational energy projects, and help transfer technology and know-how.

With a further relaxation of political tension, joint ventures between North and South Korea or Japan might be possible for petroleum exploration, production, and refining.[22] North Korea's economy is faltering, and it is desperate for energy. Problems in the energy sector include institutional weakness, an ill-defined energy policy, regular bottlenecks and poor quality of fuels, and inefficiency of energy supply to the end user. North Korea's annual energy consumption has been about 42 million tons of oil equivalent (TOE), between 1990 and 1993 with coal contributing 75 percent and oil about 10 percent. In 1990, coal production was sharply reduced to 23.1 million TOE due to flooded mines. At the same time, North Korea's oil imports fell from 3.3 million tons in 1989 to 2.5 million tons in 1990 and 1991, due to cutbacks in Russian exports. In 1991, the supply again dropped sharply, as Russia cut its supply by more than 90 percent and demanded hard currency for what was delivered. A further shock was China's demand for hard currency in exchange for oil for civilian use. Electricity production decreased in 1990 to half that in 1989, and in 1991, industries were operating at only 40 percent of capacity.

South Korea and Japan have the technology and equipment to explore and exploit offshore oil, as well as surplus refining capacity, but they have little or no petroleum resources. North Korea has some oil and gas potential off both coasts but has little or no capability to explore, exploit, or refine it. Although both South Korea and Japan have supposedly secure far-flung sources of supply, they would prefer for economic and strategic reasons to have a source of energy close to home. The parties could make a deal: South Korean and Japanese expertise to develop North Korean natural resources. This not only makes economic sense but would be a tangible expression of both sides' oft-expressed desire for closer ties.

The February 1992 nonaggression declaration between North and South Korea provides for joint development of resources and cooperation in science and technology. Joint oil exploration and development is logical for North Korea, which needs energy, sophisticated drilling equipment, expertise, and technological know-how. And South Korea may benefit by obtaining energy while enhancing rapprochement.

Cooperation in Environmental Protection

Regional environmental cooperation is a "growth industry" in Northeast Asia. The 1992 Earth Summit, officially known as the United Nations Conference on Environment and Development (UNCED), brought environmental awareness to the highest levels of government.[23] In its aftermath, China, Japan, South Korea, and even North Korea have been busy establishing new institutions, commissions, agencies, and regulations to enhance environmental protection. Even before UNCED, transnational issues—both global and regional—had begun to receive renewed attention, and the necessity of cooperation on issues such as acid rain, transportation and dumping of toxic wastes, marine pollution, and ecosystem and fisheries conservation had become obvious.[24] The motives and rationale for these initiatives may be broader than concern for the environment. By calling attention to relatively politically benign but mutually threatening environmental issues, states can sometimes achieve broader objectives. Indeed, although marine environmental protection is a peripheral issue in relations among the Northeast Asian coastal states, negotiations on environmental questions may permit parties to avoid more controversial issues such as jurisdictional or fisheries disputes by agreeing to, for example, joint contingency plans for cleaning up an open-ocean oil spill, regardless of where it is.[25] Provisional agreement on environmental issues can also improve the atmosphere for further discussion of more difficult questions in other spheres.

North Korea has recently begun to show more interest in environmental matters, particularly after it was revealed that the former Soviet Union had dumped nuclear submarine reactors in its claimed waters and that Japan regularly disposes of nuclear waste there.[26] Indeed, the news that the former Soviet navy dumped eighteen decommissioned nuclear reactors and 13,150 containers of radioactive waste from 1978 to the present, most of it in the Sea of Japan, created an uproar in the world environmental community. It particularly jolted nuclear-sensitive Japan and South Korea and even drew a rare comment from North Korea. Adding fuel to the fire, a Russian naval vessel dumped nearly a thousand tons of low-level waste in the Sea of Japan shortly after Russian President Boris Yeltsin's visit to Japan.

Japanese ex–Foreign Minister Tsutomu Hata warned his counterpart Andrei Kozyrev that if Russia proceeded with its plans to dump another 900 tons of similar waste, "the foundation of a new Japan-Russia relationship . . . will crumble." But in a stunning case of the "pot calling the kettle black," Japanese Science and Technology Agency Chief Satsuki Eda admitted that Tokyo Electric Power Company dumps ten times more radioactive waste each year into the Sea of Japan than the 900 tons dumped by the Russian navy.

South Korea strongly protested the dumping by both countries. But Russia subsequently announced that it will have to continue to dump such waste because it has no place to store the liquid waste on land. North Korea severely criticized Russia for posing a threat with both nuclear arms and radioactive waste dumping while "having the cheek" to press North Korea to accept nuclear inspections.[27] Although it may have little direct connection to environmental protection, North Korea has also been diplomatically active in seeking to halt Japan's transport of its irradiated and other nuclear materials to and from Europe using both geographic and ecological arguments.

Although most scientists agree that the dumped waste constitutes no immediate threat to the environment or humans, the longer-term effects are unknown, particularly after the containers corrode. Regardless of the facts, consumers may avoid marine products taken from the Sea of Japan. Indeed, the fisheries union in Hakodate said it feared consumers would boycott their squid, a favorite delicacy in Japan.

This shock may be the critical spur needed to forge cooperation in marine environmental protection among the coastal countries. The initial report of Russian dumping has prompted cooperation to deal with this specific issue at hastily arranged bilateral Japan/Russia meetings of relevant ministers and experts, proposals for joint South Korea/Japan/Russia surveys at specific dump sites, and a call by Japan for an international cooperative fund to help Russia treat its nuclear waste. North Korea even offered to host an international seminar on regimes for pollution control.[28]

The Law of the Sea Convention heralds a new era of transnational rule making regarding national rights and responsibilities in the oceans and serves as a framework within which nations exercise these rights and fulfill their responsibilities. It has now been ratified by the sixty countries necessary to bring it into force in November 1994.[29] But when all countries surrounding the Sea of Japan have exercised their treaty rights by extending their jurisdiction to 200 nautical miles, there will be several areas where claims overlap. And pollutants at sea are easily transported across lines drawn on a map. Recognizing this fact of nature, Article 122 of the convention calls for states bordering semienclosed seas like the Sea of Japan and the Yellow Sea to cooperate with each other in the implementation of various treaty provisions. The venue for addressing issues of ocean law and policy is thus moving from the global to the regional level as nations within regions such as Northeast Asia recognize that global standards and regimes may not adequately address their special circumstances of physical geography, uses, or policies. These factors are leading to an incipient marine regionalism and maritime regime building in Northeast Asia.

Ongoing regional cooperative environmental initiatives that involve North Korea include the following:

• The United Nations Environment Program's Northwest Pacific Region Action Plan (UNEP/NOWPAP)[30] for the wise use, development, and management of the coastal and marine environment. This project has stalled due to considerable wrangling over the plan's priorities and the allocation of its costs and responsibilities, and thus needs to be strengthened.

• The United Nations Development Program/Global Environmental Facility (UNDP/GEF) Program on Prevention and Management of Marine Pollution in East Asian Seas,[31] which includes China and North Korea in its efforts to support the participating governments in the prevention, control, and management of marine pollution at both the national and regional levels. The GEF plans to spend

$400,000 per year in North Korea. And North Korea is particularly interested in participation in the proposed network of information management and marine pollution monitoring centers and wants assistance to upgrade the equipment and facilities of its West Sea Oceanographic Research Institute.

• The Intergovernmental Oceanographic Commission's Subcommission for the Western Pacific (IOC/WESTPAC),[32] which defines regional problems, implements programs for regional marine scientific research, and facilitates regional exchange of scientific data, training, and education.

• The Northeast Asian Environment Program,[33] which promotes frank intergovernmental policy dialogue on environmental problems of common concern to the region as a whole, information sharing, joint surveys, and collaborative research and planning.

Moreover, North Korea certainly has shipping and fisheries interests in the region and is a member of the International Maritime Organization and the United Nations Food and Agriculture Organization. Future regional cooperation on environmental issues might include preventing marine pollution by harmonizing national policies, laws, and regulations and developing contingency plans for dealing with transnational oil spills;[34] ensuring sustainable development of fisheries through multilateral dialogue, research, and possibly establishment of a formal fisheries management mechanism; protection of shared vulnerable marine animals and habitat;[35] monitoring, combating, and evaluating the impact of transboundary acid rain—sourced primarily from China and deposited in North Korea, South Korea, and Japan. Cooperation in trade–environment linkages may also be possible—for example, setting and enforcing a common environmental regulatory framework for products, production processes, and resource-extraction methodologies; promoting environmentally friendly "green" industries; and establishing common environmental negotiating positions vis-à-vis trade organizations.[36]

Constraints—and Suggestions for Cooperation

The United States will probably refrain from cooperative initiatives involving North Korea until the nuclear issue is resolved to its satisfaction and the future, as well as the intentions of the post–Kim Il Sung/Kim Jong Il regime, become clearer. But in the meantime, there are several subtle policy questions that should be addressed regarding U.S. involvement in economic or environmental cooperation in the region, particularly that including North Korea. Should the United States support Japan's taking a leadership role in these sectors in the region? The Clinton administration views Japan as an increasingly important global partner in peacekeeping, in promoting democracy, in protecting the environment, and in addressing major challenges in Northeast Asia.[37] But despite stated U.S. policy, different agencies of the U.S. government may be sending conflicting signals regarding the U.S. view on Japan's taking a leadership role in some sectors. Moreover, Japan has huddled for so long under the American security and economic umbrella that it has little experience in leading multilateral initiatives. Japan may thus be reluctant to lead and its neighbors reluctant—for historical reasons—to accept its leadership. However, initiatives in environmental protection could be used as a mutual confidence builder and thus become a stepping-stone to Japan's exercising—and its neighbors' accepting—its regional leadership in more critical sectors. The economic sphere is, of course, Japan's strength, and its capacity to lead in this sector is obvious. Most of Japan's neighbors, including North Korea, desire its yen—but without too many strings or too much Japanese dominance attached. Japan's participation in cooperative economic initiatives in the region would—by virtue of its economic power—be a good test of its ability to assume its status as a major power but with an unassuming, nonthreatening posture.

A major unspoken question in Asia today is how far and how long U.S. "leadership" in the region will be accepted by Asian nations. If the United States truly wishes Japan to assert more leadership and responsibility on the world stage, it should not be seen to be competing with or undercutting Japan's leadership efforts in its own region. Consequently, as in its new policies toward European security,[38] the United States should learn how to be a good follower in the right circumstances. In Northeast Asia, it should be seen as unambiguously approving and strongly encouraging Japan's taking the lead in certain sectors.

There are other considerations regarding U.S. cooperative efforts in the region. North Korea could be a troublesome partner. It may withdraw from, reject, or greatly complicate American and others' initiatives in the chosen sectors if it feels—as it often does—that there is a "conspiracy" to engage it in order to penetrate and undermine its political and social systems. But security begins at home, and its debilitated economy is a current source of insecurity—and potential instability. Clearly, for North Korea to be productively involved in any regional economic and environmental initiative would require a sea change in its attitude and openness as well as a massive training and development effort to bring its capacity up to speed. But North Korea's attitude may be modified by the "carrots" and "sticks" of external actors. If intergovernmental agreements prove unacceptable or difficult for North Korea, then U.S. activities might be channeled through nongovernmental bodies like the East–West Center, a nonprofit Asian-oriented think tank in Honolulu. Russia's involvement in regional initiatives also makes progress unpredictable and complicated because of its own instability and tensions, as well as conflicting interests between the provinces of the Russian Far East and the center.

Given the risks associated with engaging North Korea and—if U.S. rhetoric is to have any credibility—the need to encourage and permit Japan to lead in its own region, the United States should support those environmental and economic initiatives in which North Korea is participating and that show potential for success and encourage Japan to lead new initiatives. Those ongoing initiatives that also have China's participation and support should be particularly targeted since China may be helpful in encouraging North Korea's positive and continued participation.

Thus, in the environment sector, the United States might support UNEP's NOWPAP and UNDP/GEF's program—the latter through its United States–Asia Environmental Partnership Program—while encouraging Japan or South Korea to lead and support regional cooperation on trade and environment issues, acid rain, fisheries management, and protection of valuable and vulnerable species. A current serendipitous opportunity for U.S.–North Korean cooperation might be to offer assistance in monitoring and/or retrieving the dumped Russian nuclear submarine reactors in North Korea's exclusive economic zone. This could even be a joint United States–Japan initiative under the environmental wing of its global partnership.[39]

In the economic sector, the United States might support the Northeast Asia Economic Forum and the Tumen River Area Development Project, while encouraging Japan to take the leadership in discussions on an Association of Northeast Asian Economies or a Northeast Asia Economic and Social Commission, a Northeast Asia Development Bank, or a Northeast Asia window in the Asian Development Bank (ADB); a regional labor market; a regional transportation and communication plan; Northeast Asian shipping and navigation issues; and air-traffic management. Japan should also be strongly encouraged to join the Tumen River Area Development Project, at least in a modest manner. All should support North Korea's application for membership in the World Bank and the ADB if it follows up on its preliminary inquiries about joining.[40]

North Korea is also supposedly interested in joining APEC.[41] As a longer-term goal, on the economic front, the United States should consider encouraging North Korea to eventually join the PECC, and the APEC process, initially as an observer in some of the more relevant working groups. This might include, specifically, the working group on human resource development and that on transportation, which is led by the United States. In the interim, the United States might fund the Northeast Asia Economic Forum to organize a meeting to explore the whole question of cooperation with North Korea, including North Korea's sectoral interests and priorities. And assuming the trade embargo is lifted, the United States could consider supporting the Tumen River Area Development Project by high-level participation and funding of American firms to contribute to the prefeasibility studies and the environmental impact assessments.

America's stated overall policy for the Asia/Pacific region is to help build a "new Pacific community"—a vision that sees America actively engaged in multilateral economic, political, and security processes.[42] To this end, America is supposed to promote confidence-enhancing measures and regional initiatives that reduce tensions. Potentially prominent among these are economic and environmental initiatives. However, the United States has yet to articulate specific policies for the economic and environmental sectors in Northeast Asia.

To achieve a "new Pacific community," all vestiges of the Cold War in Asia must be erased, including the tension on the Korean Peninsula. It is thus vital for regional stability that every effort be made to bring North Korea into the international community. The major carrot that is being dangled in front of Pyongyang is the prospect of diplomatic relations with the United Sates and the West, the lifting of economic sanctions, and foreign cooperation in the economic development of the country. To start the process of international socialization and normalization and to build confidence, the United States should be prepared to take a comprehensive approach that includes support for specific regional economic and environmental initiatives involving North Korea. Whatever the specific sphere chosen for cooperation, the United States, as well as Japan and South Korea—all of which are clearly bracing for the worst scenario—should also be prepared for the best.

Notes

1. " 'Source' Says Pyongyang Wants to Join APEC," *Foreign Broadcast Information Service* (FBIS)-EAS-94–023, February 3, 1994.

2. Frank Ching, "Securing Northeast Asia," *Far Eastern Economic Review*, November 11, 1993.

3. Remarks by the president to the Seattle APEC Host Committee, White House Press Office, November 19, 1993.

4. Robert Scalapino, "Northeast Asia: Prospects for Cooperation," *Pacific Review* 5, no. 2 (1992), pp. 101–11.

5. Barry Buzan, "The Post Cold War Asia–Pacific Security Order: Conflict or Cooperation?" paper presented at the Conference on Economic and Security Cooperation in the Asia–Pacific: Agenda for the 1990s, Canberra, July 28–30, 1993, p. 16.

6. Charles Morrison, "Changing Patterns of International Relations in the North Pacific," paper presented to the Conference on the Russian Far East and the North Pacific Region, East–West Center, Honolulu, August 1993.

7. Scalapino, "Northeast Asia Economic Interdependence and Challenges to the Nation State: The Emergence of Natural Economic Territories in the Asia–Pacific," concept paper for the Pacific Forum/CSIS, July 1, 1993.

8. David Wolff, "The Growth of Multilateral Organizations in the Asia–Pacific Region (Graphs and Tables)," Program on International Economics and Politics, East–West Center; Lawrence Woods, *Asia–Pacific Diplomacy: Nongovernmental Organizations and International Relations* (Vancouver: University of British Columbia Press, 1993).

9. John Merrill, "North Korea in 1992," *Asian Survey* 33, no. 1 (January 1993), pp. 43–53; Sungwoo Kim, "Recent Economic Policies of North Korea," *Asian Survey* 33, no. 9 (September 1993), pp. 864–78; Nayan Chanda and Shim Jae Hoon, "North Korea: Poor and Desperate," *Far Eastern Economic Review*, September 9, 1993, pp. 16–20.

10. Merrill, "North Korea in 1992."

11. *Foreign Broadcast Information Service* (FBIS)-CHI-94–018, January 27, 1994, p. 13.

12. Scalapino, "Northeast Asia."

13. Ministry of External Economic Relations, DPRK; Mark J. Valencia, "The Pyongyang International Conference and Field Trip," East–West Center, August 1992.

14. Mark J. Valencia, "The Proposed Tumen River Scheme," draft updated from *Pacific Review* 4, no. 3 (1991), pp. 263–71; Mark J. Valencia, "Work on Tumen River Delta Will Benefit States," *Straits Times*, November 24, 1990; John Whalen, "Status of the Tumen River Area Development Programme: Progress, Accomplishments and Remaining Tasks," paper presented to the Conference on Regional Economic Cooperation in Northeast Asia, Yongpyeong, South Korea, September 26–28, 1993.

15. Burnham Campbell, "Trade and Regional Cooperation in Developing Northeast Asia: The General Picture and the Role of the Russian Far East," draft paper submitted to the Conference on the Russian Far East and the North Pacific Region: Opportunities for and Obstacles to Multilateral Cooperation, Honolulu, August 19–21, 1993.

16. Burnham Campbell, "Financial Cooperation in Northeast Asia—An Overview of the Case for a Northeast Asian Development Bank," paper presented to the Conference on Regional Economic Cooperation in Northeast Asia, Yongpyeong, South Korea, September 26–28, 1993.

17. Kim Won Bae, "Migration and International Relations in the North Pacific," draft paper submitted to the Conference on the Russian Far East and the North Pacific Region: Opportunities for and Obstacles to Multilateral Cooperation, Honolulu, August 19–21, 1993.

18. Mark J. Valencia, "Transportation and Communication Infrastructure in Northeast Asia: Status, Plans, and Problems," paper presented to the Conference on Regional Economic Cooperation in Northeast Asia, Yongpyeong, South Korea, September 26–28, 1993.

19. Joseph R. Morgan, "An East Asian Shipping and Navigation Organization: Is One Needed?" in *Proceedings of the International Conference on the East Asian Seas: Cooperative Solutions to Transnational Issues*, ed. Hyung Tack Huh, Chang Ik Zhang, and Mark J. Valencia, Seoul, September 21–23, 1992 (Korea Ocean Research and Development Institute and East–West Center, 1993), pp. 101–104.

20. Sumner La Croix, Program on International Economics and Politics, East–West Center, personal communication.

21. Allen S. Whiting, "Yakutia Natural Gas and a Northeast Asia Energy Consortium," draft paper presented at the Conference on the Russian Far East and the North Pacific Region: Opportunities for and Obstacles to Multilateral Cooperation, Honolulu, August 19–21, 1993; Mark J. Valencia, "Oil and Gas: Possibilities of Cooperation," in *Proceedings of the International Conference on the East Asian Seas: Cooperative Solutions to Transnational Issues*, ed. Hyung Tack Huh, Chang Ik Zhang, and Mark J. Valencia, Seoul, September 21–23, 1992 (Korea Ocean Research and Development Institute and East–West Center, 1993).

22. Mark J. Valencia, "The Two Koreas: Cooperation in Offshore Oil Exploration," *The SISA Journal*, December 31, 1992, p. 74; Yonhap News Service, "Experts Discount 'Rumors' of DPRK Oil Deposits," *Foreign Bureau of Information Services*, April 21, 1993; Scott Snyder, "Possible Areas of Cooperation with the Democratic People's Republic of Korea," an Asia Society research project for the Rockefeller Foundation, November 24, 1993.

23. Peter Hayes and Lyuba Zarsky, "Regional Cooperation and Environmental Issues in Northeast Asia," Nautilus Pacific Research, October 1, 1993.

24. Mark J. Valencia, editor/author, *International Conference on the Sea of Japan*, Occasional Papers of the East–West Environment and Policy Institute, no. 10 (1989), pp. 123–53.

25. Mark J. Valencia and John Klarquist, "National Marine Environmental Policies and Transnational Issues"; and Dong Soo Lee and Mark J. Valencia, "Pollution," both in *Atlas for Marine Policy in East Asian Seas*, ed. Joseph R. Morgan and Mark J. Valencia (Berkeley: University of California, 1992).

26. Mark J. Valencia, "Nuclear Waste Dumping in the East Asian Sea: A Stimulus to Cooperation?" *SISA Journal*, December 1, 1993; the DPRK wants a joint nuclear waste probe with Russia.

27. *Foreign Broadcast Information Service* (FBIS)-EAS-93–082, April 30, 1993, p. 10; FBIS-EAS-93–127, July 6, 1993, p. 35; statement by the DPRK, plenary meeting, Maritime Safety Committee, IMO, sixty-first session, December 8, 1992.

28. International Maritime Organization, Marine Environment Protection Committee 33/WP.7/Add.1, para. 13.4, p. 21.

29. United Nations Convention on the Law of the Sea, Montego Bay, December 1982, UN Doc. A/Conf.62/122, October 7, 1982; *Journal of Commerce*, December 7, 1993.

30. United Nations Environment Program, "Draft Action Plan for the Protection and Development of the Marine and Coastal Environment of the North–West Pacific Region," September 1993.

31. Hayes and Zarsky, "Regional Cooperation and Environmental Issues in Northeast Asia."

32. Ibid.

33. Ibid.

34. Valencia and Klarquist, "National Marine Environmental Policies and Transnational Issues."

35. Glenys Owen Miller, "Vulnerable Resources," in *Atlas for Marine Policy in East Asian Seas*, ed. Joseph Morgan and Mark J. Valencia (Berkeley: University of California, 1992), pp. 36–47).

36. Hayes and Zarsky, "Regional Cooperation and Environmental Issues in Northeast Asia."

37. President Clinton, "Building a New Pacific Community," address to students and faculty at Waseda University, Tokyo, July 7, 1993. *Dispatch* 4, no. 28 (U.S. Department of State, Bureau of Public Affairs, Office of Public Communication).

38. Tyler Marshall and Paul Richter, "Clinton's Agility Makes Up for His Inexperience," *Los Angeles Times*, January 11, 1994.

39. "Miyazawa Hopes to Work with U.S. on Pollution," Kyodo News Service, *Foreign Bureau of Information Services*, June 30, 1993.

40. Snyder, "Possible Areas of Cooperation"; Peter Hayes, "The Realpolitik of the IAEA–DPRK Standoff," *Pacific Research* (February 1994), pp. 25–29.

41. " 'Source' Says Pyongyang Wants to Join APEC."

42. Winston Lord, "A New Pacific Community: Ten Goals for American Policy," opening statement at confirmation hearings for position of assistant secretary of state, Bureau of East Asian Affairs, March 31, 1993.

6

Regional Cooperation and Environmental Issues in Northeast Asia

Peter Hayes and Lyuba Zarsky

This chapter deals with the rapidly emerging agenda for regional collaboration on environmental issues in Northeast Asia. In the first section, we briefly describe some of the major transfrontier or regional environmental issues in Northeast Asia that represent a menu of opportunities for cooperation (and potential conflict) between states. These issues include transfrontier air pollution, marine pollution, migratory species, and the trend toward economic integration.

In the second section, we examine the emerging and somewhat overlapping regional environmental management regimes, which include the Northwest Pacific Action Plan (NOWPAP), the Subcommission for the Western Pacific (WESTPAC), the Northeast Asian Environment Program, and the Subregional Technical Cooperation and Development Program.

Although, due to space limitations, we cannot discuss the following additional concerns at length, these issues are important enough to warrant our mentioning them briefly.

• *Capacity building:* In addition to building capacity to deal with the cross-sectoral, complex issues of sustainable development at the national level, regional programs for environmental cooperation also entail developing regional capacities in the medium and long term.

• *Regional dimensions of global issues:* Some global issues may interrelate with regional issues in ways that cannot be ignored. Climate change, for example, may redistribute regional atmospheric circulation and precipitation patterns and thereby affect concerns such as transfrontier pollution, ecosystem management, and desertification at a regional level, which will require a regional response. The impact of climate change is a candidate for regional cooperation.

• *Monitoring, verification, and enforcement:* There are important precedents for monitoring and verifying international environmental agreements, at the regional level in Europe and globally in the ozone-depletion convention. This experience provides some guidelines for how binding regional environmental agreements in Northeast Asia might be monitored, verified, and enforced.

• *Financing:* The issue of who will pay for the costs of regional environmental cooperation is central. Donors need to recognize that resources must be provided to build requisite national and regional capacity to participate effectively in regional environmental agreements; they must incorporate environmental conditionalities into development financing; and they must recast their own organizations to ensure that they identify the benefits associated with regional environmental cooperation.

• *Nongovernmental organizations and public awareness:* Without active participation by civil society, many environmental policies are doomed to failure. Regional efforts are no less subject to this imperative than local, national, or global activities. It is therefore crucial to involve nongovernmental organizations in regional deliberations and activities in Northeast Asia at the outset rather than as an afterthought.

Critical Regional Environmental Issues

This section presents brief profiles of critical environmental issues that are amenable to regional cooperation. These issues include transfrontier air pollution (we discuss acid rain as a case in point), marine pollution (we discuss radionuclides and oil), migratory species (we discuss fish), and the trend toward economic integration (we discuss forestry).

Transfrontier Air Pollution

Transfrontier air pollution at a regional level in Northeast Asia refers primarily to the "routine" atmospheric transport and deposition of particulate matter emitted mostly in the course of energy production—a phenomenon known as "acid rain."[1]

High levels of sulfur emissions from coal-burning power plants and factories in China, North Korea, and elsewhere in the region are the main sources of acid rain. One study of China's largest coal-fired power plant showed that sulfur dioxide concentrations frequently exceed the state's permissible releases because the coal that is burned contains more than 2 percent sulfur.[2] However, even low-sulfur coals can result in absolutely and relatively high levels of sulfur dioxide emissions when the coal is burned in inefficient plants. The resulting acid rain may decrease biomass productivity (thereby reducing its carbon uptake) and degrade existing forests (thereby causing the recipient country's carbon emissions to increase).

Many scientists believe that the Korean Peninsula and Japan suffer from transfrontier acid rain originating upwind from Manchuria in China. Some have also noted that Mongolia may receive acid rains originating over its northwestern border with Russia. Depending on the time of year, some countries (especially North Korea) may be both producers and recipients of acid rain.

The precise scale and impact of transfrontier acid rain deposition remain unclear, in part due to the lack of monitoring stations and ecological studies. China itself has noted the possibility that acid rain may be transmitted long distances and that it has seriously affected areas of China.[3] About 16 million metric tons of sulfur dioxide was emitted annually in the 1980s.[4] In the area adjacent to the Yellow Sea, Chinese industry has been estimated to emit about 700,000 metric tons of sulfur dioxide per year, some of which could be transported across the Yellow Sea to Korea by the predominantly northwesterly winds.[5]

In winter (January), the airflows are generally from the Asian land mass to the ocean, whereas in summer (July), the opposite is the case. The Asian Development Bank has mapped the likely geographical distribution of acid rain by using regional sulfur dioxide emissions and regional atmospheric circulation as proxies to suggest where acid rain may occur. Acid conditions (that is, low pH values such as 4.5) occur in Japan and southern China; elsewhere, pH values are much higher.[6]

Fortunately, the problem is amenable to technological controls at the source, but at a cost. A modern power plant with glue-gas desulfurization equipment can easily remove more than 90 percent of the emissions.

Also, countries in the region are moving to establish the requisite monitoring of acid rain deposition. South Korea, for example, maintains a network of 65 acid rain–monitoring sites and has opened new sites on the southwest coast and on Cheju Island. The National Institute of Environmental Studies in Japan has convened a number of regional workshops on acid rain. Much remains to be done in terms of establishing common monitoring methodologies, comprehensive baseline monitoring, and ecosystem impact studies.

Marine Pollution

Marine pollution occurs in an area in which overlapping and contended maritime jurisdictions hinder and complicate joint environmental management.[7] East Asian seas are also semienclosed and therefore particularly subject to the effects of chemical pollutants, including hydrocarbons, heavy metals, industrial and agricultural chemicals, radionuclides, sewage, heat wastes, and many other materials. The resultant ecological and economic damage includes commercial losses from fisheries and aquaculture, destruction of flora and fauna, tourism, red tides, and so on. For reasons of brevity, we focus here on just one area of the region's seas, the Sea of Japan.

Undoubtedly, the most important sources of marine pollution in the Sea of Japan are coastal (urban, industrial, port, and riverine) inflows, the dumping of shipping and industrial wastes at sea, the disposal of radioactive wastes, and oil exploration and transport. The projected economic growth of Northeast Asia implies that all of these sources could increase exponentially, while the ocean's assimilative capacity may be stretched to its limit—or beyond. In the future, exploitation of seabed minerals may also increase the stress on marine environments. In this subsection, we address only two aspects of the issue of chemical pollution in the Sea of Japan—namely, radioactive and oil-related pollution.

Radioactive Waste Dumping. In early 1993, Russia admitted that the former Soviet Union had for decades dumped civilian and military radioactive wastes in the Sea of Japan, in violation of domestic and international laws.[8]

The total quantity of radioactive materials involved in this activity was relatively small compared with other radioactive pollution during the same period. However, the Russian activity was significant because it related to legal precedent and the integrity of the London Dumping Convention, which prohibits signatories from engaging in such wanton dumping. It also highlighted the possibility of additional uncontrolled radioactive pollution of the Sea of Japan arising from Russia's military and reactors operating in the Far East.

Russia's nuclear submarines lack funds and facilities to remove old fuel rods, let alone install new rods.[9] Russia's military forces are unable to deal with the radioactive legacy of the Cold War. It is urgent that the nuclear reactors and fuel be removed from decommissioned nuclear-powered warships, especially submarines, for safe storage and disposal. To end Russian dumping of low- and high-level wastes in the Seas of Japan and Okhotsk, Russia must choose sites for interim storage facilities on its territory and then construct those facilities. Other states in the region have capabilities that complement these needs. Japan, for example, has significant experience in decommissioning its former nuclear-powered ships.

Oil Pollution. The monitoring of chemical pollution, such as oil, in the Sea of Japan is conducted at an existing network of stations that measure pollution three times (or more) per year using standard techniques, thereby establishing the distribution of pollutants and their relationship to hydrometeorological conditions. This joint monitoring effort has been under way since 1989 and involved joint North Korean–Soviet expeditions into the Sea of Japan in 1989–90.

On the basis of one measure of oil pollution—average levels of dissolved hydrocarbons—the open areas of the Sea of Japan contain about 1.5–1.8 times more oil than do the surface waters of the Northwest Pacific Ocean. In coastal regions of the Sea of Japan, as well as in shipping lanes, the level of pollution is much higher, often 2.5 times the level in unpolluted ocean waters, and even exceeding maximum permissible concentrations on a permanent basis (for example, at Russia's Golden Horn Bay).[10] Another measure of oil pollution—the concentration of tar balls in the ocean water—ranges from 0.15–1.00 milligram per cubic meter. The concentration is high along sea-lanes, especially south of Honshu. The prevailing winds concentrate the tar balls in different parts of the Sea of Japan, depending on the season. Japan reports that, overall, the quantity of tar balls drifting or washed ashore fell between 1975 and 1985 but increased in 1990 in areas of southern Honshu, the Sea of Japan, and western Kyushu.[11]

The rate of marine oil spills appears to be increasing. South Korea, for example, reports a near doubling in the spill rate and a near tripling in the spill volume for recorded spills along its coast. There have been major oil spills, including the sinking of a tanker in February 1988, which damaged 2,000 hectares of marine aquaculture at Youngil Bay, and a tanker collision in July 1990, which released 1.5 million liters of bunker C oil.[12] In August 1993, a tanker collided with another ship off Pusan and spilled 225 metric tons of bunker oil in a nine-mile-long slick that threatened South Korea's most popular beaches.[13]

Models of oil pollution dispersal show that oil slicks in the Sea of Japan could move either onto adjacent coastal regions or out into open seas, depending on tides and winds. Data are needed on estimated spill rates and number of spills per volume of oil produced or handled, as well as mean or median size of spills for the East Asian region and the Sea of Japan to facilitate analysis of the risks of oil pollution, whether from offshore oil production, coastal refining facilities and ports, or tankers in sea-lanes. Research is also needed on (1) the physical fate of oil on surface waters, in the water column, and on bottom sediments; (2) the biological effects on fish, shellfish, seabirds, shorebirds, and waterfowl, as well as on seasonal primary, secondary, and benthic productivity; and (3) economic damages, including cleanup costs.[14]

Prevention of marine pollution is not yet a major environmental issue in the littoral states of the Sea of Japan. However, cooperation to reduce and control marine pollution could also foster a dialogue on the overarching issue of how parties that disagree on territorial boundaries and are divided over the best way to manage fisheries stocks on a sustainable basis can jointly and holistically manage an oceanic ecosystem.

These latter problems could hinder the development of collaborative approaches to reducing marine pollution because the legal status of semienclosed oceans remains ambiguous under customary law and the law of the seas. As Mark Valencia puts it:

> The most successful efforts to deal with marine environmental problems are carefully nurtured with simultaneous institution-building, scientific, and treaty-drafting activities at the regional level, but this can come about only with strong and sustained littoral state support.[15]

The scope and complexity of achieving cooperative management of the various environmental problems that afflict the Sea of Japan—all of which involve multiple economic sectors and overlapping jurisdictions, and all of which are linked to marine pollution—are daunting.

The first step must be to obtain scientifically valid data on pollution levels. Achieving this goal requires the use of sophisticated research equipment. As such equipment is available in sufficient quantity and quality only in Japan and South Korea, controlling marine pollution in the Sea of Japan must begin with a joint effort to implement a comprehensive and complete monitoring program to determine the region's ecological status. Valencia has argued that regional cooperation would be useful to intercalibrate measuring methods; determine indicator species; study the biogeochemical flows of pollutants at the river/ocean, water/sediment, and air/water interfaces; monitor dump sites for dredged materials; and automate the collection and analysis of data.[16]

Russia has proposed that a regional center be established to expand the marine pollution observation system, conduct joint research expeditions in the Sea of Japan and the Yellow Sea, and set up a database on marine environmental quality, a proposal that the Republic of Korea has also made.[17] The ROK has suggested as well that an international agreement for the prevention of marine pollution in the region be concluded and that a regional oil spill contingency plan be established to respond to accidental releases.[18]

Migratory Animals—Fish

This subsection describes the basic dilemmas involved with joint management of migratory fish species in East Asian oceans. Due to space limitations, we do not address the issues of trade in endangered species, preservation of critical habitats (especially transborder areas), or migratory bird species, although these are all important environmental priorities for regional action.

The North Pacific and the semienclosed East Asian seas are among the most heavily fished—and overfished—bodies of water. In terms of tonnage produced, the North Pacific as a whole is the most important fishing region in the world. Regional states are highly dependent on this produce. Japan and the two Koreas derive about 90 percent of their respective catches from the region, and Russia and China about 30 and 10 percent, respectively. An acute problem associated with high-seas fisheries in the Northwest Pacific and East Asian seas is that of straddling and highly migratory stocks—that is, species such as tuna and many kinds of groundfish and pelagic fish that migrate between the high seas and exclusive economic zones (EEZs) of states, as well as between EEZs.[19] Indeed, the majority of the fish now exploited by countries adjacent to the East Asian seas are shared stocks.[20]

A regional approach may be appropriate for jointly managing the fisheries of the enclosed Sea of Japan and Sea of Okhotsk as well as adjacent coastal areas. There are bilateral fishery agreements between Japan and Russia, Japan and South Korea, and Japan and North Korea, as well as between Russia and North

Korea. (A number of these agreements are nongovernmental.) The agreements establish a delicately balanced set of reciprocal fishing rights with catch quotas and specify that scientific and technical consultations be held. In some cases, joint regulatory zones are prescribed as to number and size of trawlers, type of gear, dates of operation, and catch.[21]

None of these agreements is regionwide and inclusive, and there are no regional forums in which to discuss allocation of catch. Thus, the management regime does not correspond to the inherently widely distributed and mobile fisheries resource. Consequently, a number of stocks are severely depleted. Unilateral actions to exploit or to manage the fishery stocks have even increased tensions between states—as occurred in 1993 between Russia, Japan, Poland, and South Korea over the pollock stocks in the Sea of Okhotsk.[22] Nor have larger regional or global agreements proved adequate to the task because the membership of the International North Pacific Fisheries Commission is limited to Japan, Canada, and the United States.

Some experts have proposed a Northwest Pacific approach relating to the Sea of Japan and the Sea of Okhotsk that would avoid finalizing the jurisdictional issues raised by the law of the seas and other territorial disputes but would incrementally modify existing arrangements, create regional nongovernmental arrangements, and establish a regional scientific organization. Although it would require some leadership—possibly by Japanese or Russian fishery organizations—such an approach would build on existing bilateral agreements to secure information on coastal fisheries, especially in relation to collecting statistics, performing scientific research, depicting shared stocks, identifying overfishing, and determining optimum sustainable yields from fisheries. An informal, consultative regional forum on fisheries issues along with the related fields of maritime ecology, pollution, law, and security might also be productive.[23]

Regional Economic Cooperation, Trade, and the Environment

The "environment" has typically been treated as an amenity to be balanced and traded off against economic growth. A new paradigm suggests instead that environment and development should be integrated. This notion, known as ecologically sound and sustainable development, underlies the new international consensus expressed at the 1992 Earth Summit, especially in the Agenda 21 and Rio Declarations:

> Humanity stands at a defining moment in history. We are confronted with a perpetuation of disparities between and within nations, a worsening of poverty, hunger, ill health and illiteracy, and the continuing deterioration of the ecosystems on which we depend for our well-being. However, integration of environment and development concerns and greater attention to them will lead to the fulfillment of basic needs, improved living standards for all, better protected and managed ecosystems and a safer, more prosperous future.[24]

By the same token, this perspective suggests that it is incorrect to treat environment and development as if they were separate issues. In this chapter, we adopt this perspective (shortening the concept of "ecologically sound and sustainable development" to "sustainable development") in analyzing the potential for environmental cooperation. Thus, we will discuss some of the leading economic dimensions of sustainable development in Northeast Asia as well as the more traditionally "environmental" issues of joint resource management, transfrontier pollution, and so forth.

Beyond managing common regional resources, regional cooperation in environmental management and sustainable development should be pursued when it offers net economic benefits relative to management by individual nations. Net benefits may spring from one or more of the following sources:

• Economies of scale in management, including costs of information collection, storage, and dissemination; scientific and administrative training; and establishing and operating monitoring and enforcement mechanisms

• Economies of agglomeration (the creation of one or more centers or forums for regional environmental management), including knowledge spillovers, reduced transport costs, and cheaper inputs

• Reduced transaction costs of trade stemming from a common environmental regulatory framework

• Economies of scale in capacity building, including technological, managerial, social, and physical infrastructure

• Resource pooling, which makes it possible to undertake projects in environmental management or sustainable development that would otherwise not occur

• Elimination of the "free-rider" problem, including the political, environmental, and economic costs of political conflicts arising from inadequate incentive and enforcement structures

• Elimination of standards-lowering competition

• Enhanced bargaining power in international environment, development, and trade fora, including donor agencies

Trends toward economic cooperation and integration in Northeast Asia are intensifying and create new imperatives and opportunities for regional cooperation in the pursuit of ecologically sustainable development. These trends are being pushed from three directions. First, political hostilities are softening, turning former enemies into trade and development partners. In turn, economic cooperation itself is likely to promote better regional security relations. Second, the world economy is undergoing an intensified process of economic integration. Successful development strategies in the 1990s require competitive export sectors, which can be enhanced through regional cooperation. Third, nearly all the countries in the region are undergoing a process of structural adjustment toward more market-oriented economies.[25]

Intraregional trade seems to have increased steadily throughout the 1980s and early 1990s, as regional hostilities have diminished. The precise extent of intraregional trade cannot be ascertained, since data are both hard to obtain and unreliable. According to one estimate, the (monetary) value of intraregional trade among five Northeast Asian nations increased by 225 percent between 1981 and 1989,[26] while the volume of world trade increased by only 160 percent. Trade between China and South Korea and China and Russia in the past three years has grown even faster. Intraregional trade accounted for 10.8 percent of total world trade in 1989.[27]

Links between Regional Trade and the Environment

Economic integration, especially increasing intraregional trade, presents new issues for regional environmental regulation. On the one hand, integration tends to accelerate economic growth—itself a goal of sustainable development. Without environmental controls, however, faster economic growth speeds the rate of resource depletion and generates high levels of industrial pollution.[28] Ecological degradation results both from the increased pace of growth and changes in the industry mix toward more toxic and polluting industries.[29] Besides social and environmental costs, the "grow now, pay later" strategy of development is likely to generate large environmental financing needs in the future.[30] In a feedback effect, these costs could undermine future economic growth.

On the other hand, even if nations individually strengthen environmental standards, trade-impacting local/national environmental controls will be vulnerable to standards-lowering trade competition. Environmental regulation is likely to increase production or resource-extraction costs, at least in the short term, undermining international competitiveness. In a highly competitive regional and global context, national governments are subject to economic and political pressures that push standards down. Governments may even try to gain competitive advantage by seeking foreign investment through minimal or lax environmental regulations, creating so-called pollution or resource-extraction havens. In Northeast Asia, such a strategy may be especially attractive to nations seeking to woo Japanese companies that face increasingly stringent domestic environmental regulations (as well as rising labor costs)[31] or seek foreign investment in the exploitation of forest, mineral, and ocean resources.

The pollution/resource-extraction–haven strategy in Northeast Asia is risky on three counts. First, if such a strategy is pursued by all the developing countries of Northeast Asia, a "vicious circle" of standards-lowering competition could result in an onslaught of environmental degradation. Beyond high long-term social and health costs, rapid resource depletion and ecological decline are likely to carry high opportunity costs. The income and employment stream generated by rapid and unregulated exploitation of Siberian timber resources, for example, may yield less—perhaps far less—in terms of income and employment than would the development of the Russian Far East as an international tourism asset.[32]

Second, companies and industries attracted by pollution havens are likely to be low-growth "sunset" industries, such as asbestos, which face a limited future.[33] A development strategy based on nondynamic industries is unlikely to bring technology transfer and knowledge spillovers, which are crucial to sustainable, self-generating economic growth.

Third, products manufactured in or extracted from pollution/resource-extraction havens may face import barriers in the increasingly environment- and health-conscious markets of the Organization for Economic Cooperation and Development (OECD). Northeast Asian timber resources may be especially vulnerable: global campaigns by environmentalist groups such as Greenpeace have already targeted unsustainable logging practices in the Siberian forests.

Initiatives both by governments and by voluntary national and international market-based ecolabel programs seek to discriminate among timbers on the basis of harvesting methods. Independent certifiers label suppliers or operations with an identifying mark if it can be determined that they harvest forest products according to sustainable management techniques. The global Forest Stewardship Council is seeking to go one step further and provide accreditation for local certifiers of sustainable forest products. Companies such as the consumer products giant Home Depot have announced that they will buy only from forest products suppliers whose timber can credibly be ascertained to have been harvested using sustainable management techniques. In the expectation that forest campaigns will intensify in the coming decade, Home Depot is engaging in strategic behavior and positioning itself for a market shakeout.[34]

The nations of the region could individually eschew the pollution haven strategy by imposing local/national environmental controls. However, in addition to the problem of standards-lowering competition, a patchwork of differing national regulations may impede regional trade by increasing the transaction costs of trade. Exporting companies would have to incur expenses to obtain information and adjust production specifications.

Finally, regional economic cooperation may itself create new or additional transboundary environmental externalities. Unless regulated, joint infrastructure projects such as the proposed Tumen River Area Development Project may increase the level of transboundary air and water pollution, as well as degrade cross-border habitats required to maintain the region's biodiversity.[35]

Global Trends in Trade and the Environment

Pressures for regional cooperation to manage links between trade and the environment arise at the global as well as regional level. At the General Agreement on Tariffs and Trade (GATT), a Working Group on Environmental Measures and Trade was established in October 1991. The "greening" of GATT is now on the global political agenda. Environmental groups are pushing either for greater national scope in the environmental regulation of imports or for mandatory global, minimum environment standards as a condition for accession to the global trade regime. In North America, the setting and enforcement of environmental regulations were crucial to the negotiation of the North American Free Trade Agreement (NAFTA).

The International Standards Organization (ISO) is working to develop global standards for environmental management. Although it is a voluntary organization, the ISO tends to provide many governments with both the framework and the technical specifications for setting mandatory standards. Whether through voluntary organizations or through politically pressured government regulations, the impact of environmental conditionality on traded goods and services will be of increasing importance in the 1990s.

Regional Cooperation in Trade and Sustainable Development

There are three arenas in which regional and global trends point toward the benefits of regional cooperation in managing links between trade and the environment.

First, Northeast Asian nations could cooperate in setting and enforcing a common regulatory framework for products as well as for production and extraction processes. The central aims of such a framework would be to develop common approaches to the internalization of environmental costs into output prices and to ensure that the scale of economic activity remains within ecosystem thresholds.

Environmental standards could be developed for a range of trade- and investment-impacting activities: environmental impact assessments, air and water quality, waste management, energy use, conservation of biodiversity, and so forth. The Environmental Principles articulated by the Third Program Management Committee of the Tumen River Area Development Project could serve as the foundation for a common approach to national environmental management of production.[36] The benefits of regional standards include economies of scale in information, management, and enforcement. They also eliminate the free-rider problems associated with having standards set by individual nations. It would be crucial, however, to build in mechanisms by which standards could change as new information became available or as citizen and consumer preferences changed.

Capacities for monitoring and enforcement of (regional) environmental standards could be enhanced by regional cooperation. Economies of scale could be gained through the creation of regional inspection and certification systems. A regional organizational infrastructure, such as a Northeast Asian Commission on Trade and Environment, may be needed to obtain scientific and citizen input in both the setting and the monitoring of environmental standards.

Second, Northeast Asian nations could cooperate in promoting environmentally friendly "green" industries, including export-oriented industries. Trade–environment linkages, in other words, offer not only new constraints but also new opportunities for industry growth.[37] Environmental "sunrise" industries might include environmentally sensitive tourism, forest products and fishing industries that employ sustainable harvesting methods, and environmentally sound value-added industries. Industries could be targeted with research and development support, donor support, and/or domestic credit or other subsidies. A regional ecolabel could also be developed to target "green consumers" in Japan and other OECD countries. Regional cooperation could also help to establish an international ecolabeling framework more conducive to promoting developing-country exports.[38]

Targeted industries should be dynamic, high-growth, and efficient. The additional environmental externalities justify additional support. Further research is needed to identify regional industry development projects with high technological, social, economic, and environmental spin-offs.

Third, regional cooperation in developing common negotiating postures and positions on environmental regulation within other trade organizations—including GATT, the Asia–Pacific Economic Cooperation group (APEC), and the ISO—is likely to prove beneficial. Common positions should enhance the bargaining power of Northeast Asian countries in shaping the environmental parameters of trade in the coming decade.

Emerging Regional Environmental Management Regimes

This section briefly describes four initiatives that are under way to foster cooperation on regional environmental issues in Northeast Asia: the Northwest Pacific Action Plan (NOWPAP) of the United Nations Environment Program (UNEP), the Subcommission for the Western Pacific (WESTPAC) of the Intergovernmental Oceanographic Commission (IOC), the Northeast Asian Environment Program of the Economic and Social Commission for Asia and the Pacific (ESCAP)/United Nations Development Program (UNDP), and the Subregional Program of UNDP.

Northwest Pacific Action Plan (NOWPAP)—UNEP

On the initiative of states bordering the semienclosed seas of the Northwest Pacific, the governing council of the United Nations Environment Program decided in May 1989 to prepare new action plans for seas not yet covered by UNEP's Regional Seas Program. In response, the littoral states promptly nominated national focal points to develop the NOWPAP. Officials from the six concerned states[39] met informally in Nairobi in May 1991, at which time they reaffirmed their governments' willingness to initiate the NOWPAP. Due to the wide range of early suggestions for the content of the action plan, UNDP convened an early formal consultative meeting in Vladivostok in October 1991. Experts from five national delegations (North Korea did not attend) reported on the following:

• Marine pollution monitoring in the adjacent Sea of Japan and water quality management (Japan)
• Fundamental and applied marine pollution studies, pollution-related marine ecological problems, and regional maritime pollution monitoring (the former Soviet Union, China, and the Republic of Korea)

The participants agreed that national focal points would henceforth prepare national reports for future meetings, to cover the status of the marine environment and coastal areas; national policies and measures to deal with marine pollution; and proposals for steps to be taken in a regional action plan. They noted that regional cooperation in response to a pollution emergency would be an appropriate area for joint activities in the future.[40]

At the second meeting of experts and national focal points, again held in Beijing in October 1992, all six countries were represented. At this meeting, a consultant presented a draft Regional Action Plan, which was reviewed and, in some important respects, modified (at Japan's insistence, for example, it was agreed that the section on "Biodiversity and Ecological Resources" be deleted, except for the material on wetland reserves and genetic resources).[41]

The geographical area to be covered by the action plan is not entirely clear. At the first meeting, the majority view was that it would initially cover the marine environment and coastal areas of the Sea of Japan and the Yellow Sea, without prejudice to the possibility of subsequently extending it to cover additional marine environments and coastal areas of participating states. It was also felt that the action plan would focus on marine pollution. Furthermore, the delegates reserved their right to call the Sea of Japan by different names.

Subcommission for the Western Pacific (WESTPAC)—IOC

The Intergovernmental Oceanographic Commission was established in 1960 as a functionally autonomous body within the United Nations Educational, Scientific, and Cultural Organization (UNESCO) and is charged with basic oceanographic research. The IOC's Subcommission for the Western Pacific was established in 1989. The secretariat is to be headquartered in Bangkok, which hosted the second session of the commission in January 1993.

The goals of an IOC regional subcommission are to:

• Define regional problems and develop marine scientific research programs
• Implement the IOC's global marine scientific research programs at a regional level

• Facilitate the regional exchange of scientific data, especially to developing countries
• Identify training, education, and mutual assistance needs

At its first meeting in Hangzhou, China, in February 1990, WESTPAC identified nine projects to achieve these general objectives and adopted a Medium-Term Plan (1991–95). These nine projects are as follows:

Ocean Science in Relation to Living Resources

1. Toxic and anoxic phenomena associated with algal blooms (red tides).
2. Recruitment of penaeid prawns in the Indo-Western Pacific.

Marine Pollution Research and Monitoring

3. Monitoring heavy metals and organochlorine pesticides using mussel watch.
4. Assessment of river inputs to seas in the WESTPAC region.

Ocean Dynamics and Climate

5. Banding of porite corals as a component of ocean climate studies.
6. Ocean dynamics in the Northwest Pacific.
7. Continental shelf circulation in the Western Pacific.
8. Ocean science in relation to nonliving resources—WESTPAC paleogeographic map.
9. Margins of active tectonic plates.[42]

Obviously, there may be some overlap in the activities envisaged to occur under the rubrics of WESTPAC and NOWPAP. Moreover, many of the WESTPAC activities are conducted in the South Pacific and in East and Southeast Asian oceans (thus overlapping UNEP's East Asian Regional Action Plan rather than NOWPAP). The IOC secretariat believes, however, that WESTPAC will have to draw on the stronger national marine scientific and technological capabilities in Northeast Asian states if it is to succeed.

Moreover, WESTPAC's SEAWATCH program may be helpful in the implementation of NOWPAP. Also, efforts by Northeast Asian members of WESTPAC (which includes all six states that participate in NOWPAP) on continental shelf circulation, ocean dynamics, paleogeographic mapping, tectonics and coastal zones, mussel watch, and harmful algal blooms are all either more active in Northeast Asia than in East or Southeast Asia or are implemented on a Western Pacific–wide basis without subregional focus. Although WESTPAC is less directly policy-oriented than NOWPAP, the IOC secretariat suggests that a mechanism may need to be set up to coordinate with NOWPAP, as has occurred already via the Coordinating Body on the Seas of East Asia (COBSEA) farther south.[43] WESTPAC anticipates, for example, conducting training in the field of modeling of coastal circulation in order to predict and control accidental oil spills, and is also developing a WESTPAC Action Plan as a follow-up to the United Nations Conference on Environment and Development (UNCED), both of which appear to be similar to concerns raised at NOWPAP.[44]

Northeast Asian Environment Program—ESCAP/UNDP

The Northeast Asian Environment Program initiative, which is aimed directly at policy makers in the region, arose out of a symposium held in Seoul in September 1992 that supported the development of an informal environmental network and was preceded by an earlier joint memorandum of understanding between Russia and South Korea calling for the creation of a regional environmental forum.[45] The first Northeast Asian Conference on the Environment was held in Niigata, Japan, the following October and was organized jointly by the Japanese Environment Agency and Ministry of Foreign Affairs. Delegations from China, Russia, and South Korea attended (North Korea did not attend due to sensitivities on the part of Japanese foreign affairs officials, although participants suggested that it should be invited to the next meeting, to be held in Seoul).

The first conference sought to promote a frank policy dialogue on environmental problems "of common concern to the region as a whole." To this end, the participants agreed to convene the conference regularly (in principle, annually), to be hosted by different countries in the region. In addition to emphasizing the role of local government in regional cooperation, the participants suggested the following possible priority areas for regional cooperation:

- Information sharing and exchange network
- Joint surveys and monitoring of acid rain, marine pollution, and biodiversity
- Collaborative research and training
- Case studies of economic instruments for environmental management[46]

This mandate led to the convening of the Meeting of Senior Officials on Environment Cooperation in Northeast Asia, organized by the regional United Nations Economic and Social Commission for Asia and the Pacific (ESCAP) in cooperation with UNEP and UNDP. The meeting took place in Seoul in February 1993 and was attended by the same five states (again, North Korea did not attend). The participants considered a consultant's report that listed possible areas of collaboration, and emphasized energy-related air pollution and capacity building as important cross-sectoral themes. They also suggested that only one or two substantive issues be concentrated upon at the outset in order to demonstrate the utility of cooperation and that these activities be expanded incrementally. Although they cautioned against an overly ambitious program, they also recognized that identifying priority areas necessitated the adoption of an overall strategy for regional environmental cooperation and a support arrangement.[47]

The following areas for regional cooperation were canvassed:

- Technology for sustainable development and UNEP's Regional Center on Technology Transfer at Osaka and Shiga (Japan)
- Energy issues, especially clean coal combustion (China, Mongolia, and South Korea)
- Monitoring and surveying of air pollution, especially acid rain (Japan, Russia, South Korea, and Mongolia)
- Forest decline (South Korea)
- Capacity building (South Korea)
- Information-sharing and -exchange network (South Korea)

The meeting adopted the following priority areas within which specific projects for regional cooperation could be developed:

- Energy and air pollution
- Capacity building
- Ecosystem management—in particular, deforestation and desertification
- Intercalibration of pollution measurement equipment

The meeting concluded that coastal and marine pollution issues should be addressed within UNEP's NOWPAP framework.

In mid-September 1993, in Seoul, South Korea's Ministry of Environment convened the Second Northeast Asian Conference on Environmental Cooperation at the ministerial and/or deputy ministerial level accompanied by high-level technical experts to discuss common problems, experiences with various economic instruments, harmonizing the monitoring of pollution, and so forth. The major topics considered at the Seoul meeting were as follows:

- Exploration of methods to enhance environmental cooperation in Northeast Asia, including harmonization of the ongoing environmental meetings
- Market-based policy measures for environmental management
- Pollution-measuring methods, including criteria, units, and intercalibration
- Exploration of joint research topics
- Classification of hazardous wastes
- Experiences and roles of local government in Northeast Asian environmental cooperation

These items have continued to dominate these talks at subsequent meetings in Beijing (1993), Seoul (1994), and Pusan (1995). As chair of the meetings and the lead U.N. agency for the ongoing program, ESCAP lends a more representative flavor to the deliberations, which suits foreign affairs ministries, and is less apt to take a proactive role in defining a technical basis for political consultations than would UNEP or UNDP and some national environmental agencies.

Subregional Technical Cooperation and Development Program—UNDP

In addition to UNEP and UNESCO, the United Nations Development Program (UNDP) has mediated and facilitated cooperation at a regional level. UNDP is instrumental in the Tumen River Area Development Project, which has a joint environmental component. It has also obtained agreement on two regional projects under the Global Environment Facility with developing countries of the region—one on greenhouse gases and another on marine pollution. In addition, UNDP has developed a subregional program of cooperation between six regional states on themes pertaining to sustainable development, albeit at a relatively low level of activity. These include:

• A thermal combustion and pollution reduction program, which recommended cross-border and intercountry modeling of air pollution, provision of clean coal technology, cogeneration, emission-control technologies, and so forth.[48]
• The expansion of temperate-zone food crops.[49]
• The Renewable Energy Applications for Rural Energy Supply project,[50] under which country exchanges—for example, between China and North Korea—have occurred.[51]
• The Tumen River Area Development Project, which is the most advanced of these subregional activities. It is envisaged as a multibillion-dollar project involving six regional states in which North Korea, Russia, and China will jointly develop a free economic zone.[52] The states have created a Joint Management Committee to oversee planning activities. The committee will supervise subcommissions on trade and logistics as well as on telecommunications, banking, and industry and infrastructure investment strategy.[53]

In October 1992, a preliminary environmental assessment was presented to the Management Committee's second meeting. The report stated that the hinterland, deltaic, and adjacent coastal areas were ecologically fragile and noted the paucity of environmental and resource data for the area.[54]

In May 1993, the third meeting of the Management Committee reviewed a draft set of "Environmental Principles." The following objectives were presented for consideration:

• A project goal will be to achieve "environmentally sound and sustainable development" in accordance with UNCED, international environmental laws and agreements, and multilateral donor requirements.

• Participating governments will cooperate and coordinate with each other on environmental concerns and will be responsible for preparing environmental impact assessments of projects on national territory, but coordination of environmental protection for projects undertaken within the zone by the Tumen River Development Corporation will be the responsibility of institutions specifically developed to implement that scheme.

• Member states will enable nongovernmental organizations to participate in environmental assessment procedures.[55]

Thus, the Tumen River Area Development Project may establish important legal and political precedents that will bear on other regional environmental agreements.

Notes

1. See Associated Press, "Gates Warns of Contamination in Former Soviet Union," *Washington Post,* August 17, 1992, A7; W. Potter, "The Future of Nuclear Power in the Russian Far East," paper presented to the Conference on U.S.–Japanese Cooperation in the Development of Siberia and the Russian Far East, Monterey, CA, July 22, 1993; Naoaki Usui, "South Korea and Japan Sign Nuclear Cooperation Agreement," *Nucleonics Week,* June 7, 1990, 11.

2. Fang Dong, Xu Feng-Gang, and Qui Da-Xiong, "Shentou Thermal Power Station: China," in *Energy Systems and the Environment,* ed. P. Hills and K.V. Ramani (Kuala Lumpur: Asia and Pacific Development Centre, 1990), 146.

3. People's Republic of China, "National Report of the People's Republic of China on Environment and Development," translation of a report to the United Nations Conference on Environment and Development, August 1991, 30.

4. J. Sinton et al., *China Energy Databook,* Lawrence Berkeley Laboratory, LBL-32822, rev. 2, UC-350, June 1993, VII-8.

5. M. Valencia, Chen Lisheng, and Chen Zhisong, "Yellow Sea Marine and Air Pollution: Status, Projections, Transnational Dimensions and Possibilities of Cooperation," mimeo (Honolulu: East–West Center, February 5, 1991), 5.

6. Environmental Resources Ltd., "Draft National Report: Democratic People's Republic of Korea," prepared for the United Nations Conference on Environment and Development, September 1991, 57.

7. On the jurisdictional disputes, see J. Prescott, "Maritime Jurisdiction in East Asian Seas," Occasional Paper 4 (Honolulu: Environment and Policy Institute, East–West Center, 1987).

8. See Administration of the President of the Russian Federation, "Facts and Problems Related to the Dumping of Radioactive Waste in the Seas Surrounding the Territory of the Russian Federation," October 24, 1992; translated by GreenpeaceRussia, April 22, 1993.

9. See W. Broad, "Disasters with Nuclear Subs in Moscow's Fleet Reported," *New York Times,* February 26, 1993; J. Handler, "Russian Navy Nuclear Submarine Safety, Construction, Defense Conversion, Decommissioning, and Nuclear Waste Disposal Problems," *Greenpeace Nuclear-Free Seas* report, Washington, DC, February 15, 1993.

10. "National Report from Russia Proposing UNEP Action Plan on the Natural Resources and Environment Management in the North-West Pacific," presented to the Second Meeting of Experts and National Focal Points on the Development of the North-

west Pacific Action Plan, United Nations Environment Program, Beijing, October 26–30, 1992, 4.

11. "National Report (Japan)," presented to the Second Meeting of Experts and National Focal Points on the Development of the Northwest Pacific Action Plan, United Nations Environment Program, Beijing, October 26–30, 1992, 3.

12. "Environmental Problems of the Marine and Coastal Area of Korea (National Report)," presented to the Second Meeting of Experts and National Focal Points on the Development of the Northwest Pacific Action Plan, United Nations Environment Program, Beijing, October 26–30, 1992, 17.

13. *San Francisco Chronicle*, "Oil Spill Threatens South Korean Beaches," August 3, 1993, A14.

14. D.S. Lee and M.J. Valencia, "Pollution," in *Atlas for Marine Policy in East Asia,* ed. J.R. Morgan and M.J. Valencia (Berkeley: University of California, Berkeley, Press, 1992).

15. M.J. Valencia, ed./au., "International Conference on the Sea of Japan," Occasional Papers of the East-West Environment and Policy Institute, paper 10 (Honolulu: East–West Center, 1989), 169.

16. M. Valencia, ed., "International Conference on the Seas of Japan and Okhotsk, Nakhodka, USSR, September 1989: Transnational Resource Management Issues and Possible Cooperative Responses—Summary of Soviet Papers," mimeo (Honolulu: East–West Center, April 1991), 27–28.

17. "National Report from Russia Proposing UNEP Action Plan," 14.

18. "Environmental Problems of the Marine and Coastal Area of Korea," 31–32.

19. A. Szekely and Barbara Kwiatkowska, "Marine Living Resources," in *The Effectiveness of International Environmental Agreements: A Survey of Existing Legal Agreements,* ed. P. Sand (Cambridge, United Kingdom: Grotius Publications, 1992), 270.

20. Tadashi Yamamoto and Hajime Imanishi, "Use of Shared Stocks in the Northwest Pacific Ocean with Particular Reference to Japan and the USSR," in *Resources and Environment in Asia's Marine Sector,* ed. J. Marsh (London: Taylor and Francis, 1992), 39.

21. D. Johnston and M. Valencia, "The Russian Far East and the North Pacific Region: Prospects for Cooperation in Fisheries," paper presented to the Workshop on the Russian Far East in the North Pacific Region: Opportunities for and Obstacles to Multilateral Cooperation (Honolulu: East–West Center, August 19, 1993), 3–5.

22. D. Pitt, "Fishing Countries Split on Harvests: Differences over the Pollock Catch in Russian Waters Flare at U.N. Parley," *New York Times,* August 3, 1993.

23. Johnston and Valencia, "The Russian Far East and the North Pacific Region," 29, 42.

24. United Nations Conference on Environment and Development, Agenda 21, chapter 1, Preamble, paragraph 1, June 14, 1992; emphasis added.

25. M.J. Valencia, "Economic Cooperation in Northeast Asia: The Proposed Tumen River Scheme," *Pacific Review* 4, no. 3 (1991): 263–71; Kim Sung-hoon, "Prospects for Regional Economic Cooperation in Northeast Asia: Republic of Korea's Perspectives," paper presented to Korean Options in a Changing International Order, Fifth Conference on North Korea, Institute of East Studies, University of California, Berkeley, December 11, 1991.

26. Kim Sung-hoon, "Prospects for Regional Economic Cooperation in Northeast Asia," Table 2. The five countries were China, Japan, Russia, North Korea, and South Korea. Data for Mongolia were not available.

27. Kim Sung-hoon, "Prospects for Regional Economic Cooperation in Northeast Asia," Table 1.

28. Studies of rapid growth without environmental controls include T. Panayotou and C. Sussangkarn, *The Debt Crisis, Structural Adjustment and the Environment: The Case*

of Thailand (Bangkok: Thailand Development Research Institute, October 1991); and W. Bello and S. Rosenfeld, *Dragons in Distress: Asia's Miracle Economies in Crisis,* chapters 5, 6, 11, and 12 (San Francisco: Food First, 1990). See also Republic of Korea, Ministry of Environment, "National Report of the Republic of Korea to UNCED 1992," December 1992. For a general equilibrium model of the relationship between resource depletion and increases in demand, see W. Cruz and R. Repetto, *The Environmental Effects of Stabilization and Structural Adjustment Programs: The Philippines Case* (Washington, DC: World Resources Institute, September 1992).

29. H. Hettige, R. Lucas, and D. Wheeler, "The Toxic Intensity of Industrial Production: Global Patterns, Trends and Trade Policy," *American Economic Review* 82, no. 2 (May 1992): 478–81.

30. L. Zarsky, "Lessons of Liberalization in Asia: From Structural Adjustment to Sustainable Development," paper presented to the Regional Experts Meeting on Regional Environmental Financing, Economic and Social Commission for Asia and the Pacific (ESCAP) and Asian Development Bank, Bangkok, June 15–17, 1993.

31. Byung-Doo Choi, "Political Economy and Environmental Problems in Northeast Asia," paper presented to the International Geopolitical Union conference, U.N. University, Tokyo, September 3, 1993. Choi argues that the migration of Japan's "dirty" industries is due in part to processes of capitalist development in which nations move from labor-intensive to natural resource–based processing industries, and then to capital-intensive and technology-intensive industries. Resource- and capital-intensive industries are both energy-intensive and polluting.

32. Besides the abundance of low-quality and low-value species, the exploitation of forest resources as timber in the Russian Far East is hampered by a harsh climate, resulting in slow regrowth and high operating costs See C.A. Backman and T.R. Waggener, "Soviet Timber Resources and Utilization: An Interpretation of the 1988 National Inventory," Working Paper 35, Center for International Trade in Forest Products (Seattle: University of Washington, October 1991).

33. J. Leonard, *Pollution and the Struggle for World Product* (Cambridge, United Kingdom: Cambridge University Press, 1988).

34. J. Ervin, Director, Forest Stewardship Council, interview conducted by the author, June 10, 1993; S. Rhodes, executive director, Scientific Certification Systems, interview conducted by the author, May 7, 1993. See also Forest Stewardship Council, "Fact Sheet," Richmond, Vermont, 1993.

35. A. Rosencranz and D. Gordon, "Tumen River Needs Tighter Reins," *Christian Science Monitor,* April 19, 1993, 18.

36. See United Nations Development Program (UNDP), "Memorandum of Understanding on Environmental Principles Governing the Tumen River Economic Development Area," annex B, "Environmental Principles," May 1993.

37. K. Anderson, "Economic Growth, Environmental Issues and Trade," in *Pacific Dynamism and the International Economic System,* ed. C.F. Bergsten and M. Nolands (Washington, DC: Institute for International Economics, 1993).

38. L. Zarsky, "Eco-Labels and 'Green Trade': Towards an International Eco-Labelling Framework," paper presented to the Informal Experts Workshop on Life-Cycle Management and Trade, OECD Environment Directorate, Paris, France, July 20–21, 1993.

39. That is, China, North and South Korea, the former Soviet Union, Japan, and Mongolia.

40. "Report of the First Consultative Meeting of Experts and National Focal Points on the Development of NOWPAP," Vladivostok, October 28–31, 1991, 1–5.

41. "Report of the Second Meeting of Experts and National Focal Points on the Development of the Northwest Pacific Action Plan," Beijing, October 26–30, 1992.

42. "IOC Subcommission for the Western Pacific: Second Session," Intergovernmental Oceanographic Commission Reports of Governing and Major Subsidiary Bodies, UNESCO, Bangkok, January 25–29, 1993; "Overview on IOC/WESTPAC Activities," IOC note for NOWPAP consultation, Vladivostok, October 25, 1991; "WESTPAC Information," no. 1, November 1992.

43. IOC secretariat, personal communication, September 17, 1993.

44. "IOC Subcommission for the Western Pacific: Second Session," 8, 15.

45. F. Pinto, "UNDP Environment-Related Activities and Experiences in Relation to Northeast Asian Regional Environmental Cooperation," paper presented to the Northeast Asian Conference on Environmental Cooperation, Niigata, Japan, October 13, 1992, 1.

46. "Chairman's Summary, Northeast Asian Conference on Environmental Cooperation," Niigata, Japan, October 15, 1992.

47. "Report of the Meeting of Senior Officials on Environmental Cooperation in North-East Asia," Economic and Social Commission for Asia and the Pacific, Seoul, February 8–11, 1993, 4–5.

48. G. Redding, "Reduction of Atmospheric Pollution from the Burning of Coal: Proposed Program Strategy 1992–1996 for Northeast Asia Subregional Program," report to UNDP, June 1991.

49. N. Carter, "Northeast Asia Subregional Program, Expansion of Temperate Zone Food Crops," mission report to UNDP, June 1991.

50. G. Redding, "Development of Renewable Energy Applications: Proposed Program Strategy 1992–1996 for Northeast Asia Subregional Program," report to UNDP, June 1991.

51. "Consultation Mission to Mongolia and DPR Korea, Modified Mission Report," Regional Energy Development Program, Subprogram on New and Renewable Sources of Energy, RAD/86/136, August 1990.

52. L. Kaye, "Hinterland of Hope: Regional Powers Have Ambitious Plans for Tumen Delta," Far Eastern Economic Review, January 16, 1992, 16–17.

53. M. Miller, A. Holm, T. Kelleher, "Tumen River Area Development, Report on Consultations with Governments," UNDP, October 16, 1991, 2–6.

54. Program Management Committee, "Preliminary Assessment of Natural Framework and Environment," in Infrastructure, Industry, Telecommunication and Environment, Second Meeting, Beijing, October 1992.

55. "Memorandum of Understanding of Environmental Principles Governing Tumen River Economic Development Area," draft, September 1993.

7

Will Economic Sanctions Work against North Korea?

Kimberly Ann Elliott

The debate over U.S. policy toward North Korea boils down to one deceptively simple question: what do North Korea's leaders want? No one can be sure of the answer, and different interpretations can have quite different policy implications. If the North's leadership views a nuclear weapons option as important to the survival of the regime, economic sanctions are unlikely to force them to give it up. But if they view the threat of developing nuclear weapons as a bargaining chip, a combination of carrots and sticks may induce them to trade it away. In fact, if the bargaining-chip theory is correct, the threat of economic sanctions has been useful at various stages since 1993 in signaling to the regime when it is getting too close to the edge of the cliff.

For purposes of this analysis, it is assumed that should it renege on the 1994 Agreed Framework, the North Korean regime is susceptible to external pressure that is short of military compulsion. Given that assumption, this chapter analyzes the prospects for the effective use of economic sanctions in the ongoing dispute with North Korea over its compliance with International Atomic Energy Agency (IAEA) inspection obligations. Based on available data, I first identify potential vulnerabilities in North Korea's economic structure as well as key trading partners that would have to cooperate for a sanctions effort to have a reasonable chance of success. I then present a framework developed by Hufbauer, Schott, and Elliott[1] for evaluating the circumstances under which economic sanctions are most likely to achieve foreign policy goals. I conclude with an evaluation of the specific options facing the international community in deciding whether to impose sanctions, including what products or services might be the target of effective sanctions against North Korea and whether sanctions would be more or less likely to achieve the desired outcome as a function of how they might be applied (for example, gradually or all at once).

The North Korean Economy

North Korea presents unusually difficult challenges for countries contemplating the use of economic sanctions. The North has chosen to follow an economic development strategy that emphasizes self-reliance, and with the recent opening of Albania, it is the most closed economy in the world. This choice derives in part from ideology and the political need to control information about the outside world. It is also a consequence of the U.S. decision during the Korean War to try to isolate the North, reflected today in an embargo on most trade and financial relations between the United States and North Korea, and multilateral controls on exports of dual-use and military-related technology. North Korea's external trade is also limited for commercial reasons relating to its inability to service its external debt.

Whatever the reasons for North Korea's economic isolation, the effects of that isolation are becoming increasingly serious, compounding the problems caused by an inefficient command and control economy and high military spending (perhaps as much as 25 percent of gross national product). The Bank of South Korea estimates that the economy contracted by an average of 5.5 percent annually in the period 1990–92. Sources also report that capacity utilization in manufacturing is probably no higher than 50 percent to 60 percent and may be as low as 30 percent because of petroleum shortages and general inefficiency in the energy sector.[2] These ongoing problems were exacerbated in 1995 by flooding in some areas that resulted in apparently severe food shortages. Although there is suspicion that North Korea has exaggerated the amount of damage, the United States, South Korea, and Japan all decided, for humanitarian reasons, to provide small amounts of food aid.[3]

The North's philosophy of *juche,* or self-reliance, creates several dilemmas for the international community. Because its trade and financial relations with the rest of the world are already limited, the scope and volume of potential leverage are less than in many other cases. This limits the range of sanctions options available. *Juche* also means that North Korea imports only products that it must have to keep the economy functioning and that it cannot produce domestically; it must then export to earn hard currency to pay for the imports or to provide products for barter. This deepens the dilemma for the international community since sanctions would almost inevitably affect key sectors, including the military, and might then reverberate quickly throughout the economy. Substantial economic disruption could increase the risk of either a military response by North Korea or economic collapse, both of which the international community wants to avoid.

Table 7.1 shows the distribution of North Korea's trade by partner country. Partial data for 1992 suggest that trade with Russia declined sharply again and that Russia is now North Korea's third largest trading partner, behind China and Japan.[4] Other data indicate that inter-Korean trade has grown so rapidly since it was first legally permitted in 1988 that South Korea may now be the North's fourth largest trading partner. South Korean government approvals for trade with the North through the first seven months of 1992 reportedly totaled $387 million, with perhaps $350 million being imports from the North. This would make South Korea another important source of foreign exchange for North Korea.

Oil, China, and Iran. Petroleum products supply only around 15 percent or so of North Korea's energy consumption, but shortages would affect three key sectors in particular: the military, transportation, and food production (petroleum is used in fertilizer production and to run food-processing machinery). Transportation bottlenecks also affect other sectors, including the ability to get food from the countryside to urban areas. Reuters reported in the fall of 1993 that urban workers were going into the countryside to barter "toothpaste, soap," and other items for food, with Hamhung reportedly not having received rice rations for two or three months because of transportation difficulties.[5]

Until the collapse of the Soviet Union, that country was a major source of concessional oil supplies for North Korea; since then, Russia has put trade on a hard-currency or barter basis, and oil exports to North Korea reportedly have slowed to a trickle. China has surpassed the former Soviet Union (FSU) as North Korea's largest trading partner and emerged in 1991 and 1992 as a major supplier of oil, by one estimate accounting for 40 percent of total North Korean oil imports in 1992, possibly rising to 75 percent in 1993.[6] Although no data are available, Iran reportedly concluded a deal to barter oil for Scud missiles and related technology that may have been worth several hundred million dollars.[7] North Korea also apparently has some capacity to produce oil from coal, but it is not clear how much room there is for expansion, over what period of time, and at what cost in terms of diverting coal from other uses. The United States is also committed to supplying a small amount of fuel oil each year to North Korea as part of the 1994 Framework Agreement. Shipments have been delayed from time to time over disagreement about how the oil was being distributed and could be suspended or terminated at any time North Korea is deemed not to be complying with the agreement.

Food. In recent years, North Korea's grain output reportedly has been declining and has not been sufficient to meet basic needs, even without the difficulties of transporting food from rural to urban areas. Although the data, as usual, are sketchy and of unknown reliability, some sources put grain output in recent years at less than 5 million tons per year versus estimated demand of 6.6 million tons.[8] In 1991, North Korea reportedly concluded a barter deal with Thailand for 1 million tons of rice over two to three years in exchange

Table 7.1

North Korea's Foreign Trade by Source (in Millions of Dollars)

	Exports[a]					Imports[a]				
	1989	1990	1991	1992	1993	1989	1990	1991	1992	1993
USSR/FSU[b]	891	1,047	563	N/A	N/A	1,641	1,668	858	N/A	N/A
China	167	142	85	154	297	399	403	524	541	600
Japan	268	271	284	N/A	N/A	216	194	223	N/A	N/A
A. Subtotal	1,326	1,469	932	N/A	N/A	2,256	2,265	1,605	N/A	N/A
B. All sources	1,686	1,857	1,240	916	1,020	2,905	2,930	2,280	1,500	1,620
A/B	78.6	78.6	75.2	N/A	N/A	77.7	77.3	70.4	N/A	N/A

Sources: For 1989–91, JETRO and South Korean Ministry of Foreign Affairs, as reported in Economist Intelligence Unit, *China, North Korea Country Profile, 1992–93,* 88; for 1992–93, the Central Bank of the Republic of Korea, as reported in *The Journal of Commerce,* June 20, 1994, 1A, 7A.

[a]The data for 1992 and 1993 are from a different source and thus may not be completely consistent with earlier years.

[b]The collapse of the Former Soviet Union (FSU) further complicates the problems in compiling consistent, reliable data on the North Korean economy. Among other things, the exchange rate of the ruble has depreciated significantly, and some sources suggest that the drop-off in trade with Russia when valued in dollars was even greater than indicated in the table. An article by JETRO researcher Dr. Murooka Tetsuo presents data showing two-way trade between North Korea and Russia of only $1,142 million in 1990 and $365 million in 1991 ("The Future of North Korea Trade in Agricultural Products," *Vantage Point* 16, no. 3 [March]: 1–20).

for coal, cement, and marine products. Also in 1991, China reportedly agreed to provide some $150 million in food aid over five years, while South Korea may also be providing covert financing for food (for example, paying for a shipment of rice from Vietnam) as well as providing small amounts of rice directly.[9] In 1995, North Korea suffered a major flood and launched an international appeal for food relief and rehabilitation aid. Thus, the food situation deteriorated even further in 1995–96.

Coking Coal. North Korea has large deposits of anthracite coal, which supply about 70 percent of its total energy consumption. But it has almost no deposits of coking-grade coal, which is essential in steelmaking, and must import it. As with oil, China reportedly has replaced Russia as North Korea's primary source for coking coal, accounting for nearly 90 percent of imports in 1993.[10] Output of steel reportedly dropped by half in 1992. Shortages of coking coal could further squeeze steel supplies and have serious follow-on effects for the rest of the economy, including in areas such as transportation that would also be hit by an oil embargo. Construction, which accounts for a significant portion of economic activity in North Korea, would also be hard hit.

Technology. North Korea turned to Western technology in the early 1970s when it attempted to build a light industry export sector with machinery imports from the West. Its timing was poor, however, and it was hammered by the 1973–74 oil crisis and global economic recession. It eventually defaulted on the loans used to make the purchases and has been largely shut off from Western credit and technology since.[11]

Hard Currency. North Korea exports mainly minerals and metals, such as iron and steel, and cement; agricultural products, including fish and other marine products; and a small amount of precious metals, such as gold and silver. Exports have not been sufficient to pay for needed imports, however, and North Korea runs persistent trade deficits. Russia, responding to its own problems and to North Korea's rising debts, put most trade on a hard-currency basis in 1991. China has repeatedly threatened to put trade on a hard-currency basis, but apparently has allowed trade to continue, in part through barter.

South Korea may now be the North's fourth largest trading partner and will be an important source of foreign exchange as long as it allows the North to run large surpluses. It is also an important *potential* source of trade and investment if the nuclear and other bilateral issues are resolved. The largest single source of hard currency apparently is the pro-North Korean community in Japan, which sends anywhere from $600 million to $2 billion per year in cash to Pyongyang. Much of the cash reportedly is carried in suitcases and plastic bags on the twice-a-month ferry from Niigata by Japanese North Koreans going to visit family members in North Korea.[12]

A Framework for Analyzing Economic Sanctions

In *Economic Sanctions Reconsidered,*[13] we examined 115 cases of economic sanctions, beginning with World War I. Most of the episodes studied occurred after the Second World War, and most were unilaterally imposed by the United States (77 of the 115), with only minor or no cooperation from its allies. The United Nations was constrained for much of the postwar period by Cold War politics and, prior to the 1990 embargo of Iraq (in response to its invasion of Kuwait), had imposed mandatory sanctions only twice: comprehensive sanctions against Rhodesia from 1966 to 1979 and an arms embargo of South Africa from 1977 to 1994. Since 1990, the United Nations has imposed comprehensive sanctions against Iraq, Serbia, and Haiti, and arms embargoes against a number of countries suffering from civil unrest, including Somalia, Sudan, Liberia, and Rwanda, and the UNITA rebels in Angola. The goals of economic sanctions have ranged from the relatively modest, such as the United States' seeking to settle expropriation disputes with developing countries, to the highly ambitious, such as ending apartheid in South Africa.

The present author with several colleagues made judgments about the outcome in each case—the extent to which stated foreign policy goals were achieved—*and* the contribution made to that outcome by sanctions. We then developed a set of six political and five economic variables that might be expected to affect the effectiveness of sanctions. These eleven variables are summarized in table 7.2. By comparing outcomes across cases with the values for the economic and political variables, we were able to draw conclusions about some of the factors that appear to influence the effectiveness of economic sanctions in achieving foreign policy goals.

As noted above, the data set is dominated by unilateral U.S. sanction cases, which suggests several caveats in interpreting the observed negative correlation between the probability of a sanctions success and the extent of international cooperation. First, in a great number of cases, international cooperation played no role in the outcome because the United States did not seek it. Second, cooperation was more extensive in cases involving more difficult goals, though the data suggest that it was a necessary but not sufficient condition for success in such cases. Finally, the results suggest that international cooperation has become more important over time as U.S. economic and political hegemony has declined and the global economy has become more interdependent.

Overall, we found that economic sanctions had contributed to at least partially successful outcomes in 34 percent of the 115 cases studied. The success rate for cases involving what were defined as "major" goals—such as impairing the military potential of an adversary or forcing the surrender of territory—was lower, just 23 percent. We concluded that sanctions are most likely to be effective when:

Table 7.2

Summary of Variables Analyzed

Variables having a positive relationship with success	Variables having a negative relationship with success	Variables having no clear relationship with effectiveness
Percentage of the target's total trade conducted with the sanctioner	Difficulty of the objective sought	Type of sanction imposed
Warmth of prior relations between the sanctioner and the target	Extent of international cooperation sought (correlated with difficulty of goal)	Ratio of the sanctioner's GNP to that of the target (most sanctioners in the sample are much larger than their targets)
Cost to the target as a percentage of its GNP	Cost the sanctioner imposes on itself	Use by the sanctioner of accompanying policies (covert, quasi-military, or regular military)
	Offsetting assistance received by the target from a third party	
	Economic health and political stability of the target	

- The *goal* is relatively modest, thus lessening the importance of *multilateral cooperation,* which often is difficult to obtain, and reducing the chances a rival power will bother to step in with *offsetting assistance.*
- The target is *economically weak and politically unstable* even before sanctions are imposed.
- The sanctioner and its target are *friendly* toward one another and *conduct substantial trade* (the sanctioner accounted for 28 percent of the average target's trade in all success cases but only 19 percent in failure cases; in cases involving "major" goals, the ratios were 36 percent and 16 percent, respectively).
- The sanctions are imposed quickly and decisively to *maximize impact* (the average cost to the target as a percentage of GNP was 2.4 percent in all success cases and 1 percent in failure cases; in cases involving "major" goals, the figures were 4.5 percent and 0.5 percent, respectively).
- The sanctioner *avoids high costs to itself.*

In sum, economic sanctions succeed when the economic and political costs of the sanctions to the target outweigh the costs it expects to incur from complying. Multilateral sanctions under the auspices of the United Nations typically involve ambitious objectives, which runs counter to the first finding that sanctions are a limited instrument that work best to achieve relatively modest, clearly defined goals. However, international cooperation is also likely to be more extensive under a U.N. mandate than otherwise, which may allow more ambitious objectives to be achieved. Thus, U.N. sanctions are likely to involve both higher costs of compliance, because the objective will be ambitious, and higher costs of defiance, because the sanctions are likely to be more comprehensive in scope.

A key problem in evaluating the prospects for success in a given case is that, while the costs of defiance—the likely economic impact of the sanctions—can be measured with some confidence, the costs of compliance cannot be measured in any precise way. A second problem is that the same cost, measured as a percentage of GNP, may be valued differently by different types of regimes. For example, an authoritarian government may be less responsive to the pain inflicted by economic sanctions than a democratic government whose survival depends on the support of a majority of its citizens. The normal problems associated with predicting the response of a targeted government are compounded when the regime is as secretive as that of Kim Il Sung and, now, Kim Jong Il.

Applying the Framework to North Korea

This section takes each of the five major conclusions outlined above in turn and applies them to the North Korean case.

Goals, Cooperation, and Offsetting Assistance. Inducing North Korea to abandon its suspected nuclear weapons program is a high-profile, ambitious objective. A secondary, but important, goal is preserving the integrity of the international nonproliferation regime. Thus, international cooperation is important. From the U.S. perspective, cooperation is essential because the United States already has banned virtually all trade and financial relations with North Korea since 1950 and thus has very little negative economic leverage available to it.[14]

Fears of unintended consequences, however, complicate the decision to impose economic sanctions for North Korea's immediate neighbors. South Korea and Japan would not want to provoke the North into a rash military response, and no one, especially South Korea, wants to risk an economic collapse that could make eventual reunification even more costly for the South, in relative terms, than German reunification was for the Federal Republic of Germany. In addition to these concerns, China may also be reluctant to acquiesce in U.N. sanctions to enforce antiproliferation objectives, an ongoing sore spot in its own bilateral relations with the United States. In addition to Chinese approval or abstention, multilateral U.N. sanctions would also require approval or acquiescence from Russia, which has a U.N. Security Council veto and which has expressed displeasure in past deliberations at not being consulted by the United States on this issue. Even if comprehensive U.N. sanctions were eventually imposed, however,

Iran and Libya could provide significant offsetting assistance through continued oil shipments.

Economic Health and Political Stability. North Korea's economy appears to be under severe stress, but that has not yet translated into clear signs of political instability, though there were reports of food riots in the summer of 1992 and again in the spring of 1993.[15] Visitors to Pyongyang and the countryside in 1995 reported visible signs of an energy crisis—flood damage, and food shortages. The number of defectors crossing the Chinese border has also increased.

Diplomatic and Trade Relations Prior to Sanctions. The volume of potential economic leverage is limited because of North Korea's self-imposed isolation, which has been involuntarily deepened as a result of the regime's inability to generate the hard currency needed to pay for imports and the unwillingness of China and Russia to continue providing goods on concessional terms. Still, if China, Japan, and Russia were to cooperate, the sanctions would cover probably 70 percent of North Korea's reported trade flows, well above the average in past successful cases (36 percent in difficult cases).

Potential Economic Costs of Sanctions to the Target. If North Korea's foreign trade accounts for 10 to 15 percent of GNP, comprehensive U.N. sanctions could easily impose an economic cost on North Korea at least equal to the average for past successful cases with ambitious objectives (4.5 percent of GNP), even allowing for extensive evasion and smuggling.[16]

Economic Costs to the Sanctioner. The obverse of North Korea's relative autarky is that its trade is not large enough to be of much economic importance to its partners. But the potential costs if sanctions provoke a military response from North Korea or an economic and political collapse could be quite high. Concerns about these potential costs have been a major factor dictating the cautious strategy followed to date.

Sanctions Alternatives with Respect to North Korea

The Hufbauer, Schott, and Elliott analysis revealed a strong correlation between the estimated economic costs to the target of sanctions and the probability of success. We concluded that a gradual, "turning the screws" strategy is less likely to be successful than quick, comprehensive, *decisive* imposition of economic sanctions because, "[t]ime affords the target the opportunity to adjust: to find alternative suppliers, to build new alliances, and to mobilize domestic opinion in support of its policies."[17] And to reiterate, raising the costs of defiance may be particularly important when the price the target must pay for complying with sanctioners' demands is perceived to be high.

In contrast, the sanctions strategy proposed in June 1994 by the Clinton administration would have begun with modest, primarily symbolic sanctions, which would be ratcheted up if necessary. Such cautious gradualism might be dictated in future application of sanctions by the concerns of North Korea's neighbors, who would be primarily responsible for enforcing the sanctions and who do not want to provoke either a military backlash or a destabilizing and costly economic collapse. North Korea has threatened to treat the imposition of sanctions as an act of war and explicitly threatened Japan with "deserving punishment" if it cooperated with U.S. proposals to cut off the flow of funds from the Korean community in Japan.[18]

If the DPRK reneges on the Agreed Framework, however, economic sanctions will quickly return to the agenda. If the gradual strategy proposed in 1994 were revived, the first phase would involve boycotting North Korean arms exports, which would cost the regime an estimated $50 million to $100 million a year. Other sanctions in the initial phase might include suspending all United Nations projects, as well as plans for the much larger Tumen River project. Cultural, scientific, and educational exchanges would also be cut off.[19] This first phase would also presumably include a cut-off of the fuel oil shipments, cooperation on the light-water reactors and other forms of cooperation agreed in the framework. In the second phase all financial transactions likely would be banned, including North Korea's single largest source of foreign exchange, the remittances from Koreans in Japan. A ban on financial transactions would inhibit the regime's ability to import oil, food, and other products even without imposing sanctions directly on exports to North Korea. This measure would be deferred to the second phase because of Japanese reluctance to be out front on sanctions, fearing the possibility of backlash among the Korean community there or even terrorist acts fomented by North Korea.

In 1994, the Clinton plan for sanctions did not explicitly mention moving to a full trade embargo in a potential phase three, apparently to placate China. While China might have ultimately acquiesced in the first two phases of sanctions (by abstaining on a Security Council vote), a trade embargo would directly involve China in enforcement. One way for China to finesse this problem in the future would be to refuse to continue barter trade if phase two sanctions were imposed and to insist on hard currency. North Korea would be hard-pressed to pay its bills to trade partners if the ban on financial transactions were effective.

Virtually all of the proposed sanctions would pose significant enforcement challenges. The major markets for North Korea's arms exports, primarily missiles, are Iran and Syria. Iran, in particular, would have little incentive to cooperate in the sanctions effort. Iran might also be willing to ignore broader trade sanctions and take China's place as North Korea's major supplier of oil. Although a cargo-flight ban might be imposed to enforce an arms boycott, a naval interdiction likely would be considered too provocative a step. Thus Iran potentially could poke large holes in any sanctions package. Even with naval interdiction, and assuming China formally acquiesced in a trade embargo, controlling trade across the Chinese border could be difficult given Beijing's sometimes tenuous control over its far-flung regions. Finally, money is a fungible commodity, and efforts to halt the cash flow from Japan to North Korea would require extensive global cooperation, as well as limits on the movement of people from Japan to North Korea.

A final question is whether to include food in any sanctions package, which would have an immediate impact, exacerbating shortages already plaguing the economy. For humanitarian reasons, however, food, along with medicines and other medical supplies, is typically exempted from sanctions outside of wartime. Moreover, the moral dilemmas raised by including food in an embargo are amplified when the targeted regime is an authoritarian one in which the people have no voice and where they are already malnourished.

Summary and Conclusions

Despite its relative autarky, what North Korea does import affects key linkages in its economy, and economic sanctions, reasonably enforced, could have significant economic impact. Modest sanctions, such as those proposed in phase one of the Clinton plan, might be effective in sending a signal of seriousness to North Korea if the Agreed Framework stalls or collapses. But such a move would be effective only if the threat to increase the pressure as necessary is believed in Pyongyang. In this, China is the key. Russia also has a veto in the U.N. Security Council and would need to be consulted on appropriate steps if it became necessary to move to economic sanctions, but China would be the vital link if sanctions were to be imposed.

If China were to veto a sanctions resolution in the Security Council, it could strengthen North Korea's resolve to stand fast while weakening Japan and South Korea's resolve to cooperate with the United States in a sanctions effort without a U.N. mandate. If China were to abstain on—or even better, approve—a sanctions resolution vote incorporating phases one and two as outlined above, it would bolster any sanctions effort. China could further enhance the impact of phase two financial sanctions by requiring hard currency for sales of oil, without being directly involved in imposing trade sanctions.

Assuming a sanctions package could be agreed on, would it be likely to produce the desired political results in North Korea? This brings us back to the original question: what does North Korean leadership want? If Kim Jong Il views improvement in North Korea's economic situation as critical to maintenance of his regime, a combination of carrots and sticks will probably be effective in eliciting his continuing cooperation on the nuclear issue. If he views the opening to the outside world that would accompany improved economic relations as a threat to his control, and if he believes nuclear weapons are essential to protect North Korea's security, neither carrots nor sticks will be effective. In that situation, sanctions might be necessary to protect the integrity of the international nonproliferation regime, but policy makers would need to be prepared to deal with the potential consequences, including a possible military response in the short run and probable collapse of the regime in the longer run.

Notes

1. Gary Clyde Hufbauer, Jeffrey J. Schott, and Kimberly Ann Elliott, *Economic Sanctions Reconsidered,* 2d ed., rev. (Washington, D.C.: Institute for International Economics, 1990).

2. *Oxford Analytica Daily Brief,* January 25, 1993; Park Young-ho, "Will North Korea Survive the Current Crisis? A Political Economy Perspective," *The Korean Journal of National Unification* 2 (1993), 113–15; Robin Bulman, "N. Korean Self-Reliance Is Source of Strength as Well as Weakness," *Journal of Commerce,* June 20, 1994, 7A; Australian National Korean Studies Centre, *Korea to the Year 2000: Implications for Australia,* East Asia Analytical Unit, Department of Foreign Affairs and Trade, Commonwealth of Australia, 1992, 50.

3. Jim Mann, "U.S. Trying to Prevent Tailspin by North Korea," *Los Angeles Times,* February 11, 1996, A-1.

4. *Oxford Analytica Daily Brief,* January 25, 1993.

5. Reuters, "N. Korea Barter System Born of Transport Woes," *Journal of Commerce,* November 16, 1993, 2A; Economist Intelligence Unit, *China, North Korea Country Profile, 1992–93,* 80; Peter Hayes, "Should the United States Supply Light Water Reactors to Pyongyang?" paper presented to a Carnegie Endowment for International Peace Symposium, November 16, 1993, 22.

6. John J. Fialka, "Review by U.N. in North Korea Case Requested," *Wall Street Journal,* April 2, 1993, A7; *Journal of Commerce,* June 20, 1994, 7A; *Washington Post,* June 17, 1994, A20.

7. Economist Intelligence Unit, *China, North Korea Country Profile,* 87.

8. Park, "Will North Korea Survive the Current Crisis?" *Oxford Analytica Daily Brief,* January 25, 1993, 108.

9. Mark Clifford, "Rice for Reunification," *Far Eastern Economic Review,* May 30, 1991, 38–39; Bulman, "N. Korean Self-Reliance Is Source of Strength as Well as Weakness," *Journal of Commerce,* June 20, 1994, 7A.

10. Hayes, "Should the United States Supply Light-Water Reactors to Pyongyang?" 22; Bulman, "N. Korean Self-Reliance Is Source of Strength as Well as Weakness," *Journal of Commerce,* June 20, 1994, 7A.

11. Economist Intelligence Unit, *China, North Korea Country Profile,* 86.

12. David E. Sanger, "North Korea Is Collecting Millions from Koreans Who Live in Japan," *New York Times,* November 1, 1993; Bulman, "N. Korean Self-Reliance Is Source of Strength as Well as Weakness," *Journal of Commerce,* June 20, 1994, 7A.

13. Hufbauer, Schott, and Elliott.

14. When the United States imposed the original trade embargo on North Korea at the beginning of the Korean War in 1950, it was comprehensive. In April 1989, the United States modified the embargo to allow "commercially-supplied goods intended to meet basic human needs," subject to case-by-case approval. Congressional Research Service, "Economic Sanctions Imposed by the United States against Specific Countries: 1979 through 1992," CRS Report for Congress 92–631 F, Washington, D.C., Foreign Affairs and National Defense Division, August 10, 1992.

15. R. Jeffrey Smith and Ann Devroy, "U.S. Debates Shift on North Korea," *Oxford Analytica Daily Brief,* January 25, 1993.

16. The methodology used in our analysis to estimate the costs to the target of economic sanctions involved, first, estimating the value of the trade or financial flow initially affected by the sanctions and then multiplying that figure by a fraction based on the availability of alternative sources or markets. The multiplier used in cases involving partial sanctions was typically .3 or .4; in cases of extreme dependence or tight enforcement, multipliers of .75 to .9 were used. For example, a multiplier of .9 was used for the boycott of Iraqi oil exports because Iraq's limited outlets facilitated enforcement, but a lower value of .5 was used for exports because Iraq's long land borders allowed for some smuggling. In the North Korean case, a multiplier of .5 applied to total trade flows (assuming comprehensive sanctions) would give a cost of 5 to 7.5 percent of GNP. Since many of the commodities North Korea imports tend to affect key sectors of the economy, a higher multiplier might be appropriate, which might raise the cost to as high as 10 percent of GNP.

17. Hufbauer, Schott, and Elliott, *Economic Sanctions Reconsidered,* 101.

18. David E. Sanger, "North Korea Threatens Japan over Backing U.S.-Led Sanctions," *New York Times,* June 10, 1994, A11.

19. Paul Lewis, "U.S. Offers a Plan for U.N. Sanctions on North Koreans," *New York Times,* June 16, 1994, A1; Robert S. Greenberger, "U.S. Proposes List of Sanctions for North Korea," *Wall Street Journal,* June 16, 1994, A12.

8

Enduring Legacies: Economic Dimensions of Restoring North Korea's Environment

Peter Hayes

Introduction

This chapter addresses the linkage between environmental and economic problems in North Korea. The first section provides basic environmental data for the Democratic People's Republic of Korea (DPRK), followed by a brief outline of the North Korean polity and a summary of the main factors contributing to environmental degradation in the DPRK. The second section examines four of North Korea's most pressing environmental problems. The third section reviews the DPRK's philosophy of environmental *juche* (self-reliance), its basic environmental law, and its environmental administrative system. The final section concludes by reviewing initiatives that could be taken to improve environmental management in the DPRK, as well as innovative approaches that could alleviate some of its most pressing environmental management problems.

Since the environmental crisis in North Korea is, in many respects, coterminous with the country's economic predicament, this chapter argues that environmental restoration is the key to a successful structural adjustment and economic transition in the North.

Prepared for the Fourth Annual International Symposium on the North Korean Economy, Center for North Korean Economic Studies, Korean Development Institute and *Korea Economic Daily,* Seoul, October 18, 1994.

Environmental Characteristics

The Democratic People's Republic of Korea occupies the northern parts of the Korean Peninsula, which is situated between the latitudes of 43°00' north and 33°06' north and between the longitudes of 124°10' east and 131°52' east. The land area of the entire Korean Peninsula, together with its more than 4,000 islands, is about 222,210 square kilometers, of which, the islands constitute nearly 6,000 square kilometers. The land area of North Korea is 122,762 square kilometers.

   The Korean Peninsula is very mountainous, with an average elevation of 440 meters above mean sea level. There are more than 100 mountain peaks higher than 2,000 meters, the tallest of which is Mt. Paekdu, at 2,750 meters. Mt. Paekdu is an extinct volcano containing a crater lake called Lake Chon. Most of the flat terrain in Korea is found on the western side of the country, with large plains such as the Pyongyang, Ryongchon, Unjon, Yoldusamcholli, Onchon, Chaeryong, Yonbaek, and Honam. The eastern side of the peninsula, in contrast, is quite steep, and its few plains lie along the lower reaches of rivers such as at Hamhung and Kumya.

   The Korean Peninsula joins the Asian mainland in the north. Its borders with China and the Russian Federation are delineated by the Amnok and Tumen Rivers. The peninsula is therefore "surrounded" by water—freshwater to the north and marine waters to the west, south, and east. The coastline of the Korean Peninsula is long and varied, with a total length of 8,640 kilometers (excluding islands). Of this, 2,495 kilometers belong to the DPRK. In addition to many islands, the coast includes numerous inlets, coves, and embayments. Along the west and south coasts, there are enormous intertidal flats covering some 700,000 hectares. The tidal range on the western aspect of the Korean Peninsula is some 11.0 meters. Reclamation on a vast scale has already taken place along this coast, and further reclamations are planned.

   A branch of the North Pacific Equatorial Current flows into Korean waters and raises their temperature considerably. The meeting of this warm water mass with the cold currents flowing from the north creates a highly productive front with a wide variety of fish, many of which are commercial species.

   Korea has a typically temperate climate with distinct seasons. The average annual temperature is between 8 degrees and 12 degrees centigrade. Average annual rainfall is 1,120 millimeters, most of which falls in summer. The range in latitude and in altitude provides the Korean Peninsula with a diversity of climatic conditions, which, in turn, has created a diverse flora and fauna. There are also a number of species of plants and animals indigenous to Korea, and many of them have survived in the north of the peninsula.

   The country has abundant mineral resources, including bituminous and anthracite coal, magnetite, limonite and other iron ore deposits, graphite, magnesite, gold, silver, copper, lead, zinc, and so forth.

   The land area falls into four major categories: (1) the high mountain area of the northeast, which consists mostly of forests with little or no agriculture; (2) the hilly areas around the high northern mountains and the central chain of mountains; (3) the eastern coastal region, which consists of low mountains and hilly areas with some lowlands; and (4) the western plains.

Socioeconomic Characteristics

The population of the DPRK is about 22 million, with a growth rate of about 1.8 percent annually. More than 60 percent of the population lives in cities and urban areas, and literacy is practically 100 percent.

The government states that the country is self-sufficient in food and that it enjoys full employment; full, free, and compulsory education; universal and free (or heavily subsidized) housing; comprehensive, free health services; and access to food and the means to satisfy basic material needs, such as fuel for the entire population at prices subsidized by the government.

The DPRK's per capita income has been estimated by the United Nations at around $US 1,000; the DPRK government has asserted that the correct figure is $2,000.

The DPRK has a centrally planned economy. All industry is nationalized, and land is owned either by the state or by agricultural cooperatives. Since the First Two Year Plan (1949–50), there have been a series of national plans of varying lengths. The most recent was the Third Seven Year Plan, promulgated in 1987. The government admitted in 1994 that many of the sectoral goals contained in the 1987 plan had not been achieved.

The DPRK Agenda 21 National Action Plan states that the sectoral output goals for 2000 are: electricity, 100 billion kWhe; coal, 120 million metric tons; steel, 10 million metric tons; cement, 22 million metric tons; fertilizer, 7.2 million metric tons; and grain, 15 million metric tons. In fact, the output objectives for 2000 appear to be largely the same as those promulgated in 1987.

The DPRK's gross national product (GNP) cannot be estimated accurately due to lack of data, accounting difficulties, and exchange rate uncertainties. It appears, however, that GNP growth is either stagnant or declining (some estimates put this at -5 percent per year, which represents a halving time of fourteen years). The economy is dominated by heavy industry, which accounts for more than 50 percent of total production, led by iron, steel, chemicals, food processing, and an emphasis on machine tool manufacture. According to reviews such as *Economist Intelligence Unit,* machinery manufacture and metal processing account for about 30 percent of industrial production, and textiles and food, about 18 and 9 percent, respectively.

The development of the DPRK since 1953 has been remarkable, with an impressive rate of industrialization and a very intensive agricultural system. However, these developments have threatened environmental quality due to atmospheric, liquid, and solid waste discharges from industrial complexes using obsolete and uncontrolled technology as well as from fertilizers and pesticides that support the DPRK's intensive agricultural production.

Main Factors Contributing to Environmental Degradation in the DPRK

The five main factors contributing to environmental degradation in the DPRK are as follows:

1. *Industrial geography:* Most people as well as agriculture, industry, and infrastructure are concentrated in 20 percent of the total land area, primarily in the western plains. Although Kim Il Sung directed early that industry be dispersed for strategic reasons (so it couldn't be bombed easily), in practice, the DPRK emulated the Eastern European approach of organizing industry around energy infrastructure and colocating industrial complexes with urban workforces, including residential areas.[1] This pattern of development places enormous stresses on the resource base and exceeds the environment's ability to deliver services such as waste removal, dilution, biodegradation, and disposal. Increasing amounts of chemicals must be applied to sustain agricultural productivity; industrial pollution affects human health and agriculture; and conflicting uses compete for precious land.

2. *Legacy of colonialism and war:* Japanese colonialism degraded Korean natural resources due to the careless exploitation of mines and mineral development as well as to the location of heavy industry in coastal areas with no thought for environmental considerations. Some of these impacts were exacerbated by the effects of the Korean War campaign of aerial bombing, which devastated waterworks and city environments, as well as many rural settlements and much infrastructure.

3. *Heavy industrialization:* Since the end of the Japanese occupation, the DPRK has continued to develop mining and heavy industry as the backbone of its economy, with associated environmental impacts.

4. *Technological gaps:* The DPRK has limited access to modern technology and training in industrial processes, in environmental management and pollution control, and in environmental economics, due partly to self-imposed constraints such as its trading patterns and efforts to maximize import substitution and partly to the U.S.-led de facto international embargo.

5. *Institutional framework:* The DPRK's institutional framework for environmental management, which is vertically structured to conform to the basic political hierarchy of party-led command and control, militates against lateral coordination and decentralized responsibility, both of which are integral to effective environmental management.

Although the DPRK's environmental situation is not yet quantifiable, I argue in this chapter that North Korea's accumulated and current environmental problems directly affect the productivity of its population and industries in ways that threaten its medium-term survival. The antagonistic linkages that contribute to a vicious circle of economic decline exacerbated by environmental degradation in North Korea include:

- Severe industrial pollution, including occupational hazards and uncontrolled, environmentally damaging toxic emissions to waterways
- Soil erosion and runoff due to problems with reforestation, resulting in loss of soil, siltation of waterways, and shortening of the useful lifetime of hydroelectric dams
- Inefficient use of energy, resulting in both local energy shortages and one of the highest per capita rates of carbon emission in the world
- Very high levels of fertilizer and pesticide use, resulting in nitrate pollution of groundwater and runoff, which, in turn, threatens irrigation and drinking water supplies, and results in soil acidification and declining food crop productivity
- Lack of institutional capacities to regulate or monitor environmental performance by domestic or foreign productive entities, combined with failure to enforce the rules that do exist, which, in turn, provides incentives to environmental malefactors and disincentives to potential foreign investors in the DPRK Free Trade Zone, such as soft drink manufacturers

Many of these problems are analogous to those experienced by Japan and South Korea at the end of the period of heavy industrialization. But the problems in the DPRK differ with respect to the institutional dynamics and the degree to which land-use patterns have led to extraordinarily high local pollution levels.

A strategy for economic recovery in the DPRK—and for the peaceful reunification of Korean society—will fail if it treats environmental concerns as secondary to economic objectives. Indeed, environmental restoration is the key to renovating many ailing sectors of the DPRK economy and to easing into a gradual reunification with the Republic of Korea (ROK). The following are among the steps that could integrate environmental and economic objectives:

- *Institutional reforms* are needed, with the aims of internalizing currently ignored environmental costs into domestic prices used in the DPRK to allocate goods and services, and removing intersectoral and grossly deforming subsidies from productive inputs such as coal-fired electricity used by heavy industry or households.
- *New technology* should be adopted, based on best international practice, in sectors such as forestry, mining, and transportation. This step would minimize resource use in processing industries and reduce bottlenecks in the economy.
- *Structural adjustment* is required—namely, the wholesale junking, for economic reasons, of sectors based on obsolete technology and designed to avoid dependency on imports at any cost. A structural adjustment of the DPRK's

economy is inevitable if it is to transit successfully out of its economic crisis. It makes little sense to clean up industries that are economically moribund—especially when those industries are often the heaviest polluters.

- *Pragmatic economic reforms,* such as opening North Korea to foreign investment and introducing market-based pricing, are essential to achieve resource-use efficiency in material and energetic terms, as well as rational allocation of economic and ecological resources in the DPRK's economy.
- *Building institutional capacities* to monitor and enforce environmental regulations and to integrate environmental objectives with economic strategy is critical to achieving sustainable development in North Korea. These same intangible managerial resources are also mobile and can be transferred across many sectors where they are badly needed for a range of purposes, not just environmental management. A flexible institutional framework that fosters central coordination and creative cooperation within and between public and private agencies is also essential for effective environmental management. This lateral coordination cannot be achieved in isolation from the basic structures of North Korean economic decision making. Improved environmental performance therefore requires institutional reform away from absolutist, centralized, and personalized processes in economic decision making and toward more flexible, decentralized, and bureaucratic processes. Luckily, this change is also a prerequisite for improved economic performance in North Korea.

Environmental Problems in North Korea

In this section, I review four of the most pressing environmental problems in North Korea—namely, in the agricultural, water, mining, and forestry sectors. However, the importance for the North Korean economy of the other environmental problems noted in the previous section should not be underestimated. I have merely shelved them for later consideration. Here, insofar as possible, I note the economic implications of these four problems. I wish to stress that this survey is not complete and that, due to data limitations, it is anecdotal in some respects.

The basic contours of the DPRK's environmental problems are relatively obvious, though. Its four most serious and urgent environmental challenges, in order of suggested priority, are: (1) sustainable food production, (2) water pollution and treatment, (3) restoration of past mining sites and industrial waste dumps, and (4) reforestation and afforestation.[2]

I reiterate that this section merely attempts to sketch these environmental imperatives. It does not systematically describe the various measures that the DPRK government has adopted to address them. But numerous obstacles frustrate its ability in each case to solve these problems. Indeed, the DPRK government has not been complacent in responding to these challenges, albeit their scale and complexity have often surpassed its capabilities to respond.

Agricultural Sustainability

The issue of agricultural sustainability entails shifting from current, unsustainable agricultural practices to sustainable ones, including reducing the use of pesticides, introducing integrated pest management techniques, reducing dependency on imported fertilizers, restoring acidified soils, avoiding water pollution, and overcoming land-use conflicts arising from coastal reclamation schemes.

Only about 20 percent, or 2.5 million hectares, of the DPRK's total land area is suitable for agriculture. This area is found both on the flat plains and on the lower slopes of the mountains. About 85 percent of the arable land is found on the plains, in which paddy rice predominates, although corn and millet are produced in strip cropping with vegetables. Paddy-field ridges are usually planted with soybeans. Some cotton is also grown in southern areas. The low mountains and slopes are used for growing corn, on either rain-watered or irrigated land. Pigs and poultry are also produced, as well as millet, potatoes, sweet potatoes, and tobacco. Stone terraces are common, both for orchards and for cultivated plots. In the mountainous, mostly forested areas, some sheep and goats are kept; and some vegetables are grown on terraced slopes.

To counter falling food productivity, the North has both intensified agricultural inputs and developed marginal tidal and hilly lands.[3] Fertilizer application reached about 2 metric tons per hectare on rice paddies by the early 1990s. In corn, the application is about 0.5 metric ton per hectare. In addition to urea, phosphate, and potassium sulfate or nitrate, about 20–30 metric tons of compost per hectare are spread. To counter soil acidification, urea has been substituted for ammonium sulfate, and about 0.5 metric ton per hectare of lime is spread.

This approach has resulted in declining soil fertility, lower soil organic matter content, soil salinity, acidification, pesticide contamination, and erosion (especially during the summer rains on steep slopes planted with corn). Urea and lime have increasingly replaced ammonium sulfate to offset drops in soil fertility, but the DPRK appears to have hit a point of diminishing returns. With the possible exception of tidal reclamation areas, the paddy rice sector may be less afflicted with these problems due to the inherent nature of the cultural system (except for the possible accumulation of recycled heavy metals, salinization due to rising groundwater, and pesticide contamination). The problem of soil erosion in hilly areas led to the deployment of large numbers of people to transport soil from higher slopes to cornfields in an attempt to raise soil fertility, even as 200,000 hectares of hilly land are proposed for conversion to cultivation.

In the agricultural sector, there is a trade-off between expanding production of resource-intensive and nonsustainable food crops in search of self-sufficiency on the one hand versus increasing the efficiency and sustainability of domestic production, but supplemented by increased food imports, on the other hand. Current practices entail soil erosion, soil acidification, salinity, and loss of fertility—all of which make it harder and harder to achieve self-sufficiency anyway.

The current campaign of massive tidal reclamation also poses an intractable dilemma, in that the reclaimed areas are obtained at the expense of coastal habitats that support productive fisheries and aquaculture resources, which, in turn, are important sources of scarce foreign exchange for the DPRK.

Yet another critical quandary relates to the deteriorating quality of inland waters due to agricultural runoff. This problem directly threatens human health via drinking water and the bioaccumulation of toxic materials from irrigation into food crops and marine foods, and via food tainted by untreated sewage released into rivers and coastal areas.

Water Treatment and Protection

The issue of water treatment and protection involves the introduction of wastewater treatment facilities and reduction of the pollution of inland and international waters by sewage and industrial wastes. Effluent standards have been set for all industries, for industrial wastewater discharged into sewerage systems, for treated sewage discharged into rivers, and for industrial wastewater discharged directly into rivers. These standards are applied uniformly (in principle) everywhere in the country, whatever the absorptive capacity or uses of the recipient waters. At about sixty-six wastewater-monitoring sites, pH, biological oxygen demand, chemical oxygen demand, suspended solids, free ammonia, nitrates, phenol, arsenic, and other parameters are monitored monthly.

Most major urban areas have sewage treatment plants, but only a few have biological treatment effective enough to minimize ultimate dried sludge volume, and some merely settle out major solids and release the untreated effluent into waterways in violation of standards. Moreover, modern plants, such as that in Pyongyang, have been rendered inoperable for long periods due to faulty equipment or inappropriate operating practices. Treated effluents are not disinfected with chlorine, and sludges may contain toxic heavy metals or hazardous chemicals due to the discharge of industrial effluents into sewers. Although sewage sludges are only permitted to be used in orchards and not on vegetable or cereal crops, these materials are in practice often supplied to farmers for composting, soil conditioning, or fertilizer.

Quantities of liquid effluents are not known, but the major sources of surface water pollution are probably industrial effluent, sewage, leachate from uncontrolled landfills and solid wastes (from power station ash or smelting industry slag heaps), and agricultural runoff (from fertilizer and pesticides). The Taedong River—which supplies drinking water for Pyongyang, industrial process water, and irrigation water for paddy rice fields—is a good example of the combined effects of these various sources of waterborne hazards. Not only does the 450–kilometer-long river absorb the waste flows from all the cities, towns, industries, and agriculture upstream from the west sea barrage, but the new lake created by the barrage is surrounded to the north by the city of Nampo, with its industrial complexes. Water monitoring at Pyongyang indicates that pollution levels during the spring and summer months approach national standards. Downstream, the situation may be more dire, especially as wastes accumulate in sediments and bioaccumulate in food chains in the new lake, or via irrigation onto reclaimed tidal areas or canal-irrigated rice fields.

Old industries inherited from the Japanese colonial era are particularly problematic. The coke plants at the (eighty-two-year-old!) Hwanghae Iron Works at Songrim, for example, produce highly toxic wastes containing phenols, cyanides, and naphthalene, which are discharged into the Taedong. These wastes may already exceed current water quality standards, which, in turn, may need to be strengthened in any case to protect human health and ecosystems alike.

At the Sinuiju Chemical and Fibers Complex, for example, 100,000 metric tons of effluent are released daily into the Amnok/Yalu River in the course of producing viscose rayon, paper, and cardboard from reed by treatment with caustic soda. This effluent probably contains lignite, sodium, zinc, and the like— all of which are of concern to the Chinese as well as the North Korean authorities. The four-decade-old system of primary sedimentation tanks is not working, and expensive process chemicals are not recovered before effluents are released, resulting in inefficiency as well as a degraded river system. This loss of valuable raw materials in waste streams is a story repeated in many North Korean industrial complexes.[4] In many cases, recovery and recycling systems could in large part be self-financing if the barrier of front-end costs could be hurdled.

Other industrial plants, such as the petrochemical and fertilizer complexes at Hamhung on the eastern coast, have basic wastewater treatment facilities but cannot recover trace metals and other dangerous chemicals contained in the wastewater. These wastes are released into a drain and marine outfall, and thence into the coastal marine environment. This waste stream includes organic compounds, sulfides, various dissolved solids, urea, ammonia, cyanides, arsenic, and so on. These industrial complexes also lack second lines of defense such as guard ponds in the event of equipment failure or standby equipment in the event of gaseous emissions. Not only are these plants deficient in terms of industrial health and safety (oil refineries, for example, routinely use asbestos as insulating cladding), but residential populations proximate to these plants are subject to accidental releases as well.

The large number of irrigation/hydroelectricity dams on North Korean rivers reduces the rate of flushing of various pollutants to the sea, with unknown rates of benthic accumulation and subsequent bioaccumulation of toxic materials. Also, irrigation may be raising groundwater levels and thereby increasing salinity levels in agricultural areas. The erosion is also running off into dams, which reduces the economic life or utility of irrigation and hydroelectricity investments.

Although North Korea has signed the London Dumping Convention, it has not yet provided port discharge facilities to receive oily wastes, sewage, or garbage from visiting vessels, nor does the DPRK monitor and enforce compliance with its rules in this regard by foreign vessels. Similarly, although the DPRK has basic oil spill–control boats and equipment, these systems are old and inadequate, and contingency planning and practice are not implemented. Adequate water supply is a critical aspect of infrastructure for foreign investors. At the Rajin/Sonbong Free Trade Zone, investors with significant demand for water may find supplies already so badly polluted as to be unusable—especially if they rely on waters from the Tumen River or some of its tributaries.[5] For example, the Maoshan iron mine, the DPRK's largest mine, is adjacent to the Tumen River's main channel. It has no tailings pond and discharges voluminous material directly into the river. The Awudi chemical plant in the DPRK also contributes severe water pollution to the lower Tumen River, reportedly giving fish a "kerosene" smell.

Restoration of Past Mining Sites and Industrial Waste Dumps

The rapid growth of mining since 1950 and the legacy of the industry as practiced under the Japanese occupation have degraded large areas of land and riverine systems in many areas, especially where open-pit mining is commonly combined with dumping of overburden, spoil, and tailings. Little restoration of afflicted areas has been achieved to date.

These areas are potential sources of waterborne and airborne environmental hazards, which probably have severe impacts on local soil, adjacent populations, and rivers downstream from these sites. A variety of response strategies are urgently needed, including industrial pollution control, solid-waste management, isolation of mine tailings and other solid wastes, and careful introduction of beneficiation techniques in the coal industry. Largely the same concerns apply to the waste streams of thermal power plants, the cement industry, the steel industry, and nonferrous metal–smelting plants. Coal ash, for example, contains heavy metals such as lead, cobalt, cadmium, chromium, nickel, and zinc, which threaten surface and groundwater resources if not carefully managed.

In some industries, solid wastes are successfully recycled already. At the Pyongyang Textile Complex, for example, sludges are recycled after calcination into cement block production. Sludges from other industries, however, are disposed of in landfills. A case in point is the dewatered sludges from the Pyongyang lead-battery plant, which are buried in a former coal mine, with possible impacts on groundwater and soils in the region.

Reforestation and Afforestation

Korea's forests were badly damaged in the past. In the 1940s, the tree cover had been reduced to about 12.5 cubic meters per hectare; in northern forests, the tree cover was about 15 cubic meters per hectare. Extensive reforestation efforts have been undertaken, with about 0.55 billion trees planted annually between 1987 and 1990, which amounts to about 1 million hectares over that period (at a planting density of 2,000 trees per hectare) and an annual afforestation rate of between 180,000 and 200,000 hectares per year. The government conducts campaigns involving large numbers of people in tree-planting efforts. Young people, for example, are organized into local "Green Pioneers" to plant trees.

Of the aforementioned annual afforestation rate, plantation timber forests comprised about 120,000 hectares per year, reportedly mostly coniferous plantations; protective forests for watershed protection and landscaping, about 50,000 hectares per year; and other forest types, about 10,000–20,000 hectares per year.

The government estimates that about 9 million hectares are covered with natural forest, of which only 3 million hectares are classified as productive, and that about 2.5 million hectares are covered with plantations. The 9 million hectares figure implies that three-quarters of the land area is covered by forests. Increasing this coverage seems unlikely considering the demand for land from other sectors such as agriculture, which means that most reforestation is probably occurring in already forested areas. In reality, it is more likely that only 7.8 million hectares are forested. A reasonable average standing volume for all North Korean forests based on cool temperate forests in neighboring states is 40 cubic meters per hectare. The main forest types in North Korea are cool-temperate and frigid forests.

Of the 2.2 million hectares of degraded forests, nearly 80 percent are on steep slopes, with rainfall between 30 millimeters and 1,000 millimeters (rain shadows on the leeward side of mountains, which receive little rainfall as the incoming, moisture-laden winds rain first on the windward side, are a major problem in reforestation efforts). Degraded pine forests have low productivity, with a standing volume of about 10–30 cubic meters per hectare. The vertical structure of pine forests is weak; they have low commercial value due to twisting; they are susceptible to pests; and species diversity is low.

The southwestern and southeastern slopes reportedly present particular problems due to aridity and strong sunlight. Oak forests suffer problems similar to pine forests.

Current reforestation efforts focus on converting low-yielding mixed natural forests into high-yielding conifer forests. More than 70 percent of the annually reforested areas are *Larix*-species plantations. The objective is to create a forest resource capable of meeting national industrial wood needs. Another large fraction of plantations are *Pinus korianus,* to produce pine nuts for oil extraction. The rate of coniferous reforestation may be drastically reducing the ecologically valuable mixed and broad-leaved forests.

Productive natural coniferous forests were managed until 1983 under a selective logging system with a 20–year felling cycle and a 30–centimeter minimum allowed diameter. The DPRK now uses clear-cutting and replanting to create even-aged compartments that are managed more intensively on longer (25– to 40–year) rotations to produce industrial roundwood.

Natural broad-leaved forests that are not converted into coniferous forests are managed for fuelwood production. Shrubs, coppice shoots, and small and dead timber are regularly removed in response to local demand.

No figures are available to indicate the source of wood supply by area, the type of forest, or whether the supply is obtained on a sustainable basis or by converting "natural low-productivity forests" or "well-created" and "young forests" into degraded forests. But if it is assumed that about 2 percent of sustainably managed forests are cut each year in a 50–year rotation cycle from the "well-created artificial forests," then 20,000 hectares from these forests (at 160 cubic meters per hectare) would supply only 3.2 million cubic meters per year, or about 25 percent of current wood needs in the DPRK. The difference presumably comes from cutting "low-productivity natural forests" and from imports.

Most of the wood produced by the forestry sector is consumed in the mining sector, in the pulp- and paper-processing sectors, for construction, and for fuelwood for domestic and industrial uses. United Nations Food and Agriculture Organization (FAO) data for 1988 indicate that fuelwood and charcoal production was about 4.0 million cubic meters, and that roundwood production (which includes fuelwood and charcoal production) was about 4.543 million cubic meters, implying nonfuel usage as being about 0.54 million cubic meters. However, FAO data may underestimate current DPRK fuel and nonfuel wood use by as much as two-thirds.[6]

Environmental Philosophy and Legal and Administrative Framework

The DPRK government is well aware of the current and pending negative impacts of the aforementioned environmental problems on its economy and on the quality of life of North Korean society. As with most aspects of North Korean life, the starting point for its environmental laws and administrative guidance and regulations is found in the values and norms embodied in the syncretic *juche* philosophy created by Kim Il Sung and expounded by Kim Jong Il, now leader of the DPRK.

Environmental Juche

To understand North Korean–style environmental management, it is essential to enter the North Korean worldview. The basic precepts of *juche* as applied to the environment are spelled out in the DPRK's official report to the U.N. Conference on Environment and Development, its post-Rio response to the Agenda 21 Action Plan adopted at Rio, and in various official speeches and declarations on environmental issues.

North Korean officials believe that the basic principles of *juche* were confirmed by the Rio Declaration, which asserted that humans are at the center of sustainable development due to their entitlement to a healthy and productive life. They argue that a country's environmental management capabilities are directly attributable to its political system. Because North Korean–style socialism is held to be the most advanced, human-centered social system suitable for their circumstances, so it follows (they contend) that preserving the environment conforms with what they call the "*juche*-oriented environment-protecting ideology." As evidence of their long-standing commitment to environmental protection, they cite the fact that Kim Il Sung called an early halt to the digging of gold at an important mountain site on the grounds that its cultural values outweighed the economic benefits of exploiting this resource.[7]

The North Koreans emphasize the notion of environmental improvement by human intervention, pointing to development of flood-control waterworks, reforestation, and tidal reclamation as examples of these human environmental artifacts. This notion is consistent not only with *juche* but also with the idea that protecting the environment is not just a technical or practical task, but a political task that entails indoctrination and mobilization, as in all spheres of North Korean life. It also corresponds with a phenomenon that can be termed "gigantism" that is a specialty of ministries such as the DPRK State Construction Commission and with the mass mobilization of labor, especially in the military, in massive (re)construction projects that entail "speed campaigns" and "battles" against the environment. In short, environmental protection is a means to the primary end of all state activities in North Korea: demonstrating the superiority of the North Korean–style political system, defending it, and accomplishing the goals of its revolutionary cause.

This perspective has at least two important implications for the North Korean "style" of environmental management. First, North Koreans find it difficult to grasp the concept of natural biodiversity or the need to preserve it. Thus, they can suggest that environmental management means the introduction of productive species in reclaimed tidal areas, irrespective of the natural marine ecosystems and species diversity threatened or destroyed by such projects.

Second, North Koreans have adopted the rhetoric but not yet the practice of sustainable development. Rather than viewing sustainable development as the integration of economic and environmental objectives, and as the exploitation of environmental and economic complementarities, they subscribe mostly to the orthodox paradigm wherein environment and development conflict and must be balanced and traded off against each other. Consistent with this outlook, the North Koreans view incessant technological innovation as the major solution to environmental afflictions. Consequently, they seek strong scientific and technical means with which to monitor and manage environmental problems. Finally, they put their faith in accelerated economic production and construction as providing the necessary resources to realize the first two objectives, whatever the environmental costs of doing so.

Many in the West agree with this North Korean outlook wherein nature is a subordinated means to human ends, even if they would diverge with respect to the political and ideological spin that North Koreans place on environmental concerns. Many western environmentalists, however, object to such ideas as being the original sin that led to many types of environmental abuse. Wherever one stands in this dichotomy, it must be admitted that the *juche* philosophy of environmental management has some progressive components—however difficult it is to realize them in practice. The philosophy, for example, emphasizes that the DPRK has international duties to preserve the environment (although North Koreans are quick to blame the rich industrial countries for occupying the global ecological commons and former colonial powers such as Japan for leaving behind debilitating environmental messes). Scenting the possibility of external support (and seeking international legitimacy), North Korea quickly signed the major agreements at the 1992 Rio Earth Summit on climate change, forestry, biodiversity, and the action plan and has also signed a variety of other global and regional environmental treaties.

The DPRK also stresses that environmental concerns are a social, collective matter that cannot be reduced to individual interests or merely to the interests of the current generation.

Environmental Law

In 1986, the DPRK enacted its Basic Law of Environment (see Appendix 8.1). This law requires all industries to comply with environmental standards, accords basic environmental rights to all citizens, and commits all organs of the North Korean state to preserving environmental qualities for the enjoyment of its citizenry. It lays out the basic framework for environmental administration and places the onus for environmental liability squarely on the polluter or abuser, including provision for liability, compensation, and criminal negligence. The DPRK has no formal environmental impact assessment procedure, but the Environmental Protection Law requires that major construction and development projects be thoroughly examined for any environmental impacts.

Although the law provides a legal version of the DPRK's philosophical approach to environmental problems, it is framed so generally that it provides little concrete guidance as to administrative arrangements, regulatory requirements, or enforcement procedures.

Environmental Administration

According to North Koreans, the late President Kim Il Sung "set forth the principle that the problem of environmental protection should be taken first into account ahead of socio-economic development and that every possible measure should be taken for environmental protection ahead of production and he has seen to it that the principle be kept with credit."[8]

After a series of permutations, the DPRK government restructured its environmental administration early in 1993 to better reflect its commitment to the implementation of the undertakings following the U.N. Conference on Environment and Development. This new administrative structure, in the form of the State Environment Commission, is still in the process of defining its operational procedures and other mechanisms for environmental management.

Although the DPRK has promulgated water classification standards; emission standards and maximum permissible levels; procedures for applying to set up an industrial enterprise; and permits for discharges, land development, and reclamations, little is known about how these procedures actually work or whether they work at all in most cases. It appears that these regulatory instruments are still being developed, a process hampered by two weaknesses in the DPRK's environmental administration: (1) the lack of suitably trained human resources and (2) the lack of adequate facilities and instrumentation to back up legal enforcement of those regulations that do exist.

Overall, the State Environment Commission is inadequately equipped and poorly structured to execute its broad mandate successfully. There appears to be little lateral cooperation between the different divisions of the commission, as well as overlap and competition between different components. Consequently, existing laws are not enforced, and many environmental regulations are simply unavailable to productive enterprises—including to potential foreign investors. Also, the DPRK environmental authorities tend to use Chinese legal and regulatory frameworks as models for their own. Given the limited achievements of China's environmental institutions—not to mention the extent to which its cultural and political characteristics differ from those of the DPRK—it can be argued that the North would do better to seek models elsewhere in Asia.[9]

The most urgent institutional requirement is to create an effective middle layer of management capability in the DPRK's environmental administration. North Korean environmental officials assert that they must establish a strong planning system for environmental protection and have called for environmental concerns to be integrated into the economic-planning activities of all productive units at all levels—from the central planning commission down to local factories, productive enterprises, and cooperative farms. And indeed, environmental committees are now found in most productive organizations, although their implementation record is uneven.

The paucity of management resources at this intermediate level—in terms of trained environmental policy analysts, economists, administrators, planners, and managers—is largely responsible for the gap between laudable environmental philosophies, principles, and policies and the everyday reality of lackluster environmental performance. It should be noted that the environmental authorities have acted on occasion to shut down industrial complexes that have committed egregious violations of pollution-control standards, but the impression is that such events are the exception rather than the rule and probably short-lived to boot.

These basic institutional problems are compounded by the propensity of the DPRK's economic agencies to indulge in gigantism of every imaginable kind, which reflects little concern for environmental externalities and is often achieved by mobilizing mass campaigns of unskilled workers, thereby undercutting the very professionalism needed for both economic and environmental performance.

Indeed, the DPRK Agenda 21 Action Plan promulgated in 1992 spells out an amazing array of needs for consideration by the international donor community. This set of needs can be read backward as admitting that problems pervade every aspect of environmental management in North Korea. If the list is taken as given, it is also evident that North Korea cannot hope to overcome all the obstacles that it faces without extensive international assistance.

Also, the lack of nongovernmental organizations hampers the ability of the formal apparatus to overcome the entrenched power of orthodox line agencies and the State Planning Commission itself, even though the State Environment Commission reports directly to a deputy prime minister with senior status and authority in the DPRK political system.

Conclusion

The implications of the two preceding sections on environmental problems and responses in the DPRK are rather dismal. In short, the DPRK has accumulated massive environmental costs, many of which are already undermining human and resource productivity, and many of which represent environmental bills that will fall due in the future because of the time lag and threshold effects of environmental abuse and ecosystem stress.

It is easy to list initiatives that might prevent these problems from growing even bigger. They include:

- *Providing technical assistance* in the form of overseas study tours, in-country training, and resident or visiting external experts, with particular emphasis on training environmental managers in each and every sector with major environmental impacts, as well as upgrading the skills and capabilities of the existing environmental agencies such as the State Environment Commission or the Research Center for Nature Protection and Resource Management within the DPRK Academy of Sciences.
- *Supplying badly needed equipment* for environmental purposes, bearing in mind that earlier generations of scientific equipment are generally more appropriate to basic needs as they exist in the DPRK at this time and are less difficult to transfer given the existing de facto international embargo on transferring strategic technologies (or even low-end computers for maintaining environmental databases and so on).
- *Furnishing technical and economic data* relating to environmental issues to DPRK environmental managers, who often lack even the most basic manuals

or information relating to local, regional, or global problems due to the DPRK's international isolation. It is wise to keep in mind that the continued isolation of North Korea in terms of information flows on such matters is equivalent to rendering its environmental controls virtually impotent. Although, in the past, this isolation was largely self-imposed for political reasons, a variety of conduits already exist to increase information availability. These opportunities should be exploited at every turn.

- *Transferring techniques,* such as remote sensing, which involves combining training, software, and hardware and then infusing such information and its interpretation into national, sectoral, and line agency management. In many ways, inculcating a "lateral" ethic of information sharing and lateral coordination, which is essential for effective environmental management, will be a critical test of the flexibility and resilience of the North Korean polity in the post–Kim Il Sung era.
- *Institutional innovations,* which should be pursued in addition to standard "technical assistance." It is crucial to explore innovative approaches to environmental management, financing, and education of North Korea's environmental institutions and personnel. Ensuring that DPRK environmental officials are invited to and enabled to participate in subregional environmental forums (such as the Tumen River Area Development Project environmental rules) and subregional environmental consultations (such as the Northwest Pacific Action Plan [NOWPAP] of the United Nations Environment Program [UNEP], and the Northeast Asia Environmental Coordination Program of the Economic and Social Commission for Asia and the Pacific [ESCAP] and the United Nations Development Program [UNDP]) provides them with important learning opportunities.

Insofar as these processes introduce harmonized environmental standards, common environmental–scientific terminology, or collaborative research at a subregional level, these personnel will become more proficient in ensuring that the gradual process of structural adjustment and economic reform/transition in North Korea is as environmentally sensitive as possible. Also, the DPRK shares a number of transboundary environmental resources and problems, including acid rain (as both victim and polluter), waterways, migratory species (including birds and fish), and borders (such as the demilitarized zone [DMZ]) and is also national steward for DPRK biosphere reserves under UNESCO's Man and the Biosphere Program. The DPRK and the ROK also jointly manage the demilitarized zone, which, by virtue of its militarization, has become a wildlife refuge of some importance.

All these issue areas proffer opportunities to solicit DPRK participation and contributions on the basis of mutual equality, independence, and balanced interdependence—the cardinal principles of North Korean foreign policy.

Undoubtedly, the biggest test of all will be to what extent the DPRK can introduce markets to overcome the structural rigidities of its command and control economic system and to enlist markets to improve environmental performance. The DPRK can reap many lessons from the transitional experiences of Eastern Europe, China, the former Soviet Union, Vietnam, and (given its dirigiste past) even South Korea.[10] In areas of the economy such as food production, limited markets that operate without direct reference to Pyongyang have emerged because producers and hungry consumers had no alternative but to find each other and commence internal trade due to the breakdown of national food-distribution systems. It is not enough to strengthen the ability of the State Environment Commission to grapple with the major economic ministries. It is critical that provincial environmental authorities also be endowed with authority commensurate with their responsibilities, to coevolve with the local and provincial institutional developments in the productive system in ways that will foster environmental as well as economic efficiencies. Approaches such as large-scale carbon offsets by "annex 2" countries under proposed protocols to the Climate Change Convention (which, if adopted, would enable them to fund carbon-reduction or carbon-fixing projects in states such as the DPRK and claim the credit against their own emissions account) or creative settlements of North Korea's outstanding foreign debt (such as debt-for-nature or debt-for-equity swaps) might be explored with the new regime.

It is a mistake to underestimate the stamina and resilience of the North Korean polity or the ability of the DPRK leadership to weather the storms and navigate the reefs that lie ahead. Environmental cooperation with the DPRK on a bilateral or multilateral basis can build confidence outside of the DPRK as to its ultimate intentions in coming to terms with the external world. It can also strengthen moves inside North Korea to engage the external world and to commence the transitions that it must undertake if it is to survive without collapsing, not least due to the economic pressures of a deteriorating resource base.

In conclusion, I would like to address briefly the relationship between reunification and sustainable development in Korea. The continued division of Korea is incompatible with the achievement of sustainable development on the peninsula, if only because of the ongoing risk of war and the environmental and economic devastation that such a catastrophe would bring on both sides of the demilitarized zone. Broadly, three future scenarios with respect to Korean reunification can be envisaged at this time: (1) gradual, peaceful reunification; (2) fast, violent reunification; and (3) continued division.

The second and third scenarios both entail enormous additional environmental costs that would undermine and frustrate the DPRK's economic performance and increase the cost of reunification. In the case of fast, violent reunification, enormous environmental damage would be wrought in many dimensions by military action, although the environmental assault associated with many of the most moribund sectors in the DPRK would cease almost immediately. The ROK—the likely victor in any military confrontation with the DPRK—would find itself saddled with the costs not only of the war and economic reconstruction but of the cleanup as well.

In the case of continued division, the DPRK's ability to avoid or reduce chronic, accumulated, and lagged environmental costs—let alone to restore the past damage—would be hampered greatly by the economic difficulties that would accompany continued division of Korea and isolation of the DPRK. Which would be greater—the immediate environmental costs from war followed by reunification and the eventual upgrading of the DPRK's environmental performance to that of the ROK in a forcefully reunified Korea, or the accumulated, incessant costs imposed by business as usual—cannot be determined.

What does seem obvious is that the environmental costs associated with either of these two paths are likely to exceed greatly those that would be associated with gradual, peaceful reunification. And the longer it takes to achieve peaceful reunification, the greater the environmental bill that will accrue to be paid later, by this generation or the next. In this best-case scenario, South Korea could make a big difference by providing technology and technical assistance in the hardest-hit environmental areas mentioned earlier in this chapter, by transferring the best available environmental technology via direct investment in the North, and by striving to harmonize ROK and DPRK environmental standards. The ROK could also consider investing in carbon emission–reducing or carbon-fixing activities as an "offset" in North Korea's energy and forestry sectors under the Climate Change Convention.

In short, peaceful and "fast-as-possible" reunification would appear to be the best way to achieve sustainable development in Korea.

APPENDIX 1: THE DPRK BASIC LAW OF ENVIRONMENT
[Unofficial Translation]

Chapter I: Basic Principles of Environmental Protection

Article 1

Environmental protection is the noble work to provide popular masses with environment needed for their independent and creative life.

The state always pays deep attention to the protection of country's environment so as to arrange cultural and hygienic surroundings and working conditions to the people.

Article 2

Environmental protection is the important undertaking to be carried out as a routine practice in the building of socialism and communism.

The state shall consolidate the achievements made in environmental protection and management under the leadership of the Workers' Party of Korea and take measures to improve the work keeping abreast with the modernization of relevant economic sections including industry while systematically increasing the investment of it.

Article 3

The state shall protect and manage the environment in a planned way with a perspective view, so as to create country's surroundings to meet the aspiration and requirement of the people.

The state shall build cities and villages and rationally locate factories, enterprises and other industrial establishments on the principle of environmental protection.

Article 4

It is prerequisite for the prevention of pollution and maintenance of steady rate of production to take measures for environmental protection prior to production.

The state shall guide and control factories, enterprises and co-operatives to take anti-pollution measures prior to production and to keep material and technical facilities for the environmental protection up to date.

Article 5

It is the noble obligation of the entire people to protect environment.

The state should educate the people in socialist patriotism so that they love their fatherland and their native place and take voluntary part in the protection of country's environment.

Article 6

The state shall develop scientific research to protect environment from pollution, reinforce scientific institutions of environmental protection and improve guidance on them.

Article 7

It is the unanimous aspiration and demand of the world people to prohibit the development, test and usage of nuclear and chemical weapons so as to protect environment from the damages caused therefrom.

The DPRK shall strive against environmental damage and contamination resulting from the development, test and usage of nuclear and chemical weapons on and around the Korean peninsula.

Article 8

The state shall promote scientific and technical exchanges and cooperation in the sphere of environmental protection with all countries friendly to our country.

Article 9

This law regulates the principles and rules to protect environment such as air, water, soil and living things from their damage, destruction and contamination.

The rule on maintenance, protection and management of the land, forest resources and other natural environment excluded from this law is subject to the "Land Law of the Democratic People's Republic of Korea."

Chapter II: The Preservation and Maintenance of Natural Environment

Article 10

The proper preservation and maintenance of natural environment is the requirement raised in providing the people with favorable living environment and handing down more beautiful and cultured environment to the posterity.

All the organs, enterprises, organizations and citizens should maintain, protect and manage the natural environment so as to help promote people's health and their cultural and emotional life.

Article 11

Natural environmental reserves and special reserves shall be set up to keep the natural environment under the protection of the state.

Those reserves shall be chosen by the Administration Council

Article 12

Land administration organ, scientific organs of natural reservation and local power organs should check and register in a systematic way the variations of natural environment such as animals and plantations, topography, quality of water and climate in the natural environmental reserves and the special reserves and take necessary steps for their protection and management.

Any act of hindering the preservation, protection and management of original natural environment shall be prohibited in the natural environmental reserves and the special reserves.

Article 13

The organs, enterprises, organizations and citizens should not cut down the ornamental plantations in and around the city, villages, road and railway and on lake and riverside and not damage or destroy the scenic spots, pine-tree fields on the coast of the sea, swimming beaches, mountains of marvelous mysterious shape and picturesque islands.

Article 14

The organs, enterprises, organizations and citizens should not develop collieries and mines in scenic spots, tourist centers and recreation centers and not erect the buildings and establishments affecting environmental reservation but maintain in an original shape the curves, waterfalls and sites of ancient castle and other natural monuments and places of natural beauty and historic remains.

Article 15

The organs, enterprises and organizations should take preventive measures to protect the environment from damage caused by land sinking when they develop underground resources or carry out underground constructions.

Underground water should not be extracted for use in those areas liable to the damage of sinking.

Article 16

Fowls and crawling animals bred for the maintenance of environment should not be hunted and the wild animals and animate things under water which are beneficial and growing only in our country should not be hunted or picked without permission of the environmental protection supervisory organ.

All citizens should refrain from making spoil of the habitation environment of the wild animals and aquatic lives, or picking at random precious plantations, so as not to break the equilibrium of the animate nature or disturb the cultural and emotional life of the working people.

Article 17

The city management organs and local administrative and economic guidance organs shall build everywhere parts, recreation grounds and other cultural resorts and plant trees along the roads and railroads, around buildings, on the vacant grounds within blocks and in the places for the public utility so as to expand the green belts.

The trees harmful to the environmental creation shall not be planted in the city and its surroundings.

Article 18

The organs, enterprises, organizations and citizens shall take routine part in developing their villages neatly and launch a campaign for the work with the planting month and the town beautifying month as a momentum. When buildings and facilities are under construction in towns and villages, their surroundings shall not be littered.

Chapter III: Prevention of Environment Contamination

Article 19

To prevent the environment contamination is the prerequisite for the removal of the environmental pollution.

All the organs, enterprises, organizations and citizens shall strictly observe the environmental protection limit and the standards of exhaust of contaminated materials, noise and vibration set by the state.

The Administration Council shall set the limit of environmental protection and the standards of exhaust of contaminated materials, noise and vibration.

Article 20

The relevant organs, factories and enterprises shall have the gas and dust collectors for presenting air pollution and the air filters for eliminating the bad smell reeking from the buildings and facilities, and repair and readjust in a planned way the furnaces, tanks and drainpipes and other facilities.

The local administrative and economic guidance organs shall set up hygienic protection areas between the relevant factories, enterprises and residential quarters and create forests therein.

Article 21

The excessive gas or smoke reeking rotary machines and the dirty vehicles which may raise dust due to the unpacked loads shall be prohibited from running and the machinery and equipment which make standard-exceeding noise and vibration are not allowed to be operated.

The social security organs, transport controlling organs and local power organs shall install modern gauges of exhausting gas in main streets and necessary zones to verify the exhaust of gas and smoke reeking from vehicles and take steps to prevent air pollution.

Article 22

The relevant organs, factories and enterprises shall reduce the exhaust amount of gas, dust and smoke and adjust or stop the operation of the rotary machines when they seriously contaminate the atmosphere making harm to men or animals due to the unusual meteorological conditions.

The hydrometeorological organs shall notify the organ concerned of the abnormal meteorological phenomena in good time.

Article 23

The organs, enterprises, organizations and citizens shall not incinerate leaves and garbage in the residential quarters and around major roads but dispose them in designated places.

City management organs and the organs concerned shall carry dirt away in time for the sake of environmental protection.

Article 24

The organs, enterprises and organizations shall build settling basins and purification facilities for prevention of water pollution, purify sewage and various waste waters and take measures to collect and utilize them.

Article 25

City management organs and relevant organs, enterprises and organizations shall regularly repair and maintain in good order water supply facilities and supply drinking water after properly filtering and sterilizing it.

Factories, enterprises, building and installations shall not be built nearby water intakes, reservoir and outlet; and herbicide, insecticide and other harmful chemical shall not be used there.

Article 26

All the vessels, sailing or anchoring in the territorial waters of the Republic, its economic zone, harbor and bays, port, lockgate, rivers and streams, lakes and marshes and reservoirs, shall not throw away or drop down oil, sewage and garbage.

Natural resource development organs, local administration and economic guidance organs and pertinent organs shall not pollute sea environment when they develop sea resources or undertake coastal projects.

Article 27

Shipping agencies shall have their vessels equipped with pollution protection facilities or containers; for sewage and dirt commensurate to their tonnage and pass the overhaul of maritime supervisory organ.

The maritime supervisory organs shall strictly inspect the environmental protection facilities installed in the vessels.

Article 28

The organs, enterprises and cooperatives managing and running harbor, port, lockgate and wharf shall have sewage and garbage disposal facilities, carry away sewage and dirt from vessels and purify or scoop up the oil and dirt dropped down in the sea or river.

Article 29

Relevant organs, enterprises and organizations shall install settling basins and purification beds of sewage and waste water and sanitation facilities and disposal beds and industrial waste in the places which will be kept out of polluting the sea, rivers and streams, lakes and marshes, reservoirs and drinking water resources.

Overburden heaps, refuse dump, coal depot, soot and slag disposal beds shall be properly built so as to protect environment of their surroundings from contamination, and after their use they shall be covered with soil for three planting and crop cultivation.

Article 30

Agricultural chemicals on state prohibition list for their contamination of atmosphere, water and soil or affection of the human body, shall neither be produced nor imported.

Toxicity of the agricultural medicines shall be checked by the Hygienic Quarantine Organ.

Article 31

The agricultural guidance organs and the institutions enterprises, organizations and citizens that deals with agricultural medicines shall take steps to prevent the blow-off of chemicals in the air, their flowing into rivers, lakes and ponds, reservoirs and the sea and their accumulation in the soil.

When agricultural medicines are to be sprayed by aircraft, they shall receive permission of the environmental protection supervisory institution.

Article 32

Those institutions, factories and enterprises that produce or deal with radioactive substances shall set up percolation and purification facilities and lower the radioactive density below the discharge standard to protect environment from contamination by radioactive gas, dust, sewage and waste.

The aforesaid institutions, factories and enterprises shall regularly check and measure the level of radioactive contamination to prevent the damage by pollution.

Article 33

Those institutions, factories and enterprises that produce, supply, transport, handle, use or abolish the radioactive substances shall receive the permission of the treatment of radioactive materials from the Radioactive Supervisory Institution or the Social Security Organ.

The Radioactive Supervisory Institution shall normalize the survey of the factors that may cause environmental pollution and take relevant measures.

Article 34

The contaminated foodstuffs and fodder as well as fish and fruit shall not be imported.

The institutions, enterprises, organizations concerned and citizens shall take care of the foodstuffs in process of production and treatment so as not to be polluted.

Article 35

The facilities and technology that cause damages to the health of the people and environment for the discharge of harmful substances, noise and vibration shall neither be imported nor introduced into production.

Article 36

The institutions, enterprises and organizations shall check frequently the discharge quantity and density of the harmful substances and strength of noise and vibration caused in process of production, lower them in phase and receive the permission from the Supervisory Institution for the Environmental Protection.

The noxious materials shall not be discharged when they are not permitted by the above mentioned institution or exceed the permitted standard.

Article 37

The local power organs, land administration, institutions and relevant organs shall shift out of the city the factories and enterprises harmful to the health of residents and the freight transportation road and rail tracks be remote from the residential quarters or built underground. The dwelling houses affected by pollution shall be shifted to the place nice to live in.

Contaminative factories and enterprises and those dealing with a great volume of freight shall not be built in downtown, and the buildings and establishment without anti-pollution facility shall not be utilized.

Chapter IV: Guidance and Management on Environmental Protection

Article 38

Strengthening of the guidance and management on the environmental protection is the important requirement in carrying through the environmental protection policy of the state.

The state shall properly establish the environmental protection system and strengthen guidance and supervision on environmental protection to improve its management and thus meet the requirement of the reality.

Article 39

The Administration Council shall give coordinated guidance to the environmental protection.

A non-standing (ad hoc) committee for environmental protection shall be established in the Administration Council in order to ensure collective guidance and take necessary steps for the environmental protection.

Article 40

The supervision over the environmental protection shall be carried out by the land administrative bodies, and departmental bodies such as sanitary and anti-epidemic organs and the radiation supervisory institutions and other competent authorities.

Article 41

The relevant organs, enterprises and organizations shall provide the supervision and measurement organs for the environmental protection with materials and working conditions needed in the supervision and measurement of environmental protection.

The state planning board, material supply organs, financial and banking institutions and labor administrative bodies shall satisfactorily provide in time the equipment, materials, funds and manpower necessary for the environmental protection.

Article 42

The relevant central bodies and land administrative organs and local power organs shall carry out their overall investigation over the environmental damages and pollution and take measures for the improvement of environmental protection by drawing up a yearly plan.

Article 43

The land planning bodies and relevant design examination commissions shall examine, in accordance with the requirement of the environmental protection, the hydrometeorological, topographical and oceanographical conditions to choose the residential and industrial areas and examine for approval only those technical subjects and design which have been agreed upon by the public health organs, hydrometeorological institutions and relevant specialized agencies.

Article 44

The completion checking organs and those organs participating in this checking shall not give pass to the capital construction projects devoid of the anti-pollution fittings.

Article 45

The Administrative Council shall establish a national environmental pollution observation system, enhance the role of the observation and measurement bodies to carry out normal observation and measurement on the environmental changes, and take scientific and technical steps to dispose sewage, various wasted water and industrial leftovers.

Article 46

Educational institutions and publication and press bodies shall disseminate technical know-how and conduct mass education in various forms and ways for the environmental protection and widely introduce and propagandize the successes achieved in this field.

Chapter V: Compensation for Damages and Punishment on Environmental Damages

The organs, enterprises, organizations and citizens who damaged the health of the people and properties of state and social cooperative organizations and citizens by damaging, destroying and contaminating environment shall pay compensation for damages.

Article 48

The organs, enterprises, organizations and citizens suffering from the damages caused from the violation of the rule of the environmental protection shall claim compensation for damages from their counterparts.

Article 49

The environmental protection supervisory bodies shall let offenders compensate for equivalent losses when the latter damage land and natural resources in violation of the rule of the environmental protection.

Article 50

When foreign country's vessel or people contaminate the atmosphere and water in the territory and economic zone of our country, the supervisory bodies in the ports and other competent authorities shall detain the vessels or people and let them compensate or pay their penalty for damages.

Article 51

The environmental protection supervisory bodies shall ban the project, operation of the factories and rotary machines and withdraw the relevant buildings and establishments when they carry out them in violation of the rule of the environmental protection and confiscate the materials and products used in such illegal acts.

The environmental protection supervisory bodies shall let the offenders restore to the original state the environment damaged, destroyed and polluted.

Article 52

The officials of the organs and enterprises and responsible citizens who have brought considerable loss by seriously damaging, destroying and polluting the country's environment shall be accused of the administrative or criminal punishment on account of their circumstances.

Notes

1. See M. Feshbach and A. Friendly, *Ecocide in the USSR: Health and Nature under Siege* (New York: Basic Books, 1992), for an account of this situation.

2. Secondary environmental problems in the DPRK not covered here include: management and disposal of toxic and hazardous materials; reduction of emissions from thermal power stations and industry; environmental occupational health and safety; biodiversity protection, land-use planning, and nature reserves; and tidal area reclamation–related environmental problems, including estuarine losses, fishing impacts, water quality problems, and long-run viability of these coastal barriers and low-lying hinterlands in the face of possible climate change–induced sea-level rise over the next century.

3. See Hy-Sang Lee, *Supply and Demand for Grains in North Korea: A Historical Movement Model for 1966–1993,* draft, Department of Economics, University of Wisconsin, 1994.

4. Environment Protection Bureau, *National Report of the D.P.R. of Korea,* report to U.N. Conference on Environment and Development, Pyongyang, April 24, 1991, 17.

5. Ma Jiang, *Tumen River: Environmental and Tourism Guidelines for Development Planning,* paper presented to the workshop on Trade and Environment in Asia–Pacific: Prospects for Regional Cooperation, Honolulu, September 23–25, 1994.

6. The estimate of nonenergy industrial wood use in FAO statistics is a residual category derived by subtracting total energy-related uses from total production after adjusting the latter figure for starting balance and net imports. It appears that the total production figure for the DPRK is understated by an order of magnitude.

7. Environment Protection Bureau, *National Report of the D.P.R. of Korea,* 3.

8. *National Action Plan for "Agenda 21" of the United Nations Conference on Environment and Development,* DPRK State Environment Commission, 1993.

9. See V. Smil, *China's Environmental Crisis: An Inquiry into the Limits of National Development* (Armonk, NY: M.E. Sharpe, 1993); and J. Goldstone, *Imminent Political Conflicts Arising from China's Environmental Crises,* Occasional Paper 2, Peace and Conflict Studies Program, University College, University of Toronto, December 1992.

10. D. Fisher, *Paradise Deferred: Environmental Policymaking in Central and Eastern Europe* (London: Royal Institute of International Affairs, Energy and Environmental Programme, 1992); J. Russell, *Energy and Environmental Conflicts in East/Central Europe: The Case of Power Generation* (London: Royal Institute of International Affairs, Energy and Environmental Programme, 1991); "Environmental Action Programme for Central and Eastern Europe," paper submitted to the Ministerial Conference, Lucerne, Switzerland, April 28–30, 1993; M. Simons, "West Offers Plan to Help Clean Up East Europe," *New York Times,* May 4, 1993, A8.

9

Engaging North Korea on Energy Efficiency

Peter Hayes and David F. Von Hippel

The Yalta Conference at the end of World War II resulted in the partitioning of Korea. Though the boundary thus created was altered slightly by the agreement that ended the Korean War, the Korean Peninsula was left divided. The two Korean states thus created—the Republic of Korea (ROK), often referred to as South Korea, and the Democratic People's Republic of Korea (DPRK), or North Korea—went on to rebuild their shattered economic infrastructure and pursue development in very different ways, aided by different economic partners. The DPRK's economic rise from the ashes of war was impressive, particularly given its political isolation from the West. Recently, the end of the Cold War and of economic aid from the former Soviet bloc, together with other world and regional events, have put the DPRK's economy in what most observers agree is either a downward spiral or, at best, a state of stagnation.

A recent study by the authors estimated the prospects for energy efficiency improvements in the DPRK economy. In the process, we derived a detailed estimated supply and demand balance for fuels used in North Korea, which is shown in Table 9.1. We would encourage readers interested in a detailed discussion of how this balance was compiled to consult that study.[1] In this chapter, we touch on some of the problems faced by the DPRK in its energy sector, describe our indicative estimates of the potential for implementing energy efficiency and renewable energy measures in the DPRK, and discuss some of the means whereby the DPRK's energy problems can be addressed through international cooperation.

Energy Sector Problems

In this section, we briefly discuss some of the energy sector problems in North Korea. In some cases, evidence of these problems is gleaned from various project descriptions and mission reports filed by recent visitors to the DPRK. In other cases, there is clearer evidence for energy sector problems. In either case, problems in the DPRK energy sector must be considered (and in some cases addressed) before meaningful progress can be made on implementing energy efficiency or renewable energy measures.

Key Resource and Technological Bottlenecks

Though the evidence for key resource and technological problems is largely anecdotal, there have been reports of "bottlenecks" in the DPRK energy system that have the effect of impeding the flow of goods and materials. In some cases, these bottlenecks interact to form cycles that further constrict the DPRK economy. For example, coal shortages at power plants have been caused—at least partly—by a lack of iron and steel to maintain the rail system that brings the coal from the mines to the power stations.[2] The iron and steel deficiency is, in turn, the result of the lack of coal to fuel metals production as well as rail transport difficulties in moving ore from the mines to the mills.

Similarly, lack of spare parts for certain imported infrastructure may constrain production in some industries. Downstream industries dependent upon the output of the upstream industries are affected in turn. Lack of fuel for trucks and other transport equipment delays delivery of parts and other inputs to factories, resulting in lower overall productivity.

The DPRK electricity generation and distribution system is outdated, with a fairly complex grid of sixty-two power plants, fifty-eight substations, and eleven regional transmission and dispatching centers operated literally by telephone and telex, without the aid of automation or computer systems. This system results in poor frequency control, poor power factors, and frequent power outages.[3] The power generation system suffers from a lack of spare parts in some instances as well as from a lack of testing equipment for use in maintenance activities.

Low Rate of Utilization of Energy Facilities

In part because of resource bottlenecks such as those described above, the rate of utilization of key energy facilities in the DPRK is reportedly relatively low. If official DPRK electricity generation figures are correct, the capacity factor for electricity generation facilities (computed as the output of power plants divided by what their output would be if they operated 100 percent of the time at full power) was on the order of 50 to 60 percent in 1990. On the other hand, if estimates by outside observers are more accurate, capacity factors could have

144

Table 9.1

Estimated Detailed DPRK Energy Balance for 1990

Units: Terajoules (TJ)*	Coal and coke	Crude oil	Refined products	Hydro/nuclear	Wood/biomass	Charcoal	Electricity	Total
Energy supply	1,355,048	119,261	26,604	240,180	382,050			2,124,044
Domestic production	1,317,960			240,180	355,383			1,913,624
Imports	68,392	119,261	26,604		26,667			240,923
Exports	30,403							30,403
Inputs to International Marine bunkers								
Stock changes								—
Energy transformation	(461,938)	(119,261)	91,639	(240,180)	(10,667)	3,520	147,728	(589,148)
Electricity generation	(381,683)		(20,851)	(240,180)			199,800	(442,914)
Petroleum refining		(119,261)	112,489					(8,771)
Coal production/ preparation							(8,664)	(8,854)
Charcoal production					(10,667)	3,620		(7,147)
Coke production								—
Other transformation								
Own use	(63,000)						(14,955)	(76,855)
Losses	(18,343)						(28,466)	(44,809)
Fuels for final consumption	894,023		118,243		371,383	3,520	147,726	1,534,896
Energy Demand	894,301	—	118,529	—	387,528	3,435	147,663	1,531,454
Industrial sector	558,979	—	51,728	—	1,600	—	91,740	704,047
Iron and steel	275,821						24,671	300,592
Cement	95,660						5,504	101,174
Fertilizers	23,994						21,409	45,403
Other chemicals	10,474		41,728				6,616	58,818
Pulp and paper	4,026						932	4,959
Other metals	25,804						3,421	29,228
Other minerals	—							—
Textiles	29,385						2,497	31,882
Building materials	37,204						189	37,393

Non-specified industry	56,500	10,000	—	1,600	26,500	94,800
Transport sector	—	33,794	—	—	7,882	41,675
Road	—	24,387	—	—		24,387
Rail	—	1,301	—	—	3,882	6,282
Water		940	—	3,435		940
Air		2,088	—	3,436		2,088
Non-specified	—	5,000	—	—	4,000	9,000
Residential sector	233,899	6,503	—	202,310	13,398	519,545
Urban	117,958	6,503	—		9,276	137,170
Rural	115,843	—	—	262,310	4,122	382,376
Agricultural sector	9,750	5,005	—	44,950	2,672	62,277
Field operations	—	2,619	—	—	907	3,526
Processing/other	9,750	2,388	—	44,950	1,664	58,760
Fisheries sector	—	1,073	—	—	100	1,173
Large ships	—	873	—	—		873
Processing/other	—	200	—	—	100	300
Military sector	38,467	17,425	—	—	24,039	79,932
Trucks and other transport		5,926				5,926
Armaments		2,368				2,368
Air force		2,299				2,299
Naval forces		6,731				6,731
Military manufacturing	887				79	987
Buildings and other	37,680	100			23,980	61,640
Public/commercial sectors	34,915	—		—	7,932	42,847
Non-specified/other sectors		3,000				3,000
Non-energy use	18,290			58,667		78,957
Electricity General (Gross TWhe)	28.31	1.51	26.69			66.60

*One Terajoule is equal to one trillion joules, which is the equivalent of approximately 24 tonnes of crude oil (tonnes of oil equivalent). Figures in this table should be considered accurate to at best two significant digits.

been in the 30 to 40 percent range and may have been even lower in more recent years (for example, 1991–1993). Capacity factors of 50 to 60 percent are low, but not extremely so, for a modern electrical grid, whereas average capacity factors of 30 to 40 percent would be quite low.

There are several different estimates of DPRK oil refining capacity. If the higher estimates are correct, refining capacity in North Korea is probably under-utilized, whereas the lower estimates would imply that refineries ran at near full capacity in 1990. In either case, reportedly lower oil imports since 1990 have probably caused one or both of the DPRK's refineries to be operated at subopti-mal rates, which typically results in lower operational efficiencies (due to the facilities being operated at partial load and/or being started and stopped more often).

Industrial boilers and furnaces are probably also operated at suboptimal rates due to the types of feedstock and fuel constraints. Like refineries and power plants, these industrial devices typically perform at lower average efficiencies when operated at lower rates.

Underdevelopment of Key Subsectors

Economic development in the DPRK in the last few decades has focused on extractive and other heavy industries. Partly as a consequence of this focus—and partly as a result of North Korea's political isolation from much of the industrial-ized world—some key sectors of the DPRK economy remain underdeveloped or produce goods that are effectively obsolete.

Unlike many Asian countries, the DPRK does not have a semiconductor industry. As a result, and because importing computer equipment into the DPRK is difficult at best, the country lacks the electronic automation and control sys-tems that could markedly improve the efficiency of its industrial processes, boilers, and other equipment.

The DPRK produces a number of medium and heavy trucks. Chief among these is a 2.5–metric ton vehicle that is apparently a crude copy of a Soviet truck from the 1950s and 1960s. This truck reportedly has a carburetor that wastes a considerable amount of fuel at low speeds. More modern, efficient, and reliable truck designs would enhance efficiencies in the transport sector and in the many other sectors of the DPRK economy that rely on truck transport of goods.

With the exception of some small-scale manufacturing of coal briquettes, coal preparation (which involves pulverizing and washing coal to reduce impurities such as ash and sulfur) is apparently not practiced in the DPRK. The power plant and industrial boilers, and even the smaller boilers in residential and public/com-mercial buildings, would be more efficient and easier to operate and maintain if they were fueled with prepared coal.

Other key processes that have been underdeveloped in North Korea include coal-mining technologies—the DPRK lacks the technology to mine coal at more than moderate depths—and oil and gas exploration. There may be oil and gas reserves in offshore areas of North Korea, but the country lacks the technologies to explore and develop these resources effectively and has yet to secure an international partner to aid in such an effort.

Limits on Coal Resources

Although the DPRK has substantial coal reserves, the varying quality of its coals, and the location of some of its better coal reserves, limits their utilization. Some of the coals mined in Korea have ash contents as high as 65 percent and heating values as low as 1,000 kilocalories per kilogram (roughly one-sixth the energy content of high-quality coals). Untreated coals of this quality can be expected to have a low efficiency of combustion. The large volumes of bottom and fly ash generated when these coals are burned create a disposal problem.[4]

Approximately one-half of the coal reserves in the important Anju mining area (northwest of Pyongyang) are located under the seabed. Although this deposit includes some of the higher-quality coal in the area, the DPRK currently lacks the technology to extract this coal effectively and safely. In mines in the Anju district that are close to the sea, it is reported that miners must already pump six metric tons of seawater per metric ton of coal mined, due to saltwater intrusion into the low-lying coal seams.

Low Efficiency of Energy-Transforming Processes and Equipment

The reported low efficiency of energy-transforming processes and combustion equipment has been noted earlier in this chapter. Low-efficiency energy sector devices in the DPRK reportedly include the following:

- Industrial boilers, which suffer from a lack of spare parts, inadequate maintenance and control systems, suboptimal fuel quality, and antiquated design.
- Boilers in residential and public/commercial buildings, which have the same general problems as industrial boilers.
- Utility boilers and generators, which not only have the same types of efficiency problems as industrial and other boilers but also have problems with the electrical components of the generating facilities (including reports of degraded insulation on generator windings) and experience emergency power outages.
- The electricity transmission and distribution systems. Official estimates of losses in these systems total 16 percent of generation, which would be high for a modern system of a size similar to the DPRK grid but not unreasonably so. Other observers, however, suggest that these losses comprise a

higher fraction of generation. In either case, it is clear that the efficiency of the electricity transmission and distribution system has room for marked improvement.

Fragmentation of Institutional Responsibility for Key Parts of the Energy Sector

The fragmentation of institutional responsibility in the energy sector inhibits efforts to upgrade the DPRK's energy systems. There is no single institution in North Korea that is responsible for energy analysis, integrated planning, and management. Ministries and other government organizations involved in the energy sector include:

- The Ministry of Coal Mining (coal exploration, mining, and supply)
- The Electric Power Industry Commission (electricity generation, dispatching, sales, and development)
- The State Planning Commission, Central Statistics Bureau, and Commission for Science and Technology (energy statistics and energy-planning activities)
- The Transport Commission (energy use in the transport sector)
- The Ministry of Atomic Energy (nuclear energy research)
- The External Economic Affairs Commission (purchase of crude oil and refined products, and purchase of imported equipment for use in the energy sector)
- The Ministry of Machine Building Industry (domestic manufacturing of power generation equipment)
- Institutes within the Academy of Sciences (research and development activities; R&D activities are also carried out by the individual ministries)
- The State Committee for Energy (major decisions in the energy sector)
- The military (army, air force, and navy, as well as reserve units), which accounts, by our estimate, for a significant share of fuels used in the DPRK, particularly petroleum products

Coordination between the various institutions involved in energy sector activities should be improved to enable North Korea to take advantage of the energy efficiency opportunities and energy-planning resources that could become available (through bilateral and multilateral aid, for example) in the near future.

Demographic and Workforce Issues

The North Korean workforce is literate, disciplined, and hardworking; these attributes have been key in allowing the DPRK to make the economic strides that it did in (particularly) the two decades following the Korean War. The DPRK workforce, however, suffers from a lack of technological training as a result of

North Korea's political isolation. In addition, the relatively low rate of growth of the population means that the workforce is aging. This trend may cause average workforce productivity to decline over the long term (all else being equal, as the ratio of active workers to retirees declines) and may present problems in retraining workers for new, higher-technology jobs (for example, to make goods that would be competitive in the export market). Academics and engineers involved in the basic sciences and in applied research and development probably also suffer lower productivity due to limited and tightly controlled contact with their peers in other countries.

Another workforce issue is the significant fraction (probably on the order of 17 percent) of potentially economically active males that are in the armed forces of the DPRK. Although soldiers apparently participate in public works projects and in some other civilian economic activities (such as the harvesting of crops), the proportion of workers in the active armed forces (and the time spent by the 5 million reservists in military training) undoubtedly acts as a drain on the overall DPRK economy.[5]

Suppressed and Latent Demand for Energy Services

Lack of fuels in many sectors of the DPRK economy has caused demand for energy services to go unmet. Electricity outages are one obvious source of unmet demand; but portions of the North Korean fishing fleet have been idled for lack of diesel fuel. Residential heating is reportedly restricted in the winter to conserve fuel, resulting in uncomfortably cool indoor temperatures.

The problem posed by suppressed and latent demand for energy services is that when and if supply constraints are removed, there is likely to be a surge in energy use, as residents, industries, and other consumers of fuels increase their use of energy services toward desired levels. This probable surge in energy use makes it even more important to enhance the energy efficiency of equipment and appliances in the DPRK as much as possible but will limit any net savings in fuels.

Compounding the risk of a surge in the use of energy services is the virtual lack of energy product markets in the DPRK. Without fuel-pricing reforms, there will be few incentives for households and other energy users to adopt energy efficiency measures.

Energy consumers are also unlikely, without a massive and well-coordinated program of education about energy use and energy efficiency, to have the technical know-how to choose and make good use of energy efficiency technologies.

Potential for Energy Efficiency and Renewable Energy Measures in the DPRK

In a recent study,[6] we described an estimated energy supply and demand balance for North Korea (shown earlier, in Table 9.1). In the first part of this chapter, we have already related some of the energy sector problems facing the country. In this section, we use the estimated energy balance as a starting point for an indicative-though quite admittedly very approximate and not at all exhaustive—quantitative analysis of some of the energy efficiency and renewable energy options that could be implemented in the DPRK as well as a more qualitative discussion of some of the alternatives available.

In the following subsections, we describe the goal of our analysis, present the approach and data sources used, describe the overall results of the analysis, and present the specific assumptions used and study results obtained for the key subsectors and end uses addressed.

Goal of the Study

The preparation of a full-fledged analysis of the energy efficiency and renewable energy opportunities for a country like the DPRK is a large undertaking and is not only well beyond the scope of this study but even further beyond the limitations of the data on the North Korean energy situation that we have had available. As a consequence, our modest goal was to prepare indicative quantitative analyses of energy efficiency options for a number of key sectors and subsectors. Although these analyses are necessarily built on a number of assumptions, they are designed to provide order-of-magnitude estimates for the energy savings potentially available and of the costs of achieving those savings. Furthermore, we hope that this analysis will help to indicate fertile areas where additional work is needed to evaluate energy efficiency and renewable energy opportunities in North Korea, while suggesting specific near- and medium-term opportunities for energy efficiency measures.

Approach and Data Sources

Our general approach to preparing the analysis of North Korea's energy efficiency opportunities can be described as follows:

• Use the estimated DPRK energy balance data as a guide to indicate key sectors and subsectors where fuel demand could be significantly reduced by energy efficiency measures.

• Use the energy balance results, together with data from the international energy literature and where necessary (that is, often) rough estimates of key parameters, to estimate end-use shares for key technologies.

• Use cost and performance data on energy efficiency and renewable energy technologies from international literature sources to estimate potential fuel savings in key subsectors and the investment costs that would be required to achieve those savings. In many cases, we have been fortunate to be able to draw on the large body of work on energy efficiency programs in the People's Republic of

China that has been published by the Energy Analysis Program of Lawrence Berkeley National Laboratory (LBNL) and its Chinese collaborators. In many of these cases, the cost and performance data are based on actual Chinese experience obtained during the 1980s.

• Formulate viable assumptions regarding the future. A full-fledged analysis of the achievable potential for energy efficiency measures requires a host of assumptions about the future. Population growth rates, economic growth rates, and underlying, ongoing structural changes-such as changes in the housing stock, shifts in industrial output, and changing patterns of personal consumption (among many others)-form the backdrop against which energy efficiency opportunities should be considered. For this analysis, however, and for a variety of reasons, we have chosen, for the quantitative portion of our analysis, to let our estimate of potential energy sector improvements stand for the achievable savings over the next decade. Our reasons for this assumption, in addition to the paucity of reliable data that the reader will by now recognize is endemic to our topic, include the following:

• Since our study derived a 1990 energy balance, and the North Korean economy has reportedly been either static or in decline in the years since 1990, it would seem that even an immediate turnaround would be unlikely to result in 1990–2005 fuel consumption levels that, on average, greatly exceed 1990 levels. Realistically, political considerations would appear to make a complete and immediate turnaround less likely than a slow recovery.

• Evaluate and aggregate the potential impacts and costs of the energy efficiency and renewable energy technologies quantified and suggest other key measures that are likely to be broadly applicable in North Korea.

• Evaluate, briefly, the potential environmental and other impacts of implementing energy efficiency measures.

Although complete implementation of a particular energy efficiency measure in a subsector is unlikely, the pathways for technology dissemination in North Korea—if there is committed support from national leaders and financial and technical support from the international community—have the potential to allow the rapid implementation of energy efficiency measures.

We believe that our assumptions as to the energy savings achievable from the technologies we address (quantitatively) are more likely to prove to be underestimated rather than overestimated. This belief is informed by the large number of anecdotal reports of vast waste of energy in the DPRK, even when compared with early 1980s conditions in China.

Overall Results for Energy Efficiency Measures Evaluated

We chose the following set of energy efficiency and renewable energy measures for our initial analysis:

Measures That Would Save Coal

- Industrial boiler improvements
- Residential (multifamily) and public/commercial/military boiler improvements
- Domestic coal stove/heater improvements
- Residential (multifamily) and public/commercial/military building-shell improvements
- Electric utility boiler improvements

Measures That Would Save (or Generate) Electricity

- Improvements in industrial electric motors
- Improvements in electric motors in other sectors
- Improvements in residential lighting
- Improvements in nonresidential lighting
- Reduction in "own use" at coal-fired electric utility plants
- Reduction in "emergency losses" at coal-fired electric utility plants
- Reduction in electricity transmission and distribution losses
- Generation of wind-powered electricity

A Measure That Would Save Petroleum Products

- Replacement of the existing fleet of 2.5–metric ton trucks

The details of the process we used to estimate the impacts and costs of these measures are provided in the Von Hippel and Hayes study mentioned previously.[7]

Table 9.2 shows the overall results of our evaluation of these measures. We have assumed that under an aggressive program with both strong leadership commitment inside the DPRK and technical and financial cooperation from other countries, these measures (or some of these measures and others with similar per-unit costs and impacts) could be implemented over the next ten years. In total (that is, in year ten of a crash program), they save approximately 390 petajoules[8] per year of coal (about 29 percent of the 1990 DPRK coal supply) at a cost of about $US 1.3 billion (1990 dollars), plus more than 50 petajoules per year (about 25 percent of 1990 generation) of electricity supply (electricity saved plus new wind-powered generation) at a cost of approximately $1.7 billion. Replacement of the DPRK fleet of 2.5–metric ton trucks, as we have modeled it, is unlikely to be cost-effective (for reasons explained in the next subsection) but would save approximately 4.4 petajoules of refined products (somewhat less than 4 percent of total national oil use and 18 percent of road transport oil use as we have estimated it) at an investment cost of $0.82 billion.

As noted below, the key assumption that we have made in estimating the costs and performance of most of the coal- or electricity-saving energy efficiency measures is that the costs and performance of these measures, when implemented in the DPRK, would be similar to the costs and performance of the

Table 9.2

Summary of Quantitative Evaluation of Energy Efficiency and Renewable Energy Options for DPRK

Measure	Estimated energy savings potential TJ*/yr	Total estimated investment cost $US 1990
Measures to save coal:		
Industrial boiler and furnace improvements	158,267	610,400,542
Residential and public/commercial military boiler improvements	41,091	88,480,469
Building envelope improvements	27,513	54,306,490
Domestic stove/heater improvements	31,935	22,921,595
Electric utility boiler improvements	114,505	441,621,174
Totals	373,310	1,217,730,269
Avoided losses of coal during transport	3,733	
Total coal supply savings	377,043	
Fraction of 1990 total coal supply	28%	
Investment required, $ per GJ/yr of coal supply savings		3.23
Investment required, $ per tce/yr of coal supply savings		95
Measures to save/generate electricity:		
Industrial motors and drives	8,719	339,561,095
Motors and drives in other sectors	1,574	61,311,299
Residential lighting	2,572	100,182,798
Non-residential lighting	10,267	285,183,258
Own use reduction in power plants	2,752	128,592,305
Reduction of emergency use in power plants	6,420	187,530,445
Transmission and distribution improvements	10,675	311,801,170
Wind-powered electricity generation	3,942	200,000,000
Totals	46,921	1,614,162,370
Additional avoided T&D losses (based on 1990 rates)	4,211	
Total electricity supply savings/generation	51,132	
Fraction of 1990 total electricity generation	25.6%	
Investment required, $ per GJ/yr of electricity supply savings/generation		32
Investment required, $ per MWh/yr of electricity supply savings/generation		114
Measure to save petroleum products:		
Improvements in 2-1/2 tonne truck fleet	4,379	824,815,770
Fraction of 1990 total refined products use	3.7%	
Fraction of 1990 total refined product use in road transport	18.0%	
Investment required, $ per GJ/yr of refined products savings		188
Investment required, $ per toe/yr of petroleum products savings		7,882

*One Terajoule is equal to one trillion joules, which is the equivalent of approximately 24 tonnes of crude oil. Tce is tonnes of standard coal equivalent.

Figures in this table should be considered accurate to *at best* two significant digits.

Table 9.3

Cost of Greenhouse Gas Reductions in DPRK

Measures	GHG savings	Cost ($US 1990 per metric ton per year
Measures to save coal	36 million metric tons CO_2	35
	210,000 metric tons methane	6,090
Measures to save electricity	9.7 million metric tons CO_2	165

measures as experienced in the People's Republic of China during energy efficiency programs carried out there in the 1980s. It could be argued that the costs of the measures in China might be lower than in the DPRK, due to lower labor rates and a larger manufacturing base in China. Conversely, the opportunities for savings with the measures we have evaluated may be greater in the DPRK than they were in China, due to the older capital stock found in the DPRK.

The transfer of LWR (light-water reactor) technology is a political prerequisite to starting bilateral or multilateral initiatives in energy efficiency (or other types of projects and trade, for that matter) with the DPRK. Nonetheless, we cannot resist the temptation to compare the costs and impacts of our list of measures with the costs and impacts of the proposed nuclear power plants. A pair of LWRs with a combined electricity generation capacity of 2 gigawatts (or 2 billion watts, the current LWR transfer proposal) would, if run reasonably efficiently, produce roughly 12,000 GWh per year of electricity. This is about 44 petajoules per year of electricity supply. The cost of the reactors (probably about $US 4.5 billion in 1995 dollars) would be a bit less than 50 percent higher than our estimates for the costs of both the electricity- and coal-saving measures we evaluated (factoring inflation into our cost estimates in 1990 dollars).[9] Like the energy efficiency and renewable energy measures, the LWR scheme would likely take nearly ten years to provide its full capacity, even if construction were to start today (1995). Unlike the energy efficiency options, however, none of the LWR capacity will be available until the year in which the plants are complete and fueled, whereas some of the energy efficiency savings would be available in the first year of the program (with more available each year thereafter).

Not coincidentally, the energy efficiency and renewable energy measures that we have evaluated will also reduce greenhouse gas (GHG) emissions per unit of energy service provided.[10] Based on the emissions calculations detailed in the study referenced earlier, we estimate that GHG savings (and costs per metric ton of carbon reduced) would be as shown in Table 9.3.

In reviewing the cost figures presented above, the reader is urged to keep several considerations in mind:

- The CO_2 cost figures are expressed in dollars per metric ton of carbon dioxide, not per metric ton of saved carbon (as is also common in the literature). To express these figures in dollars per metric ton of saved carbon, one would multiply by $44/12$.
- The cost figures are expressed as *total* investment (over ten years) per metric ton of annual emission reduction. In order to express these figures in terms of dollars per metric ton of total emission reduction, one would probably divide them by a factor of 10 to 20 (to account for the fact that savings would accrue over the project's life cycle—say ten to twenty years—assuming a low, zero, or negative discount rate is applied to future GHG emissions). In the former case, the cost of CO_2 reduction by coat-saving measures would fall to $3.50 per metric ton, and that of electricity-saving measures to $16.50—both quite cheap by international standards.
- The cost figures are given on a gross basis and are thus not adjusted for the fuel, operations and maintenance, and other types of economic and environmental benefits that would accrue from the energy efficiency and renewable energy investments we have evaluated.
- The costs for carbon dioxide and methane savings shown for coal-saving measures are not additive. The same efficiency investment outlay provides savings of both gases.
- In estimating the GHG savings from electricity generation measures, we have assumed that the electricity saved would have been generated by the combination of coal-fired, hydroelectric, and oil-fired plants currently operating in the DPRK. If the thermal plants are "on the margin"—that is if electricity savings through efficiency measures and renewable sources displaced electricity generated by coal- and/or oil-fired plants first—then GHG emissions savings would be greater (and their costs lower) than shown above.

Sectoral Results

In this subsection, we present our performance and cost assumptions for those energy efficiency and renewable energy measures that we have evaluated quantitatively and discuss other measures that could be applied (and should be evaluated in a more detailed study) in the various sectors and subsectors of the DPRK energy economy.

Measures for the Electricity Generation Sector

Our quantitative analysis of energy efficiency and renewable energy measures in the electricity generation sector of the DPRK includes the following measures:

• *Electric utility coal-fired boiler improvements:* Utility boilers in the DPRK reportedly have minimal (if any) insulation, are poorly operated, suffer from steam tube cracks and other maintenance problems, and are often antiquated. We assumed that a combination of measures that have been applied to industrial boilers in China could be applied to utility boilers in the DPRK at similar costs to obtain similar results. We have assumed that a combination of microcomputer boiler control, insulation of piping, and renovation of boilers could raise the average boiler efficiency (heat energy output divided by fuel energy input) from about 60 percent to near 85 percent, reducing coal consumption by about 30 percent.[11] We assumed that these measures would be available for about the same cost as similar industrial boiler improvements in China—approximately $3.86 per gigajoule per year of coal saved.[12] In fact, economies of scale may make efficiency improvements for utility boilers less costly per unit of energy saved than similar measures for generally smaller industrial boilers.

• *Reduction in "own use" at coal-fired electric utility plants:* We have assumed that the in-station use of electricity at coal-fired power plants is 7.2 percent of gross generation. Based on cost and savings estimates from Sathaye,[13] we estimate that own use can be reduced to 4.5 percent at a cost of $46.30 per gigajoule per year of electricity saved.

• *Reduction in electricity transmission and distribution (T&D) losses:* Official DPRK estimates place transmission and distribution losses of electricity at 16 percent of net generation (electricity leaving the power plant), although, as noted earlier, this figure may well be low. We have assumed—again, based on performance and cost data in Sathaye[14]—that it would be possible through a combination of measures to reduce combined T&D losses to 10 percent of net generation at an average cost of $29.20 per gigajoule per year. T&D improvements would include better system control facilities, improved transformers, the addition of capacitance to the system, and other measures to improve power factors and reduce voltage fluctuations.

• *Reduction in "emergency losses" at coal-fired electric utility plants:* We have assumed, based on anecdotal reports, that emergency losses of power at coal-fired power plants in the DPRK average about 7 percent of gross generation. We assume that these losses can be reduced by 90 percent through the application of measures available at a cost per unit of energy saved similar to that for T&D improvements. It may well be, however, that the combination of boiler improvements and T&D improvements will by themselves reduce or eliminate emergency losses, with little or no additional efficiency investments required.

• *Wind-powered electricity generation:* Wind power is one of the major renewable resources readily available to the DPRK, though the wind resources in the country remain, to our knowledge, largely unmapped.[15] We have assumed that 500 megawatts of wind generation capacity (for example, 500 machines per year of 100 kilowatts or 250 machines per year of 200 kilowatts) could be installed in the DPRK over the next ten years (with machines manufactured in the DPRK and/or imported) and that the average capital costs of the machines would be similar to those for wind machines produced in joint ventures in Eastern Europe, about $400.00 per kilowatt. We assumed a capacity factor of 25 percent for machines installed in the DPRK, yielding an investment cost of $51.00 per gigajoule per year of electricity generated. Note that this cost does not include fixed or variable operating and maintenance costs, but these are typically a small fraction of annualized capital cost for wind power generation.

Other potential energy efficiency improvements addressing the electricity generation sector that seem promising but that we have been unable to evaluate quantitatively include:

• *Coal preparation:* Grinding and washing coal to remove ash and sulfur would improve the efficiency of coal combustion in utility boilers. Such preparation would reduce the load of ash in the bottom of boilers and provide a more homogeneous coal particle size, allowing for cleaner and more complete combustion. The environmental benefits of such measures (including reduced particulate and sulfur oxide emissions to the air) could be considerable, and by-products of coal cleaning (inert material removed from coal and elemental sulfur) could be used in the building and other industries. In addition, coal preparation, if done near the coal mines, should reduce coal transport costs by increasing the energy content of the coal per unit mass.

• *Expansion of electricity metering:* At present, there is reportedly little or no metering of electricity consumption in North Korea. Metering the electricity used by industrial facilities, residences, and buildings would not only provide valuable information on the use of electricity in the DPRK but would also, if coupled with per-unit electricity pricing, provide electricity users with an incentive to use electricity efficiently.

• *Cogeneration:* The energy literature on China and the former Soviet Union[16] cites examples of industrial boilers and furnaces that have very high exhaust gas temperatures, indicating the availability of a substantial amount of waste heat. Assuming that such situations are also common in North Korea, the waste heat from industrial and other large boilers could be used to generate electricity.

• *Gasification combined-cycle electricity generation/retrofits:* The efficiency of electricity generation from coal could be increased dramatically in the DPRK by first converting the coal into a gas, combusting the gas in a turbine that turns a generator, and then routing the exhaust gases from the turbine to a boiler to raise steam for a second cycle of electricity generation. Gasifiers could be added as "front ends" to existing (renovated) coal-fired boilers in the DPRK. The efficiency of gasification combined-cycle plants can be more than 40 percent,[17] a vast increase from the probable 20 to 25 percent efficiency in existing DPRK plants. There should also be substantial emissions benefits from employing this technology. Coal preparation may be a prerequisite for implementing this technology in North

Korea. Repowering of the DPRK's oil-fired utility boilers (more than 200 mega-watts) to make them combined-cycle plants is also a strong possibility.[18]

Measures for the Industrial Sector

Our quantitative analysis of efficiency and renewable energy measures in the industrial sector of the DPRK includes the following measures:

• *Improvements in industrial coal-fired boilers and furnaces:* Like utility boilers, industrial boilers and furnaces in the DPRK reportedly have very low average efficiencies, perhaps as low as 50 percent for boilers. Using the same set of improvements assumed for utility boilers (see above), we assumed that the average boiler efficiency could be raised from about 50 percent to about 80 percent, reducing coal consumption by about 37.5 percent.[19] We assumed that these mea-sures would be available for approximately the same cost as similar industrial boiler improvements in China—approximately $3.86 per gigajoule per year.

• *Improvements in industrial electric motors:* Electric motors in the DPRK may be made domestically or imported from China, or they may be constructed from a combination of domestic and Chinese materials. In any case, the stock of motors in the DPRK is highly likely to be both aging and inefficient. We have prepared rough estimates of the fraction of electricity use, by subsector, that is consumed in motors and drives. These estimates vary from as low as 50 percent, for subsectors in which we felt electricity was likely to be used intensively in end uses other than motive power (such as electrolytic refining of metals), to as high as 95 percent, for subsectors (such as the cement industry) in which we felt that motor-driven applications such as grinding and sizing of cement "clinker" (raw cement) would likely be the dominant use of electricity. As a point of reference, note that 65 percent of the electricity used in the entire Chinese economy has been estimated to be consumed in electric motors.

Based again on Chinese experience, we have assumed that it would be possi-ble to increase the average motor efficiency from approximately 75 percent to approximately 88 percent.[20] The latter efficiency (which corresponds to higher-efficiency new motors produced in China as of 1990) is similar to that for standard new electric motors sold in the United States and Japan, so efficiency improvements beyond what we have assumed are definitely possible.[21] We have assumed that the cost of this efficiency improvement would be on the order of $39.00 per gigajoule per year of electricity savings.

• *Industrial lighting improvements:* We have assumed that lighting accounts for a relatively modest 5 percent of electricity use in the DPRK. Based on the cost and performance of nonresidential lighting improvements in industrialized countries, we have estimated that it would be possible to save 50 percent of the industrial lighting electricity used through a variety of measures (including im-proved bulbs and ballasts, more efficient fixtures, replacement of incandescent lamps with fluorescent lamps, and lighting controls) at a cost of about $28.00 per gigajoule per year of electricity saved.[22]

As in the electricity generation sector, there are a wealth of opportunities for saving energy in the industrial sector that we have not been able to evaluate quantitatively. These include:

• *Industrial process improvements:* It is likely that a considerable amount of electricity and coal could be saved by improvements in industrial processes. These opportunities are available in many subsectors. In the DPRK cement industry, for example, the coal consumption per unit of output is 6.9 gigajoules per metric ton of "clinker."[23] This can be compared with an average coal use of 6.1 gigajoules per metric ton in China in 1980, 5.2 gigajoules per metric ton in China in 1992,[24] and 3 gigajoules per metric ton in modern plants in industrialized countries. These figures imply that coal use in the cement subsector could be reduced by between 12 percent to more than 50 percent. Similar opportunities exist in the iron and steel, other metals, fertilizer, textiles, and other industrial subsectors. In the important iron and steel subsector, possible process improvements include integrating steel production and forming processes (thus eliminating the need to cool and reheat the steel), continuous casting and forming, electricity generation using top pressure in blast furnaces, use of coal gas for electricity generation, and other technologies.[25] Generic efficiency improvements applicable to many industries include insulating product pipelines; using better refractory materials (special ceramics used as, for example, furnace linings) that last longer and have better insulating properties; using variable-speed drives to reduce the electricity used in electric motors; modifications to reduce friction in piping, valves, and conveyance systems; and using harder, longer-lasting materials in cutting and grinding applications.

Note that process improvements can be geared not only toward improving the efficiency of fuel use but also toward reducing materials waste. Improving chemical reactors so that there is less waste of reactants, using better-quality raw materials to improve product yield, and recycling waste materials from production processes and product refining can reduce both waste and energy consumption.[26] Product modifications that result in the reduction of raw materials (and thus energy) used per unit of product are also possible.[27] Not coincidentally, these improvements also typically reduce process effluents to the environment.

Process improvements also could be directed toward the 30 percent of DPRK petroleum demand that is reportedly used in carbide manufacturing. So little is known about how this petroleum is used in carbide manufacture (if the report of such use is in fact correct) that it is impossible to say what the prospects for savings are in this sector.

• *Coal processing:* As for electricity generation, coal washing and other methods of coal preparation could help to improve the combustion efficiency of coal-fired boilers and furnaces in the industrial and other sectors dramatically. It is likely that coal processing could also improve the efficiency of industrial processes in which coal is used as a feedstock—including fertilizer (ammonium) and synthetic fiber manufacture.

• *Construction industry modifications:* The massive scale of construction projects in the DPRK, coupled with the use of manual design and construction methods, results in a wastage of building material relative to more updated methods. Considerable savings in steel and cement—and thus savings in the energy needed to produce these materials—are possible through the use of improved construction practices.[28]

*Measures for the Residential and
Public/Commercial/Military Sectors*

Our quantitative analysis included the following efficiency measures for the residential sector:

• *Boiler improvements:* For small and medium-sized space-heating (and possibly water-heating, in some instances) boilers of the type found in urban residential and other buildings, we assumed, based roughly on the same sources we used for our industrial boiler measure estimates, that a 15 percent improvement in efficiency (starting from an average boiler efficiency of 50 percent; thus, a 23 percent reduction in coal use) would be available for approximately $2.15 per gigajoule per year of coal saved. Note that the boiler improvements included here are unlikely to exhaust the opportunities for improving boiler energy efficiency through equipment upgrades and improved operations and maintenance.

• *Building-envelope improvements:* We have included two simple building-envelope improvement measures in our estimate of possible energy efficiency savings. These are: (1) the application of a 30–millimeter coat of concrete containing perlite—a lightweight mineral with insulating properties—to the inside of the typical concrete-slab walls of residential and other buildings and (2) double glazing of windows. Combined, these two measures are estimated—based on simulations for Chinese buildings—to save 20 percent of heating energy.[29] The cost of these savings is estimated at slightly under $2.00 per gigajoule per year. Note that in applying this measure to coal use in buildings, we have assumed that boiler improvements would take place before (or at the same time as) building-envelope improvements—that is, the savings fraction for building-envelope improvements was applied to the total energy use after boiler efficiency improvements had been factored in.

The two building-envelope improvements can be considered a minimal simple start to the list of potential measures of this type. Other measures include caulking and weather stripping to reduce air infiltration, insulation of water piping, improved radiator controls (in fact, visitors to the DPRK report that the only heat-control measure available to residents of typical North Korean apartment buildings is the opening and closing of windows and doors), interior and exterior wall and roof insulation, roof coatings, and others.

• *Rural residential coal stove/heater improvements:* We have assumed that the average residential stove/heater could be improved from an average of 30 percent efficiency to 40 percent efficiency, thus saving 25 percent of initial coal use. This is a rough estimate on our part. The estimates that we have found of coal stove efficiency in the DPRK and China range from 20 to 50 percent; 30 percent was cited as an estimate for the DPRK by an informed visitor to the country.[30] We have assumed that this efficiency improvement would be available for the same cost cited for coal stove improvements in China[31]—namely, $0.72 per gigajoule per year.

• *Electric motor improvements in urban residential and nonresidential buildings:* Electric motors are typically used in multifamily apartment buildings and in nonresidential buildings for a variety of purposes, including ventilation, refrigeration, and water pumping (for heating and potable water). We have assumed that 10 percent of the electricity used in the urban residential subsector, and 30 percent of that used in the public/commercial and military sectors, is used in electric motors. These estimates are admittedly rough guesses at best but are lower than the fraction of electricity used in motors in similar sectors in many other countries. We have assumed that the average cost and performance of measures that increase the efficiency of these motors would be roughly the same as in the industrial sector.

• *Improvements in residential and nonresidential lighting:* We have assumed that the fraction of residential electricity employed in lighting end uses is 40 percent. This figure is somewhat higher than lighting electricity fractions quoted for Thailand and the former Soviet Union (28 and 33 percent, respectively), but both of those societies employ electricity for end uses—including air-conditioning and water heating—that reportedly are uncommon in DPRK residences. We have assumed that 80 percent of lighting electricity use in residences in the DPRK powers incandescent bulbs, that compact fluorescent (CFL) bulbs could save 75 percent of the electricity used by incandescent bulbs (while providing similar or enhanced light output), and that compact fluorescent bulbs could reasonably be substituted for incandescent bulbs for 80 percent (by energy) of lighting uses. Taken together, these three assumptions result in a 48 percent reduction in electricity use in residential lighting. As an estimate of costs, we have assumed that, as other authors have suggested for China, a factory producing 3 million CFL bulbs per year could be built in North Korea at a cost of $5 million.[32] The cost of conserving electricity by producing and using these bulbs would be approximately $39.00 per gigajoule per year. We should note that since the lifetime of CFLs is shortened if they are operated on a grid with fluctuating voltage and low power factors, transmission and distribution improvements would probably have to go hand in hand with the introduction of CFLs in the DPRK.

Our assumption for nonresidential buildings is that 50 percent of the electricity consumed is used in lighting. As for industrial lighting, we assume that 50 percent of this amount could be saved by a package of lighting energy efficiency measures, at a cost of about $28.00 per gigajoule per year. Since these cost and savings estimates are based on figures for industrialized countries, our guess is that similar improvement would cost less and save more in the DPRK, particularly if quality lighting components could be produced with a substantial contribution of domestic (versus imported) labor and materials.

Other possible energy efficiency measures for the residential and nonresidential buildings sector include the following:

• *Improvements in electric appliances:* The fraction of residences in the DPRK with refrigerators is unknown but is likely to be small. Those refrigerators that are in use in the DPRK are probably similar to Chinese models and thus up to 50 percent less efficient than those manufactured in industrialized countries. Liu et al.[33] report that Chinese refrigerators in the 200–liter size range consumed 365 kilowatt-hours per year, whereas South Korean models of similar capacity used 240 kilowatt-hours per year. To the extent that refrigeration is used in buildings other than private residences (for example, in communal kitchen facilities), similar savings may be possible. Improvement of the efficiency of refrigerators manufactured in or available to the DPRK could be increasingly important, as a refrigerator is probably one of the first appliances in which households will invest if economic conditions in North Korea begin to improve markedly.

A substantial fraction of households in the DPRK have television and/or radio. Recent improvements in electronics technology to which the DPRK does not currently have access have reduced the hourly energy consumption of these devices markedly, though the aggregate amount of electricity saved by such improvements may be small due to the limited power consumption of radios and small televisions. Other improvements in appliance efficiency in North Korea may well be possible, but their evaluation must await better information on the stock of electricity-using appliances in the household and other sectors. Microwave ovens, for example, accomplish many cooking tasks more efficiently than simple electric resistance burners, but the penetration of the latter in the DPRK residential housing stock is currently unknown (we assume that penetration of microwaves in North Korea is near zero).

• *Improvements in cooking efficiency (noncoal fuels):* Urban households in the DPRK reportedly use charcoal, liquefied petroleum gas (LPG), and kerosene stoves for cooking in addition to coal stoves. Rural households use wood and other types of biomass for cooking and heating. Efficiency improvements in all of these technologies are possible, though the percentage improvements (and the aggregate amount of fuel savings) is likely considerably higher for devices using solid fuels. Reduction in the use of wood and biomass fuels through the use of more efficient stoves and heaters would help to make wood and biomass available for other applications and/or reduce harvest pressures on forests.

• *District heating:* District heating of homes and other buildings using heat from power plants, industrial facilities, and stand-alone central steam plants is apparently practiced in North Korea (as it is throughout Eastern Europe), but the extent to which it is practiced is unknown. Switching to an efficient district heating network from a system of dispersed small boilers and stoves could result in substantial coal savings.

• *Building-shell improvements in rural homes:* Potential improvements include caulking and weather stripping, insulation, and glazing, but any definitive list of measures will have to wait until a better description of the rural housing stock in the DPRK is in hand.

• *Use of biogas:* Biogas produced via anaerobic fermentation of human night soil, animal manures, and agricultural wastes could be used as a clean cooking fuel in rural areas or could contribute to small-scale power production (with cogenerated heat for agricultural processing or other applications). The biogas production process also has the potential to yield important by-products such as animal bedding, soil amendments, and organic fertilizer as well as potentially (depending on the state of current waste-disposal practices) reduce environmental impacts.

Measures for the Transport Sector and Other Sectors

We have evaluated only one energy efficiency measure in the transport sector in a quantitative manner:

Replacement of medium-duty trucks: Trucks of 2.5 metric tons are the workhorses of the military ground transport fleet in the DPRK and are reportedly widely used for civilian goods as well. We have assumed that all the gasoline used for civilian freight transport by road in the DPRK is used in such trucks, and assuming that the freight transport provided by each vehicle is on the order of 30,000 metric ton–kilometers per year, we calculate that there are slightly fewer than 60,000 civilian 2.5–metric ton trucks, together with a similar number of military trucks in active service. If the most heavily used two-thirds of these trucks (which we assumed to use 90 percent of the fuel) were replaced with new vehicles similar to the Isuzu FRR model, a fuel savings of about 43 percent would result. We have assumed that these vehicles could be manufactured in the DPRK at a cost of $10,000.[34] At this cost, however, replacement of the truck fleet is not likely to be cost-effective. Note, though, that we have assumed that the existing trucks would be replaced regardless of whether they are at the end of their useful life. If one assumed only an incremental cost for the trucks (the difference between the costs of producing a standard DPRK truck and one similar to the Isuzu model), and/or if one assumed a substantially heavier usage (in metric ton–kilometers per year) for the new trucks, this measure would appear more cost-effective. Whether these changes would make this measure sufficiently cost-effective to pursue is impossible, with the data at hand, to ascertain.

Other potential improvements in the transport and other sectors might include the following:

• *Electric motor and drive improvements for electric locomotives:* Electrified rail is the backbone of the DPRK transit system. Though we have no data on the efficiency of electric locomotives in North Korea, potential efficiency improvements on the order of those described above for industrial motors seem plausible.

Substantial improvements in electric rail efficiency might come about simply as a result of transmission and distribution improvements on the electric grid as a whole. Other options for increasing rail efficiency might include updated rail control and scheduling systems, track improvements to reduce friction (and forced halts), and optimization of freight loads.

• *Updating other transport fleets:* Updating the road passenger transport, water transport (including the fishing fleet), and air transport fleets might as much as double their efficiency, but any fuel savings would be highly likely to be offset by increased use of these transport modes as they became more efficient and reliable.

• *Biofuels for transport:* In various documents, the DPRK government has expressed an interest in increasing self-reliance by replacing petroleum-based transport fuels with liquid fuels derived from biomass. Although the greenhouse gas and pollutant reduction benefits of such a program are important, we are reluctant to endorse this idea enthusiastically at present because of the following considerations: (1) All DPRK agricultural land appears to be needed and fully employed just to feed people; thus, production of motor fuels from agricultural crops such as corn would appear to be ruled out. (2) There appears to be relatively little extra wood or crop wastes available for use as cellulosic feedstocks for biofuels production (via either fermentation or thermal liquefaction). If the biomass resource situation changes in the future, however, biofuels would become a more attractive option.

• *Improving agricultural tractors:* Specific fuel consumption in tractors in China, reported to be 195 grams per horsepower-hour in the 1980s, was some 10 percent greater than for similar tractors in industrialized countries.[35] Tractors in the DPRK are unlikely to be more efficient than the Chinese average and are likely to be less efficient.

• *Reducing fertilizer use:* Fertilizer application in North Korea is reported to be excessive for some crops. On rice, for example, it has been suggested that the typical-practice nitrogen fertilizer application in the DPRK could be reduced by 25 percent.[36] If so, then significant reductions in energy use in the energy-intensive ammonia manufacturing industry in the DPRK should be possible, as well as (probably minor) reductions in the need for tractor fuel for fertilizer application.

Institutional Issues and Policies Affecting Implementation of Energy Efficiency Measures

If simply estimating the potential for energy efficiency improvements for an economy were all one had to do to convince policy makers to implement such measures, then fuel use in the world would be markedly less than it is now. In reality, institutional issues and national policies affect the implementation of energy efficiency and renewable energy measures in any country. Although unique in many ways, North Korea is no exception.

In this section, we discuss some of the types of institutional and policy issues that affect implementation of energy efficiency measures; review some of the recent lessons learned from nascent and ongoing energy efficiency programs in Eastern Europe, China, and the former Soviet Union; examine some of the existing bilateral and multilateral energy efficiency–related initiatives under way in the Northeast Asia region; present some potential strategies and mechanisms for implementing such measures in the DPRK; put forward suggestions for how to build and strengthen North Korean institutions so as to enhance their ability to carry out energy efficiency, renewable energy, environmental protection, and other sustainable development–related activities; and hint at ways in which organizations inside and outside North Korea might lend support to the implementation of energy efficiency and renewable energy measures in the DPRK.

Introduction: Issues in Implementing Energy Efficiency and Renewable Energy Measures in the DPRK

A host of issues—some unique to North Korea and some generic to the situation in many countries—affect which energy efficiency programs and measures[37] are implemented, as well as how they are implemented and on what time frame. We discuss some of these issues briefly below.

• *Institutional weaknesses and fragmentation:* The institutional arrangements in the energy sector are complicated and reflect a high degree of functional fragmentation.[38] Since there is no single specialized institutional authority or ministry that is responsible for energy analysis, integrated planning, and overall energy sector management, it is difficult to know which of the many institutional players in the DPRK energy sector should be responsible for implementing energy efficiency programs. Although many energy efficiency programs could be restricted in scope to, for example, a single economic sector, the need to coordinate activities by both suppliers and consumers of energy argues for the creation of a single authority (or a coordinated consortium of authorities) in the DPRK if effective programs are to be implemented. China's experience in coordinating planning and policy organs with line ministries to achieve energy efficiency goals is relevant in this respect.

• *Lack of information:* One universal barrier to implementing energy efficiency measures is the lack of information—on the part of residential customers, industrial plant managers, building superintendents, transport decision makers, midlevel bureaucrats in energy sector institutions, upper-level government officials, and others—as to the benefits, relative costs, and potential impacts of these technologies.[39]

• *Lack of energy markets:* The lack of meaningful pricing of most energy commodities in the DPRK, combined with the insensitivity to prices common to planned economies, creates an indifference to energy efficiency measures. If, for example, coal for an industrial plant is supplied as a matter of course according to a fixed allocation schedule, the plant manager has relatively little incentive to try to increase energy efficiency. Although true market pricing of goods, especially energy goods, is probably at the very least several years away in North Korea, some sort of pricing reform will be necessary to encourage energy users to increase the efficiency of their energy use.

• *Access to funding:* Although they result in cost savings in the medium to long term, many energy efficiency measures will require an initial outlay of capital. For the DPRK, this capital will be needed either to import efficient equipment or to retool its industries to produce efficient equipment. In either case, internal DPRK funds will be hard pressed to meet the needs of an aggressive energy efficiency program such as the effort we have described. Some countries—Thailand and China are examples—have set aside significant sums for energy efficiency programs. But North Korea, which lacks the vibrant economic growth of some other developing nations in the region, would have difficulty doing the same, and initial funding would have to be provided from external sources. On the other hand, China began funding its energy efficiency programs at the beginning of the 1980s, at a time when the leadership was laying the groundwork for economic growth but before the current phase of rapid growth had been established. Such experience highlights the difference that a committed leadership can make, even when money is tight.

• *Access to technology:* In countries with open trade policies, access to funding is most of what it takes to have access to technology. In the case of the DPRK, however, the issue is more complex, as some nations with energy-efficient technologies to export—the United States is an example—have less than open policies with regard to technological exports to North Korea. The prospective thawing of the DPRK's political relations with the United States, South Korea, and others could quickly change this situation. In the meantime, China may be a good source of inexpensive and easily adopted technologies that, even though not the most advanced, would represent significant improvements over those currently used in North Korea.

• *Institutional motivation:* Effective implementation of energy efficiency measures in the DPRK will require that officials at all levels of government perceive a mandate for energy efficiency and a benefit to themselves or their institutions. This means that (1) a clear and detailed mandate to implement energy efficiency measures aggressively must be issued at the highest level of the North Korean government; (2) any institutional disincentives to energy efficiency must be dismantled; (3) a system of clear, verifiable (to the extent practicable) energy efficiency goals must be set up to reward officials for program performance; and (4) the status of energy efficiency activities in the rankings of institutional activities must be high enough to encourage officials to pursue their targets aggressively.

• *Energy supply bias:* Many officials and other decision makers in developing nations (and developed nations, for that matter) see energy sector problems as primarily a matter of ensuring an adequate supply of fuels rather than simply providing energy services in the most efficient manner available. As a consequence, officials may tend to be either blind to or suspicious of the benefits of energy efficiency measures.[40] Efforts must be made to persuade key individuals that efficiency improvements are complementary to supply expansion.

• *Project scale bias:* Unlike energy supply projects, which tend to be large in scale (and large-scale undertakings are a North Korean specialty), energy efficiency projects vary widely in scale but often involve many small installations. The incremental nature of these investments may appear unfamiliar and thus daunting, from the bureaucratic and/or job-prestige perspective, to the officials who would be charged with implementing them.

• *Lack of skills and training—government-level:* Effective implementation of energy efficiency programs will require that government energy planners be well versed in the concepts of energy efficiency. This is almost certainly not the case in the DPRK at present. Even in countries where officials can be expected to be technically competent, continued training and exposure to new developments is desirable.

• *Lack of skills and training—program implementation–level:* In addition to the government officials who must support, sanction, and guide the implementation of energy efficiency programs, a cadre of trained engineers and technicians would be required to survey preinstallation energy performance and actually design, install, and monitor applications of energy efficiency equipment. This cadre of skilled individuals does not exist in the DPRK at present, though there are doubtless many trained people in the DPRK with sufficient basic skills in engineering and technology to learn the "trade" relatively rapidly. These people, or the trainers who would run in-country courses, must be trained before energy efficiency measures could be implemented on a broad scale.

• *Relative status of sectors:* Even if resources to implement energy efficiency and renewable energy programs in the DPRK became available, and assuming that the issues presented here could be adequately resolved, there would remain a question of which energy efficiency measures would be implemented first. Although yardsticks such as fairness across sectors and overall cost-effectiveness might be considered, it is likely that the political status of different ministries (and even that of industries within a given ministry) and the personal status within the governmental hierarchy of key officials would influence the selection of projects for implementation.

• *Prospects for reunification:* An additional layer of complexity in deciding which DPRK sectors and subsectors to target for energy efficiency improvements is posed by the prospects for and possible modes of reunification of North and South Korea. For example, would it make sense to undertake energy efficiency modifications in the North Korean motor vehicle industry when South Korea's infrastructure in the subsector is both much more modern and probably adequate for both Koreas? Would it not make more sense to target industries that complement the industrial strengths of the South? These questions, unfortunately, cannot be answered in a straightforward fashion as they are inextricably linked to political issues such as national sovereignty, self-reliance, and pre-reunification military sustenance.

Lessons from Ongoing Examples of Energy Efficiency Technology Transfer

Given the unique nature of North Korean society, one could expect that implementing energy efficiency measures in the DPRK would require somewhat different techniques and approaches than those appropriate to promoting energy efficiency in a Western nation or in a developing market economy. Happily, research on the implementation of energy efficiency measures in the republics of the former Soviet Union, Eastern Europe, and China provides some insight into what sorts of approaches appear to be effective in countries that have some economic, political, and infrastructural similarities with North Korea. The brief review of these lessons and insights presented in this subsection leans heavily on the work of the researchers in the Energy Analysis Program at the Lawrence Berkeley National Laboratory in Berkeley, California, and the reader is urged to consult the LBNL work for further elaboration on the topic.[41]

The approaches and insights from efforts to implement energy efficiency and renewable energy measures in other countries that are likely to be applicable to the DPRK include those discussed in the following subsections.

Promote Changes in Physical Infrastructure That Facilitate Energy Decision Making. We have discussed earlier the types of energy-using equipment and other infrastructure in the DPRK that could be targeted for replacement or rehabilitation. What has been emphasized relatively less, but is at least as important, is the need to invest in equipment that allows flows of energy to be controlled and quantified adequately. Such equipment includes electricity, heat, and hot-water meters; steam- and process-control valves and shunts; and dimmers and other equipment for controlling lighting. Applications for such equipment exist throughout the residential, public/commercial/military, and industrial sectors. Without such equipment—which typically is inexpensive and relatively easy to install and operate—any attempt to institute price signals in energy markets, or even to reward reduced energy use in other ways, will be futile as end users will lack the ability to control energy flows, will not have the quantitative feedback that tells them whether efforts to reduce energy use have succeeded, or—worst of all—will not have either type of information.

Implement Institutional Changes to Spur the Adoption of Energy Efficiency Measures. At present, the prices for energy commodities in the DPRK—to the extent that they are priced at all—need not bear any resemblance to their cost of production. Although pricing reform in the energy sector is further off in the DPRK than in the economies of Eastern Europe, the former Soviet Union, and China, some revision in how fuels are distributed will clearly be necessary. Schipper and Martinot[42] also note that energy quotas may work against energy efficiency because a factory (for example) which implements energy efficiency measures—to the extent that it uses less than its energy quota—may simply have its quota reduced by the utility, forcing it to reduce output and devaluing its efficiency investment. This "ratchet effect" was found to be a barrier to efficiency improvements in China as well. It was at least partly addressed through modifications to the incentive system—for example, preventing the ratcheting downward of energy allocations to enterprises that successfully improved efficiency, allowing such enterprises to resell unused allocations or awarding them a portion of the cost of saved energy, and providing efficient enterprises with preferential access to material and energy inputs and investment funds. Although it is not clear to us exactly how energy quota systems work in the DPRK, similar issues are likely to arise there.

Standards for specific energy consumption (that is, the amount of energy needed to produce a unit of physical output) have long been used in China to gauge performance of and within industrial and other enterprises. Issued nationally, and often tailored to conditions specific to individual enterprises, these standards have been used to measure progress in improving efficiency and have formed the basis of a system of financial and other awards. It is, in effect, a system of performance evaluation that parallels those systems based on output levels and product quality. This system is losing its effectiveness as China's transition to a market-oriented economy progresses and the central-planning apparatus weakens, but it may still be quite appropriate for North Korea at this time.

Another necessary institutional change concerns access to energy-efficient products, materials, and parts. Since these items probably will be imported, a successful program will entail a loosening of restrictions on imports. China, already one of North Korea's largest trading partners, would be a good source of efficient technologies and equipment that might be more easily absorbed (and more affordable) than those available from already-developed countries. China has been a major energy supplier to North Korea in the past and may have an interest not only in marketing equipment but in reducing North Korea's dependence on energy imports.

Changing energy policies to shift from a focus on maintaining and increasing fuel supplies to increasing energy efficiency while maintaining or increasing energy services will also be necessary. Although the DPRK government has released a general statement of support for energy efficiency (published as "Let Us Further Strengthen the Struggle to Conserve Power" in *Nodong Sinmun,* January 21, 1995), these policies should be expressed in more concrete terms.

Make Available Government-Backed Loans and Grants for Energy Efficiency Improvements. Organizations in North Korea—factories or local housing authorities, for example-will need access to capital or credits that will enable them to obtain energy—efficient equipment and devices. The success of energy efficiency and conservation projects in China during the 1980s is attributable at least in part to the availability of substantial amounts of money for energy efficiency investments from the central government.[43] Originally in the form of grants, such funding gradually gave way to low-interest loans, matched by funds from local governments and enterprises that leveraged limited central-government monies. Funding was targeted at measures that the central government wished to demonstrate. Once end users saw the benefits to be gained from adopting the measures so demonstrated (and became willing to adopt them without further encouragement from the government), funding was then shifted to other priority technologies.

Provide Training and Information on Energy Efficiency Measures and Technology. The decentralized nature of energy efficiency investments, as pointed out by Schipper and Martinot,[44] requires that adequate information and training be provided in a timely manner to all of the various government officials, plant operators, ministry planners, equipment suppliers and installers, and others who must help to bring energy efficiency measures through the planning, program delivery, and installation phases. Among the major tasks of China's network of more than two hundred energy conservation service centers are the training of officials, plant personnel, and auditors in energy measurement and management techniques and the dissemination of information on the availability, application, and operation of various classes of energy-efficient equipment. In the DPRK, personnel will need to be trained for the (probably entirely new to North Korea) classifications of energy auditors, equipment installers, demand-side management planners, equipment operators, maintenance personnel for specific energy efficiency technologies, and last but certainly not least, teachers to train all of the types of personnel just mentioned. As in China and the former Eastern bloc, this training must be provided to people working at the operational level. Unlike much of present-day Eastern Europe, however, decision making in North Korea remains a centralized activity; therefore, it is essential to provide as much information and training to high-level government officials as the leadership will allow.

Obtain Quantitative and Qualitative Information on Existing "Energy Markets." Although we are confident that there exist in North Korea much energy data to which we (and probably anyone else outside of the DPRK) have not had access, it is virtually certain that the specific energy end-use data that are required for accurate planning and evaluation of energy efficiency options have not been collected (and/or gleaned from existing information). As a consequence, extensive energy demand surveys and equipment audits will be required in every sector before energy efficiency programs on a broad scale can be implemented in the DPRK. This assumes the availability of trained people (see above) who can carry out audits and surveys and evaluate their results.

Pursue Sector-Based Implementation of Energy Efficiency Measures. One point made forcefully by Schipper and Martinot is the need to pursue energy efficiency opportunities on a sector-by-sector basis, as opposed to through an overarching "least-cost planning" style of analysis as has been practiced for electric and gas utility service areas.[45] It is people at the sectoral level who must work with energy-using equipment daily to do their jobs, rather than planners in a central ministry, who are more likely to be interested in energy efficiency opportunities.

One way to gain support for energy efficiency measures is to emphasize those that achieve multiple goals. Energy-efficient technologies can be combined with building retrofits that increase the comfort of residents, the rebuilding of factories to improve output, the renovation of power plants to cut down on forced outages, and other upgrading efforts that have little—explicitly—to do with energy efficiency. China, in the 1980s, introduced a major process improvement to the steel industry—continuous casting—primarily as an energy efficiency measure and supported its introduction with funding from the national program of efficiency investments. In China's other energy-intensive industries, such as chemicals and cement manufacturing, measures to increase energy efficiency have typically produced greater output and higher quality as well, resulting in high rates of adoption.

To the ultimate users of energy efficiency measures, the relative costs per unit of energy savings of the various possible industrial process, transport, and energy supply improvements is less than meaningful: what matters is how energy efficiency opportunities stack to up to other potential uses for the investment funds that they have available (for example, investment funds allocated from the central government). In addition, it is likely to be a mistake to place personnel from the typically supply-oriented energy sector in charge of equipment decisions—energy-related though they may be—in other sectors of the economy since they would bring with them a strong supply-side bias.

Carry Out Demonstration Projects. The most effective way to convince decision makers in the DPRK-at both the national and local levels-that energy efficiency measures and programs are worthwhile will be to show that they work in specific North Korean situations. Carefully designed, effective demonstrations of energy efficiency and renewable energy technologies that involve local actors as much as possible are likely to catch the interest of North Koreans. Given the good system for technology dissemination in the DPRK, this approach is likely to lead to the adoption of energy efficiency measures into the North Korean way of doing things. One word of caution here is to make sure that any demonstration projects carried out can be replicated elsewhere in the DPRK: measures unique to one or a few specific industrial plants, for example, are not likely to be widely replicated.

Promote Domestic Production of Energy-Efficient Products. This measure would involve ventures such as the establishment of foreign-owned factories for making appliances, lighting products, and other types of energy efficiency equipment, as well as joint ventures between foreign companies and North Korean concerns (probably state-owned but perhaps eventually parastatal or private) in which foreign technology is licensed to North Koreans. Examples of foreign-owned factories and licensing of technologies abound in the developing world, including a number of ventures in Eastern Europe and the former Soviet Union[46] as well as in China. It is likely that the earliest examples of such technology transfer to the DPRK will come in the context of ventures in the Tumen River Economic Development Zone. If they do, efforts will probably have to be made to ensure that a significant portion of the output of energy-efficient devices remains in the country for use by North Koreans rather than simply being exported to generate (much-needed) hard currency.

Potential Strategies for Implementation of Energy Efficiency Measures in North Korea

Building on the experience and research in similar countries, as well as on the ongoing energy sector–related projects involving the DPRK, we present below our suggestions for key strategies to promote the implementation of energy efficiency and renewable energy measures in the DPRK. Admittedly, some of these strategies will take time to implement (or even to start), and some are more likely to gain the approval of DPRK officials than others.

• *Provide information and general training to high-level government officials.* Getting energy efficiency programs off the ground in the DPRK will be impossible without top officials embracing the concept, as virtually all policy changes in North Korea, at present, must have clear direction from the very top. Consequently, the advantages and local/international opportunities provided by energy efficiency and renewable energy programs and measures must be presented to top officials in a manner that is both forceful and forthright.

• *Provide specific information and training to local actors.* Training of a very specific and practical nature must be provided to personnel at the local level. Examples here are factory energy plant managers, boiler operators in residential and commercial buildings, power plant and heating system operators, and new job classifications such as energy efficiency equipment installers and energy auditors.

• *Implement standards and enforce them.* DPRK officials have made general statements about their support for energy efficiency and environmental protection. The next step is to codify these in terms of quantitative standards for the efficiency of new appliances and equipment as well as effluent standards for new—and perhaps eventually existing—factories, power plants, residential heating boilers, vehicles, and other major sources of pollution. Once standards are set, it will be necessary to create the capability to enforce them by recruiting and training enforcement personnel and supplying them with the tools required to do their job (testing equipment and adequately equipped labs, for example) and the high-level administrative support needed for credible implementation of sanctions.

• *Establish a program of grants and concessional loans.* Experience in China has shown that such a program in itself can have a significant positive impact on overall sectoral energy efficiency. The benefits of institutionalizing support for efficiency, however, would go beyond those obtained through the various individual projects themselves. Creating a government agency or corporation with its own budget would signal a strong commitment to efficiency on the part of the government and would create a constituency within official circles for promoting energy efficiency goals.[47] Moreover, by establishing a pool of funds for which government ministries, sectors, and/or individual enterprises could compete, it would stimulate at all levels awareness of energy efficiency potential, methods, and technologies. Eliciting proposals would encourage end users (including those whose proposals were ultimately rejected) to translate general concepts of energy efficiency into actual changes in equipment and operating procedures, thus bringing them one step closer to practical implementation.

• *Modify existing incentives.* Despite some problems, quota management and administrative measures were key to China's success in eliminating many of the worst energy inefficiencies in its industrial sector and in stimulating the adoption of relatively more advanced techniques and technologies. Although inappropriate to a market economy, a well-designed program of administrative measures would effectively utilize the strengths of North Korea's current form of government.

• *Reform energy pricing.* Before market forces of any kind can help to spur the implementation of energy efficiency measures, the prices for energy products in the DPRK must be adjusted toward their actual costs of production. This, of course, includes products that are currently not priced at all. Pricing of some energy products, particularly electricity, will require the implementation of metering and billing systems. To be effective, parallel reforms that sensitize local decision makers to prices (that is, that allow them to benefit from cost savings) must also be implemented.

• *Promote joint ventures and licensing agreements.* The government of the DPRK, and other interested parties, should promote joint ventures and licensing agreements between DPRK concerns (governmental or otherwise) and foreign firms with energy-efficient technologies to produce. Compact fluorescent light-bulb factories are a commonly cited example of potential energy technology transfers.[48] A wide variety of efficient industrial equipment and controls (including adjustable-speed drive motors and improved industrial and utility boilers), efficient household appliances and components, and efficient building technologies have already been introduced to China through commercial channels and are being or will be manufactured there. Wind turbine generators are another intriguing possibility, given the apparent success of such ventures in former Eastern bloc nations[49] and the North Koreans' historical emphasis on machinery manufacture. Foreign firms that have successfully transferred efficient and renewable technologies to China, Russia, and Eastern European nations represent a valuable repository of experience that could be applied to similar efforts in North Korea. Depending on how fast the Tumen River Economic Development Zone develops (infrastructure in the zone is not yet adequate to support major industry), this area could be the location most acceptable to the DPRK for the first such ventures. It is likely that the first few foreign companies to participate in joint ventures in the DPRK will require guarantees not only from the DPRK government but also from their own government or another industrialized nation or a multilateral donor.

Notes

1. D. Von Hippel and P. Hayes (1995), *The Prospects for Energy Efficiency Improvements in the Democratic People's Republic of Korea: Evaluating and Exploring the Options.* Nautilus Institute Report, Nautilus Institute for Security and Sustainable Development, Berkeley, California, USA.

2. P. Hayes (1993c) *Should the United States Supply Light Water Reactors to Pyongyang?* Nautilus Institute, Berkeley, California. October 29, 1993.

3. "Electric Power Management System," a project funded by the United Nations Development Program (UNDP), will only address control systems at four critical power plants and four substations.

4. Combustion efficiencies decline in part because a large volume of inert material (ash) must be heated up by the burning coal. "Fly ash" denotes that fraction of coal ash that leaves the boiler with the hot exhaust gases and is trapped by ash-collection devices or emitted to the atmosphere. "Bottom ash" is that fraction of the inert material in the coal that remains in the bottom of the boiler after the coal is combusted.

5. This cost is in addition to the direct financial outlays for maintenance of the armed forces.

6. Von Hippel and Hayes (1995), *The Prospects for Energy Efficiency Improvements in the DPRK, op cit,* see Executive Summary.

7. Ibid.

8. A petajoule is equal to 10^{15} (1 million billion) joules. By way of comparison, a metric ton of crude oil (1 metric ton of oil equivalent) is equal to approximately 41.8 billion joules (gigajoules).

9. This comparison is admittedly simplistic, as it leaves out operating and mainte-nance (O&M) costs for both the LWR and the energy efficiency/renewable energy op-tions, as well as fuel- and decommissioning-related costs for the LWR. If all of these costs were included, however, the comparison would probably be even more favorable to the energy efficiency options, since the incremental O&M costs of energy efficiency options are likely to be low (perhaps negative in many instances), whereas the O&M costs for the reactor are decidedly non-negligible. Also, the lifetimes of the energy efficiency technologies and the lifetime of the LWR are likely different, although many of the energy efficiency investments—boiler improvements, for example—may ultimately have lifetimes ap-proaching that of the LWR. As one final note, it is probable that some of the energy improvements on our list—the transmission and distribution improvements, at least—will be necessary in order to enable an LWR to be operated effectively on the DPRK grid.

10. Net greenhouse gas emissions may not be reduced to the same extent, however, because the consumption of energy services in the DPRK will probably rise as energy efficiency measures effectively increase the supply of fuel available.

11. M. Levine and L. Xueyi (1990), *Energy Conservation Programs in the Peoples Republic of China*. Applied Science Division, Lawrence Berkeley Laboratory, Berkeley, California, and Energy Research Institute, Peoples Republic of China. LBL-29211. D. Yande (1992) *An Analysis of the Potential in Investment-Cum-Energy Conservation in Chemical Industry in China*. Energy Research Institute, The State Planning Commission, The People's Republic of China. M. Levine, F. Liu, and J. Sinton (1992), "China's Energy System: Historical Evolution, Current Issues, and Prospects." *Annu. Rev. Energy Environ.* 1992. 17:405–435.

12. We have used a conversion rate of 4.755 1990 Chinese yuan to the 1990 U.S. dollar to convert quoted costs for Chinese energy efficiency investments to U.S. dollars. Microsoft Corporation (1994), *Microsoft Encarta, 1994* (CD-ROM software). Because the yuan was not as of 1990 a floating currency, this assumption may introduce some inaccu-racy in converting Chinese costs.

13. J. Sathaye (1992), *Economics of Improving Efficiency of China's Electricity Sup-ply and Use: Are Efficiency Investments Cost-effective?* (Mimeo), Lawrence Berkeley Laboratory.

14. Ibid.

15. Analysts of wind resources in the DPRK have referred to Chinese border area and offshore islands as the only likely sites for wind energy development; but it appears that such assessments consider wind-generated electricity to be primarily an off-grid resource. Our assessment that wind is probably an attractive resource for the DPRK is based on the country's rugged topography and strong seasonal (winter/summer) weather patterns.

16. For example, Levine and Xueyi (1990), *Energy Conservation Programs in the People's Republic of China*.

17. R.H. Williams and Larson, E.D. (1993), "Advanced Gasification-Based Biomass Power Generation." in *Renewable Energy: Sources for Fuels and Electricity*, edited by T.B. Johansson, H. Kelly, A.K.N. Reddy, and R.H. Williams. Island Press, Washington, D.C.

18. Repowering existing 20– to 30–year-old oil-fired boilers to create combined-cycle plants figures prominently in the future plans, for example, of the major electricity utility in Hawaii.

19. Levine and Xueyi (1990), *Energy Conservation in the People's of Republic China;*

Yande (1992), *An Analysis of the Potential;* Levine et al. (1992), *China's Energy System.*

20. Sathaye (1992) *Economics of Improving Efficiency of China's Electricity Supply and Use.*

21. Note that motor efficiencies vary by size class, with larger motors (for example, 100 to 200 horsepower or 75 to 150 kilowatts) having efficiencies generally a few percent higher than smaller motors of similar types. The efficiencies presented here can be thought of as rough weighted averages over the stock of electric motors in use.

22. D. Von Hippel and R. Verzola (1994), *Indicative Study of the Potential Economic and Environmental Impacts of Demand-Side Management in the Philippines.* Nautilus Institute Report. Nautilus Institute, Berkeley, California.

23. Data obtained from DPRK sources and in authors' files.

24. J. Sinton (1995), "Physical Intensity of Selected Industrial Products." Spreadsheet printout. LBL Lawrence Berkeley Laboratory, Berkeley, California.

25. Z.P. Liu, J.E. Sinton, F.Q. Yang, M.D. Levine, and M.K. Ting (1994), *Industrial Sector Energy Conservation Programs in the People's Republic of China during the Seventh Five-Year Plan (1986–1990).* Lawrence Berkeley Laboratory, Berkeley, California, and Energy Research Institute, Peoples Republic of China. LBL-36395.

26. For example, valuable metals such as gold, zinc, and cadmium can be recovered from the flue gases and liquid effluents of metal-smelting industries, and sulfuric acid could be recovered from steel and nonferrous metal plants. The latter modification would not only remove SO_x from flue gases but would also serve as a source of sulfuric acid for the chemical industry, reducing energy use in that subsector.

27. As an example (though one unlikely to be directly germane to North Korea at present), by carefully controlling the aluminum rolling and forming process, U.S. manufacturers have been able to reduce the thickness and weight of aluminum cans markedly.

28. Data obtained from DPRK sources and authors' files.

29. S. Lang, Y.J. Huang, and M. Levine (1992), *Energy Conservation Standards for Space Heating in Chinese Urban Residential Buildings.* Energy Analysis Program, Energy and Environmental Division, Lawrence Berkeley Laboratory, Berkeley, California.

30. Data obtained from DPRK sources and in authors' files.

31. Levine and Xueyi (1990) *Energy Conservation Programs;* Yande (1992) *An Analysis of the Potential in Investment-Cum-Energy Conservation;* Levine et al. (1992) *China's Energy System.*

32. Sathaye (1992) *Economics of Improving Efficiency of China's Electricity Supply and Use.*

33. F. Liu, W.B. Davis, and M.D. Levine (1992), *An Overview of Energy Supply and Demand in China.* Energy Analysis Program, Energy and Environment Division, Lawrence Berkeley Laboratory, Berkeley, California. LBL-32275 UC-350.

34. This figure is based on the fact that the Isuzu truck model cited is available in the United States for roughly $30,000 (retail). Assuming that (1) a large portion of this cost is dealer profit, profit for Isuzu, import costs and duties, and other nonproduct costs, and (2) such trucks could be built in the DPRK at DPRK labor rates, but with Japanese technology (presumably under license), we have guessed at a DPRK production cost of $10,000.

35. Liu et al. (1992), *An Overview of Energy Supply and Demand in China.*

36. Personal communication with a U.N. agricultural sector expert with experience in the DPRK.

37. Here we distinguish between energy efficiency measures, which can be thought of as the technologies or techniques that can be employed to increase the efficiency with which fuels are used, and energy efficiency programs, which are institutional arrangements for implementing energy efficiency measures.

38. P. Hayes (1993b), *Cooperation on Energy Sector Issues with the DPRK*. Nautilus Institute, Berkeley, California. October 29, 1993.

39. A. Reddy (1991), *Barriers to Improvements in Energy Efficiency*. Lawrence Berkeley Laboratory, Berkeley, California. LBL-31439.

40. Ibid.

41. L. Schipper and E. Martinot (1993), *Energy Efficiency in Former Soviet Republics: Opportunities for East and West*. International Energy Studies, Energy Analysis Program, Energy and Environment Division, Lawrence Berkeley Laboratory, Berkeley, California. LBL-33929. Prepared for U.S. Department of Energy; E. Martinot (1994), *Technology Transfer and Cooperation for Sustainable Energy Development in Russia: Prospects and Case Studies of Energy Efficiency and Renewable Energy*. Energy and Resources Group, University of California at Berkeley, Berkeley, California, (summary of a Ph.D. Dissertation—Draft); Liu et al. (1992), *An Overview of Energy Supply and Demand in China*; Levine, Liu, and Sinton (1992), "China's Energy System."

42. Schipper and Martinot (1993), *Energy Efficiency in the Former Soviet Republics*.

43. For example, Levine and Xueyi (1990). *Energy Conservation Programs in the People's Republic of China*.

44. Schipper and Martinot (1993), *Energy Efficiency in the Former Soviet Republics*.

45. Ibid. Schipper and Martinot also point out two disadvantages of least-cost planning in the context of the former Soviet Union that are probably equally relevant to North Korea. First, stable energy markets and prices (which are inputs to least-cost planning) do not exist as they do (for the most part) in the West, and data on energy end uses, as noted earlier in the chapter, as well as cost data for domestic and imported equipment, are problematic. Second, least-cost planning is sufficiently similar to the system of planning formerly in use in the USSR (and still used in the DPRK) that it would provide a comfortable and familiar retreat for central planners and thus could be considered a step away from, rather than toward, economic reform.

46. Martinot (1994), *Technology Transfer and Cooperation for Sustainable Energy Development in Russia*.

47. Bringing together a large number of relatively small-scale demand-side projects under the umbrella of a single program may also go some way toward mitigating the bias toward large-scale projects.

48. J. Sathaye, R. Friedmann, S. Meyers, O. de Buen, A. Gadgil, E. Vargas, and R. Saucedo (1994), "Economic Analysis of Ilumex: A Project to Promote Energy-Efficient Residential Lighting in Mexico." *Energy Policy*, February 1994, pp. 163–171.

49. Martinot (1994), *Technology Transfer and Cooperation for Sustainable Energy Development in Russia*.

Part 3

Strategy: Calculus and Confidence-Building Measures

10

Confrontation or Compromise? Lessons from the 1994 Crisis

Young Whan Kihl

Confrontation and accommodation represent two mutually exclusive and contrasting methods of dealing with international conflict. Whereas confrontation clearly connotes an overt act of escalating tension and military showdown, backed up by the use of force—or the threat of force—accommodation leading to compromise is clearly an obtrusive method of diplomacy aimed at peaceful settlement of international disputes. The attempt to resolve the North Korean nuclear issue in 1994 went through, and alternated between, two separate stages of confrontation and accommodation as ways of containing and resolving the conflict on the Korean Peninsula. Whereas confrontation entails a military showdown possibly leading to war, compromise or accommodation involves diplomatic bargaining and negotiation, with a gamelike situation, which has the possibility of resulting in peace and stability.[1]

This chapter first reviews the background of the 1994 Korean crisis and also evaluates how the Korean Peninsula conflict began in confrontation but was turned toward compromise and accommodation. What explains the temporary reprieve from the Korean crisis? How realistic and how feasible is the idea of settling the conflict based on a quid pro quo resolution of the North Korean nuclear controversy? What are the future prospects of a lasting peace on the Korean Peninsula in the post–Cold War security environment, reflecting the dynamics of both regional and global politics?

An earlier version of this chapter appeared as "Confrontation or Compromise on the Korean Peninsula: The North Korean Nuclear Issue," *Korean Journal of Defense Analysis* 4, no. 2 (winter 1994): 101–29.

Context of the 1994 Korean Crisis

As tension mounted on the Korean Peninsula in the early summer of 1994, the possibility of another Korean War was openly debated in the media.[2] It was during the Panmunjom meeting on March 19, 1994, that the North Korean negotiator (Pak Yong-su) walked out of the conference room after making some highly inflammatory, "threatening" remarks to his southern counterpart. In his statement, which was subsequently retracted by North Korean leader Kim Il Sung, Pak overreacted: "Seoul is not far away from here. If a war breaks out, Seoul will turn into a fireball. . . . Mr. Song, you will never survive the war, either."[3] North Korea's Army Chief of Staff Choe Gwang, on April 8, denounced the United States, Japan, and South Korea for "engaging in a vicious attempt to provoke a war against us" and claimed that his army would "give them a decisive counterblow and annihilate them mercilessly."[4]

These bellicose and ominous postures had a chilling effect in South Korea. The Seoul government reacted with heightened defensive measures, including intensified civil defense exercises throughout the land. The U.S. Clinton administration also reacted to the North Korean negotiator's March 19 outburst and walkout by announcing, on March 21, that Patriot missiles would be sent to South Korea, in response to a request by U.S.–Korea Combined Forces Commander General Gary Luck, and that work would start on a U.N. resolution to apply economic sanctions against North Korea.

Pyongyang's Suspected Nuclear Weapons Program

The 1994 Korean crisis was prompted by North Korea's "suspected" nuclear weapons program. North Korea is known to have a rather extensive and ambitious program of nuclear reactors and has been reprocessing the spent fuel for possible weaponry use. According to a U.S. Central Intelligence Agency report to the president in December 1993, North Korea had probably already produced one or two nuclear bombs.[5] Therefore, the international community, led by the United States, began to address the danger of nuclear proliferation and the challenge that North Korea posed internationally.

In 1985, North Korea (the Democratic People's Republic of Korea, or DPRK) signed the Nuclear Non-Proliferation Treaty (NPT) but did not become a party to the International Atomic Energy Agency (IAEA) safeguard measures until January 1992. In the meantime, in 1989, North Korea extracted an unknown quantity of spent fuel from its 5–megawatt electric experimental reactor at Yongbyon, admitting that a tiny amount of plutonium had been obtained from what it calls a radioactive chemical laboratory in the Yongbyon complex. Furthermore, the DPRK has additional reactors and reprocessing plants under construction, which, when put into operation, would make North Korea a formidable nuclear power.[6]

In 1992, under considerable international pressure, North Korea agreed to allow IAEA on-site inspections of its nuclear reactors. IAEA field inspections in 1992, however, revealed certain anomalies in North Korea's claims regarding plutonium extraction. Although the IAEA, in February 1993, requested "special inspections" of two undeclared sites containing nuclear wastes, to resolve the issue of plutonium extraction, North Korea denied the IAEA access to waste sites and, on March 12, 1993, suddenly announced that it was giving the required ninety-day notice for withdrawal from the NPT, thereby creating a crisis mood in the region. This unprecedented North Korean move enhanced suspicions that North Korea was indeed engaged in a nuclear weapons program and that it wanted to hide the evidence from international inspection.[7]

On June 11, just one day before the announced withdrawal from the IAEA was to take effect, North Korea reversed its stance by announcing that it had now decided to "suspend its withdrawal." This was timed to coincide with the calling of the first high-level U.S.–DPRK meeting in Geneva. In exchange for the DPRK's agreeing to "suspend" its withdrawal from the NPT, the United States set five preconditions for continuation of high-level negotiations with North Korea: (1) the DPRK would not leave the NPT; (2) there would be no more reprocessing of spent fuel while the talks were proceeding; (3) the DPRK would not refuel the 5–megawatt electric reactor without IAEA supervision; (4) there would be progress in North–South Korean discussions; and (5) the U.S.–DPRK talks would make progress.

In July 1993, at the second high-level U.S.–DPRK meeting, the United States offered to help shift North Korea's nuclear power program from graphite-moderated reactors to light-water reactors (LWRs). The DPRK, in turn, agreed to allow the "continuity of safeguards" inspections by the IAEA to continue, to discuss with the IAEA the requested "special inspections," and also to engage in discussions with the government of the Republic of Korea (ROK). In August, the IAEA was able to conduct only partial and unsatisfactory continuity of safeguards inspections. Since the DPRK also refused to meet with the ROK government, to discuss a promised exchange of envoys, the U.S. government concluded that there was no basis on which to proceed with the third round of bilateral dialogue with North Korea in September, as originally planned.

In the remainder of 1993, IAEA–DPRK negotiations were deadlocked over the issue of access to two nuclear waste sites that North Korea refused to open on the ground that they were military bases.[8] In late December, however, North Korea made a conciliatory gesture by permitting IAEA inspection activities to resume and changing the film in the cameras installed to monitor the reactor activities. This was arranged through the U.S.–DPRK channel in New York, via the DPRK diplomatic mission to the United Nations. The U.S. government now agreed to enlarge the next high-level bilateral talks to include a "broad and thorough" discussion of economic and political issues as well as the security issues that had been the subject of discussion thus far.

The IAEA and the DPRK, since December 1993, had been discussing parameters for effective continuity of safeguards inspections—that is, to assure that no further reprocessing had taken place since the original IAEA inspection in 1992. In fact, the IAEA and the DPRK, in February 1994, came to agree on inspection arrangements. On March 3, 1994, for the first time in more than one year, North Korea allowed the IAEA to resume nuclear inspections, but once again, the North Koreans refused complete access to all declared and undeclared sites.

During the first half of 1994, North Korea continued to renege on its agreement with the IAEA. Since its inspection of all declared facilities was incomplete, the IAEA announced that it could not assure continuity of safeguards. This led the United Nations Security Council president to issue a unanimously approved statement, on March 31, 1994, calling on the DPRK to permit full safeguards inspections. On the eve of the May 1994 crisis, therefore, no meaningful progress had been made on the issue of the IAEA continuity of safeguards inspections.

U.N. Sanctions Triggered by IAEA Withdrawal

The 1994 Korean crisis erupted with the official North Korean announcement, in April 1994, that it would refuel the Yongbyon 5–megawatt electric reactor in May. While the IAEA and the DPRK were engaged in discussions on modalities for IAEA supervision of refueling, U.S. government officials confirmed that unsupervised refueling would result in their breaking off ongoing efforts to negotiate with the DPRK. On May 14, the North Korean official news agency reported that replacement of fuel rods at the Yongbyon experimental nuclear reactor had begun without IAEA inspectors present to determine whether plutonium had been extracted from the spent fuel. As the DPRK refused to allow the IAEA to take samples of fuel rods, the IAEA announced that it could not reach an agreement with North Korea on satisfactory arrangements to supervise refueling.

On May 17, U.S. Defense Secretary William Perry publicly warned that North Korea was diverting fuel rods from its Yongbyon reactor into enriched plutonium production. Unless IAEA inspectors were able to intercede, this would allow North Korea to acquire enough plutonium to build five or six new nuclear bombs over the next two years.[9] On May 28, the U.N. team of inspectors decided to leave North Korea because its proposals for monitoring the refueling operation were rejected.

The IAEA board of governors adopted a resolution, on June 10, invoking the first formal sanctions against North Korea for barring full inspections of its nuclear facilities. IAEA Director General Hans Blix, in a letter to the United Nations Security Council, reported that the continuity of the DPRK's compliance with the NPT safeguards measures could not be guaranteed and that his team of inspectors was unable to verify whether North Korea was diverting the spent fuel and reprocessing it. This IAEA letter cleared the way for United Nations Security Council deliberations regarding the possibility of imposing sanctions on North Korea.

On June 13, North Korea announced its withdrawal from the IAEA in an act of defiance over the IAEA report to the United Nations Security Council. This announcement was met, on June 14, by a joint pledge on the part of the United States, South Korea, and Japan to impose sanctions against North Korea; the United States also sought a mandatory arms embargo against North Korea as a first phase of sanctions. The United Nations Security Council met to consider the U.S.-drafted resolution.

The Clinton administration decided to press for two-stage sanctions against North Korea. If the Pyongyang government did not give IAEA inspectors access to its nuclear plants, limited economic sanctions would be imposed initially, to be followed by a total trade embargo. The DPRK Foreign Ministry reiterated its earlier statement that North Korea would consider the imposition of economic sanctions to be a hostile act tantamount to a declaration of war. Threatening rhetoric and gestures reached such a point that the 1994 Korean crisis might, indeed, have gotten out of hand and plunged the Korean Peninsula into the tragedy of another hot war.

The 1994 Crisis in Perspective

What was the reason behind North Korea's March 1994 threat of war against South Korea? Evidence shows that Pyongyang's "war threat" of turning "Seoul into [a] Sea of Fire" was a premeditated act based on a carefully orchestrated scenario.[10] The North Korean delegate read a prepared text at a formal negotiating table in Panmunjom rather than making spontaneous remarks. The threat was therefore part of the psychological warfare directed against the South Korean population. By making this war threat, North Korea hoped to spread fear and anxiety among the South Korean people. The threat was also used to divide opinion in the South by polarizing it between hawks and doves and also by driving a wedge between the governments of South Korea and the United States.

The threat of war was also directed toward North Korea's own population at home. The regime wanted to strengthen domestic control. By putting the country on a semiwar footing, it was trying to overcome economic hardship and international isolation. In a time of difficulty, a population will typically stay unified and disciplined.

For North Korea to go to war made little sense from a military standpoint. For North Korea to start a war that it could not win in the end would be a foolish act, even if it could succeed in heightening tension. If North Korea really wanted war, its negotiators would never have mentioned the word *war* and would have begun a peace initiative, as the North did before the 1950–53 Korean War.

Finally, the war threat and brinkmanship were also directed against the international community, including the United States. It was apparent that the North Korean regime wanted to squeeze the maximum amount of concessions out of the United States by playing its nuclear card. In 1995, the NPT was scheduled to undergo a revision. Since the United States wanted to maintain the existing NPT system, North Korea could raise the stakes and plunge the world into chaos by threatening to leave the IAEA. North Korea gambled that the Clinton administration did not, and would not, want war. The threat to go to war, or to use force, was a strategic move utilized by Pyongyang in order to achieve its policy objective. Its strategic calculus was to maximize its security interest and also to extract the utmost concessions from the United States.[11]

The IAEA, the DPRK, and the NPT

The DPRK, as the rogue state with nuclear ambitions, was clearly the culprit, inviting international condemnation and moves toward sanctions. The international community's response to the North Korean nuclear challenge was conducted at two levels. The first was the multilateral channel via the IAEA and the United Nations Security Council, and the second was the bilateral and region-wide dealings with North Korea led by the United States via military and diplomatic pressure. The DPRK's dealings with the IAEA over on-site inspections are recounted first in this section, to be followed later by the discussion of U.S.–DPRK bilateral talks and negotiation to settle the North Korean nuclear issue.

Whereas the IAEA acts as an executive arm of the United Nations that carries out on-site inspections on nuclear safeguards, the United Nations Security Council is the decision-making body of the United Nations that adopts appropriate resolutions on matters of maintaining international peace and security. When and if the Security Council's resolutions are not complied with, it has the power to recommend enforcement measures, including sanctions and the use of force, as in the case of the Gulf War following the Iraqi aggression against Kuwait. Hence, the DPRK's confrontation with the IAEA and the United Nations Security Council was a serious matter of fulfilling the DPRK's legal obligations under the NPT and the United Nations charter.

IAEA Inspection of Suspected Nuclear Sites

In September 1974, North Korea joined the IAEA for the purpose of receiving atomic power–related benefits that go with membership. To improve safety measures at North Korea's atomic reactor in Yongbyon, for instance, the facility has been inspected by the IAEA since December 14, 1977. North Korea also received IAEA technical assistance to improve the uranium-mining and enrichment facilities in Pyongsan and Paekchon.

It was not until December 12, 1985, however, that North Korea joined the NPT at the urging of the former Soviet Union, from which it was receiving atomic energy–related technology and equipment. Six years later, on January 30, 1992, North Korea signed the IAEA FSA (full safeguard accord), which was required of all NPT members within eighteen months after admission into the NPT. North Korea's Supreme People's Assembly, on April 9, 1992, ratified the accord.

The IAEA guidelines (document IFNCIRC/153) specify three separate stages and procedures for investigating the overall safety of member countries' nuclear facilities.[12] First, a member state must prepare a list of facilities subject to inspection and, within two months, submit a design information report answering fifty-eight questions for each facility to be included in the list. Second, the IAEA carries out a preliminary inspection in order to cross-check the list against the facilities. Third, the IAEA proceeds with periodic inspections of facilities in accordance with the inspection schedule agreed on with the respective member state.

In its initial report submitted on May 4, 1992, North Korea identified facilities at sixteen locations that are subject to IAEA inspection. These included two research reactors, one each in Yongbyon and at Kim Il Sung University, respectively; a nuclear fuel processing plant, a nuclear fuel storage facility, a 5–megawatt electric experimental nuclear reactor, a radiochemical laboratory (under construction), and a 50–megawatt electric nuclear reactor (under construction)—all in the Yongbyon complex; a 200–megawatt electric atomic power plant (under construction) in Taechun; a uranium mine in Pyongsan; uranium refineries in Pyongsan and Paekchon; and a 635–megawatt electric atomic power plant (under construction) in Shinpo.[13]

The IAEA team of inspectors, led by Director General Hans Blix, visited North Korea's nuclear facilities from May 11 to 16, 1992, followed by the first preliminary inspections from May 25 to June 6. An auxiliary agreement between the IAEA and North Korea on nuclear inspection procedures was signed on July 10, 1992. A total of six preliminary inspection visits took place thereafter, the second from July 6 to 16, 1992; the third from September 1 to 15; the fourth from November 2 to 12; the fifth from December 14 to 22; and the sixth from January 26 to February 6, 1993.

As the IAEA on-site inspections progressed, questions and discrepancies began to emerge. For instance, North Korea stated in its initial report to the IAEA that, in 1990, a tiny amount of plutonium (90 grams) had been extracted from its experimental reactor in Yongbyon. However, initial analysis of samples taken during the IAEA's inspections showed that at least three times the reported amount had been extracted. North Korea claimed that an IAEA technical error in calculation might account for the discrepancy, but the IAEA demanded that North Korea provide a full explanation within a month. The IAEA proceeded on the assumption that North Korea was hiding evidence of having extracted additional plutonium from the experimental reactor.

National Security, Sovereignty, and a Legal Loophole

The IAEA–DPRK controversy then became deadlocked, with the North Koreans charging that the IAEA was unfair and biased against the North.

The IAEA demanded access to two unreported facilities in the Yongbyon nuclear complex whose presence subsequently became known via satellite photography undertaken by the U.S. military early in 1993. This information, relayed to the IAEA by the U.S. government, was condemned by North Korea as a violation of its sovereignty and national security. A heated verbal battle ensued between the IAEA and North Korea over the fact that photographic evidence had been obtained via satellite.

In February 1993, the IAEA demanded a special inspection of these two facilities, which might be hiding the waste from the plutonium extraction. North Korea, however, claimed that these were military facilities that had nothing to do with nuclear development. It refused the IAEA's demand on the ground that the IAEA was acting on behalf of a third country, the United States, and that it was unfair for the IAEA to demand an unprecedented special inspection only of North Korea.

Since it was difficult for North Korea to refute the IAEA position, Pyongyang declared its intention to withdraw from the NPT on March 12, 1993, although, as noted earlier in the chapter, it reversed this stance on June 11, on the eve of the U.S.–DPRK high-level talks. In so doing, it invoked the provision of the NPT that recognizes a country's right to withdraw on the ground that "extraordinary events . . . have jeopardized [its] supreme interests." According to the NPT, Article 10, Section 1,"[E]ach Party shall in exercising its national sovereignty have the right to withdraw from the Treaty if it decides that extraordinary events, related to the subject matter of this Treaty, have jeopardized the supreme interests of its country . . . [and] shall give notice . . . three months in advance."[14]

The IAEA–DPRK stalemate persisted until May 1994, when North Korea acted to sabotage the work of IAEA inspectors in North Korea by accelerating the refueling of the reactor in Yongbyon. North Korea defended its act for reasons of safety, claiming that the reactor's fuel rods had to be replaced on time, although it did so in the absence of the IAEA inspectors, who wanted to take samples. It also defended its act on legal grounds, based on its claim of sovereignty, declaring that nothing in the NPT treaty and the IAEA safeguard accord would prevent it from exercising its sovereign power.

In defense of its act, the DPRK charged that the IAEA was not impartial. It pointed out that because other countries such as Japan were already engaged in IAEA-monitored plutonium extraction, North Korea should have the same rights as they did. They asked why the IAEA allows Japan to extract plutonium, and without U.S. objections.

The DPRK appeared therefore to be proceeding with the separation of plutonium from the spent fuel with or without IAEA inspectors present. In this sense, the

IAEA allows a legal loophole.[15] The fact is that all the advanced states, subject to IAEA inspection, are allowed to operate breeder reactors and employ other plutonium-using technologies, as long as IAEA inspectors are present to monitor the activities.[16] The only catch is that, in reprocessing the spent fuel, the extracted plutonium will not be diverted for use in weapons. This is the point that North Korea wanted to keep secret. Therefore, for political and strategic reasons, the DPRK will continue to resist the international pressure and will object to application of the transparency rule to its nuclear program.

North Korea's unexpected IAEA withdrawal announcement, the first of its kind, took the international community by surprise. It also raised questions regarding the effectiveness of the IAEA's inspection efforts, with broader implications for the viability of the NPT as an international regime for nuclear safeguards.

The Nuclear Non-Proliferation Treaty came up for revision in 1995. According to Article 10, Section 2 of the NPT, which was signed in 1968 but went into effect on March 5, 1970, "Twenty-five years after the entry into force of the Treaty, a conference shall be convened to decide whether the Treaty shall continue in force indefinitely, or shall be extended for an additional fixed period or periods. This decision shall be taken by a majority of the Parties of the Treaty." The hour of decision on the NPT revision was rapidly approaching, and the DPRK knew that others were apprehensive.

The DPRK judged that the United States, as one of the key, founding members of the NPT, could not afford to see a country like North Korea sabotage and undermine the effort to save the structure by reforming the international nuclear nonproliferation regime. This was the reason behind the DPRK's using its bargaining chip to seek direct access to the United States.

Pyongyang thus used both formal and informal channels in its attempt to promote what it called "a package deal." Pyongyang clearly wanted to use the nuclear issue as leverage or a bargaining chip in its negotiations with the United States on a host of security and political issues. North Korea relied on a strategy of linkage of issues. Former U.S. President Jimmy Carter's June 1994 Pyongyang trip could therefore be examined from the broad perspective of the DPRK's strategic and political calculation.

Two-Track and Back-Channel Diplomacy

Apart from the multilateral channel of IAEA on-site inspections, the international response to the North Korean nuclear intransigence was also conducted at a bilateral level, and in a regional context, led by the United States in consultation with its allies in the region, South Korea and Japan. In this endeavor, the United States relied on two-track diplomacy: via official and nonofficial channels. Before recounting the official channel—that is, how the U.S.–DPRK high-level talks were conducted in 1993–94—the episode of Jimmy Carter's "personal diplomacy" should be explained, with a view to placing the outcome of Carter's Pyongyang mission in its proper perspective in the context of the 1994 Korean crisis.

The danger of a second Korean war was somehow averted and had subsided by late summer 1994. This was largely the result of the efforts of Jimmy Carter during his successful four-day mission to Pyongyang on June 15–18. Coinciding with Carter's planned trip, the Clinton administration decided on June 15, in drafting its Security Council resolution, to allow North Korea a grace period to settle its dispute over international nuclear inspections before the first stage of mild U.N. sanctions would take effect. However, on June 16, China rejected a U.S. draft resolution calling for U.N. sanctions against North Korea over the nuclear issue.

Carter's "Private" Mission to Pyongyang

Although former U.S. President Jimmy Carter's trip to Pyongyang was touted as a "private" mission, his status and prestige as a former president of the United States clearly carried weight and produced an impact on the Clinton administration. It is therefore inconceivable that there had been no prior consultation and coordination between the two presidents regarding the diplomatic initiative to be undertaken by Carter. For this reason, Carter's trip to Pyongyang can be regarded as supplementing the official U.S. government policy toward North Korea with a second-track and back-door channel of diplomacy.

As the North Korean crisis erupted in 1994, Jimmy Carter was concerned about the danger that the conflict could escalate into a full-scale war over the nuclear issue. He was particularly concerned about "the apparent lack of an avenue of communication with the top leader of North Korea," Kim Il Sung.[17] Carter was convinced that Kim was "the only one who could make the decisions to alleviate the crisis and avoid another Korean war." With this in mind, Carter telephoned President Bill Clinton about one hour before Clinton was to depart for Europe to participate in a ceremony marking the fiftieth anniversary of the Normandy invasion in World War II. As Carter expressed his concern over the developing crisis with North Korea, President Clinton agreed to send someone to give him a background briefing on the issue. This person turned out to be Robert Gallucci, assistant secretary of state for military and security affairs, who came to Atlanta, Georgia, to brief Carter. Gallucci also carries the rank of ambassador-at-large and served as chief U.S. negotiator in the second U.S.–DPRK high-level talks.

For several years, Jimmy Carter had had a standing invitation to visit Pyongyang. He therefore initiated a call, one day after he spoke with President Clinton, to reconfirm that invitation and verify that the invitation came from President Kim Il Sung himself. Carter then called Vice President Al Gore to inform him that he was strongly inclined to accept the North Korean invitation. The next morning, Gore assured Carter that President Clinton and his top advisers approved of his Pyongyang visit.

In the meantime, Carter, in Atlanta, received a number of briefings from his own sources, including one from a Georgia Institute of Technology nuclear engineer and from a CNN news reporter who had recently been to North Korea. On Friday afternoon, June 10, Carter flew to Washington, with his wife and his aide (Marion Creekmore), for additional briefings on the subject.[18] On June 11, Carter reviewed all the information, wrote out his own itinerary for the trip, and then read his plans over with Ambassador Gallucci, who had no suggestions for changes.

Carter left Atlanta on June 12, accompanied by his wife Rosalynn, Marion Creekmore, and Dick Christenson of the U.S. State Department, who would act as an interpreter. Except for official briefings that he received, Jimmy Carter was "without any clear instructions or official endorsement" from the U.S. government. In effect, he was on his own, Carter claims.[19]

Carter arrived in Seoul on June 13 and stayed at U.S. Ambassador James Laney's official residence. He had talks with President Kim Young Sam the next day and discovered that most of Kim's top advisers seemed somewhat troubled about Carter's planned visit to Pyongyang. The exception was Deputy Prime Minister Lee Hong-koo, who was in charge of reunification talks and, Carter says, was more positive and helpful and had more objective views toward North Korea. Carter also talked with U.S. General Gary Luck, commander of the U.S.–ROK Combined Forces, who said he was deeply concerned about the consequences of another Korean war. General Luck's estimation, according to Carter, was that "the costs [of another Korean war] would far exceed those of the 1950s."[20]

Carter's Meeting with Kim Il Sung

From Seoul, Jimmy Carter traveled to the truce village of Panmunjom and crossed the demilitarized zone (DMZ). He arrived in Pyongyang on June 15 and met with North Korean President Kim Il Sung on June 16 to open a round of talks aimed at easing the crisis.

Carter's first day in Pyongyang obviously did not work out as well as expected. He had his first meeting with Kim Yong-nam, Pyongyang's foreign minister, but their discussion did not go very far toward resolving the conflict. In response to Carter's proposal on how to end the impasse, Kim Yong-nam told him that convening a third round of U.S.–DPRK talks was a prerequisite to any affirmative move by North Korea. Carter also realized that the threat of sanctions would get nowhere because the North Koreans considered it an "insult, branding North Korea as an outlaw nation and their revered leader as a liar and criminal." The foreign minister's comments, although moderate in tone, seemed to Carter as if the North Koreans "would go to war rather than yield to international condemnation and economic pressure."[21]

As he was somewhat distressed, Carter woke up in the middle of the night to ponder what he should do next. In the absence of instructions or authority from his government, Carter decided to send Marion Creekmore to Panmunjom with instructions to transmit a secure message from South Korea to Washington explaining the situation and also seeking authorization from President Clinton to propose a third round of talks in order to defuse the crisis.

On June 16, Carter met North Korean President Kim Il Sung. To his surprise, Carter found Kim Il Sung "to be vigorous, alert, intelligent, and remarkably familiar with the issues." Although Kim consulted frequently with his advisers— including Foreign Minister Kim, Vice Foreign Minister Song Ho-kyong, and First Vice Minister Kang Sok Ju—it was clear to Carter who was in full command and who made the final decisions. Kim thanked Carter for accepting this three-year-old invitation but asked that Carter speak first.

Carter described his "unofficial role," the briefings that he had received, and his visit with South Korean President Kim Young Sam before presenting the position that he had carefully prepared before leaving Atlanta. He outlined the entire situation as he saw it in such a way as to make Kim Il Sung fully aware of "all concerns about North Korean nuclear policies." On occasion, Kim would nod or ask Carter to pause while he talked to his advisers. Dick Christenson, Carter's State Department interpreter, later reported that Kim Il Sung was obviously not thoroughly briefed on "one important problem: IAEA inspectors being expelled."

Kim Il Sung, in effect, accepted all of Carter's proposals, with two major requests. The first was that the United States support Pyongyang's acquisition of light-water reactor technology, realizing that the funding and equipment could not come directly from the United States. The second was that the United States guarantee not to stage a nuclear attack against North Korea. All the outstanding nuclear issues, Kim insisted, could be resolved at the third round of U.S.–DPRK talks when they resumed. During the talks, he was willing to freeze North Korea's nuclear program and to consider a permanent freeze if its aged reactors could be replaced with modern and safer ones.[22]

Carter assured Kim Il Sung, in turn, that there were no nuclear weapons in South Korea or tactical weapons in the waters surrounding the Korean Peninsula, and that the U.S. intention was to see North Korea acquire light-water reactors. Both leaders agreed that the Korean Peninsula should be made nuclear-free. Now that Carter was able to get the North Korean commitment, he had Dick Christenson call Marion Creekmore to tell him to return to Pyongyang without sending his message to Washington.

When Carter called Robert Gallucci from Pyongyang, on an open line, to report the apparent agreement with the North Korean leader, he was told that a high-level meeting was in progress in the White House and that his report would be discussed. After telling Gallucci of his plan to give CNN an interview, while promising to refrain from speaking for the U.S. government, Carter said from Pyongyang that the North now agreed not to expel international inspectors, as long as "good-faith efforts" were made to resolve the dispute. He was later contacted by Anthony Lake, Clinton's national security adviser, to clarify certain points and to go over a statement that the U.S. government was proposing to make.

On June 17, Jimmy Carter announced in Pyongyang that the Clinton administration was now "ready to suspend the U.N. sanctions effort." He met Kim Il Sung again, on June 17, for three and a half hours on a yacht sailing on the Taedong River. He told the North Korean leader that Washington "provisionally agreed" to a third round of high-level talks with Pyongyang to discuss, among other points, the issue of the light-water reactor requested by North Korea. Reacting to this claim, President Clinton said to a reporter while visiting Chicago that "nothing has changed" in his policy of pursuing U.N. economic sanctions against North Korea.[23]

Impact of Carter's Mediator Role

One of the accomplishments of Jimmy Carter's Pyongyang mission was the role he played as mediator between South and North Korea. Upon his return to Seoul, on June 18, Carter conveyed a message from Kim Il Sung to South Korean President Kim Young Sam. Carter related that the North Korean leader was willing to meet the South Korean president "anywhere, at any time and without any conditions." Although the proposal sounded more like a propaganda ploy, it was identical to what Kim Young Sam had already proposed during his presidential campaign in December 1992. South Korean President Kim accepted the proposal immediately.[24]

As a gesture of good faith, on June 21, North Korea extended the visas of two IAEA nuclear inspectors, allowing them to continue monitoring the refueling of its reactor. As the Korean crisis was defused by Carter's Pyongyang visit, the Clinton administration, on June 22, also announced that the third U.S.–DPRK high-level talks would be held in Geneva on July 8.[25]

As a follow-up to Carter's mediation of the North–South Korean summitry, preliminary talks were held in Panmunjom regarding the details of the proposed Korean summit. On June 28, the two sides sent delegates of deputy prime ministerial rank, who agreed that the first summit would be held on July 25–27 in Pyongyang. On July 1, delegates from both sides held a working-level meeting at Panmunjom to settle procedural matters related to the forthcoming summit. They agreed to hold at least two one-on-one summit sessions, with only a handful of ministerial-level officials. The two sides also agreed that 100 South Korean officials and 80 journalists would accompany President Kim Young Sam. The stage was set for the historic summit to take place in Pyongyang, in a forward-looking and anticipatory atmosphere.[26]

The unexpected death of North Korean leader Kim Il Sung on July 8, however, led to an indefinite postponement of the first-ever, historic summit between North and South Korea. On July 8, the third U.S.–DPRK high-level talks in Geneva also convened, but the meeting was suspended until a later date as the

DPRK delegation returned to attend Kim Il Sung's funeral. The meeting was subsequently resumed on August 5–13, producing a four-part preliminary agreement, discussed later in the chapter.

Clearly, the Carter visit to Pyongyang gave North Korea an opportunity to reconsider its hardened stance and priorities. With a United Nations Security Council resolution on imposing economic sanctions imminent, North Korea needed a face-saving way to reverse its bellicose, hard-line position on the nuclear issue. Before passing the "point of no return" on the question of war or peace, North Korea clearly hesitated and blinked, retreating from its brinkmanship position in its showdown of force with the United States. The logic of moderation won the day over that of extremism.

The significance of Jimmy Carter's mediator role is that his Pyongyang visit put the brakes on the downward spiral into which the 1994 Korean confrontation had been locked ever since the reactor fuel imbroglio in May triggered the crisis. It was fortunate because Carter prompted Kim Il Sung to commit to keeping IAEA inspectors at DPRK nuclear facilities; he also carried a list of DPRK offers back to the United States.

The key factor influencing Kim Il Sung was the apparent divergence between Carter and Clinton over the efficacy of sanctions. This enabled Carter to maintain his own credibility both in the United States and in the DPRK. Kim Il Sung perceived that Carter was not simply an emissary of Clinton.[27]

Carter's visit also indicated to the DPRK that Seoul's views would hereafter play a lesser role in American decisions. This factor had increased the DPRK's desire to have Carter visit in the first place. The same logic may work again when and if Carter decides to accept an invitation to revisit North Korea.[28]

Carter's Pyongyang visit made the South Korean government nervous and was at first strongly opposed by Seoul. Many expressed the concern that Carter might easily fall victim to the North Korean leader's hypnotizing ploys. One commentator, for instance, wrote that Carter "was too quick in his assessment of Kim Il Sung" when he stated, during a press conference in Seoul, that he found Kim Il Sung to be "vigorous, intelligent and, above all, surprisingly well informed" about the somewhat complicated nuclear issues. The fact that a former U.S. president would come up with such a definitive assessment after seeing a person for only several hours was considered shocking.[29]

U.S.–DPRK Geneva Talks and Negotiations

The U.S.–DPRK confrontation, precipitated by the reactor fuel imbroglio of May 1994, was thus eased by Carter's successful "personal diplomacy." The call for the third U.S.–DPRK high-level meeting in Geneva, on July 8–9 and August 5–13, 1994, was clearly one tangible accomplishment of Carter's Pyongyang mission. This section examines what took place at the official, government-to-government channel of negotiations in Geneva. What difference, if any, did this meeting make in resolving the North Korean nuclear issue? How should we characterize the bargaining at the Geneva talks and their accomplishments? Were the talks an act of compromise or accommodation? Was it Carter's trip to North Korea that led to a kind of breakthrough on the 1994 Korean crisis? Was that trip closer to compromise and appeasement, or was it a genuinely positive step toward the final resolution of the Korean conflict based on accommodation?

There is a basic difference between compromise and accommodation as diplomatic tools and methods for settling international disputes. Both approaches clearly rest on the assumption of seeking peaceful alternatives to war and conflict. Whereas compromise is clearly a more direct and unobtrusive form of settlement, accommodation is a more deliberate and public form of settlement.[30] The U.S.–North Korea talks and negotiations in Geneva reflect elements of compromise and accommodation as a way of settling international disputes.

To be successful, both compromise and accommodation must start from the premise of striking a deal and obtaining a quid pro quo resolution of conflict. Accommodation is a clean and clear resolution, based on the mutual recognition of rival interests; compromise is likely to be less clean and clear because it often entails concession and give-and-take trading. Both of these methods are ultimately a political act. Compromise and concession are often criticized by purists as acts of appeasement and unnecessary giving in to the opponent, even if the payoff from a settlement may be so much more tangible that it cannot be dismissed lightly.[31]

The Logic of Accommodation

Strategic calculus was the deciding factor behind the eruption of the 1994 crisis to begin with, just as it was the deciding factor behind the attempt to resolve the conflict, whether via informal channels of diplomacy, as in Pyongyang, or official channels, as in Geneva. Both sides to the dispute were engaged in the task of advancing their security interests. This aspect of reliance on the strategic calculus was clearly evident, especially in the conduct of the high-level talks in Geneva in 1993–94.

As a strategic move, the United States continued to pursue the possibility of U.N. sanctions as if Carter's mediating efforts had produced no results. The United States increased the pressure on the DPRK to conform to its demands and those of the United Nations Security Council and the IAEA. The United States also reiterated its official position, offering assurances that the door was still open for the DPRK to walk through at any time, while taking time to clarify exactly what North Korea had meant by its declarations to Carter.

From the U.S. perspective, the ingredients of a compromise settlement were finally placed on the table. The Carter mission succeeded in extracting a significant concession from North Korea. The DPRK now hinted that it would trade away its reprocessing plant if conditions were right. It would also put its construction program for 50– and 200–megawatt electric plutonium production reactors on hold. The fact that these two issues were now open for discussion indicated to the U.S. negotiator that the DPRK was putting all its cards on the table. From the U.S. point of view, restoring full-scope safeguards was the only matter that remained to be settled. Therefore, the Clinton administration had to move rather quickly to strike a deal. Timing is always an important variable in successful bargaining.[32]

Once this break in the logjam occurred, the possibility of a breakthrough settlement of the nuclear issue based on a quid pro quo or win-win formula began to emerge. What precipitated this sudden breakthrough besides the obvious fact of Jimmy Carter's mediating role? What was the logic of a dramatic settlement of the North Korean nuclear issue?

Since Carter's successful mediation in June 1994, the two sides' mutual interests began to converge. U.S. interests clearly lay in stopping North Korea's extraction of plutonium by reprocessing spent fuel, while the DPRK had a series of demands on its shopping list, which included a negative security guarantee from the United States (i.e., assurances that the United States would not initiate a nuclear attack against North Korea), a U.S. guarantee that North Korea could acquire light-water reactor technology, a U.S. guarantee that North Korea's fuel needs would be met in the interim period until the light-water reactors were put into operation, and the establishment of a liaison office preparatory to an eventual normalization of U.S.–DPRK diplomatic relations. These were all substantive demands by North Korea that, if fully met, would give the North tangible benefits and rewards for having played the nuclear card with skill and tact.

Analysis of the "Win-Win" Propositions

The North Korean strategy for achieving these objectives was to conduct direct talks with the United States. It wanted to strike a package deal with the United States on a host of issues as preconditions for resolving the nuclear issue. North Korea also wanted to bypass both South Korea and the IAEA in its dealings with the United States on the nuclear matters.

The U.S. strategy, on the other hand, was to pressure and persuade North Korea to abandon its nuclear ambitions, by modifying its program away from the development of weaponry and toward the peaceful use of atomic energy. To achieve this objective, the U.S. position all along had been to involve the IAEA in the process of verifying the present and past history of Pyongyang's nuclear industry.

Whereas North Korea proposed a package deal to settle the nuclear issue, the United States was not willing to accept it unless the nuclear safeguards issue was settled first. It then suggested that the next stage of political settlement, including the eventual normalization of diplomatic relations, would naturally follow. Another important reason why the United States was reluctant to make a political settlement with North Korea was the alliances that the United States maintains with South Korea and Japan. The United States had to coordinate its policy change with allied countries.

In the end, a compromise was struck between the respective North Korean and U.S. versions of settlement proposals. The third high-level talks, in 1994, thus show a desire to attain a compromise settlement that reflects at least the public positions already articulated in 1993. At the end of the second round of the second U.S.–DPRK talks in Geneva, on July 19, 1993, a joint statement was issued on a three-point agreement, thereby setting the benchmark for the subsequent U.S.–DPRK talks and negotiations in 1994.

Prior to the breakthrough agreement on August 13, 1994, two prior U.S.–DPRK high-level talks had been held. The first, held in New York in January 1992, were attended by U.S. Under Secretary of State Arnold Kantor and North Korean Workers' Party Secretary Kim Yong-sun. This session provided the forum for airing the official position of each side and for discussing a wide range of issues of mutual concern to the two countries. However, it did not produce any tangible agreement. Nor was there any follow-up meeting between the two countries.

The second U.S.–DPRK high-level talks on the nuclear issue took place in 1993. Two rounds of meetings were held, the first in New York City, on June 9–11, 1993, and the second in Geneva, on July 16–19. It was at the end of the second round of the talks that a joint statement was issued on the three-point agreement.[33] These points were that (1) North Korea would begin talks with the IAEA regarding the question of outstanding safeguards—that is, special inspections; (2) inter-Korean talks would be reopened to discuss matters of mutual concern, including the nuclear issue; and (3) a third round of high-level talks would be held within two months to discuss possible U.S. assistance for North Korea to replace existing graphite-moderated reactors with light-water reactors. Because of lack of progress on the first two items, however, the third round of talks did not take place on time. Despite the lack of progress, Jimmy Carter informed Kim Il Sung in Pyongyang, as previously noted, that the Clinton administration was now willing to hold such bilateral talks.[34]

The third U.S.–DPRK high-level talks were more substantive and succeeded in producing concrete agreements that were important enough to serve as the benchmark for the subsequent U.S.–DPRK negotiations. The third round of talks began in Geneva on July 8, 1994, but was suspended on July 9 because of the death of North Korean leader Kim Il Sung on July 8. The talks resumed on August 5 and produced a breakthrough agreement on August 13 on steps to ease nuclear tensions and on the establishment of liaison offices in each other's capitals, with further talks scheduled for September 23 in Geneva.[35]

A four-point joint statement reaffirmed the principles of the June 11, 1993, U.S.–DPRK joint statement. The four specific elements, which constitute an integral part of a final resolution of the nuclear issue, were then identified in the

U.S.–DPRK agreement of August 13, 1994. These elements were substantively important enough to merit the following detailed listing:[36]

1. The DPRK promised "to replace its graphite-moderated reactors and re-lated facilities with light-water reactor (LWR) power plants," and the United States was prepared "to make arrangements for the provision of LWRs of approximately 2,000 MWe to [North Korea] as early as possible" and "to make arrangements for interim energy alternatives to the DPRK's graphite-moderated reactors." Upon receipt of U.S. assurances regarding the provision of LWRs and arrangements for interim energy alternatives, the DPRK would then "freeze construction of the 50 MWe and 200 MWe reactors, forgo reprocessing, and seal the radiochemical laboratory, to be monitored by the IAEA."
2. The United States and the DPRK were prepared "to establish diplomatic representation in each other's capital and to reduce barriers to trade and investment, as a move toward full normalization of political and economic relations."
3. To help achieve peace and security on a nuclear-free Korean Peninsula, the United States was prepared "to provide the DPRK with assurances against the threat or use of nuclear weapons by the United States," and the DPRK remained prepared "to implement the North–South Joint Declaration on the Denuclearization of the Korean Peninsula."
4. The DPRK was prepared "to remain a party to the Treaty on the Non-Pro-liferation of Nuclear Weapons and to allow implementation of its safe-guards agreement under the Treaty."

In addition, both sides agreed that expert-level discussions were necessary to advance the issues of replacing North Korea's graphite-moderated reactor pro-gram with LWR technology, safely storing and disposing of the spent fuel, providing alternative energy, and establishing liaison offices. Accordingly, both sides agreed that expert-level talks would be held in the United States and the DPRK, or elsewhere, as agreed, and that they would recess their own talks but resume in Geneva on September 23, 1994.[37]

In the subsequent press conference held early August 12, at North Korea's mission to the United Nations in Geneva, U.S. chief negotiator Robert Gallucci stated that "the agreement that we reached . . . we both regard as a very useful one, one that advances objectives that we both share" and that "there are many important issues that remain to be resolved."[38] North Korean negotiator Kang Sok Ju, in turn, said that "the agreement we have reached is a weighty and significant document" and that "we will freeze our graphite-moderated nuclear power plants, [while] we will be given alternatives for an interim period before we get the light-water reactor." He added that "this is [the] most important and essential element in resolving the so-called nuclear issue."[39]

Two separate meetings of experts were subsequently held, in Pyongyang on the question of establishing liaison missions and in Berlin on the question of light-water reactor construction. The second round of the third U.S.–DPRK high-level talks was then held in Geneva, from September 23 to October 17, 1994, to make further progress before finalizing and implementing the four-point agreement already reached. After seeking further consultation with their home governments, while the technical-level meetings were still going on in Geneva, delegations from both sides met on October 21 to sign an "Agreed Framework between the United States and the Democratic People's Republic of Korea." The agreement states that both sides will (1) "cooperate to replace the DPRK's graphite-moderated reactors and related facilities with light-water reactor (LWR) power plants," (2) "move toward full normalization of political and economic relations," (3) "work together for peace and security on a nuclear-free Korean Peninsula," and (4) "work together to strengthen the international nuclear non-proliferation regime."[40]

Regarding the first point, the United States agreed, "[i]n accordance with the October 20, 1994 letter of assurance" written by U.S. President Bill Clinton, to "make arrangements for the provision to the DPRK of a LWR project with a total generating capacity of approximately 2,000 MW(e) by a target date of 2003" and, for this purpose, to "organize under its leadership an international consortium to finance and supply the LWR project to be provided to the DPRK." The United States also agreed to "make arrangements to offset the energy forgone due to the freeze of the DPRK's graphite-moderated reactors and related facilities, pending completion of the first LWR unit," and to provide the DPRK, during this interim period of energy needs, with an annual supply of 500,000 tons of heavy oil for heating and electricity production purposes.[41] The DPRK agreed, as these conditions are met, to "freeze its graphite-moderated reactors and related facilities. . . . within one month of the date of this Document" and allow the IAEA to monitor this freeze. Dismantlement of the graphite-moderated reactors, however, will not be completed until the LWR project is completed. On the question of disposal of the spent fuel from the 5–megawatt electric experimental reactor, the DPRK agreed to cooperate with the United States "in finding a method to store [it] safely . . . during the construction of the LWR project, and to dispose of the fuel in a safe manner that does not involve reprocessing in the DPRK."

On the remaining points, both sides agreed to "reduce barriers to trade and investment, including restrictions on telecommunications services and financial transactions," and to "upgrade bilateral relations to the Ambassadorial level" as works of the liaison offices progress. To realize a nuclear-free Korean Peninsula, the United States agreed to "provide formal assurances to the DPRK, against the threat or use of nuclear weapons by the U.S.," while the DPRK agreed to "take steps to implement the North–South Joint Declaration on the Denuclearization of the Korean peninsula" and, for this purpose, to "engage in North–South dialogue." The DPRK also agreed to "remain a party" to the NPT and to comply with its IAEA safeguards obligations. Finally, on the question of verifying the DPRK's "past" nuclear reactor activities, the DPRK agreed to "come into full compliance" with the IAEA requirements "[w]hen a significant portion of the LWR project is completed, but before delivery of key nuclear components."

An appendix was also attached to provide further technical details regarding the agreement. This agreement does not explicitly use the words *special inspection,* but the DPRK's "full compliance with [the IAEA]) safeguards" includes "taking all steps that may be deemed necessary by the IAEA, following consultations with the Agency with regard to verifying the accuracy and completeness of the DPRK's initial report on all nuclear material in the DPRK." The agreement reportedly contains certain secret protocols, but their contents have not been made public.[42]

Prospects for Settlement of the Korean Conflict

Future prospects for U.S.–DPRK negotiations on the nuclear issue, based on the Geneva Agreed Framework, are uncertain. Unlike the IAEA–DPRK multilateral negotiations, the U.S.–DPRK bilateral talks made some progress, it is true, but this was due, primarily, to the timely intervention by Jimmy Carter. Despite the limited progress, the success of these bilateral talks depends on the fostering of mutual trust, which is yet to be tested. The IAEA–DPRK multilateral negotiations, moreover, have reached the point of mutual distrust rather than the working relationship that is essential for the successful implementation of the IAEA safeguards.[43]

How Viable Is Quid pro Quo Resolution of the Nuclear Issue?

Despite the difficulty of conducting negotiations in a multilateral diplomatic forum, it is important that progress also be made at the IAEA–DPRK level. Without success on the multilateral front, in connection with IAEA on-site inspections and the DPRK's full compliance with the IAEA safeguards requirements, the U.S.–DPRK agreement will remain hollow and meaningless. So far, the nuclear dispute has been well managed, but it is premature to celebrate the breakthrough based on compromise because the ultimate test comes when and if the DPRK complies with the nuclear safeguard regulations within the context of IAEA activities.

A multilateral framework for U.S.–DPRK relations is also important if the terms of the agreement are to be carried out successfully. Realizing the first point of agreement, on the light-water reactor construction, will depend on a smooth relationship between the DPRK and an international consortium, to be established for the purpose of financing and providing a technology appropriate to North Korea's needs. Unless and until the DPRK proves by words and deeds that it is willing and able to work within the multilateral framework of the international consortium, even if it is underwritten by a U.S. guarantee, implementation of the Geneva Agreed Framework provision regarding the construction of a light-water reactor may not be successful.

The U.S.–DPRK high-level talks in Geneva almost failed due to a reported deadlock over the old issues and new problems arising from North Korea's demands. Difficulty arose over the questions of whether (1) South Korea will be allowed to participate in the international consortium as a key member over North Korea's strenuous objection; (2) North Korea will allow IAEA special inspections at two "suspected" nuclear waste sites, in a clear reversal of its earlier indication of concession; and (3) the United States will go along with North Korea's new demand for $2 billion, in cash, to compensate Pyongyang for what it has already invested in the construction of new reactors and "reprocessing" facilities.[44]

Although these talks were depicted by U.S. chief negotiator Robert Gallucci as "businesslike and serious," there are bound to be new obstacles and a danger of the Geneva Agreed Framework not being implemented due to North Korea's new and changing expectations as well as changes in domestic political support both in the United States and among its allies South Korea and Japan.

Lessons from the North Korean Crisis

Now that the North Korean nuclear challenge has successfully been met and contained, within the framework of both the IAEA and an international consortium for providing North Korea with light-water reactor technology, it is high time to draw some conclusions from the case study of the 1994 North Korean nuclear crisis. What appropriate lessons can we learn from the crisis and its successful resolution?

Major lessons and findings regarding the North Korean case may be broadly stated in three areas. First, regarding *the behavior of North Korea as a surviving Leninist state,* we can draw the following conclusions:

- Confrontation breeds the grounds for either war or peace.
- When Pyongyang is pressed to defend itself from an external threat, the logic of nuclear brinkmanship and regime survival sets in.
- To disguise its sense of insecurity, the North Korean regime utilizes extreme forms of brinkmanship, following hyperbolic threats and intimidation with more tenable bargaining overtures.
- It remains a mystery why North Korea used the rhetoric of "war threats and intimidation" against South Korea in the summer of 1994. But the fact is that North Korea announced its withdrawal from the NPT, in 1993, and from the IAEA, in 1994, for mixed motives.

Second, regarding *the controversy over North Korea's nuclear program,* we can draw the following conclusions:

- Nuclear nonproliferation continues to preoccupy the United States as a superpower in the post–Cold War environment of global politics. To achieve this objective, the United States is prepared to use dual-track diplomacy in bargaining with the non–nuclear weapon state. As long as North Korea adheres to a rational strategy, the logic of accommodation and interest convergence will set in to shape the bargaining process in U.S.–DPRK negotiations.
- The impending reform of the NPT in 1995 gave North Korea a window of opportunity to play its nuclear card correctly to its advantage. This is why North Korea was able to extract concessions from the United States directly, or indirectly via other countries such as South Korea and Japan, in the form of greater financial payoffs and undiminished political gain.
- North Korea also adopted a negotiating strategy of linkage of the issues in an attempt to strike a package deal compromise settlement.
- The IAEA is strong and viable as long as the member states are willing to abide by the international rules. If any member, such as North Korea, is determined to break away from the international regime, by blocking the IAEA's routine and special inspections, the IAEA alone cannot enforce its will without the support of the United Nations Security Council and General Assembly.

Third, regarding the broader *issue of war and peace* in the post–Cold War era, we can draw the following conclusions:

- A small nonweapon state, such as North Korea, can learn to play a strategic game of nuclear brinkmanship to its advantage with a superpower.
- Diplomatic accommodation can still work as a technique of conflict settlement in the nuclear age. The resolution of conflict in the strategic realm, including nuclear crisis, can still proceed rationally, in post–Cold War global and regional politics.
- For nuclear diplomacy to succeed as a high-risk and high-stakes game, it must be based on and backed up by military power and preparedness. The nuclear weapon states must be ready to go to war, if necessary, in order to defend their national interests and strategic position. The threat of retaliatory strikes must be credible.

Finally, what is the future of accommodation, and how viable is quid pro quo resolution of the nuclear issue? Despite the passing of the Cold War era globally, Korea has remained the last, glacial frontier of the Cold War battles, primarily due to North Korea's ambitious nuclear development program. However, with the settlement of the North Korean nuclear controversy, prospects for maintaining peace and security on the Korean Peninsula are now enhanced. The secret and key to success are the diplomacy of accommodation and reconciliation, based on a willingness to compromise and attain quid pro quo resolution of the conflict. In this age of transnational and intergovernmental bargaining, there is still room for personal diplomacy, which Jimmy Carter's successful mission to Pyongyang so aptly demonstrated in defusing the 1994 Korean conflict.

Notes

1. For an analysis of the use of force versus diplomacy in recent history, see Gordon A. Craig and Alexander L. George, *Force and Statecraft: Diplomatic Problems of Our Time* (New York: Oxford University Press, 1990).

2. Jim Hoagland, "Thinking about Korean War II," *Washington Post,* May 12, 1994, A27. Also see *Time*'s cover story, "Korean Conflict: Is Kim Il Sung Bluffing, or Would He Go to War?" June 13, 1994. Also, in this same issue, see: Bruce W. Nelson, "Down the Risky Path," 24–28; J.F.O. McAllister, "Pyongyang's Dangerous Game," *Time,* April 4, 1994, 60–61.

3. "Pyongyang Breaks Off Inter-Korean Contacts," *North Korea News* (Seoul), no. 728, March 28, 1994, 1.

4. "We Will Annihilate the Enemy Mercilessly," *North Korea News* (Seoul), no. 731, April 18, 1994, 1.

5. This classified assessment was supported by virtually all intelligence agencies but disputed by the State Department's analysts. Steven Engelberg, "Intelligence Study Says North Korea Has Nuclear Bomb: A Dilemma for Clinton: Four U.S. Agencies Agree that Pyongyang Has Arms, but State Department Disagrees," *New York Times,* December 26, 1993, A1, 8.

6. For an excellent and timely account of the Korean nuclear issue, see Andrew Mack, "The Nuclear Crisis on the Korean Peninsula," *Asian Survey* 33, no. 4 (April 1993): 339–59. Also see Andrew Mack, "North Korea and the Bomb," *Foreign Policy* no. 83 (summer 1991): 87–104.

7. Kongdan Oh and Ralph C. Hassig, "North Korea's Nuclear Program" (233–50), and Young Whan Kihl, "Epilogue: Korean Conundrum in the post–Cold War Era" (329–38), in *Korea and the World: Beyond the Cold War,* ed. Young Whan Kihl (London and Boulder, CO: Westview Press, 1994).

8. There is no reason why military bases should be excluded from international inspection. In fact, North Korea argued in 1992, during talks on the nuclear issues with South Korea, that military bases in the South should be open for on-site inspection.

9. Reuters report, May 17, 1994.

10. Park Kwon-sang, "What's behind North Korea's 'Seoul-into-Sea-of-Fire' Threat?" *Dong-A Ilbo,* March 26, 1994.

11. Craig and George, *Force and Statecraft,* 169–170, 179.

12. Kim Tae-woo and Kim Min-seok, "The Nuclear Issue of the Korean Peninsula," *Bukhan Yon'gu* (fall 1993), as cited in *Korea Focus on Current Topics* 1, no. 6 (1993): 57–70.

13. Ibid.

14. 21 UST483: TIAS 6839, as reprinted in Peter A. Clausen, *Nonproliferation and the National Interest: America's Response to the Spread of Nuclear Weapons* (New York: HarperCollins, 1994), 208–13.

15. Leonard S. Spector, "Kim Il Sung's Legal Loophole," *Far Eastern Economic Review,* July 7, 1994, 30.

16. Ibid.

17. Jimmy Carter, *Report on Our Trip to Korea,* June 1994. Carter Report remains as unpublished. This document, prepared by Jimmy Carter for internal use, was reportedly circulated by the Carter Center but not released to the public. Subsequent attempts to verify the authenticity of this document with the Carter Center in Atlanta, however, were unsuccessful on the ground that the document should not have been made available to unauthorized personnel. My access to this document is from the newsletter printed and distributed by the Greater Cleveland Area Association of Korean-Americans, Fall 1994.

18. Ibid. He later discovered, to his dismay, how sharply some of the assessments of the U.S. and North Korean experts differed from his own subsequent on-site observations.

19. Ibid.

20. Ibid.

21. Ibid.

22. Kim Il Sung told Carter that Brezhnev had promised a 2,000–megawatt electric reactor to North Korea in the late 1970s but that Chernenko subsequently reneged on this promise.

23. David Sanger, "Carter Visits to North Korea: Whose Trip Was It Really?" *New York Times,* June 18, 1994, A6.

24. Ibid., "Two Koreas Plan Summit Talks on Nuclear Issue," *New York Times,* June 19, 1994, A1, 12.

25. Douglas Jehl, "Clinton Says the North Koreans Really May Be Ready for Talks," *New York Times,* June 23, 1994, A1, 5.

26. Interview with South Korean Deputy Prime Minister Lee Hong-koo, Seoul, July 8, 1994.

27. Peter Hayes, "Impact of Carter's Visit to the DPRK," June 20, 1994. *NPR Daily Report,* June 22, 1994. *NPR Daily Report* is compiled by Nautilus Institute, Berkeley, CA, for members of the Northeast Asia Peace and Security Network.

28. The possibility of Carter's returning to Pyongyang, and Seoul, was openly mentioned in newspapers. See, for instance, *Hanguk Ilbo,* September 23, 1994.

29. Yang Sung-chul, "The Carter Shock: Five Surprises," *Chosun Ilbo,* June 22, 1994.

30. Both compromise and accommodation, as types of agreements, entail bargaining and negotiation between the parties to a conflict. Martin Patchen, *Resolving Disputes between Nations: Coercion or Conciliation?* (Durham, NC: Duke University Press, 1988). Accommodation of rival interests, as diplomatic procedures, takes various forms: detente, rapprochement, entente, appeasement, alliance, etc. Each of these forms of diplomatic accommodation, however, may or may not progress itself to the next level or form of accommodation. This question is addressed by Craig and George, *Force and Statecraft,* 247–51.

31. For an analysis of negotiation in general, see Fred C. Ikle, *How Nations Negotiate* (New York: Praeger, 1964). Also see Roger Fisher and William Ury, *Getting to Yes: Negotiating Agreement without Giving In* (Boston: Houghton Mifflin, 1981).

32. Craig and George, *Force and Statecraft,* 163–77.

33. For the complete text of this agreement, see Peter Hayes, "Should the United States Transfer Light-Water Reactors to North Korea?" *Korean Journal of Defense Analysis* 6, no. 2 (winter 1994): 217. Also see Richard W. Stevenson, "U.S.-North Korea Meeting Yields Some Gains on Arms," *New York Times,* July 20, 1993, A2.

34. Michael R. Gordon, "Clinton May Add G.I.'s in Korea While Remaining Open to Talks," *New York Times,* June 17, 1994, A1.

35. Alan Riding, "U.S. and North Korea to Resume Negotiations," *New York Times,* August 5, 1994, A3.

36. Alan Riding, "U.S. and N. Korea Say They'll Seek Diplomatic Links," *New York Times,* August 13, 1994, A1, 10; David E. Sanger, "Carter Optimistic After North Korea Talks," *New York Times,* June 17, 1994, A10.

37. Ibid.

38. *NPR Daily Report,* August 12, 1994. The *New York Times* editorial praised the U.S. negotiator and his North Korean counterpart: "Diplomacy with North Korea has scored a resounding triumph." "Nuclear Breakthrough in Korea," editorial, *New York Times,* October 19, 1994, A22.

39. "Kang's Remarks at October 21 Press Conference in Geneva," *Korean Report* (Tokyo), no. 291, October 1994, 6–8.

40. See appendix A for the text of the "Agreed Framework between the United States of America and the Democratic People's Republic of Korea," which does not require U.S. Senate ratification.

41. For the text of Bill Clinton's letter of assurance, see the Annex to Appendix A in this volume.

42. The existence of "confidential minutes" attached to the agreement, as part of the settlement, was noted by Robert Gallucci during his press conference in Geneva on October 21, 1994.

43. Gallucci, speaking at the Foreign Press Center on October 27, 1994, characterized the framework agreement as based not on "trust" but on "verification," as discussed in *NPR Daily Report,* October 28, 1994.

44. McAllister, "Back to Square One," *Time,* October 10, 1994, 51.

11

Beyond the Geneva Agreed Framework: A Road Map for Normalizing Relations with North Korea

Scott Snyder

The presidents of the United States and South Korea unveiled the Korean War Memorial during the summer of 1995 in honor of American soldiers who fought for freedom in Korea more than four decades ago. While commemorating past losses and triumphs, the ceremonies also served to remind us that the Korean War is not yet over. Neither has the end of the Cold War restored conditions of peace to the Korean Peninsula. Almost 2 million soldiers—including 37,000 Americans—remain stationed along the demilitarized zone (DMZ) separating the two Koreas. Despite progress in freezing North Korea's nuclear program, the United States remains concerned about North Korea's long-range ballistic missile program, its conventional forces, and chemical weapons stockpiles. The War Memorial ceremonies in Washington remind us that the United States still has considerable influence on, responsibility for, and interest in the future of Korea. The Geneva Agreed Framework—supported by extensive policy coordination among the governments of the United States, the Republic of Korea (ROK), and

An earlier version of this chapter entitled "A Framework for Achieving Reconciliation on the Korean Peninsula: Beyond the Geneva Agreement" appears in *Asian Survey* 35, no. 8 (August 1995): 699–710. © 1995 by the Regents of the University of California. The views presented here are the author's own and do not represent those of the United States Institute of Peace.

Japan—has laid a foundation for relieving tensions on the Korean Peninsula, but lasting peace and regional stability will not be assured until a road map for normalizing relationships on the Korean Peninsula has been developed and implemented.

The Geneva Agreed Framework One Year Later

The Geneva Agreed Framework between the United States and the Democratic People's Republic of Korea (DPRK), signed on October 21, 1994, has passed three critical tests during its first year of existence. A failure in any of these three areas would have ripped up the agreement and sent American, South Korean, and Japanese officials back to the drawing board, with the uncertain prospects that would have accompanied a renewed drive for economic sanctions against North Korea through the United Nations. Despite the fact that the Geneva Agreed Framework has thus far survived these three challenges to its viability, there should be no illusion that the successful implementation of the agreement will be easy or that it fully addresses the root causes of conflict on the Korean Peninsula.

The first challenge to the Geneva Agreed Framework was from the U.S. Congress, which held at least seven congressional hearings through March 1995. A January 1995 *Wall Street Journal* editorial concluded that despite the generosity shown to an undeserving regime, the Geneva Agreed Framework offered some potentially important advantages by capping and promising eventually to eliminate North Korea's nuclear weapons program. By choosing not to challenge the Geneva Agreed Framework, the *Journal* and members of Congress initially appear to have accepted the prospect that implementation of the Agreed Framework may halt and eventually dismantle North Korea's nuclear weapons program—if North Korea fulfills its obligations under the agreement. This means that the DPRK will not refuel the 5–megawatt electric experimental reactor at Yongbyon nor reprocess more than 8,000 fuel rods removed from the reactor in May 1994, which contain enough plutonium to make up to six nuclear weapons. In addition, the North Koreans have halted construction of two larger reactors that might have produced enough plutonium to manufacture dozens of bombs per year.

The second challenge to the Geneva Agreed Framework was from North Korea. In return for North Korean commitments to freeze its nuclear program, the United States has agreed to oversee the delivery of two 1,000–megawatt electric proliferation-resistant light-water reactors (LWRs)—pending North Korea's full acceptance of its obligations as a member of the Non-Proliferation Treaty (NPT)—and to provide 500,000 tons of heavy oil annually as compensation for fuel production capacity forgone by the halt in construction of North Korea's graphite reactors. However, the type of light-water reactor to be supplied to Pyongyang was left ambiguous in October 1994 in Geneva, with Ambassador Robert Gallucci insisting that the only financially, technically, and politically viable option was for South Korea to play a central role in providing the reactor, while Pyongyang insisted that it would never be willing to accept a light-water reactor from its erstwhile adversaries in the South.

Negotiations between U.S. and North Korean negotiators in Berlin failed to resolve the issue, and the "target date" of April 21, 1995, for signing the light-water reactor contract passed without a rupture in the basic conditions underlying the Geneva Agreed Framework. The DPRK failed to follow through on threats to reload its experimental reactor, and the United States offered to continue negotiations at a higher level in an effort to resolve the dispute. Deputy Assistant Secretary Tom Hubbard and his North Korean counterpart Kim Kye-kwan spent more than three weeks in Kuala Lumpur in May and June 1995 trying to iron out a compromise that would be acceptable to North Korea while also satisfying the requirements that the light-water reactor be based on a South Korean model and that South Korea would play a central role in the project. The result was encapsulated in simultaneous announcements on June 12, 1995, in Kuala Lumpur and Seoul. The agreement allowed South Korea a central role in providing a "South Korean–model" light-water reactor to the North while allowing Pyongyang to accept a reactor that is based on an "original U.S. design."[3]

This complex compromise was made possible by the creation in March 1995 of the Korean Peninsula Energy Development Organization (KEDO), a multinational organization mandated under the Geneva Agreed Framework to provide the DPRK with a light-water reactor. Under the KEDO charter, an executive board consists of Robert Gallucci, Choi Tong-Chin, and Tetsuya Endo, the representatives, respectively, of the U.S., ROK, and Japanese governments, which are directly concerned with the North Korean nuclear issue. Under the executive board, an American executive director, Stephen Bosworth, and two deputy directors from South Korea and Japan, Choi Young-jin and Itaru Umezu, respectively—with the assistance of an American engineering firm playing the supervisory role of program coordinator—will undertake the task of negotiating a supply contract with the DPRK. In turn, it was announced on June 12, 1995, that KEDO will select the Korean Electric Power Company (KEPCO)—a South Korean firm—as the primary contractor to fulfill its obligations to supply a light-water reactor to North Korea based on the Ulchin-3 and -4 designs currently being completed in South Korea. Thus, KEDO—an international organization under American leadership—has the responsibility of ensuring that a South Korean reference model light-water reactor will be built in the DPRK.

The third challenge to the Geneva Agreed Framework has been whether the South Korean government is capable of maintaining sustained popular support for the agreement during the course of implementation. Thus far, South Korean public support for the Agreed Framework has been fluid and uncertain, and shifts in South Korean public opinion appear to be reflected—rather than led—by statements of a senior leadership in South Korea that is driven more by domestic political sensitivities than by a consistent, goal-oriented policy toward North Korea.[4]

South Korean ambivalence toward the Geneva Agreed Framework appears to be directly proportional to the extent to which South Korea is perceived to be either empowered or sidelined by its implementation at any particular moment. Despite official acceptance in Seoul of the Geneva Agreed Framework prior to its unveiling (without which it would have been politically impossible for the United States to formally conclude an agreement with North Korea), President Kim Young Sam's comments to the *New York Times* criticizing the agreement just days prior to its signing was a reflection of deep South Korean public ambivalence that the South had been sidelined from the official negotiations on an issue that directly affected its national security interests.[5]

Public support for the agreement grew in South Korea during the months of scrutiny given to the nuclear framework by a skeptical U.S. Congress: the benefits of the agreement were more widely recognized by the Korean public in contrast with the alternative in the event the agreement were to unravel. But public attitudes hardened when it became necessary for the United States and North Korea to return to the negotiating table (again, without South Korea) for additional discussions to settle issues related to North Korea's central role.

Although the Geneva and Kuala Lumpur agreements benefited in the eyes of South Korean analysts following the successful negotiation of a rice deal with North Korea in June 1995 (supporters of the rice deal argued that the U.S.– DPRK agreements laid the groundwork for success in the inter-Korean negotiations, whereas critics asserted that U.S. negotiators achieved clearly defined objectives while ROK negotiators failed to demonstrate that they made any strategic gains in the rice talks), public support turned negative in the initial stages of the KEDO negotiations as the focus shifted to South Korea's central role, not in building the reactors but in financing a deal that had been negotiated by the United States rather than by South Korea.[6]

Of the three challenges that the Agreed Framework has faced thus far, the need for South Korean public support for the implementation of the agreement is most critical; otherwise, the political and financial backing necessary to support the project will disappear, and the United States—rather than North Korea, as many critics have predicted—will find itself unable to fulfill its obligations under the Agreed Framework.

KEDO and the Implementation of the Agreed Framework

As KEDO fulfills its responsibilities, it will be very important for the United States government to extricate itself from being cast as an intermediary or "honest broker" between the two Koreas. As a mediator, the United States would be vulnerable to false charges that it was being manipulated by either side, and such a role risks compromising the U.S.–South Korean security alliance. Although KEDO is headed by an American, South Koreans and Japanese will also be at the table at every stage of KEDO negotiations with North Korea to implement the provision of a light-water reactor to the North. This structure should dilute criticisms at earlier stages that by negotiating directly with North Korea, the United States had effectively sidelined its South Korean allies from the negotiations, indirectly assisting North Korea's strategic objective of avoiding interaction with South Korea while improving relations with the United States. The United States must stand firm in insisting that all future negotiations on technical issues related to the provision of light-water reactors to the North be handled through KEDO, not by falling back on bilateral negotiations between the United States and North Korea.

The initial work of KEDO has begun with one round of negotiations in Kuala Lumpur in September of 1995 and one round in New York from October to December of 1995. The focus of these talks was on the conclusion of a supply contract with North Korea and on the terms of repayment by North Korea for KEDO's provision of light-water reactors. These negotiations defined the scope of KEDO's supply responsibilities as part of the LWR project. In addition, the terms of repayment by North Korea were agreed upon to ensure that financial contributors will be able to support the project. Even with the successful resolution of these issues following the December 15, 1995 signing of a supply contract, KEDO could become a hostage at any time to political/security issues not fully addressed by the Geneva Agreed Framework—including the necessity to resume dialogue between North and South Korea—that underlie the resolution of complex technical issues on which the success of the agreement will ultimately depend.

North Korea's Current Options and Prospects

The major unknown that has inhibited our ability to define clearly strategic objectives on the Korean Peninsula has been our limited understanding of North Korea's internal politics. While our understanding of domestic political factors in Pyongyang remains opaque, enough circumstantial evidence can be deduced from the available facts to give us a basic understanding of the DPRK and its policies now that Kim Il Sung has passed from the scene.

First, we know that Kim Jong Il, whose public appearances became somewhat more regular since the beginning of 1995, appears to be in charge and that the decisions emanating from Pyongyang are rational and even pragmatic. The decisions to go ahead with the U.S.–DPRK negotiations in the summer of 1994, to accept the final iteration of the Geneva Agreed Framework and Kuala Lumpur negotiations, and to release Chief Warrant Officer Bobby Hall in December of 1994 are all indications of a coherent policy and political order in Pyongyang. Contrary decisions in each case might have led to direct threats to the survival of the North Korean regime. In addition, decisions have been made to proceed apace with efforts to attract foreign investment to the northeastern corner of the DPRK—the Rajin–Sonbong area near the mouth of the Tumen River—and to encourage processing-on-commission trade. Thus far, an authoritative internal decision-making process for certain large matters appears to be in place, though we cannot predict its future stability or longevity.

Second, the North Korean economy continues to suffer from serious bottle-necks, and production shortages in the area of foodstuffs are severe. These short-ages have clearly been exacerbated by the extraordinary rainfall and subsequent flooding caused in North Korea by Typhoon Janis in August of 1995. Even prior to this severe natural disaster, the external economy of North Korea had shrunk by one-quarter from 1989 to 1993, and the DPRK has failed for decades even to service its external debt. Following the most severe flooding in living memory in North Korea in August 1995, the leadership in Pyongyang took the unprece-dented step of requesting external humanitarian assistance from the United Na-tions and other international relief organizations. The initial U.N. assessment projected that the structural deficit in North Korea's grain production would increase in 1995–96 from an average of 1.5–2 million tons to more than 3.5 million tons and made an initial appeal for more than $US 15 million in assis-tance to meet initial emergency food, shelter, and medical needs.[7] Prior to the floods, the recent grain deals with South Korea, Japan, and others had suggested the seriousness of the food shortfall the DPRK faces and raised new fears among some analysts about the near-term stability of the North Korean regime. North Korean attempts to attract outside investors continue to go unanswered, and Pyongyang has still not improved its poor credit record or reduced its $US 10.3 billion external debt, which remains unserviced from loans made to North Korea in the mid-1970s. Although the ROK has only twice the population of the DPRK, the South Korean economy is estimated to be eighteen times the size of the North Korean economy.[8]

Third, regime survival is unquestionably the primary goal for North Korean leaders, who have witnessed the fall of communism in Eastern Europe and the collapse of the Soviet Union, and now must face an uncertain future—having lost the leadership of the man who founded the DPRK and led it for almost half a century. Moreover, the DPRK has been losing the diplomatic battle, having been isolated by South Korea's successful Nordpolitik policy. Since 1990, "coexist-ence" with the ROK and protestations that one side should not "try to eat the other side" have gradually replaced more aggressive themes in North Korean rhetoric.[9] The major exception has been a voluble and sustained attack on ROK President Kim Young Sam—particularly after President Kim Young Sam criti-cized Kim Il Sung as a war criminal instead of offering condolences following the death of Kim Il Sung on July 8, 1994—but the nature of these attacks can correctly be attributed to internal political needs during the leadership transition as well as fear of South Korea's considerable economic and political advantages vis-à-vis the North. The last available countermeasure at the North's disposal has been an attempt to seek cross-recognition with South Korea's old allies by im-proving its relations with the United States and eventually Japan while avoiding contact with the ROK government as much as possible. Perhaps fearing that

Seoul will try to take advantage of its superior power and absorb the North, Pyongyang will likely continue to implement a strategy that attempts to improve its relations with the United States while holding South Korea at bay unless it can be assured that improved relations with the ROK won't endanger the survival of the regime in Pyongyang.

Fourth, as global communism has failed, the foundational elements of the North Korean regime have shifted away from an emphasis on Marxism–Leninism to Kim Il Sung thought and the principle of *juche,* or self-reliance. The tenacity with which the DPRK holds on to the trappings of the socialist state is reminiscent of the misplaced loyalties held by some seventeenth-century Koreans who continued to carry out rituals in honor of the "true" Chinese Ming leaders decades after the Ching dynasty leaders had wiped out the traces of their Chinese predecessors. Students of traditional Korean history will readily recognize that the Marxist–Leninist bureaucratic structures of North Korean institutions have failed to obscure the influence of Confucianism in North Korean culture and thought. Adherence to strict standards of "principle" and "morality" in world view, the peculiar nature of the succession process, and even the overwhelmingly agricultural structure of North Korean society reinforce one's impression that the traditional aspects of this society remain strong, despite the influence of modernization in some key areas.

On the basis of these facts, one might draw some conclusions about the likelihood of a North Korean collapse at this time. Barring a serious breakdown in the political leadership or an unusual combination of external pressures, a full collapse of the North Korean state or its absorption by the ROK is unlikely, and the possibility of our being able to control such an outcome through the available policy tools—either by stabilizing or undermining the North Korean regime—is even more remote.

The variables that led to a collapse of the East German state do not appear to exist in the DPRK at this time. The traditional elements of this isolated society are themselves too stable to allow naturally for the kinds of changes that might presage a collapse. Although the North Korean leadership is well aware of global trends, the populace has been relatively isolated from the outside world and simply cannot compare the difference in living standards between South and North Korea. Moreover, the level of political control and penetration into North Korean society by internal security networks remains much higher than it was in the former East Germany. Even the occasional reported food riots in the DPRK will remain a localized phenomenon since the horizontal organizational structures that might allow such riots to spread do not exist in North Korean society due to severe travel restrictions imposed on the general populace. For these reasons, the danger of a North Korean collapse will be much higher after a partial opening of North Korean society has begun. Even if there is a regime transition, South Korea, China, and others will shrink from direct involvement in North Korean domestic instability, allowing a transition to proceed without external interference.

Lessons from the North Korean Nuclear Crisis

The media focus on U.S. policy toward Korea has reached its highest level of intensity in over forty years, but most Americans are relatively unfamiliar with the complex history of one of our most serious alliance commitments to grow out of the Cold War.[10] Despite the extensive media coverage given to the North Korean nuclear issue, there has been no serious attempt to encourage a sustained debate or to forge a policy consensus on the strategic aspects of a shared U.S.–ROK policy toward the Korean Peninsula. As a result, opinion continues to be divided among policy makers in the United States, the ROK, and Japan with regard to whether it is possible to influence the future of the North Korean regime without incurring unacceptable costs. To the extent that a shared strategy for dealing with security on the peninsula remains undeveloped, we will continue to hand a relatively weak DPRK the initiative to set the agenda and pace of implementation of the Geneva Agreed Framework, most likely with serious negative consequences for long-standing U.S.–ROK and Japan–ROK ties.

In this respect, the experience gained in negotiating the Geneva Agreed Framework, the strengths and weaknesses of the outcome, and the questions that will inevitably arise over the course of the ten-year-plus implementation phase should provide us with a strong foundation on which to consider some fundamental questions regarding our policy toward North Korea. First, the nature of the jointly identified solution embodied in the Geneva Agreed Framework between the United States and the DPRK was the result of a commitment to a "broad and thorough" approach—or "package solution"—in which each side was able to identify objectives that were sufficiently important to induce parallel concessions while avoiding setting preconditions that could become obstacles to progress. The key to making such an approach succeed in practice is the ability to identify with sufficient specificity the interim steps required to ensure that neither side attempts to backtrack on or reinterpret any part of the agreement.

Second, the structure of the agreement—in which a series of parallel movements are made on the basis of clearly delineated, concrete steps—provides verifiability and helps to ensure that neither side will pocket a concession by taking unfair advantage. Of course, beyond the vague threat that nonimplementation of the agreement will return both sides to a confrontational path that includes sanctions, the mechanisms necessary to prevent misunderstanding have not been clearly defined thus far. Nonetheless, if the main steps necessary to reach parallel objectives are clearly identified and reversible, each side will have a measure of leverage available in the absence of mutual trust. In this respect, the process of implementation itself is an important confidence-building measure.

Third, the Geneva Agreed Framework's focus on solving a clearly defined problem facilitates the setting aside of "red herring" issues that are extraneous to the agreement's implementation. As a result, attempts by either side to introduce inappropriate elements to the negotiations are obvious and clearly noticeable.

This decreases the likelihood that incrementalism can be used to pursue objectives that are not embodied in an agreement if the boundaries of the negotiations have been properly marked. For instance, the North Koreans initially raised the question of replacing the armistice with a peace treaty during the negotiations in Geneva but dropped those demands when U.S. negotiators emphasized that this subject was outside the bounds of the problem under discussion.

Finally, the weakest parts of the agreement—and the area in which it appears that North Korean commitments are most likely to falter—are the commitment to North–South dialogue and problems related to South Korea's central role in providing "South Korean–style" LWRs to the DPRK. Congressional resolutions under consideration[11] call for "strengthening" the Geneva Agreed Framework by insisting on substantive progress in North–South dialogue and implementation of the major provisions of the 1991 North–South Agreement on Reconciliation, Nonaggression, Exchanges, and Cooperation (hereafter referred to as the North–South Agreement). Despite the North's resistance to engagement with the South in a substantive dialogue thus far, the United States was prepared to walk away from the table in Geneva if the DPRK had failed to include the agreement's provisions requiring North–South dialogue.[12] In the end, North Korean diplomats have had to swallow both of these concessions because South Korea's central involvement is critical to the viability of the agreement, and there is simply no other satisfactory option available to the DPRK but to resume contacts with the ROK; however, the likelihood of significant substantive progress in any North–South discussions under these circumstances remains unclear.

With the exception of issues related to North–South interactions, the substantive steps that the DPRK has taken thus far in accordance with the Geneva Agreed Framework have been striking, given familiar past patterns in its dealings with the ROK in which the DPRK has sought general agreements based on principle and later willfully misinterpreted key provisions as a pretext to avoid implementation. This pattern of deception by the DPRK has been deeply ingrained in the North–South negotiating record. In contrast with past North Korean behavior, U.S. negotiators have been pleasantly surprised thus far with the level of cooperation and openness that has been afforded to technical teams who have visited Yongbyon in order to stabilize and encase the stored spent fuel rods for eventual shipment from North Korea. There has also been sporadic progress in working-level talks that will lead to the establishment of liaison offices in Washington and Pyongyang. Most notable as a sign of the importance attached to the Geneva Agreed Framework is the assertion in some North Korean editorials that the DPRK is dutifully fulfilling its obligations, coupled with the "expectation" and insistence that the United States follow suit.[13]

Assessing Our Shared Objectives

What, then, are the parameters for determining U.S. objectives for the future of the Korean Peninsula, and how might we work with our South Korean and

Japanese allies to achieve those objectives? The United States should not hesitate to exercise leadership in coordination with our allies to define a strategy that addresses the significant remaining challenges on the peninsula. The future of North–South reconciliation and eventual reunification, possibilities for conventional arms-control and other tension-reduction measures, the extension of economic prosperity and regional cooperation, and ultimately, the shape of the Northeast Asian security environment and the U.S. role in this region will all be determined by our ability to work with our South Korean allies to define a security strategy for the future of Korea and Northeast Asia.

The foundation of any discussion of U.S. security interests on the Korean Peninsula must start with the need for close coordination with our South Korean allies in designing an appropriate strategy for dealing with the DPRK. The level of political and military cooperation—including through the Joint U.N. Command and consultations on policy toward the DPRK—with the ROK is higher than with almost any other American ally. Dealing with remaining challenges vis-à-vis the DPRK will require a sustained, integrated, and highly disciplined diplomatic approach. The initial progress that has resulted from the Geneva Agreed Framework underscores the need for and potential advantages of such an approach. The DPRK has begun to respond, but there is a need to bolster opportunities for interaction between North and South Korea, particularly since the ultimate disposition of security issues on the Korean Peninsula will depend on the Koreans' ability to work out their own problems directly.

The United States should neither stand between the two Koreas in the role of intermediary nor take any action that would compromise our alliance with the ROK. We can do more, however, than simply provide passive support while waiting for the Koreas sort out the possibilities for reunification. The U.S. policy toward Korean reunification—that it is up to the Koreans themselves to decide how and when to achieve reunification—is correct. However, given the foundations of our policy, described above, and the new possibilities for reducing tension that have accompanied the end of the Cold War, there is a need for us to work with our South Korean allies to develop a road map for inter-Korean reconciliation through which the United States might assist in promoting an atmosphere conducive to substantive inter-Korean dialogue and tension reduction on the Korean Peninsula.

Elements of a Road Map for Peace on the Korean Peninsula

Drawing on the analytical conclusions of the preceding discussion, the approach outlined below for shaping a strategic policy toward the Korean Peninsula is based on the following assumptions: (1) the cornerstone of U.S. policy toward the Korean Peninsula is the enduring value and strength of the U.S.–ROK alliance; (2) the United States should bolster efforts at inter-Korean reconciliation, but it should not take the lead in mediating or brokering an inter-Korean settlement; (3) the DPRK seeks a guarantee that U.S.–ROK aims do not threaten its primary strategic objective of regime survival; (4) the Geneva Agreed Framework provides an effective model for moving forward in small, interlocking steps toward the broader goals that will result in settling the nuclear issue, but the aspects that deal with strategic or regional issues—such as the need for North–South dialogue—require strengthening, or the success of the Geneva Agreed Framework will be threatened; (5) a road map toward inter-Korean reconciliation is a prerequisite for forward progress in regional security and the promotion of economic prosperity and stability in Northeast Asia.

The United States, Japan, and South Korea should carry out consultations to develop a road map toward the eventual normalization of relations with North Korea that will parallel the implementation of the Geneva Agreed Framework and provide a timetable for the resolution of security issues between the two Koreas. This timetable would lay out an integrated approach consisting of steps designed to move toward tension-reduction on the Korean Peninsula in parallel with implementation of the Geneva Agreed Framework.

The formulation of such a road map will require extensive consultations in advance between the United States, Japan, and the ROK to determine an appropriate sequence of actions needed to achieve reconciliation and to clearly define a joint position on all issues involved. In addition to coordinating our respective policies effectively to avoid future differences that might provide the DPRK with the opportunity to exploit undeserved leverage, the creation of such a road map will keep the initiative in the hands of the United States, Japan, and the ROK and will be designed to reassure the DPRK that its goals of regime survival are not threatened by engaging in a genuine reconciliation process.

The first set of interlocking steps envisioned as part of a road map is the achievement of substantive progress in North–South dialogue through the resumption of North–South Korean Joint Committee talks on political and security issues and exchanges and cooperation between North and South Korea. Although the Military Armistice Commission (MAC) remains the legally proper mechanism through which military issues are handled, if the MAC fails, it may be necessary to seek a tripartite interim arrangement for dealing with these issues until the conclusion of a peace treaty and full normalization of relations among all countries in the Northeast Asian region, the ultimate destination of our combined road map.

One possibility for restoring the MAC in the near term while inducing dialogue on political and security issues might be to offer to implement a phased dismantling of the U.N. Command, as North Korea has demanded, in return for North Korean pledges to cease its efforts to undermine the MAC, return to negotiations through the MAC, and restore the status quo ante. In addition, North Korea should agree to tripartite negotiations on an interim peace mechanism and conventional arms reductions that, when fully implemented, would lay the foundations for negotiation of formal peace arrangements with South Korea and the United States.

As substantive progress is made in political and military talks to reduce conventional military tensions, resulting in a measurable level of progress to be determined, a gradual lifting of the U.S. economic embargo should occur, and discussions to resolve U.S. concerns about the North Korean ballistic missile program should be conducted and progress achieved. Since the lifting of economic restrictions is reversible, this is one area in which the United States might take the lead. Diplomatic discussions on normalization between the DPRK and Japan should also be resumed at this time. It is anticipated that this phase of events might occur within five years and would accompany parallel progress made in implementing the Geneva Agreed Framework prior to the delivery of key nuclear components for the construction of LWRs. Throughout this period, one would expect that inter-Korean economic cooperation would continue to grow steadily. Full normalization between Japan and the DPRK may occur in parallel with concrete improvement in North–South dialogue and measurable progress in conventional arms reductions on the peninsula, but full compensation accompanying Japan–DPRK normalization should be delayed until after the DPRK has returned fully to the NPT by accepting special inspections, further reinforcing a key provision of the Geneva Agreed Framework.

The second broad set of interlocking steps, projected to occur during the second half of the implementation of the Geneva Agreed Framework (in five to ten years), should include substantive progress in arms reduction as a result of North–South Korean Joint Committee meetings and the broader implementation of cooperation and exchange efforts between the two Koreas through the Joint Cultural Committee. These steps would proceed in parallel with discussions on outstanding issues in the U.S.–DPRK dialogue; support for DPRK membership in the Asian Development Bank, the World Bank, the International Monetary Fund (IMF), and other international financial and trade organizations on the appropriate terms; and the upgrading of U.S.–DPRK relations. It is unlikely, however, that the United States could move to full normalization of relations with the DPRK in the absence of a peace agreement.

Pending measurable progress in demilitarization and overall implementation of the North–South Agreement, it will be necessary to initiate discussions with the DPRK designed to replace the armistice agreement with a formal peace treaty. During any peace treaty discussions that might be held, it would be made clear that the question of U.S. troop presence in the ROK is to be decided between the United States and the ROK and is not an appropriate issue for discussion with the DPRK. A peace treaty, projected to occur in a time frame of about ten years, would not be concluded until after the full implementation of the North–South Agreement, meaning that a more normal relationship between South and North Korea would be established prior to the signing of a peace treaty.

Since some restrictions by the ROK on economic cooperation have already been lifted, one immediate area for coordination and progress might be simultaneous progress in lifting restrictions on U.S.–ROK joint ventures in North Korea.

In addition, nongovernmental cultural and educational exchange between the United States and North Korea and Japan and North Korea should be encouraged, particularly if it is possible to find ways to involve representatives from both North and South Korea in constructive unofficial dialogue, cooperation, or exchange activities in either Japan or the United States. The DPRK should be encouraged to join the ASEAN Regional Forum (ARF), the Asia–Pacific Economic Cooperation group (APEC), or other multilateral dialogues apart from any timetable as part of the suggested framework. Participation in cultural and other nongovernmental exchange activities should be delinked from political conditions and promoted separately as a means of expanding our mutual understanding and knowledge of respective cultures and political and economic conditions.

We certainly cannot expect that the development of a road map for normalization of relations with North Korea will be easy. In fact, it will take at least a decade and possibly longer. But if such a road map is developed properly and North Korea can be encouraged to forge close relations with its neighbors, inter-Korean tensions might be lessened; other forms of economic, political, and security cooperation in Northeast Asia are likely to flourish; U.S. interests in regional stability will be achieved; and economic prosperity may be extended throughout the region.

Notes

1. The Geneva Agreed Framework was a primary subject of discussion at the following hearings: "North Korea and Nuclear Weapons," Senate Foreign Relations Subcommittee for East Asian and Pacific Affairs, December 1, 1994; "The North Korean Nuclear Agreement," Senate Energy Committee, January 19, 1995; "The U.S. Agreement with North Korea," Senate Foreign Relations Committee, January 24 and 25, 1995; "Defense Issues Overview," Senate Armed Services Committee, January 26, 1995; "The Nuclear Agreement with North Korea," House Subcommittee for International Relations and East Asian and Pacific Affairs, February 23, 1995; "Justice/State/Appropriation for FY96," House Appropriations Committee for Justice/Commerce/State, March 2, 1995.

2. *Wall Street Journal*, "North Korea's Bombs," January 30, 1995, A20.

3. Joint U.S.–DPRK press statement, Kuala Lumpur, June 13, 1995, U.S. Department of State; Resolution 1995–12 of the Executive Board of the Korean Peninsula Energy Development Organization, June 13, 1995.

4. John Burton, "Survey of South Korea," *Financial Times*, June 26, 1995 as cited by Nexis; and conversations with South Korean analysts in Seoul, June 1995.

5. James Sterngold, "South Korean President Lashes Out at U.S.," *New York Times*, October 8, 1994, 3.

6. Agence-France Press, "LWR Talks with North Korea Positive: Bosworth," September 15, 1995; "Editorial Protests Light Water Reactor's Financial Burdens," *Hanguk Ilbo*, Seoul, September 17, 1995, 3, as cited by Nexis.

7. "Assessment of Damage and Immediate Relief Requirements following Floods: Preliminary Findings of United Nations Assessment Mission," United Nations Department of Humanitarian Affairs, September 12, 1995.

8. Judy Lee, "North Korea Sees Contradiction for Fifth Straight Year in 1994: South," Agence-France Presse, June 20, 1995.

9. Chong-sik Lee, "North and South Korea: From Confrontation to Negotiation," in *Korea Briefing, 1990,* ed. Chong-sik Lee (New York: Asia Society and Boulder, CO: Westview Press, 1991).

10. Don Oberdorfer, "Report on a Visit to North Korea," Asia Society lecture, Washington, D.C., January 1995.

11. House Joint Resolution 83, "Relating to the United States–North Korea Agreed Framework and the Obligations of North Korea under That and Previous Agreements with Respect to the Denuclearization of the Korean Peninsula and Dialogue with the Republic of Korea," is the resolution most likely to receive positive consideration.

12. Kyodo, "Inter-Korean Dialogue Almost Killed Nuke Talks: Perry," October 22, 1994.

13. Korean Central News Agency, "North Reports on Berlin Talks on Reactors," March 25, 1995; "North on Rejection of South's Reactors and KEDO," March 10, 1995, as cited by Nexis.

North Korean Decision-Making Processes Regarding the Nuclear Issue at Early Stages of the Nuclear Game

Alexandre Y. Mansourov

Is North Korean behavior in the triple-track negotiations with the United States, the Republic of Korea (ROK), and the International Atomic Energy Agency (IAEA) concerning the notorious nuclear issue strategic or erratic? Are the moves that North Korea makes in this respect based on a calculus of its national interests, and if so, who determines this calculus and how? Or are these decisions driven by domestic politics, and if so, what are these internal political dynamics and how are they related to North Korean foreign policy making? Or is Pyongyang's behavior totally erratic—based on some blind passions and paranoia of its leaders and their followers, obscure standard operating procedures of its obsolete decision-making apparatus, and a variety of misperceptions and misunderstandings about the world around it? In short, does North Korea have a nuclear game plan, what are its modalities, who draws its outlines, who implements it and how, and what might account for its discrepancies, if any? These are the issues I address in this chapter.

Who Devises the Nuclear Game Plan in Pyongyang?

The end of global East–West confrontation in 1991 presented new opportunities and posed new challenges on the Korean Peninsula: a long-standing uneasy but

---

*This chapter was written before Kim Il Sung's death. As it was an influential paper in the West that shed light onto the North Korean "black box" of decision-making, we are presenting the paper in its original form.—Eds.

peaceful coexistence of two belligerent Korean states may soon either end with reunification of Korea or degenerate into a heated nuclear arms race both between North and South and in the Northeast Asian region as a whole. Many argue that this choice is for Pyongyang to make. To be prepared for any contingency, one needs to know the true intentions of the leadership of the Democratic People's Republic of Korea (DPRK), where policy initiatives come from, who formulates North Korean priorities and how, and what accounts for variations between policy guidelines and their implementation.

The evidence strongly suggests that it was the Great Leader Kim Il Sung himself who originally conceived and defined the North Korean nuclear program.[1] Though for decades the program's actual progress has been determined mainly by technical and technological developments and the availability of financing, its practical utility was defined by political considerations. There is little doubt in my mind that as long as the DPRK was under the nuclear umbrella of the former Soviet Union and had credible guarantees regarding its national security from its Soviet and Chinese allies, Kim Il Sung did not contemplate using the nuclear program for anything other than the officially stated purpose of the peaceful generation of atomic energy.[2]

Today, however, quite a different set of nuclear intentions is attributed to the Great Leader. In particular, there is reason to believe that sometime in 1990, or maybe even in 1989, after consultations with Defense Minister O Jin-u and Science Adviser Yi Sung-gi, President Kim ordered the Ministry of Atomic Energy Industry (MAEI) to study the issues related to the possible military applications of the North Korean nuclear program. Consequently, later in 1990, the MAEI personnel extracted some plutonium from damaged fuel rods installed at the experimental 5–megawatt electric nuclear reactor built in 1986.[3] It was this incident that led the U.S. and South Korean intelligence communities to conclude in 1992, on the basis of IAEA nuclear inspection results, that the odds were better than even that Pyongyang had already produced enough plutonium to build one or perhaps two atomic bombs.

These developments led to growing speculation about Pyongyang's nuclear ambitions, and since late 1991, scholars and policy makers in the West and in East Asia have been pondering possible motives for such a dramatic shift in the North Korean nuclear policy. On the one hand, Donald Zagoria provides an excellent summary of very rational exogenous motives related to the changing security environment around the DPRK that may have influenced Kim Il Sung's decision:

1. *The "pariah state" syndrome:* Overnight, the DPRK lost its major security allies and hence had to defend itself entirely by its own means.
2. *The need to maintain the balance of forces on the Korean Peninsula:* The DPRK was faced with adversaries armed with nuclear weapons; therefore, it had to develop its own nukes to counterbalance this threat.

3. *Enhanced security through nuclear deterrence.*
4. *"Low price tag":* Once nuclear weapons have been developed, they become relatively cheap, much cheaper than conventional arms.
5. *The "nuclear card":* Pyongyang could draw international attention to its domestic problems and acquire some diplomatic and political clout in order to negotiate economic and political concessions from the West. In other words, if a nuclear bomb is the "perfect weapon for the poor outcasts," Pyongyang is said to be the ideal candidate for it.[4]

On the other hand, Kongdan Oh, at RAND, stresses endogenous motives related to the following domestic factors. First, North Korean leaders are trying insofar as possible to avoid forfeiting the sunk costs of the nuclear program: it is too expensive an acquisition to be abandoned easily.[5] Second, the Great Leader saw these "family jewels" as guarantees of the continuity of the Kim dynasty as the heir apparent, Kim Jong Il, consolidates his grip on power. Finally, nobody in Pyongyang wants to lose face and be seen as yielding to outside pressures, which may undermine their position in domestic politics.[6]

Setting aside the question of their validity, these analyses are, admittedly, deductive, somewhat speculative in their origins, and static by nature. Their main shortcomings are twofold. First, while accounting for some apparent reasons, they stop short of identifying the sources of the emergence of a "new strategic thinking" in North Korea's nuclear policy sometime in the early 1990s. In particular, they do not account for the evolution in the official Pyongyang line on the nuclear issue: from an adamant denial of having anything to do with a nuclear program (until 1990) to an admission of the program's existence and an emphasis on its exclusively peaceful nature (1991) to a "neither deny nor confirm" policy on the military aspect of its nuclear program (from mid-1992 on). Second, given the fact that the above-mentioned strategic and domestic concerns and priorities are more or less constant over time, they fail to explain considerable vacillations in North Korea's behavior in its nuclear negotiations with the IAEA and the international community—from intimate cooperation in the first nine months of 1992 to growing bickering over the scope and character of the IAEA inspections during the five months thereafter to outright defection from the nonproliferation regime in March–May 1993 to the reluctant return to the negotiating table with the United States and the IAEA in mid-1993 to an overeager and almost euphoric midnight run to a "package deal" in late 1993–early 1994 to another collapse of all the agreements made in Vienna and New York on February 15 and 25, 1994, respectively, and a new escalation of war rhetoric on the Korean Peninsula. What is going on here? Clearly, knowledge of Pyongyang's strategic intentions per se, whatever those intentions may be, does not provide much help in accounting for its day-to-day negotiating behavior.

As for the sources of policy initiatives, some evidence points toward rather nontraditional developments in the foreign policy–making process in the DPRK recently. First of all, there is the rise of the Institute of Peace and Disarmament (IPD) as the principal think tank formulating new foreign policy approaches and proposing new policy implementation ideas. This is an elitist establishment research institution generously funded and relatively free to discuss in confidential memos any foreign policy issues of the day. Its senior research personnel, in part educated abroad, have free access to information about the external world, travel widely overseas and often float trial balloons regarding future North Korean positions, advise the Korean Workers' Party (WPK) and different bureaucracies that are in charge of foreign affairs, and usually participate as experts in DPRK delegations at almost all international conferences and talks. The fact that the Institute of Peace and Disarmament is not formally part of the state or party apparatus allows it to stay above parochial organizational interests and to claim implicitly that it can discuss the country's national interests. In short, the IPD appears to perform a function remotely resembling the one played by the Moscow-based Institute of World Economy and International Relations, Russian Academy of Sciences (IMEMO) under Gorbachev.

Indeed, once the security environment around the DPRK dramatically changed in 1991 (North Korea lost its Moscow ally and principal donor just as its estrangement from its Beijing ally was growing, and hence, it was basically left alone to defend itself against the U.S. nuclear shield and sword in South Korea), strategic thinking in Pyongyang was forced to change. In their confidential memos, analysts at the Institute of Peace and Disarmament began to urge the International Department of the WPK to adopt a new strategic posture vis-à-vis the international community. Their proposals included: (1) normalization of relations and diversification and improvement of economic ties with the West by cooperating with the IAEA and establishing diplomatic relations with Japan, and in the long run, with the United States; (2) engaging the ROK in comprehensive security, political, economic, and cultural dialogue; and (3) adopting a new policy stance on the nuclear issue. Instead of adamant denial of the existence of a nuclear program, which was characteristic of all the prior years, they urged WPK leaders to admit the program's indigenous origins as an achievement of socialist construction, to stress its peaceful purposes aimed at solving the energy problem, and to seek cooperation with the IAEA in order to alleviate international fears.

Second, most analysts are aware that North Korea has a highly compartmentalized institutional structure. As Dr. Steven Linton, who visited the DPRK fourteen times in a recent three-year period, put it, "North Korean society often evokes the image of a bicycle wheel with thin spokes radiating out from a small hub at the center and extending all the way out to a narrow rim."[7] There appear to be relatively few formal lateral connections between the "spokes." So on the one hand, the DPRK bureaucracy has a clear chain of command and a concentrated leadership structure; but on the other hand, decisions do not come quickly and easily or in the most efficient form because of the lack of consultations across the bureaucratic lines. Rigid hierarchical vertical subordination blocks any horizontal coordination of policy.

However, as far as the nuclear issue is concerned, almost nothing has been written about the recent cracks in policy, shifts of decision-making authority, and reallocation of resources and responsibilities in the North Korean state and party bureaucracy, which seem to be an adaptive response of the state to changing external demands. Until early 1992, when it was still a no-priority question, all issues related to the Non-Proliferation Treaty (NPT) were handled by the Ministry of Foreign Affairs (MOFA) Department for Treaties and Laws and the General Department of the MAEI. As the nuclear issue was brought into the limelight and Pyongyang became heavily engaged with the IAEA regarding negotiations and inspections, it was handed to the MOFA International Organizations Department, with direct political guidance being provided by the International Department of the WPK Central Committee. The more politicized, intrusive, and contentious the IAEA inspections became in 1992–93, the higher the level of the Pyongyang government that considered decisions on their modalities. The Great Leader himself even participated.

Furthermore, later on, issue linkages advocated by the United States at its talks with DPRK representatives in New York and Geneva—that is, for the North to resume North–South dialogue and open its nuclear sites for IAEA inspections simultaneously as preconditions for the third round of U.S.–DPRK high-level talks—literally forced North Korea to reorganize part of its foreign policy–related bureaucratic apparatus in a way that attempted to break through this tight compartmentalization in order to enable it to deal with the issues under consideration in a coordinated and expeditious manner. Institutionally, it is not surprising that there was no entity in the MOFA or any other ministry to deal with the United States. The Committee for the Peaceful Reunification of the Fatherland and the Reunification Policy Committee of the Supreme People's Assembly, both headed by Yun Gi-bok, who protects his turf as vigorously as he can, are in charge of the North–South dialogue. IAEA-related questions are to be handled by the MAEI and MOFA International Organizations Department. The International Department of the WPK Central Committee seems to have failed to perform the policy coordination function because its personnel and resources were disproportionately oriented toward the Soviet Union and China, which were rapidly losing diplomatic significance for the North Korean nuclear and security problems, and it simply lacked the expertise to handle the nuclear and U.S.–related issues.

From late 1991 on, not only did Pyongyang have to find somebody, and establish some entity, to deal with the United States, but it also had to set up some new coordinating mechanisms within its foreign policy bureaucracy to enable it to draft and negotiate in tandem and jointly implement mutually agreed upon policies. Apparently, it was not easy because of the bureaucratic inertia and resistance from the International Department of the WPK Central Committee,

North Korean–style turf battles, ideological reservations, and personal ambitions. However, in the fall of 1993, word got out that Kim Il Sung appointed three "policy steering teams." The first is a U.S.-oriented group, headed by Kim Yong Sun, which is in charge of all IAEA-related matters and DPRK–U.S. relations. The inter-Korean relations lobby seems to have managed to keep the North–South dialogue separated from all other interests and concerns, and it is President Kim's younger brother, Kim Yong-ju, who heads the ROK-oriented team. Last, the "Japan team" is reportedly headed by the newly elected vice president of the DPRK, Kim Byung-sik, a Japanese Korean and former deputy head of the "Chosen Sōren."

Third, as foreign policy problems continued to mount in 1991–92, with North Korean alliances becoming crippled and pressures from the West on the nuclear issue growing, President Kim Il Sung, who was always in charge of strategic foreign policy making, reportedly became more and more interested in day-to-day tactical issues as well. As a result, the stature of the person responsible for formulating foreign policy proposals within the WPK, Director of the International Department of the Central Committee Kim Yong-sun, grew considerably. In May 1990, he was promoted to the position of member and secretary of the WPK Central Committee (international affairs). In April 1992, in recognition of his success in getting the United States to cancel the 1992 "Team Spirit" exercise and other progress at the talks with the West, he was promoted to the position of Alternate Member of the Politburo of the WPK (international affairs).[8] As a result, not only did he get frequent access to the Great Leader and his son, but given his extensive ties with the Institute of Peace and Disarmament, he was exposed to new ideas himself and did not hesitate to urge foreign policy innovations upon both leaders, bypassing traditional bureaucratic channels of decision making.

However, this kind of high visibility and frequent access to the Great Leader is tricky and could prove fatal in the domestic political climate of North Korea. For a North Korean politician, being assigned to handle the nuclear negotiations and DPRK–U.S. relations is a high-risk, high-stakes gamble. For as these talks proceed, the American side tends to sort out its North Korean negotiating partners into "moderates" and "conservatives," "soft-liners" and "hard-liners," and demand that all the contacts be channeled through those in Pyongyang whom it perceives as falling into the category of "progressive reformists," despite the official DPRK hierarchy. Obviously, at this moment, there could be nothing worse for a regime insider in Pyongyang than to be labeled a "progressive reformer" by the enemy and subjected to these kinds of attempts to be drawn into the antiregime limelight, which usually results in charges of "state treason and counter-revolutionary activities." On the other hand, whenever these talks stall and tensions mount, those politicians who are in charge of dealing with the IAEA and the United States get blamed for lack of competence, skills, and so forth and are often transferred to other jobs. In short, given the highly unpredictable nature and high stakes of the DPRK nuclear game with the international community, it is tantamount to political suicide for a North Korean party politician to be appointed to this job.[9]

Paradoxically, since high-ranking party officials try to avoid these assignments by all means, despite their enormous significance, the jobs are basically left to the state bureaucrats from the MOFA and the MAEI. However, given the nature of their institutional position, the latter are not entitled to make strategic or even tactical decisions by themselves. Therefore, their approach to the nuclear-related issues is very cautious and piecemeal. They have neither the authority nor the reputation to introduce or promote policy changes. So the North Korean nuclear policy evolves in a slow, incremental way within the parameters set forth by the Great Leader at the Central People's Committee (CPC). Let me stress, though, that this does not mean that bureaucrats receive orders from Kim Il Sung or Kim Jong Il on every petty issue involved. This is not necessary, because the bureaucrats already have mind-sets that make them hypersensitive to political opinions: while formulating policies, they are driven not only by their past negotiating experience and policy agenda but also by their anticipation of possible political reactions at the top.

Fourth, although there is almost no official information on the meetings of the CPC, sometimes it is compared to the Meiji-period "Genro," the Council of the Elderly Rulers, and is reported to rival the institutional position of the Politburo of the WPK in the North Korean power structure. In particular, its role, albeit somewhat enigmatic, is always of paramount importance in forging strategic consensus among the top national leadership in Pyongyang—including the top military brass, security officials, and political leaders—on matters related to national security issues and regime survival. The Great Leader is said to prefer to rely on the CPC's apparatus and his old comrades in arms, most of whom are members of the CPC, as well as his personal Bodyguard Service, rather than on the much younger Politburo Secretariat or the Administrative Council. One could argue that after Kim Jong Il secured the first vice chairmanship of the National Defense Committee of the CPC in May 1990 and its chairmanship in April 1992, he was more inclined to use the CPC rather than the Politburo, Administrative Council, and various state bureaucracies in promoting his policies while still relying on his power base at the WPK Central Committee. Evidently, it was the narrow circle of the CPC members that considered the issues related to the DPRK's nuclear program and adopted and amended Pyongyang's nuclear strategy. The more institutionalized Kim Jong Il's position became within the CPC in 1990–93, the more respect and authority his views on the nuclear issue commanded. It was at the ninth term, seventh session, of the Central People's Committee, held on March 11, 1993, that the decision to withdraw from the NPT was debated and made. The next day, Kim Jong Il announced it on behalf of the CPC.

In short, by late 1991, a set of new policy ideas advocated by the IPD had emerged, institutional changes within the foreign policy bureaucracy were under way, new access to the nexus of power had been opened by the promotion of

Kim Yong-sun to the WPK Central Committee's secretariat, and a new source of decision-making authority had been provided by the elevation of Kim Jong Il to the chairmanship of the key body in charge of formulating the DPRK's nuclear policy—that is, the CPC's NDC. In early 1991, after some prodding by Kim Yong-sun and at Kim Jong Il's insistence, these new proposals were brought to Kim Il Sung's attention. After emotional consideration at a number of meetings with members of the Central People's Committee, President Kim blessed the new course sometime in late 1991.

There are two extreme views on the Great Leader's involvement in making these strategic decisions. One holds that he is totally "out of the loop," whereas the other contends exactly the opposite—that the entire country from top to bottom breathes, eats, and sleeps at Kim Il Sung's whim and command. Neither is true. Scores of foreign delegations, including those from the United States, that have visited Pyongyang since 1991, testify that President Kim, despite his age, not only is in full control of his faculties and the country but also has a firm grip on the issues related to the nuclear problem. Talks with foreign visitors—in particular with President Kim's longtime friend Prince Norodom Sihanouk, known for his pragmatism and realpolitik mentality; U.S. congressional representatives who like to shoot from the lip regarding American concerns; and Japanese businessmen wary of further involvement in the North Korean economy because of lingering clouds of political instability—provide Kim with an indispensable "reality check." On the other hand, time and again we witness that policy innovations are adopted in the DPRK only after some consensus-building process has taken place at the level of the Central People's Committee; they are not mandated by the Great Leader alone. Moreover, as Dr. Linton argues, "[W]hile impossible to quantify with precision, public opinion is a factor in policies adopted by the DPRK leadership . . . and when there is a change of policy the DPRK government must explain it to their population in a way that is palatable."[10] I would add that usually this is done through the state-controlled news media and internal news releases, as well as during the consideration and approval of a new policy line by the Supreme People's Assembly, which functions more as a mechanism for informing the population about major changes in policy than as a policy-making institution.

In short, this radical shift in the North Korean nuclear policy from moral indignation at "groundless accusations of us developing nuclear weapons by malicious imperialists" to a more open, pragmatic, and sustainable policy of "neither confirm nor deny" regarding the military aspects of its nuclear program (which basically was mimicking the U.S. policy at the time on nuclear weapons in South Korea) should be seen as the result of a new strategic consensus that formed among the top leadership in Pyongyang around the ideas proposed by a nontraditional analytical source—namely, the IPD backed by the International Department of the WPK Central Committee—was blessed by President Kim, and was made palatable to broad public opinion.

Psychodynamics of the Nuclear Game

However, new foreign policy priorities and corresponding intellectual and institutional developments alone do not suffice to explain the dynamics of nuclear policy making in the DPRK. Psychological perceptions and appearances seem to matter as much in Pyongyang as they do in Washington. In particular, the changing perception of threat to the survival of the regime plays an extremely important role in determining the tactics and modalities of North Korean negotiating behavior.

According to the tenets of *juche,* voluntary isolation is good because self-reliance underpins national security. However, forced abandonment is judged to be bad because it leaves North Korea alone against its will, and the regime will have to struggle for survival on its own. In the same vein, mutual dependence is seen in a positive light because it enables North Korea to retain control over its decisions and attend to its sensitivities and vulnerabilities. Entrapment is feared because it forces Pyongyang to lose face, leaves the impression that it is bullied into submission, and puts the regime's stability to the test. These distinctions are subtle, but nevertheless very real in psychological terms and in policy-making processes. For external security is tightly linked to the survival of the Kim Il Sung regime, or as Paul Bracken at Yale put it succinctly, "[A] threat of implosion is linked with a threat of explosion in North Korea."[11]

My hypothesis is that when a perception of threat to national security and hence to the survival of the domestic regime increases, feelings of entrapment are exacerbated, which leads North Koreans to stall on cooperating with the IAEA, the United States, and the ROK. Conversely, when a perception of threat to national security and hence regime survival is declining, feelings of abandonment by the international community grow, which leads Pyongyang to make more concessions to the IAEA, to talk business with the United States and South Korea, and to scale down its belligerent rhetoric so as to avoid abandonment. In other words, North Korea does not want to be abandoned, but it does not want to be entrapped either—quite reasonable desires, right? This accounts for the gyrating pattern in the DPRK's negotiating behavior.

What might cause these fluctuations in the perception of threat to the regime's survival? I would argue that these factors include: (1) the health of the top two leaders; (2) challenges to Kim Jong Il's succession bid and problems with both legitimacy and the transfer of charisma; (3) the regime's performance in managing the economy; and (4) the politics of transition.

First, in the short term, if the Great Leader's or Dear Leader's health deteriorates (the recent rumors about the son's failing health made me question who will outlive whom), the perception of threat will rise, exacerbating the fear of entrapment, which is likely to lead to Pyongyang's periodic failure to cooperate in the nuclear game.

Second, in the medium term, if political challenges to Kim Jong Il's succession mount, or if he continues to face a legitimacy problem, the regime's perception of threat is sure to be heightened. As Kim Jong Il is faced with growing latent pressures from his domestic critics and opponents, he is likely to feel increasingly entrapped and besieged, which may cause him to turn to some kind of reckless behavior, including on the nuclear front.

Also, it is worth mentioning that every time the United States and the ROK hold the Team Spirit joint military exercises or escalate the military buildup in South Korea, the North Korean military seems to get the upper hand vis-à-vis the civilian elites in strategic and tactical decision making on foreign policy matters, including the nuclear issue. Even after Kim Jong Il was appointed the supreme commander in chief of the KPA in December 1992, top North Korean generals still got direct and preferential access to President Kim in emergency situations. Consequently, any new "defensive measures" by the United States in the South are likely to exacerbate the military paranoia and fears of entrapment in Pyongyang, which tends to result in the DPRK's stonewalling or canceling the talks with the IAEA, the ROK, and the United States again and again.

Third, also in the medium term, if the economy continues to stagnate at its current rock-bottom level or deteriorates further, the political elite in Pyongyang is likely to become increasingly frustrated at the state bureaucracy for its inability to handle the economic situation "correctly," which may lead to attempts to reorganize or reform the latter, which, in turn, may provoke greater bureaucratic resistance to change. This schism is likely to induce splits within the state and party bureaucracy on how to proceed, which may lead to growing re-evaluation of domestic economic and ideological orthodoxy and reassessment of threats posed to the regime by the external world. Therefore, the perception of threat is likely to decline, which should increase the fears of abandonment and, hence, lead to greater North Korean cooperation with the IAEA, the United States, Japan, and the ROK.

Fourth, in the long run—insofar as the political transition from an exclusively totalitarian regime based on communist ideology, dictatorial one-man–one-party rule, and no political pluralism to an inclusive, hard-type, bureaucratic, authoritarian regime based on market-oriented modernizing, nationalistic, and populist appeals, advocated by a new breed of enlightened pragmatists in Pyongyang, proceeds in a smooth and peaceful way without mass political mobilization and social upheavals—the regime's perception of threat is likely to decline, which will fuel the fears of abandonment and consequently force North Korea to cooperate more eagerly and fully with the international community and the IAEA.

To sum up, from the standpoint of compelling domestic factors, theoretically, the best hope for successful resolution of the nuclear issue, paradoxically, seems to lie in the good and lasting health of both the father and the son, a smooth leadership transition, with Kim Il Sung's charisma being fully transferred to his son, and North Korea's peaceful and rapid transition to a new type of regime amid continuing sluggish economic performance.

How do these predictions hold up in reality? Let's consider several key decision points from summer 1991 to May 1994 in the DPRK's nuclear diplomacy. First of all, I think that the original cooperation with the IAEA—the decision to sign the Nuclear Safeguards Accord (NSA) and open the Yongbyon nuclear complex for IAEA inspections—may be largely attributed to a somewhat declining perception of threat to the regime's survival. Indeed, the initial shock of a virtual cutoff of political and economic ties with the former Soviet Union and deteriorating relations with the People's Republic of China (PRC) had passed, albeit bitterness and sense of betrayal remained. After the breakdown of their alliance system, North Koreans felt abandoned. Therefore, they decided to explore new routes to security.[12] In September 1991, the DPRK was admitted to the United Nations. Throughout 1991 and most of 1992, the North Korean party and state bureaucracy (the WPK International Department, Administrative Council, Ministry of Foreign Affairs, Ministry of Atomic Energy Industry, and Committee for the Peaceful Reunification of the Fatherland) were busy trying to break new ground with new counterparts. By mid-1992, the MOFA had already held seven rounds of normalization talks with Japan in Beijing. Representatives of the Administrative Council and the CPRF had held eight rounds of Pyongyang–Seoul talks, and the North and South Korean prime ministers had signed an "Agreement on Reconciliation, Nonaggression, and Exchanges and Cooperation between the South and the North" (December 13, 1991) and a "Joint Declaration on the Denuclearization of the Korean Peninsula" (January 20, 1992). On January 22–29, 1992, Secretary Kim Yong-sun held a series of talks in New York with Arnold Kanter, U.S. undersecretary of state for political affairs, and forged a compromise agreement with the United States on opening the North Korean nuclear sites in exchange for assurances of American removal of nuclear weapons from South Korea and the cancelation of the 1992 annual Team Spirit military exercise. Finally, Hong Gun-pyo, North Korean vice minister of the Ministry of Atomic Energy Industry, after yearlong negotiations with Hans Blix, director general of the IAEA, signed the NSA in Vienna on January 30, 1992. Afterward, the IAEA conducted five ad hoc inspections of nuclear facilities at the Yongbyon complex in 1992 and one in February 1993. By and large, expectations in Pyongyang were flying really high in 1991–92, and North Koreans were willing to increase their overall cooperation with the IAEA and the international community as a whole even further.

Second, contrary to what many in the West believe, Pyongyang's confrontational policy of March–May 1993 was not founded in its reluctance to accept "special inspections" of two undeclared nuclear sites at Yongbyon. That was a precipitating event, not the cause. The problem developed much earlier—in October–December 1992—and was the result of an increasing perception of threat to the integrity and stability of the regime, which spurred fears of entrapment among North Korean leaders. We may disagree about the results of the meetings between Kanter and Kim Yong-sun in late January 1992, but there is clear evidence that the North Korean side interpreted the compromise as a quid pro quo deal that set the modalities of all further developments: the DPRK's permanent entrance into the NSA and acceptance of continuous IAEA inspections in exchange for permanent U.S. cancelation of the Team Spirit exercises and removal of its nuclear threat to the DPRK. This was Kim Yong-sun's understanding of the "deal" he brought home, and this was the palatable policy that he sold to Kim Il Sung and Kim Jong Il and that kept the conservatives and the military contented and off the backs of the moderates in Pyongyang. Thereafter, all the skirmishes with the IAEA about the scope, timing, and regularity of inspections were considered of minor significance and manageable as long as the overall parameters of the "deal" were holding. This was because a fragile domestic consensus had been reached in Pyongyang that, in order to consolidate its achievements at the talks with its new Western counterparts, it was necessary to maintain the safeguards and allow the IAEA access to its already declared and undisputed nuclear facilities.

However, when the United States and the ROK, in their twenty-fourth annual Security Consultative Meeting (SCM) in Washington, D.C., agreed to resume the joint Team Spirit military exercises on October 7, 1992, it was a "deal breaker" for many and the beginning of the end of many diplomatic and political careers. First, North Korea tried to save the game by denouncing this decision.[13] Then it threatened to break off all North–South contacts.[14] Neither ploy worked. Instead, the ROK added fuel to the fire by accusing the North of running a sixty-two-member spy ring in the South Korean government establishment. As tensions grew, neither the MOFA nor the CPRK could contain the dispute with the ROK and the United States within their bureaucratic realms: tentative consensus among conservatives and pragmatic moderates, the military, and civilian elites was eroding rapidly. So while on the defensive, the politicians who were behind the "new strategic thinking" were compelled by their opponents to start renegotiating the original domestic "pact" with the aim of narrowing its scope and hardening its underpinnings but broadening its base of political support. Prime Minister Yon Hyong-muk, parts of the Administrative Council, and the WPK Central Committee were drawn into the battle. The prime minister–led North–South dialogue seems to have been slated to be the first victim of this process. On October 14, 1992, Yon expressed his indignation at the decision of the twenty-fourth SCM in a letter to his South Korean counterpart, Hyun Sung-jong. On October 27, 1992, a joint meeting of the government, the WPK, and various organizations adopted a resolution that threatened to call off the ongoing inter-Korean dialogue and demanded that the United States and the ROK cancel their decision to resume the Team Spirit exercises. On October 31, 1992, in a telephone conversation with his South Korean counterpart, Prime Minister Yon Hyung-muk demanded that the ROK suspend all other military drills, including "Hwarang" and "Foal Eagle," which were scheduled to begin November 2 and 3, 1992, respectively. But all Pyongyang's concerns and demands were falling on deaf ears.

As a result, domestic pressure to halt the IAEA inspections began to pick up steam. So on November 3, 1992, Pyongyang issued two statements simultaneously: one by the MOFA spokesman warning that the North would refuse to permit future IAEA inspections if Team Spirit were resumed and a joint statement by the chairmen of the North's delegations to the North–South Joint Reconciliation, Military, Economic, and Social and Cultural Subcommittees announcing that the North would boycott the first session of the North–South joint committees scheduled to meet weekly at Panmunjom starting on November 5, 1992. Later in November, the inter-Korean JNCC talks stalled, and the DPRK government representatives in Moscow, New York, and Beijing made a number of statements that explicitly said that the North would boycott the ninth inter-Korean high-level talks scheduled for December 21–24, 1992, unless South Korea and the United States scrapped their decision to resume Team Spirit. Their efforts were in vain.

Apparently, by early December 1992, the political consensus in Pyongyang that then–Prime Minister Yon Hyung-muk, Secretary Kim Yong-sun, and their supporters could negotiate successfully with the international community and keep their end of the bargain with the hard-liners about the cancelation of Team Spirit had completely broken down. The fears of entrapment rose sharply, and the effectiveness and viability of the policy of cooperation with the IAEA were increasingly challenged. At meetings of the CPC, reportedly, course correction was urged, and heads began to roll. On December 10, 1992, at the twentieth plenary meeting of the sixth Central Committee of the WPK, a dozen generals were promoted to Central Committee membership, and a recommendation was made to remove Yon Hyung-muk from power. The next day, at the fourth session of the ninth Supreme People's Assembly, the government was reshuffled, and a new prime minister, Kang Song-san, was appointed, with Yon being relegated to head of the Jagang provincial chapter of the WPK. Curiously, at that time, only those who were in charge of the North–South dialogue suffered demotions. Kim Yong-sun and others responsible for the DPRK–U.S. contacts were allowed to make a comeback. This may reflect a long-standing belief in Pyongyang that the ROK government was in any case a U.S. puppet and that it was a mistake from the very beginning to have taken the North–South talks seriously as long as the DPRK–U.S. disputes remained unresolved. So while Yon was demoted, Kim was promoted to alternate member of the WPK Politburo at the same plenum. Besides, there was still some bleak hope in Pyongyang that the incoming Kim Yong Sam administration in Seoul could be induced to become more cooperative by intimidation or persuasion (even Kim Il Sung alluded to this in his 1993 New Year's address).

These hopes were dashed when, on January 26, 1993, the South Korean Defense Ministry and the U.S. forces in Korea announced that they would conduct the seventeenth Team Spirit exercise in mid-March 1993. Moreover, it was announced that B-1B bombers capable of carrying nuclear bombs would participate in the war games. At the same time, the IAEA stepped up its pressure on Pyongyang to open two undeclared nuclear sites to its ad hoc inspections and insisted on its right to conduct "special inspections" without prior notice. What is surprising is that, at this late stage of the game, there were still those in Pyongyang who tried to save the situation. A six-member North Korean parliamentary delegation, headed by Kim Yong-sun, hoped to participate in a congressional meeting scheduled for February 3–4, 1993, in Washington, but the delegation was denied visas by the U.S. State Department. Ultimately, the last attempt of North Korean doves to avert the confrontation was undercut by American hawks.

From then on, every politician in North Korea realized that a showdown was inevitable, whereupon it became a matter of principle for the Great Leader to stay the course and not blink first. Once Kim Il Sung asked his son "to do something about it," it became almost fatal for people to find themselves on the wrong side of the issue. I disagree with those who argue that it was Kim Jong Il who instigated the confrontation over the nuclear inspections in order to "crack the heads of the entire elite." Yes, Kim Jong Il took personal responsibility for initiating the showdown with the IAEA on March 12, 1993. But I believe it was masterminded by the risk-prone Great Leader himself, was debated several times at the Central People's Committee, and reflected an emerging new political consensus, supported by a new coalition in power tilted in favor of conservative patriarchs and the military. This coalition took the position that the U.S.-backed IAEA's plotting and bullying must not continue and that the regime's survival was again at stake. Yes, heads rolled—but much earlier and very much later, so that from mid-March to late May, the peak of the confrontation, there were no reports of the "executioner" at work. On the contrary, my impression is that political elites jumped on the bandwagon of the seemingly winning course of adversarial engagement, and most of them survived. It was only later, when Kim Il Sung decided to ease up and come back to the negotiating table with the United States, that government and party reshuffles were resumed. Did Kim Jong Il use the showdown to his benefit? Of course he tried to, but not by chopping off the heads (and brains) that were in scarce supply and that he needed so badly in a time of crisis. He did it by using the occasion to boost his legitimacy, by showing his potential rivals and opponents, as well as the North Korean public at large, that he could also be tough, stand up to external pressures, and lead the country through its hardships and challenges. Did he succeed? I believe he did, partially, although some people feel that Kim Jong Il's handling of the whole matter was simply a disaster, which further contributed to his reputation as a reckless and unreliable statesman.

Third, why did North Korea decide to return to the negotiating table with the United States in May–June 1993 and eventually suspend temporarily the "effectuation of its withdrawal from the NPT"? Some explain this move from the viewpoint of strategic interaction—that is, that the nuclear standoff was a kind of game of chicken, and Pyongyang, albeit bullish at the beginning, swerved first. However, if anything, (1) some sort of mutual blinking occurred; (2) although the United States did some pushing, it was too eager to accommodate Pyongyang's basic concerns quickly in order to bring it back to the NPT; and (3) later on, North Korea did not hesitate to disengage again whenever its sensitivities were disregarded. So since there was in reality no tremendous external pressure of a credible nature (such as economic sanctions or the threat of a military strike), the answer may involve mainly domestic politics and only partially the strategic interaction between the United States and the DPRK.

In my view, having successfully suppressed the internal opposition to the decision to gamble on the DPRK's future status in the NPT, having created a new military-tilted support coalition for tougher policies toward the IAEA, and having sustained the initial shock of the international outcry over these moves, Kim Jong Il and his supporters may have felt more secure by mid-May 1993 than they did in February of that year when the nuclear-related domestic policy debate was at its peak. In a sense, the perception of threat to the regime's survival among the top leadership might have declined far enough to make President Kim Il Sung worry about the excesses of this new policy and the prospects of abandonment of the DPRK by the international community. These fears of growing abandonment reportedly were also expressed at the April meetings of the Central People's Committee. This may be one of the reasons why Kim Il Sung is reported to have told his son, and ordered bureaucrats around him, to go the extra mile in order to reopen the channels of dialogue with the United States and the IAEA and to revive the negotiating process, following the guidelines established in the past. He may have hoped that the engagement per se could alleviate these fears of abandonment and that if it could somehow produce any positive results, so much the better.

Indeed, if one looks at the content of the agreements arrived at by the DPRK and U.S. sides at the high-level talks in New York between the vice foreign minister of the DPRK, Kang Sok-ju, and U.S. Assistant Secretary of State Robert Gallucci on June 2–11, 1993, at the eleventh hour before the June 12 deadline on which the DPRK's announced withdrawal from the IAEA would go into effect, they are basically limited to a reiteration of compromises reached eighteen months earlier at the Kim Yong-sun–Kanter talks in New York in January 1992. That is, the United States agreed not to threaten the DPRK with the use of force and reiterated that it did not pose a nuclear threat to North Korea, while Pyongyang agreed to suspend "the effectuation of its withdrawal from the NPT" and to allow the IAEA to conduct inspections to assure the "continuity of the nuclear safeguards." But at the Geneva high-level talks, held the following month (July 14–19, 1993), both sides, represented by the same people, dramatically expanded the negotiating agenda and for the first time put on the table issues related to the future political and diplomatic settlement of the nuclear issue (including the transfer of a light-water reactor [LWR]) and normalization of their bilateral relations. With joint efforts, the dialogue, albeit lacking mutual trust and vulnerable to political manipulations on both sides, was put back on the right track. In August 1993, IAEA inspectors went to Yongbyon to verify the continuity of the nuclear safeguards. In October 1993, low-level DPRK–U.S. and DPRK–IAEA contacts were resumed in New York and Vienna, respectively. In late February 1994, after some pulling and hauling, the parties signed a broadly based agreement on the immediate resumption of the IAEA inspections, their timing and scope, and the resumption of the North–South dialogue in exchange for the outright cancelation of the 1994 Team Spirit joint military exercise and agreement on the date and mandate of the third round of the U.S.–DPRK high-level talks. As a guarantee against unilateral cheating, all steps were to be announced and taken simultaneously.

Fourth, why did the "small deal" break down? The official line from Washington is as follows. After the February 15 and 25, 1994, accords were signed, a seven-member IAEA team went to the DPRK from March 1 to 15, 1994, to check the continuity of the safeguards but, upon their return, declared that North Korean cooperation had been unsatisfactory. In addition, eight South–North contacts in Panmunjom failed to lead to any agreement on the exchange of special envoys. Therefore, the United States accused the DPRK of intentionally violating the agreements reached in February and said it was no longer bound by its commitments. Instead, the IAEA referred the matter for resolution to the United Nations Security Council, which issued a Security Council president's statement (March 31, 1994) urging the DPRK to permit completion of the agreed-upon inspections and to continue to cooperate fully with the IAEA toward a comprehensive resolution of the nuclear issue as a whole.

From the North Korean perspective—as expressed in statements from the DPRK's Ministry of Atomic Energy Industry (March 18, 1994), the MOFA (March 21, 1994), and the North's delegation to the working-contact meetings on the exchange of special envoys (March 21, 1994)—these developments were another example of the "widening partiality of the IAEA," U.S. attempts "to stifle the North Korean regime," and South Korea's "deliberate attempts to put the brakes on the DPRK–U.S. talks by abusing the idea of exchange of special envoys."

In particular, the MAEI General Department spokesman stated that the DPRK fulfilled all its obligations to the IAEA under the February 15 agreement—that is, it allowed the IAEA inspectors, unhindered, to reload and service containment and surveillance devices, verify physical inventories, examine a number of records and documents, verify design information, and take samples and measurements. However, the IAEA inspectors went beyond the agreed procedures and insisted on taking samples from the input accountability tank, whose IAEA seals were certified as unbroken; on gamma mapping at most points instead of at a few selected points as agreed earlier; and on verification of cooling systems, which was never part of the agreement. In other words, Pyongyang claims that the procedures agreed to earlier in Vienna and fully implemented by the IAEA inspectors were "sufficient to enable the agency to fully verify nondiversion of nuclear material at our nuclear facilities and definitely ensure the continuity of safeguards as well." In short, such a discrepancy between what the IAEA agreed to in Vienna and what its inspectors actually tried to do in Yongbyon, the fact that the IAEA bombarded Pyongyang with three telexes during the fourteen-day inspection period threatening to ask the United Nations for sanctions if it did not allow IAEA inspectors to take extra samples, as well as the total disregard for the DPRK's "special status" as a country that "only temporarily suspended the effectuation of its withdrawal from the NPT"—all these events could not but make the North Koreans feel cheated on and frustrated.

In the meantime, Pyongyang's frustration also grew as South Koreans insisted in Panmunjom, in contact after contact, that the main purpose of the exchange of special envoys be to talk about the nuclear issue or Seoul would not agree to the exchange at all, and then the North would not be able to tell the United States that it had fulfilled its second obligation under the February 25, 1994, accord with Washington. In an effort to beat the March 21, 1994, deadline and to break the impasse, at the sixth round of working contacts, on March 12, 1994, the North's delegate, Pak Yong-su, dropped all the North's previous preconditions and proposed to sign a joint communiqué pledging an early exchange of envoys. But his South Korean counterpart, Song Young-dae, rejected the proposal after Seoul decided that same day to adopt a "tough reaction policy" toward Pyongyang.

It was unfortunate that the United States jumped into the fray hastily rather than sitting it out: even before the IAEA inspection was over and while the South–North contacts were still under way, some key U.S. policy makers indicated that the United States was likely to reconsider its promise to cancel the Team Spirit exercise and to hold the third round of high-level U.S.–DPRK talks. I consider this move ill-timed because, at that moment, there were bureaucrats in North Korea's MOFA, the CPRK, and the MAEI who believed that they could still salvage the situation without political interference and a renewed confrontation with the international community. However, after the U.S. announcement, the regime's security and stability were put in question again. The military and hard-liners in Pyongyang, who were closely watching the developments, immediately got excited. They began to display growing fears of entrapment. As a result, the bureaucratic players were excluded from the policy-making process. Kim Jong Il stepped in and orchestrated a traditional "face-saving" exit for domestic consumption in North Korea, basically saying, "We don't want to talk to you either, cheater."

Conclusion

My main argument in this chapter has been as follows. As a rule, the general parameters of Pyongyang's policy toward the IAEA are considered and decided at the Central People's Committee meetings chaired by President Kim Il Sung and/or his son, Kim Jong Il. Decisions are made with strategic considerations and concern for bargaining reputation in mind, and are not driven by passions or other ulterior motives. A newly powerful think tank with close links to the CPC, the Institute for Peace and Disarmament, has had considerable intellectual input into the reformulation of the DPRK's nuclear strategy and in providing justification for its negotiating behavior recently. However, there is a certain degree of bureaucratic autonomy regarding nuclear policy making in North Korea, especially as far as the activities of the Ministry of Atomic Energy Industry and the Ministry of Foreign Affairs are concerned.

This limited bureaucratic autonomy stems from two sources. On the one hand, a growing interagency coordination and cooperation—ironically, imposed on a highly compartmentalized and rigidly hierarchical North Korean bureaucracy by issue linkages advocated by U.S. negotiators—made different ministries more aware of both the plays around them and of the game as a whole, expanded information available to them, enabled them to produce more realistic policy outputs when requested by the top political leadership, and also allowed them to band together to press policy positions they deemed rational whenever they were faced with political challenges from the WPK Central Committee International Department and other players. On the other hand, this relative bureaucratic autonomy regarding North Korean tactics during the negotiations with the IAEA and the United States stems from the fact that party politicians in Pyongyang consider close involvement with the whole nuclear issue to be too tricky and risky for their political careers. Hence, they try to keep their distance from the issue until a rallying battle cry is issued from the very top. This leaves bureaucrats alone to handle the dialogue. They have little latitude to change the course of events, except in a minor, very incremental way; however, neither are they burdened with particularly heavy responsibilities. As a result, we witness a slow, piecemeal kind of evolution of the nuclear policy within very general parameters set forth previously at the top.

Furthermore, this slow policy evolution tends to be very sensitive to the prevailing concerns in Pyongyang about threats to the regime's survival and stability. Whenever a perception of threat to the regime's survival increases, the fears of entrapment grow, and a coalition tilted in favor of the positions advocated by the military and hard-liners is formed. Consequently, the DPRK's disengagements mount and negotiations stall, if they do not totally break down. In contrast, whenever the perception of threat declines and the Kim family feels more secure, the DPRK tends to experience a growing fear of abandonment, which leads to the redistribution of influence back to the civilians and pragmatic soft-liners. Consequently, North Korea's cooperation with the IAEA increases, and its attitude becomes more flexible and forthcoming.

As for the future, I think the patterns of North Korean behavior analyzed above will last for some time. Hence, we should expect no breakthroughs in the

DPRK's talks with the IAEA and the United States beyond the parameters already established in the form of a so-called package deal. The United States would be well advised not to do anything hasty that could increase the fears of entrapment in Pyongyang and provoke the consolidation of the belligerent defense coalition, which might risk total isolation or war in order to prolong its stay in power. Also a piece of advice from the scores of textbooks on the art of diplomacy is appropriate: if you want the accords to be implemented, make them as specific as possible and adhere strictly to their provisions. Do not shift your gears at the crossroads. If you yourself cheat, you cannot expect full cooperation from others, especially when verification is available and goodwill is such a scarce resource on both sides.

Notes

1. A 2–to-4–megawatt electric nuclear research reactor that the USSR delivered to the DPRK in August 1965 under the terms of the 1959 agreement actually became operational in 1967. For a cross-reference, see Joseph S. Bermudez, Jr., "North Korean Nuclear Infrastructure," *Asia-Pacific Defence Review* (June 1993), 6. In 1984, the DPRK began construction of a 50–megawatt electric nuclear power reactor (G-2, gas-graphite type). It was scheduled for completion in 1995 or 1996. But all the work on it was frozen after the Geneva Agreement in October 1994. In January 1986, the DPRK commissioned a 5–megawatt electric indigenous experimental nuclear power reactor (gas-graphite design of the 1940s, calder type) which was in operation until October 1994. Lastly, construction of a 200–megawatt electric nuclear power reactor was also interrupted by the conclusion of Geneva accords in October 1994. For more details on the evolution of the North Korean nuclear program, see Alexandre Mansourov, "The Origins, Evolution, & Current Politics of the North Korean Nuclear Program," *The Non-Proliferation Review,* Vol. 2, no. 3, Spring–Summer 1995, 25–39.

2. Suffice it to say that, in September 1974, the DPRK joined the IAEA. In December 1985, under heavy pressure from Moscow, Kim Il Sung agreed to sign the Non-Proliferation Treaty and re-emphasized the peaceful purposes of North Korea's nuclear research efforts.

3. A Carnegie Endowment team of nonproliferation experts who visited the DPRK in May 1992 and had talks with Choe Chong-sun, an official of the Ministry of Atomic Energy Industry, cited him in their report as saying that North Korean nuclear scientists extracted spent fuel "to produce a little bit of plutonium for experimental purposes and to study the nuclear reprocessing cycle sometime in 1989–1990." Earlier, at a briefing for the Japanese reporters visiting Pyongyang on the occasion of President Kim Il Sung's eightieth birthday, Choe made similar comments. Nicholas Kristoff, *New York Times,* April 16, 1992, 3.

4. From Professor Zagoria's presentation at a research seminar sponsored by the Center for Korean Research, East Asian Institute, Columbia University, March 1993.

5. Overall, it is rumored that North Korea might have spent almost $US 10 billion on its nuclear program. For comparison, the size of its GNP was estimated at $23 billion in 1992.

6. From author's interview with Kongdan Oh in New York City in April 1993.

7. Linton's presentation at a resarch seminar on Contemporary Korean Affairs sponsored by the Center for Korean Research, East Asian Institute, Columbia University, February 1993.

8. Also in April 1992, he was appointed chairman of the Foreign Affairs Committee of the Supreme People's Assembly in order to smooth the ratification of the Nuclear Safeguards Accord (NSA), due in May 1992, as well as other pending legislation aimed at establishing "free-trade economic zones" in the DPRK.

9. Kim Yong-sun was among those who lost his title and job in December 1993, apparently for his failure to achieve the kind of outcomes at the talks with the IAEA and the United States that Kim Il Sung and Kim Jong Il wanted.

10. From author's interview with Linton in March 1993.

11. Paul Bracken, "The North Korean Nuclear Program as a Problem of State Survival," in *Asian Flashpoint: Security and the Korean Peninsula*, ed. Andrew Mack (Camberra, Allen & Unwin, 1994), 85–86.

12. Interestingly, the defeat of the anti-Gorbachev coup in August 1991 in Moscow reportedly accelerated the new policy formation in Pyongyang.

13. On October 12, 1992, the Ministry of Foreign Affairs of the DPRK issued a statement denouncing the ROK and the United States for deciding to resume the Team Spirit exercise.

14. The spokesman for the CPRF issued a statement in Pyongyang on October 13 that said, "If the United States and the South Korean authorities go down the road toward the intensification of tensions through any resumption of the joint military exercise called 'Team Spirit,' all the dialogues including the inter-Korean high-level talks will be deadlocked and the implementation of the North–South agreements will be suspended." *North Korea News,* October 26, 1992, no. 654, 4.

The Future of the
U.S.-ROK Alliance

Peter Hayes and Stephen Noerper

The alliance between the United States and the Republic of Korea (the ROK, or South Korea) is situated in a security environment characterized by prevailing uncertainty over four critical factors: (1) leadership in the Democratic People's Republic of Korea (the DPRK, or North Korea); (2) the multiple implications of the October 1994 U.S.-DPRK Agreed Framework; (3) an increasingly complex political equation in both the ROK and the United States; and (4) conflicting strategic priorities within the national security community of each country.

Compounding these challenges are several others not necessarily unique to U.S.-Korea relations—namely, a declining U.S. military budget base, calls for U.S. force reductions, changes in military strategy to suit the post–Cold War era, and greater politicization of military issues. The defense establishments in both countries are not united on the balance to be stuck between military defense versus deterrence versus reassurance; on the role of military force in supporting bilateral or multilateral diplomacy and arms control; on the military's mission in achieving "comprehensive security"; and so on. Of course, many of these options are not mutually exclusive. But a consensus has yet to emerge as to how to achieve security in the flux in interstate relations that ensued after the end of the Cold War.

Paper presented to the International Workshop on the U.S.-ROK Alliance, Seoul, October 5, 1995, sponsored by Strategic Studies Institute, U.S. Army War College; Institute for Far Eastern Studies, Kyungnam University; U.S. Defense Nuclear Agency; and Korea Society of the United States.

Our analysis rests on the premise that a security alliance is strong to the extent that each partner perceives that the benefits obtained via the alliance outweigh the costs incurred due to the alliance. If the benefits outweigh the costs for both partners, and if the domestic distribution of costs and benefits resulting therefrom is supportable politically, then joint interests in maintaining the alliance will converge and the alliance will cohere. Of course, the converse is equally true: if costs predominate between and within alliance partners, so joint interests will diverge and the alliance may dissolve.

Ultimately, each alliance partner measures interests with respect to fundamental values and norms that underlie its political culture, including the value placed on democracy, human rights, market capitalism, and observance of international norms concerning stability, peace, and nonaggression. In reality, security partners may not concur completely on these latter values and norms, and contending policy currents may capture the security relationship on one or both sides and define national interest in narrower and more mundane or lower-level values and norms (for example, in terms of primacy in various aspects of alliance relationships, choice of weapons systems, or the well-known phenomenon of service rivalry over missions and budgets).

Broadly, such converging and diverging interests may be analyzed with respect to the following three dimensions in a modern security alliance:

1. Common alliance ideology
2. Institutional integration fostered by the alliance
3. Unique capabilities imparted by one or both partners

Obviously, the interests of each alliance partner can move in contrary directions in each of these three dimensions at the same time—as well as differentially between alliance partners. Thus, determining whether a security alliance is stronger or weaker at a point in time is not a simple matter because simultaneous impulses to reinforce the status quo or to initiate change are inherent in such relationships and are complex in nature.

In this chapter, therefore, we ask the following question in relation to recent trends in the U.S.-Republic of Korea (ROK) alliance: in terms of ideology, institutional integration, and capabilities, whose interests are affected, and who gains and who loses? We conclude with an appraisal of future issues that will affect the U.S.-ROK alliance. In short, we foresee that the alliance will become a much looser arrangement than in the past. Along the way, the two partners will be forced to adjust their mutual postures in terms of institutional integration and capabilities, given the shifting rationale for the alliance.

Alliance Ideology

Any security alliance based on free choice requires that the partners enunciate the rationale for alliance in ways that evoke support from the political elite.

Without a convincing ideology to legitimate an alliance, the political basis for alliance will crumble with time whatever the extent of institutional integration or capabilities provided by an allied state. For an alliance to succeed, both sides must consent to the arrangement and it must be perceived as legitimate by security elites and other, politically salient publics.

Militant Containment

During the Cold War, the joint rationale for the alliance was straightforward: to contain the military threat posed by the DPRK, as part of the global struggle between the U.S.-led "free world" and the Soviet-led "communist world." On the U.S. side, profound debates occurred as to whether the U.S. strategic goal was immediate or eventual rollback of the Soviet empire (and/or, circumstances permitting, its local allies such as the DPRK), the militant containment of the Soviet Union and its allies, or the engagement and eventual transformation of these adversaries.

For the most part, militant containment of the DPRK was the core of U.S. security policy in Korea. This goal was embodied in declared doctrines of mutual assured destruction; U.S. nuclear first use and neither-confirm-nor-deny policy in Korea; the primacy of ground forces in U.S.-ROK military strategy on the peninsula and related forward deployment of U.S. troops and nuclear weapons in Europe and the Far East and on U.S. warships and aircraft; joint exercises, war-planning, and targeting activities; and military training, military aid, military technology transfer, and arms sales between the United States, as patron state, and its allies such as the ROK.

In Northeast Asia, Japan is (and has been since 1945) the "cornerstone" of U.S. strategy, while U.S. Forces Korea (USFK) served as a symbolic U.S. "anchor" on the Asian mainland. In this fashion, the U.S. commitment to the ROK was viewed as a critical indicator of U.S. credibility with respect to its other security allies in the region as well as important in its own right. This interest justified massive U.S. military aid to the ROK, which played a crucial role in its economic growth in the sixties and seventies. From the early seventies, a third major rationale emerged for the alliance, albeit from very different perspectives for each partner—namely, to avoid the proliferation of nuclear weapons in Korea and the Asia–Pacific region.

In the aftermath of the Cold War, the situation has both simplified and become more complicated at the same time. The Korean Peninsula is no longer at risk of being swept up in a global conflagration of the kind envisaged during the mid-eighties in notions such as "horizontal escalation" or "theater nuclear war."

For the ROK, the ending of the Cold War also meant that its importance in U.S. strategy may have dwindled because U.S. interests in the peninsula are no longer defined with respect to Russia, the People's Republic of China (PRC), or Japan, except as part of an ambiguous U.S. regional "balance of power" strategy.

On the other hand, the risks associated with U.S. unilateral action in Korea have fallen as a result of delinkage from U.S. global security strategy. The long-standing ROK concern that the United States might be constrained in Korea by the risk of escalation involving China or the former Soviet Union now has little basis in reality. Moreover, the credibility of U.S. military capabilities has increased arguably since the Gulf War victory, although differences between the situation in the Persian Gulf and in Korea should not be underestimated (see the subsection entitled "U.S. Conventional Force Improvements" below). Arguably, the nuclear nonproliferation goal is now as important as defense against and deterrence of the DPRK by the two allies—especially now that ROK-DPRK economic relations are developing.

In public, both U.S. and ROK officials pronounce the alliance to be alive and well. The United States has reiterated its commitments to the ROK on many occasions. But both public and private tensions have emerged within the alliance over how to deal with the North Korean nuclear challenge.

For its part, the United States emphasizes a three-tiered policy of forward deployment, comprehensive force upgrade options, and maintenance of key regional alliances. The Clinton administration declared a new commitment to maintaining the U.S. troop presence during visits to the ROK in 1994 and 1995 U.S.-ROK presidential meetings. The February 1995 East Asia Security Review (EASR) also reiterated the U.S. commitment to ROK security. The post–Cold War rationale for U.S. security alliances now rests on the ambiguous notion of a regional "balance" of power—albeit one in which the competition is nonideological when compared with the Cold War.

The July 1995 visit to Washington by ROK President Kim Young Sam reaffirmed the strength of the U.S.-ROK alliance and provided assurances in the wake of bilateral discord on the DPRK nuclear talks. These events, coupled with the May 1995 Kuala Lumpur agreement and the subsequent launch of the Korean Peninsula Energy Development Organization (KEDO) put the ROK in the driver's seat in the relationship, especially in further dealings with the DPRK. The problem has emerged, however, that the ROK has not been willing to steer at crucial junctions, but has resisted the United States role as "back seat driver."

Seoul and Washington diverged most dramatically over the U.S.-DPRK nuclear dialogue. The two sides disagreed publicly on the handling of the DPRK at various points in the negotiations. The relationship has shifted onto a new plane as the ROK adjusts to the fact that its archenemy has established relations with its security patron. Indeed, within the ROK, some voices emerged arguing that the development of a Washington–Seoul–Pyongyang "Korean triangle" fundamentally alters the U.S.-ROK alliance. Undeniably, most security analysts believe that these tensions did not seriously threaten the U.S.-ROK alliance. Nonetheless, the fact that these policy debates sometimes erupted into public view suggests that—at least at the tactical level—U.S. and ROK approaches do not always move in tandem. In this vein, ROK officials expressed anxiety in

1995 as to the size and nature of the U.S. presence and U.S. congressional realignment. The ROK press and public seized upon incidents involving U.S. troops on the ground and urged a review of the Status of Forces Agreement, a phenomenon that also emerged recently in U.S.-Japan relations.

Countering the Conventional Military Threat from the DPRK

In spite of these frictions, the enduring, rock-solid foundation of the U.S.-ROK alliance relationship remains the conventional military threat posed by the DPRK. It is the DPRK's conventional military force that commands attention in spite of all the drama associated with its nuclear challenge in recent years.

At present, the ROK faces four major and simultaneous military threats from the North: a massive conventional force of 1.2 million troops, the vast majority of which are deployed close to the demilitarized zone (DMZ); a growing ballistic missile threat; greatly improved special forces (some 100,000) with the ability to filter rapidly into key political, industrial, and otherwise critical sectors within the ROK; and at least until the DPRK nuclear freeze imposed by the Agreed Framework, the specter of a nuclear-armed North Korea.

Complicating the nuclear issue was and remains the ongoing North Korean ballistic and cruise missile program, which makes the averted nuclear and projected chemical and biological weapons (CBW) threat even more disturbing. On May 29, 1993, North Korea successfully test-fired the 1,000–1,300–kilometer-range, liquid-fueled Rodong-1 missile over the East Sea of Korea (commonly known as the Sea of Japan). A follow-on version, the Rodong-2, with a range of 1,500–2,000 kilometers, is being developed. South Korean analysts believe it could carry a 50–kiloton nuclear device or a VX chemical warhead.

The Washington media reported on September 29, 1995, that the western United States "could be within range" of the DPRK's Taepo Dong-2 by the year 2000.[1] Senator John Kyl noted that "if the information is even close to the truth, it presents for the first time a very serious and relatively quick challenge to U.S. sovereignty." These statements appear to be worst-case positions, as other, less alarming evaluations of DPRK capabilities over time have been made by high-level authorities. In the September 29 report, in fact, a U.S. intelligence official cautioned that "it will take a lot longer than the year 2000" for the DPRK to develop long-range missile capability, "although there is no question they would like to achieve that."

Static Comparison

The 1995 ROK *Defense White Paper* assessed the DPRK threat as being much greater than in 1994. In terms of total forces, no change was evident over the previous year, although one additional corps was formed. But the DPRK has added about 500 new artillery pieces. Overall, North Korean forces continued to outnumber the South Korean forces by a factor of 1.6 while registering a twofold advantage in the number of arms (see Table 13.1).

Table 13.1

DPRK-ROK Military Balance (excluding U.S. forces)

Forces	DPRK	ROK	Ratio (DPRK/ROK)
Total active armed forces	1,206,000	655,000	1.8
Ground Forces			
Personnel	1,066,000	550,000	1.9
Reserve—infantry divisions	22–26	23	1.3
Reserve—infantry brigades	18	0	18
Infantry divisions	30	21[a]	1.4
Truck mobile divisions	1	0	1/0
Infantry brigades	4	2[b]	2
Truck mobile brigades	20	0	20
Armored brigades	15	4	3.75
Special operations brigades	22	7	3.1
Medium/light tanks	3,500	1,800	1.9
Armored personnel carriers	4,000	1,750	2.3
Artillery	8,400	4,500	1.9
Multiple rocket launchers	2,400	114	21
Surface–surface missiles	54	24	2.3
Antiaircraft artillery	8,800	600	14.7
Surface–air missile sites	54	34	1.6
Surface–air missiles	800	250	3.2
Air Forces			
Personnel	80,000	45,000	1.8
Bombers	82	0	82/0
Fighters	748	480	1.6
Helicopters	275	530[c]	0.5
Transports	310	40	7.8
Naval Forces			
Personnel	60,000	60,000[d]	1
Major surface combatants	3	36	0.1
Attack submarines	23	1	23
Missile attack boats	39	11	3.6
Patrol boats	388	140	2.8
Mine warfare type	23	10	2.3
Amphibious craft	194	34	5.7

Source: Joint Intelligence Center—Pacific (at Pacific Command in Honolulu) (ONK), "Republic of Korea/North Korea, Military Capabilities," September 27, 1993; released by CINCPAC under a U.S. Freedom of Information Act request to the author.

[a] Includes two marine divisions.

[b] Includes one marine brigade.

[c] Includes helicopters organic to the ROK Army and Navy.

[d] Includes ROK marine corps.

Since 1984, two-thirds of the 1.2 million–strong Korean People's Army (KPA) has been located within 50 miles of the DMZ, a figure estimated to have reached nearly 70 percent by the early nineties. In terms of troop deployment, 65 percent of land, 60 percent of naval, and 40 percent of air assets are deployed along the Pyongyang–Wonsan Line, in close proximity to the DMZ. The KPA's 100,000–strong special forces could infiltrate ROK defenses in the rear in waves of 20,000 with the assistance of some 2,300 S-type bridge-laying vehicles, AN-2 aircraft, and minisubs.

In recent years, North Korea has moved to replace its towed artillery with self-propelled artillery, including 4,500 self-propelled howitzers, 2,300 towed guns, and 2,400 multiple rocket launchers ranging in caliber from 107 millimeters to 240 millimeters. The U.S. Defense Intelligence Agency (DIA) reported in April 1994 that North Korea deployed eighteen pieces from its first indigenously produced turreted self-propelled artillery system, the M-1992 130–millimeter gun, as well as an M-1992 30–millimeter cannon. The DIA also released imagery indicating a more aggressive forward deployment of the 240–millimeter M-1991 MLRS and an increase in the number of launchers in some M-1991 MLRS batteries from four to six.

Qualitative Factors

Military analysts have long recognized that simple force ratios provide little insight into either the qualitative factors or the strategic capabilities that would determine the outcome of a conflict such as might erupt on the Korean Peninsula. Recent American assessments make it feasible to grasp the qualitative aspects of potential conflicts between North and South Korea.

A September 1993 net assessment by the Joint Intelligence Center at Pacific Command (JICPAC) in Hawaii states that although the military balance in Korea still favors the North, situational elements "would make any North Korean attack on South Korea a very difficult operation."[2] These situational factors include the following:

- The strength of ROK defensive positions
- The size and potential of the ROK economy
- The sheer size advantage of the ROK population (40 million versus 20 million)

Although the DPRK has only a quarter of the ROK's gross national product (GNP), it devotes as much as 20–25 percent of its GNP to the military to keep an estimated 1 million plus men under arms. However, recent recalculation of the DPRK's GNP by economists at the Institute of International Economics in Washington, D.C., suggests that the DPRK's GNP may be more on the order of $50 billion—reducing the fraction spent on the military to a high but more likely 10 percent of GNP.[3]

Whatever the reality in relation to the DPRK economy, the ROK spends only 5 percent of its GNP on the military but still dwarfs North Korea's military expenditures. The ROK has opted to build a strong defensive position dependent on technology and U.S. treaty commitments (which entail a U.S. military expenditure in and around the Korean Peninsula of about $11–12 billion per year) rather than on numbers per se. JICPAC notes that the ROK's demographics and economic base could support a significant expansion of the armed forces if the military situation so dictated.

As noted above, the DPRK's ground forces are well equipped and trained, and most are forward deployed. The DPRK army has a well-known numerical advantage in artillery and surface-to-air missiles (SAMs) (see Table 13.1). JICPAC states that the North has the capability "to insert by air or sea about 2,500 men in a single lift to operate in ROK rear areas to impede mobilization and other vital defense efforts."

JICPAC also notes that the DPRK's larger air force is offset by the ROK air force's qualitative advantages, whereas its sheer numbers of naval forces still outweigh the ROK's naval forces despite the South's recent production of frigates and corvettes.

Overall, JICPAC draws the following conclusions:

- The North has significant logistics stockpiles that are "somewhat offset by the ROK's superior transportation infrastructure and modern production facilities."
- Both countries have considerable industrial potential to support their military forces.

The ROK's basic defensive situation consists of the following factors:

- The terrain north of Seoul is dominated by rice paddies offering limited off-road mobility.
- The terrain west of Seoul is a wide coastal plan with main invasion routes to Seoul.
- There is extensive tunneling under the DMZ by the DPRK.
- The mountainous central DMZ area offers a prime DPRK infiltration route.
- The narrow eastern coastal plain is lightly settled and less heavily defended.
- Some 40 percent of the ROK population resides within 40 miles of Seoul.
- The mountains make it difficult to move forces to and from the east coast.

The DPRK's defensive situation may be described as follows:

- The central mountains contain key industries.
- The narrow eastern coastal plain contains several key urban areas.
- The mountainous terrain along the eastern DMZ renders operations difficult.
- There are small hills and very channelized terrain north of Kaesong.

Dynamic Comparisons

Static balances based on simple force ratios can be very misleading in the case of the two Koreas, where geography and qualitative differences would greatly affect how any war would unfold. A better way to evaluate the military balance is with dynamic, scenario-driven analyses.

Strategic analysis provided by Rand to annual war games conducted at the U.S. Naval War College provides just such a review.[4] According to Rand analysts, the DPRK's military objectives in a conventional attack on the ROK are fairly obvious and include a main offensive north of Seoul, a pinning attack down the eastern coastal plain, the mining of ROK ports, the restriction of sea-lanes of communication, and the reduction of ROK and U.S. air sortie generation over the DPRK.

Because of its bearing on the security dilemma that exists on the peninsula (and that informs the worst nightmares of DPRK military planners), the most interesting scenario for the analysis of a dynamic balance in Korea is a variant of the U.S.-ROK Combined Forces Command (CFC) basic war plan, *Oplan 5027*, wherein the ROK would blunt a DPRK offensive, stabilize the defensive line in *FEBA Bravo* (20–30 miles below the DMZ), and execute a retaliatory offensive once U.S. reinforcements arrive.

In this variant, a U.S. marine expeditionary force (about a division) and air assault division along with ROK divisions would assemble on the east coast to launch an overland offensive north toward Wonsan. A little later, a combined U.S.-ROK force would land amphibiously near Wonsan and advance to Pyongyang. Finally, a combined U.S.-ROK force would execute a major counteroffensive in the area north of Seoul aimed at reaching Pyongyang, either linking up with the force interposed at Wonsan or meeting it in Pyongyang. To this end, substantial mechanized ROK forces would have to be available for these offensives to punch through hardened DPRK forces. Thus, a major aerial campaign to attrite these northern forces would be required before such a counteroffensive could begin.

A crucial external variable that would affect the success of such a U.S.-ROK counteroffensive against the DPRK is whether U.S. or ROK marine or army forces were committed elsewhere. Also, U.S. aircraft carriers might be unavailable, and U.S. strategic lift might be insufficient to provide the requisite additional support. Overall, these factors could make a counteroffensive impossible or seriously delay it.

Rand analysts believe, however, that the balance would swing in favor of the South so long as two other conditions held. First, the ROK forces would have to be able to withstand DPRK forces over the first 5–15 days.[5] Second, they would have to hold the line while U.S. and ROK forces were mustered for the counteroffensive for another 15–20 days. Such a campaign would also entail their joint air forces controlling the air and neutralizing DPRK attacks against southern air bases as well as successful aerial interdiction of DPRK ground force movements.

To pull off such a countervailing strategy, ROK and U.S. forces would need to improve their perimeter control against DPRK special forces, have effective antiballistic missile systems in place, and be able to "sterilize" areas by destroying mobile threats such as Stingerlike missiles. Implementing this strategy would also require the combined southern forces to obtain better means to identify fortified defensive positions north of the DMZ without having to assault them directly, including a rock-penetrating munition to kill opposing forces in underground facilities. Finally, CFC forces would have to find ways to overcome the likely destruction of North Korean roads if they were to advance quickly on Pyongyang. In short, a sure-fire offensive capability to march into North Korea and crush its defensive forces is a long way off in the future and cannot be assured today.

To these strictly military considerations must be added the "balance of morale." North Korea's military is largely composed of uniformed civilians dragooned into gargantuan corvée labor projects. Thus, it is grossly bloated for reasons related to internal political control, and its very size and centralized and brittle command-and-control and communications-and-intelligence systems may undermine its fighting capabilities.

Also, the declining standard of living in North Korea cannot be hidden from its people, who endure daily privations. The ROK government today is at least as legitimate and probably less politically fragile than its northern counterpart. In wartime, it is likely that the southern population would unite behind the ROK government, whereas civil war could erupt in the North and rapidly degrade its military machine. In short, the psychological balance would likely favor the South in any prospective war.

Regional Security Issues

Even as the ROK faces the threat from the North, it is adjusting its mid- to long-term defense planning to address the multiple challenges of the post–Cold War environment. However, the future security imperatives are highly uncertain given the flux in domestic, regional, and global security relationships. In addition, the ROK faces the uncertainty associated with the leadership successions in all the great powers related to the peninsula, as well as that associated with Kim Jong Il's rule in the DPRK.

Beyond the DPRK

ROK defense planning of the 1980s and early 1990s focused almost exclusively on the threat from the North. Since 1993, the ROK *Defense White Papers* have focused more on regional issues and the ROK's regional security role. Seoul's fundamental external security concerns arise from continuing instability in Russia and the former Soviet republics; China's significant defense expansion and rapid force modernization; and Japan's qualitative force structure improvements, nuclear development; and economic and political competition throughout Asia.

Russia and Korean Security

Although Russia has forsworn the former Soviet Union's expansionary military policy, it remains a Eurasian power with historical interests in the region. It is revamping its military presence in the Russian Far East even as it is reducing that presence. Russia lost some of its largest ice-free ports when Ukraine and the Baltic States left the former Soviet Union, thereby increasing the strategic importance of Vladivostok and the nearby port of Nakhodka as key centers for the export of raw materials. Although the ROK has greatly increased its trade and improved its diplomatic relations with Russia, the ROK Defense Ministry (MND) is concerned about ongoing deployments of T-72 and T-80 Main Battle Tanks (MBTs), MiG-29 and MiG-31 combat aircraft, and surface-to-air missile (SAM) 5/10/12s as well as the likely deployment of T-82 MBTs and Su-35 combat aircraft.[6]

In the area of defense cooperation, Russia will deliver sophisticated weaponry to the ROK in late 1995 as partial payment against the former Soviet Union's $1.56–billion debt to the ROK, according to Itar-Tass news agency. A spokesman for Rosvooruzheniye, Russia's "monopoly arms exporter," stated that it would provide the ROK with modern T-80U tanks, BMP-3 armored vehicles, Metis-M antitank guided missiles, and Igla antiaircraft missiles.[7] These deals-in-the-making reflect how far Russia has moved away from its former embrace of the DPRK, including provision of much of its arsenal during the Cold War.

ROK defense planners remain cautious about Russia given its military presence in the region. They observe Russia's ongoing dispute with Japan over rights to the Kurile Islands and its dispute with China over the right to control parts of the Amur and Ussuri Rivers—both of which are under negotiation and still to be settled in bilateral Sino-Russian and Sino-Japanese agreements in draft as of mid-1996. They also note that pro-DPRK elements still influence Russian policy on Korea in Moscow and in the Far East, and that Russia has not simply supported U.S.-ROK positions in negotiations with the DPRK due to continuing great-power aspirations to affect the course of events on the peninsula. The fact that Moscow does not wish to lead in Asia ahead of the Commonwealth of Independent States (CIS) Asian republics also complicates any evaluation of Russian intentions. Given the chance of reunification due to the possible—however improbable—collapse of the DPRK, ROK military planners must also ponder on sharing a border with Russia. Russia's domestic instability and significant military transfers to China without regard to regional concerns about China's increasing power projection capabilities also worry ROK security analysts.

The Rise of Japan

Japan continues to modernize its security forces. Insofar as Japan's basic security posture is concerned, three elements have been stressed: (1) assumption of new responsibilities based on "creative initiation" in the post–Cold War era, (2) adherence to the tenets of the U.S.-Japan security relationship, and (3) maintenance of flexible defense assets.

Seoul is concerned about the Japanese Self-Defense Forces' (SDF's) force-upgrade programs, which include plans for acquiring Aegis cruisers, AWACS (airborne warning and control systems), combat helicopters, advanced Patriot surface-air missiles, and F-15 aircraft. ROK officials privately express concern over Japan's plutonium fast-breeder reactors at Monju and Joyo, the legacy of Japanese involvement in Korea, and the U.S. contention that Japan's host-nation support (HNS) far exceeds that of the ROK. Among ROK defense and foreign policy elites, there is a widespread view in Seoul that Japan will acquire great-power status militarily. Such a view is balanced by a web of increasing ties between Korea and Japan, including important links in the security arena. Many ROK analysts are much less complacent than their American counterparts about Japan's "virtual" nuclear weapons capabilities, with the U.S. insistence that the ROK abandon plutonium-reprocessing technology a particularly sore point in some quarters in Seoul who advocate Korean "nuclear sovereignty" to achieve equal nuclear fuel cycle status with that of Japan.

China's Challenge

The 1994 visit of China's President Jiang Zemin to Moscow symbolized a new era in Sino-Russian relations. Military cooperation will constitute part of that new relationship and will include personnel exchanges, the joint development of a new Chinese fighter, and arrangements for the further transfer to China of Russian defense technology in rocketry and advanced air defense. Beijing has taken advantage of tension within the former Soviet Union to modernize its military through the selective purchase of Russian, Kazakhstani, and Ukrainian arms and technology, thereby gaining access to equipment one or two generations in advance of its own. China's enormous military leap in such a short period concerns strategists in Seoul and elsewhere.

The ROK military observes that although the Chinese People's Liberation Army (PLA) is downsizing as a whole, PRC defense spending increased in 1994–95. China's primary preoccupation is domestic modernization of its economy. The PRC believes that it can achieve thereby the economic wherewithal to become a first-rate power by strengthening its military. Military upgrades include procurement of T-72 Main Battle Tanks and MiG-29/31 and SU-27 combat aircraft, as well as plans to procure two to four type-877 Kilo-class submarines. As China expands its blue-water capabilities, some military planners in Beijing regard aircraft carrier technology as essential.

From Seoul's perspective, the major insecurity arising from China's defense modernization is that the PRC might lend its passive or active support to the DPRK in a conflict involving the two Koreas. The prospect of increased security coordination and even military–military cooperation between the PRC and Russia probably works to the ROK's advantage by reducing the DPRK's remaining room to play off Beijing and Moscow against each other.

Many ROK officials regard China as posing the most significant threat to Korean security in the long term. This view accords with U.S. defense priorities. Despite historical animosities toward Japan, this threat perception motivates ROK military planners to look favorably on the creation of an active Washington–Tokyo–Seoul strategic triangle to offset any expansionist tendency on the part of Beijing.

At least until 2000, ROK strategic planners (like their U.S. counterparts), will be greatly unsettled by China's robust military buildup in the region, especially as it could affect the Korean peninsula. An important goal of the new Association of Southeast Asian Nations (ASEAN) Regional Forum or ARF (in which the DPRK also has expressed interest) is to counter the perceived threat of Chinese expansion amid any possible reduction of the U.S. military presence in the region. Conversely, no one believes that the ARF—or any of the other semiofficial multilateral security forums supported by the United States and the ROK—will engender a multilateral collective security system in the region in the short to medium term. Multilateral efforts to contain security threats—as occurred in relation to the DPRK proliferation threat—are feasible in specific instances. But most observers believe that national and bilateral approaches will remain predominant given historical divisions and enduring security dilemmas in the region.

Given these emerging regional perspectives, the 1994–1995 ROK *Defense White Paper* highlighted for the first time the goal of developing limited blue-water ROK naval capabilities to protect vital sea lines of communication, together with the ability to project power offshore from the peninsula. The ROK's interest in sea power derives from concern about the U.S. "Bottom-Up Review" and unrestrained naval modernization in neighboring countries. Given the ROK's substantial political and economic investment in good relations with the PRC, it remains doubtful that the ROK will align itself with any future U.S. campaign to "contain" rather than merely to "engage" the PRC—even though the ROK is disturbed by PRC military power projection capabilities. A difference in this regard is a potential point of major strategic divergence between the two allies, second only to that regarding possible developments in relation to normalization of U.S.-DPRK relations.

Institutional Integration

Institutional integration engendered by a security alliance provides multiple benefits: constant diplomatic consultation in relation to strategic objectives of the alliance; high-level political consensus arising from regular security consultations; precise and efficient command and control systems; more effective communications and intelligence capabilities; and a variety of burden-sharing and cost-minimization arrangements relating to the production, sales, re-export, and stockpiling of arms and materiel; training and exercises; and the matching of complementary national military capabilities.

Conversely, tight integration can generate political unrest and alienation among nationalist and isolationist sectors of public opinion in the ROK and the United States; concern about the relative significance of the alliance to the two partners; and accusations that one party or the other is obtaining unfair side advantages by virtue of the other's commitment to meeting strategic imperatives.

U.S. Arms Sales and Technology Re-export

The ROK purchases the largest portion of its foreign arms from U.S. companies, with major cooperative defense efforts aimed at development of the F-16/Korea Fighter Plane (KFP), the K-1 Main Battle Tank, various helicopters, and the P-3C antisubmarine warfare (ASW) aircraft. The ROK purchased a total of $6.77 billion of U.S. weapons systems ($4.58 billion in FMS and $2.19 billion commercially) between 1988 and 1993, 80.1 percent of its total overseas military purchases.

The ROK has complained vociferously about barriers to technology transfers established by U.S. firms under U.S. government regulations. Consequently, the ROK has looked elsewhere for arms supplies. In December 1990, for example, the ROK awarded the French firm Matra a $185.2–million contract for Mistral antiair missiles. The French contract transferred technology along with the missile system. ROK officials contend that technology transfer cost in the acquisition of defense systems will affect procurement decisions for the foreseeable future.

The U.S. government has agreed, in principle, to ease its controls over South Korea's re-exports of U.S. technology–based military goods to third countries. At ROK-U.S. Security Consultative Meetings, the ROK notes that the Pentagon has reviewed positively the ROK's proposal for ROK re-export of items no longer produced in the United States without prior U.S. consent, but with after-export notice to the U.S. government. Another proposal considered entails U.S. approval of the re-export of items produced in the United States within forty-five days of an official ROK request. The ROK views any such changes in U.S. policy as significant, given that the United States approved only 14 percent of ROK applications for re-export approval between 1989 and 1993, with only three items actually re-exported. This figure was much lower than during the 1988–1989 period, when 34 out of 41 items were approved prior to the conclusion of the 1989 memorandum of understanding (MOU). The United States consented to only 2 of 101 re-export requests in 1993 and 1994.

Host-Nation Support

Despite the tremendous level of U.S.-ROK defense cooperation, debate continues between the United States and the ROK over issues such as the level of host-nation support (HNS). The ROK's direct contribution to maintaining U.S. Forces Korea (USFK) was $105 million in 1991, $180 million in 1992, $220 million in 1993, $260 million in 1994, and $300 million for 1995. The ROK agreed to this figure only after considerable pressure from the United States for the ROK to meet one-third of won-based costs for the USFK by 1995. As the agreement was hammered out in Washington, a ROK National Assembly hearing revealed that the ROK spent about $322 million to service U.S. Air Force aircraft deployed outside of the peninsula. Under the Status of Forces Agreement, ROK servicing of USAF aircraft is limited to those deployed in the ROK. Apparently, USAF aircraft deployed in Guam and Okinawa as well as other aircraft not based in Korea but under the command of CINCPAC were serviced by the ROK military, an indication that the U.S. contribution to the alliance from forward-deployed forces external to the peninsula is considerably greater than the direct costs of maintaining USFK.

The annual ROK expenditure to support the U.S. Forces Korea was estimated at $0.9 billion in 1995 by the office of the U.S. secretary of defense. The U.S. Congress accepts only six categories as HNS-related expenses—namely, Combined Defense Improvement Projects (CDIPs); ROK military construction, storage, and management of U.S. war reserve stockpiles; maintenance of U.S. equipment; combined defense activities; and indigenous labor costs.

The ROK regards other expenses as valid contributions, citing burden-sharing costs such as operations and maintenance expenses for ROK-U.S. joint forces ($10.3 million), rental fees for training fields ($10.7 million), reduction or exemption of taxes and housing support ($116.2 million), human resources support ($126.7 million), real estate support ($1.84 billion), and the Yongsan base relocation ($12.8 million)—totaling $2.1 billion, or more than double what the United States counts toward HNS.

To reduce the possibility of U.S. troop reductions if and when the DPRK threat subsides, the ROK government has no alternative to persuading the United States to include indirect support in HNS calculations; increasing the South's HNS to entice U.S. forces to remain; or increasing ROK defense spending to achieve greater self-sufficiency. Burden-sharing will become an increasingly thorny issue for both sides in the coming years.

Operational Control

Despite contention over HNS and technology transfers, the United States and the ROK have made substantial progress on resolving the issue of operational control. By mutual agreement, the ROK assumed operational control over the defense of the entire 155–mile-long DMZ after the ROK military regained peace-time operational control of ROK forces committed to Combined Forces Command (CFC), which took place on December 1, 1994. An ROK spokesman emphasized that the new operational structure will have "many positive impacts on readiness, thereby enhancing the overall deterrence posture of the CFC."[8] In practical terms, the ROK control of defense along the DMZ did not change how coordination is achieved with the USFK in wartime via the CFC. But politically, the ROK's resumption of peacetime operational control over its own forces represented a major political breakthrough. The DPRK can no longer beat the drum that the ROK does not exercise operational control over its own forces as an excuse for not entering into meaningful discussions with the ROK.

Capabilities

A standing security alliance serves joint interests if it permits the partners to minimize the capabilities—and therefore the cost—required to achieve a given set of strategic objectives, or to maximize joint capabilities to avoid a potentially catastrophic outcome (that is, to avoid an infinite cost).

The military equation that represents the relationship between ROK and U.S. forces is well known. On the U.S. side, ground forces serve as a political trip wire but constitute a small fraction of fighting forces unless supplemented by massive reinforcements from the continental United States, which would take time. U.S. in-theater aerial and naval forces are important contributors to timely fighting power, but of themselves are unlikely to turn a DPRK tide. U.S. communications-and-intelligence capabilities are critically important to the combined capabilities of both partners.

The U.S. ability to project a nuclear threat against the DPRK, either as a latent form of deterrence or in an immediate crisis, is unique, as is its leadership role representing the ROK's interests in a host of international institutions—most importantly, the U.N. Security Council, the G-7, and the International Atomic Energy Agency (IAEA).

On the ROK side, the center of gravity lies in its massive active and reserve ground forces, complemented by marines, potent aerial strike forces, and special forces.

The most important changes in this equation affecting stability on the peninsula arise from ROK force acquisitions and buildup on the one hand and adjustments to the U.S. force structure on the other—in particular, the removal of U.S. nuclear weapons from Korea.

ROK Force Improvements

In recent years, a major arms buildup and modernization of ROK forces have been of great concern to the DPRK. The ROK military have sought qualitative enhancement and the effective integration of deployed forces to achieve a more balanced force structure.

In the past, the ROK has invested primarily in human resources rather than equipment, and resources continue to flow in that direction. Of the $12.4-billion 1994 defense budget, 51 percent was allocated to human resources–related accounts, including $5.7 billion for human resources, $130 million for training and education, and $602 million for facilities designed primarily to enhance morale. An additional $350 million was designated for police functions. However, infantry divisions have been reduced in accordance with greater emphasis on augmented firepower and enhanced mobility for ground force units. The defense budget for fiscal year 1995 was set at approximately $14.48 billion, or an increase of 10 percent from 1993. Operations and maintenance constituted $10 billion and spending on "maintenance for war potential" $4.4 billion.

Although defense remains the single largest portion of the government budget, defense spending as a percentage of overall government spending has fallen in the past half decade. Since 1989, it has declined from its long-held position at one-third of central government spending to less than one-quarter. Budgetary constraints work against ROK modernization options and have led to implementation of a full-time reserve forces system, wherein soldiers discharged from short-term active duty serve in the reserve forces. MND officials hope that savings from reductions in active military personnel will be reinvested to strengthen new force structures. Moreover, several internal and external factors may preclude further substantial reductions—namely, U.S. pressure for increased burden sharing, ROK interest in the development of a modern indigenous arms industry, and uncertainty over threats from the DPRK as well as developments in China and Japan.

The ROK military expects to spend some 34–36 percent of its budget on force upgrades and modernization efforts throughout the remainder of the decade of the nineties. At the same time, the ROK military is striving to achieve closer civilian-defense technology collaboration to increase self-sufficiency in weapons design and development. This emphasis on national defense production over imports has affected the alliance with the United States because of the switch to local suppliers. As of 1990, the MND has held that preference should go first to domestic research and development of weapons systems or their licensed production. Only when those two methods are judged impractical are negotiations permitted for foreign purchases.

Although indigenous arms production accounts for more than 80 percent of ROK defense procurements, many local armaments are produced under license with U.S. or other foreign companies. A primary characteristic of ROK domestic defense production in the 1990s has been specialization by industries in one specific area of military research. The selective defense procurement policy was developed to increase specific technological knowledge. In 1994, the MND designated 284 items for procurement, with eighty-four national firms responsible for their development and production. Nineteen defense technology projects were launched under government direction, whereas thirteen were allocated to civilian firms. Some $61.4 million has been invested in the development of 143 of the items.

In short, dependence on the United States as the main supplier of arms and arms technology is falling year by year, and with it, the ability of the United States to influence political and military decisions relating to ROK force levels and structure.

U.S. Conventional and Nuclear Capabilities

As is well known, the USFK has undertaken a variety of measures to enhance forces in response to increased tensions and the threat of war surrounding the sanctions issue with the DPRK.

U.S. Conventional Force Improvements

Measures to increase readiness and augment combat power included the transfer of Patriot SAMs; the replacement of two squadrons of Cobras with thirty-six AH-64 Apache attack helicopters; Global Positioning System (GPS) receivers supplied to Second Infantry Division maneuver units; the addition of sixteen OH-58D Kiowa Warrior observation helicopters; the replacement of twenty-four M113 APCs with twenty-nine TOW-capable Bradley Fighting Vehicles; the fielding of Contingency Air Control System/Automated Planning System to automatic air tasking order production and dissemination; and the upgrading of all maneuver and support forces with frequency-hopping radios.

The Clinton administration also initiated a high-level review of flexible deterrence options for strengthening U.S. Forces Korea. The United States is positioning more supplies, munitions, and logistics and support equipment at its bases in Korea in advance of any reinforcements. Moreover, the U.S. Army is accelerating work on its four-year endeavor designed to locate and hit DPRK multiple rocket launchers when they emerge from underground shelters behind the DMZ.

In reality, U.S. force improvements will have only a marginal impact on the balance of military power in the Korean Peninsula. One lesson of the political confrontation with Pyongyang over its nuclear program since 1993 is that the U.S. high-technology war against Iraq has very limited applicability to the situation in Korea. Superficially, the lessons that could be derived for Korea from Operation Desert Storm were that the United States has:

- Overwhelming combat advantage
- Deep strike capability with precision-guided munitions
- Airpower that sets conditions for ground maneuver
- The ability to conduct a successful indirect approach to ground maneuver and to move, concentrate, and counterconcentrate

- The ability to isolate an operational theater politically and militarily
- The ability to conduct successful coalition warfare
- Defined national and military objectives
- The ability to employ capable forces with superior firepower and high-technology weapons

A war in Korea, however, would differ from that in the Gulf in terms of weather and terrain, the force structure and weapon technologies, and opposing doctrine and operational concepts that would determine how forces would be employed.

Physically, the mountains of Korea would greatly restrict the kind of open-area armor operations used in the deserts during the Gulf War. There are few · roads in Korea, and off-road driving is difficult due to mountains and agricultural activities. It would be hard for any kind of armor or mechanized force to cross these areas except for brief periods in winter. Moreover, air forces are constrained in Korea by narrow valleys that would make it hard to hit targets with free-falling weapons. Low-altitude haze and clouds complicate matters. Shallow waters around Korea also favor diesel submarines, mines, and smaller combatants rather than the open-ocean operations conducted during the Gulf War.

Operation Desert Storm required months of U.S. buildup in the theater to bring overwhelming U.S. power to bear on Iraq. This pattern appears to have confirmed the DPRK leadership's belief that if a war is to be fought successfully, it must be initiated with little or no warning, and it must be concluded rapidly and decisively. U.S. ground reinforcement would take weeks and months, whereas the pace of renewed war in Korea would be measured in days and weeks.

The DPRK military could also reduce the ability of the United States to strike deeply with precision-guided missiles (PGMs) by heavy use of surface-to-air missiles and guns to attrite directly incoming PGMs, especially where terrain dictates that these be delivered through a limited corridor; by hardening sites and forces, and by dispersing and hiding others; by limiting the warning of attack and seeking to win quickly, as this would limit the number of PGMs that could be brought to bear against the North; and by attacking ports and air bases with special forces to reduce the flow of PGMs into Korea and their use in aircraft against the North.

The combination of terrain and sheer densities of DPRK forces at possible entry points would also make it difficult for CFC forces to achieve operational maneuver. Indirect approach to ground maneuver is highly limited on the peninsula, making air assault and amphibious operations desirable for the CFC. But the DPRK could offset these options, too, by using special forces, arrays of surface-to-air missiles, mines, coastal artillery, hardening positions, and limited warning.

The DPRK could also counter CFC operational maneuvers in the North by deploying mechanized forces in which it would combine infantry tactics with advanced infantry weapons, heavy use of artillery, land mines and barriers, and hardened positions.

It is true that the increasingly meager forward-deployed U.S. forces are still equipped with far higher technology weapons than their DPRK adversaries. However, the DPRK could slowly acquire many U.S. capabilities, including offensive capabilities, and turn these against the United States unless the United States strives for technologies that are difficult for the DPRK military to assimilate or sustains a substantial technological edge in countervailing weapon systems deployed against the DPRK.

Thus, the North might be able to neutralize key apparent U.S. military advantages shown in Operation Desert Storm. The North's most likely response would be to strive for a further reduction in any warning of attack, as this would counter virtually all American strengths. Hardening of the North's military sites, combined with attacks on U.S. air bases and ports in the ROK, would also follow logically from a concerted effort by the DPRK to offset American strengths exhibited in the Gulf War.

The international support for the DPRK relative to that which might be obtained by the United States and the ROK would also greatly affect the DPRK's ability to sustain a war against the South. It is impossible to predict this intangible factor with certainty; however, it implies that remaining on excellent terms with China would be essential to any successful DPRK war effort, whatever steps it might take in narrow military terms to offset American military advantages. Again, a short war would be necessary for the DPRK to obviate the likely greater ability of the United States to bring a powerful international coalition to bear in a second Korean War.

Perhaps the biggest DPRK advantage might arise from international perceptions of who started a war. Obviously, for the United States, the most difficult environment in which to wage an effective war against the DPRK would be one in which it did not appear that the North was responsible for the conflict.

No matter who started such a war, the United States and the ROK could also differ over what objectives to pursue in the course of a successful campaign against the North. Most Americans who contemplate a renewed war in Korea consider the restoration of the DMZ to be an appropriate objective, whereas the ROK would be likely to aim to extinguish the DPRK as a separate state.

U.S. Nuclear Withdrawal

Some Koreans still wonder whether U.S. nuclear weapons are located on the Korean peninsula, and DPRK allegations are still made in this regard. In 1992, both U.S. and ROK leaders stated publicly that the U.S. tactical nuclear weapons stored at Kunsan Air Base had been pulled out of the ROK. The media has also reported that U.S. officials have given the DPRK private assurances that the weapons have been removed and that the DPRK is welcome to inspect U.S.

forces on bases in the ROK to reassure itself as to their departure—as part of a negotiated package of inspections under the North–South nuclear inspection arrangement.

Until recently, however, there was no independent way to confirm the presence or absence of U.S. nuclear weapons in the ROK. Now it is possible to clarify this issue publicly based on a U.S. Army response to the authors' U.S. Freedom of Information (FOI) Act request. The army stated that "All documentation relating to Personnel Reliability Program, Nuclear Surety, and the Weapons Support Detachment has been destroyed."

Grasping the full significance of this statement requires a basic understanding of how U.S. nuclear weapons were deployed in the ROK. As of the mid-1980s, there were reportedly about sixty nuclear gravity bombs stored at Kunsan for loading onto nuclear-capable F-4 and F-16 fighter-bombers. There were also about forty 203–millimeter and thirty 155–millimeter nuclear artillery shells stored at Kunsan. As U.S. forces in Korea had only fifty-four 155–millimeter artillery tubes and twelve 203–millimeter tubes, the United States planned to use ROK artillery units to actually fire the weapons at advancing DPRK forces if war had broken out. The smaller shells would have been fired at frontline units (especially tanks), and the bigger shells at rear elements, especially massed troop concentrations and command and control posts.

These weapons required a substantial organizational infrastructure under the Plans and Operations Nuclear Division of U.S. Forces Korea. The division had three branches, which covered nuclear plans and operations, control of the weapons, and emergency disposal of nuclear weapons. The USFK also had an infrastructure dedicated to commanding and controlling nuclear operations. The Eighth U.S. Army Headquarters was responsible for operations and training involving Emergency Action Messages (nuclear fire orders) and procedures, the physical security of the weapons, and the reliability of the personnel.

The Eighth Army's Nuclear Surety Program conducted Nuclear Surety Program inspections, nuclear program management evaluations, and unit-level nuclear technical proficiency evaluations, and it appointed nuclear surety boards and surety officers in nuclear weapons–related units.

The most important U.S. unit in nuclear weapons operations in Korea was the U.S. Weapons Support Detachment–Korea or WSD-K. The WSD-K, created in March 1973, fielded nuclear support teams (NSTs) whose task was to transport nuclear artillery shells to artillery tubes and fire them in battle. The NSTs of the WSD-K were to ensure that U.S. custody of nuclear weapons was always maintained and that nuclear weapons would only have been used with validated authorization involving multiple codes.

As its name implies, the Personnel Reliability Program, or PRP, ensures that U.S. personnel handling nuclear weapons are trustworthy and that the American command keeps absolute control over nuclear weapons at all times. The PRP involved extensive annual checks on the status of psychological profiles of military personnel involved with nuclear operations.

The USFK's PRP was coordinated by the Eighth U.S. Army's nuclear surety team, supported by Eighth Personnel Command. According to the Eighth Army, in 1988, there were 644 PRP positions in the U.S. Second Division. Thus, about 5 percent of U.S. ground forces in Korea were devoted to the nuclear mission at that time.

That no documentation is now available under FOI on these units indicates that they have been deactivated. It follows that nuclear weapons cannot be located in the ROK, as U.S. law requires that all nuclear-armed forces have nuclear surety units, PRPs, and delivery teams such as the WSD-K. Thus, we conclude that there are no U.S. nuclear weapons in Korea today.

This conclusion does not mean that such weapons could not be reintroduced in the future, although this contingency is highly unlikely for two reasons. First, the organizational infrastructure would have to be re-established, which would take time. Second, fundamental U.S. interests preclude reintroducing nuclear weapons into Korea, where they would be subject to seizure and/or loss of control to either North or South Koreans.

Continuation of U.S. Nuclear War Planning

In spite of the documented withdrawal of nuclear weapons from Korea, other documents released under the U.S. Freedom of Information Act show that the USFK continues to maintain the organizational infrastructure needed to conduct offensive and defensive nuclear operations in and around Korea.

In particular, the January 19, 1993, version of the USFK's *Organization and Functions Manual* known as USFK Memo 10–1 describes this infrastructure as follows: "In conjunction with Nuclear Operations Branch and J2," the Fire Support Branch of USFK's Operations Division "targets, performs target analysis for all nuclear weapons systems" in accordance with requirements defined by the U.N. and Combined Forces Commands, the commander of U.S. Forces Korea, as contained in the current versions of *Operation Plans 5027* and *5047*.

The assistant chief of staff J5 "provides recommendations concerning the formulation of nuclear weapons policy for NEA [Northeast Asia], including guidance for general and limited employment of strategic and nonstrategic forces," under the direction of and as tasked by the commander in chief of the USFK.

In response to requirements specified by the commander in chief of Pacific Command in Hawaii, the Plans Division assistant chief of staff J5 "initiates and participates in special studies on matters concerning nonstrategic nuclear force structure and special weapons policy and planning" and, as directed by the commander of the USFK, "provides liaison with appropriate agencies for nuclear weapons policy matters and development of nuclear options for USFK in accordance with nuclear weapons guidance."

This official also perform the following functions:

- "Provides policy recommendations concerning theater deployment of nuclear forces and composition of theater stockpiles, including quantitative warhead requirements and employment strategies."
- "Consolidates and submits all USFK staff inputs addressing joint and Army concerns on the Korean peninsula during execution of all Joint Strategic Capabilities Plan category taskings to HQ USCINCPAC for the CINC's preparedness assessment report." This latter plan refers to the central, global U.S. strategic nuclear war plan maintained by Strategic Command and implemented via the SIOP, or Strategic Integrated Operational Plan.

The USFK continues to run its Nuclear-Biological-Chemical (NBC) Defense School and plans to train about thirty personnel a year in radiological and chemical monitoring, decontamination procedures, and so forth. The Chemical Branch of the USFK Plans Division is responsible for planning, coordinating, and supervising the execution of NBC defense and chemical warfare operations, including Appendix 2 on NBC defense and chemical operations in Annex C of the USFK war plan, and the NBC defense, intelligence, and chemical warfare portions of the USFK Standard Operating Procedures.

Compared with the extensive and byzantine nuclear war infrastructure of the USFK before nuclear weapons were withdrawn from the Korean Peninsula in early 1992, these capabilities are not very impressive. There has been a distinct organizational shift away from the command and control and communications and intelligence, logistical, and allied dimensions of nuclear war planning in the USFK. What is left is minimalist and focuses on generic planning, targeting, and policy analysis for future contingencies.

It is not surprising that the USFK still plans to fight a nuclear war in Korea. The doctrine and practices associated with nuclear war planning and exercising were deeply integrated into all U.S. military forces during the Cold War. It is hard for some in the U.S. military to give up the "great equalizer" as it faces down the DPRK's massive conventional forces to the North and as sections of the U.S. intelligence community advise that the DPRK may already have obtained a crude nuclear device, if not a deliverable nuclear weapon.

The continuing planning, targeting, and policy analysis for nuclear war in Korea also may be justified internally as necessary in order to advise the U.S. national command as to the practicalities involved in reintroducing nuclear weapons into Korea and in employing nuclear weapons against the DPRK should war erupt—in accordance with declared U.S. policy reserving the right to reintroduce withdrawn theater nuclear weapons in contingencies, and consistent with its global policy of no first use against Non-Proliferation Treaty (NPT) members in compliance with their NPT obligations—except in cases in which they are engaged in aggression and allied with a nuclear-armed state.

In reality, it would be extremely difficult to reintroduce U.S. nuclear weapons into the Korean Peninsula now that the key units needed to store, guard, and deliver tactical and theater nuclear weapons have been removed from Korea, and the units that linked U.S. nuclear delivery teams to ROK artillery units (from which nuclear artillery shells would have been fired) have been denuclearized.

Conversely, these residual activities (if they still exist in the mid-nineties) may also send a highly undesirable gung-ho "bathroom" message to the ROK military as to the utility of nuclear weapons. Given that the U.S. nuclear threat against threatened or actual aggression on the part of the DPRK can and most certainly would be realized only from offshore (or even home-based) nuclear weapons, there is no strategic reason for the USFK to go through these motions.

If the actual rationale for continuing is to restrain any residual South Korean military desires to obtain nuclear weapons by co-opting them in ongoing U.S. nuclear war planning and to reassure the ROK leadership that the United States still holds a nuclear umbrella over the ROK, then the United States is sending a mixed message to its partner about the primacy of nonproliferation goals in allied strategy. Of course, if this activity is simply the outcome of bureaucratic momentum, or a global requirement placed on all commands regardless of local circumstances, then nuclear war planning in the USFK should be terminated immediately.

Provided that the nuclear freeze on DPRK nuclear activities is kept in place, it is unlikely that the nuclear issue will be divisive as it was in the eighties. Rather, the nuclear issue may just fade away with time.

Conclusions

This review of critical issues affecting the U.S.-ROK alliance today implies that it will become looser rather than tighter in the future. Since 1992, the DPRK nuclear threat justified the alliance by conflating the ongoing containment of the DPRK conventional threat with that of heading off its nuclear proliferation. But the increasing institutional distance between the two partners—manifested in the alliance in the form of mutual irritation with respect to host-nation support, re-export of U.S. arms technology, and the SOFA—reflects the underlying shift in economic relations.

If the DPRK's nuclear threat subsides—and with it, its conventional military threat as envisaged by the United States as the Agreed Framework is implemented (see below)—then even the major military rationale for the alliance, the DPRK threat, may also recede in significance (at least in terms of justifying a continuing U.S. presence).

Undoubtedly, the biggest test of the U.S.-ROK alliance is the fact that the United States is now dealing politically with the DPRK independently of the

ROK. Equally, the ROK's dealings with the DPRK are also complex and affect vital interests of the United States in ways that Washington cannot control. This challenge boils down to two issues: the U.S.-DPRK Agreed Framework and the future of the armistice.

The Agreed Framework

The October 1994 U.S.-DPRK Agreed Framework is the main bulwark stopping North Korea from developing nuclear weapons. The Agreed Framework specifies a decade-long schedule of steps that must be taken in Washington and Pyongyang to ensure that each side fulfills its agreements in tandem. If implemented, the Agreed Framework requires the DPRK to freeze its indigenous nuclear fuel cycle option; to allow the United States to stabilize and eventually remove spent fuel containing plutonium from North Korea; to allow IAEA routine safeguards on declared facilities; to dismantle its locally manufactured reactors; and to resolve the inconsistency between its declared past reprocessing of plutonium and the evidence gathered by the IAEA that North Korea is lying. For its part, the United States is obliged to arrange the supply of 500,000 metric tons of residual oil per year to fuel a power plant and to transfer 2 gigawatts-electric of light-water reactors (LWRs) to the DPRK.

For the ROK, the impact of the U.S.-DPRK Agreed Framework has been complex. Seoul is confronting the reality that its strongest ally is developing multi-layered diplomatic relations with its arch-enemy. Furthermore, the Seoul government has found itself caught between Washington's evolving stand on the nuclear issue and a domestic conservative coalition opposed to any compromise with the North. Ultimately, the Kim administration has had little room to maneuver, although it insisted that North Korea accept a South Korean light-water reactor and obtained assurances from the United States that it will pressure Pyongyang to move forward in dialogue with Seoul.

It is difficult to forecast just how the political mood will continue to shift in either Washington or Seoul. But it is clear that the U.S. administration's flexibility on the DPRK issue will be limited by the curbs that the U.S. Congress has placed on the implementation of the Agreed Framework. And increased nationalist sentiments so evident in Seoul may reinforce those who argue for moving faster (or slower) with respect to economic or political relations than is preferred by the United States. Relatedly, the two partners may collide over the extent to which the DPRK is forced to deal directly with the ROK, versus having its contact via multilateral institutions led by the United States.

In relation to the U.S.-ROK alliance, perhaps the most important outcome of U.S.-DPRK negotiations is that the United States has opened its own window to look into Pyongyang instead of automatically identifying with the perspective from Seoul. Interpretation of DPRK motivations is now a small cottage industry in the United States, where many believe that the game now is how to facilitate

DPRK dealings with the ROK via Washington rather than, as is still held widely in the ROK, how to force Pyongyang to go to Washington via Seoul. The United States is hampered in such a role, however, by the dominance of security concerns in its policy apparatus for Northeast Asia and the lack of a subregional vision concerning economic integration or almost any other issues—including even a definition of strictly U.S. security interests at a sub-regional level.

The Armistice Issue

Both the United States and the DPRK are committed in the Agreed Framework to normalizing their relationship at a rate determined by progress in relation to a set of issues that each side holds important. On the U.S. side, this item refers to four main issues. (1) restarting the stalled ROK-DPRK dialogue and the ROK as the primary supplier of the LWR via the Korean Peninsula Energy Development Organization; (2) stopping DPRK missile exports; (3) resolving the issue of recovering the remains of U.S. servicemen missing-in-action in the Korean War; and (4), conventional arms control starting with the DMZ. On the DPRK side, this item refers to lifting of U.S. sanctions and progress toward a peace treaty and normalization of relations.

Should the Agreed Framework collapse because either or both sides fail to perform to the other's satisfaction, then the DPRK has retained the option of restarting its nuclear power and weapons program, and the United States has kept its nuclear umbrella over the ROK (even though all its nuclear weapons have been withdrawn from the peninsula). The United States is also committed to reviving economic sanctions against the DPRK should the situation revert to confrontation combined with challenge to the NPT regime. Such a stance always includes the prospect of war on the peninsula, as the DPRK has stated that it views the imposition of U.N. sanctions as an act of renewed war by the United States (both sides are technically at war, as the 1953 armistice only suspends hostilities). It was just such a slide to the brink that brought former U.S. President Jimmy Carter into the picture in June 1994 before Kim Il Sung died—a slender thread indeed on which to hang peace in Korea.

The critical litmus test of American intentions from the North Korean perspective is its stance in relation to normalization and a peace treaty. The DPRK has already made it impossible to operate the armistice organizational infrastructure for routine and crisis management of the demilitarized zone—first, by withdrawing access for parties to the already moribund Neutral Nations Supervisory Commission and, second, by rejecting even low-level military contacts at the Military Armistice Commission (the MAC) at Panmunjon. This stance was underscored in 1996 by a series of North Korean incursions into the DMZ, and the DPRK's declaration that it no longer recognized the implementing organs of the Armistice. It is prudent to redress this situation from a strictly military stance, as inadvertent transgressions by either side (such as the U.S. helicopter's straying into DPRK airspace in December 1994) could escalate rapidly into war.

The DPRK leadership, however, understands that the U.S. side will not end the Korean armistice and sign a peace treaty—or even normalize relations—for some time. DPRK leaders have dropped their long-standing objection to U.S. troops in the ROK and want less hostile relations with Washington.[9]

Thus, the DPRK has begun to seek what it terms "an interim peace mechanism" to replace the MAC and get the ball rolling. Unfortunately, it has not spelled out what it has in mind other than showing some interest in exploring this agenda. One possibility is a set of simultaneous nonaggression pacts between the parties to the Korean conflict (Beijing and Seoul, Washington and Pyongyang) that would establish a new, truly peacekeeping function for U.N. troops rather than the military role of U.S. Forces Korea (nominally, U.N. Command).[10] This deal might be the outcome of four power talks proposed by the U.S. and ROK presidents in 1996.

In Washington, the Korean armistice is regarded as the cornerstone of the U.S. alliance system in East Asia and therefore untouchable. It is still virtually heresy even to raise the issue, let alone discuss a detailed road plan toward ending the armistice. Yet achieving normalization and a peace treaty are integral to the DPRK's willingness to forgo its nuclear weapons option and to return to the NPT regime, including resolution of the discrepancies in relation to past reprocessing that compelled the IAEA to demand special inspections of sites in the DPRK. In the long run, there can be no nonproliferation without full normalization and a peace treaty. But almost no one in Washington takes the DPRK seriously on this central point because the issue appears to lie in the distant future rather than the hurly-burly of presidential, party, and bureaucratic politics.

In reality, positions taken now will predispose politicians to adopt policies in the future. By default, these issues are being decided now on the basis of short-term political expediency. The virtual refusal of the United States policy establishment to transcend the armistice and to envisage a post–Cold War, post–nuclear-threat-based relationship with the DPRK will lead to the unraveling of the U.S.-DPRK Agreed Framework as surely as night follows day. This outcome could again unleash a DPRK nuclear weapons threat as soon as in one or two years. How long it would take for Japan and South Korea to follow suit is anyone's guess.

Implications for the Non-Proliferation Regime

The U.S.-DPRK Agreed Framework is also an important test case for the limits of coercive enforcement of the NPT regime on the one hand and the potential for positive inducements to obtain compliance from potential proliferators on the other. Some argue that the DPRK is so unique that no precedents are set in relation to the treatment of other hard-core proliferating states such as Iran.

Conversely, if cooperative engagement as embodied in the Agreed Framework proves successful, it will have demonstrated to the nuclear powers that the NPT regime must be built on positive as well as negative power capabilities, with all that this result implies for the removal of extended deterrence to allies, no first use, economic benefits, technology transfer, and so on. Thus, the ending of the Korean armistice is also about removing a vestige of the Cold War in Asia, ending a forty-five-year-long policy of militant containment in that region against U.S. adversaries, and removing 43,000 U.S. troops from being in harm's way in Korea itself. There are no shortcuts to nuclear nonproliferation on the Korean Peninsula. The only way to ensure nuclear nonproliferation in Northeast Asia is to resolve the Korean conflict, to end the armistice, and to construct a new set of regional and bilateral cooperative security relationships. The question is how best to achieve each of these necessary conditions for regional nuclear nonproliferation.

The United States had to force both the ROK and the DPRK to accept KEDO as a multilateral mechanism to contain a clear and present security threat. Ironically, it is an open question whether the United States is willing to follow the ROK's diplomatic lead in the search for multilateral frameworks in which to realize comprehensive security in the region. To date, the bulk of the U.S. foreign policy establishment has neglected the emerging regional and subregional agendas relating to political, economic, and environmental conflict and cooperation.[11] Undoubtedly, bilateral security alliances remain the primary instrument of U.S. policy in the region. But in the long term, the United States runs the risk of missing the boat in Northeast Asia by insisting on the primacy of military alliances born in the Cold War.

Notes

1. Northeast Asia Peace and Security Network (NAPSNet), *Daily Report,* Berkeley, California, September 29, 1995; available at WWW.Nautilus.org.

2. Joint Intelligence Center at Pacific Command (ONK), "Republic of Korea/North Korea, Military Capabilities," September 27, 1993; released by CINCPAC under a U.S. Freedom of Information Act request to the author.

3. Such calculations depend on the method used to calculate per capita GNP equivalent in the DPRK and on what fraction of the DPRK military force is corvée labor used in state infrastructure works such as canals and monuments and for domestic political mobilization and control purposes, versus professional fighting personnel. Our own guess is that about 56 percent of the DPRK military are rear-based and, in any case, would be of low operational utility in wartime due to low motivation, poor equipment, lack of training, failures of logistical support, and vulnerability to combined operations.

4. *Global 92 Analysis of Prospective Conflicts in Korea in the Next Ten Years,* RAND N-3544–NA, prepared for the Office of Net Assessment, Office of the Secretary of Defense, Rand, Santa Monica, California, 1993.

5. As presented by Nick Beldecos and Eric Heginbotham at the Brookings Institution symposium "Regional Policies and the U.S.-North Korean Nuclear Agreement," June 26, 1995. See also Beldecos and Heginbotham, "The Conventional Military Balance in

Korea," *Breakthroughs* 4, no. 1 (spring 1995): 1–8. These authors used war-gaming models for conventional combat developed by Joshua Epstein at Brookings to model a Korean conflict. They concluded that the line would hold north of Seoul whatever the DPRK military forces might throw at the combined forces.

6. Ministry of National Defense, Republic of Korea, *Defense White Paper 1994–1995,* Seoul, 53.

7. NAPSNet, *Daily Report,* September 27, 1995.

8. NAPSNet, *Daily Report,* December 1 and 5, 1994.

9. NAPSNet, *Daily Report,* September 28 and 29, 1995.

10. This formula is the "2 + 2" approach. Other approaches include the "2 + 1" approach (the two Koreas and the United States as broker), the "2 + 4" approach (the two Koreas and the four great powers involved with the peninsula), the "2" approach (the two Koreas only), and the "1" approach (induce the DPRK to participate in multilateral regional security arenas such as the ARF). See Tae Hwan Ok, "The U.S.-ROK Relationship in Times of Change," paper presented to the Conference on Change and Challenge on the Korean Peninsula, Center for Strategic and International Studies, Washington, D.C., September 20, 1995, 14.

11. C. Johnson and E. Keehan, "The Pentagon's Ossified Strategy," *Foreign Affairs* 74, no. 4 (July–August 1995): 112.

14

Confidence-Building Measures: Bilateral versus Multilateral Approaches

Janice M. Heppell

Introduction

The Challenge of Confidence Building in Northeast Asia

The Asia–Pacific region has witnessed remarkable changes over the past few decades. Most states in the region have posted double-digit economic growth, developed more representative political institutions ("democracy" in Asia has its own flavor), and improved relations among themselves. However, the post–Cold War era, while bringing many positive developments, has also led to uncertainty, as the once-familiar playing field has become one with new and unfamiliar parameters, leaving nations to speculate as to the primary threat to their security.

As countries in the region struggle to identify and address these ill-defined threats, some misperceive the resultant actions as offensive preparations, based in part on logical calculations but often to a degree on underlying mistrust related to historical, economic, or diplomatic factors. To prevent a buildup of weapons in a time of relative peace, it is essential for nations of the region to begin dismantling the barriers to better understanding of their neighbors. Although many have called for a multilateral framework within which to undertake such

Prepared for the Conference on Peace and Security in Northeast Asia and the Nuclear Issue, East–West Center, Honolulu, July 17–20, 1994.

confidence-building measures (CBMs), others have argued that too many barriers exist for a multilateral framework to be effective.

Confidence building is not simply the negotiation or adoption of specific measures, but rather, it is the *relationship* between negotiation and implementation that is the key and ultimately leads to a transformation in threat perceptions. Although recent history has demonstrated that some confidence-building measures can be replicated, it is ineffective simply to apply a blanket package of confidence-building measures to a situation and expect them to be effective, even if they had been completely successful in previous circumstances.

Over the past five or six years, a variety of proposals have been made to transfer the structures and measures of the Conference on Security and Cooperation in Europe (CSCE) to the Asia–Pacific region. However, controversy has arisen because those specific arrangements cannot effectively address the distinct differences in history, culture, force structure, domestic politics, and levels of economic development nor account for the intraregional animosities and rivalries, noncontiguous nature of states, or divergent threat perceptions. As James Macintosh notes, "disassociated from the larger political process and purpose, confidence building loses much of its meaning and becomes a narrow, information enhancing activity incapable of fundamentally altering a security relationship."[1] However, this is not to say that the lessons learned cannot be applied with care and attention.

In a multilateral framework like the CSCE, positive developments in some areas can be held up by unrelated problems existing between other countries. Consensus is not easily achieved, and the timing for solving these problems is critical; the resolution of issues may be impeded if efforts are not actively pursued at the bilateral level, where a "window of opportunity" may exist for solving each problem. It is unlikely that these opportunities will occur simultaneously in a multilateral context. As an example of the difficulty of reaching consensus on anything in Northeast Asia, I will examine the attempt by the United Nations Security Council (UNSC) to agree upon and pass a resolution on the application of sanctions to North Korea in June 1994, in response to its recalcitrance on the nuclear issue. These events highlight the challenges inherent in multilateral problem-solving efforts and illustrate the fact that the June 1994 North Korean nuclear crisis was ultimately solved along bilateral lines. Additionally, the reasons why consensus was impossible to reach—or in other words, the individual reasons for each country to support or not support sanctions—will be put forth, showing the complexity of the competing interests in the region.

For this reason, it is essential to continue to pay heed to the importance of bilateral relationships in the region, not only to maintain the good ones but to seek to improve those characterized by some degree of strain. Relying only on a web of bilateral alliances would be regressive whereas active pursuit of problem-solving efforts at the bilateral level—in order to facilitate the development of a cooperative security regime—is the only way to effectively address the *common* problems that exist in the Northeast Asian region. In this vein, the third section of this chapter examines the bilateral relationships in the region, identifies the stumbling blocks to confidence and trust, and gives suggestions for modest CBMs.

Common security problems—such as environmental degradation, migration flows, security of the sea lanes of communication (SLOCs), resource claims, drug trafficking, proliferation of weapons of mass destruction, sustainable energy (nuclear), safety of nuclear facilities, and storage of nuclear waste—all require cooperative efforts to be addressed effectively. Some can function as catalysts in the development of a multilateral consultative structure, whereas others will need to be settled within such a structure once it develops. Although problems such as the aforementioned pose a security risk to all, a conflict of interest is likely to develop in many of the cases, between polluters and the polluted or between proliferators and nonproliferators.

Those issues that have the potential to be catalysts in the development of a regional security regime demonstrate the necessity of giving equal attention to both function and form. In fact, function should receive even more attention than form at the outset. The terms *architecture* and *structure* receive a great deal of ink, whereas practical assessments of the functional utility—and therefore, feasibility—of such proposals receive insufficient consideration. Cooperative security should be "issue-driven" and realistic. The last section of this chapter suggests a project that could meet the criteria involved in this line of thinking.

Confidence-building measures will have to be modest at the outset, as they were in the European context twenty years ago when the institutionalized process began, involving primarily informational and communication-related military CBMs that were implemented against the backdrop of increased cultural contacts between adversaries. Their value will be as much in the process of consultation that develops as in the value of the information exchanged, laying the groundwork for a regular dialogue channel in the event of heightened tensions in the future. However, if the confidence-building efforts are truly successful, such a tense situation might never develop.

The Challenges of Problem Solving in a Multilateral Context

In June 1994, a crisis mounted over North Korea's suspected nuclear weapons program and its continued refusal to submit to inspectors from the International Atomic Energy Agency (IAEA). Its actions had many implications: (1) they challenged the integrity of the nonproliferation movement and the Nuclear Non-Proliferation Treaty (NPT), then up for renewal in 1995; (2) they threatened the security environment of the entire Asia–Pacific region, but especially Northeast Asia; and most directly, (3) they put the safety of 70 million people on the Korean Peninsula at great risk.

Here, the events of June 1994 will illustrate the articulation between multilateral and bilateral processes at work in the Northeast Asian region. From there, factors will be suggested that may have encouraged or prevented the support of sanctions by each of the main actors in the conflict, illustrating the difficulty of establishing an effective multilateral political/military framework in Northeast Asia.

The June 1994 Crisis

To set the stage, on May 27, 1994, Pyongyang refused to shut down the refueling of its nuclear reactor or identify the critical eighty-nine fuel rods that replaced the ones broken in 1989, which the IAEA needed to analyze the history of the reactor. It is suspected that North Korea reprocessed rods removed in 1989, the last time that the reactor was reloaded, and a time when the International Atomic Energy Agency inspectors had not yet obtained access to the DPRK. The United Nations Security Council warned North Korea to cooperate with the inspectors and cease changing fuel rods without inspectors present. A veiled reference to mild economic sanctions was made, which North Korea rejected.[2]

On May 30, South Korean President Kim Young Sam ordered case-by-case countermeasures against North Korea's possible nuclear weapons program, noting that upon entering a serious stage in relations, the South Korean government should prepare itself for the possibility that the UNSC would take up the problem.[3] It didn't ease matters when North Korea test-fired a Silkworm missile into the Sea of Japan.[4]

By the first of June, Seoul was ready to consider sanctions, although lawmakers were divided over their effectiveness. The South Korean government began to consider banning trade and other forms of contact with the North but was still looking for a negotiated settlement with Pyongyang. While visiting in Seoul, China's Vice Foreign Minister Tang Jiaxuan showed reluctance to join international pressure against North Korea, emphasizing that "a superpower like the United States should not wield its power ruthlessly against a small power" like North Korea.[5] Despite such statements in Seoul, China did not try to tone down the strongly worded statement issued by the UNSC in New York on May 30, which was a significant departure from its previous performance in the Security Council Meetings. This position could be viewed as a means of demonstrating some semblance of a compromise with the West. In cooperation, it also pledged to stop supplying food and oil to North Korea in addition to halting border trade, a promise that, if carried out earnestly, would have significant impacts on North Korea. Russian President Boris Yeltsin also threw Russia's support into the international community's camp when he promised Kim Young Sam that he would support sanctions if negotiations were unsuccessful. Russia's idea of convening an eight-party conference to deal with the nuclear issue was again floated by Russian Ambassador Yuli Vorontsov in Seoul, but without much response.[6] Some degree of consensus regarding the seriousness of the situation seemed to be taking shape, and on the surface, it appeared that an agreement on sanctions might be possible. However, in reality, at this point it was quite clear that a meaningful sanctions package would be unlikely to get China's or even Russia's approval.

On June 2, Washington pledged to seek sanctions and canceled the third round of high-level talks with North Korea, after the IAEA reported that it could no longer guarantee that Pyongyang had not diverted plutonium, given that the North had already removed all but 1,800 fuel rods from its reactor. With tensions soaring, Pyongyang reiterated its previous warning that sanctions would be tantamount to a declaration of war. During talks with Kim Young Sam, Yeltsin officially stated that Moscow would not extend its military treaty with Pyongyang.[7] This was particularly significant, as it came at a time of high tensions on the peninsula.

On June 3 (in Washington), the IAEA offered another possible route by which Pyongyang could comply, by allowing special inspections of the nuclear waste sites, since it could not examine the used fuel rods, now almost entirely in the cooling pond. At the same time, the United States began intensive consultations with Tokyo, Moscow, and Seoul. Discussions touched on the option of "allied sanctions" in the event that Beijing vetoed U.N. sanctions. Japan, under mounting pressure to show its solidarity with the international community's commitment, prepared a ten-point package of economic sanctions that it could enforce against North Korea,[8] although the government was clearly apprehensive about possible retaliation by its pro-Pyongyang Korean community.[9] Sanctions also posed difficulty for the shaky minority government of Prime Minister Tsutomu Hata, which was treading carefully so as not to alienate the large Japan Socialist Party (JSP), which has significant backing from the pro-Pyongyang Korean minority.

June 6 brought some very serious statements. U.S. Secretary of Defense William Perry, although not recommending such action at the time, stated that a pre-emptive strike on North Korea's nuclear installations was not out of the question, a reversal of his stance two months earlier. While South Korean Foreign Minister Han Sung-joo was on his way to New York to address the UNSC, President Kim Young Sam also came out with a stiff and terse warning for the neighbor to the North, stating that North Korea would face destruction if it didn't abandon its nuclear program. "We will not tolerate North Korean possession of even half a nuclear bomb,"[10] he threatened, which was the first time that he had retaliated verbally against the North on the issue. This show of solidarity was underscored by a joint statement issued by the United States, Japan, and South Korea, declaring that the international community should make the appropriate responses, including sanctions.[11] The result was a draft for a two-stage embargo against North Korea, beginning with limited economic sanctions and moving to a total trade stoppage. The resolve of the "allies" appeared strong.

Not to be pushed around without a fight, Pyongyang the following day threatened to quit the Nuclear Non-Proliferation Treaty, declaring that it would no longer feel the need to be part of the IAEA if it came under too much pressure.

Conflicting sentiments regarding Russia's eight-party conference proposal were registered: North Korea's Foreign Minister Kim Young-nam said that he was considering the idea, although another North Korean diplomat in Geneva said that the standoff it was not a matter for an international conference because the issue was between North Korea and the United States—if it were a general nuclear disarmament matter, such a conference might have been possible, but on this issue, it was not a suitable approach to pursue, he stated. Russia did not take the side of its former ally either. In the recently concluded meetings with President Kim Young Sam, Russia had promised to participate in international sanctions.[12] Back in Seoul, Kim Young Sam called a National Security Council meeting.[13] The objectives were threefold: to show the world, the North Korean administration, and the South Korean people the seriousness with which Seoul was approaching this situation.

However, despite what appeared to be consensus among "the players," there was still one holdout. As Foreign Minister Han Sung-joo was on his way to Beijing to discuss the nuclear issue, Chinese President Jiang Zemin was pledging to Choi Gwang, chief of the general staff of the Korean People's Army, Beijing's unwavering friendship with Pyongyang. Without mentioning the nuclear crisis, he proclaimed, "Our two communist parties, two countries and two armies have a tradition of friendly relationships."[14] These sentiments were echoed by Choi's Chinese counterpart, Zhang Wannian, who reportedly said: "The traditional friendship between China and North Korea has been formed by the blood of the Chinese people and the military, and the heroic people of the Democratic People's Republic of Korea who achieved a great success in building a nation and military under the leadership of President Kim Il-sung."[15]

June 8 saw a significant split in the international resolve on the sanctions issue, basically between China and "the others" in the international community. China slammed the idea of sanctions, saying that they would aggravate the situation. It is possible that China was attempting to increase its influence over Pyongyang by assuming a more sympathetic attitude, in order to reach a negotiated settlement, and/or it believed that the "cure" (sanctions) was more dangerous than the "disease" (North Korea's suspected nuclear weapons capability). Effective sanctions could have precipitated a collapse of the North Korean regime, bringing about instability on the peninsula, which is one of China's backyards. North Korea's envoy to the IAEA reiterated North Korea's firm stance against inspections of the two nuclear waste sites. On the other side of the field, South Korean officials called for joint readiness of South Korean and American forces, increased surveillance activities, and strengthened early-warning capabilities. Sanctions were seen as unavoidable by both South Korea and the United States, which would not be intimidated by threats. President Yeltsin, using a hot line set up on the basis of agreements made the previous week in Moscow, called President Kim Young Sam to reiterate his continued support for sanctions. In short, the structure of the situation had become: All for one and one for all, except China.

By June 9, the IAEA had drafted its own set of sanctions against North Korea, to freeze about $500,000 to $600,000 worth of annual technical aid to North Korea. After promising the visiting Foreign Minister Han Sung-joo its "best efforts" to resolve the nuclear standoff, China abstained during the vote on the IAEA's draft resolution, which was significant because some members might have been reluctant to support the motion if China had directly opposed it. In response, the North Korean envoy, Yun Ho-jin, emphatically stated that North Korea would not allow any more inspections and suggested that the IAEA inspectors in North Korea would have to leave. Washington continued to talk tough about pushing ahead with a U.N. resolution. Perhaps in the hope of securing Russia's declared support for sanctions, Washington finally endorsed Russia's eight-party conference plan. In this heightened state of tension, the "powers" appeared to have a fairly strong front, although China was a question mark.

On June 14, in preparation for unforeseen developments at the heightened level of tension, Seoul ordered civil defense drills involving 6.6 million civil defense corps members, to organize evacuations and provide first aid for air raid victims. These beefed-up drills, which had been held regularly in the past, though on a much smaller scale, captured the attention of the international media, which focused on a "frenzied situation" in South Korea, where all South Koreans were said to be stocking up on ramyon (instant noodles) and buying gas masks. Of course, the recent events had been serious enough to catch the attention of the South Koreans, who are usually quite complacent regarding any imminent threat from the North, something that has become part of their daily lives. Certainly, many started making preparations (although not at the level depicted in the media). That hype, combined with the usual North Korean rhetoric, generated North Korean verbal attacks on the South for drumming up tension on the peninsula. The following day, North Korea announced its intention to pull out of the IAEA, although no mention of the fate of the inspectors was made.

This statement increased the stakes. North Korea called for direct talks with the United States on June 14. Russia's Foreign Minister Andrei Kozyrev said that he saw sanctions as only a last resort. China, continuing to maintain its somewhat ambiguous position, made a statement declaring, "We hearby deplore the adverse turn of events. The Chinese government once again appeals to all parties concerned to be cool-headed and to exercise restraint."[16]

At this critical juncture of June 14, under great pressure, the fissures in the multilateral effort began to grow. Pyongyang went ahead and officially withdrew from the IAEA, the first country ever to quit the international agency. The United States presented a draft at the UNSC, delineating a two-phased approach and giving Pyongyang a month to comply with the safeguards accord and implement the inter-Korean 1992 non-nuclear declaration.[17] Reaction to the proposal was the least supportive compared to any of the previous drafts. The South Korean opposition objected to using neighboring countries to push through an embargo that could lead to war, challenging South Korea to lead the way. China rejected the draft, urging further negotiations. It also emphasized that "China, in principle, doesn't subscribe to the involvement of the Security Council in the nuclear issue of the Korean peninsula or resorting to sanctions to solve it. The only way is direct dialogue."[18] Russia withheld its support, not because it opposed the contents of the draft but rather because it was angry about not being consulted in advance during its preparation.[19] Japan, although supportive, would certainly have preferred not to have to enforce sanctions. This was the last true test of the will to cooperate on sanctions. It failed.

In the end, the visit by former U.S. President Jimmy Carter eased tension considerably.[20] Where did the idea of Carter's visit come from? It is not certain, but in mid-May, during the visit to Washington of former South Korean opposition leader/human rights champion Kim Dae-jung, he brought up a possible role for Carter to Washington officials. To defuse the crisis with North Korea, he suggested dispatching "an elder statesman, respected internationally, trusted by the Chinese and North Koreans and sharing the views of President Clinton." He noted that face-saving is "even more important in dealing with North Korea, a country ruled for five decades by one man with absolute authority, Kim Il-sung."[21] He remarked that dispatching the Reverend Billy Graham in early February with Clinton's personal message apparently increased Kim Il Sung's readiness to negotiate and the latter mentioned that North Korea had long admired President Carter.

On June 16, taking a more moderate approach, Washington offered Pyongyang a grace period to settle the dispute before sanctions would be activated and indicated that it would impose tougher measures only if Pyongyang took further steps to threaten security. In addition, the South Korean ruling Democratic Liberal Party (DLP) asked the government to reconsider the denuclearization policy, which is based on the joint Declaration on the Denuclearization of the Korean Peninsula, given the fact that North Korea clearly appeared to have violated it and looked unlikely to abide by it in the future after its announced withdrawal from the IAEA.[22]

After arriving in Pyongyang on June 15, by June 17, Carter and Kim Il Sung were making promises. Kim authorized a joint search for Americans missing in action from the Korean War and agreed to freeze nuclear activities and allow international nuclear inspectors to remain in North Korea. On the other side, Carter announced that the movement for sanctions had been suspended and that Washington had provisionally agreed to a third round of talks and support for North Korea's acquiring a light-water reactor.

Washington, however, denied that sanctions were on hold and stated its commitment to pursue them until Kim's pledges could be measured in deeds. Reaction from Seoul was also reserved, based on years of deep feelings of distrust and a belief that Carter's visit was more of a photo opportunity than a chance for a resolution to the conflict. Carter explained his opposition to sanctions: declarations of sanctions would be considered as an insult to North Korea, by branding it an outlaw country, and an insult to its so-called Great Leader, by branding him a liar and a criminal.[23] Although many people would suggest that past deeds warrant just such a characterization of Kim Il Sung, Carter's face-saving treatment of Kim Il Sung earned a lot of mileage. However, it is certain that many South Koreans and Washington officials considered Carter's approach and moves naive in dealing with someone such as cagey as Kim Il Sung. In his recommendations to Washington to establish formal relations with Pyongyang, Carter added, "Diplomatic relations are not a gift or favor or reward to be handed out between two countries. It's a common belief that the exchange of ambassadors and opening of relations is of mutual benefit. My opinion is that it would be of great mutual benefit to have open communication and better understanding between my country and North Korea."[24] During Carter's meeting with Kim Young Sam on June 18, he delivered a proposal by Kim Il Sung to meet with his South Korean counterpart "anywhere, at any time, without any conditions," which Kim Young Sam accepted immediately, indicating the sooner the better.

Although it cannot be determined whether Carter's visit significantly changed Kim Il Sung's position in the nuclear standoff or whether it was more of a face-saving "out" of an increasingly hopeless situation for both sides, it was later learned that days prior to Carter's visit, China's Foreign Ministry in Beijing called in the North Korean ambassador and warned that his government could not depend indefinitely on Chinese support in the confrontation with the United States over the nuclear issue, and that it would be in Pyongyang's best interests to cooperate more with international efforts to inspect its nuclear facilities. Not only was this a significant move on China's part after opposing the international call for sanctions, but it also marked a big change in China's previously stated stance that it maintained little or no influence over North Korea.[25]

Over the next week, while the parties involved were trying to establish the sincerity of recent pledges, tension eased gradually, and offers for bilateral improvements in relations began to flow in. Japan's then Foreign Minister Koji Kakizawa offered to help Pyongyang convert its nuclear facilities to a light-water reactor in a gesture aimed at normalizing bilateral relations, coming the day after Carter returned to Seoul. In a possible return gesture, Pyongyang lifted a ban on Japanese tourists, implemented in June 1993, although this cannot be seen as purely a goodwill gesture, given that Pyongyang desperately needs foreign exchange. Once the moves were afoot to realize the historic North–South summit, Seoul offered to encourage phased economic cooperation, beginning with small-sized joint ventures in light industry; leading to cooperation in the fields of mining, agriculture, and communications; and ultimately fostering an economic community. The development of rail links and direct navigation routes was also proposed. Private businesses, anxious to implement long-awaited plans for joint ventures or investment, began to talk seriously again of the possibilities. The issue of sanctions fell to the background as tensions subsided. Everyone breathed a sigh of relief. All parties were let off the hook.

Factors Promoting and Preventing Multilateral Consensus on Sanctions

In the Northeast Asian region, the circumstances that drive policies in each country are far from homogeneous, which is one of the reasons why the establishment of a multilateral security forum is so challenging. Consensus is often almost impossible to reach. This section *suggests* (the lists are not exhaustive) each country's possible reasons for supporting or opposing sanctions, illustrating the challenges to multilateralism in the security field.

China

Reasons for Supporting Sanctions

- *To preserve the great strides made between 1991 and 1994 in its relationship with South Korea:* Particularly in the area of economic cooperation and trade, China and South Korea had become valuable partners. In order to preserve this important relationship, China did not want to be drawn into a situation in which it had to play its last card. Although, if push came to shove and China had to choose one of the two with which to be partners, it would almost certainly give the nod to Seoul, it did have an interest in maintaining relations with Pyongyang. China played a much greater role in cooperating with the international community against its formerly close ally than it would have a few years ago, although it was the main holdout in the search for a consensus on sanctions.
- *To prevent North Korea from going nuclear:* A nuclear-armed North Korea would force both South Korea and Japan to reconsider their non-nuclear pledges.
- *To prevent friction with the United States, after tensions regarding most favored nation (MFN) trading status, human rights, arms sales, and recent underground testing:* China didn't need another flare-up with the United States.[26]

Reasons for Opposing Sanctions

- *To preserve stability on its frontier:* Nuclear weapons on the Korean Peninsula would alter the security equation in the region. However, more important from China's perspective, a North Korea with nuclear weapons would not pose as much of a threat to China as a collapsing North Korea. China has an interest in preventing a hard landing for North Korea as it enters the international arena. In the event of collapse, China would be forced to consider intervention lest the United States and South Korea move in to establish order, removing the buffer area on that Chinese border. Whether one regards sanctions as preserving or threatening stability really depends upon one's perspective.

- *To prevent further feelings of isolation by Pyongyang, which could provoke a rash response:* North Korea's isolation, upon Seoul's normalization of relations with both the Soviet Union/Russia and China, was cited as one cause for Pyongyang's recalcitrance and pursuit of nuclear weapons as an equalizer in response to the unfavorable shift in the military balance.
- *The possibility of gaining more leverage by being on Pyongyang's side rather than against it:* Beijing continually denied having any significant leverage over Pyongyang, although it appeared that its actions behind the scenes just prior to Carter's visit may have laid the foundation for a more receptive Kim Il Sung.
- *Feelings of kinship for its comrades in arms:* The octogenarian leaderships of both China and North Korea had an enduring relationship for more than forty years. Although not always on the best of terms, the octogenarian set in China was possibly the only group in the world to know the North Korean leadership well. Despite their differences, they may have felt great difficulty in completely abandoning their former comrades in arms.
- *Inability to enforce sanctions effectively along the border:* Trade along the remote border of Jilin Province, formed by the Tumen River, accounts for more than 40 percent of North Korea's trade with China. The trade is important to the local economy on the Chinese side, which is home to most of China's Korean minority. Attempts to enforce the sanctions would have been difficult at best.
- *Irritation over Washington's continued interference on human rights:* It could be said that Beijing threw its support behind sanctions after Washington granted MFN privileges at the end of May. However, if the United States had irritated China enough, China could have used the sanctions card to frustrate the United States and demonstrate its strength.
- *China's dual role as both an emerging superpower and a representative of developing nations:* China declared that the United States shouldn't push around smaller nations like North Korea.
- *China's willingness to support arms control relative to other countries, coupled with its unwillingness to draw attention to its own program or set a precedent for retaliation:* China wished to continue its own nuclear testing and force modernization.

Japan

Reasons for Supporting Sanctions (Basically International)

- *To demonstrate commitment to the U.S.–Japan relationship and follow the U.S. lead in security issues, despite trade tensions.*
- *To show commitment to international security efforts after its hesitancy to respond during the Gulf War and international criticism of its checkbook diplomacy.*
- *To demonstrate its commitment to the nonproliferation movement:* There

were suspicions that if North Korea were proved to have a nuclear capability, Japan would entertain the thought of developing its own arsenal.[27]

- *To ensure that it has a place at the table regarding issues related to Korea:* If Japan didn't support sanctions and contribute to solving the proliferation issue, its role in contributing to the Korean problem in the first place as a colonial power could have been emphasized.
- *To preserve the modest improvements made in Japanese–South Korean political and economic relations, despite their still suffering a lack of trust in military and social relations.*

Reasons for Opposing Sanctions (Basically Domestic)

- *Political instability of Japanese domestic politics:* On its third prime minister in almost as many months, Japan was led by a shaky coalition government, which affected the consistency of its foreign policy.[28]
- *Strong influence of the Japan Socialist Party:* The then leader, Tomoiichi Murayama, was the first socialist leader in four decades. Although he was considered a moderate, the JSP did not support sanctions.
- *Difficulty in controlling remittances to North Korea:* Although Murayama was seen as a moderate, the Japan Socialist Party receives a significant amount of support from the pro-Pyongyang Korean minority and would have faced great opposition from that small but quite powerful group if it supported sanctions.
- *Threats by Pyongyang that any moves to cut off remittances would result in retaliation:* Many people felt that Japan was a primary target for North Korean missiles, possibly more so than the Korean brethren in the South.
- *Domestic opposition to participation of the Self-Defense Forces (SDF) in an international embargo:* Japan's current constitution would not allow Japan to participate in a U.N. embargo. The issue of constitutional revision is a hot topic both in Japan and within the region.
- *Fears of reprisal for "squeezing" the Korean minority in Japan:* By attacking the pro-Pyongyang Korean community in Japan, Tokyo could have had a significant "minority" issue on its hands if the pro-Seoul Koreans had rallied behind their pro-Pyongyang brethren, seeing the issue as another slap in the face to the ever-oppressed Koreans in Japan.[29]

Russia

Reasons for Supporting Sanctions

- *To demonstrate commitment to burgeoning Russian–South Korean relations:* Seoul and Moscow had made great strides in economic, diplomatic, and military cooperation in a very short time.
- *To demonstrate commitment to its place in "the Western camp" and try to*

hold onto a role as a political power, if it could be an economic power at that point.

- *To demonstrate commitment to the NPT and prevent being blamed for already having contributed to North Korean nuclear weapons development.*
- *To keep the West happy:* Russia's reliance on Western aid/support for its political and economic survival limited its ability to take stands against those supplying such aid.

Reasons for Opposing Sanctions

- *Retaliation for not being consulted on the draft resolution in mid-June 1994.*
- *Desire to demonstrate that its vote still counted and that it had some clout.*

South Korea

Reasons for Supporting Sanctions

- *To take an active role in drafting sanctions rather than being marginalized by Pyongyang.*
- *To reassert and maintain its coleadership in the negotiations with North Korea, vis-à-vis the United States:* Not only did North Korea succeed in marginalizing Seoul, but the United States effectively marginalized South Korea as well.
- *To assure South Korea of its coleadership of any regional negotiating forum, either during the push for sanctions or in a postsanctions situation.*

Reasons for Opposing Sanctions

- *Fear of retaliation by Pyongyang if sanctions were imposed:* The "sea of fire" comment would not soon be forgotten.
- *To give Pyongyang "a way out" by dealing with South Korea, despite constant marginalization by Pyongyang as it dealt primarily with the United States.*
- *Fear of economic collapse and a subsequent hard landing:* South Korea was keenly aware of the costs of unification, which would have been significantly higher in the event of collapse in the North. After tasting the benefits of economic growth and prosperity, many South Koreans did not wish to lower that standard of living, a situation sure to arise if the North experienced a hard landing.

United States

Reasons for Supporting Sanctions

- *To show strong resolve in foreign policy, an area in which the Clinton administration had been under fire for being too weak and inconsistent.*

- *To demonstrate commitment to the security of the Asia–Pacific region in general and South Korea in particular:* Had concerns regarding the future of the U.S. military presence and security guarantee in the Asia–Pacific region.
- *To show strong resolve for enforcing the NPT and the global nonproliferation regime, by demonstrating to cheaters that they could not avoid serious consequences, and to deter threshold states from entertaining ideas of following North Korea's lead:* The NPT extension conference and the drive for a CTBT weighed heavily on Washington's mind.

Reasons for Opposing Sanctions

- *The feeling that, if Washington was not 100 percent certain that it could (1) get consensus on sanctions and (2) ensure their effectiveness, sanctions should not have been pushed for:* Sanctions are better as a threat than as a reality. If sanctions are implemented and fail, the bargaining leverage is lost.
- *The feeling that, if sanctions succeeded, they could have caused either implosion (collapse) or explosion (retaliation):* Both situations would have been extremely dangerous.
- *To avoid conflict with China.*

Lessons from the Drive for Sanctions

We can see a direct relationship between the increasing prominence of the sanctions issue and the growing tensions on the peninsula and among the participants. However, as sanctions grew in importance, the consensus began to wane as individual factors or conditions affecting each player were brought into starker reality. Although there was unanimity on the severity of the situation, it was impossible to reach a consensus on the appropriate response, due to the marked differences in the circumstances related to their respective domestic and foreign policies.

The "sanctions of June issue" was in reality an attempt that was made to alleviate the problem multilaterally but that was played out and ultimately solved along various bilateral lines, with both positive and negative results. As the tension reached its peak, the exercise became one of a bilateral showdown between North Korea and the United States, resulting fortunately in an improvement in their very strained relationship and subsequently breathing new life into North–South dialogue, IAEA–North Korean dialogue, and further U.S.–North Korean dialogue.

The complexity of the Northeast Asian region makes it difficult to reach multilateral consensus in a timely fashion. In this case, the value of the multilateral effort lay in its success in (1) defining the severity of the issue, (2) defining the priorities of the major players, and (3) maintaining pressure while bilateral dynamics played out. In reality, despite how successfully the international community could rally together, what Pyongyang wanted was direct, high-level talks with the United States, which is exactly what it ultimately got. The nuclear card allowed the North Korean leadership to attain and sustain (sometimes off and on) high-level dialogue at the international negotiating table, most often with its desired partner, Washington.

It appears that bilateral efforts made the difference at critical junctures. But bilateral relations also served to derail the process from time to time, such as U.S.–China tensions over MFN and both Moscow's and Washington's protests of not being consulted prior to the issuing of their respective proposals. The Carter visit let everyone off the hook. With the July 1994 death of Kim Il Sung, the situation was frozen in time, giving all parties, including those of us who were trying to keep up with the situation, some time to breathe.

The Application of CBM Menus in Bilateral Contexts

In attempting to improve relations, timing is everything. What can be offered or agreed upon by one party may not be acceptable or interesting at the same time for all involved. In general, by continuing to strive for improvements in bilateral relationships, it is possible to take advantage of the "windows of opportunity" that may exist for solving a long-standing problem or building confidence—windows which are unlikely to all be open at the same time for all parties involved. By earnestly pursuing policies to understand and address the individual needs and concerns of Northeast Asian neighbors, and in conjunction with efforts to establish regular channels of multilateral dialogue, it is possible to work toward an official multilateral dialogue in the future. However, the latter will always be a difficult struggle.

The bilateral relationships of Northeast Asia are characterized by an intricate blend of political/diplomatic, economic, and military stumbling blocks, while different priorities (economic growth, political reform, military modernization) exist within each country each year.[30] Based on the five Northeast Asian states (China, Japan, North Korea, Russia, and South Korea), there are ten different bilateral relationships, only two of which have any current or previous alliance affiliation (North Korea–China and North Korea–Russia).[31] As a result, there are eight independent relationships, falling at different points along the friend–enemy spectrum, which require the development of measures to promote trust and solve some persistent problems, so that central decision makers will come to see that neighbors are neither the threat they once were nor the threat they might become.

By initially utilizing a combination of basic informational, communication-related, and constraint-oriented CBMs, it is possible to attempt to negotiate what Gerald Segal refers to as an effective menu of à la carte measures.[32] For the

Northeast Asian region, it is also important to include a category of nontraditional CBMs, either quasi-military or nonmilitary CBMs, to deal with comprehensive security concerns, including economic, political, environmental, and cultural security issues. Although the latter category were not part of the European experience, they would prove useful in the intricate Northeast Asian security context.[33] The measures proposed here are very modest in nature. Yet, like the Helsinki CBMs of 1975, they could provide a starting point in developing a habit of dialogue and allow individual pairs of countries to move at their own pace in improving their relations and addressing issues of mutual concern.[34] As most of the threats at this point are not imminent, this exercise has value in establishing avenues of dialogue *before* crisis situations occur and provides a foundation for a regional security dialogue and broader CBM regime in the future. This section traces recent developments in the eight bilateral relationships and delineates modest packages of CBMs that could form the foundation for a more comprehensive regional security mechanism in the near future.

Russian–Japanese Relations

The Northern Territories dispute serves as a diplomatic stumbling block to building confidence as it impedes developments in both the military and economic arenas; consequently, many have argued for delinking the territorial dispute from efforts to develop contacts in other areas. However, some progress has been made. Indeed, after failing to show for two previously scheduled summit meetings, Russian President Boris Yeltsin finally visited Tokyo in October 1993 for a long-awaited summit, at which Yeltsin and then Japanese Prime Minister Morihiro Hosokawa discussed a proposal for the transfer of two of the four disputed islands. If realized, such a development would be the most significant in Japanese-Russian relations to date and would pave the way for greater cooperation, particularly economic, which Japan had stated cannot be fully realized until the dispute is resolved.[35] Returning the disputed Northern Territories has met with strong opposition from within Russia for two reasons: (1) nationalist resistance to losing yet another piece of Russian territory and, more important, (2) reluctance to relinquish the strategic advantages provided by the islands. The islands screen the Sea of Okhotsk, which hosts Russian submarine bases and a ballistic missile–firing area, serve as bases for advanced jet fighters and signals-intelligence posts, and bestow valuable mineral and fishing rights. Although there is little likelihood of Russian military aggression against Japan, the presence of Russian naval, air, and ground forces within sight of Hokkaido coupled with uncertainty in Russia's domestic politics is of concern to Tokyo.[36]

An additional stumbling block in Russian–Japanese relations is Russia's persistent dumping of nuclear waste at sea, which has been carried out for more than twenty years and continues due to the "lack of funds" necessary to establish suitable land-based storage.[37] The dumping endangers both Japanese and South

Korean waters, and Russia has been pressuring Japan for aid in establishing a comprehensive waste-disposal system.

Russia and Japan already signed an agreement on the *Prevention of Incidents at Sea* in September 1992, and military officials have been engaging in a bilateral security dialogue leading to an agreement in 1996 to explore bilateral military CBMs.[38] The two countries have agreed to increase high-level exchanges of officials, promote nonproliferation, enhance the role of the United Nations, and work to make Russia a part of the Asia–Pacific community. Further confidence-building measures could include the following:

- *"No first use of force" declaration.*
- *Exchange of data on defense spending, force structure, and deployment:* Japan is still concerned about Russian deployments in the Far East, especially after the conclusion of the CFE Treaty, and the fate of the Russian Pacific fleet.
- *Exchange of military officials:* This item should include contacts with both central and regional officials, as authority within Russia is steadily devolving to regional administrations and many decisions are increasingly being made by regional commands.[39]
- *Notification of air force and particularly naval maneuvers and movements:*[40] Japan's concern over security of the sea lanes of communication makes this a particularly vital issue. The observation of military maneuvers could be negotiated in the near future, after the mutual dialogue process is under way.
- *Establishment of a hot line and a cool line.*
- *Establishment of a nuclear consultative group:* This group would discuss issues of nuclear nonproliferation, nuclear waste disposal, nuclear safety, and nuclear power. These issues are of mutual concern to both countries and could provide a focus for unofficial discussions of concerns and strategies regarding these issues. The findings could be communicated to the respective governments, providing an unofficial and nonconfrontational dialogue channel between administrations.

Japanese–North Korean Relations

Negotiations on the normalization of relations between Japan and North Korea broke off at the eighth round of talks in Beijing in November 1992, when Pyongyang refused Tokyo's demand for an investigation into the alleged abduction of a Japanese national.[41] However, when there seemed to be an easing of Pyongyang's recalcitrant attitude toward nuclear inspections by the IAEA early in 1993. Tokyo stated in mid-February that it would seek to resume negotiations with Pyongyang, although this was sidelined by the negative events beginning in March 1994, when Pyongyang prevented the IAEA from completing thorough inspections of North Korean nuclear facilities. Nonetheless, Japan is in a good position to participate in economic cooperation with North Korea since it has the money and is not hindered by the intricacies of the reunification issue. Possible confidence-building measures could include the following:

- *"No first use of force" declaration:* Although both North Korea and Tokyo fear the use of nuclear weapons more than conventional weapons, the inclusion of "nuclear" in such a declaration would imply (1) Japan's undeclared intention to develop a nuclear capability and (2) North Korea's current development or possession of nuclear weapons. Discussion of that issue would only serve to impede other CBMs, and thus, a general declaration covering all types of weapons (conventional, chemical, biological, and nuclear) would be more effective.
- *Consultation between defense officials:* Such consultation should be encouraged if only because it establishes a channel for dialogue, available for use in the event of a crisis situation.
- *Notification of military maneuvers in the Sea of Japan:* Although North Korea's cash-strapped economy precludes large-scale military maneuvers at this time, such a promise would be a good place to begin a reciprocal agreement. Japan staged its largest military exercise in postwar history during early October 1993, and the first combined exercise since 1983.[42] Pyongyang would not agree to observation of maneuvers, for fear of revealing weaknesses more than strengths.
- *Consultations on economic cooperation and tourism:* Pyongyang is appealing for foreign investment in free-trade zones, and although the conditions are not favorable for investment due to lack of infrastructure, it is an opportunity for Japan to encourage North Korea out of its isolation, while the cooperative experience could be the basis for greater developments in the political or military realms.[43]

These measures are extremely limited but do represent a start to the process. Basic communication measures are the only reasonable steps that can be suggested at this time.

Japanese–South Korean Relations

Despite a continued underlying lack of trust, relations and cooperation between Japan and South Korea continue to improve. South Korean President Kim Young Sam hosted Japanese Prime Minister Morihiro Hosokawa for a successful summit meeting in November 1993, at which Hosokawa delivered a clear apology to Koreans for Japan's aggression during the colonial period and World War II, the first time a Japanese politician had sufficiently addressed the issue. However, former Justice Minister Shigeto Nagano did significant damage to the goodwill that was engendered by Hosokawa's remarks. Confidence-building measures that have been agreed upon to date include frequent meetings of defense ministers and ranking defense officials; agreements for reciprocal goodwill port calls by naval vessels, which carried Korean Naval Academy cadets to Japan in 1993 while a Japanese warship was scheduled to make a return visit in 1995; and the exchange of flight schedules of military aircraft to aid in avoiding collisions.[44] During the 1994 Rimpac exercises, which ended in late June, the United States, Japan, and South Korea exercised as a team against the Canadian-Australian team, a first but not something that was easily agreed upon. Such agreements represent significant developments in the military sphere, if they are indeed carried out, but compared to bilateral economic and political cooperation, military and cultural exchanges[45] still lag far behind.

Further confidence-building measures could include the following:

- *"Nonuse of force" declaration.*
- *Direct exchange of military information, including published white papers, defense budgets, force structures, weapons systems, and weapons system development information:* As both countries have mutual security treaties with the United States, there is little threat of short-term military confrontation, but the act of exchanging information is more important than the actual information exchanged in establishing the process of information sharing.
- *Exchange of defense officials and defense ministers:* Such an exchange would establish communication on a high level and provide an opportunity to clarify misplaced threat perceptions and discuss mutual concerns.
- *Exchange of military delegations of midranking and lower-ranking military personnel:* Such an exchange would provide the opportunity for better understanding the fundamental nature of each group. This should be conducted on the basis of invitation, demonstrating goodwill and a desire for better relations. The inclusion of naval cadets on warships conducting port calls is an important step.
- *Establishment of hot lines and cool lines:* In the short run, these might serve more as a communication link relating to the North Korean crisis rather than an emergency link between the two countries.
- *Notification of military activities, particularly naval and air, in the Sea of Japan.*
- *Observation of military activities:* This measure could be undertaken by joint teams of Korean and U.S. Forces Korea military personnel and Japanese and U.S. Forces Japan military personnel, with the U.S. forces acting as a buffer between direct Japan–South Korean activity. The U.S. forces, having a working understanding of both militaries, might be well positioned to clarify misunderstandings or aid in communication. This step should be undertaken at first by invitation, along the lines of the Helsinki CBMs, later expanding to obligatory observation.

- *Promotion of the cultural exchange of high school and university students:* Such exchanges would be sponsored by both government and business groups with commercial interests in the other country. Emphasis should be placed on visiting a variety of historic and culturally important sites, providing students the opportunity to understand the foundations of the other culture better and to dispel persistent disdain. In addition, students should be asked to identify issues that they consider to be important on a regional or global scale. Issues of common interest could then serve as a focal point for an ongoing and task-oriented project addressing the concerns. Access to quality mass culture (such as movies, music, and the arts) should be permitted and promoted jointly. This unconventional measure is important to address the persistent lack of accurate understanding about each country. Prejudices persist and will continue to breed suspicions in the future unless they are addressed now.

After implementing these basic information and communication CBMs and developing a habit of consultation, South Korea and Japan could move to apply constraint CBMs. The following inspection CBM might also become feasible:

- *Mutual inspection of facilities related to nuclear energy, the nuclear fuel cycle, and nuclear weapons development capability:* It would be useful to discuss implementation of such an inspection regime, given that both South Korea and Japan are concerned about future weapons development spurred by changes in the international environment.

Sino-Japanese Relations

Both China and Japan share suspicions about each other's aspirations for economic and military dominance in Northeast Asia in the twenty-first century. However, China and Japan have made moves to establish links between both their foreign and defense ministries. In December 1993, inaugural security talks were held, at which Japan's defense policy and China's rapid equipment modernization program were discussed, providing a good starting point from which to proceed with modest CBMs. CBMs that might be considered include the following:

- *"No first use of force" declaration.*
- *Publication and exchange of defense budgets, force structures, and deployment:* China recently issued a white paper in 1992 on defense, although it was a very brief document that contained basically the same information found in the International Institute for Strategic Studies (IISS) *Military Balance.* However, the fact that Beijing produced such a

document at all was a significant step. China's defense budget does not include revenue earned from the production of civilian goods or arms sales, nor does it include arms purchases. Efforts should be made for standardization of this information and subsequent direct exchange.

- *Continued exchange of high-level defense officials:* The military still has a great deal of influence politically in China, and thus, it is important to establish positive relations with those in charge at the higher levels. In addition, the military has become involved in business and development projects. *Economic cooperation* in general, but particularly with *military enterprises producing civilian goods*, could establish a mutually beneficial relationship.
- *Establishment of hot and cool lines.*
- *Notification of naval and air maneuvers or movements:* China, Japan, and Taiwan all claim the disputed Senkaku Islands in the East China Sea.[46] Beijing's recent bold reassertion of its sovereignty over the Senkakus, the Spratly Islands, and the Paracels and subsequent stationing of additional troops in the Spratlies has alarmed many in the region, fearing that Beijing might be willing to take the islands by force. This casts suspicion over unexpected maneuvers or deployments, making advance notification by both parties very important.

The Chinese have been known to value their secrecy, which, although it makes a good case for transparency, necessitates development in a very gradual manner. China staunchly advocates noninterference in the internal affairs of other countries and thus would resist implementation of intrusive measures, at least in the formative stages of a relationship.

Sino–South Korean Relations

Seoul and Beijing have witnessed bilateral trade soar, particularly since they normalized relations in August 1992. Memorandums of understanding have been signed in telecommunications cooperation, joint development of natural resources in the Yellow Sea, high technology, aerospace and automobiles, cultural exchanges, and fisheries concerns. On the diplomatic front, in 1993, China returned the remains of five Korean independence fighters to South Korea, and the two countries have agreed on a joint public servant training program. On the military side, the foreign ministers agreed to exchange military attachés between embassies: four South Korean attachés were sent to Beijing in 1993, while two Chinese army colonels have recently been stationed at a military attaché office in Seoul. Although most of the developments between the two former enemies are in the economic sphere, small steps are being made in the security arena. This heightened interdependency certainly contributed to China's moderating role in the sanctions debate.

CBMs that should also be considered include the following:

- *"Nonuse of force" declaration.*
- *Publication and exchange of defense budgets and force structures.*
- *Notification of naval and air force maneuvers, particularly in the East China Sea.*
- *Hot lines and cool lines:* Such communication channels, for immediate consultation in a crisis, could be most useful in dealing with developments in the North Korean situation.

As Pyongyang's lone remaining ally, Beijing has been sensitive not to alienate Pyongyang by undertaking significant steps in the area of military confidence building and cooperation with Seoul, lest it isolate Pyongyang further and prompt it to resort to drastic measures.[47] By the same token, an exceptionally weak stance on Pyongyang's intransigence could adversely affect the budding Seoul–Beijing relationship. For the time being, a bilateral relationship fostered by economic and industrial cooperation would seem more prudent than seeking far-reaching methods of military cooperation. One area slated for industrial cooperation is the construction, operation, and management of nuclear power plants, which could provide the foundation for a trilateral or multilateral cooperation project with North Korea, which is desperately in need of electricity.[48]

Sino-Russian Relations

The current relationship between Beijing and Moscow is one of the most active of the previously antagonistic relationships in the region and one that has displayed the most characteristics of traditional and successful European-style confidence-building measures. Since the early 1980s, significant unilateral, non-negotiated cuts in border troops and tanks have been made by both Beijing and Moscow.[49] The first formal agreement was not signed until April 24, 1990, when Li Peng visited Moscow to discuss further border reductions. Currently, senior Ministry of Defense officials exchange visits, and officials at the political level meet regularly to discuss issues of regional and global concern.

In December 1992, Boris Yeltsin and Chinese President Yang Shangkun signed a memorandum of understanding, agreeing to accelerate work on a mutual reduction of armed forces in the border region and building confidence in the military sphere across the border, culminating in an agreement by the end of 1994. In 1996, they agreed to reduce armed forces in the designated border region to a minimum level, give remaining troops a clearly defensive nature, and commit to "no first use" of nuclear weapons and refrain from using the threat of nuclear weapons against any non-nuclear state.[50] Prior to the Yeltsin–Yang meeting, the eighth round of Sino-Russian disarmament talks was held, resulting in a commitment to eventually withdraw both parties' main forces back 100 kilometers on each side of the border to establish a 200 kilometer stability zone of decreased military activity.[51] In November 1993, Russian Defense Minister Pavel Grachev met with his Chinese counterpart, Chi Haotian, in Beijing, the first visit by a Russian defense minister to China since the Soviet breakup. In establishing further confidence-building measures, they agreed to send three additional military attachés to each capital; exchange military delegations; jointly develop a new jet fighter for China, the Super 7, based on the Russian MiG-21; and signed a five-year agreement on military cooperation and the promotion of friendly relations between the two armies. The most recent agreement is the accord on the Prevention of Dangerous Military Activities (PDMA) along the border during maneuvers, accidental missile firings, or unintended frontier violations.[52]

Ironically, the success of these bilateral confidence-building measures can have a potentially adverse effect on other regional players, which might view the new relationship as a little too cozy for comfort. Pyongyang has certainly been isolated by this evolution, as it can no longer play China and Russia off against each another. Japan and South Korea may also be threatened by such a development in the future. Such is the paradox of bilateral confidence building in a regional context: confidence building in one case can stimulate confidence erosion in another.

Russian–South Korean Relations

Russia has eyed South Korea as a possible substitute economic partner for Japan, yet despite surging two-way trade, which has doubled between 1989–1994, the economic and political cooperation foreseen when diplomatic relations were restored in 1990 has failed to materialize for two main reasons: (1) Seoul's suspension of economic aid due to Moscow's tardy servicing of interest payments on previous loans and (2) Russia's refusal to pay compensation for victims of the Korean Air Lines (KAL) flight shot down in 1984.[53] However, the successful summit meetings between Kim Young Sam and Boris Yeltsin held in June seem to have served to kick-start an increasingly cooperative relationship.[54]

Military ties have been expanding rapidly, and Russia is hoping to expand military cooperation with South Korea. In August 1993, a Russian flotilla paid a goodwill visit to Pusan, the first since 1904, while two South Korean ships made a return port call in Vladivostok one month later. Russia has proposed joint naval drills, but Seoul has yet to agree. An agreement for personnel exchanges, including defense ministers and ranking military officials, has been signed. Russia envisages increased military exchanges, leading to joint rescue exercises for fishing boats and ultimately combined drills.[55] The two countries have agreed to coproduce modern weapons, utilizing South Korean capital and marketing expertise and Russian technological expertise. They have established a hot line between the Kremlin and the Blue House, which was used one week after installation during the mounting crisis in June 1994. During Kim Young Sam's summit trip, he visited the Russian fleet in Vladivostok—a very symbolic end to Russian–South Korean Cold War tensions, which sent a strong message to North Korea.

Russia seems to have little concern for the impact that closer relations with Seoul will have on Pyongyang. Although North Korea still permits Russia over-flight rights en route to Vietnam, the two countries have ceased joint naval maneuvers since 1990. Russia has also terminated nuclear and military assistance to its former close ally. Although the Treaty of Friendship, Cooperation and Military Assistance signed in 1961 remains in effect, Article 1, which promises military intervention in the event of conflict, is essentially null and void.[56]

North–South Korean Relations

The North–South relationship is currently at an impasse, as Pyongyang insists on dealing directly with the United States on the NPT issue. However, North and South Korea had made progress in the realm of confidence building by agreeing to the Agreement on Reconciliation, Non-Aggression, and Exchange and Coop-eration at the sixth inter-Korean prime ministers' talks in 1990.[57] During the talks, Seoul indicated its acceptance of Pyongyang's proposal for simultaneous, mutual inspections and went further to propose a simultaneous trial inspection at the end of January 1992. In addition, it signed the joint North–South Declaration on the Denuclearization of the Korean Peninsula, on December 31, 1991, pledg-ing the renunciation of nuclear processing and uranium enrichment facilities and a North–South reciprocal inspection, to be carried out by the Joint Nuclear Control Commission (JNCC). Disagreements over the scope of inspections and the necessity of challenge inspections prevented progress of the JNCC and served as a warning sign to Seoul that Pyongyang was stalling for time to develop its nuclear weapons capabilities.[58] However, regardless of previous steps and agree-ments relating to arms control and confidence building, it would seem that there is little hope for the resumption of positive steps until the NPT crisis is resolved.

There has been endless debate in Seoul regarding the use of carrots and/or sticks in dealing with Pyongyang's intransigence. The main carrot to be offered by both Seoul and the international community would be economic assistance, whereas the primary stick would be economic sanctions. Although investment is desperately needed, it would almost certainly be accompanied by a foreign pres-ence, which would bring both polluting influences to North Korean society and potential witnesses to North Korea's decay and suspected human rights viola-tions, thereby "poisoning" this particular carrot.[59]

The challenge for Kim Jong Il is how to attract desperately needed foreign investment and aid without allowing information from the outside world to filter in or permitting the international community to truly witness the state of internal affairs. Confirmation of reported human rights violations would almost certainly pose barriers to valuable economic aid, and Pyongyang must surely be sensitive to Washington's policy toward China, linking the renewal of most favored nation status with an improvement in its human rights record. There is clearly an inverse relationship between the amount of information that seeps in or out and the prospects for the survival of the Kim regime. However, the situation will be even more of a question mark until it is determined just what strategy Kim Jong Il will utilize to hold onto power, openness or isolation, and if indeed he survives at all.

Bilateral Confidence-Building Measures: A Summary

Bilateral confidence-building measures can be useful in dealing with the issue-specific nature of relations in Northeast Asia, and they provide flexibility in circumventing stumbling blocks that would otherwise be roadblocks in a multilateral confidence-building regime. The proposals that have been suggested here are extremely modest and militarily insignificant, primarily utilizing informational and communication-related CBMs, while leaving verification and constraint CBMs for application after some barriers of mistrust and misperception have been broken down. Verification plays a vital role in confidence building, but at the outset, it is important for nations to get to the table and establish channels for dialogue. There is reason for caution, however. With every improvement in bilateral relations, there is the possibility of a counter-reaction by another regional member, which may feel threatened when a previously adversarial or benign relationship improves, as evidenced by North Korea's mounting feeling of isolation. For this reason, it is important to work simultaneously toward enhancing a regional security dialogue process as well.

An Exercise in Regional Cooperation

For a number of years now, a host of proposals have been advanced to establish a framework for a multilateral security dialogue in Asia, at both the regional and subregional levels. Although opposed at first by the Americans, Japanese, and Chinese, the idea has been gradually accepted, but difficulties have arisen over the form. Finally, on a large regional scale, there is now the Association of Southeast Asian Nations (ASEAN) Regional Forum[60] at the governmental level and the Conference on Security and Cooperation in the Asia–Pacific (CSCAP) at the nongovernmental level[61] as venues for dialogue. Establishing a consensus or implementing confidence-building measures on such a wide scale, however, is difficult at best due to the large number of countries involved and their divergent interests.

The difficulty in establishing a regional security framework is in trying to find a common, tangible interest from which all states benefit and from which none suffers. As Stewart Henderson notes: "States do not base their security on altruistic, unfounded notions of cooperation. It is only through an appeal to national interests that the building blocks of a cooperative security system will be put in place. Cooperative security is not a theory but a practical method of dealing with important issues."[62]

Arguably, the North Korean NPT crisis could have served as a focal point for regional cooperation since it was the greatest threat to regional and quite possibly international security.[63] This issue, more than any other issue, demonstrated the perils associated with lack of trust, the absence of reliable information, and insensitivity to the fears of other states. However, as described earlier in this chapter, although the NPT crisis served as a catalyst in bringing together nations that would otherwise not have cooperated on international foreign policy, it also served as a divisive issue, underscoring the difficulties inherent in the multilateral approach to problem solving. Therefore, although it is in the interests of all to continue to work together to improve the situation on the Korean Peninsula, the NPT crisis did not quite fit the necessary criteria for a multilateral solution.

It is a tall order to find such a common problem acceptable for cooperation by all Northeast Asian states. But one exists now that is a threat to all in the region, and that all states—even North Korea—could cooperate in addressing—namely, the dumping of nuclear waste (primarily and most extensively by Russia) into the Sea of Japan.

In April 1993, it was revealed that Moscow had been dumping nuclear waste into the Sea of Japan at least since the earliest records were kept in 1966. Public outcry has been especially loud in Japan, as the dumping is practically on its doorstep, but both Koreas and China have also condemned the dumping.[64] Tokyo was particularly enraged that Moscow would dump nuclear waste on Japan's doorstep, seemingly without any warning, only days after Yeltsin had visited Japan to improve bilateral relations.[65]

Russia claims that it has no choice but to dump the waste at sea because it lacks the storage capacity on land, and the amount currently stored on floating tankers is growing as submarines and other atomic-powered navy vessels are being decommissioned. In late February, 1994, Russia said that it could not ratify the permanent ban on nuclear dumping but would "endeavor to avoid pollution of the sea by dumping of wastes and other matter," according to the International Maritime Organization.[66] However, subsequent reports indicated that Russia continued dumping. Japan has recently pledged $100 million to help with the construction of storage facilities. Japan also agreed to finance the construction of a reprocessing plant by Japanese firms in Russia's Far East if Russia stops the dumping, although this plant would take two years to construct.

Although numerous multilateral environmental and economic cooperative projects are already under way in the region, the radioactive waste problem is unique in that it is highly visible, politically significant, and cuts across political, environmental, security, and nuclear safety concerns, thus providing a good opportunity for joint cooperative efforts in achieving a common goal. This issue overlaps a wide range of government agencies and officials from departments of foreign affairs, environment, science and technology, national security, and maritime and port administrations. Cooperation by similar ministries of the regional members could be a prime example of a nontraditional CBM, as it would establish a channel for dialogue in which all have a common goal. Perhaps 80 percent of the people who would be involved in an arms-control and confidence-building dialogue would have to be involved in such a project.

The issue involves not only the dumping of low-level radioactive waste—which is a highly visible, political, and psychological issue—but also dealing with the spent fuel rods upon decommissioning. These rods, which are highly radioactive and can be reprocessed for use in a bomb, pose both a safety and a safeguards risk. Finally, there is the issue of the reactors, which must be physically extracted from the vessels and dealt with effectively. In the past, they have been dumped in the ocean as well. With a hundred more ships to be decommissioned in the near future, thirty to forty of which use nuclear propulsion, this issue is timely and a time bomb, not only in the environmental sense but as it affects Russia's relations with its neighbors. It is critical to view such an approach not as an opportunity to condemn Russia for what it has done, for this would be a confidence-destroying measure. Rather, it should be viewed as a constructive way to improve the situation for all in the region by mobilizing financial resources, technology, and enthusiasm from where they exist and utilizing them to jointly address a regional problem that affects everyone.

The public perception of nuclear issues, whether they involve weapons or energy or waste, is of great concern to all the Northeast Asian administrations, which are all committed to nuclear energy. Negative press on this issue could pose domestic challenges as people question the safety of the nuclear energy option. This could provide the Northeast Asian states with a viable, necessary, and mutually beneficial project for cooperation. Coupled with efforts to improve bilateral relations, an issue-driven framework could be expanded into a regional security dialogue in the future, once efforts on the bilateral side level address the stumbling blocks to larger cooperation and facilitate the view of a common house.

Notes

1. James Macintosh, "Key Elements of a Conceptual Approach to Confidence Building," in *Arms Control in the North Pacific: The Role for Confidence Building and Verification* (Ottawa: Verification Research Unit, Non-Proliferation, Arms Control and Disarmament Division, External Affairs and International Trade Canada, April 1993), 65.

2. *Korea Herald,* June 1, 1994, 1.

3. Ibid., May 31, 1994, 1.

4. Washington reacted with "deep dismay," whereas Japan voiced little concern, as "the very old missile" was not considered to be too threatening. *Korea Times,* June 2, 1994, 1.

5. Son Key-young, *Korea Times,* June 2, 1994, 2.

6. The idea of an eight-way conference on the North Korean nuclear issue was first

suggested in late March 1994. It would include the two Koreas; the neighboring countries of Japan, China, and Russia; the United States; and representatives from both the United Nations and its nuclear agency, the IAEA. The proposal, issued without prior consultation with the United States, caused great consternation in Washington, as it saw Russia trying to flex its diplomatic muscles like a superpower, which, in Washington's opinion, it clearly was not. See Stephane Bentura, "Russia's Diplomatic Assertiveness Troubles U.S.," *Korea Herald,* March 27, 1994, 5. At that time, Japan gave the idea a guarded welcome, appreciating Russia's interest and pledging to study the idea further. The United States was cool to the idea, stating that the United Nations was the best venue through which to resolve the issue. South Korea echoed Washington, noting the intention but advocating the UNSC as the appropriate channel.

7. At the Yeltsin–Kim Young Sam summit in Moscow, Yeltsin said that Article 1 of the (North) Korea–Soviet Treaty of Friendship, Cooperation, and Mutual Assistance, signed in 1961, which promises military intervention upon an attack against North Korea, was dead. Statements had been made in late April that the obligation was nonbinding given the change in the international political environment. See *Korea Herald,* June 3, 1994, 1. The summit was a feather in the cap of Kim Young Sam, as it served to further enhance an already cooperative relationship with North Korea's former ally. Great strides were made in the areas of military confidence building and defense, science, and technical cooperation, despite the sticky issue of Russia's remiss loan repayments to South Korea.

8. Japan's package included: (1) a ban on trade, including commerce through third countries; (2) a ban on government officials' traveling to North Korea; (3) a ban on allowing North Korean officials to come to Japan; (4) strict control of immigration procedures; (5) restrictions on cultural, sports, and scientific exchanges; (6) a ban on flights between the two countries; (7) an export ban on weapons and weapons-related goods and materials; (8) a ban on investments and loans, including bank transfers; (9) restrictions on cash carried to North Korea by Koreans from Japan. See Walter Mears (AP), "Sanctions on N.K. Imperative: Clinton," *Korea Herald,* June 5, 1994, 1. Prior to this declaration, Japanese banks blocked the flow of U.S. dollars to North Korea, although they continued to remit other currencies such as the yen and mark. The government did not accept responsibility for the decision; instead, it stated that the banks acted autonomously. Under U.S. law, U.S. banks have been prohibited from remitting dollars to North Korea, and Japanese banks feared the case would become a diplomatic issue. See *Korea Times,* May 20, 1994, 1.

9. There are approximately 260,000 pro-Pyongyang Korean residents in Japan, largely concentrated in Osaka, who reportedly take or remit between $700 million and $1 billion in cash and goods each year to North Korea. Given the rise of the yen in recent years and the shrinking of the North Korean economy, the annual inflow from Japan would have exceeded the entire 1990 North Korean budget and may now represent two years' worth of Pyongyang's budget. Katsumi Sato, "Japan Stop Funding Kim Il Sung," *Far Eastern Economic Review (FEER)* 156, no. 36 (September 9, 1993), 23. See also David E. Sanger, "Cash for N.K. N-Plant Traced to Osaka," *Korea Herald,* November 2, 1993, 1; and Charles Smith, "Cash Lifeline," *FEER* 156, no. 30 (July 29, 1993), 23. One source noted, "It is true that there are numerous [North Korean] agents in Japan, and it is extremely difficult to keep track of them. That is more disturbing than missiles." Mears, "Sanctions on N. K. Imperative," 1.

10. *Korea Herald,* June 7, 1994, 1.

11. According to Teruaki Ueno (Reuters), pro-Pyongyang ethnic Koreans bitterly criticized Japan on Monday, June 6, 1994 over the threat to impose economic sanctions against North Korea for refusing to submit to nuclear inspections. [R]estrictions on cash remittances and travel by Koreans between Japan and North Korea would raise a grave

human rights issue," said a representative for the General Association of Korean Residents in Japan. *Korea Herald,* June 8, 1994, 1.

12. Russia further showed where its allegiance lay by (1) returning Korean War documents to South Korea, proving once and for all that North Korea launched the Korean War; (2) promising to stop selling weapons to North Korea; and (3) possibly undertaking joint military cooperation. *Korea Times,* June 8, 1994, 1.

13. Conditions for such a meeting are stated under Article 91 of the constitution. Such meetings are called at times of crisis and policy decisions forged at these meetings generally carry substantial weight. This was the first such meeting to be called by Kim Young Sam since he took office.

14. *Korea Herald,* June 8, 1994, 1.

15. Ibid.

16. *Korea Times,* June 16, 1994, 1.

17. Phase one included a mandatory arms embargo; a ban on all traffic except passenger flights; suspension of financial assistance; a ban on scientific, technological, and cultural cooperation; and a reduction in diplomatic ties. Phase two, which would require an additional resolution to implement, would freeze Pyongyang's overseas assets, cut off remittances, and perhaps place a ban on China's crude oil supplies. No mention is made of Russia's suggested eight-party conference. *Korea Times,* June 17, 1994, 2.

18. *Korea Herald,* June 17, 1994, 1.

19. The issue is a reverse of the situation in March 1994, when Russia proposed its conference idea without prior notification to Washington. At times, it seemed like children's play: one would not have known that the stakes were so high only from observing the behavior of the two.

20. There are a host of questions surrounding the Carter visit that are puzzling: (1) Was Carter a truly independent agent? (2) Did the White House use him as the one acceptable high-profile intermediary? (3) The State Department is staffed by ex-Carterites. Who approached whom? (4) Was there a physical obstacle to communication with Carter in Pyongyang? (5) Did Carter overstep his bounds in terms of what he promised? (6) Was the White House distancing simply a result of lack of unanimity in the State Department and the Pentagon? (7) Were Carter/Clinton naive in the sense that the visit simply provided Kim Il Sung with a photo opportunity and propaganda mileage? (8) Was the "private citizen" argument simply a ploy to enable the White House to disown Carter if the trip went poorly? (9) Did Carter provide a way to allow Clinton to extricate himself from the sanctions impasse?

21. *Korea Times,* May 14, 1994, 1.

22. Calls were made on May 12 and May 24 to reconsider the joint Declaration on the Denuclearization of the Korean Peninsula, which, among other things, prohibits the possession of any facilities to reprocess or enrich uranium. The radiochemical laboratory would violate that provision. However, the government reaffirmed its commitment to denuclearization on May 27.

23. *Korea Herald,* June 19, 1994, 1.

24. Ibid.

25. *Korea Times,* June 30, 1994, 1.

26. The United States and China had recently gone head-to-head recently on a number of issues. Washington continued to tie renewal of China's most favored nation trading status to China's human rights violations and ballistic missile sales, particularly the shipment of M-9 and M-11 missiles to Pakistan, Iran, and Syria.

27. Comments by former Prime Minister Tsutomo Hata on June 17, 1994, brought this issue to center stage. He remarked, "It's certainly the case that Japan has the capability to possess nuclear weapons but has not made them" due to its obligations under the

NPT. *Korea Herald,* June 22, 1994, 1. Hata later denied having made the remarks. Such comments, combined with the large stockpile of plutonium that Japan had to fuel its fast-breeder reactor, led many to speculate that, given a change in the security situation or the political winds, Japan would "go nuclear" in a snap.

28. Comments by former (and extremely short-lived) Justice Minister Shigeto Nagano of the Hata government nearly obliterated the positive steps that former Prime Minister Hosokawa took in late March 1994, by sincerely apologizing for Japan's World War II aggression. Nagano, a former army captain during the war who rose to army chief of staff before entering politics, commented that the Nanjing massacre was a "fabrication" and that it was "wrong" to say that the Pacific war was waged with the aim of aggression, but rather, it was an effort to liberate Asia from European colonialism. Despite a retraction, and Nagano's resignation, Asian nations responded with great fury and protests. See *Korea Herald,* May 5, 8, and 12, 1994.

29. During the June crisis, Japanese authorities attempted to discover the pro-North Korean Residents Association or Chosen Soren's records of remittances to North Korea. After a significant chase from chapter to chapter of the Chosen Soren, Japanese authorities raided a North Korean middle school looking for the records. Huge bipartisan demonstrations erupted, with Koreans seeing the issue as an affront to their race. During the same period, as tensions were mounting, there were frequent attacks against North Korean schoolgirls, easily identified by their distinctly Korean school uniforms. Their dresses were slashed, and some were physically attacked by Japanese fed up with the North Korean nuclear standoff.

30. For example, South Korean President Kim's priority in 1993 was domestic political reform and the eradication of corruption; in 1994, it was economic revival through internationalization and globalization.

31. This also excludes the two most important bilateral relationships, those existing between the United States and both Japan and South Korea. Their maintenance is critical to the security of the Northeast Asian subregion and the Asia–Pacific region as a whole.

32. Gerald Segal, "Northeast Asia's Common Security or à la Carte?" *International Affairs* 67, no. 4 (October 1991), 755–767.

33. For a comprehensive explanation of CBMs and the additional category of nontraditional CBMs, see Macintosh, "Key Elements of a Conceptual Approach to Confidence Building," 57–78.

34. For the purposes of this chapter, the suggestions for bilateral confidence–building measures are mostly confined to transparency measures (information, notification, and exchange measures). Of course, developments in the areas of economic and environmental cooperation are invaluable to promoting shared interests and should be strongly encouraged.

35. Yeltsin articulated his strategy on the normalization of Russian-Japanese relations in a plan proposed in 1990, in which he envisaged a progression through five stages: (1) official recognition of the territorial problem; (2) demilitarization of the four disputed islands; (3) establishment of a zone of free enterprise on the islands with an agreement to cooperate on trade, economic, techno-scientific, cultural, and humanitarian matters; (4) signing of a peace treaty; and (5) resolution of the territorial issue over a period of fifteen to twenty years. Although Russia claimed that this approach could make the islands a uniting rather than a divisive factor, such a protracted solution did not satisfy Tokyo.

36. See Robert R. Rau, "Japan's Growing Involvement," *U.S. Naval Institute Proceedings* 119, no. 12 (December 1993): 66.

37. A Russian government report, produced by environmentalists and other officials, indicated that the Soviet Union and its successor Russia tossed more than 144,000 cubic meters of liquid and solid radioactive waste into the East Sea and waters near Kamchatka

between 1966 and 1992, on 216 occasions. See "Soviet Union Dumped N-Waste in Far Eastern, Arctic Seas," *Korea Times,* April 4, 1993, 1.

38. Russia also has bilateral INCSEA agreements with Canada, the United States, and Korea.

39. In addition, the Russian Far East administrations are increasingly participating in independent commercial ventures and retaining the receipts for use in the region. This could lead to differences between official policy or figures flowing from Moscow and actual activity occurring in the Far East. The potential for illegal entrepreneurial activity exists, including the smuggling of consumer goods from Japan, South Korea, and China. Reports have indicated that Pacific fleet personnel actively smuggle goods or help civilian smugglers violate borders.

40. Providing one day of notice, Russia dispatched a cruiser into the South China Sea, near the disputed Spratly Islands, on the pretext of protecting Russian vessels from pirate attacks. Japanese officials suspected that the piracy patrols could be a rationale for future naval buildup in the area, given that Russian vessels have not been subject to pirate attack for some time. Japan was notably disturbed by such unexpected action. *Japan Times,* August 25, 1993, 2.

41. North Korean terrorist Kim Hyun-hee, who planted a bomb on a South Korean airplane that exploded off Myanmar in 1987, confessed that she had learned Japanese from a Japanese woman who had been abducted from Japan by North Korean agents. *Korea Herald,* February 18, 1994, 2.

42. The exercise involved 9,000 ground self-defense force (GSDF) members, 37,000 maritime SDF (MSDF) personnel, and 46,000 air SDF (ASDF) personnel, operating a total of 120 ships and 760 aircraft. The navy and air force held joint antisubmarine and antiaircraft exercises with the U.S. Navy and Air Force. *Korea Times,* October 3, 1993, 1.

43. The Ranjin–Songbong special economic zone is located in the northeast corner of North Korea and is part of the Tumen River development area, a "grandiose" project backed by the United Nations Development Project, intended to open up the hinterland of China, North Korea, and Russia. According to Mark Clifford, the Tumen River project is a pipe dream in search of money. However, there are a number of interested investors, but the NPT crisis slowed progress. See Clifford, "Send Money," *FEER* 156, no. 39 (September 30, 1993), 72; and Ed Paisley, "White Knights," *FEER* 157, no. 9 (March 3, 1994), 46.

44. These agreements were made by South Korean Defense Minister Rhee Byoung-tae and his Japanese counterpart, Kazuo Aichi. See *Korea Herald,* May 7, 1994, 1.

45. To date, Japanese mass popular culture, including music and films, is prohibited by law from entering South Korea. Although there have been discussions for some time directed toward lifting the ban, opposition is strong.

46. The Senkakus lie approximately equidistant from Okinawa and Taiwan, bestowing more than 21,000 square kilometers of continental shelf, believed to contain one of the last unexplored sources of oil and natural gas in maritime Asia. Sovereignty would extend to the airspace above the claim as well. See Rau, "Japan's Growing Involvement," 66.

47. China and North Korea still maintain their relationship as allies, requiring each to intervene automatically if the other is engaged in war against a third country, although, in reality, China's ties with Seoul have become increasingly stronger and Beijing would not blindly support adventuristic action by Pyongyang.

48. For further details, see Yu Kun-ha, "Seoul, Beijing Seek Industrial Alliance," *Korea Herald,* February 20, 1994, 8.

49. For more detailed discussion of the unilateral reductions along the border by both China and the Soviet Union, see Gerald Segal, "A New Order in Northeast Asia," *Arms Control Today* 17, no. 7 (September 1991): 14.

50. Pledges were also made to improve trade and cooperation in the conversion of

defense industries, construction of atomic power plants, and outer space research, to name a few.

51. See Bonnie S. Glaser, "China's Security Perceptions: Interests and Ambitions," *Asian Survey* 33, no. 3 (March 1993): 256.

52. The agreement was signed by defense ministers Pavel Grachev and Chi Haotian on July 12, 1994. In addition, Russia offered to help with training for the operation of Russia's Sukhoi-27 warplanes, which China purchased in 1993, and with the S-300 air defense missile system, which it is trying to sell to China. *Korea Times,* July 14, 1994, p.1.

53. Although Russia has offered to settle some of its debts through weapons transfers, Seoul would be unlikely to accept because of incompatibility with U.S. equipment and Washington's obvious opposition. Regarding the airliner issue, Russia has failed to reveal whether it recovered any of the bodies or belongings from the crash and accepts no responsibility, citing the jet's failure to respond to warnings, a claim staunchly disputed by Seoul. For details, see Shim Jae Hoon, "Russian Roulette," *FEER* 156, no. 40 (October 7, 1993), 30.

54. Seoul welcomed the efforts of the Russian government initiated by Yeltsin to clear past issues. These efforts included: (1) restoration of the dignity of ethnic Koreans in Russia; (2) publication of documents related to the KAL incident; and (3) delivery of the archive documents on the Korean War, proving that North Korea started the war. See "Text of the Joint Declaration," *Korea Herald,* June 3, 1994, 2.

55. South Korea has only one chopper and one boat for rescue operations. The boat tragedy of October 10, 1993, which left 200 people dead or missing, proved that the maritime police were incompetent in rescue operations. New attention placed on joint search and rescue operations could be of benefit in preventing of future tragedies.

56. Russia reportedly sold twelve submarines to North Korea in 1993–1994, allegedly for use as scrap metal. However, some analysts feel that North Korea might use the old Russian subs to upgrade its own fleet. Russia reserves the right to sell parts to North Korea, although it is not likely to do so in the near future.

57. The basic agreement on nonaggression contains the following provisions: (1) no use of force and no armed aggression against the other side; (2) peaceful settlement of differences and disputes through dialogue and negotiation; (3) designation of the military demarcation line and zone of nonaggression; (4) establishment and operation of a North–South Joint Military Commission to implement and guarantee nonaggression along with confidence-building matters; (5) installation of a telephone hot line between the military authorities of both sides; and (6) formation of a North–South Military Commission to discuss concrete measures for the implementation and observance of the agreement and the elimination of military confrontation. See Tae Hwan Kwak, "Inter-Korean Military Confidence Building: A Creative Implementation Formula," *Korea Observer* 24, no. 3 (autumn 1993): 381.

58. See Paik Jin Hyun, "Nuclear Conundrum: Analysis and Assessment of Two Koreas' Policy Regarding the Nuclear Issue," *Korea and World Affairs* 17, no. 4 (winter 1993): 632.

59. See Paul Bracken, "Nuclear Weapons and State Survival in North Korea," *Survival* 35, no. 3 (autumn 1993): 150.

60. The foreign ministers of the ASEAN announced the establishment of an official forum for the purpose of developing a constructive pattern of political and security relationships and dialogue on Asia–Pacific issues. Participants include ministers from the ASEAN, its dialogue partners, and ASEAN Post-Ministerial Conference (PMC) observers (China, Russia, Vietnam, Laos, and Papua New Guinea). In conjunction, a Senior Officials Meeting (SOM) is held a few months prior to the ASEAN Regional Forum (ARF),

involving representatives from all countries participating in the ARF. On the agenda at the 1994 meeting were topics of preventative diplomacy, conflict management, nonproliferation, confidence-building measures, and Northeast Asian security.

61. The CSCAP is the newest and most wide-reaching nongovernmental avenue for dialogue. The concept was developed in 1992, and the forum was officially announced in June 1993. The CSCAP consists of ten founding institutions from around the Asia–Pacific rim. They include: (1) the Strategic and defense Studies Centre, Australian National University; (2) the University of Toronto–York University Joint Centre for Asia–Pacific Studies, Canada; (3) the Center for Strategic and International Studies, Indonesia; (4) the Japan Institute for International Affairs; (5) the Seoul Forum for International Affairs, Korea; (6) the Institute of Strategic and International Studies, Malaysia; (7) the Institute for Strategic and Development Studies, the Philippines; (8) the Singapore Institute of International Affairs; (9) the Institute for Security and International Studies, Thailand; and (10) the Pacific Forum/CSIS, United States. Each institution is charged with coordinating academics, specialists, and officials operating in their private capacities to collaborate in working groups to address specific issues related to security (widely defined) in the region. Topics currently being addressed in these working groups and on the agenda for the first meeting include maritime cooperation in Southeast Asia, security cooperation in the North Pacific, defining cooperative and comprehensive security, confidence- and security-building measures, transparency, and preventing the proliferation of weapons of mass destruction. The CSCAP also seeks to coordinate its efforts with those of the ASEAN Regional Forum by conveying to the ARF research on issues under current examination and of particular concern to the CSCAP. This coordination of efforts is particularly important in order to prevent the duplication of research, disseminate research findings, and provide a channel for enhanced communication among institutions in the region.

62. Stewart Henderson, *Canada and Asia–Pacific Security—Recent Trends,* NPCSD working paper 1 (Toronto: York University, 1991), 2.

63. According to CIA Director James Woolsey, North Korea represents the highest potential for instability in the world, cited in *Korea Herald,* February 26, 1994, 1. The comment was made prior to the IAEA's unsuccessful attempt to carry out desired inspections fully, the subsequent referral of the situation to the U.N. Security Council, and North Korea's comment that Seoul would turn into a "sea of flames" if Pyongyang were provoked by sanctions or the resumption of the Team Spirit military exercises.

64. China announced a ban on nuclear waste dumping on February 18, 1994. The new rules conform to the three resolutions approved in 1993 by the international Convention on the Prevention of Marine Pollution. Beijing stated that "disposing of wastes without a license or dumping irresponsibly at sea will be punished severely." *Korea Herald,* February 20, 1994, 5.

65. However, Moscow did inform one of the three nuclear watchdogs, the IAEA, two weeks in advance of its plan, but the international body failed to pass on the information. The dumping occurred at precisely the same time that IAEA Director General Hans Blix was in Seoul participating in the IAEA-sponsored International Symposium on Advanced Nuclear Power Systems. Greenpeace condemned Blix and the IAEA, stating, "The IAEA's failure to inform the governments involved clearly shows where its intention lies—not in environmental or human protection, but in promotion of nuclear power and radioactive waste dumping." That same day, Blix met with President Kim Young Sam, expressing his concern over North Korea's nuclear weapons program, which Greenpeace called a terrible contradiction. See *Korea Times,* October 20, 1993, 4.

66. *Korea Herald,* February 23, 1994, 1.

Part Four

External Challenges:
Korea and the Major Powers

15

Nuclear Forces in Northeast Asia

Gerald Segal

By nearly common consent, the uncertainty over the status of nuclear forces in Northeast Asia is the most dangerous feature of Asia–Pacific security. Although most attention has been paid to the status of North Korea's nuclear program, too little attention has been paid to the way in which the status of existing nuclear forces in the region affects the North Korean problem. It is true that the two largest acknowledged nuclear powers, Russia and the United States, have been reducing their forces in recent years, but they still remain by far the largest nuclear powers in the region.[1] The main focus of this chapter is to assess the status of nuclear forces in Northeast Asia in order to identify ways in which the great powers and the states of the region can help limit the risks derived from North Korea's apparent attempt to acquire a nuclear weapons capability.

At the outset, it should be acknowledged that this chapter is not about the complete denuclearization of Northeast Asia. Although that may be an eventual objective, it will only come about as part of a broader denuclearization by the acknowledged nuclear powers. The United States, Russia, and China deploy nuclear weapons in the region because they see it as a vital arena of international affairs. All three powers have territory and vital interests in the region. The future of the nuclear weapons of these powers involves the problem of denuclearization, whereas the concerns over North Korea and Japan involve threats of nuclear proliferation. These issues are distinct, but linked, and it is the linkage that motivates and animates this chapter.

The Status of Nuclear Forces

This section is intended to set out the facts as we know them, but in truth, there are few "facts" that can be reliably described.[2] One clear fact is that there are only three nuclear weapons powers in Northeast Asia (Russia, the United States, and China). But even this statement contains ambiguities, for it is impossible to offer a tight definition of Northeast Asia. For the purposes of this chapter, "the region" is defined as a circle that stretches out 1,500 kilometers in all directions and whose center is the middle of the Korean demilitarized zone (DMZ). (The reason why this zone is selected is discussed later in this section.)

A second uncertainty is that it is impossible to know what cuts have been made as part of the continuing Strategic Arms Reduction Talks (START) process. This chapter offers some guesses, but they are no more than that. Some Russian officials suggest that even they do not know how many nuclear weapons they deploy in the region at any one time, so a civilian analyst working with public sources will know even less. It is chilling to recall the "discovery" of a wagonload of nuclear missiles near Kurgan (western Siberia) that were "mislaid due to the negligence of railway staff."[3]

Finally, for the purposes of this chapter, we assume that, as the United States and Russia assert, there are no sea-based tactical systems on operational duty in the region. We assume that there are tactical systems in store. Weapons can be on "inactive reserve" or "retired," which means that although not operational, they have not been destroyed.[4]

The United States apparently has no operational deployment of tactical systems in Northeast Asia, nor are there any operational land-based or air-launched strategic systems in the region. Tactical systems are unlikely to be stored in the region, although the phrase "stored centrally" probably does include Hawaii. There are eight Ohio-class SSBNs (*SSBN*, or strategic submarine ballistic nuclear, is the U.S. Navy's term for a ballistic missile submarine), each with twenty-four missiles. The SLBMs (submarine-launched ballistic missiles) are Trident 1 C-4s, first deployed in 1980. They have a range of 7,400 kilometers, a throw weight of 15,000 kilograms, and carry eight 100–kiloton warheads with a circular error probable (CEP) of 450 meters. Under START II, these missiles are to be downloaded to about half their current number of warheads.

The Russians, unlike the United States, have territory in Northeast Asia, and therefore, they have a different configuration of forces. Tactical systems are present in both land-based and air-launched form, but reliable data on these forces are impossible to obtain. Some analysts suggest that one can assume that roughly a third of all Russian tactical nuclear weapons are in the region, but this assumption is usually based on the rather dubious comparison with strategic nuclear systems, in which a third of the capability can be found in the region. We assume there are at most 1,000 tactical warheads in the Russian portion of Northeast Asia.

Russian strategic weapons are both land- and sea-based. It is difficult to be certain about the number of SSBNs deployed in the region. Russia apparently deploys twenty SSBNs at two bases (Pavlovskoye and Ribachiy). There appear to be two Yankee-class SSBNs, each carrying sixteen SS-N-6 Serb missiles. They were deployed in 1974 with a range of 3,000 kilometers and a throw weight of 6,500 kilograms. There are two multiple re-entry vehicle (MRV) warheads, each of 500 kilotons with a CEP of 1,300. The nine Delta 1 SSBNs each have twelve SS-N-8 Sawfly missiles, first deployed in 1973, with a range of 9,100 kilometers and a throw weight of 11,000 kilograms. They each carry two MRV 800–kiloton warheads with a CEP of 900. The nine Delta III SSBNs each have sixteen SS-N-18 Stingray missiles, first deployed in 1978, with a range of 6,500 kilometers and a throw weight of 16,500 kilograms. They each have three –kiloton warheads with a CEP of 900. The Deltas are likely to be eliminated under START II. The intercontinental ballistic missiles (ICBMs) are deployed in the Transbaykal and Far East MDs, but it is hard to be sure about which systems are still operational and which will be eliminated or changed in the START II regime. The twenty-seven SS-25s in Irkutsk are likely to remain. First deployed in 1985, they have a 10,500–kilometer range and a throw weight of 10,000 kilograms. They carry one 750–kiloton warhead with a CEP of 200. More problematic is the rest of the force. In 1993, it included some of the one hundred SS-11s, first deployed in 1975 but expected to be eliminated under START II. One report suggested that by the year 2000, the Russians will have disposed of thirty SSBNs and 1,800–2,000 ballistic missiles.[5] In any case, it is pointless to provide too much detail as ICBMs can be targeted from sites outside the region.

China, like Russia, is a local power, and therefore, there are special problems in counting its capability in the region. Land-based missiles include up to sixty intermediate range ballistic missiles (IRBMs) (DF-3), CSS-2, first deployed in 1970. They have single warheads with a 3–megaton yield and a range of 2,800 kilometers. ICBMs include up to twenty CSS-3s (DF-4), first deployed in 1978, with a range of 7,000 kilometers. They carry a single warhead of 3 megatons. The four CSS-4s (DF-5) were first deployed in 1981 with a range of 15,000 kilometers. Their single warheads have a 5–megaton yield. It has been suggested that China has a reload capability for these missiles as spares are kept. The thirty-six solid-fueled, mobile CSS-6s (DF-21) were first deployed in 1985 with a 1,800–kilometers range and a single warhead of up to 300 kilotons yield. There may be up to two SSBNs with twelve submarine-launched ballistic missiles (SLBMs) (CSS-N-3), first deployed in 1986 with a range of up to 3,000 kilometers and a single warhead of up to 300 kilotons. The CEPs of Chinese systems are not known. Half the DF-5s (two) are deployed in Luoning, and some DF-4s are deployed at Sundian, both within our Northeast Asian zone. Other systems are deployed in southern and western China. The SSBNs are believed to be deployed with the North Sea fleet. Not much is known about China's tactical systems, said to number 150 warheads. China is said to have multiple independently targetable re-entry vehicle (MIRV) capability, but there are no deployed systems.

In sum, these data, as with those for conventional weapons, should be treated as at best suggesting general features rather than providing hard and complete evidence. The first feature is that the great powers deploy large numbers of nuclear warheads with massive destructive potential. This power far outweighs anything likely to be deployed by any other state for a long time to come. Second, the number of warheads has been reduced in recent years, the first time this has happened in the nuclear age. Third, China is the smallest nuclear power, but considering the potential level of destruction, deterrence among the three powers remains robust. Fourth, although Russia and China are local powers with borders with North Korea, the United States deploys most of its nuclear forces at sea and has no land frontier. But the United States does have two key allies in the region, South Korea and Japan, whereas neither Russia nor China apparently has security treaty relationships with North Korea (or any other state).

When discussing deterrence and alliances, we need to explain the definition of the region. *Northeast Asia* is not a scientific term (nor is there even an agreed spelling).[6] The best that one can do is to set out the current assumptions of this chapter. My starting point is a sense that weapons, in and of themselves, are not the problem. Rather, the issue is how they are perceived and used by political leaders. Thus, judgments are just that—judgments—about political issues. My working definition focuses on the middle of the Korean DMZ because the most pressing tension is that between the two Koreas and the concern over North Korea's nuclear weapons capability. If there were no tension surrounding North Korea's nuclear weapons program, then it is a safe bet that there would be little international concern about the status of nuclear weapons in Northeast Asia. Once that assumption is made, the facts of geography dictate that the territory of China and Russia be included in the Northeast Asian zone but not that of the United States.

It can be argued that a more politically correct definition of the region should include Guam and Alaska. That is certainly one way to tie in American forces, and it is certainly true that American forces based in these places do operate in the Northeast Asian region. But Anchorage is as far from Seoul as Moscow is; and if the definition of Northeast Asia is widened this far, it takes in nearly all of European Russia, as well as Central and South Asia.

In essence, the argument about a wider regional definition is part of a broader point often made by both the Chinese and critics of nuclear-free zones. It is argued that nuclear weapons, and especially strategic weapons, are global in reach and therefore should be counted globally, not regionally. It is argued that nuclear-free zones are not the same as nuclear-safe zones because weapons can be targeted from well outside any region, no matter how it is defined. Thus, the fact that American forces in Alaska or Guam operate in Northeast Asia is little different than saying that American ICBMs in the Midwest or bombers based around the world are or could be targeted on Northeast Asia. Russian missiles in Northeast Asia did and could again target Alaska; but they also have targeted—and could do so again—the continental United States. Chinese DF-5 missiles in Northeast Asia apparently target the United States and European Russia, although de-targeting agreements are under discussion.

This complex and global interconnection exists largely because the deployment of weapons essentially serves national strategies, and these strategies have operated primarily with a view toward global threats. If we consider the threat assessments of the great powers, it is clear that Northeast Asia has long been seen as part of a global strategic problem. Of course, we all remember those debates in Europe about whether one could fight a limited nuclear war, and we should recall the absence of any firm conclusion. For those who always thought it improbable that nuclear war could be contained, it is clear that any discussion of Northeast Asian nuclear matters cannot be separated from global issues.

Thus, we focus on Northeast Asia because of the Korean problem, and we draw our regional boundaries from the center of the DMZ. We broaden the range to include neighboring countries that are players in the dispute. But we recognize that any proper consideration of the security problems in the region requires consideration of more global factors. In the end, we are more concerned about the "software" of politics than the hardware of nuclear weapons technology.

For the United States, deployment of nuclear weapons in the Pacific region during the Cold War served a number of roles. The primary enemy was the Soviet Union, but as part of a global struggle.[7] There was regular talk about escalation scenarios for war in Europe that assumed the United States would compensate for Russian advantages in Europe with strikes against Pacific parts of the Soviet Union. The United States was also concerned about China after 1964, and Chinese targets began appearing on the Strategic Integrated Operational Plan (SIOP) in their own right and not as part of a Sino-Soviet alliance.[8] The United States also had concerns about how to defend its allies South Korea and Japan. These two were seen as threatened by the Soviet Union and/or China, and thus, the United States had to consider problems of extended deterrence, much as it did in Europe.[9] The United States was also concerned about North Korea, although not as a nuclear power. Scenarios concerning North Korea assumed a version of the Korean War that involved great powers with nuclear capabilities.[10]

With the end of the Cold War, there have been important changes in the American strategic calculation.[11] Most important, the risks of nuclear war with the main enemy, Russia, are seen as sharply reduced—hence, the major reduction in forces in recent years. Although it is true that, unlike in Europe, the presence of the Russian empire in East Asia has not changed, the political and economic reality is a Russian basket case that poses little immediate threat. The rise of Russian nationalism is certainly a worry for the future, but the decline in Russian power is real and long-lasting. Nevertheless, the nuclear arsenal is less affected by this process of decline, and the United States must guard against the scenario of an anti-American Russian nationalism armed with nuclear weapons. There is even the remote scenario of a disintegrating Russia in which the successor regime in the Far East inherits a nuclear capability. Thus, Russia will continue to feature in the American SIOP, but at a much reduced state of readiness.

China has always figured at a much lower level in American planning, and little has changed in recent years. China's nuclear capability modernizes at a very slow level, and it makes no major effort to deploy large numbers of any nuclear weapon.[12] The United States continues to find it prudent to deter China but sees no reason for anxiety. The United States once considered China as a reason to deploy an antiballistic missile (ABM) system, but current discussions about defensive systems do not refer primarily to a China threat. If China is seen in a nuclear context, then it is primarily in terms of its continuing nuclear-testing program and the effect that has on the prospects for renewal of the Non-Proliferation Treaty (NPT) and negotiations for a Comprehensive Test Ban Treaty (CTBT). China is also seen as a main player in persuading North Korea to abandon its nuclear program and as a contributor to possible proliferation in a range of other countries such as Pakistan, Syria, Iran, or Algeria.

From Russia's point of view, the nature of the threat has also changed with the end of the Cold War.[13] Not only is the United States seen as less threatening, but so is China. Much as in the American calculation, there are residual and new concerns but at nothing like the level of intensity seen during the Cold War. Given all that has been happening in Russian society and the armed forces, the status of nuclear forces ranks very low on the agenda, and even lower if the specific issue is forces in Northeast Asia.[14] There are worries about Kazakhstan, but not many about Korea. In the longer term, there are worries about how Japan will cope with the North Korean issue and a possible removal of the American nuclear umbrella. But for the time being, Russia feels it has more than enough nuclear weapons to deal with Northeast Asian contingencies.

China has long demonstrated such a laid-back attitude toward nuclear weapons. It has never deployed large numbers of any type of nuclear weapon, and there are no signs of change in such a policy.[15] It is true that the reduction in Russian and American arsenals has added pressure on China to do the same, but the gap remains large, and China can properly claim to have a minimum deterrent. China's persistent testing of nuclear weapons while the other powers edged toward a comprehensive test ban treaty was a bigger problem in public relations terms, but it was not specifically a Northeast Asian issue. China continues to modernize its nuclear weapons gradually, but détente with Russia has made the process far from urgent. Periodic failures by the civilian version of its missiles suggest that China is still struggling with technical problems. In the context of Northeast Asia, China, like the other powers, is concerned about North Korea's intentions. It is unlikely that China wants to see a nuclear-armed North Korea, but neither does it wish to see Pyongyang humiliated by Western pressure. The result is a China in a difficult political position, which, if badly handled, might lead to war on its Korean frontier and/or a nuclear-armed South Korea and Japan in due course. The political stakes are high, and higher than at any time since the end of the Korean War.

In sum, it is clear that any discussion of nuclear forces in Northeast Asia has to take place in a global context. Any drawing of lines defining the region is arbitrary. But it is somewhat less arbitrary to argue that there is a concern with nuclear issues in Northeast Asia and that it is focused on the risks of proliferation in Korea. There are risks in Japan as well, but they have existed for a long time, and the most likely trigger for them to be activated is events in Korea. Nevertheless, because the great powers have nuclear weapons in the region and they are acutely involved in the resolution of the Korean issue, the disposition of their own forces in the area is important. Few people seriously believe there is much risk of conflict between the acknowledged nuclear powers in Northeast Asia, but there is much that these powers can do to help resolve the Korean issue. If proliferation is prevented in Northeast Asia, then few will worry about the status of nuclear forces in Northeast Asia. Hence, we turn to a discussion of the links to the proliferation problem in Korea and Japan.

Links to Proliferation in Korea and Japan

This is not the place to discuss why North Korea seems to be acquiring nuclear weapons, but it is necessary to discuss the linkages between the Korean problem and the great powers. One of the few things that does seem clear about the Korean problem is that North Korea is motivated primarily by worries about the survival of its regime. It finds itself increasingly falling behind the South in all forms of competition and, most important, in economic competition. Whether North Korea is actually acquiring nuclear weapons or not, it apparently feels that the threat of doing so seems to get American and Japanese attention. The danger is that by engaging in such a high-risk strategy of survival, it may bring about a major political and military crisis that will engulf the region.[16]

Of course, part of the reason for North Korea's brinkmanship is recent changes in great-power policies toward Korea. Chinese and then Russian détente with South Korea made it plain that the North had fewer and less warm friends. The fate of communist regimes elsewhere in the world, and even the reforms in China and Vietnam, suggested that the North was under heavy pressure to change. Had China and Russia remained stalwart friends competing for North Korean favors, it is unlikely that we would be facing a crisis in Northeast Asia. But there is no turning back that particular clock, and we live in an environment in which it is a fact of life that China and Russia will want to grow closer to South Korea. No great power wants to see a nuclear-armed North Korea, although China is less intensely opposed than Russia, which is less intensely opposed than the Japanese or the Americans.[17]

A range of reasons are advanced by China and to some extent Russia for not being too worried about North Korea. There is the argument that North Korea does not want to acquire nuclear weapons; it only wants to be loved. There is the view that even if North Korea did go nuclear, it would be no more serious a problem than living with Russian or Chinese nuclear power, so it is not worth a crisis. There is also the view that the nonproliferation regime has already been perforated by the likes of Israel, India, and Pakistan.

If China and Russia could know that a nuclear-armed North Korea would not provoke either a conflict or proliferation in South Korea or Japan, then they might be more relaxed about the Korean crisis. But China and Russia are less willing to sit back and watch because no one can have such assurances, and the Americans and to some extent the Japanese are not prepared to take the chance. The European powers, and most notably France, have, if anything, taken a tougher line in the International Atomic Energy Agency (IAEA) about the need to deal with this risk of proliferation. France sees obvious chain-reaction effects in North Africa or even in Eastern Europe.

Now that the Western powers and the IAEA have committed so much prestige to halting a North Korean program, firm linkages have been established between the Korean problem and wider regional and global security. There is unlikely to be any going back to a less worried mode of thinking without undermining regional and global antiproliferation regimes. The linkages between the levels of policy have already operated, sometimes with great effect. The Russians and Americans feared proliferation, so they made serious efforts to reduce their nuclear arsenals and to withdraw sea-launched tactical systems. There has been more nuclear disarmament on the part of the Russians and Americans in recent years than at any other time in the nuclear age. What is more, North Korea demanded the withdrawal of American nuclear weapons in South Korea before serious talks could take place, and the Americans eventually agreed to do so albeit as part of a global policy shift on toward deployment of American nuclear weapons. It can be argued that this concession to common sense looked a bit too much like a concession to North Korea, which only encouraged Pyongyang to ask for more. But it certainly established a process whereby the Korean and wider issues of nuclear weapons were linked.

The link now focuses on the need to counter proliferation by stopping the North Korean program. Most of North Korea's demands before it accepts full inspections concern nonmilitary linkage (trade, recognition). Pyongyang demands an end to the Team Spirit military exercises but rarely sees these exercises as a specifically nuclear threat. From North Korea's point of view, the current standoff concerns much wider issues.

But from the point of view of the wider world, the issue is precisely one of proliferation. The Europeans certainly saw this matter in the run-up to the NPT Extension Conference in 1995 as critical to holding the nonproliferation regime in place at a time of great strain. The Americans have similar concerns but, unlike the Europeans, also have close alliance ties in Northeast Asia. Many American policy makers fear the long-run consequences of proliferation for Japan, not to mention the damage it might do to regional security in an area of vital economic interest. Americans would like to withdraw conventional forces from Japan and South Korea but cannot do so in the current environment. They see this crisis as a test of American commitment to East Asia after the Cold War.

During 1993–1994, American policy was to pressure China in order to see whether Beijing could produce North Korean compliance with the IAEA. In so doing, the Korean problem became wrapped up with broader Sino-American relations, including debates over trade and human rights. China was offered a reason both to play hardball in order to get greater concessions on trade and human rights issues; and to cooperate in order to prove that it is worthy of most-favored nation (MFN) status and a more positive American attitude. China was offered the opportunity to demonstrate that it is a responsible great power in the U.N. Security Council and not just a reactive power that adjusts to agendas set by others. The fact that China drafted a Security Council Presidential Statement critical of North Korea demonstrated both of these Chinese impulses, with all the inherent contradictions.

Not far behind in China's motivation for dealing with the North Korean issue at the height of the nuclear confrontation was its uncertainty about relations with Japan.[18] Some—including the Chinese—argued that it is unfair to be so concerned about North Korea's nuclear program when we ignore Japan's efforts. Of course, Japan has long had the option of going nuclear fairly rapidly, and its recent accumulation of plutonium and new processing capacity merely makes the process a bit shorter and the potential arsenal much larger. But the essential risks have been present for some time and were never activated because the political conditions did not make it necessary. In the post–Cold War world, China, like other powers, recognizes that it is precisely the political conditions that seem to be changing.[19]

Today, China can see that Japan has greater doubts about the American guarantee now that the common Russian threat has eased. It can see that Tokyo is increasingly alarmed at China's own growth and its doubled defense budget from 1989 to 1993. China can also see that Japan regards North Korea as a different, and far less sane, sort of power than China or Russia, and thus, proliferation by North Korea is far more dangerous than living with a nuclear-armed Russia or China. Japan reads the same signals about North Korea promising not to threaten South Korea but issuing no such promises to Japan. Tokyo worries about the growing reach of North Korean ballistic missiles and sees China as in part responsible for this problem. Finally, Japanese domestic politics is in upheaval, and what were once considered fixed points on its political agenda are rapidly changing.

In short, despite growing Sino-Japanese economic relations, the strategic picture is worsening, and North Korea is seen as a large part of the problem. It is very much in China's interest to remove the North Korean problem and perhaps ease Japan's concerns. China does not want Japan to embark on a major military program and certainly not to acquire a nuclear weapons capability. One of China's current advantages over Japan is its superiority in military, and especially nuclear, capability. If the next century is really going to include a confrontation between Japan and China, then China has every reason to lull Japan into a sense a calm about the future so that the Chinese economy can grow strong. Even if the future is less nasty, China still has no interest in a worried Japan that builds up its military forces and unleashes its pent-up nationalism.

In short, the uncertainties about Korea and Japan are the prime motive for worry about nuclear forces in Northeast Asia. All the great powers have an active interest in preventing drastic change in the military status quo in Northeast Asia. All three nuclear powers can agree that if they could reduce concern about North Korea, they could lessen the incentive for Japan to change its policies. If all this could take place, then the great powers could go back to minimizing the attention paid to Northeast Asian security. But if they fail to deal with Korea, then they will all be forced to pay close attention to Northeast Asia, and even the status of great power nuclear forces might come into play. So what can be done to deal with the risks?

An Arms-Control Agenda

Sensible arms control begins with an assessment of the main problem and an understanding of what is achievable. It may be that a nearly nuclear-free Northeast Asia is the objective, but it is not achievable without at least a nearly nuclear-free world. A more achievable, but still difficult, goal is to prevent further proliferation of nuclear weapons in Northeast Asia so that the process of reducing nuclear forces and tension can continue. Approaching this goal requires action that sometimes might be unilateral and more often would be better for being negotiated, verifiable, and multilateral. The absence of any effective multilateral mechanism for arms control in Northeast Asia is a problem much lamented of late, but with little indication that progress is being made to meet the challenge.[20]

Of course, any strategy that might be adopted depends on an assessment of the nature of the problem with North Korea. If the problem is essentially one of how to reassure North Korea about its continuing existence, then the problem barely concerns changes in nuclear policy and relates much more to trade deals and diplomatic niceties as were outlined in the October 1994 US-DPRK Agreed Framework. If the problem is about ascertaining whether North Korea has a nuclear weapons program and, if so, how much it has achieved, then the arms-control agenda is far more concerned with nuclear issues. This chapter assumes that the problem is about both, in that regime survival is what has motivated North Korea to acquire nuclear weapons. But it also assumes that North Korea, like others before it, can step back from the brink of nuclear weapon status, and to that end, there are steps that the international community can take to make this outcome more likely.

At the global level, the following actions are vital:

- Russia and the United States must continue to demonstrate their seriousness about reducing their nuclear arsenals. If the Russians and Americans were really in a state of nuclear tension, the reductions of the past few years would not have taken place. The cuts demonstrate that the international trend is toward the reduction in nuclear arsenals and that those who seek to go the other way should be stopped. For too long, the superpowers were not serious about nuclear arms control, which undermined their ability to limit nuclear proliferation. The fact that some previous efforts to limit proliferation failed is no reason to sanction new failures, especially when important successes have been chalked up (South Africa, Latin America). From the point of view of Northeast Asia, it is important that further reductions in Russian and American arsenals include, if not feature, reductions in weapons deployed in Northeast Asia.
- As the nuclear superpowers (and in this respect, there are still two superpowers) reduce their arsenals, the need for medium nuclear powers to join the process of reduction becomes all the more important. In Northeast Asia, the main attention focuses on China. The Chinese, like the Russians before them, should be encouraged to restructure their arsenal to rely less on land-based systems and more on SLBMs. China still has technological problems in this respect, and arms control might involve measures of "positive conditionality" that include technology transfer in exchange for serious arms control. If even China is seen to be reducing its nuclear arsenal, the NPT regime will be strengthened.
- Strengthening the NPT regime requires a series of more specific measures, including serious progress on a CTBT.

At the regional level, there seems to be far less that can be done concerning current stockpiles of weapons but more that can be done in the wider diplomatic realm. The problem is that, as far as Russia and the United States are concerned, the Northeast Asian region cannot be divorced from global strategies, and therefore, it makes little sense to limit Northeast Asian nuclear forces specifically. China may find it easier to reconfigure forces in the long run, but then if it faces similar demands from other neighbors, its national security would be severely affected. Thus, any Chinese, American, and Russian systems above tactical range are unlikely candidates for further reductions. Nevertheless, there is much that can be done in arms control at the regional level. Measures might include some of the following:

- A register of nuclear arms in the region would be most welcome. Anyone who has tried to compile a list of nuclear weapons deployed in the region, as we tried earlier in this chapter, will know how much suspicion would be cleared up by this simple act of transparency. The Russians and the Americans are perhaps closest to achieving such openness, and the American neither-confirm-nor-deny (NCND) policy seems more flexible than ever before. China's surprisingly cooperative behavior regarding the U.N. Conventional Arms Register suggests that the optimists might be right and China is prepared to cooperate on arms control once it learns the advantages of the system.

- Transparency might also be extended to more basic aspects such as military doctrine, threat perceptions, and/or priorities of defense industries. A great deal of this already takes place in the post–Cold War dialogues between Americans and Russians. Specific efforts can be made at the regional level, and they might seek the participation of China and perhaps other states. China is especially reticent on these matters—hence, the wildly varying estimates of such basics as Chinese defense spending. Specific dialogues might be held to include civilian nuclear programs so as to ease concern about Japanese intentions. There are clearly many steps that could be taken under the guise of improving the safety of civilian nuclear plants that would also have a military confidence-building spin-off. Once again, positive conditionality could be useful to encourage cooperation. By offering access to new technologies, the likelihood of cooperation could be increased.

It is true that none of these measures would deal directly with the problem of North Korea. In essence, the time has passed for such direct linkages, if only because the credibility of the entire nonproliferation system is on the line when North Korea defies the IAEA. But these other arms-control measures might be useful in a more general way if the North Korean problem is primarily about reassuring the North. If Pyongyang fears that once it lets the IAEA carry out full inspections, then the West will no longer pay attention to North Korea if it finds nothing to worry about, then the arms-control process may require some apparent detours from the IAEA's agenda in order to reassure North Korea about continuing cooperation. It is in this respect that positive conditionality as proposed in the 1994 Agreed Framework offers much hope, for it promises North Korea real cooperation if it undertakes certain actions. North Korea's failure to cooperate fully with the IAEA does not bode well, but if it should fully cooperate, then it becomes all the more important to demonstrate that good behavior brings rewards. Of course, if North Korea is really seeking nuclear weapons as a way to ensure the survival of the regime, then there is little that these measures, or any others, will do to prevent the nuclear problems in Northeast Asia from getting much worse.

Notes

1. In 1986, the U.S. warhead stockpile was 23,400, compared to 45,000 for the Soviet Union and 425 for China (6.1 percent of the world total). In 1993, the United States held 16,750 warheads, Russia held 32,000, and China held 435 (8.7 percent).

2. The numbers presented in this chapter are derived from a variety of sources, few of which agree on specifics but most of which broadly reflect the same trends. Apart from the annual volumes of *The Military Balance,* published by Brassey's for the International Institute for Strategic Studies (IISS), and the *SIPRI Yearbook,* published by Oxford University Press for SIPRI, there is also the *Nuclear Weapons Databook,* vol. 5, by Robert Norris et al. (Boulder, CO: Westview Press, 1993).

3. *Guardian,* February 3, 1994.

4. In 1993, the United States had 400 warheads on inactive reserve and 5,850 retired warheads. Russia had 17,000 inactive and retired warheads. See "Nuclear Notebook," *Bulletin of the Atomic Scientists,* July and December 1993, both on p. 57.

5. *Jane's Defence Weekly* 19, no. 23, June 5, 1993.

6. On the debates, see Gerald Segal, *Rethinking the Pacific* (Oxford, United Kingdom: Oxford University Press, 1990).

7. Robert Art, "The US: Nuclear Weapons and Grand Strategy," in *Security with Nuclear Weapons?* ed. Regina Cowen-Karp (Oxford, United Kingdom: Oxford University Press for SIPRI, 1991).

8. Michael Mazarr, *Missile Defences and Asian-Pacific Security* (London: Macmillan, 1988).

9. Michael Mazarr, "The INF Treaty and Asia-Pacific Security," *Pacific Review* 1, no. 3 (1988), pp. 248–256.

10. Sang Hoon Park, "The US, South Korea, and the North Korea Problem," *Survival* (summer 1994).

11. CSIS Nuclear Strategy Group, *Towards a Nuclear Peace* (Washington, D.C.: CSIS, June 1993).

12. Gerald Segal, "China," in *Security with Nuclear Weapons?*

13. Dunbar Lockwood and Jon Wolfsthal, "Nuclear Weapons and Proliferation," *SIPRI Yearbook, 1993* (Oxford, United Kingdom: Oxford University Press for SIPRI, 1993).

14. Renée de Nevers, "Rethinking Russian Security" (London: Brassey's for the IISS, Adelphi Paper, 1994).

15. John Lewis and Hua Di, "China's Ballistic Missile Program," *International Security,* 17, no. 2 (fall 1992); and John Hopkins and Weiming Hu, "Strategic Views from the Second Tier," and Litai Xue, "Evolution of China's Nuclear Strategy" (based on John Lewis and Xue Litai's *China's Strategic Seapower* [Stanford, CA: Stanford University Press, 1994], both in *Strategic Views from the Second Tier,* ed. John Hopkins and Weiming Hu (San Diego: IGCC, January 1994).

16. See the author's contribution to *Jane's Intelligence Review,* "North Korea: A Potential Time Bomb" (Special Report no. 2, April 1994).

17. James Hoare, "Korea and the Great Powers" (London: Brassey's for the IISS, Adelphi Paper, 1994).

18. Gerald Segal, "The Coming Confrontation between China and Japan?" *World Policy Journal* 10, no. 2 (summer 1993).

19. See generally Ron Matthews and Keisuke Matsuyama, eds., *Japan's Military Renaissance* (London: Macmillan, 1993).

20. Paul Evans, "The CSCAP Process," *Pacific Review* 7, no. 2 (1994).

16

The Status of U.S., Russian, and Chinese Nuclear Forces in Northeast Asia

*Dunbar Lockwood**

Since the Cold War ended, it is quite difficult to envision a realistic scenario in which any of the five declared nuclear weapons states would deliberately initiate the use of nuclear weapons against each other. Conversely, the international community is increasingly concerned about the spread of nuclear weapons to developing countries where they might be used in regional conflicts. Of these regional concerns, Northeast Asia has recently vaulted near to the top of the list. The historical animosities, the territorial disputes, the potential power vacuum created by the disengagement of the superpowers, the region's growing import- ance as a trading partner, the general economic dynamism accompanied by in- creasing defense expenditures and acquisition of high-tech weaponry, the imminent leadership changes, and the political isolation of North Korea, com-

*Dunbar Lockwood currently works for the U.S. Arms Control and Disarmament Agency (ACDA). He wrote this chapter in 1994 when he was Assistant Director for Research at the Arms Control Association (ACA)—a private nongovernmental organiza- tion (NGO) based in Washington, DC. The views expressed in this chapter are his own and do *not* reflect those of ACDA or the U.S. government.

Any of the numbers that have been updated in this chapter since 1994 have been done so exclusively with the use of *unclassified* written data, which is cited wherever possible, e.g., the START I Treaty's January 1, 1996, Memorandum of Understanding (MOU).

The author would like to thank Adam Grissom, Stan Norris, Jack Mendelsohn, and Jon Wolfsthal for their generous assistance in helping prepare this paper in 1994. Any errors, of course, are solely the responsibility of the author.

bined with its development of new, longer-range ballistic missiles and possibly nuclear weapons, have all contributed to fears that Northeast Asia could potentially become a nuclear powder keg.

The current and future deployment of nuclear weapons in Northeast Asia by the United·States, Russia, and most particularly, China—each with vital interests in the region—will play a critical role in determining how the region's other states plan their military programs. The calculus of deterrence and defense postures of the three declared nuclear-weapon states with a military presence in the region are inextricably interrelated and will also affect the way security planners in the states of East Asia make budgetary and military calculations.

It is clear to the United States, Russia, and China that it would not be in their respective interests for any additional state in the region to develop a nuclear weapons capability in the near or distant future. Although a consensus exists among the governments in Washington, Moscow, and Beijing that they should try to dissuade other states in Northeast Asia from "going nuclear," there is no discernible consensus on the appropriate means for achieving that goal.

North Korea's perceptions of U.S. global nuclear capabilities and intentions as they pertain to the Korean Peninsula are certainly an important factor in Pyongyang's decision about whether to pursue (or continue to pursue) nuclear weapons. Similarly, Japan's perceptions of North Korea's nuclear capabilities and intentions, as well as those of Russia and China, will be an important factor in Tokyo's longterm decision about whether to remain a non–nuclear weapons state.

With these calculations and perceptions in mind, this chapter looks at: (1) the current status of U.S., Russian, and Chinese nuclear forces (e.g., numbers, types, locations, operational characteristics, targets, trends in force structure, the impact of recent arms-control agreements and unilateral initiatives); and (2) global, regional, and unilateral arms-control measures that the three major nuclear powers could implement to help reduce the likelihood of nuclear proliferation in the region.

U.S. Nuclear Forces

New Policy Debate on the Purpose of U.S. Nuclear Weapons

Since 1990, a number of important factors have changed the U.S. government's perspective regarding its nuclear weapons programs. The end of the confrontational relationship with Moscow, the lack of a clear and present security threat, progressively declining defense budgets, and the negotiation of the Strategic Arms Reduction Talks (START) Treaties have compelled the United States to reduce the size of its nuclear arsenal, spend less on nuclear weapons, and curb modernization programs. Despite these developments, it is clear that the United States will continue to maintain thousands of nuclear weapons, with some limited modernization, for the foreseeable future. More broadly, there is no consensus in the United States on the purpose of these weapons in the post–Cold War era, and a new debate has begun in Washington. The outcome of this debate will likely have implications for international nuclear non-proliferation regime, including efforts to stop the spread of nuclear weapons in Northeast Asia.

With the passing of the Cold War, two separate schools of thought on the future of U.S. nuclear weapons have emerged. First, there is the school that believes that: (1) the role of nuclear weapons in international relations has diminished dramatically; (2) the exclusive, or at least primary, purpose of U.S. nuclear weapons is to deter or respond to the use of nuclear weapons against the United States or its allies; and (3) strict constraints on U.S. nuclear weapons (e.g., a ban on nuclear testing) could help the United States strengthen its efforts to curb proliferation of nuclear weapons in the developing world as well as in the former Soviet Union.

Second, there is the school of thought that believes that (1) increased "instability and uncertainty" in the developing world, coupled with the spread of "weapons of mass destruction," necessitate an expansion of the role of U.S. nuclear weapons to deter or respond to chemical and biological weapons or even conventionally armed ballistic missiles; and (2) the development of "mini" or "micro" low-yield nuclear weapons would be useful for attacks against "rogue states" such as Iraq whose leaders might take refuge along with their senior military officers in reinforced underground bunkers during a conflict with the United States.

In addition, there is another group, which includes members in both of the first two schools of thought, that believes the United States must maintain its nuclear forces at their current number with a modest level of modernization as a "hedge" against retrograde leaders' coming to power in the Kremlin. To add to the cacophony in the U.S. debate, there is frequent disagreement within the same schools of thought about the degree to which their policy formulations should be carried out. In this context, it is worth noting the precedent of the 1991 Gulf War. When Iraq attacked U.S. troops with conventionally armed Scud missiles and posed the potential threat of using chemical or biological weapons, the United States decided not to respond with nuclear weapons.

The conclusions of the Defense Department's "Nuclear Posture Review," which were publicly released in September 1994, stayed silent on the question of whether the United States should use or threaten to use nuclear weapons in response to chemical and biological weapons threats. (Rather than announcing changes in U.S. declaratory policy on use, the NPR focused largely on projecting the U.S. strategic force structure in the year 2003, if START II is implemented.) It remains to be seen, however, whether the government can arrive at a consensus about the future role of U.S. nuclear weapons.

Reductions in the Number of Strategic Nuclear Weapons

Since 1991, the United States has removed all of its oldest strategic weapons from operational service, including Minuteman II intercontinental ballistic missiles (ICBMs), Poseidon submarines, and B-52G bombers. Consequently, the number of deployed U.S. strategic nuclear warheads declined by about one-third from September 1990 to January 1, 1996—from 12,646 to 8,205.[1] (Under START I, the United States and Russia must reduce the number of warheads deployed on their strategic systems to 6,000 each by December 2001. If the START II treaty is ratified and implemented, that number will drop to 3,500 by no later than 2003—a 72 percent decrease from the September 1990 level.

START I entered into force on December 5, 1994. START II, which was signed on January 3, 1993, was approved by the U.S. Senate on January 26, 1996. But Russian ratification of START II is not a foregone conclusion, and the United States has said that it is not prepared to go down to START II levels unilaterally.[2]

Spending on Nuclear Weapons

With the end of the Cold War and the continuing economic burden of a large federal budget deficit, the U.S. government has found that it cannot justify allocating scarce resources to its nuclear programs at the levels it maintained in the recent past. A decade ago, strategic nuclear programs accounted for 11 percent of the Department of Defense (DOD) budget when the Reagan administration's strategic modernization program was being implemented. But by 1994, strategic nuclear programs represented only 3 to 4 percent of the DOD budget.[3] Admiral Henry Chiles, then commander in chief of the United States Strategic Command (STRATCOM), told Congress in April 1994 that spending on U.S. strategic forces over the last decade has declined far more rapidly than the U.S. defense budget as a whole in the same period. Chiles said that although the Defense Department's total obligating authority declined by more than 33 percent (in constant fiscal year 1993 dollars), "the portion of the overall defense budget dedicated to nuclear forces declined over 74 percent in FY93 dollars."[4]

Status of Strategic Weapons Programs

In recent years, the United States has also curtailed the development, testing, and production of new nuclear systems. With respect to nuclear warheads, the United States has not conducted any underground nuclear tests since 1992 and, with the closing of Rocky Flats' plutonium pit fabrication unit in November 1989, has not produced any new warheads since the summer of 1990.[5] It shut down its last plutonium production reactor in 1988 and has not enriched any uranium for weapons purposes since 1964.

Regarding nuclear delivery vehicles, Admiral Chiles told Congress in his April 1994 testimony that "There are no new . . . ballistic missile programs on the drawing boards to replace our current systems,"[6] and the Defense Department said in 1994 that "development of a new intercontinental ballistic missile (ICBM) is not anticipated for at least 15 years."[7]

Some strategic modernization, however, is proceeding. The United States continues to build B-2 bombers and Trident submarines—two programs for which Congress has already appropriated the vast majority of the funding. In addition, the Clinton administration is seeking funding to build additional Trident II (D-5) submarine-launched ballistic missiles (SLBMs) and upgrade the accuracy and extend the life of the Minuteman III ICBM.

ICBMs

U.S. ICBM plans are quite straightforward: all of the remaining Minuteman II missiles, have been removed from operational service; when and if START II is implemented, all of the Minuteman III missiles will be downloaded from three warheads each to one, and all 50 of the ten-warhead MX missiles will be eliminated. The Nuclear Posture Review called for the U.S. ICBM force to consist of 450–500 single-warhead Minuteman IIIs by the year 2003, provided that START II is implemented.

SSBNs and SLBMs

U.S. nuclear-powered ballistic missile submarines (SSBNs) are considered to be the heart of the U.S. strategic deterrent. The last three Poseidon submarines were removed from patrol status on April 1, 1994. Trident submarine production continues on schedule. By 1997, the United States plans to have a total of eighteen SSBNs—ten in the Atlantic based at King's Bay, Georgia, carrying twenty-four Trident II missiles each and eight in the Pacific based at Bangor, Washington, carrying twenty-four Trident I missiles each.

In the Nuclear Posture Review, DOD decided that if START II is implemented, it will reduce the total number of Trident submarines from 18 to 14, all of which would be armed with the Trident II missile. Under START II, the United States will be permitted to deploy up to 1,750 warheads on its SLBMs.

Strategic Bombers

With respect to strategic bombers, the Pentagon concluded in its Nuclear Posture Review that the Air Force: (1) required no more than twenty B-2s for nuclear missions; (2) should convert its B-18s to a non-nuclear role; and (3) should maintain sixty-six B-52Hs. The B-2 deployments and the B-18 conversion are scheduled to be completed by the late 1990s.

Tactical Nuclear Weapons

Tactical Nuclear Weapons Withdrawn from South Korea

Less than a month after President George Bush's September 27, 1991, announcement that the United States would withdraw all of its ground- and sea-launched tactical nuclear weapons, press reports cited anonymous Bush administration officials as saying that the United States planned to remove all U.S. nuclear weapons from South Korea, including air-delivered nuclear weapons.[8] (At that time, Robert S. Norris, a senior analyst for the Natural Resources Defense Council, estimated that there were approximately one hundred U.S. nuclear weapons based in South Korea—sixty B-61 gravity bombs available for delivery by several squadrons of nuclear-capable F-16s located at Kunsan Air Base plus forty W-33 nuclear artillery shells.)[9]

On December 18, 1991, then President of South Korea Roh Tae Woo announced in a televised speech that "As I speak, there do not exist any nuclear weapons whatsoever, anywhere in the Republic of Korea."[10] Subsequently, senior U.S. officials stated that "U.S. policy is consistent with" President Roh's statement.[11]

Tactical Nuclear Weapons Withdrawn from Ships in the Pacific

Between September 1991 and June 1992, the United States withdrew all tactical nuclear warheads routinely deployed at sea on surface ships, attack submarines, and aircraft carriers, including those that patrol in the Western Pacific. These withdrawals consisted of: B-57 depth strike/bombs for S-3 jets and SH-3 helicopters; B-61 gravity bombs for A-6, A-7, and F/A-18 planes deployed on aircraft carriers; and W-80 warheads for Tomahawk sea-launched cruise missiles (SLCMs) deployed on cruisers, destroyers, and attack submarines. In addition, the United States removed from service 350 B-57 depth bombs deployed with land-based naval antisubmarine warfare (ASW) aircraft, including B-57 depth bombs reportedly deployed in Alaska, California, Guam, and Hawaii.[12]

Current Operational Tactical Nuclear Weapons

Since 1984, the United States has reduced the number of operational tactical nuclear warheads in its arsenal by more than 90 percent. The retired tactical nuclear weapons that have not yet been dismantled either are stored in depots in the United States or have been shipped to the Department of Energy's (DOE's) Pantex facility near Amarillo, Texas, where they are being dismantled at a rate of up to 2,000 per year.

The United States, however, plans to maintain some tactical nuclear weapons well into the future. In January 1992, General Colin Powell, then chairman of the

Joint Chiefs of Staff, announced that the United States planned to reduce its tactical nuclear weapons to 1,600. At the time, Powell made it clear that this number included B-61 gravity bombs for naval carrier-based aircraft—apparently about 650. But in October 1993, the Pentagon stated that the navy and marine corps "can prudently do away with the tactical nuclear mission of their air components."[13] Consequently, the number of tactical nuclear warheads remaining in the active stockpile dropped to approximately 950, according to some nongovernmental analysts.[14]

In 1993, the Clinton administration confirmed some earlier projections about the types of tactical nuclear weapons that the United States plans to keep when it told Congress that the only tactical nuclear warheads the United States currently plans to maintain in its active stockpile after September 30, 1996, are three variants of the B-61 gravity bomb (mods 3/4/10) and the W-80 warhead for Tomahawk SLCMs.[15] Based on these developments, Robert S. Norris and William Arkin estimated that the United States would maintain approximately 600 B-61 gravity bombs stored in the United States and Western Europe for the U.S. Air Force (and other NATO squadrons) and about 350 W-80 Tomahawk SLCM warheads stored in the United States for the U.S. Navy.[16]

In 1978, the Carter administration announced U.S. policy on "negative security assurances"—a policy that has been reaffirmed by all subsequent administrations, including the Clinton administration. (Although the principal aim of the original U.S. 1978 statement on negative security assurances was to encourage countries to join the NPT as non-nuclear weapon states, the purpose of the qualifying clauses was, inter alia, to preserve the option of using or threatening to use nuclear weapons against non-Soviet Warsaw Pact countries or against North Korea which was "allied" with China.)

The September 1994 Nuclear Posture Review's findings did not directly address the question of negative security assurances, but in April 1995, just prior to the NPT Review and Extension Conference, the United States reaffirmed its policy with the following statement:

> The United States reaffirms that it will not use nuclear weapons against any non-nuclear weapon States Parties to the Treaty on Non-Proliferation of Nuclear Weapons except in the case of an invasion or any other attack on the United States, its territories, its armed forces or other troops, its allies, or on a state towards which it has a security commitment, carried out or sustained by such a non-nuclear-weapon State in association or alliance with a nuclear weapon State.[17]

Therefore, as it stands now, U.S. declaratory policy on the employment of nuclear weapons would preclude the United States from initiating the use of nuclear weapons against North Korea (an NPT party), *unless* Pyongyang carried out or sustained an attack against the United States or its allies "in association or in alliance" with a nuclear weapons state, (e.g. if North Korea carried out an attack across the demilitarized zone "in assistance or alliance" with China).

Russian Nuclear Forces

The end of the Cold War, the virtual free fall in the Russian economy, the signing of strategic arms reduction agreements with the United States, and the unilateral initiatives taken first by Mikhail Gorbachev and later by Boris Yeltsin have clearly had an enormous impact on the status of Russian nuclear forces.

The production of nuclear weapons systems has ground almost to a halt. Russia has stopped producing ballistic missile submarines, strategic bombers, and all intercontinental ballistic missiles, except for the SS-25. Development of new nuclear weapons has also been curtailed. For example, in 1991, the United States estimated that Moscow had "five or six" new types of long-range ballistic missiles under development.[18] But in 1994, U.S. intelligence officials told Congress that the number is down to two or three—testing of nuclear weapon systems has also declined. Russia has not conducted an underground nuclear test since becoming the successor state to the former USSR (which conducted its last test on October 24, 1990). The flight-testing of strategic ballistic missiles has also dropped precipitously in recent years.[19]

Although the retirement of older Russian strategic nuclear weapons has thus far been carried out at a relatively slow pace, the operational readiness or alert levels of existing Russian strategic forces have dropped precipitously.

Russia has made a commitment to dismantle a significant portion of its tactical nuclear warheads and asserts that this process is well under way.

ICBMs

ICBMs in 1990

See table in Appendix, "Former Soviet Union ICBMS: Sept. 1990 and Jan. 1996."

Russian ICBM Deactivations

As of January 1, 1996, Russia had eliminated all 326 of its SS-11s, all of its forty SS-13s, forty-six of its forty-seven SS-17s, and eighteen of its 204 SS-18s.[20] In addition, all of the warheads from 104 SS-18s in Kazakhstan, and the forty-six SS-24s and 130 SS-19s in Ukraine had been withdrawn to Russia by mid 1996, according to public statements by U.S. and Russian officials.

Based on their location, it seems likely that the two hundred SS-11s based at Drovyanaya, Yasnaya, and Svobodnyy were targeted on China prior to their retirement.[21] Most of the other ICBMs that have been deactivated were probably targeted on the United States.

ICBMs in 1994 and Projections for START

As of January 1, 1996, START-accountable ICBMs in the former Soviet Union consisted of: one SS-17, 186 SS-18s, 170 SS-19s, ten silo-based SS-24s, thirty-six rail-based SS-24s, and 351 SS-25s in Russia plus twenty-four SS-18s in Kazakhstan, one hundred twenty-eight SS-19s and forty-six silo-based SS-24s in Ukraine, and eighteen SS-25s in Belarus—for a total of 970 ICBMs with 5,181 warheads. Since 1990, this represents a 31 percent cut in missiles and a 22 percent cut in warheads.

Under START I, Russia is expected to retain some SS-19s, SS-24s, and SS-25s, and no more than 154 SS-18s. Under START II, Russia will be required to eliminate all of its SS-18 and SS-24 ICBMs and is expected to field no more than 105 SS-19s downloaded to one warhead each plus a total of 500–1,000 single-warhead SS-25–type missiles, both in silo- and mobile-basing modes.[22]

ICBM Production

Russian ICBM production has continued to decline in the early 1990s.[23] In February 1993, the CIA's national intelligence officer for strategic programs, Dr. Lawrence Gershwin, said, "today the only strategic missile in production at all is the SS-25 road mobile ICBM, and that production is down from what it historically has been. We are really at a rather low point in missile production."[24]

Development of New ICBMs

The U.S. intelligence community now expects that Russia will deploy a variant of the SS-25 sometime "during this decade" both in silos and in a mobile-basing mode.[25] Reportedly, the new "Topol M" was first flight tested in December 1994.[26]

SSBNs

SSBNS in 1990

In the START I January 1, 1996, Memorandum of Understanding (MOU), Russia declared a total of forty-three SSBNs, divided as follows: twenty-six in the northern Atlantic fleet on the Kola Peninsula and seventeen in the Pacific fleet—twelve based at Rybachiy some 15 kilometers southwest of Petropavlosk on the Kamchatka Peninsula; and five at Pavlovskoye, some 65 kilometers southeast of Vladivostok.

Among other things, the January 1, 1996 START I MOU revealed that almost two-thirds of the most modern SSBNs (i.e., subs armed with MIRVed missiles) were based in the northern Atlantic fleet. The twenty-six on the Kola Peninsula included six Typhoons, seven Delta IVs, four Delta IIIs, four Delta IIs, and five

Delta Is. The twelve at Ribachiy included nine Delta IIIs, two Delta Is, and one Yankee I. The Pavlovskoye fleet consisted of five Delta Is. As of that date, the Russian *Pacific* fleet (i.e., Ribachiy and Pavlovskoye) had 532 SLBM warheads accountable under START I—down from 636 in September 1990 as a result of the elimination of two Delta Is and five Yankee Is.

In 1988, Rear Admiral William Studeman, then director of U.S. Naval Intelligence, told Congress that Yankee-class SSBNs had stopped patrolling off the U.S. coast in late 1987 and were "conducting combat service patrols against theater targets," compensating for the projected loss of SS-20 missiles under the Intermediate-Range Nuclear Forces (INF) Treaty. He added that the Yankee Is, equipped with sixteen 3,000–kilometer-range SS-N-6 missiles each, "can reach . . . Asian targets while alongside their piers."[27] Specifically, a Yankee I based at Ribachiy could launch missiles from port and hit Japan, while a Yankee-I based at Pavlovskoye could hit China, North Korea, or Japan. (The SS-N-8 and SS-N-18, carried by the Delta I and Delta III, respectively, have greater range than the SS-N-6.) It should also be noted that it is extremely unlikely that all seventeen Russian SSBNs in the Pacific fleet (or all of the twenty-six in the northern fleet, for that matter) are fully operational given Russia's economic crisis and the numerous press reports that Moscow maintains only one or two SSBNs on patrol at any given time.[28]

SSBN Production and Projected SSBN Reductions

Admiral Felix Gromov, commander in chief of the Russian Navy, said in 1993 that "the construction of new strategic submarines is not planned for the near future, although designers continue to work in this field."[29] Admiral Gromov added that, by the year 2000, Russia would reduce the number of its SSBNs to twenty-four,[30] presumably six Typhoon-, seven Delta IV–, and eleven Delta III–class submarines. (If this is the case, it seems likely that Russia would decide to close down the Pavlovskoye base near Vladivostok since none of these submarines is based there.)[31] U.S. intelligence officials echoed Admiral Gromov in their public statements to the U.S. Congress in 1993. CIA analyst Gershwin said in February 1993 that, for the first time since the 1960s, Russia has stopped producing ballistic missile submarines and the U.S. intelligence community does not "anticipate a resumption of the production of ballistic missile submarines until . . . sometime after the year 2000."[32] In June 1994, Rear Admiral Sheafer said that, under START II, the Russian SSBN force "will decrease by 50 percent from its current level of 48 submarines."[33]

SLBMs under Development

Various developments in Russian SLBMs are in the works.[34] Russia is developing a new SLBM for deployment on Typhoon-class submarines.[35] According to an April 1993 Russian press report, the SS-N-20 follow-on development is slated to be completed by 1996. U.S. Naval Intelligence expects that all six of the Typhoon SSBNs will be backfitted with the follow-on to the SS-N-20 by the late 1990s. It seems likely that the follow-on to the SS-N-20 based on Typhoon submarines on the Kola Peninsula would be used for U.S. targets rather than Asian targets.

Bombers

Bombers in 1990

In the January 1, 1996 START MOU, Russia declared eighty-nine deployed heavy bombers; sixty-three Bear-Hs, twenty Bear-Gs, and six Blackjacks. Ukraine, for its part, declared twenty-five Bear-Hs and 19 Blackjacks.

It now appears that the forty-two Bear-Hs located in the Far East Military District at Ukrainka, are the only START-accountable bombers based in the Asian part of Russia (i.e., east of the Ural Mountains).

Given that almost 80 percent of the former Soviet Union's Blackjacks and almost 30 percent of its Bear-Hs were still located in Ukraine as of January 1996, and that Russia lacks the number of tankers needed for a robust aerial refueling capability, it seems unlikely that Moscow would be able to bring many of its most modern strategic bombers to bear in a conflict in Northeast Asia.

Projected Strategic Bomber Forces

Moscow's strategic bomber production declined sharply in the early 1990s[36] and has now ceased altogether.[37] The number of heavy bombers Russia will retain in the future will probably depend not on the numerical limits imposed by START I and START II on Russian strategic forces but rather on how many Blackjacks and Bear-Hs it can retrieve from Ukraine and how many aircraft it can afford to maintain.

In addition, the role of Russian strategic bombers is expected to change dramatically in the future. Reportedly, the Russian Air Force has recently been restructured in order to conform with the new military doctrine which stresses preparation for tactical missions around Russia's periphery. Blackjack, Bear, and Backfire bomber crews have begun training as a "composite force" to deliver conventional weapons against targets near Russia's borders.[38]

Soviet INF Treaty Implementation East of the Urals

The INF Treaty,[39] which was signed in December 1987 and entered into force on June 1, 1988, required the United States and the Soviet Union to dismantle all of their land-based missiles with a range of 500 to 5,500 kilometers within three years. In implementing this treaty, the Soviet Union dismantled a significant number of nuclear-armed missiles that were certainly targeted against China and a few that may have been targeted against North Korea.

These mobile missiles included the 5,000–kilometer-range three-warhead SS-20s, the 900–kilometer-range SS-12s, and the 500–kilometer-range SS-23s. The SS-20s within range of China included forty-five at Novosibirk, forty-five at Drovyanaya, forty-five at Barnaul, and thirty-six at Kansk. The SS-12s within range of China included thirty-six at Gornyy, nine at Kattakurgan, and forty at Novosyoyevka. (The Novosyoyevka base, just north of Vladivostok, put the 900–kilometer-range SS-12s within range of Pyongyang as well as northeastern China.) The SS-23s within range of China included twenty-two in Semipalatinsk, Kazakhstan.

Ground-Launched Nuclear Weapons with a Range of Less Than 500 Kilometers

On October 5, 1991, then Soviet President Mikhail Gorbachev declared that the Soviet Union would eliminate all of its existing nuclear artillery projectiles and warheads for tactical nuclear missiles.[40] On January 29, 1992, Russian President Boris Yeltsin said that Russia had stopped the production of nuclear warheads for nuclear land mines as well as for artillery and tactical missiles. He added that "stocks of such nuclear devices will be eliminated."[41] Russian officials have said that they plan to dismantle all the nuclear land mines by 1998 and all the tactical warheads associated with Russia's short-range missiles and artillery by the year 2000.[42]

Naval Tactical Nuclear Weapons and the Pacific Fleet

In his October 5, 1991, initiative, Gorbachev said that "all tactical nuclear weapons shall be removed from surface ships and multi-purpose submarines." (In February 1993, the Russian Ministry of Defense announced that this initiative, which had been reaffirmed by Yeltsin, had been carried out.)[43] In his January 29, 1992, initiative, Yeltsin said that Russia would dismantle one-third of its naval tactical weapons formerly deployed on ships, submarines, and aircraft. Subsequently, Russian officials indicated that they plan to fulfill this pledge by 1996.[44]

Presumably, the two-thirds of Russia's naval tactical nuclear warheads that are not slated for dismantlement will remain in storage facilities near existing naval bases, including those in the Pacific fleet. Although Russia has been reducing the number of nuclear-capable ships, submarines, and aircraft in the Pacific fleet, a significant residual nuclear capability remains, and some modernization appears to be taking place. For example, in the early 1990s, Moscow began replacing obsolete Tu-16 Badger medium-range bombers with the modern, supersonic Tu-22M/Tu-26 Backfire strike aircraft.[45] The International Institute for

Strategic Studies (IISS) estimated in 1993 that seventy Tu-26s in two regiments are based at Alekseyevka naval airfield north of Vladivostok. Backfires can carry nuclear payloads of AS-4s, AS-16s, or nuclear gravity bombs.[46]

IISS estimated that the Tu-26s are supported in the strike role by fifteen Su-24 Fencers and thirty-five Su-17 Fitter fighter-bombers,[47] both of which can carry nuclear gravity bombs.[48]

Pacific fleet surface combatants are also capable of nuclear surface strike operations. As of 1994 the fleet had a single Slava-class cruiser and six Sovremenny-class destroyers.[49] The Slava (*Chervona Ukraina*) can carry sixteen SS-N-12 antiship missiles with an estimated range of more than 500 kilometers. The Sovremennys are capable of carrying eight 90–kilometer-range SS-N-22 antiship missiles each.[50]

As of 1994, the surface ships were augmented by about ten cruise missile submarines (SSGNs), including two Oscar II boats capable of fielding twenty-four SS-N-19 SLCMs.[51] SS-N-19s are antiship cruise missiles with an estimated range of 550 kilometers. Additionally, the Sierra I–class and the Akula-class SSNs assigned to the Pacific fleet are able to carry the 3,000–kilometer-range SS-N-21 SLCM for land-attack missions.[52]

A host of Pacific fleet units can conduct nuclear antisubmarine operations. IISS estimated in its 1993–1994 Military Balance that airborne ASW forces include fifteen Il-38 May, thirty-five Be-12 Seagull, and twenty Tu-142 Bear-F aircraft. Sixty Ka-26 and Ka-27 Hormone helicopters supplement this force. All of these units are able to carry nuclear torpedoes and depth charges.[53]

At least twenty-two surface combatants can conduct nuclear ASW operations, although primary responsibility would fall to the two Kara-class cruisers and three Udaloy-class destroyers that are dedicated to ASW. These ships can carry nuclear-tipped ASW torpedoes.[54] Pacific fleet attack submarines are also able to carry nuclear torpedoes. Additionally, Akula- and Sierra-class SSNs can carry the SS-N-15 nuclear depth charge and the SS-N-16 ASW rocket.[55]

Notwithstanding this extensive nuclear-capable force structure, the Pacific fleet is a hollow force. The U.S. director of naval intelligence's 1994 "Posture Statement" reported that the fleet was suffering severe supply and financial problems.[56] Four Pacific fleet conscripts reportedly starved to death in 1993 in a scandal that prompted one of several fleet command changes.[57] In July 1993, oil and lubricant shipments to fleet bases were halted because the fleet could not pay its bills.[58] Many of the Pacific fleet's ships are unfit to go to sea due to a lack of spare parts and maintenance.[59] Finally, numerous reports indicate that the operating tempo for all of Russia's major fleets, including the Pacific fleet, has dropped precipitously.

Nuclear-Armed SAMs in the Far East Military District

In 1990, the Pentagon said, "The Soviets are . . . substantially upgrading their Far East air defense capabilities with the rapid buildup of SA-10 Grumble surface-to-air missile sites." At that time, the DOD projected that a total of twenty-seven SA-10 battalions would eventually be deployed in the Far East.[60] It is estimated that at least one out of every three SA-10 launchers has nuclear-armed interceptor missiles.[61] (In 1993, the IISS estimated that there were 570 SAMs in the Far East Military District but did not provide a breakdown by type.) According to Russian officials, Moscow plans, in accordance with President Yeltsin's January 29, 1992, initiative, to dismantle half of the warheads associated with antiaircraft missiles by 1996 or 1997.[62] Presumably, the warheads that will be dismantled will be those associated with the older SA-2 and SA-5 SAMs rather than the SA-10s.

Air-Launched Tactical Nuclear Weapons

Russia has said that it plans to dismantle half of the nuclear munitions for tactical aircraft by 1996.[63] Presumably, the other half will remain in storage depots near existing depots, including those at bases in the Asian part of Russia. According to IISS, Russian attack aircraft based in the Far Eastern TVD include the MiG-27 Flogger and the Su-24 Fencer E,[64] both of which can carry nuclear gravity bombs.[65] In 1988, the Pentagon said that the Soviet Union's Strategic Air Army (SAA) at Irkutsk, just north of the Mongolian border near Lake Baikal, was "arrayed against . . . China/East Asia." At that time, nuclear-capable Backfire, Bear-G, Badger, and Blinder bombers were based at Irkutsk.[66] Today, the status of the Irkutsk Air Army is unclear.

Russian Brain Drain to China and North Korea

The continued political and economic turmoil in Russia has intensified international concerns about the prospect for a "brain drain" in which former nuclear weapons scientists and engineers sell their expertise to the highest bidder.

Then CIA Director James Woolsey told Congress in July 1993 that "delays in pay, deteriorating working conditions, and uncertain futures are apparently spurring Russian specialists to seek emigration despite official restrictions on such travel."[67] Woolsey added that China has been "aggressively recruiting" weapons scientists from Russia, and his aide Gordon Oehler said, "there is evidence the North Koreans would like to have them [too], but the Russians are unwilling to go."[68]

In January 1993, Yevgeny Primakov, then head of the Russian Foreign Intelligence Service (FIS), said that "as of the beginning of 1993, the FIS had no data indicating that Russian specialists of this kind were working in Third World countries which are producing or starting up the production" of weapons of mass destruction. In February 1994, the Russian Security Ministry announced that North Korea had tried to recruit sixty engineers from Makeyev Design Bureau in Miass, which is responsible for Scud missiles and SLBMs. Russian police, however, prevented the group from boarding a plane in Moscow bound for Pyongyang in October 1992.[69]

In January 1994, the Japanese weekly *Shukan Bunshun* published what it claims is an official Russian government assessment of the brain drain to North Korea. According to this document, 160 Russian specialists have participated in the North Korean nuclear weapons and ballistic missile programs and 9 nuclear weapons scientists and 17 missile engineers are currently taking part.[70]

Scenarios for Russian Use of Nuclear Weapons

In a press conference on November 3, 1993, Russian Defense Minister Pavel Grachev made it clear that Russia's newly adopted military doctrine does not reaffirm the pledge made in 1982 by Leonid Brezhnev that the Soviet Union would not be the first to use nuclear weapons under any circumstances.[71] Grachev said that "there is absolutely nothing in the doctrine about non-use of [nuclear] weapons."[72]

The change in Russia's declaratory policy on no first use may reflect, *inter alia,* a general sense in Moscow that because of the recent sharp decline in its conventional forces and its overall economic and political situation, Russia must now rely more on nuclear weapons both for deterrence and for its status as a major world power.[73] With respect to nuclear deterrence, Moscow may be particularly concerned that if its relations with Beijing take a dramatic turn for the worse in the next ten to twenty years, Russian conventional forces east of the Urals might not be able to counter those that China could bring to bear. Sergei Rogov, deputy director of the Institute for the Study of USA and Canada in Moscow, recently wrote: "While relations with China today are pretty good, a military conflict with China has been and will always be a nightmare for Russian military planners. Concerns about whether Russia is capable of fighting a conventional war with China lead to an emphasis in Russian military circles on the need to keep some tactical nuclear weapons."[74]

Chinese Nuclear Forces

China's nuclear weapons program remains shrouded in secrecy, but it appears that Beijing is continuing to upgrade and expand its forces slowly with the development of new types of ballistic missiles and the acquisition of nuclear-capable aircraft from Russia.

Unlike the United States and Russia, China has not yet agreed to subject its nuclear forces to legally binding limits in any international agreements. But China, of course, has a much smaller force—roughly 300 deployed nuclear warheads and possibly another 150 ground-launched tactical nuclear warheads in storage, according to Robert S. Norris, Andrew S. Burrows, and Richard W. Fieldhouse, authors of the *Nuclear Weapons Data Book,* Volume 5, *British, French, and Chinese Nuclear Weapons.*

The Rationale behind Chinese Nuclear Forces

China began a program to develop nuclear weapons in the mid-1950s and exploded its first nuclear weapons device in 1964. Since then, it has continued to give the maintenance and development of nuclear weapons a high priority. There appear to be four major reasons why Beijing continues to dedicate a substantial amount of resources to its nuclear weapons programs. First, China seeks to deter U.S. and Russian aggression or political intimidation. (Of course, if deterrence failed and the United States or Russia initiated the use of nuclear weapons against China, Chinese nuclear forces would give Beijing the capability to retaliate and punish the aggressor and/or deny the aggressor victory.) China intends to make sure that it will never again be subjected to what it calls "nuclear blackmail."[75] This concern stems directly from Chinese experience in the 1950s and 1960s. China reportedly believes that it was subjected to nuclear threats by the United States during the Korean War and during the Taiwan–Formosa Strait crises (Quemoy and Matsu) in 1954–1955 and 1958, and by the Soviet Union during the Sino-Soviet border clashes in 1969.

Today, even if the United States and Russia were to eliminate their tactical nuclear weapons and ratify and implement the START II Treaty, they would each still have more than ten times more nuclear weapons than China has today. Moreover, China knows that both Russia and the United States have targeted China in the past with nuclear weapons and could do so again in the future. In a sentence that seems representative of Beijing's view, a former member of the General Staff and the Ministry of National Defense of China's People's Liberation Army (PLA) recently wrote: "Before the total elimination of the superpowers' nuclear arsenals, it would be suicidal and reckless for China to give up its own limited nuclear retaliatory capability."[76]

Second, China's robust nuclear weapons program also appears to be part of an effort to increase Beijing's international prestige and status, as well as its influence over both regional and international security issues.[77] Although China has the world's largest population and fastest-growing economy, it is still a relatively poor country and would probably not be considered a major power with status comparable to the other permanent members of the U.N. Security Council without nuclear weapons.

In a related reason, over the last three decades, China—like France—has apparently seen its nuclear weapons as a way to remain politically autonomous from Washington and Moscow. By developing its own nuclear weapons, China—unlike Japan and Germany—has not had to join a security alliance and rely on another state's "nuclear umbrella."[78] Thus, in some ways, China's nuclear forces serve a political purpose similar to France's *force de frappe.*

China also probably seeks to maintain and upgrade its nuclear forces so that it can settle regional security issues (e.g., border disputes with India and Vietnam, disputes over claims to the Spratly Islands, the status of Taiwan) on its own terms without concern that it could be politically coerced by any of its neighbors that currently have nuclear weapons or may have them in the future.[79] In addition to the United States and Russia, China must be concerned about many of its neighbors: India currently has the capability to assemble a relatively small number of nuclear weapons quickly; North Korea may have or may be pursuing nuclear weapons capability; and Japan, South Korea, and Taiwan have the technology to develop nuclear weapons relatively quickly.[80] Thus, China may believe it is necessary to maintain and upgrade its nuclear arsenal as a hedge against nuclear proliferation in Asia.[81]

Trends in Chinese Nuclear Forces

China has developed a nuclear "triad," but with far more emphasis on land-based ballistic missiles than on submarines or bombers. The technology of these systems lags far behind U.S. and Russian nuclear weapons systems. For example, China's ballistic missiles are believed to be far less accurate than U.S. and Russian ballistic missiles. In addition, Beijing has not yet deployed missiles that can deliver warheads to separate targets (i.e. MIRVed missiles).

As mentioned above, China's nuclear arsenal is far smaller than the U.S. and Russian arsenals and will not come anywhere near those levels for the foreseeable future. China's force structure and operations, as well as its declaratory policy, reflect a countervalue, "city-busting," second-strike strategy that can be fulfilled with a relatively small force.

Although it seems clear that China does not seek to field large numbers of nuclear weapons, the People's Liberation Army continues to work on many different types of nuclear weapons—a guideline referred to as "small but all-inclusive."[82] Consequently, Beijing appears to have numerous development programs under way to improve its nuclear forces in qualitative terms. The pace of Beijing's modernization programs, however, is extremely gradual and slow. For example, as a rule of thumb, many years pass between the first flight-test of a new ballistic missile and the actual deployment of that missile. With China's growing economy, it will probably have sufficient resources to raise its defense budget, including increased expenditures for nuclear weapons, for many years to come.

Improving Survivability

In order to deter a U.S. or Russian nuclear attack against China, Beijing has focused its efforts on developing a secure strategic retaliatory capability. To increase the survivability of its nuclear forces, China has tried to make its ballistic missiles more difficult to locate and target by storing them in caves and tunnels, using camouflage, deploying them on mobile land-based launchers, and deploying them on submarines. Current modernization efforts—e.g., the development of solid-fuel mobile ICBMs and lighter, more compact warheads—seem geared to reduce the vulnerability of China's nuclear forces to a first strike.

Land-Based Ballistic Missiles

Land-based ballistic missiles are the mainstay of China's nuclear forces. These systems vary in range from 1,000 to 13,000 kilometers. Between the mid-1960s and the early 1970s, China developed the Dong Feng, or "East Wind," family of four land-based missiles: the DF-2, DF-3, DF-4, and DF-5. All four missiles were reportedly intended to have the capability of striking U.S. targets. The DF-2, first successfully flight-tested in 1964, has a range of 1,000–2,000 kilometers—sufficient range to hit Okinawa, Japan. (The DF-2 has now been removed from service.) The DF-3, first successfully flight-tested in 1966, has a range of 2,600–2,800 kilometers—enough range to strike the (former) U.S. bases at Clark and Subic Bay in the Philippines. The DF-4, first successfully flight-tested in 1970, has a range of 4,700 kilometers—sufficient range to reach Andersen Air Force Base on Guam. Finally, the DF-5, first successfully flight-tested in 1971, has a range of 12,000–13,000 kilometers and was apparently designed with the intention of being able to hit the continental United States.[83]

After the Sino-Soviet border clashes in 1969, however, Beijing reportedly decided to retarget most of its nuclear forces on the Soviet Union. According to John Lewis and Xue Litai, Soviet cities became the designated targets of Chinese missiles in the early 1970s.[84] It is believed that most Chinese land-based missiles are deployed in the northwestern part of China, from where they would only have the range to hit targets in Russia.[85]

The missiles in the DF series have a slow response time, vulnerable basing modes, and poor accuracy.[86] Consequently, the Chinese leadership has decided to develop new solid-fuel, mobile, land-based ballistic missiles, including the DF-21, DF-31, and DF-41.

DF-3 (CSS-2)

According to some standard public reference sources, China deploys forty to eighty DF-3[87] missiles.[88] The road-mobile DF-3, which was the first Chinese missile to use storable liquid fuel, has a single warhead with an estimated yield of 1–3 megatons. It was initially deployed in 1971. Reportedly, the DF-3s are deployed at launch sites near Dalong, Liuchingkou, X'ian, Kunming, Jianshui, Liankengwang, Xuanhua, Fengrun, Itu, and Tangdao, with most of the missiles in the northwestern part of China near the Soviet (now Russian) border.[89] Many of the DF-3s are stored in caves and valleys in order to conceal their locations and enhance their survivability. In a report published in 1976, the U.S. Defense Intelligence Agency (DIA) said that the DF-3 is "probably intended for relatively large population targets in central and eastern Russia."[90] According to a 1994 report by the U.S. Congressional Research Service (CRS), the deployment of the DF-3 "provides the PRC with a capacity to hit static targets such as population and industrial centers in central and eastern Russia, for example, as well as similarly close targets elsewhere in East and South Asia."[91]

DF-4 (CSS-3)

Approximately ten to twenty DF-4 missiles are now deployed in China.[92] This liquid-fuel missile, which is housed in both silos and tunnels, was first deployed in 1980. The DF-4's warhead has an estimated yield of 1–3 megatons. The silo-based versions are reportedly located in China's central and southeast region near Sundian and Tongdao.[93] The tunnel-based versions are located in the northwestern region on erector launchers in Qinghai (Xiao Qaidam, Da Qaidam, and Delingha), where they were moved in 1971, when they were retargeted against the Soviet Union.[94] The DF-4 is probably targeted against Russian military-industrial and population centers.[95] According to the U.S. Air Force, it "can reach targets throughout European Russia, including Moscow."[96]

DF-5 (CSS-4)

Today, China reportedly deploys four to ten DF-5A missiles in silos.[97] (These are deployed among a large number of fake silos to make them more surviv-able.)[98] China has the capacity to build many more DF-5s, as has been demonstrated by the production of CZ-2 and other space-launch vehicles, but appears content to demonstrate ICBM capability with a small number of missiles.[99] This liquid-fuel system, whose warheads have an estimated yield of 3–5 megatons, first became operational in 1981.[100] Two of the DF-5As are located near Luoning in Henan Province.[101] The DF-5A, with a range of up to 13,000 kilometers, is China's only missile capable of hitting the continental United States. According to a 1994 edition of *Jane's Strategic Weapons Systems*, the DF-5 has a circular error probable (CEP) of 500 meters.

DF-21

Reportedly, China deploys roughly twenty-five to fifty DF-21s.[102] This mobile missile, which has a range of 1,800 kilometers, was first deployed in 1988. The DF-21, which has a warhead with an estimated yield of 200–300 kilotons, is China's first land-based intermediate-range ballistic missile with solid fuel.[103] (The JL-1 SLBM, which is essentially the same missile as the DF-21, was China's first ballistic missile with solid fuel.)[104]

According to one press account, the DF-21s are deployed in the northwest province of Qinghai and the southwest province of Yunnan.[105] Presumably, those DF-21s based in Qinghai are targeted against urban industrial areas in

Russia, and those in Yunnan are targeted against northeastern India and Southeast Asian countries.[106] *Jane's Defence Weekly* reported in January 1994 that some of the DF-21s have recently been equipped with conventional warheads "so they can be more effectively employed in limited local wars."[107]

ICBMs under Development

In order to improve the reliability and survivability of its land-based nuclear forces, China is now trying to develop solid-fuel, mobile ICBMs.[108] Currently, all of China's land-based nuclear missiles except for the DF-21 have liquid fuel. These missiles are not only more difficult to maintain than solid-fuel missiles, but they have slow reaction times as well. For example, in order to launch the DF-4 tunnel-based missiles, the PLA must roll the missiles out to the launch pad, place them on the launch stand, and fuel them—a process that requires several hours.[109] Furthermore, China has only a handful of ICBMs, and these are all liquid-fuel, silo-based systems. In addition to the development of ICBMs with solid fuel and mobile basing modes, many analysts believe that China is trying to give its new land-based missiles increased range and the capability to carry multiple independently targetable re-entry vehicles (MIRVs).

In order to develop solid-fuel mobile ICBMs with greater range and MIRVs, it appears likely that China would have to decrease the size and weight of its current warheads. According to U.S. government officials and private analysts, China's recent underground nuclear tests at Lop Nor were probably part of a series of tests to develop smaller, more compact warheads for its new mobile ICBMs,[110] possibly for the single-warhead DF-31 ICBM or for the DF-41, which may carry MIRVs.[111] (U.S. Senator Larry Pressler has compared the DF-31 and DF-41 to the Russian single-warhead SS-25 and ten-warhead SS-24 ICBMs, respectively.)[112] China's commitment to negotiate a comprehensive test ban (CTB) by 1996—a commitment undertaken in 1993—may have represented Beijing's estimate of how long it would take China to complete the test program for the development of new warheads with higher "yield-to-weight ratios" for these ICBMs. (Chinese officials, however, claim that the purpose of recent tests was to incorporate safety features into their warheads, such as insensitive high explosives.)[113]

According to John Lewis and Hua Di, the new DF-31 and DF-41 solid-fuel mobile ICBMs will have ranges of 8,000 and 12,000 kilometers and become operational in the mid-1990s and late 1990s, respectively. They also assert that the warhead originally designed for the DF-31 and DF-41 has a yield of 200–300 kilotons, but the 660–kiloton underground blast at Lop Nor on May 21, 1992, may indicate that the Chinese are trying to develop a higher-yield warhead for these two missiles.[114] On May 4, 1994, Senator Pressler, using the New Delhi–based Institute of Defense Studies and Analysis as his source, cited the same ranges and deployment dates for the DF-31 and DF-41 as Lewis and Hua but estimated that they will have yields of 100 kilotons and 1 megaton, respectively.[115] Pressler also said that these ICBMs will probably be MIRVed and "can be raised and launched in thirty minutes."[116]

Reported Help from Russian Scientists in Developing New ICBMs

It appears that, as part of its effort to develop solid-fuel, mobile ICBMs, Beijing has actively recruited former Soviet weapons scientists and engineers to come work in China. James Woolsey, then director of U.S. Central Intelligence, told Congress on July 28, 1993, that China is "the country that is probably most aggressively recruiting CIS [Commonwealth of Independent States] scientists to help in a wide number of weapons programs." Woolsey added, "there is substantial movement along those lines."[117] Subsequent to Woolsey's statements, a spate of press reports indicated that the flow of CIS weapons designers to China continued on a large scale in late 1993.[118] China seems interested in acquiring technology from the CIS, particularly from Russia, to improve the range and accuracy of its ballistic missiles, especially technology that would help Beijing design the DF-31 or a follow-on version so that it is similar to Russia's SS-25 mobile, solid-fuel ICBM.[119] In the spring of 1996, U.S. Secretary of Defense William Perry confirmed press reports that Washington had "information that China was seeking SS-18 technology from Russia." China has also reportedly approached Ukraine seeking help to improve Beijing's ballistic missile technology.[120]

In addition to the unsanctioned help from Russia, there appears to be a fair amount of sanctioned help. Reportedly, Russia's Atomic Energy Minister Viktor Mikhailov visited China in November 1992 as part of an initiative to broaden nuclear cooperation between Moscow and Beijing.[121] Reportedly, China has also contracted with Russia to buy three diesel-powered Kilo-class submarines[122] and purchased a "sizable force of SA-10 SAMs."[123]

SSBNs and SLBMs

Current SSBNs and SLBMs

China has built two Xia-class SSBNs, which can carry twelve Julang-1 (JL-1) SLBMs each.[124] Although Beijing has declared both of these submarines to be operational, some in the West continue to question whether both SSBNs have actually conducted patrols with their missiles. According to the 1994 CRS report, "It is uncertain if the second Xia-class submarine can be considered fully operational."[125] Furthermore, in his June 1994 "Posture Statement," the director of U.S. naval intelligence said that China had "commissioned" only one SSBN.[126] The SSBNs are believed to be deployed in the North Sea fleet, possibly at Quingdao or Ningbo on the Yellow Sea.[127]

The JL-1, which was developed and tested during the 1980s,[128] was China's first ballistic missile to use solid fuel. Reportedly, the JL-1 has not been flight-tested since 1988.[129] With a range of just 1,700 kilometers, the JL-1 could only strike Moscow from the Baltic Sea—an unlikely location for a Chinese submarine. Presumably, the JL-1 is designed to be deployed on submarines patrolling in the Western Pacific, from where it could target urban industrial areas in the eastern part of Russia.[130]

SSBNs and SLBMs under Development

The U.S. intelligence community apparently now believes that China has, at least for the near future, halted or slowed SSBN production. In May 1993, Rear Admiral Edward Sheafer told Congress that China's "nuclear-powered submarine construction program effort has probably at least temporarily ended at the current half dozen ballistic missile and attack units"[131] ("the current half dozen" apparently refers to one operational Xia-class SSBN and five Han-class SSNs.)[132] But in his June 1994 "Posture Statement," Admiral Sheafer said, "China is believed to be working on an indigenous design for a second generation nuclear-powered ballistic missile submarine to carry a new SLBM also in development; the new SSBN may be launched by the turn of the century." The "new SLBM . . . in development" to which Sheafer referred is the JL-2, which is a variant of the DF-31 ICBM.[133] Like the DF-31, it is expected to use solid fuel and have a range of 8,000 kilometers.

The relatively slow pace of SSBN development and production may be due, *inter alia*, to technical difficulties China has experienced in developing nuclear reactors for its submarines and solid fuel for its SLBMs.[134] Robert S. Norris, Richard Fieldhouse, and Andrew Burrows—authors of *Nuclear Weapons Databook*, Volume 5, *British, French, and Chinese Nuclear Weapons*—project that China will eventually build "perhaps four to six" SSBNs.[135]

Bombers

Current Bombers

There is considerable uncertainty about the number and types of Chinese aircraft that are equipped to carry nuclear weapons. Norris, Burrows, and Fieldhouse estimate that China currently fields approximately 180 nuclear-capable aircraft: 120 Hong-6s, thirty Hong-5s, and thirty Qian-5s. They estimate that a total of approximately 150 nuclear gravity bombs are available to arm these aircraft.[136] The CRS, on the other hand, estimates that the Chinese nuclear bomber forces consist of thirty Hong-6s, whereas the IISS says only that "some [H-6s] may be nuclear-capable."

These planes are based on Soviet technology from the 1950s and 1960s. (Specifically, the designs of the H-6, H-5, and Q-5 were based on the Soviet

TU-16 Badger, the IL-28 Beagle, and the MiG-19, respectively.)[137] The Hong-6 and Qian-5, however, are still under production.[138] In the last two decades, bombers have received less emphasis in China's nuclear forces than ballistic missiles, presumably because of their limited range and vulnerability to Soviet/-Russian air defense.[139] According to the CRS, "it is often claimed that these obsolescent aircraft would have great difficulty penetrating sophisticated air defenses. At least some observers speculate that it is improbable that China's air force has a nuclear delivery mission against either Russia or U.S. forces in Asia."[140] Little is publicly known in the West about the locations of Chinese bomber bases. The Hong-6s may be based at Datong (Qinghai).[141]

Bombers under Development

The Hong-7 bomber, which is China's only modern bomber, was first flight-tested in 1988. In 1992, the aircraft entered series production at the Xian Aircraft Factory.[142] In a development that suggests that the Hong-7 may finally be nearing operational status, it was reported in March 1994 that, as part of a marketing effort to sell the aircraft to Tehran, Xian Aircraft would fly the Hong-7 to Iran for a series of flight demonstrations.[143]

China, however, may have decided that it is cheaper and faster to purchase nuclear-capable aircraft from Russia and other foreign countries than to develop new planes indigenously. Beijing has recently purchased a number of Su-27 Flanker fighters from Moscow. The first of these were initially delivered in January 1992.[144] *Jane's Defence Weekly* reported in early 1994 that China was operating a squadron of twenty-six Su-27s at Wuhu, a base near Shanghai.[145] According to U.S. intelligence and press accounts, Beijing will probably exercise its option to purchase one or two more squadrons, eventually giving China a total of fifty to seventy-five Su-27s.[146] (According to a May 1993 report from the director of U.S. naval intelligence, "the Chinese Air Force has experienced training and maintenance problems in integrating the Flanker into its technologically obsolescent aircraft order-of-battle.")[147] Reportedly, China is also interested in buying four or more nuclear-capable Tu-22M Backfire bombers from Russia.[148] China has also demonstrated interest in purchasing Soviet-built Su-24 Fencers and MiG-29 Fulcrums from Iran.[149]

Land-Based Tactical Nuclear Weapons

There is some controversy over whether China has any tactical nuclear weapons. Norris, Burrows, and Fieldhouse assert that China introduced approximately 150 tactical nuclear weapons into its arsenal in the late 1970s, possibly including atomic demolition munitions, nuclear artillery, or multiple-rocket system (MRS) shells or tactical missiles. They base their conclusion in part on the fact that China has conducted several nuclear tests with yields well below 20 kilotons and conducted military exercises in which Beijing reportedly simulated the use of tactical nuclear weapons. Norris, Burrows, and Fieldhouse note that the worsening relations between China and the Soviet Union in the late 1960s and early 1970s may have spurred Beijing's tactical nuclear weapons program. They also suggest, however, that recent improvements in the relationship between China and Russia could lead China to retire its tactical nuclear weapons.[150] Jonathan Pollock of the Rand Corporation has written, "Given that the prospect of a Soviet attack diminished appreciably during the mid- and late-1980s, it is possible that the Chinese have already begun to quietly dismantle [their tactical nuclear weapons] which they have been loath to even acknowledge or confirm in the first place."[151]

Scenarios for Chinese Use of Nuclear Weapons

Although Chinese military planners will continue to be concerned about the United States, Russia, India, and Japan, it seems very unlikely that China would get involved in a nuclear conflict with any of these three countries. In June 1994, Admiral Sheafer gave what seems to be an accurate assessment when he said that China "does not perceive any large-scale threat from either global or major regional powers through the next decade. Intra-regional conflicts—mainly in southern Asia—are seen as more likely, largely revolving around disputed claims in the South China Sea (such as those to the Spratly Islands)." Another plausible regional scenario might involve a military conflict between China and Taiwan if Taipei declared independence. But neither seizing the Spratly Islands nor preventing Taiwan's independence would justify the political, economic, and environmental costs that China would bear if it used nuclear weapons. Furthermore, Beijing would have no reason to use or threaten to use nuclear weapons in these scenarios because it could ultimately prevail in both cases with conventional forces.

Recommendations on Regional Bilateral Initiatives

It is difficult to identify viable proposals to limit U.S., Russian, and Chinese nuclear forces that would directly affect North Korea, Japan, or other Northeast Asian countries. For example, a "zonal" approach—prohibiting the deployment of U.S., Russian, and Chinese nuclear weapons in a designated area—would be problematic for a number of reasons. To begin with, such an arrangement would be extremely difficult to negotiate and implement due to the geographical and numerical asymmetries. With the implementation of then U.S. President George Bush's September 27, 1991, initiative, the United States no longer deploys any tactical nuclear weapons in or near Northeast Asia (see the subsection entitled "Tactical Nuclear Weapons Withdrawn from South Korea"), nor does the United States have any strategic nuclear weapons based in Asia (unless one counts Trident submarines that patrol in the Pacific Ocean), but this is irrelevant because strategic weapons could hit targets in the region, regardless of where they are based. This latter point applies to Russia as well. In China's case, all of its nuclear weapons are based in Northeast Asia. Furthermore, Beijing does not appear to be willing to limit the number and types of its nuclear weapons until the United States and Russia make reductions to or near China's level—a development that is not in the offing.

Although a far-reaching nuclear-free zone in Northeast Asia covering U.S., Russian, and Chinese nuclear weapons deployments in any meaningful way is probably not viable, some regional initiatives targeted on individual states could make a positive impact, especially in the short term. The following subsections list proposals for bilateral measures intended to help prevent nuclear proliferation in Northeast Asia.

Bilateral Initiative That the United States Could Take with North Korea

The United States should take the following action: continue to fund and implement the U.S.-DPRK October 1994 Agreed Framework to contain and ultimately, reverse the North Korean nuclear proliferation threat.

Bilateral Initiatives That the United States Could Take with Japan

The United States should take the following actions:

1. Encourage Japan to abandon its breeder reactor program and stockpile low-enriched uranium (LEU) for fueling existing light-water reactors
2. Reassure Japan that strains in U.S.-Japanese relations over trade issues and the dissolution of the Soviet Union will not reduce the U.S. commitment to Japan's security

Bilateral Initiatives That the United States Could Take with Russia

The United States should take the following action: Continue to help Russia improve security and accounting for nuclear material through the Nunn–Lugar program, lab-to-lab cooperation and other similar initiatives. (If reprocessed plutonium can easily be diverted from Russia to North Korea then Pyongyang would not need to maintain any of its nuclear facilities to build a bomb.)

A Bilateral Initiative That Russia Could Take with North Korea

Russia should take the following action: Stop Russian weapons scientists and engineers from emigrating to North Korea by creating expanded opportunities to apply their expertise to peaceful purposes.

Bilateral Initiatives That Russia Could Take with Japan

Russia should take the following actions:

1. Encourage Japan to establish a regular government-funded program, similar to the Nunn–Lugar program, to help Russia control and account for its nuclear materials. (In 1994, Japan, which has significant expertise in this area, committed $17 million for the International Science and Technology Center in Moscow and pledged an additional $80 million for other denuclearization activities,[152] including funding to help build a storage facility for plutonium from dismantled warheads.)
2. Seek financial assistance from Japan to dismantle Russian nuclear submarines (SSBNs, SSNs, and SSGNs) in the Pacific fleet. This would include assistance to:

   - Dispose of spent fuel from naval nuclear reactors.
   - Dispose of solid radioactive waste, including defueled reactor compartments from decommissioned submarines.
   - Cut up the submarines themselves. (Russia and Japan are currently holding negotiations for an agreement in which Moscow would make a commitment not to dump liquid nuclear waste from decommissioned submarines in the Sea of Japan in exchange for assistance from Tokyo in building a new sea-based facility to store and dispose of that waste.[153]

3. Sell Japan low-enriched uranium blended down from HEU recovered from dismantled warheads—similar to the agreement with the United States.[154] Tokyo could use the LEU to fuel its existing light-water reactors.

A Bilateral Initiative That China Could Take with North Korea

China should take the following action: Make it clear to North Korea that if it continues to renounce its nuclear weapons program, Beijing will push Western countries hard to normalize economic and political relations with Pyongyang.

General, Global Commitments That the United States, Russia, and China Could Make

Although bilateral regional measures and initiatives are worth pursuing, some of them have the potential danger of appearing, at least implicitly, discriminatory by singling out a nation (e.g., North Korea or Japan) as unfit to possess nuclear weapons. Arms-control measures will be more enduring if they help promote a world in which it is universally recognized that nuclear weapons have very limited political and military utility and that the political, economic, and environmental costs of developing nuclear weapons will almost certainly exceed the benefits.

Therefore, the arms-control steps that the United States, Russia, and China can take that will have the greatest impact in the long run will probably be steps that will strengthen the international nuclear nonproliferation regime as a whole. In this context, it is crucial that the United States, Russia, and China take concrete initiatives to implement nuclear disarmament commitments undertaken at the 1995 NPT Extension Conference. By helping create an international environment in which nuclear weapons are seen as more of a liability than an asset and their acquisition a violation of an international norm, an NPT supported by almost all of the world's nations indefinitely would make it easier for the post–Kim Il Sung/Kim Jong Il regime (or a united Korea with nuclear weapons) to follow the precedent that South Africa set by dismantling Pretoria's nuclear weapons and becoming a non–nuclear weapons state.

The United States, Russia, and China should take the following actions:

1. Strengthen long-standing negative security assurances.
2. Continue to refrain from nuclear testing, sign, and ratify a Comprehensive Test Ban Treaty in 1996.[155]
3. Stop the production of fissile material for weapons and negotiate and sign a fissile material cutoff treaty (FMCT), placing—at a minimum—all plutonium-reprocessing and uranium enrichment facilities under IAEA safeguards.
4. Follow through on the implementation of various U.S.-Russian nuclear transparency agreements that have already been agreed in principle, e.g., exchanges of data on warheads and fissile material and reciprocal monitoring initiatives.
5. Allow some international monitoring of warhead dismantlement. (In practice, this would probably be a bilateral agreement between the United States and Russia.)
6. Make a commitment to dismantle all naval nuclear warheads carried on attack submarines, surface ships, and aircraft (i.e., all naval nuclear warheads except for those that arm SLBMs).
7. Make (or reaffirm) a commitment to dismantle all ground-launched tactical nuclear warheads.
8. Establish and institutionalize a multilateral forum—including the United States, Russia, China, Japan, and South and North Korea—to discuss nuclear security issues in Northeast Asia.

APPENDIX

Table 16.1

Former Soviet Union ICBMs: September 1990 and January 1996

September 1, 1990	Jan. 1, 1996	Change
• 326 SS–11s at bases in Russia:	0	–326
60 at Bershet	0	–60
26 at Teykovo	0	–26
40 at Krasnoyarsk	0	–40
50 at Drovyanaya	0	–50
90 at Yasnaya	0	–90
60 at Svobodnyy	0	–60
• 40 SS–13s at Yoshkar-Ola, Russia	0	–40
• 47 SS–17s at Vypolzovo, Russia	1	–46
• 204 SS–18s in Russia:	186	–18
64 at Dombarovskiy	58	–6
46 in Kartaly	46	0
64 in Uzhur	52	–12
30 in Aleysk	30	0
• 104 SS–18s in Kazakhstan:		
52 in Derzhavinsk (which the United States formerly referred to as Imeni Gastello)	total of 24*	–80
52 in Zhangiz-Tobe		
• 170 SS–19s in Russia:	170	0
60 in Kozel'sk	60	0
110 in Tatishchevo	110	0
• 130 SS–19s in Ukraine:	128**	–2
40 in Pervomaysk	128**	–2
90 in Khmel'Nitskiy		
• 234 SS–25s in Russia:	351	+117
36 in Teykovo	36	0
18 in Yoshkar-Ola	36	+18
45 in Yur'Ya	45	0
45 in Nizhiniy Tagil	45	0
27 in Novosibirsk	45	+18
27 in Kansk	45	+18
36 in Irkutsk	36	0
0 in Drovyanoya	18	+18
0 in Barnaul	36	+36
0 in Vypolozovo	9	+9
• 54 in Belarus:	9	+9
27 in Lida	total of 18	–36
27 in Mozyr		
• 33 rail-based SS–24s in Russia:	36	+3
12 in Kostroma	12	0
12 in Krasnoyarsk	12	0
9 in Bershet	12	+3
• 10 silo-based SS–24s in Tatishchevo, Russia	10	0
• 46 silo-based SS–24s in Pervomaysk, Ukraine	46**	0**

Table 16.1 *(continued)*

Note: These numbers are for deployed land-based missiles, *not* warheads; these figures are based on START I definitions and counting rules.

*24 SS–18 silos remained in Kazakhstan as of January 1, 1996, but all of the warheads associated with those missiles had been withdrawn to Russia by 1995, according to U.S. and Russian officials.

**Although none of the (as of January 1996) 46 SS–24 silos and only 2 of the 130 SS–19 silos in Ukraine had been dismantled, all of the warheads from these missiles had been removed and withdrawn to Russia by mid–1996, according to public statements by U.S. and Russian officials.

Sources: START MOU September 1, 1990; START MOU January 1, 1996.

Table 16.2

Deployed Soviet/Russian Heavy Bombers

Bomber Type	Sept. 1, 1990	Sept. 1990 Total	Jan. 1, 1996	Jan. 1996 Total
Bear-Gs:	46 in Ukrainka, Russia	(46)	4 in Engels; and 16 in Ryazan	(20)
Bear-Hs: (w/ALCMs)	21 in Uzin, *Ukraine;* 22 in Mozdok; 40 in Semipalatinsk, Kazakhstan; 1 in Kubyshev	(84)	25 in Uzin, *Ukraine;* 21 in Mozdok; 42 in Ukrainka	(88)
Blackjacks:	2 in Kazan, Russia; 13 in Priluki, *Ukraine* (plus 6 test planes at Zhukovsky)	(15)	6 at Engels; 19 at Priluki, *Ukraine* (plus 6 test planes at Zhukovsky)	(25)
		(145)		(133)

Table 16.3

Soviet/Russian ICBM Warheads

	Sept. 1, 1990	Jan. 1, 1996	Change
SS–11	326	0	–326
SS–13	40	0	–40
SS–17	188	4	–184
SS–18 in Russia	2,040	1,860	–180
SS–18 in Kazak	1,040	240*	–800
SS–19 in Ukraine	780	768**	–12
SS–19 in Russia	1,020	1,020	0
SS–24 rail	330	360	+30
SS–24 silo (Ukraine)	460	460**	0
SS–24 silo (Russia)	100	100	0
SS–25 Belarus	54	18	–36
SS–25 Russia	234	351	+117
Grand Totals	6,612	5,181	–1,431

Note: All numbers are based on START I counting rules.

*Although 24 SS–18 silos (and therefore 240 SS–18 warheads) in *Kazakhstan* were still START I accountable as of January 1, 1996, all of the warheads had been removed from their missiles and withdrawn to Russia by 1995, according to public statements from U.S. and Russian officials.

**Although 128 SS–19 silos (768 warheads) and 46 SS–24 silos (460 warheads) in *Ukraine* were still START I accountable as of January 1, 1996, all of the warheads had been removed from their missiles and withdrawn to Russia by mid–1996, according to public statements from U.S. and Russian officials.

Sources: START I MOU, September 1, 1990 and January 1, 1996.

Table 16.4

Soviet/Russian Submarine-Launched Ballistic Missiles (SLBMs)

Deployed SLBMs

Missile Type	Sept. 1, 1990	Jan. 1, 1996	Change
SS-N–6	192	16	–176
Ss-N–8	280	232	–48
SS-N–17	12	0	–12
SS-N–18	224	208	–16
SS-N–20	120	120	0
SS-N–23	112	112	0
Totals:	940	688	252

Table 16.5

Soviet/Russian SSBNs (nuclear-powered ballistic missile subs)

	Sept. 1, 1990	Jan. 1, 1996	Change
Yankee I	12	1	−11
Yankee II	1	0	−1
Delta I	18	12	−6
Delta II	4	4	0
Delta III	14	13	−1
Delta IV	7	7	0
Typhoon	6	6	0
Totals:	62	43	19

Table 16.6

Kola Peninsula (North Atlantic) Deployed Russian SLBMs and SSBNs (Jan. 1, 1996)

Nerpichya (Kola Peninsula)
120   SS-N-20 SLBMs   6   Typhoons

Yagel'Naya (Kola Peninsula)
112   SS-N-23 SLBMs   7   Delta IVs
 64   SS-N-18 SLBMs   4   Delta IIIs
 64   SS-N-8 SLBMs   4   Delta IIs
 24   SS-N-8 SLBMs   2   Delta Is

264   17

Ostrovnoy (Kola Peninsula)
48   SS-N-8s*   3   Delta Is

Totals:
432 SLBMs   26   SSBMs

*Includes 12 SS-N-8s at Nerpa elimination/conversion facility.

Table 16.7

Russian SLBMs and SSBNs in the Pacific Fleet (Jan. 1, 1996)

Pavlovskoye (Kamchatka Peninsula)				
60	SS-N-8	on	5	Delta Is

Rlbachiy (Petropavlovsk)				
16	SS-N-6	on	1	Yankee I
36	SS-N-8*	on	2	Delta Is
144	SS-N-18	on	9	Delta IIIs
196			12	

Totals:				
256	SLBMs*	on	17	SSBMs

*Includes 12 SS-N-8s at "Zvesda" conversion or elimination facility.

Table 16.8

Russian SLBM Warheads in the Pacific Fleet

Sub Type	Sept. 1, 1990				Jan. 1, 1996			
	SSBNs	Missiles		Warheads	SSBNs	Missiles		Warheads
Delta Is	9	×	12	=	108	7	×	12	=	84
Yankee Is	6	×	16	=	96	1	×	16	=	16
Delta IIIs	9	×	16 × 3	=	432	9	×	16 × 3	=	432
	24				636	17				532

Delta Is carry 12 SS-N-8s each.
Yankee Is carry 16 SS-N-6s each.
Delta IIIs carry 16 SS-N-18s each.

Table 16.9

Russian Bombers, January 1996

Mozdok	19 Bear-H-16 2 Bear H-6 --- 21
Ukrainka	16 Bear-H16 26 Bear-H6 --- 42
Engels	6 Blackjack 4 Bear-Gs --- 10
Ryazan 6 Blackjacks, 35 Bear-H16s 28 Bear H-6s 20 Bear-Gs --- 89	16 Bear-G

Bombers in Ukraine:
19 Blackjack (Priluki)
25 Bear-H (Uzin)

Notes

1. September 1, 1990, is the date that corresponds to the data the United States provided in the START I memorandum of understanding (MOU). For a breakdown of the 12,646–warhead number by weapon system, see "Factfile: Past and Projected Strategic Nuclear Forces," *Arms Control Today* (July–August 1992): 35–36; and "U.S. Strategic Nuclear Forces," Department of Defense Fact Sheet, Office of the Secretary of Defense, Public Affairs, June 1992. January 1, 1996 is the date that corresponds to the data the United States provided in the START I MOU. For a breakdown of the 8,205 warhead number by weapon system, see ACDA Fact Sheet, April 2, 1996.

2. On March 14, 1994, at George Washington University, U.S. Secretary of Defense William Perry said that although the United States has come down to the START I level unilaterally, "as a hedge," it has "not begun implementing the START II reductions and will not do so until Russia undertakes comparable reductions."

3. Les Aspin, U.S. secretary of defense, "Annual Report to the President and the Congress," January 1994 (Washington, DC: U.S. Government Printing Office, 1994), 150.

4. Admiral Henry G. Chiles Jr., U.S. Navy, commander-in-chief, United States Strategic Command, written statement submitted to the Senate Armed Services Committee, April 20, 1994, 3.

5. "Nuclear Notebook: U.S. Nuclear Weapons Stockpile," July 1994, *Bulletin of the Atomic Scientists* (July–August 1994): 61.

6. Chiles, written statement submitted to the Senate Armed Services Committee, 3.

7. Aspin, "Annual Report to the President and the Congress," 148.

8. Don Oberdorfer, "U.S. Decides to Withdraw A-Weapons from S. Korea," *Washington Post,* October 19, 1991, A1; David Rosenbaum, "U.S. to Pull A-Bombs from South Korea," *New York Times,* October 20, 1991, 3.

9. Don Oberdorfer, "Airborne U.S. A-Arms to Stay in South Korea," *Washington Post,* October 12, 1991, A20; Robert S. Norris, personal communication with the author, June 21, 1994.

10. Robin Bulman, "No A-Arms in S. Korea, Roh Says," *Washington Post,* December 19, 1991, A38; James Sterngold, "Seoul Says It Now Has No Nuclear Arms," *New York Times,* December 19, 1991, A3.

11. See, for example, Pete Williams, assistant secretary of defense for public affairs, Department of Defense news briefing, July 2, 1992.

12. United States Arms Control and Disarmament Agency (ACDA), "Annual Report to the Congress," 37; William M. Arkin and Robert S. Norris, "Taking Stock: US Nuclear Deployments at the End of the Cold War" (Washington, DC: Greenpeace/Natural Resources Defense Council, August 1992), 4.

13. U.S. Department of Defense, "The Bottom Up Review," October 1993, 88; see also "Nuclear Notebook: U.S. Nuclear Weapons Stockpile, July 1994," 63.

14. "Nuclear Notebook: U.S. Nuclear Weapons Stockpile, July 1994," 61, 63.

15. "Report to the Committees on Armed Services and Appropriations of the Senate and the House of Representatives on Nuclear Weapons Testing," required by Section 507 of the fiscal year 1993 Energy and Water Development Appropriations Act (the "Hatfield Amendment"), July 1993, 7.

16. "Nuclear Notebook: U.S. Nuclear Weapons Stockpile, July 1994," 61.

17. Department of State, statement of Secretary of State Warren Christopher, April 5, 1995.

18. Dick Cheney, U.S. secretary of defense, "Annual Report to the President and the Congress," January 1991, viii.

19. Robert Gates, director, U.S. Central Intelligence, testimony before the Senate Armed Services Committee, January 22, 1992, as cited in "Threat Assessment, Military Strategy, and Defense Planning" (Washington, DC: U.S. Government Printing Office, 1992), 60.

20. *START 1 MOU, January 1, 1996.* Available from ACDA Public Affairs, U.S. ACDA, 320 21st St., NW, Washington, DC 20451.

21. U.S. Department of Defense, *Soviet Military Power, 1984,* 21, 23; Robert Berman and John C. Baker, *Soviet Strategic Forces: Requirements and Responses* (Washington, DC: Brookings Institution, 1982), 111.

22. See Dunbar Lockwood, "Strategic Nuclear Forces under START II," *Arms Control Today* (December 1992): 10–14; Alexei Arbatov, ed., "Implications of the START II Treaty for U.S.-Russian Relations" (Washington, DC: Henry L. Stimson Center, October 1993), report no. 9, 6.

23. William Grundmann, director for combat support, Defense Intelligence Agency, written statement submitted to the Joint Economic Committee, June 11, 1993, 18; see also Evgeni Shaposhnikov, "The Armed Forces: To a New Quality," in *Russian Security after the Cold War,* ed. Teresa Pelton Johnson and Steven E. Miller (Washington, DC: Brassey, 1994), 192.

24. Dr. Lawrence Gershwin, hearing before the Senate Armed Services Committee, February 3, 1993, as cited in "Current Developments in the Former Soviet Union," Senate Hearing 103–242 (Washington, DC: U.S. Government Printing Office, 1993), 30.

25. Dr. Lawrence Gershwin, hearing before the Senate Governmental Affairs Com-

mittee, February 24, 1993, as cited in "Proliferation Threats of the 1990s," Senate Hearing 103–208 (Washington, DC: U.S. Government Printing Office, 1993), 41; Gershwin, hearing before the Senate Armed Services Committee, February 3, 1993, 8; "CIA Expects Russia to Deploy Three New Ballistic Missiles by 2000," *Aerospace Daily,* February 4, 1993, 195; Lieutenant General James Clapper, director, U.S. Defense Intelligence Agency (DIA), as cited in "The START Treaty," hearings before the Senate Foreign Relations Committee, Senate Hearing 102–607 (Washington, DC: U.S. Government Printing Office, 1992), part 2, 163.

26. See, for example, *Jane's Intelligence Review,* vol. 7, no. 5: 195–200.

27. Rear Admiral William Studeman, director, U.S. Naval Intelligence, written statement submitted to the House Armed Services Committee, Subcommittee on Seapower and Strategic and Critical Materials, 22.

28. Rear Admiral Edward Sheafer, director, U.S. Naval Intelligence, "Posture Statement" (mimeo), May 3, 1993, 46; John H. Cushman Jr., "U.S. Navy's Periscopes Still Follow Soviet Fleet," *New York Times,* February 23, 1992, A14; Bruce Blair, *The Logic of Accidental Nuclear War* (Washington, DC: Brookings Institution, 1993), 103; see also "No New Subs," *Aviation Week & Space Technology,* November 23, 1992, 25.

29. Admiral Felix Gromov, commander in chief of the Russian Navy, "Reforming the Russian Navy," *Naval Forces* 14, no. 4 (1993): 6.

30. Ibid., 10.

31. See Handler, "Russia's Pacific Fleet," 167.

32. Gershwin, hearing before the Senate Armed Services Committee, February 3, 1993, 31.

33. Rear Admiral Edward Sheafer, director, U.S. Naval Intelligence, "Posture Statement," June 1994. (In May 1993, Admiral Sheafer said that "the Russians will still retain nearly two dozen SSBNs . . . after the year 2000." See Sheafer's "Posture Statement," May 3, 1993, 40.)

34. Unless otherwise indicated, all the information in this subsection comes from Sheafer, "Posture Statement," May 3, 1993, 44.

35. Gershwin, hearing before the Senate Armed Services Committee, February 3, 1993, 163.

36. Grundmann, written statement submitted to the Joint Economic Committee, June 11, 1993, 18.

37. "Production of TU-160 Strategic Aircraft Discontinued," Moscow Television, June 3, 1994, as cited in FBIS-SOV-94–107, June 3, 1994, 23; A. Velovich, "Kazan Produces Final Batch of Blackjacks," *Flight International,* August 12–18, 1992, 22.

38. Covault, "Russian Bomber Force Seeks Tactical Role," 44.

39. The source for the numbers and locations of the INF missiles listed in this subsection is the INF Treaty's June 1, 1988, memorandum of understanding.

40. Mikhail Gorbachev, televised statement, October 5, 1991, as cited in *SIPRI Yearbook 1992* (Stockholm, Sweden: Stockholm International Peace Research Institute, 1992), 87; see feature articles on "President Bush's Nuclear Weapons Initiatives," in *Arms Control Today* (October 1991), 3–13.

41. Boris Yeltsin, televised statement, January 29, 1992, as cited in *SIPRI Yearbook 1992,* 90.

42. National Academy of Sciences, *Management and Disposition of Excess Weapons Plutonium* (Washington, DC: National Academy Press, 1994), 40 n. 1; Blair, *Logic of Accidental Nuclear War,* 105–106.

43. Margaret Shapiro, "Russian Navy Rids Itself of Tactical Nuclear Arms," *Washington Post,* February 5, 1993, A31; "Tactical Nuclear Arms Removed from Vessels," Itar-Tass, February 4, 1993, as cited in FBIS-SOV-93–022, February 4, 1993, 1.

44. National Academy of Sciences, *Management and Disposition of Excess Weapons Plutonium*, 40 n. 1; Blair, *Logic of Accidental Nuclear War*, 105–106.

45. U.S. Department of Defense, *Soviet Military Power, 1990*, Washington, DC: U.S. Government Printing Office, 1990, 98.

46. Backfires can carry two AS-4 antiship missiles with a 560–kilometer range or nuclear gravity bombs. Alternatively, they can carry up to ten AS-16s—six in a rotary launcher plus another four under their wings. Cochran et al., *Nuclear Weapons Databook*, vol. 4, *Soviet Nuclear Weapons*, 164, 243; see also "Nuclear Notebook: Estimated Russian (CIS [Commonwealth of Independent States]) Nuclear Stockpile (July 1993)," *Bulletin of the Atomic Scientists* (July–August 1993): 57.

47. Handler and Arkin, "Nuclear Warships and Naval Nuclear Weapons, 1990," 32.

48. Numbers of Su-24s and Su-17s come from IISS, *Military Balance, 1993–1994*, 103; nuclear armaments for Su-24s and Su-17s come from Cochran et al., *Nuclear Weapons Databook*, vol. 4, *Soviet Nuclear Weapons*, 251, 258.

49. Ship types and classes come from John Jordan, "The Russian Navy in Transition," *Jane's Intelligence Review* (April 1994): 159; see also Handler and Arkin, "Nuclear Warships and Naval Nuclear Weapons, 1990," appendix B.

50. Norman Polmar, *The Naval Institute Guide to the Soviet Navy*, 5th ed. (1991), 155, 168.

51. In 1993, IISS estimated that there were nine SSGNs in the Pacific fleet. Source for Oscar II nuclear armaments, Polmar, *Naval Institute Guide*, 107; source for two Oscar IIs in the Pacific fleet, Jordan, "Russian Navy in Transition," 159.

52. U.S. Department of Defense, *Soviet Military Power, 1990*, 53. See also Cochran et al., *Nuclear Weapons Databook*, vol. 4, *Soviet Nuclear Weapons*, 180. According to John Jordan, there are four Akula-class SSNs in the Pacific fleet.

53. Aircraft numbers and types are from IISS, *Military Balance, 1993–1994*, 103. Nuclear payloads are from Cochran et al., *Nuclear Weapons Databook*, 264–269.

54. Handler and Arkin, "Nuclear Warships and Naval Nuclear Weapons, 1990," 30–31.

55. Ibid., 29.

56. Sheafer, "Posture Statement," June 1994.

57. Ibid.; see also Aleksandr Maltsev, "Third Serious Fire This Year at Pacific Fleet," *Kommersant-Daily*, May 24, 1994, 14, in FBIS-SOV-94–101, May 25, 1994, 35.

58. Jordan, "Russian Navy in Transition," 154.

59. IISS, *Military Balance, 1993–1994*, 97.

60. U.S. Department of Defense, *Soviet Military Power, 1990*, 98. According to Steven Zaloga's "Soviet Air Defense Missiles," a regiment of SA-10s has two battalions; each battalion has three batteries; each battery has three launchers; and each launcher has four missile canisters.

61. Cochran et al., *Nuclear Weapons Databook*, vol. 4, *Soviet Nuclear Weapons*, 32; John Pike, personal communication with the author, June 28, 1994.

62. National Academy of Sciences, *Management and Disposition of Excess Weapons Plutonium* (Washington, DC: National Academy Press, 1994), 40 n. 1; Blair, *Logic of Accidental Nuclear War*, 105–106.

63. National Academy of Sciences, *Management and Disposition of Excess Weapons Plutonium*, 40 n. 1.

64. IISS, *Military Balance, 1993–1994*, 104.

65. Cochran, et al., *Nuclear Weapons Databook*, 251, 253.

66. U.S. Department of Defense, *Soviet Military Power, 1988*, Washington, DC: U.S. Government Printing Office, 1988, 79.

67. James Woolsey, director, U.S. Central Intelligence, written statement submitted to the House Foreign Affairs Committee, Subcommittee on International Security, Interna-

tional Organizations and Human Rights, July 28, 1993, as cited in "U.S. Security Policy toward Rogue Regimes," (Washington, DC: U.S. Government Printing Office, 1994), 79.

68. Ibid., 33.

69. "DPRK Reportedly Sought Russian Scientists to Modernize Missiles," Itar-Tass, February 10, 1993, in FBIS-SOV-93–026, February 10, 1993, 11; Steven Zaloga, "Russian Reports," *Armed Forces Journal International* (April 1993): 17.

70. Steven Zaloga, "Russian Military Readiness Nosedives," *Armed Forces Journal International* (May 1994): 55.

71. For a discussion of the Soviet Union's no-first-use policy, see Raymond L. Garthoff, *Deterrence and Revolution in Soviet Military Doctrine* (Washington, DC: Brookings Institution, 1990), 80–88.

72. Fred Hiatt, "Russia Shifts Doctrine on Military Use," *Washington Post,* November 4, 1993, A33.

73. Lieutenant General James. R. Clapper, Jr., director, U.S. Defense Intelligence Agency, statement before the Senate Select Intelligence Committee, January 25, 1994, *Federal News* transcript, 40–41; Fred Hiatt, "Russians Favoring Retention of Nuclear Deterrent," *Washington Post,* November 25, 1992, A1.

74. Sergei Rogov, "Russian Views of Nuclear Weapons," in *Toward a Nuclear Peace,* ed. Michael J. Mazarr and Alexander T. Lennon (New York: St. Martin's Press, 1994), 208.

75. Paul Godwin and John Shulz, "Arming the Dragon for the 21st Century: China's Defense Modernization Program," *Arms Control Today* (December 1993): 6; Zhai Zhihai, "The Future of Nuclear Weapons: A Chinese Perspective," in *Nuclear Weapons in the Changing World: Perspectives from Europe, Asia, and North America,* ed. Patrick J. Garrity and Steven A. Maaranen (New York: Plenum Press, 1992), 170; Song Jiuguang, "START and China's Policy on Nuclear Weapons and Disarmament in the 1990s," Stanford University, Center for International Security and Arms Control, May 1991, 8, 10.

76. Richard K. Betts, "Nuclear Blackmail and Nuclear Balance" (Washington, DC: Brookings Institution, 1987); for the Korean War, see 32–33, 42; for the Taiwan–Formosa Straits crises, see 59, 68; and for the 1969 Sino-Soviet border clash, see 79–81, and Raymond L. Garthoff, *Detente and Confrontation: American-Soviet Relations from Nixon to Reagan,* rev. ed. (Washington, DC: The Brookings Institution, 1994), 237–238. See also Godwin and Shulz, "Arming the Dragon for the 21st Century," 6; Robert S. Norris, Andrew S. Burrows, and Richard Fieldhouse, *Nuclear Weapons Databook,* vol. 5, *British, French, and Chinese Nuclear Weapons* (Boulder, CO: Westview Press, 1994), 324; Zhai Zhihai, "Future of Nuclear Weapons," 170.

77. Robert G. Sutter, "Chinese Nuclear Weapons and Arms Control Policies: Implications and Options for the United States," Congressional Research Service (CRS), 94–422 S, March 25, 1994, CRS-6; Shen Dingli, "Toward a Nuclear-Weapon-Free World: A Chinese Perspective," *Bulletin of the Atomic Scientists* (March–April 1994): 53–54; Zhai Zhihai, "Future of Nuclear Weapons," 169–170.

78. Jonathan D. Pollack, "The Future of China's Nuclear Weapons Policy," in *Strategic Views from the Second Tier: The Nuclear Weapons Policies of France, Britain, and China,* ed. John C. Hopkins and Weixing Hu (San Diego: University of California, Institute on Global Conflict and Cooperation, 1994), 157.

79. Godwin and Schulz, "Arming the Dragon for the 21st Century," 6–7; Desmond Ball, *MacNeil–Lehrer News Hour,* WNET New York, show 4800, November 17, 1993.

80. Sutter, "Chinese Nuclear Weapons and Arms Control Policies, CRS-6; Zhai Zhihai, "Future of Nuclear Weapons," 170.

81. Pollack, "Future of China's Nuclear Weapons Policy," 161, 165; Song Jiuguang, "START and China's Policy on Nuclear Weapons and Disarmament in the 1990s," 10.

82. Song, "START and China's Policy on Nuclear Weapons and Disarmament," 12; Xue Litai, "Evolution of China's Nuclear Strategy," in *Strategic Views from the Second Tier*, 178.

83. John Lewis and Xue Litai, "China Builds the Bomb," 212; Norris, Burrows, and Fieldhouse, *Nuclear Weapons Databook*, vol. 5, *British, French, and Chinese Nuclear Weapons*, 361–362; prepared statement by Joseph S. Bermudez Jr., submitted to the House Foreign Affairs Committee, Subcommittee on International Security, International Organizations and Human Rights, July 28, 1993, as cited in "U.S. Security Policy toward Rogue Regimes," 104.

84. Lewis and Xue, "China Builds the Bomb," 213; Norris, 324, 362.

85. See, for example, Sutter, "Chinese Nuclear Weapons and Arms Control Policies," passim.

86. Xue Litai, "Evolution of China's Nuclear Strategy," 175; Sutter, CRS-6, CRS-12–CRS-13.

87. The DF-1 was renamed the DF-3.

88. Norris, Burrows, and Fieldhouse, *Nuclear Weapons Databook*, vol. 5, *British, French, and Chinese Nuclear Weapons*, 363, 381; Ministry of Defence, "Statement on Defence Estimates 1992" (London: HMSO, 1992), 21; Sutter, "Chinese Nuclear Weapons and Arms Control Policies," CRS-9; IISS, *Military Balance 1993–1994*, 152. Norris estimates 50–80; Sutter estimates 40–50; and the IISS estimates 60 plus.

89. Clare Hollingworth, "China's Growing Missile Might," *Defense & Foreign Affairs* (March 1985): 28–29, as cited in Norris, Burrows, and Fieldhouse, *Nuclear Weapons Databook*, vol. 5, *British, French, and Chinese Nuclear Weapons*, 363, 380; "Chinese Flight Test New Missile Version," *Aviation Week & Space Technology*, June 30, 1986, 16, as cited in Norris, Burrows, and Fieldhouse, *Nuclear Weapons Databook*, vol. 5, *British, French, and Chinese Nuclear Weapons*, 380.

90. Defense Intelligence Agency, *Handbook on the Chinese Armed Forces*, DDI-2682-32–76 (Washington, DC: U.S. Government Printing Office, 1976), 8–2, as cited in Norris, Burrows, and Fieldhouse, *Nuclear Weapons Databook*, vol. 5, *British, French, and Chinese Nuclear Weapons*, 363.

91. Sutter, "Chinese Nuclear Weapons and Arms Control Policies," CRS-8.

92. Norris, Burrows, and Fieldhouse, *Nuclear Weapons Databook*, vol. 5, *British, French, and Chinese Nuclear Weapons*, 363, 382; Sutter, "Chinese Nuclear Weapons and Arms Control Policies," CRS-9; IISS, *Military Balance 1993–1994*, 152. Norris estimates "not more than 15–20"; Sutter estimates "less than 20"; and the IISS estimates 10 plus.

93. Hollingworth, "China's Growing Missile Might," 28–29, as cited in Norris, Burrows, and Fieldhouse, *Nuclear Weapons Databook*, vol. 5, *British, French, and Chinese Nuclear Weapons*, 382, 340.

94. Lewis and Hua, "China's Ballistic Missile Programs: Technologies, Strategies, Goals," *International Security* 17, no. 2 (fall 1992): 10, as cited in Norris, Burrows, and Fieldhouse, *Nuclear Weapons Databook*, vol. 5, *British, French, and Chinese Nuclear Weapons*, 363, 382.

95. Norris, Burrows, and Fieldhouse, *Nuclear Weapons Databook*, vol. 5, *British, French, and Chinese Nuclear Weapons*, 382.

96. U.S. Air Force, Tactical Air Command, TAC Intelligence Briefing 79–3, "People's Republic of China Armed Forces," February 8, 1979, 5, as cited in Norris, Burrows, and Fieldhouse, *Nuclear Weapons Databook*, vol. 5, *British, French, and Chinese Nuclear Weapons*, 382.

97. Lewis and Hua, "China's Ballistic Missile Programs," 19, as cited in Norris, Burrows, and Fieldhouse, *Nuclear Weapons Databook*, vol. 5, *British, French, and Chinese Nuclear Weapons*, 385; Sutter, "Chinese Nuclear Weapons and Arms Control Poli-

cies," CRS-9; IISS, *Military Balance 1993–1994,* 152. Lewis, Hua, Norris, and the IISS all estimate 4; Sutter estimates "about 10."

98. Lewis and Hua, "China's Ballistic Missile Programs," 19, as cited in Norris, Burrows, and Fieldhouse, *Nuclear Weapons Databook,* vol. 5, *British, French, and Chinese Nuclear Weapons,* 385.

99. Norris, Burrows, and Fieldhouse, *Nuclear Weapons Databook,* vol. 5, *British, French, and Chinese Nuclear Weapons,* 364.

100. Ibid., 363, 385.

101. Ibid., 347, 364.

102. Norris, Burrows, and Fieldhouse, *Nuclear Weapons Databook,* vol. 5, *British, French, and Chinese Nuclear Weapons,* 388; Sutter, "Chinese Nuclear Weapons and Arms Control Policies," CRS-9; IISS, *Military Balance 1993–1994,* 152. Norris estimates 25–50; Sutter estimates 30.

103. Norris, Burrows, and Fieldhouse, *Nuclear Weapons Databook,* vol. 5, *British, French, and Chinese Nuclear Weapons,* 388.

104. Ibid., 396.

105. "China Switches IRBMs [intermediate-range ballistic missiles] to Conventional Role," *Jane's Defence Weekly,* January 29, 1994, 1.

106. Ibid.; Norris, Burrows, and Fieldhouse, *Nuclear Weapons Databook,* vol. 5, *British, French, and Chinese Nuclear Weapons,* 388; see also David Shambaugh, "Growing Strong: China's Challenge to Asian Security," *Survival* 36, no. 2 (summer 1994): 56.

107. "China Switches IRBMs to Conventional Role," 1.

108. Lewis and Hua, "China's Ballistic Missile Programs," 28–29; K. Yan and T. McCarthy, "China's Missile Bureaucracy," *Jane's Intelligence Review* (January 1993): 41; Jim Mann, "China Upgrading Nuclear Arms, Experts Say," *Los Angeles Times,* November 9, 1993, 2; Godwin and Shulz, "Arming the Dragon for the 21st Century," 7; Dr. Lawrence Gershwin, national intelligence officer for strategic programs, Central Intelligence Agency, "Threats to U.S. Interests from Weapons of Mass Destruction over the Next Ten to Twenty Years," September 23, 1992; Robert Gates, director, U.S. Central Intelligence, spoken testimony before the House Armed Services Committee Defense Policy Panel, December 10, 1991, *Federal News Service Transcript,* 11–1.

109. Norris, Burrows, and Fieldhouse, *Nuclear Weapons Databook,* vol. 5, *British, French, and Chinese Nuclear Weapons,* 363.

110. Patrick E. Tyler, "China Explodes H-Bomb Underground as Test," *New York Times,* June 11, 1994, 7; Mann, "China Upgrading Nuclear Arms," 2C; R.A. Taylor, "Test Ban Flouted by China," *Washington Times,* November 6, 1993, A1; L.H. Sun, "China Resumes Nuclear Tests; U.S. Prepares to Follow Suit," *Washington Post,* October 6, 1993, A23; V. Gupta, "Assessment of the Chinese Nuclear Test Site near Lop Nor," *Jane's Intelligence Review* (August 1993): 379; Lewis and Hua, "China's Ballistic Missile Programs," 30; Godwin and Shulz, "Arming the Dragon for the 21st Century," 7.

111. Lewis and Hua, "China's Ballistic Missile Programs," 11, 30; "Nuclear Notebook," *Bulletin of the Atomic Scientists* (November 1993): 57.

112. Senator Larry Pressler, *Congressional Record,* November 20, 1993, S16655.

113. *The Comprehensive Test Ban: Views from the Chinese Nuclear Weapons Laboratories* (Washington, DC: Natural Resources Defense Council, 1993), ii, 26; see also Dingli, "Toward a Nuclear-Weapon-Free World," 52–53.

114. Lewis and Hua, "China's Ballistic Missile Programs," 30.

115. Senator Larry Pressler, "Pressler Charges New Chinese Weapons Threaten United States," press release, May 4, 1994. It should be noted that the range and deployment date estimates are very similar to those published by John Lewis and Hua Di, "China's Ballistic Missile Programs," 11.

116. See n. 115.

117. Woolsey, as cited in "U.S. Security Policy toward Rogue Regimes," 33. (See the subsection on the Russian "brain drain" above.)

118. See, for example, J.J. Fialka, "U.S. Fears China's Success in Skimming Cream of Weapons Experts from Russia," *Wall Street Journal,* October 14, 1993, 12; T. Atlas, "Russia's Brain Drain Has Fallout," *Chicago Tribune,* October 24, 1993, section 1, 7; P.E. Tyler, "Russia and China Sign a Military Agreement," *New York Times,* November 10, 1993, A15; Alfred D. Wilhelm Jr., "China and the Region: Facing a Decade of Challenges," *Arms Control Today* (December 1993): 12. In addition to the apparently unsanctioned transfer of expertise to China, Moscow has sanctioned the sale of Su-27 fighter planes and SA-10 surface-to-air missiles (SAMs) to China and is reportedly negotiating the sale of Kilo-class diesel-powered submarines and marine gas-turbine engines.

119. Fialka, "U.S. Fears China's Success," 12; M. Sieff, "Missile Buildup in China Could Threaten U.S.," *Washington Times,* November 12, 1993, A16; Atlas, "Russia's Brain Drain Has Fallout," section 1, 7; Mann, "China Upgrading Nuclear Arms," 2C; Tyler, "Russia and China Sign a Military Agreement," A13; Sheafer, "Posture Statement," May 3, 1993, 30.

120. P.B. de Selding, "China Seeks Ukraine's Expertise," *Space News,* November 29–December 5, 1993, 1. See also Evan Mederios, "U.S. Warns Russia, Ukraine, on Missile-Related Sales to China," *Arms Control Today,* (May–June 1996): 24.

121. Sheafer, "Posture Statement," May 3, 1993, 30.

122. Sheafer, "Posture Statement," June 1994.

123. Norris, Burrows, and Fieldhouse, *Nuclear Weapons Databook,* vol. 5, *British, French, and Chinese Nuclear Weapons,* 369, 396; Sutter, "Chinese Nuclear Weapons and Arms Control Policies," CRS-13.

124. Norris, Burrows, and Fieldhouse, *Nuclear Weapons Databook,* vol. 5, *British, French, and Chinese Nuclear Weapons,* 369. In its most recent edition of *Military Balance,* IISS lists only one Xia-class SSBN; see IISS, *Military Balance 1993–1994,* 152.

125. Sutter, "Chinese Nuclear Weapons and Arms Control Policies," CRS-13.

126. Sheafer, "Posture Statement," June 1994.

127. Norris, Burrows, and Fieldhouse, *Nuclear Weapons Databook,* vol. 5, *British, French, and Chinese Nuclear Weapons,* 396.

128. Ibid., 359, 396; Lewis and Hua, "China's Ballistic Missile Programs," 30.

129. John Jordan, "The People's Liberation Army Navy (PLAN)," *Jane's Intelligence Review* (June 1994): 279, 282.

130. Norris, Burrows, and Fieldhouse, *Nuclear Weapons Databook,* vol. 5, *British, French, and Chinese Nuclear Weapons,* 364, 396.

131. Sheafer, "Posture Statement," May 3, 1993, 30.

132. IISS, *Military Balance 1993–1994,* 15.

133. Lewis and Hua, "China's Ballistic Missile Programs," 28–29.

134. "Nuclear Notebook" (November 1993): 57; Lewis and Hua, "China's Ballistic Missile Programs," 26–27; Jordan, "People's Liberation Army Navy," 282.

135. Norris, Burrows, and Fieldhouse, *Nuclear Weapons Databook,* vol. 5, *British, French, and Chinese Nuclear Weapons,* 373; see also *Jane's Strategic Weapon Systems,* "China: Offensive Weapons," issue 4, which says that "up to four modified 'Xia' class boats may be planned."

136. Norris, Burrows, and Fieldhouse, *Nuclear Weapons Databook,* vol. 5, *British, French, and Chinese Nuclear Weapons,* 359.

137. Ibid., 365, 366–367, 394.

138. Ibid., 390, 394.

139. Ibid., 365.

140. Sutter, "Chinese Nuclear Weapons and Arms Control Policies," CRS-7.

141. Norris, Burrows, and Fieldhouse, *Nuclear Weapons Databook,* vol. 5, *British, French, and Chinese Nuclear Weapons,* 392.

142. Prasun Sengupta, "China Expands Air Forces," *Military Technology* (August 1992): 51.

143. David Boey, "Chinese Firm Seeks Bomber Sale in Iran," *Defense News,* March 28–April 3, 1994, 38.

144. Sengupta, "China Expands Air Forces," 49.

145. "First Picture of Chinese 'Flanker,' " *Jane's Defence Weekly,* February 12, 1994, 6.

146. Sheafer, "Posture Statement," May 3, 1993, 29; J.A. Ackerman and M.C. Dunn, "Chinese Airpower Revs Up," *Air Force Magazine,* July 1993, 59.

147. Sheafer, "Posture Statement," May 3, 1993, 29.

148. Ackerman and Dunn, "Chinese Airpower Revs Up," 59; "Chasing the 20th Century," *Jane's Defence Weekly,* February 19, 1994, 26.

149. "Nuclear Notebook," (November 1993): 57.

150. Norris, Burrows, and Fieldhouse, *Nuclear Weapons Databook,* vol. 5, *British, French, and Chinese Nuclear Weapons,* 370–371; see also Pollack, "Future of China's Nuclear Weapons Policy," 159–160.

151. Ibid., 160.

152. Japan has reportedly earmarked $80 million for Russia and $20 million for Ukraine, Kazakhstan, and Belarus combined. *Defense News,* April 11–17, 1994, 2; "Nuclear Successor States of the Soviet Union," Carnegie Endowment for International Peace/Monterey Institute of International Studies, no. 1, May 1994, 21.

153. According to Greenpeace, the Japanese newspaper *Yomiuri* reported on June 3 that Japan and Russia had agreed to build a floating facility to store and dispose of liquid radioactive waste. This facility would be funded by part of the $100 million that Japan has pledged to the former Soviet Union in denuclearization assistance. The states hoped to begin construction this summer and complete the facility six months after that.

154. The United States has agreed to purchase 500 metric tons of HEU from Russia. In September 1993, Viktor Mikhailov, the head of MINATOM, stated that "500 metric tons of HEU represents [only] about 40 percent of Russia's total reserves." See Elizabeth Martin, "A Conversation with Viktor Mikhailov," *NUKEM Market Report* (October 1993).

155. In March 1994, President Clinton extended the U.S. moratorium through September 1995; it remains intact as of mid-1996. U.S. law prohibits testing after September 30, 1996, unless another country tests after that date. Russia, for its part, has not conducted a single nuclear test since becoming an independent state. (The last Soviet test took place in 1990.)

17

Nuclear Forces in the Far East: Status and Implications for Proliferation

Ralph A. Cossa

Since the dawn of the nuclear age, Northeast Asia has traditionally been a strategic afterthought in the minds of nuclear strategists; European and global issues and considerations have largely preoccupied the minds of these experts and arms-control advocates. Although three of the five declared nuclear powers are located in or adjacent to this region, only one—China—is thought of primarily in an Asian context. During the Cold War era, the United States and the Soviet Union were viewed primarily in the global context. When nuclear issues were thought of regionally, the spotlight invariably focused on the European theater.

Historically, there have been very sound reasons for this. Preoccupation with the global aspects of the nuclear weapons challenge requires little explanation or justification, given the ability of both the United States and the Soviet Union "to destroy the world several times over"—a capability that will remain even if all planned strategic force reductions through 2003 take place as scheduled. It was also clear that the primary dividing line between East and West during the Cold War ran through Germany. Given the Warsaw Pact's conventional firepower advantage, nuclear weapons figured significantly in the North Atlantic Treaty Organization's (NATO's) strategic calculus and gave rise to the U.S. refusal to make any "no-first-use" pledges.

Northeast Asia was very much a secondary theater in the Cold War, especially after Sino-U.S. rapprochement essentially neutralized the Soviet Union's Far Eastern forces. Indeed, in the mid-1980s, when the United States and the

Soviet Union engaged in intermediate-range nuclear forces (INF) discussions, the United States focused on SS-20s east of the Urals until Japan complained bitterly that simply shifting these weapons westward hardly made the world (especially their world) safer. The talks eventually took on a global dimension.

There is a certain irony in all this since the nuclear age dawned over Hiroshima and Nagasaki and the world's most pressing "nuclear crisis" today centers on the Korean Peninsula. The period in between has also seen some potentially tense Asia-oriented nuclear moments. In fact, Lawrence Freedman from King's College in London argues that the most complex nuclear relationships have centered not around Europe or elsewhere, but on Asia.[1]

Nuclear strategy has always been developed with Europe more than Asia in mind, yet the most complex nuclear relationships have existed in Asia. The crises over Berlin and Cuba in the early 1960s produced some tense moments, yet it remains the case that the only nuclear weapons ever used in anger were those dropped on Japan in August 1945. At different times, both the United States and the Soviet Union actively considered nuclear strikes against China, and there were advocates of tactical use in the Pentagon during both the Korean and Vietnam Wars.

I would also note that during the 1991 Gulf War, little consideration was given to using nuclear weapons against Iraq (although it was made clear to Iraq that if it employed chemical weapons or other weapons of mass destruction, the United States would retaliate using "all available means"). However, many defense planners and pundits openly spoke about using nuclear weapons against North Korea if it were to attempt to capitalize militarily on America's preoccupation with the Middle East. It is easy to speculate (but impossible to prove) that the fear that America would resort to nuclear weapons if North Korea opened a "second front" during the Gulf War helped deter North Korean aggression during this period; it could even have had a role in stimulating Pyongyang's nuclear appetite (as the Gulf War in general no doubt did).

Regardless of one's interpretation of history, it is clear that the nuclear spotlight today is focused on Northeast Asia, thanks to North Korea's reluctance, at least until recently, to adhere to International Atomic Energy Agency (IAEA) safeguards. As this chapter is being written, the crisis appears to be "on hold," given the sudden death of North Korean President Kim Il Sung. Even before the "Great Leader's" death, it was unclear whether North Korea would ultimately permit IAEA special inspections and, of equal or greater importance, live up to the December 1991 North–South "Joint Declaration for a Non-Nuclear Korean Peninsula"—an agreement that, if honored, would also put an end to nuclear reprocessing on the peninsula.

There is at least one other reason why the United States should cast a nuclear eye in the direction of Northeast Asia. Now that the United States and Russia have agreed to aim their intercontinental ballistic missiles (ICBM)/submarine-launched ballistic missiles (SLBM) "at the sea" rather than at each other, the only missiles still presumably aimed at the United States are those based in the People's Republic of China (PRC). Although few would view China as a serious threat to U.S. security today (and I am certainly no advocate for changing this mind-set), China's nuclear capabilities—and its importance as one of the world's five declared nuclear powers—should not be overlooked.

Status of Nuclear Forces

A review of nuclear forces in Northeast Asia today should, by definition, focus almost exclusively on China and Russia. Nonetheless, a few words about the United States nuclear posture appear in order at the outset since its "nuclear umbrella" over Asia plays a significant role in maintaining peace and stability in the region. In the interest of completeness, Japan and the Korean Peninsula are also included briefly in this discussion.

United States

The United States was widely believed to have had tactical nuclear weapons deployed in the Republic of Korea (ROK) and aboard U.S. Seventh Fleet assets afloat in the Western Pacific during the Cold War. Although Soviet defense specialists identified South Korea as "the only place in Asia where the United States has its nuclear warheads practically without concealing the fact,"[2] the United States has never confirmed this worst kept of all nuclear secrets.

The question of whether the United States maintained nuclear weapons on the Korean Peninsula became moot in 1991, when U.S. President George Bush announced his decision to remove tactical nuclear weapons from all overseas bases and from deployed tactical ships and aircraft—an initiative that, not coincidentally, was followed a week later by a similar pledge by Soviet President Mikhail Gorbachev. Given the U.S. military's "neither confirm nor deny" (NCND) policy regarding the presence of nuclear weapons (at home, abroad, afloat, or elsewhere)—a policy that remains in effect today—Bush could not officially announce the withdrawal of nuclear weapons from Korea. This dilemma was solved in December 1991, when South Korean President Roh Tae-woo certified (without actually confirming their earlier presence) that there were no U.S. nuclear weapons currently situated on Korean soil.

There are some today who speak of Bush's 1991 decision to bring deployed nuclear weapons home as if it were largely driven by events on the Korean Peninsula. Gerald Segal, for instance, in his review of nuclear forces in Northeast Asia, states that "North Korea demanded the withdrawal of American nuclear weapons in South Korea before serious talks could take place, and the Americans eventually agreed to do so."[3]

Although the "bring them home" decision has had a profound impact on the

Korean Peninsula and added considerable flexibility (and a new moral high ground) to the U.S.-ROK negotiating position, it would be a mistake to view Bush's decision in such terms. It was the overriding need to consolidate all of the former Soviet Union's tactical nuclear weapons within the Russian Federation (i.e., to retrieve them from the other increasingly independent members of the emerging Commonwealth of Independent States, or CIS) that provided the strategic rationale (and sense of urgency) behind the near-simultaneous U.S.-Soviet announcements. To imply that North Korean demands drove this decision sends a false message to Pyongyang.

This decision notwithstanding, America's still-massive strategic and tactical nuclear arsenals, and its ability to deploy forces rapidly (including tactical nuclear assets if necessary), keeps the United States nuclear umbrella over Asia intact. According to the International Institute for Strategic Studies (IISS), the United States strategic arsenal today is comprised of 1,524 launchers (ICBMs, SLBMs, and strategic bombers) armed with 9,970 warheads.[4] Even upon completion of START II in 2003, the United States could possess up to 1,047 launchers while limiting itself (and the Russians) to 3,500 strategic warheads each. According to the Defense Department's "Bottom-Up Review," this will equate, in 2003, to eighteen Trident submarines equipped with C-4 and D-5 missiles, 500 Minuteman III missiles carrying a single warhead each, up to ninety-four B-52H bombers equipped with air-launched cruise missiles, and twenty B-2 bombers.[5]

The United States also has a wide variety of potential delivery systems should it feel compelled to employ tactical nuclear weapons. These include everything from 155–millimeter artillery (firing .1–kiloton shells) to cruise missiles (which can carry 200–kiloton warheads) to bombs dropped by a variety of tactical aircraft. Future inventories were not specified in the Bottom-Up Review, although it was noted that a comprehensive Department of Defense (DOD) follow-up review of U.S. nuclear forces was being conducted. A recent Heritage Foundation report aimed at influencing that DOD review argued that the United States should retain 1,000 air-launched cruise and attack missiles, 500 sea-launched cruise missiles, and 1,000 tactical nuclear bombs, in order to "deter not only Russian use of tactical nuclear weapons and other weapons of mass destruction, but also those of any other potential enemy in a regional conflict."[6] The actual U.S. tactical nuclear force is likely to be about half this size.

Korean Peninsula

North Korea currently has no demonstrated nuclear capability and only limited means of delivery should such a capability be verified. Most estimates suggest that Pyongyang has enough plutonium secreted away (about 12 kilograms) for two crude nuclear devices. Even if all future reprocessing is halted and full IAEA safeguards are restored, some uncertainty will remain about North Korea's ability to produce up to two weapons, and North Korea seems intent on preserving this ambiguity.

North Korea's current operational missile inventory, comprised of 300–kilometer-range Scud missiles, allows Pyongyang to seriously threaten South Korea and U.S. facilities based in the ROK. Missiles currently on the drawing board will permit Pyongyang to extend this threat. The Nodong-1, with its 1,000–kilometer range, can reach many targets in Japan, whereas the experimental Taepo Dong-1, with its 2,000–kilometer estimated range, encompasses all of Japan and beyond (to as far south as Taiwan). Meanwhile, a suspected Taepo Dong-2, with an estimated range of up to 3,500 kilometers, could extend the threat to as far away as Guam.[7] But these systems are still on the drawing board, years away from achieving operational status, and with assessed accuracies that will make their value more psychological than military, even if the North can develop a nuclear warhead for these missiles.

South Korea has neither a nuclear weapons program nor any indigenous nuclear capability. It was widely believed that a nuclear weapons program was under way in the ROK in the early 1970s under President Park Chung-hee. Park apparently planned to construct a nuclear reprocessing plant (employing French technology) in order to produce the necessary plutonium until pressure from the United States forced him to cancel the project. There was also a report, attributed to Korean Democratic Liberal Party chief policy analyst Suh Su-jong, that President Roh Tae-woo also contemplated embarking on a nuclear weapons program as late as 1991, in response to North Korean nuclear developments, in order "to reduce [South Korea's] over-whelming military dependence on the United States."[8] Once again, pressure from the United States is reported to have halted the program.

At present, South Korea seems content to remain under the U.S. nuclear umbrella and to work closely with its American allies to eliminate North Korea's nuclear weapons program. There is little talk emanating from official channels about the ROK's reinstituting an indigenous nuclear weapons program in the face of the potential North Korean challenge. Public opinion in the ROK seems to be putting a curious twist on this, however. There appears to be a growing mood among many in South Korea—and particularly among the younger generation—that too much attention is being paid to the nuclear issue. They not only see little likelihood of a nuclear attack from North Korea but also talk openly about the prospects of the South's one day "inheriting" a nuclear weapons capability when their nation—as it surely will—eventually absorbs the North.[9]

China

China conducted its first nuclear test in 1964 and today fields a modest strategic nuclear force. According to the Chinese, this force exists only as a deterrent. China stands alone today in its pledge not to initiate the use of nuclear weapons.

China develops and possesses a small number of nuclear weapons solely for the purpose of self-defense. On the very day that China acquired a nuclear weapon in 1964, the Chinese government solemnly declared that at no time and under no circumstances would the country be the first to use, or threaten to use, nuclear weapons.[10]

This pledge notwithstanding, Chinese military specialist Tai Ming Cheung notes that Chinese military strategists have traditionally argued that this would not prohibit the use of nuclear weapons to repel a conventional Soviet invasion of their homeland. The defensive use of nuclear weapons, "if confined strictly to Chinese territory," would not violate China's no-first-use pledge since the Chinese actually mean "no first use on enemy territory."[11]

Given the lack of transparency involving most aspects of the People's Liberation Army (PLA), but particularly when it comes to its nuclear forces, estimates regarding exact inventory and capabilities vary.[12] Most estimates put the total Chinese nuclear weapons inventory at between 250 and 350 deployed warheads (or roughly one-tenth the size to which the United States the size that the U.S. and Russia have agreed to limit themselves by 2003).

According to the IISS, the Chinese possess two types of land-based ICBMs (the CSS-4 [DF-5] and CSS-3 [DF-4] and one SLBM (the CSS-N-3 [JL-1]). All are assessed to carry a single warhead, with yields in the 2- to 5-megaton range. Only the four CSS-4 sites, with their 15,000–kilometer-range missiles, are capable of striking targets in North America, whereas the ten CSS-3 missile launchers can target locations as far away as Europe. The Chinese also have up to sixty CSS-2 (DF-3) intermediate-range ballistic missile (IRBM) launchers capable of striking targets throughout Asia with their 2,700–kilometer-range missiles.[13]

Rounding out the Chinese strategic missile arsenal, according to the IISS, is a single Xia-class SSBN (nuclear-powered ballistic missile submarine), with its twelve 2,200 to 3,000 kilometer-range missiles.[14] Other sources indicate that a second Xia has also become operational, with another two currently under construction.[15] Attempts to develop a follow-on, longer-range SLBM appear to have been hampered by technical difficulties relating to the use of solid propellants. As a result, both at present and for the foreseeable future, it appears highly likely that the Chinese will rely on ground-based ICBMs for the bulk of their nuclear deterrence.[16]

The Chinese also have up to 120 Hong-6 (TU-16/Badger-type) strategic bombers capable of carrying two warheads each with ranges from 2,000 to 4,500 kilometers. Older Hong-5 (IL-28/Beagle) bombers and MiG-19–derivative Qian-5 fighters also have a nuclear weapons delivery capability. China has an estimated stockpile of 150–200 or more nuclear fission and fusion aerial bombs.

Very little is known regarding China's tactical nuclear capability, beyond the belief that Qian-5 tactical fighters are capable of delivering low-yield aerial bombs on a battlefield. The IISS states that tactical nuclear weapons have been reported but that no details are available.[17] On the other hand, Richard Field-house, from the Nuclear Weapons Databook Project, while reporting a suspected Chinese test of a "neutron bomb design" in 1988, notes that "whether the Chinese have tactical nuclear weapons or neutron bombs is unclear."[18] Tai Ming Cheung acknowledges this ambiguity but, as early as 1989, suspected that tactical nuclear weapons had already been added to the Chinese arsenal.[19]

Although China has not officially confirmed that it has tactical nuclear weapons, its efforts to miniaturize nuclear warheads and develop missiles suitable for delivering such weapons suggest that the weapons are already in its arsenal.

Cheung points to tests of low-yield (less than 20–kiloton) weapons, including the suspected 1988 neutron device test, which he equates to Chinese discussions of developing "third-generation nuclear devices." His assessment of Chinese military exercises indicates that these tactical weapons would be used "to support infantry against the enemy's forward lines, rather than on crucial rear units," thus complying with the "no-first-strike-on-enemy-territory" principle.[20]

Little is known about the command and control of Chinese nuclear forces other than that it is exercised, as is control over the PLA in general, through the Chinese Communist Party's (CCP's) Central Military Commission (CMC). Within the CMC, ultimate authority rests with senior leader Deng Xiaoping, while day-to-day authority rests with CCP Chairman (and Chinese President) Ziang Zemin. Two other senior military leaders, Vice Chairmen Liu Huaqing and Zhang Zhen, also wield considerable influence within the CMC.

Operational control of nuclear forces is apparently exercised through the PLA's General Staff Department (GSD). Land-based strategic and suspected tactical nuclear weapons fall under the Second Artillery, which, until the late 1980s, evidently reported directly to the CMC, bypassing the GSD completely. The suspected introduction of tactical nuclear weapons increases the command-and-control challenge and the need for strict procedures and constant monitoring. As Cheung notes: "With the development of tactical doctrine and weapons, and their increasing integration into general military operations, more military officers at lower levels of the command chain have their hands on a nuclear button. Strict command procedures, however, are designed to prevent field commanders from acting on their own initiative."[21]

The spectacle of the Soviet Union's breaking up into several nuclear-capable states has also raised questions about the safety and accountability of China's nuclear inventory should China suffer a similar fate in the post-Deng era. No doubt the PLA has made provision for this, but no details are available. In my assessment, fears of China's disintegrating, à la the USSR, are largely unfounded. At any rate, given the modest size of the PRC's nuclear inventory and the general cohesiveness of the PLA, the problem of nonaccountability or dispersal of nuclear weapons should not be as serious as that experienced in the former Soviet Union (FSU).

Russia

Determining the current size and disposition of Russia's nuclear arsenal in general, much less the portion that may reside in the Northeast Asian region, is a difficult task, given questions about just how much has been decommissioned and/or turned over for destruction. All Russian ICBMs/SLBMs can reach targets throughout the globe, and (except for ICBMs in hardened fixed silos) land-based and air-launched strategic and tactical nuclear assets can easily be shifted from one region to another.

According to the IISS, the Russian/CIS strategic arsenal (including assets in Belarus, Kazakhstan, and Ukraine nominally under Russian military control), at last count, was comprised of 2,162 launchers (ICBMs, SLBMs, and strategic bombers) armed with 10,456 warheads.[22] Even upon completion of START II in 2003, Russia would likely possess up to 917 launchers while limiting itself to 3,500 strategic warheads.

No Bottom-Up Review or comparable official Russian forecast is available, but the IISS estimates that, given START II reductions, the Russian nuclear arsenal in 2003 is expected to include 105 downloaded SS-19 ICBMs and 340 or more SS-25 mobile ICBMs, with some of the latter also deployed in silos. The air leg of the strategic triad is forecast by the IISS to be comprised solely of ALCM-equipped TU-95/Bear bombers since the more modern TU-160/Blackjacks are largely in Ukrainian hands and are not likely to be turned over to the Russians. The IISS also expects the Russians to keep their two most modern SSBNs in service, pointing out that Russia could field six Typhoons (each of which carries twenty SS-N-20 SLBMs with ten warheads each) and seven Delta IVs (sixteen SS-N-23 SLBMs with four warheads apiece) and still meet START II SLBM limits.[23]

The number, type, and disposition of the SSBN force are highly speculative. Gerald Segal, for instance, states that the Deltas are likely to be eliminated under START II, presumably in favor of the more capable Typhoons.[24] At least one Russian strategist, however, expects both Delta IIIs and IVs to remain in the inventory, along with the Typhoons, while predicting a force of eighteen to twenty-three SSBNs by 2003.[25] Meanwhile, the Russian admiral in charge of shipbuilding, speaking in 1992 and not referring to specific types, reportedly stated that the future Russian force would consist, by the year 2000, of approximately seventeen SSBNs and that, beyond that date, Russian submarine construction would occur only to replace decommissioned boats.[26]

There has also been some speculation (particularly among Far East nuclear-free zone advocates) that this future Russian SSBN force would be based entirely in the northern fleet. Although this cannot be ruled out, at least one Russian strategist thinks that the likelihood that SSBNs will remain in the Far East is "far greater than not." In fact, Dr. Vladimir Ivanov asserts that "when START II is implemented, the strategic value of the Sea of Okhotsk is likely to increase."[27] This is not to say that the Russians cannot be induced to forgo deploying SSBNs in the Far East, but only to note that the prospects of this happening naturally do not appear high.

It does appear, however, that the Russians will soon stop producing submarines in this region. Greenpeace investigators were told that submarine production was bring phased out in the Far East. The sole production facility at Komsomolsk had been 20 percent converted to civilian use by 1992 and was to be fully converted by the end of the decade, after which the facility would produce "river and sea ships for transport" rather than submarines.[28]

As far as the present is concerned, most estimates point to twenty SSBNs in the Pacific fleet inventory today, at Pavlovsk (at the eastern edge of Strelok Bay) and Rybachiy (in Krashenininkova Bay near Petropavlovsk). Segal breaks these down as follows: nine Delta IIIs, nine Delta Is, and two Yankee SSBNs, the latter a 1974-vintage boat carrying sixteen SS-N-6 3,000-kilometer-range missiles.[29] This compares favorably with the SSBN inventory of nine Delta IIIs, nine Delta Is, and six Yankee-class submarines acknowledged in the Soviet Pacific fleet at the onset of the START negotiations.

The head of the Press Center for the Russian Pacific Fleet acknowledged to Greenpeace that there were twenty SSBNs in the Pacific fleet as of 1992. Captain First Rank Victor Ryzhkov also stated that there were twenty SSNs/SSGNs (cruise missile submarines) (and fifty-five diesel-powered submarines) in the Pacific fleet inventory at that time.[30] Other Russian naval officers complained to Greenpeace about extremely low operational tempo rates among the SSN/SSGN fleet due to maintenance and sustainability problems and "the poor state of refit technology." However, they claimed that the SSBNs "had a better refit capability and systems of support" and that "the 'coefficient of use' of SSBNs was comparable to the United States."[31]

Greenpeace's unprecedented Far East nuclear inspection trip also revealed considerable problems regarding operational safety and even greater problems when it came to the dismantling of decommissioned nuclear-powered submarines.[32]

Visits to the Pacific fleet, however, indicate that funds are inadequate for the immediate problem of defuelling and safely storing the dozens of submarines that have been taken out of service in the past few years. Also, there is a lack of capacity for scrapping the decommissioned submarines. Finally, neither the land-based storage facilities for defuelled reactors nor the transport system to carry the reactor vessels to such sites exists.

The chief of the Russian Pacific fleet's Department of Exploitation and Technical Service of Nuclear-Powered Submarines also expressed concern that decommissioned submarines might sink at dockside and cause major ecological problems. These problems are likely to be around for some time, since he also estimated that it would take thirty to forty years to scrap the anticipated sixty decommissioned Pacific fleet submarines.[33] Protests by concerned residents residing near nuclear submarine facilities have further complicated navy decommissioning plans. When these (often legitimate) expressions of public concern about nuclear safety are added to the history of at least eight submarines lost to sinkings or reactor meltdown, it is easy to conclude, as did the Greenpeace study, that "Soviet nuclear submarines were at times as much a threat to Soviet sailors and to the environment as they were to western navies."[34] In the future, this promises to become even more true.

One action that has reduced the (accidental or deliberate) threat potential of Russian tactical nuclear submarines has been the removal of all nuclear cruise missiles and torpedoes from the fleet. In accordance with the 1991 Bush–Gorbachev initiatives, the Russian Defense Ministry announced in February 1993 that all nuclear warheads had been removed from Russian ships and submarines (except SSBNs). The Russians have also stated that all ground and air-launched tactical nuclear warheads have been retrieved from other states of the FSU and are now situated on Russian soil.

Nonetheless, the Russians possess a wide variety of potential delivery systems should they ever elect to employ tactical nuclear weapons. These include everything from 152–millimeter artillery to a full range of rockets, missiles, and bombs. The Heritage study credits the Russians with 3,800 tactical nuclear weapons, while Segal speculates that, at most, about 1,000 of these are situated in the Far East.[35]

Throughout the Cold War, the Soviets claimed a no-first-use policy, in contrast to the United States and NATO. Ironically, at a time when the likelihood of nuclear confrontation is diminishing, the Russians have renounced this pledge.[36] Russian Defense Minister Pavel Grachev, in describing his nation's new military doctrine in November 1993, announced that Russia was abandoning the old Soviet no-first-use policy and would no longer rule out the possibility of first use against other nuclear weapons states or against non-nuclear nations allied with nuclear states.[37] Although directed primarily at Ukraine, this policy shift adds a new dimension to Russian nuclear strategy.

The disintegration of the Soviet Union (and the subsequent recognition that the successor Commonwealth of Independent States had little in common beyond a distrust for, and desire to be independent from, Moscow) had raised serious concerns about command and control and accountability of former Soviet tactical and strategic warheads. With the alleged return of all tactical warheads to Russian soil and the existing de facto Russian control over all ex-Soviet strategic rocket forces (with the added safety valve of having a second finger on the button of non-Russian-based ICBMs), these fears have been significantly reduced—but they have not been eliminated.

Even if every single Soviet/Russian tactical nuclear warhead is now accounted for (a very big "if"), concerns remain over these stockpiled weapons' finding their way into the black market. Add to this the fact that there exist in the FSU about 1,000 tons (1 million kilograms) of weapons-usable, highly enriched uranium and 160–200 tons of weapons-grade plutonium and the magnitude of the potential problem becomes clear. As one observer notes, "the leakage of one-hundredth of one percent of the plutonium stockpile would be enough to provide a Third World country with a nuclear arsenal."[38]

Noted proliferation expert Leonard Spector asserts that "a minor but unmistakable amount of leakage" has occurred,[39] while an analyst at the Natural Resources Development Council puts it this way: "Without any hype you can say that kilogram-quantities of nuclear weapons material have been taken out of [Russian] institutions, and some fraction of that has crossed the international border."[40]

There is also a genuine concern regarding the lack of control and accountability of Russian nuclear knowledge, with stories too numerous to recount (or discount) about Russian nuclear scientists' selling their services to countries such as North Korea, Iran, and other nuclear wanna-bes (not to mention known sponsors of international terrorism).

Japan

Japan has no nuclear weapons program and is constitutionally prohibited, under Article 9, from possessing the long-range, offensive, power-projection weapons systems needed for their delivery. Tokyo remains committed today to its three non-nuclear principles, which prohibit the manufacture, possession, or introduction into Japan of nuclear weapons. The Atomic Power Basic Law (Article 2) also limits Japan's use of nuclear energy to peaceful purposes. However, few doubt (and the Japanese themselves admit) that—given Japan's advanced nuclear and rocket technologies and vast stockpiles of tons of plutonium—a nuclear weapons capability (complete with delivery systems) is well within Tokyo's ability to achieve rapidly, if situations warranted.[41] Such situations are discussed in the following section.

Inter-relationship with Nuclear Proliferation Dynamics

The most pressing regional nuclear proliferation questions emerging from this review of Northeast Asia's nuclear capabilities deal not with the existence of, management of, or control over existing regional/global nuclear force but with the aspirations of the region's current non-nuclear players. Although the spotlight most frequently shines on North Korea, the more far-reaching (and potentially disruptive) question is "whither Japan?"

Japan

There has been a great deal of speculation that the development of a nuclear capability on the Korean Peninsula will drive Japan into developing nuclear weapons. In my view, the logic behind such assessments is seriously flawed. The single determinant of Japan's nuclear future can be summed up in one phrase:

"the U.S.-Japan security alliance." As long as this alliance remains firm (that is to say, as long as Tokyo believes that the U.S. nuclear umbrella will not be withdrawn), there is virtually no chance that Japan will elect to develop nuclear weapons. If a massive nuclear arsenal in the hands of one traditional rival and a modest (yet formidable) nuclear arsenal in the hands of a second historic foe have not, over the past four decades, driven Japan to develop an independent nuclear capability, why would a rudimentary capability in the hands of a nation that in the past has been more the prize than the threat now drive such a decision?

The Japanese realize that the development of a power-projection capability (with or without nuclear weapons) would cause such distrust and paranoia among its neighbors that the likely results would be, in military/security terms, a massive arms buildup and a closer accommodation between China and Japan's World War II victims. In economic terms, the result would likely be the withdrawal of the welcome mat that has currently been put out for Japanese businessmen and investors regionwide. Neither Japan's military security nor its economic security would be enhanced by obtaining a nuclear weapons capability.

Although beyond the scope of this chapter, it is important to note at least briefly that there are a number of events that could strain or even rupture the United States–Japan alliance, including disagreement over broader policy issues regarding China, Russia, or events on the Korean Peninsula, most specifically to include a Japanese refusal (or lukewarm effort) to support U.S. forces in the event of hostilities on the Korean Peninsula. United States–Japan trade frictions, although insufficient in and of themselves to rupture the alliance, do add straw to the camel's back. The alliance remains in need of—and generally receives—constant nurturing to keep it healthy. The soundness of this alliance is critical to regional stability and nonproliferation efforts since it obviates the need for Japan to "go nuclear."

The reverse is also true. Should the alliance for any reason crumble and the nuclear umbrella be removed (which I see as extremely unlikely), Japan would invariably feel compelled to develop a nuclear deterrent capability, regardless of developments on the Korean Peninsula. Considerable distrust for China lies just below the surface in Japan today despite the generally hospitable current state of Sino-Japanese relations, and it requires no digging at all to find Japan's anti-Russia sentiment. The latter should not be surprising since the Russo-Japanese rivalry predates the establishment of the Soviet Union, and the crumbling of the Soviet empire has changed neither the geopolitical landscape nor past attitudes between these two old adversaries.[42]

For Japan to place its security in the hands of either China or Russia is even more unthinkable than for Japan to arm itself with nuclear weapons; the Japanese would build their own nuclear umbrella before they would rely on one made in China or Russia. Japanese possession of nuclear weapons would also drive Koreans on both sides of the demilitarized zone (DMZ) (but particularly in Pyongyang) to pursue a nuclear weapons capability vigorously.[43]

North Korea

North Korea's apparent quest to develop nuclear weapons appears to be happening more in spite of, than because of, the nuclear developments described earlier. The ROK pledge that there are no U.S. nuclear weapons in the South, when added to its willingness (endorsed by the United States in the context of the on-again, off-again North–South talks) to open U.S. as well as ROK military bases in the South to North Korean inspection, should have reduced North Korean paranoia about U.S.-ROK intentions and capabilities.[44] These overtures appear to have had little positive impact on North Korea's behavior, however.

Even if the North Koreans mistakenly assumed that the reported removal of nuclear weapons from South Korea was in response to their demands, their subsequent actions have clearly worked against their declared ultimate goal of removing all U.S. forces (nuclear and otherwise) from the peninsula. Their refusal to cooperate with the IAEA has already caused the scheduled withdrawal of 6,500 U.S. troops from Korea to be placed on hold. And until former U.S. President Jimmy Carter at least temporarily defused the situation, many in the United States were calling for the immediate reintroduction of U.S. tactical nuclear weapons onto the peninsula as well.

Nuclear weapons–related developments in China and Russia also appear to have had little bearing on North Korean behavior. Political developments in both capitals undoubtedly have had an impact, however, as has the growing economic and (conventional) military might of South Korea. Russian President Boris Yeltsin has made it clear to Pyongyang that it can no longer rely on Russian support in the event of hostilities on the peninsula, especially if such activity is instigated by the North. Russian arms are also no longer readily available, and their purchase requires hard currency—a commodity in rare supply in Pyongyang.

China remains North Korea's closest (only?) friend in the region, but "socialism with Chinese characteristics," as now practiced by Beijing, no doubt frightens Pyongyang, given the degree of outside exposure that it requires to succeed. China's decision to establish diplomatic relations with South Korea, and its backing of the entry of both Koreas into the United Nations, also raises concerns in Pyongyang over the reliability of the Sino–North Korean special "close as lips to teeth" relationship.

Meanwhile, the Republic of Korea has expanded its political, economic, and military might over the past decade at the same time that the North has slid consistently downhill in all three categories. As a result, even with the presumed withdrawal of U.S. nuclear forces from the ROK, the North could see itself as more vulnerable today than ever before. North Korea could be pursuing a nuclear capability today based on what appear, at least to the leadership in Pyongyang, to be legitimate security concerns.

If this is the case, then China may hold the key to finding a possible solution.

In addition to oil and food (both precious commodities in short supply in North Korea), China has something that may be even more important to offer Pyongyang in return for genuine concessions and cooperation—namely, the same kind of security assurances that the United States currently offers Seoul. A Chinese "nuclear umbrella" could help prod North Korea along the path toward genuine rapprochement with South Korea and the United States.

In this regard, China's nuclear capability could become a source of regional stability if Beijing were willing to offer, and Pyongyang were willing to accept, a Chinese security guarantee in return for strict North Korean adherence to IAEA safeguards and a resumption of the North–South dialogue (including a mutual commitment to the no-reprocessing agreement). The United States should encourage this approach.

Arms Control and Disarmament

There are many arms-control and disarmament issues that grow out of the above discussions. Some take on a global dimension, whereas others are more regional in nature. This section provides a brief broad-brush review, in an effort to stimulate debate and (hopefully) offer some new approaches or perspectives. I will start where I just left off, with a few more thoughts on the challenges emanating from the Korean Peninsula.

North Korean Situation

One reason that the current situation is so difficult to deal with is that North Korea's motives and intentions remain unclear (and may shift in the wake of Kim Il Sung's death). Quite frankly, I haven't a clue as to what really lies behind North Korea's actions over the sixteen months before October 1994 (since its decision, subsequently suspended but not rescinded, to withdraw from the Non-Proliferation Treaty, or NPT)—and am highly skeptical of anyone who claims to understand its logic.

It is quite possible (perhaps even most likely) that North Korea is determined to develop nuclear weapons at any cost. If so, then efforts to prevent this from happening, short of a military invasion, are destined to fail. On the other hand, the North could be bluffing; it could merely be trying to play the only card that remains in its hand—the threat of "going nuclear"—in order to see what kind of concessions or package deals this might gain it.[45] Or it could be searching for security in the face of its declining geopolitical position, in which case the aforementioned Chinese umbrella might help bring it in from the rain.

As the North Korean leadership regroups in the wake of Kim Il Sung's sudden death, the rest of the world waits to see whether the post-Kim era will be one of reconciliation or renewed confrontation. Fortunately, the elder Kim (with considerable help from Jimmy Carter) set the stage for a genuine rapprochement between Pyongyang and both Washington and Seoul. The new leadership could justify abrupt changes in past practices merely by claiming to be fulfilling the Great Leader's last wishes. This, of course, assumes that the leadership that ultimately emerges (which may or may not include Kim Jong Il at the helm) will have reconciliation and economic recovery as its primary goals.

It is at least equally possible that the new leadership will be as untrustworthy and belligerent as the old one, especially if the Dear Leader is calling the shots and his behavior remains consistent with past practices. If so, there will probably be a tendency on the part of the United States to pick up the crisis where it left off immediately before the Carter visit and press once again for international sanctions. This, in my view, would be self-defeating in the long run.

Sanctions (gradual or otherwise) will likely prove counterproductive for several reasons. First, they create yet another source of tension between the United States and both China and Japan, relationships that need fewer, not more, points of contention.[46] Second, there is the more familiar argument that sanctions won't work, especially if the PRC and Japan fail to enforce them vigorously. More important is the possibility that, international precedents notwithstanding, sanctions in this instance might actually work.

North Korea, by most accounts, is already on the brink of economic collapse. What happens if sanctions succeed in driving it over the edge? The two most likely outcomes are implosion (an internal collapse, possibly to include anarchy, civil war, and the need for someone—South Korea, the United States?—to come in, restore order, and bail out the North à la West–East Germany) or explosion (in the form of a desperate military thrust south toward Seoul—a move that would be destined to fail but that would cause untold death and destruction before it was over). This constitutes a lose–lose situation, not only for North Korea but for the United States and all of Northeast Asia.[47]

If all that is desired is for North Korea to gradually feel enough pressure to come to the conclusion that an opening to the West is the only way out, then a better alternative could be a return to the postcrisis policy of containment and isolation rather than renewed brinkmanship.

How, then, do we deal with North Korea's threat (on hold since June 1993) to withdraw from the Non-Proliferation Treaty? The answer is, we don't. In fact, if North Korea abandons the IAEA safeguards program and—in defiance of its NPT obligations—once again refuses to honor its IAEA obligations, then it should be expelled from the NPT. North Korea's leaving the NPT is not going to cause the international agreement to collapse; allowing Pyongyang to stay in and openly flaunt its rules and international norms could—and would further destroy the credibility of the IAEA as well.

If North Korea returns to its old tricks, then the United Nations Security Council should make it clear to the North that its continued refusal to cooperate with the IAEA means continued international isolation and, more important, that any attempt to test, deploy, or export nuclear weapons would result in its expulsion from the United Nations. The Security Council should also reiterate U.S. President Bill Clinton's message that any use of such weapons would result in the destruction of North Korea.

China or other sanctions opponents should not balk at such an initiative; they could also be more easily convinced to increase pressure on Pyongyang privately once the spotlight is turned off. This course of action denies Pyongyang the limelight and leverage it so desperately seeks and serves notice that North Korea can expect nothing from the civilized world until it clearly demonstrates its willingness to follow international standards of behavior. It also avoids idle or unenforceable threats that merely perpetuate an atmosphere of crisis.

While waiting to see what Pyongyang is going to do, Beijing should be encouraged to take more initiative in developing long-term solutions and offering them to North Korea. Although North Korea will no doubt remain fiercely independent, China's historically close ties with the senior leadership in Pyongyang still provide Beijing an entry that few other nations enjoy. The time for Beijing to use its influence, limited as it may be, is now, to help ensure that the window of opportunity for dialogue with the North remains open.

Other Peninsula Issues

While dealing with today's alligators, it is important not to forget the overall swamp. Most analysts agree that one day there will be reunification—or at least a confederation of sorts—between North and South. A reunion today would leave the peninsula with one of the world's largest and most overly equipped militaries—one that would have almost ten times as many forces under arms as does Japan. One of the initiatives mentioned by Jimmy Carter that must be seized now is North–South discussions aimed at lowering force levels on both sides of the DMZ. Again, mutually supportive security guarantees by the United States and China could play a positive role.[48]

All the major players in this drama (even North Korea) profess to be in favor of a nuclear weapons–free peninsula. Over the long term, therefore, a Korean Peninsula nuclear weapons–free zone (KP-NWFZ) concept should be developed. This should be the focus of any "four plus two" dialogue and should be built upon the 1991 North–South "Joint Declaration for a Non-Nuclear Korean Peninsula."

Proposals have also been offered from time to time for a broader Northeast Asia (NEA) NWFZ, which, in most instances, would also entail the removal of Russian tactical and strategic nuclear assets (including SSBNs) from the Far East. An NEA-NWFZ might also entail China's restricting the employment of its nuclear forces, an action that Beijing would likely see as an unacceptable infringement on its sovereignty. Some proposals also raise freedom of the seas concerns and could otherwise restrict operations of the U.S. Navy, given its insistence on clinging to the NCND policy.[49] One proposal, by Australian defense specialist Andrew Mack, also encompasses Taiwan and plutonium reprocessing in Japan, which further complicates the task.[50] It seems advisable to learn to walk first—via a KP-NWFZ—before attempting to run toward broader NEA-NWFZ proposals.

Broader Proposals/Initiatives

Many nations, China conspicuous among them, have called for total nuclear disarmament. Such proposals appear unrealistic and could prove destabilizing; they could actually provide incentive to renegade states to produce a few crude devices—weapons whose military and psychological worth would be enhanced in a nuclear weapons–free world.

There is a need, however, for a START III to continue the downward trend in the U.S.-Russian overall nuclear inventories. As one Japanese nuclear specialist commented, "that the superpowers agreed to leave only some 3,000–3,500 strategic warheads in Russia [and, in fairness, we should add in the United States] is no 'favor' to the rest of the world."[51]

Eventually, China and the other declared nuclear states will need to be brought more fully into the dialogue, although the Chinese maintain that U.S.-Russian force levels will have to be reduced dramatically before China would seriously enter into nuclear arms–reduction talks. China has, however, signaled its willingness, beginning in 1996, to participate in a Comprehensive Test Ban Treaty (even as it remains the sole nuclear power that still conducts tests), and this initiative should be pursued.

More important than new initiatives, in many respects, is the need to assist the Russians in the elimination of weapons systems and warheads already committed to destruction. The security problems outlined by Spector, Cochran, and others, and the environmental hazards documented by Greenpeace, demand that greater international attention (including financial support) be directed toward the Russian decommissioning effort.

It may also be time for the nuclear powers to review their stands on the no-first-use issue. Before doing so, however, the terms of reference should be broadened to include chemical and biological weapons (the "poor man's nucs") as well. What appears desirable is an agreement forswearing the use of any and all weapons of mass destruction that carries with it the implicit warning that the use of chemical or biological agents could draw a nuclear response.

The renewal of the NPT in 1995 proved to be another watershed event. The nuclear states looked to strengthen the treaty by including penalties both for withdrawal and for nonmembership. It seems somewhat hypocritical (even if logical or understandable) for the United States to demand that North Korea be punished for wanting out of an agreement that some of its closest friends and allies (including Israel) have refused to join. In order to make the NPT meaningful, the U.N. Security Council should declare that nonsignatories will be expected to subject all shipments even remotely suspected to contain nuclear technology or weapons to search (and seizure, if appropriate). It should also warn NPT signatories and nonsigners alike that they could face international censure (and perhaps even expulsion from the United Nations) if they are caught exporting nuclear weapons technology or hardware. This does not interfere with internal domestic prerogatives (which would ensure a Chinese veto) but does draw the line at the water's edge to halt proliferation, an international concern.

More responsible action on the part of the "haves" might also help encourage more "have-nots" to sign up for an unlimited extension of the NPT. A Comprehensive Test Ban Treaty, a broad-based no-first-use agreement, and a commitment in principle to a START III (along with dedicating more assets to bringing START II to fruition) would all be helpful and set some meaningful examples.

Other Topics for Discussion and/or of Concern

I believe it useful at the end of this analysis to take a step back and examine the broader geopolitical environment, the one in which the nonproliferation dynamic must operate. Quite frankly, if we don't first work on the broader relationships, we will never create the atmosphere of trust that makes immediate problems more manageable and genuine progress in the arms-control and disarmament arenas possible.

Over the longer term, there are two priority tasks that, if successfully accomplished, could make the greatest contribution to regional security and nonproliferation: one is the maintenance of a constructive, cooperative relationship among Asia's three major powers—the United States, Japan, and China; the other is to foster and advance the growing trend toward multilateralism in Asia.

United States–Japan–China Relationship

More than anything else, the security environment of the twenty-first century will be shaped by the three-way inter-relationship among the United States, Japan, and the People's Republic of China. To the extent that the three can cooperate, we will have a generally secure environment in which to deal with all the challenges sure to come our way. Conversely, tensions among the three will have an unsettling effect regionwide, if not globally.

I am not referring to any type of strategic triangle or security condominium, but merely to a healthy three-way relationship in which no participant is aligned with another specifically to counter the third. Such a relationship essentially exists today but is historically atypical; basic antagonism and distrust between China and Japan (with the United States siding with one or the other) is the more "normal" occurrence. The return of such a regional bipolar struggle pitting any two against the third serves no one's interests.

This in no way argues against the maintenance of strong bilateral security ties between the United States and Japan. This linkage must be the strongest, thickest arm of any trilateral relationship and, as argued earlier, is a prerequisite for ensuring a non-nuclear Japan. But the United States–Japan security relationship must focus on the promotion of regional security, stability, and prosperity. Although clearly providing for the defense of Japan, it must not be viewed as aimed at countering or containing China.

All three nations must devote considerable diplomatic effort in order to keep this three-way relationship in harmony. They must continue to seek out opportunities for greater bilateral and trilateral dialogue, including discussions on sensitive, potentially divisive economic and security issues.

Multilateral Cooperation

The need for enhanced dialogue is not restricted to the United States–Japan–China relationship. More bilateral and especially multilateral dialogue is needed regionwide across a broad political, economic, and security spectrum to create greater regional confidence and awareness. There are still many real or potential threats to regional security, despite the lack of a global Cold War enemy. Expanded multilateral dialogue can help to defuse potential problems before they are realized. Such dialogue, to be credible, must be as inclusive as possible and involve the active participation of the United States, Japan, and China.

Several successful multilateral initiatives are currently under way at both the official and nongovernmental levels. The most successful official forum is the ASEAN Post-Ministerial Conference and its soon-to-be-created extension, the ASEAN Regional Forum (ARF). At the nongovernmental level, the Council for Security Cooperation in the Asia–Pacific (CSCAP), which links broad-based member committees in eleven Asia–Pacific nations, shows great promise. Organizations such as ARF and CSCAP can provide a useful venue for the discussion of Asian arms-control and nonproliferation issues.

Conclusion

This is a time of great hope and great challenge when it comes to arms control and nonproliferation in Asia. Relations among the three nuclear powers are less competitive and seemingly more cooperative than at any time since the dawn of the nuclear age. Many opportunities are available to reduce the threat of nuclear confrontation further between these states and to support initiatives that will make it less likely that new members will join the nuclear club. Nonetheless, a great deal of uncertainty remains, especially regarding nuclear inventories and locations. Greater nuclear transparency on the part of all three nations would help build confidence among the three and throughout the region.

The most pressing problem, the apparent effort by North Korea to develop nuclear weapons, defies simple solution (or even basic understanding). There seems to be an inverse relationship (if, indeed, there is any relationship) between nuclear developments involving the three major nuclear powers and North Korea's drive for the bomb. Rather than respond positively to the withdrawal of U.S. nuclear warheads from overseas bases, ships, and aircraft, the North has become, at least until immediately before Kim Il Sung's death, more recalcitrant. Where it will go from here remains unclear.

China's status as a nuclear power may, in the long run, prove stabilizing if it will provide, and North Korea will accept, Chinese nuclear assurances in return for genuine reconciliation and progress toward a denuclearized Korean Peninsula. The United States' over-the-horizon nuclear capability remains the most credible deterrent to North Korea's use of nuclear weapons, if Pyongyang cannot be dissuaded from its current course.

Notes

1. Lawrence Freedman, "Nuclear Strategy and Asia," *Korean Journal of Defense Analysis* Vol. 5, No. 1 (summer 1993): 41.

2. Vladimir Ivanov and Victor Vrevsky, *Asia–Pacific in 1990s: Soviet Security Perceptions* (New Delhi: Allied Publishers, 1989), 131.

3. Gerald Segal, "Nuclear Forces in Northeast Asia," Northeast Asia Peace and Security Network paper (Berkeley, CA: Nautilus Institute for Security and Sustainable Development, May 1994), 8.

4. *The Military Balance, 1993–1994* (London: Brassey's for the International Institute for Strategic Studies, 1993), 235.

5. Les Aspin, "Report on the Bottom-Up Review," U.S. Department of Defense, October 1993, 26.

6. Baker Spring, "What the Pentagon's Nuclear Doctrine Review Should Say," Heritage Foundation Backgrounder 987, May 26, 1994, 9–10.

7. Barbara Starr, "No. Korea Casts a Longer Shadow with TD-2," *Jane's Defence Weekly,* March 12, 1994, 1. See also Art Pine, "CIA Reports New Korean Missiles," *Los Angeles Times,* March 18, 1994, 5.

8. Paul Shin, "U.S. Said to Stop South Korea's Nuke Bomb Plans," *Washington Times,* March 29, 1994, 11.

9. These attitudes were relayed by a visiting group of prominent Korean journalists during roundtable discussions at Pacific Forum CSIS in Honolulu on June 16, 1994. The journalists cautioned that this was far from being a majority or an official view. It was, however, a viewpoint frequently expressed primarily (but not exclusively) by the younger generation.

10. Col Xu Xiaojun, "China's Grand Strategy for the 21st Century," in *Asia in the 21st Century: Evolving Strategic Priorities,* ed. Michael D. Bellows (Washington, DC: National Defense University Press, 1994), 39.

11. Tai Ming Cheung, "New Bomb Makers," *Far Eastern Economic Review,* March 16, 1989, 27–28.

12. For more information on Chinese military transparency (or the lack thereof), including suspected Chinese rationale, see Ralph A. Cossa, "Chinese National Security Objectives in the Post–Cold War Era and the Role of the People's Liberation Army," paper prepared for the Twenty-third Sino-American Conference on Contemporary China, Taipei, Taiwan, June 7–8, 1994.

13. *Military Balance, 1993–1994,* 244.

14. Ibid.

15. See, for example, Richard Fieldhouse, "China's Mixed Signals on Nuclear Weapons," *Bulletin of the Atomic Scientists* (May 1991): 41; and Segal, "Nuclear Forces in Northeast Asia," 3. These sources also credit China with twenty rather than ten CSS-3 launchers. Segal also identifies thirty-six mobile CSS-6 (DF-21) 1,800–kilometer-range missiles with a single 300–kiloton warhead each and indicates that China may have developed (but not yet deployed) a multiple independently targetable re-entry vehicle (MIRV) capability.

16. Paul Godwin and John J. Schulz, "Arming the Dragon for the 21st Century: China's Defense Modernization Program," *Arms Control Today* (December 1993): 6.

17. Ibid. Also Fieldhouse, "China's Mixed Signals on Nuclear Weapons," 41; and *Military Balance, 1993–1994*, 244.

18. Fieldhouse, "China's Mixed Signals on Nuclear Weapons," 41. Segal, "Nuclear Forces in Northeast Asia," 3, reports that China has 150 tactical warheads, but he is most likely referring to aerial bombs and not missile or rocket warheads or artillery shells. He also reports that "not much is known about China's tactical systems."

19. Cheung, "New Bomb Makers," 28.

20. Ibid.

21. Tai Ming Cheung, "Who's in Charge?" *Far Eastern Economic Review*, March 16, 1989, 27.

22. *Military Balance, 1993–1994*, 235.

23. Ibid., 231.

24. Segal, "Nuclear Forces in Northeast Asia," 2.

25. Vladimir I. Ivanov, "Russia's New Military Doctrine: Implications for Asia," in *Asia in the 21st Century*, 218.

26. Joshua Handler, "Nuclear Free Seas: Greenpeace," a trip report on a July–November 1992 Greenpeace visit to Moscow and the Russian Far East, February 15, 1993, 13, citing a conversation with Contre-Admiral Leonid Belyshev, chief of shipbuilding and armaments for the Russian Navy, in Moscow.

27. Ivanov and Vrevsky, *Asia–Pacific in the 1990s*, 221–222.

28. Handler, "Nuclear Free Seas," 14.

29. Segal, "Nuclear Forces in Northeast Asia," 2.

30. Handler, "Nuclear Free Seas," 3. Ryzhkov also stated that another nuclear-powered and thirty-five diesel submarines had been removed from the fleet since 1985.

31. Ibid., 20.

32. Ibid., 25.

33. Ibid., 16–17, citing Russian Captain First Rank Pavel Smirnov.

34. Ibid., 1.

35. Spring, "What the Pentagon's Nuclear Doctrine Review Should Say," 9; and Segal, "Nuclear Forces in Northeast Asia," 2.

36. Fred Hiatt, "Russia Shifts Doctrine on Military Use," *Washington Post*, November 4, 1993, A1, A33. See also Michael R. Gordon, "The Guns May Be a Bit Rusty but the Nuclear Arms Are Still Polished," *New York Times*, November 29, 1993, A10. For a broader discussion of the new Russian military doctrine, also see Ivanov and Vrevsky, *Asia–Pacific in the 1990s*, 211–213.

37. To ensure that Ukraine (and the other states of the former Soviet Union) did not miss the message, Grachev also emphasized that the new doctrine sanctioned the use of troops both at home and "beyond Russia's borders" to protect national interests.

38. Paul Quinn-Judge, "Russia Called Fertile Ground for Nuclear Proliferation," *Boston Globe*, July 3, 1994, 12, citing U.S. nuclear specialists and CIA Director James Woolsey's June 28, 1994, testimony to a House subcommittee.

39. Ibid.

40. Ibid., citing Spector and Thomas Cochran, director of the nuclear program at the Natural Resources Development Council (NRDC).

41. For an excellent review of Japan's capabilities, attitudes, and (lack of) intentions, see Kumao Kaneko, "Nukes as Flukes: Suspicious World Sizes Up Japan's Nuclear Intentions," *Japan Times Weekly,* June 20–26, 1994, 8, international edition.

42. Unlike the European and Central Asian fronts, where former staging areas have become buffer zones (if not sources for partners in future anti-Russian alliances), in Northeast Asia, Russia remains as close and as potentially threatening to Japan as the Soviet Union ever was, while the major Cold War point of contention—the Japanese Northern Territories—remains firmly in Russian hands.

43. The determining factor for Seoul would be the viability of the ROK–United States security alliance and the degree of pressure applied by the Unted States not to respond in kind to either Tokyo or Pyongyang.

44. Although the massive North Korean hardware inventory continues to provide Pyongyang with a significant numerical edge, Pyongyang's ability to feed, fuel, and otherwise sustain this force, even in peacetime, has been seriously questioned.

45. Pyongyang today, in my assessment, faces a lose–lose situation. It can attempt to remain a hermit kingdom and eventually collapse of its own weight—and most forecasts suggest that the North Korean economy is not far from this point. Or it can attempt to save its economy by gradually opening up its society and, in so doing, run the risk of its leaders' suffering the same fate as their East European communist colleagues. As a result, the North will approach any package deal with much care and with the intent of cutting as many as possible of the strings that are certain to be attached.

46. The proposed imposition of international sanctions had become a major point of contention between the United States and China since China believed that this American "cure" was worse than the disease being treated. The Chinese are not convinced that a North Korean nuclear capability is imminent (or even likely) but, even before Kim's untimely death, believed that the North was unstable and capable of either lashing out suddenly or collapsing into a state of chaos if sanctions were applied.

47. For more on this line of argument, see Ralph A. Cossa, "Sanctions on North Korea Are a 'Lose–Lose' Strategy," *Christian Science Monitor,* June 17, 1994, 19.

48. Russia might also have a role to play here as well, but it would likely be more symbolic than substantive

49. A U.S. unilateral review of this policy also appears in order in the wake of the removal of all nuclear warheads from U.S. tactical ships and aircraft.

50. Andrew Mack, "A Northeast Asia Nuclear Free Zone: Problems and Prospects," paper presented at Nuclear Policies in Northeast Asia, a UNIDIR conference, Seoul, May 25–27, 1994.

51. Ryukichi Imai, "Asian Ambitions, Rising Tensions," *Bulletin of the Atomic Scientists* (June 1993): 34.

18

Great-Power Nuclear
Forces Deployment and
a Limited Nuclear-Free Zone
in Northeast Asia

John E. Endicott

The idea of nuclear-free zones (NFZs) in Northeast Asia (NEA) is not new. In fact, there have been numerous references to such an idea in the speeches and declaratory policies of the leaders of North Korea, the former Soviet Union, and the Socialist Party of Japan ever since the late 1970s. These ideas will not be reviewed in detail in this context, but normally, they were general, encompassed vast regions of operating area of the Pacific Ocean, and were not believable or realistic given the political rhetoric and invective of the Cold War era in which they were generated.

This chapter reviews the impact of a concept, born in late 1991 and tested in U.S. government and academic circles as early as February 1992, that would attempt to limit the deployment of nuclear weapons within a described zone of Northeast Asia—a circle 1,200 nautical miles in radius and centered in the middle of the demilitarized zone (DMZ) of the Korean Peninsula. Central to the idea is the creation of a multinational verification agency, based in Vladivostok, that would oversee implementation and execution of the agreement. This organiza-

Georgia Institute of Technology Center for International Strategy, Technology, and Policy (CISTP). Paper prepared for the Conference on Peace and Security and the Nuclear Issue in Northeast Asia at the East–West Center, Honolulu, July 17–19, 1994.

tion would become the first operating regional institution with security responsibilities that would meet at a working level on a regular—perhaps daily—basis. Its responsibilities would be to ensure that nuclear weapons-possessing states with forces in the region—Russia, the People's Republic of China (PRC), and the United States—have, indeed, removed weapons as promised. Further, however, the verification organization, staffed by specialists from all the areas in the zone (China, Japan, North and South Korea, Mongolia, Russia, Taiwan, and the United States), would be authorized and expected to inspect the nuclear power and research programs of the non-nuclear weapons possessing states—Japan, the two Koreas, Mongolia, and Taiwan—to ensure that pledges not to weaponize their programs are being honored.

While the region would enjoy the benefits of having nuclear weapons removed from the immediate area of the zone, realization of the concept would also accelerate the development of a cooperative regional security community that would replace the confrontation of the Cold War era with a sense of developing cooperation. Reciprocal access to military and nuclear installations throughout the zone, as found in the 1991 North–South bilateral denuclearization agreement for the Korean Peninsula, would begin to build a sense of trust, offer a reassuring transparency regarding hitherto secret defense facilities, and most important, provide a supportive environment for the final realization of the denuclearization of the peninsula. The isolation and political paranoia of the leaders of the Democratic People's Republic of Korea (DPRK) could indeed be reduced in the near and midterm. Of critical importance to the long term is the creation of a regional security community that has as its long-term partner the United States, working with its Asian neighbors to ensure a stable security environment for the general prosperity of the entire region.

Central to the success of such a concept is the commitment of Japan, especially, to open its plutonium-reprocessing facilities and nuclear storage areas to the multinational inspectors. No one factor is more destabilizing to the states of East Asia than the 8 tons of plutonium held by a dynamic and vibrant Japan. Even though Japan's reprocessing program is under full International Atomic Energy Agency (IAEA) safeguards, conversations with policy makers of the states of the region reveal a very deep and abiding concern over this program for an energy alternative for the future. Japan's leadership in this effort is a natural outgrowth of its worldwide commitment to see the nuclear weapons threat disappear from the earth. This would be a step that the new prime ministers of Japan could begin during their respective tenure as leader of a new and remarkable coalition of political forces in Japan.

The enthusiastic involvement of all the states mentioned above is required, however, and could be realized as a result of the "window of opportunity" offered to the international community by President Jimmy Carter's bold trip to North and South Korea. When the author exposed military and civilian policy makers, academics, and civic bodies in the nations mentioned above to the concept, it received a consistently positive, if cautious, reception. However, for this chapter, it is appropriate to examine what impact such a concept would have on the deployment patterns of the nuclear weapons states and what might be the feasible ways to approach actual implementation after having heard the critique of the security communities of the countries concerned.

Deployment Patterns of Nuclear Weapons States within the Zone

Russia

Until the *Nuclear Weapons Databook*, volume 5, was published in April 1994, the most difficult nuclear weapons deployment pattern to describe was China's; however, since this much-needed book reached our hands, only one nation in the Northeast Asian region stands out as difficult to project. That country, unfortunately for this chapter, is Russia. However, parameters can be outlined, and maximums can probably be described with some degree of reliability. Precise data, which capture the ongoing reduction and modernization of strategic systems in this area due to Strategic Arms Reduction Talks (START) reductions, are difficult to obtain. In any case, what can be shown is the nature of the impact of the realization of a limited NFZ, even if we cannot, at this juncture, identify each and every nuclear weapons site and describe the kind of systems present.

One of the problems is, of course, the increasingly chaotic nature of the Russian state and the manner in which it supports its military establishment. From recent preliminary studies by Barry Blechman, Gerald Segal, and William Arkin and Robert Norris, a very unclear and changing picture of Russian nuclear forces can be gleaned. Segal presents us with the reported finding of a "wagon-load of nuclear missiles near Kurgan (western Siberia) which were 'mislaid due to the negligence of railway staff.' "[1] Although western Siberia is not within the limited nuclear-free zone (LNFZ), the notion that tactical missiles can be "found" in railway cars at random marshaling yards throughout Russia does not build confidence in the reliability of our regional accounting.

The most recent publication of the International Institute for Strategic Studies, or IISS (a map of strategic systems published in 1992), showing the placement of Russian strategic nuclear weapons indicates that there are five principal nuclear installations in the zone. Beginning with the SS-11 base at Drovyanaya, just east of Lake Baikal, with fifty launchers and one warhead per launcher,[2] the facilities progress eastward in the following manner:

- Yasnaya SS-11 base, with 90 launchers
- Svobodnyy SS-11 base, with 60 launchers
- Ukrainka Air Base, with forty-five TU-95 Bears (with sixteen ALCMs per aircraft)
- Pavlovskoye Naval Base, with six Delta 1 SSBNs (nuclear-powered ballistic missile submarines) and possibly three Yankee SSBNs

Outside the zone, at 1,500 nautical miles from the DMZ, is the Ribacniy Naval Base, with three Delta 1 subs and nine Delta 111 SSBNs. The Delta 1s carry twelve SS-N-8 missiles with one warhead each; the Delta 111's carry sixteen SS-N-18 missiles with three warheads per launcher. The Yankees have sixteen SS-N-6 missiles with one warhead apiece.[3]

If the above figures are correct, Russian strategic warheads number approximately 1,040 within the zone. Tactical warheads have been estimated at 1,000 for "the Russian portion of Northeast Asia."[4] Thus, in a very rough way, we can estimate that somewhat more than 2,040–2,050 Russian warheads are within the zone depicted as the LNFZ for Northeast Asia. Given the range of the various strategic systems involved, all members of the NFZ are at risk from these strategic forces. The tactical weapons will be assumed to threaten only immediate border areas but could actually threaten areas as much as 500 nautical miles from their location if tactical airforces are the method of employment.

Although counting installations and projecting range capabilities for hardware depicts one kind of image, there is another side of the Russian East Asian deployment profile that needs to be appreciated fully to understand why Russia may be interested in adherence to a limited nuclear-free zone in Northeast Asia. Since 1989 and the fall of the Soviet Union, a dramatic transformation of the military instrument in Russia, especially in the Russian Far East, has occurred. This transformation is not pretty. It includes the aforementioned discovery of an abandoned railway car with tactical missiles aboard,[5] air force pilots not being paid for more than five months, "the virtual disappearance of the ex-Soviet Pacific Fleet," and extremely low states of operational readiness by Russian nuclear submarines.[6] A visit to Vladivostok[7] reveals a fleet and its personnel reduced to very low operational standards. The overall cumulative impact of these individual events will have the probable effect of reducing the corporate effectiveness of the nuclear instrument in the Russian Far East while increasing the likelihood of specific and discrete unauthorized events involving nuclear weapons. It would seem imperative to reduce these risks as fast as possible. Thus, the LNFZ may prove to be useful to the Russian government domestically by reducing the presence of a very worrisome element and internationally by providing a new leadership role for the Russian government in East Asia. This is especially important in assuring the economic revitalization of the Russian Far East by providing an additional tie to the vibrant economies of the nations involved in the zone.

China

The location of Chinese nuclear weapons within the zone has become known through the excellent scholarship of the *Nuclear Weapons Databook,* volume 5. From the information available in this new publication, and other sources, especially the IISS's *Military Balance, 1993–1994,* it is clear that the People's Republic of China has an intercontinental ballistic missile (ICBM) force of four to six DF-5 missiles with a range of at least 13,000 kilometers, ten to fifteen DF-4 missiles with a 4,750–kilometer range, and approximately sixty DF-3 missiles capable of reaching 2,800 kilometers. Warhead yields for the three classes of missiles are estimated to be 5 megatons for the DF-5, 3 megatons for the DF-4, and 2 megatons for the DF-3.[8] As Victor Gilinsky has opined, just focusing the world's attention on the inordinate size of the Chinese operational warheads would be a useful endeavor.

Although the author agrees that the use of such warheads is unconscionable from a tactical standpoint, they substantiate the declaratory statements of the PRC government regarding a no-first-use policy; the Chinese have, in essence, operationalized a minimum deterrence policy by employing such warhead sizes. More will be said later about the unique nuclear weapons program pursued by the PRC.

The various range capabilities of the missiles reflect an evolution of PRC threat perception and, of course, available technology. The DF-3 was capable of reaching Clark Air Field in the Philippines. The DF-4 was designed to bring Guam and U.S. military facilities there under attack but was later adapted to the need to be able to threaten Moscow with nuclear weapons. The DF-5 has a range of between 13,000 and 15,000 kilometers and can reach any target in Russia or the United States.

All known locations of the DF-4 missile can place at risk all the major U.S. bases in East Asia, and even the DF-3 can challenge most U.S. forces based in Japanese installations. Of special note, again, is the fact that the Chinese have exercised a considerable degree of restraint in deploying their strategic systems. Over a period of possibly eight years or more, they have chosen to produce and deploy approximately four to six ICBMs when their capability far exceeded that number. Only two of these ICBMs have they placed in hardened underground silos.[9]

The total deployment of nuclear weapons within the limited nuclear-free zone reveals the following:

- Six sites of DF-3 missiles for approximately forty-eight warheads
- Two (possibly three) DF-4 sites for nine warheads
- Three (possibly two) DF-5 sites for six warheads
- Two SSBNs, each with twelve DF-21 submarine-launched ballistic missiles (SLBMs), nine with a range of approximately 1,700 kilometers
- Thirty-six road-mobile DF-21A missiles with a 1,700–kilometer range
- 150 tactical warheads

Within the limited NFZ, we can assume a total of approximately 273 nuclear warheads possessed by the People's Liberation Army (PLA). Fewer than 40, approximately 36, weapons can be located outside the zone, making the total impact of the LNFZ regime very severe on the PRC deterrent system if implemented in its original form—that is, that all weapons within the zone be relocated or removed.

In the Russian case, interest in a limited nuclear-free zone can be shown to be consistent with past declaratory policies and current internal imperatives. However, in the Chinese case, there has historically been little or no interest in regional arms-control efforts—with the exception of a willingness to negotiate regarding the Sino-Russian border. Beijing's stance regarding nuclear weapons arms control has long been that until the major nuclear powers significantly reduced their inventories, the PRC would not be interested in nuclear arms-reduction talks. Beijing has also, since the end of the Cold War, increased its defense budget at least 10 percent each year[10] and has adopted a new defense doctrine more outwardly oriented or aggressive than Mao's completely defensive "people's war." This new "partial war" planning concept emphasizes "preparing for a war with one of China's other neighbors" (not Russia).[11] In this new concept, the PLA is to seize the initiative at the outset of a conflict and defeat the enemy as rapidly as possible. Holding in mind China's often-repeated pledge of no first use with regard to nuclear weapons, we must assume that nuclear weapons are not integrated into the concept of partial wars unless something unforeseen were to occur.

China at this time may, however, be interested in a limited nuclear-free zone. When this LNFZ proposal was first presented in Beijing at a March 1992 conference cosponsored by the Institute for Global Concerns and the CISTP, the Chinese response was acute, adamant, and severe. No Chinese involvement! However, a year later, in March 1993, a perceptible and positive change had taken place (one week prior to the North Korean announcement of possible withdrawal from the Non-Proliferation Treaty [NPT] regime). Thus, even though the LNFZ concept involves a disproportionate number of its limited nuclear resources, the PRC may be willing to discuss such a concept (with the aim of minimizing the LNFZ's impact on its deterrent forces) in order to be assured that the other nations in East Asia, especially Japan and North Korea, would not opt for a full nuclear weapons program in the future. Of course, involvement as a major player in such a regional or subregional system would assure the PRC formative access to a new process that would ultimately pay back handsome economic development dividends.

The United States

In recognition of a new international situation after the end of the Cold War, President George Bush in September 1991 made the unilateral decision to remove tactical weapons from U.S. ground and naval forces worldwide. This new policy removes operational deployments of tactical nuclear weapons—both land- and sea-based—from Northeast Asia.[12] U.S. strategic systems are not located in the zone, but eight Trident submarines do operate out of Bangor, Washington, with the Trident 1 C4 missile.[13]

It is unlikely initially that official U.S. policy will support the creation of a limited NFZ in NEA without some significant groundswell of support for the idea coming out of Asia first. With regard to nuclear-free zones, it has long been U.S. policy to support those that are developed, mature, and are supported by the states of the region involved. In this case, the states of the region are focusing on possible nuclear proliferation in the DPRK and are not looking at the root causes of the North Korean action. Also, there is no developed track record of these particular states' working closely in such a venture. Although this author has heard the notion that such a regime cannot be attempted in Asia, it does involve certain evidence of mental entrapment. Additionally, there are issues involving the "innocent free passage" of naval vessels through the zone that will make the United States reluctant to declare this status when traveling in international waters but still within the zone. The U.S. Navy will have to be convinced that, in essence, the restrictions that such a zone might entail are in the national interest, even though some slight operational restrictions might have to be endured.

The United States must address the limited nuclear-free zone concept as a method to begin the building of a security community in NEA so that American influence can remain supportive over the long term but not "overly" involved. It is a way to begin sharing leadership through, first, the mechanism of the verification agency and, later, other security areas as trust and transparency materialize from the day-to-day operation and interaction of the agency staff.

A Realistic Limited NFZ for NEA

When the LNFZ concept was presented to specialists of the two nuclear weapons states of the region, it became clear that a total ban on nuclear weapons and the removal of all such weapons from the zone would not initially be acceptable. Exceptions would have to be made for certain weapons systems. These modifications in the original total ban could include all SSBNs and their associated SLBMs. Thus, in the case of Russia, the approximately nine SSBNs reportedly operating out of Pavlovskyoe, near Vladivostok in the Maritime Province, would be exempted from the first phase of regime implementation and would be permitted to remain in the zone.

In the Chinese case, it would be appropriate to exempt the two SSBNs possibly operating out of Qingdao, as submarine-launched missiles admittedly are a more stable and generally recognized retaliatory form of weapons system. However, in the Chinese case, it will be noticed that all of the sites identified as DF-5 (ICBM) installations are quite within the zone. If this is, in truth, the case, it would seem very unlikely that the PLA and PRC would ever agree to the inclusion of such installations in the first phase of a limited NFZ. Likewise, the two DF-4 sites, with missiles having a range of approximately 4,800 kilometers, would be likely candidates for exemption from the first phase. To those who ask, "Why exempt DF-4s and DF-5s?" the author would reply that these systems place at risk U.S. forces and political centers in the United States itself. To realize their elimination, of course, is in the long-term interest of U.S. national security; however, initially, the concept of "shared risk" must be applied to zone implementation so that we may transit via transparency and trust building to ultimate reciprocal weapons reduction. The PRC nuclear retaliatory systems that include the forty-eight DF-3s, the thirty-six DF-21A road-mobile 1,700-kilometer-range missiles, and the approximately 150 tactical (air-delivered and artillery-fired) weapons comprise more than 70 percent of the nuclear systems within the zone. Under the current concept of the limited NFZ, these weapons could be relocated outside the zonal boundary. (Of course, this is the case in the Russian situation as well; however, the existence of agreed-upon weapons-reduction goals under START II makes it less likely that the Russians would take the opportunity to relocate strategic resources, just take credit for early achievement of the year 2003 goal. This is not necessarily the case for tactical weapons. An incentive program for the turning in of special nuclear materials could be the international equivalent of the gun-buyback programs now seen throughout cities in the United States.)

Readers may be asking why the LNFZ concept permits relocation of weapons not exempted within the zone rather than mandating their destruction. Ultimately, their destruction is the goal, but the object initially is to create a working confidence-building measure (CBM) that could more accurately be termed a confidence-building mechanism. The fact that an international organization would be created, operate out of Vladivostok, and bring together, on a regular basis, military and civilian specialists of the countries concerned cannot be stressed enough. This does not exist in Asia. In Europe, we see deep redundancy in this regard. Even Russia is becoming a Partnership for Peace partner of the North Atlantic Treaty Organization (NATO). And to some observers, I would maintain that this is not a cultural difference but the legacy of unfortunate historic political involvement and events over the past century. The fact that nuclear weapons brought together such intractable foes as the United States and the Soviet Union should not be overlooked. The same fundamental interest in controlling one of humanity's most devastating inventions can function to create a new security system for Northeast Asia. To finally institutionalize the process of substantive arms control and arms reduction in the Asian area—the only area where they have been used in anger—and to employ this process to build a stable security environment certainly must be a policy goal for all nations of the region as we approach the twenty-first century.

In discussions in April 1994 with members of the Russian General Staff, Russian Security Council, Foreign Ministry, and security academics in Moscow and Vladivostok, excitement and interest in the LNFZ concept were evident, but as mentioned above, a total ban on weapons within the zone was seen as premature. However, the deputy director of the Russian Security Council, Colonel General Valeri Manilov, termed the concept "a marvelous idea that must be operationalized."[14] His concept of operationalization was to focus immediately on the area of and adjacent to the Korean Peninsula. In fact, if we were to examine the accompanying chart of 500–nautical mile circles emanating from the Korean Peninsula, we would observe what Manilov more or less considers the "operationalization" of the idea. His suggestion would be to establish a non-nuclear zone right away in a circle immediately surrounding the Korean Peninsula, possibly involving some territory of Russia, China, and Japan. A circle that fully inscribes all of the Korean Peninsula could also include Vladivostok, Qingdao, Shenyang, Hiroshima, Nagasaki, Kobe, and Osaka and would also include the U.S. base at Sasebo. There would be two SLBM test centers in the Chinese area as well as one DF-4 installation. Of course, the Chinese and Russian SSBN bases mentioned above would be within this circle but possibly exempted.

Creating such a first phase would allow for all the required infrastructure to be developed and for the all-important administrative day-to-day meetings to begin. It would also have most of the ingredients of the more expanded zone, which could be implemented by an agreed schedule—possibly five or ten years. Such a delay in full zonal implementation would also provide the PRC with a vantage point to see whether the United States and Russia achieve their agreed-upon cuts for the year 2003.

Next Steps

It is clear from discussions in China, Japan, South Korea, Mongolia, Russia, and the United States[15] that there is considerable positive interest in a limited NFZ for Northeast Asia. However, it is also clear that the details of such a concept must come "out of Asia" and not be seen as the child of the United States. The member states of the proposed zone must be present at the formulation of such an accord.

In this light, four retired general officers from China, Japan, South Korea, and Russia agreed to join CISTP and Georgia Tech and their American colleagues in a three-month examination of Pacific security issues and focused on creating a draft agreement that was placed before a student simulation of a regional LNFZ negotiating conference in March 1995. Once this was done, the four general officers joined in briefing interested government and academic circles in Washington, Boston, and San Francisco on their recommendations and the results of the simulation.

After such a draft agreement has been vetted throughout the American security studies community, it would be appropriate to hold an international conference on neutral ground where this draft agreement might be debated and a possible new and further consensus derived.

Much work has been done to realize a limited NFZ in NEA, but as all recognize, it will take much more. Ultimately, there is no insurmountable reason why nuclear arms control and nuclear arms reduction should not be on the official agenda of the nations of East Asia. Further, there is no insurmountable reason why the United States should not play a supportive role in husbanding this effort. In an era when big-power rivalry has given way to increasingly effective regional arrangements in other areas of the world, it is time to set our policy objectives higher than in the past or at present. In this new era, we must free ourselves of foreign policy that approaches nearsighted myopia; we must strive to create an international security system built on cooperation, not confrontation. As the Chinese say, the journey of 20,000 li (about 10,000 kilometers) must begin with the first step.

It's time to begin.

Notes

1. Gerald Segal, "Nuclear Forces in Northeast Asia," Northeast Asia Peace and Security Network paper (Berkeley, CA: Nautilus Institute for Security and Sustainable Development, May 1994), 1–2.

2. According to *The Military Balance, 1993–1994* (London: Brassey's for the International Institute for Strategic Studies [IISS], 1993), the total number of SS-11s in the Russian inventory has dropped to 100. That makes it difficult to have 200, as indicated above in the named complexes.

3. See Segal, "Nuclear Forces in Northeast Asia," 2. The IISS's *Military Balance, 1993–1994*, pp. 1–2, lists only one warhead for the SS-N-6 and SS-N-8 in contrast to two as found in Segal's May 1994 paper. Of course, if the Segal figure is correct, the figures above increase further.

4. Segal, "Nuclear Forces in Northeast Asia," 2.

5. Ibid.

6. Presentation by Barry Blechman, May 6, 1994.

7. As the author did in April 1994.

8. IISS, *Military Balance, 1993–1994*, 244.

9. Again, according to the *Nuclear Weapons Databook*, vol. 5, *British, French, and Chinese Nuclear Weapons,* ed. Robert S. Norris, Andrew S. Burrows, and Richard W. Fieldhouse (Boulder, CO: Westview Press, 1994, 338–41).

10. Ministry of National Defense, Republic of Korea, *Defense White Paper, 1993–1994,* 47.

11. John Garver, "Organizational Capabilities of the Chinese PLA," *Project on the Capacity of Military Organizations: Selected Asian Nations* (Atlanta, GA: Joint Management Services, January 14, 1993, 7).

12. See Gerald Segal's assumptions regarding this matter in his "Nuclear Forces in Northeast Asia." In light of the U.S. policy of neither confirming nor denying this situation, it will be assumed that tactical weapons have been removed from South Korea—as asserted by the president of the Republic of Korea (ROK)—and are not anywhere in the area.

13. See William M. Arkin and Robert S. Norris, "Nuclear Alert after the Cold War," *Nuclear Weapons Databook,* Working Papers, NWD 93–4, October 18, 1993, 2.

14. Interview in Moscow, April 1994.

15. Positive discussions have also been conducted with U.S.-based representatives of North Korea and Taiwan.

19

Regional Non-nuclear Options from South Korea's Perspective

Seongwhun Cheon

With the end of the Cold War, bipolar conflicts centered around the two pillars of world politics, the United States and the Soviet Union, disappeared. However, various regional disputes with long traditions that were previously overshadowed by the superpower competition have emerged as renewed threats to international peace and security. In the post–Cold War era, therefore, conflicts are diversified in their nature and magnitude.

In Northeast Asia, problems that had been discounted during the Cold War—for example, territorial disputes among the regional powers—became pending and important issues in the region. Traditional competition, together with war memories and undisplayed hostilities among the regional players, have increased the potential for political conflicts, now mostly dominated by economic fervor. There are signs of instabilities in the future. In particular, China and Japan, with their economic boom, have kept increasing their military expenditures.

China, with the largest army in the region, is increasing its military budget—for example, by 12 percent in 1992. Although the Chinese cut their troops by 1 million in 1985–1987 and are planning to cut their troops further to about 2 million over the next ten years, this quantitative reduction has been offset by qualitative improvements. As part of its massive modernization program, China purchased Su-27 and MiG-29 fighter aircraft from Russia, as well as new destroyers and frigates, and reportedly introduced new classes of amphibious assault and supply ships that can be used for long-range operations.[1]

Japan's expansion of conventional military capabilities and its pursuit of a more active role in international disputes are becoming particularly worrisome.

Although the ratio of the increases in its military expenditures is shrinking, its defense budget is increasing. The 1992 budget of $US 36.2 billion was the world's sixth largest.[2] As part of its defense modernization program, Japan is planning to buy F-15s, ten destroyers, ninety tanks, and five conventional submarines, as well as develop an advanced FSX fighter aircraft with the United States and improve its antisubmarine warfare capability.[3] In addition, in 1992, both houses of the Japanese Diet passed a bill to allow Japan's armed forces to participate in U.N. peacekeeping missions. China and the two Koreas are vocal opponents of any extension of Japanese overseas military activities. They expressed concern that peacekeeping operations (PKOs) were the beginning of an inevitable resurgence of Japanese military might.

There are also security concerns in the Northeast Asian region with respect to Russia. In the last few months before the CFE I Treaty was signed, the Soviet Union shipped tens of thousands of weapons beyond the Urals, where they did not need to be destroyed or even counted. According to one estimate, the tanks, armored combat vehicles, and artillery withdrawn beyond the Urals totaled 57,300 pieces.[4] Old equipment in the Far East could be replaced with the new withdrawn equipment, and new units could be formed and equipped with weapons moved from Europe.

Compared with Europe, a significantly different geopolitical situation prevails in Northeast Asia. There exist diverse political systems and cultures, as well as considerable variations in population size, territory, and the degree of economic strength. Furthermore, there are important interstate conflicts such as the North–South Korean confrontation and the Japanese-Russian territorial dispute. Indeed, there has been little change in the Cold War mentalities of the states in the region. Security cooperation among the states is virtually nil, and no regional security forum like the Conference on Security and Cooperation in Europe (CSCE) exists. At the moment, regional players seem indifferent to, or at least not very concerned about, enhancing military stability in the region.

Under the circumstances, North Korea's nuclear program, which was first publicized in 1991,[5] has been a source of concern among the states in the region. The refusal of the Democratic People's Republic of Korea (DPRK) to accept International Atomic Energy Agency (IAEA) special inspections and its March 1993 announcement that it would withdraw from the Non-Proliferation Treaty (NPT) have drawn closer international attention to the Korean Peninsula than at any other time since the Korean War. North Korea's decision not to live up to the NPT has a significant impact on the international nonproliferation regime and is regarded as a serious challenge to that regime. Regional powers have held virtually identical positions on the North Korean nuclear issue—that is, they strongly support the denuclearization of the Korean Peninsula and feel that the issue should be resolved through dialogue rather than by imposing sanctions upon Pyongyang.

Assuming that the Joint Declaration on the Denuclearization of the Korean

Peninsula signed by the two Koreas in December 1991 will be effective in the future, this chapter examines various measures that could facilitate and support the denuclearization status of the Korean Peninsula. The first section reviews the history of the debates over nuclear issues between North and South Korea. The second section describes how the joint declaration was agreed upon and examines progress toward its implementation. The third section illustrates options that can be taken by the two Koreas to facilitate denuclearization of the Korean Peninsula. The final section considers regional powers' options for supporting the denuclearization of the peninsula.

Nuclear Debates between North and South Korea

North Korea's Nuclear Weapons–Free Zone (NWFZ)

Historically, the DPRK has strongly denounced the presence of U.S. nuclear weapons on the Korean Peninsula while advocating the conversion of the peninsula into a nuclear weapons–free zone. The first official statement of the North's antinuclear sentiment was a November 7, 1956, letter from the Supreme People's Assembly of the DPRK to the members of the South Korean National Assembly and the general public. The letter accused the South of violating the military armistice agreement and trying to introduce nuclear weapons on the Korean Peninsula.[6] Since then, the North intermittently raised the nuclear weapons issue in the 1960s and 1970s.

Pyongyang's antinuclear campaign intensified with concrete proposals in the 1980s. At the Sixth Congress of the DPRK Workers' Party, held in December 1980, North Korean President Kim Il Sung proposed the establishment of a nuclear weapons–free/peace zone on the Korean Peninsula as one of the measures to implement the North's unification formula—the "Democratic Confederal Republic of Koryo" (DCRK).[7] In June 1986, Pyongyang suggested a tripartite meeting among the two Koreas and the United States to discuss the establishment of a nuclear weapons–free/peace zone on the peninsula. In the arms-reduction proposal issued on July 23, 1987, Pyongyang called for tripartite talks at the foreign ministerial level to discuss a four-year process of North–South mutual force reductions down to the level of 100,000 troops, together with the parallel withdrawal of U.S. forces and nuclear weapons from the peninsula. The updated and more comprehensive proposal made on November 7, 1988, suggesting a three-year timetable, spelled out detailed measures that would take place at each stage of the process. According to the proposal, the United States would pull back its forces and nuclear weapons to south of 35° 30' north latitude (a line running between Pusan and Chinhae in the South) by the end of 1989, and United States ground forces and nuclear weapons would be completely withdrawn from the Korean Peninsula by the end of 1990. The proposal also suggested trilateral talks at which verification, among other issues, could be discussed.

In the 1990s, North Korean proposals have taken more refined and concrete shape. In the "Disarmament Proposal for Peace on the Korean Peninsula," issued on May 31, 1990, Pyongyang presented a ten-point plan for confidence building and arms reduction. Concerning the nuclear problem, the North proposed that the North and South should convert the Korean Peninsula into a nuclear-free zone by taking the following measures:

- Joint efforts should be made to get all the nuclear weapons deployed in South Korea withdrawn immediately.
- Nuclear weapons should not be produced or purchased.
- Foreign planes and warships loaded with nuclear weapons should be banned from entering or passing through Korea.

On July 30, 1991, the North Korean Foreign Ministry proposed that the two Koreas jointly declare an NWFZ by the end of 1992, which would be guaranteed by neighboring nuclear weapons states by the end of 1993. The proposal has drawn attention because there was no request for trilateral talks, and the withdrawal of U.S. forces was implicitly mentioned as a follow-up measure rather than as a precondition for the pursuit of an NWFZ.

At the Fourth Inter-Korean High-Level Talks, held October 22–25, 1991,[8] the North proposed a draft "Declaration on Establishing a Nuclear Weapons Free Zone (NWFZ) on the Korean Peninsula" and linked its acceptance of the IAEA safeguards inspections to the withdrawal of U.S. forces and nuclear weapons from South Korea. The nine-point proposal

- Forbids the testing, manufacture, introduction, possession, and use of nuclear weapons
- Prohibits the transit, landing, and visiting of nuclear-capable aircraft and ships
- Prevents any agreement guaranteeing a nuclear umbrella and prohibits deployment and storage of nuclear weapons on either side's territory
- Bans military exercises involving nuclear weapons
- Demands simultaneous inspections of North Korea's nuclear facilities by the IAEA and South Korea's military bases by the North

It was not until the signing of the Joint Declaration on the Denuclearization of the Korean Peninsula that Pyongyang suddenly changed its position and withdrew the NWFZ proposal.

South Korea's Denuclearization

The Republic of Korea (ROK) hardly responded to Pyongyang's nuclear initiatives. In marked contrast to Pyongyang's aggressive antinuclear proposals, in the mid-1970s, then President Park Chung-hee even hinted at the possibility of South Korea's developing nuclear weapons in case the United States withdrew its forces.[9] No proposals concerning nuclear issues were advanced by the South Korean government until recently. On August 1, 1991, the Foreign Ministry made a statement saying that representatives from the two Koreas could discuss military matters, including the issue of nuclear nonproliferation, in order to reduce tensions and build confidence between the two.[10] There seemed to be many factors behind the South's indecisive position, of which the presence of U.S. nuclear weapons on the Korean Peninsula was probably the most important.

At the Fourth High-Level Talks, the South Korean prime minister urged that Pyongyang, without any conditions, first stop developing nuclear weapons and accept international safeguards inspections. South Korea's position on the nuclear issue, though not explicitly declared at that time, was that even if U.S. nuclear forces were withdrawn, Seoul would need U.S. nuclear protection and would therefore allow U.S. ships and aircraft to pass through or visit South Korean territory, including sea and airspace. According to this position, the North's proposal—particularly the second and third points—was hardly acceptable.

The year 1991 was a turning point for nuclear debates on the Korean Peninsula. Following U.S. President George Bush's initiative to eliminate tactical nuclear weapons on September 27, 1991, and Soviet President Mikhail Gorbachev's reciprocal step on October 5, 1991, South Korean President Roh Tae-woo issued a "Declaration on Denuclearizing and Building Peace on the Korean Peninsula" on November 8, 1991, which was the beginning of Seoul's diplomatic campaign to deter Pyongyang from developing nuclear weapons. The declaration, the first official nuclear policy announced by the ROK government, is as follows:

1. The Republic of Korea will use nuclear energy solely for peaceful purposes, and will not manufacture, possess, store, deploy or use nuclear weapons.
2. The Republic of Korea will continue to submit to comprehensive international inspection all nuclear-related facilities and materials on its territory in compliance with the NPT and with the nuclear safeguards agreement it has concluded with the IAEA under the treaty, and will not possess nuclear fuel reprocessing and enrichment facilities.
3. The Republic of Korea aspires for a world of peace that is free of all nuclear all weapons of mass destruction, and we will actively participate in international efforts toward the total elimination of chemical and biological weapons and observe all international agreements thereon.

The most important part of President Roh's November 8 declaration was the ROK government's voluntary renouncement of its right to possess nuclear reprocessing and enrichment facilities. Although it was sharply criticized by pronuclearists in South Korea, Seoul's decision seemed inevitable at that time. The DPRK's nuclear program was full of ambiguities and suspicions, and in particular, Pyongyang was suspected of building and running a large-scale reprocessing plant at Yongbyon. Later, that suspicion proved to be accurate.[11] South Korea seemed so desperate to prevent North Korea from becoming a nuclear power that it had to take the initiative to renounce its right to possess important nuclear capabilities and had to appeal to Pyongyang to forgo its nuclear weapons program.

At the Fifth Inter-Korean High-Level Talks, held December 10–13, 1991, North Korea tabled its previous nuclear weapons–free zone proposal, and South Korea put forward a draft "Declaration on Denuclearizing the Korean Peninsula," which was an expanded version of President Roh's November declaration. At the meeting, the two sides reached an agreement on fundamental issues and goals, known as the "Agreement on Reconciliation, Nonaggression, and Exchanges and Cooperation." This twenty-five–point basic agreement provides a framework for improving relations between the two sides. Acting on the belief that the two Koreas themselves should inspect each other's nuclear-related installations and materials in order to build confidence in the military area, the South Korean prime minister proposed, at the Fifth High-Level Talks, North–South reciprocal inspections. He also called for each side to carry out simultaneous pilot inspections of one military and one civilian site that it had designated on the other side by January 31, 1992, on the condition that the two sides first agree to scrap nuclear reprocessing facilities. South Korea offered to submit Kunsan air base and one civilian nuclear facility to inspection by the North and proposed Sunchon air base and the Yongbyon nuclear complex for inspection by the South.

Pyongyang was obviously not prepared to respond to Seoul's offer and put off further discussions on the nuclear problem until later talks. The two sides just agreed to hold an ad hoc meeting on the nuclear issue.

Joint Declaration on the Denuclearization of the Korean Peninsula

Agreeing on the Denuclearization of the Korean Peninsula

The international community was concerned about the nuclear issue, and South Korea took more active measures to push North Korea to abandon its nuclear ambitions. On December 18, 1991, President Roh declared a nuclear-free South Korea, saying that "there do not exist any nuclear weapons whatsoever, anywhere in the Republic of Korea." A practical implication of Roh's declaration was that U.S. nuclear weapons had been completely removed from the peninsula. Seoul also urged Pyongyang to sign and ratify the IAEA safeguards agreement and accept international inspections. South Korea even hinted that the annual Team Spirit ROK-U.S. joint military exercises might be canceled, depending on the North Korean attitude toward the nuclear problem.[12]

The first ad hoc meeting on the nuclear issue was held on December 26, 1991. To the South's surprise, the North withdrew its own proposed draft "Joint Declaration on Denuclearizing the Korean Peninsula" and adopted, instead, many points from the draft of South Korea's denuclearization proposal. For example, the North's proposal forbade the possession of nuclear fuel reprocessing and enrichment facilities. Furthermore, it referred neither to the prohibition of a treaty guaranteeing a nuclear umbrella nor to the transit, landing, or visiting of nuclear-capable aircraft and ships.

There has been much speculation about why the North changed its position and virtually copied that of the South. North Korean leaders were well aware of the urgent need to normalize diplomatic ties with the United States and improve relations with Japan to overcome their economic, political, and diplomatic difficulties. Since the United States and Japan had maintained their positions that Pyongyang should settle the nuclear issue, the North had to take some positive steps.

After intense negotiations, the two sides finally came to an agreement on the "Joint Declaration on the Denuclearization of the Korean Peninsula" at the third ad hoc meeting on December 31, 1991. The declaration contains the following six points:

1. The South and the North shall not test, manufacture, produce, receive, possess, store, deploy, or use nuclear weapons.
2. The South and the North shall use nuclear energy solely for peaceful purposes.
3. The South and the North shall not possess nuclear reprocessing and uranium facilities.
4. The South and the North, in order to verify the denuclearization of the Korean Peninsula, shall conduct inspection of the objects selected by the other side and agreed upon between the two sides, in accordance with procedures and methods to be determined by the South–North Joint Nuclear Control Commission.
5. The South and the North, in order to implement this joint declaration, shall establish and operate a South–North Joint Nuclear Control Commission within one month of the effectuation of this joint declaration.
6. This joint declaration shall enter into force on the day on which the South and the North exchange notifications of completion of the formalities for the entry into force of the present declaration.

Immediately after signing the agreement, on January 7, 1992, South Korea announced that the 1992 Team Spirit military exercises would be canceled. At the same time, North Korea promised to sign the IAEA safeguards agreement and accept its inspections. Pyongyang did sign the full-scope safeguards agreement on January 30, 1992. The denuclearization declaration established a legal and moral basis upon which South Korea could take appropriate measures vis-à-vis North Korea to counter its proliferation attempts. The Joint Nuclear Control Commission, established on March 19, 1992, became the official body for implementing the terms of the declaration.

Inter-Korean Negotiations on Reciprocal Inspections: Temporary Failure

To verify denuclearization, the two Koreas were to inspect objects or sites chosen by the state conducting the inspection but agreed to by both sides. The JNCC served as a forum for negotiating and implementing these reciprocal inspections. But the two parties could not agree on the objects and methods of the inspections, and the negotiations were stalemated.

Since the beginning of the inter-Korean discussions on nuclear matters, the two Koreas had held different views on many aspects of verifying what they would agree on. As the IAEA inspection of its nuclear facilities became more imminent with the initialing of the safeguards agreement on July 15, 1992, North Korea began to mention asymmetrical inspections. As a condition for accepting the IAEA inspections, the North argued that military bases in the South should be inspected by the North to enable the North to see for itself whether U.S. nuclear weapons had been removed. President Kim Il Sung first raised the asymmetrical inspections issue during an interview on September 26, 1991. Regarding the international inspections of North Korea, Kim Il Sung made the following remarks:

> Therefore, we do not object to nuclear inspection. What we are against is not the nuclear inspection itself but the unreasonable attitude of some people who are trying to impose nuclear inspection on us unilaterally contrary to international justice. We have never put nuclear threat to anyone but, instead, we are exposed to nuclear threat. It is no secret that more than 1,000 US nuclear weapons are actually deployed in South Korea. Thus, if a fair inspection is to be carried out, it should be made not only on us but also on nuclear bases in South Korea.[13]

At the Fourth High-Level Talks, Pyongyang proposed simultaneous implementation of the IAEA's inspections of North Korean nuclear facilities and of the North's inspections of military bases in the South.[14] In a Foreign Ministry statement issued on November 25, 1991, North Korea responded positively to President Roh's November 8 declaration and made the following proposals.

> First, if the United States begins the withdrawal of nuclear weapons from South Korea, we will sign the IAEA safeguards accord.
>   Second, both an inspection to confirm US nuclear weapons in South Korea and an inspection of our nuclear facilities should be carried out simultaneously.
>   Third, DPRK-US negotiations to discuss simultaneous nuclear inspection and removing the nuclear danger against us should be held.[15]

Meanwhile, North Korea welcomed President Roh's announcement on a nuclear-free Korean Peninsula. The North, however, argued that it could not know for sure whether the nuclear weapons had been withdrawn based merely on the word of South Korean authorities who had no control over U.S. nuclear weapons. Pyongyang reiterated that the IAEA inspections of its nuclear facilities and its inspections of the U.S. bases in South Korea must be conducted simultaneously. North Korea threatened to discontinue negotiations while proposing to conduct simultaneous inspections of nuclear facilities.[16]

At the Fifth High-Level Talks, South Korea proposed, on a reciprocal basis, symmetrical inspections of each side's nuclear facilities versus nuclear facilities and military bases versus military bases. Furthermore, the South, as a trial measure, suggested that each side conduct a pilot inspection of one nuclear facility and one military base of the other side.[17]

The South's argument for symmetrical inspections was based on the idea that an inspection object should be chosen based on whether the object had already been opened to the outside world. The South has been adhering to the IAEA full-scope safeguards agreement since 1975. Seoul stressed that nuclear facilities already opened to the IAEA could not be traded for military bases that had never been revealed to the outside. The ROK maintained that it should be able to inspect North Korean military bases if the DPRK wanted to inspect U.S. military bases in South Korea.

The North signed a full-scope IAEA safeguards agreement on January 30, 1992. Therefore, the IAEA's inspections of North Korean nuclear facilities were de facto allowed. With these developments (the South's symmetrical inspection proposal and the North's acceptance of IAEA inspections), the North Korean concept of asymmetrical inspections was modified. At the Sixth High-Level Talks, Pyongyang proposed a new version of the asymmetrical inspection scheme: the South would inspect the Yongbyon nuclear complex, and the North would carry out simultaneous inspections of all U.S. military bases in South Korea.

In order to support its modified asymmetrical inspection scheme, at the first round of the JNCC meetings in March 1992, the DPRK began to insist on the principle of simultaneous dissolution of suspicions. With this principle, North Korea emphasized that the two sides must dissolve mutual suspicions. But the DPRK contended that, in fact, nuclear weapons had existed in the South and Seoul had more nuclear facilities than Pyongyang. Therefore, to dissolve mutual suspicions simultaneously, North Korea argued that the South's inspection of North Korean nuclear facilities at Yongbyon and the North's full-scope inspections of U.S. military bases in South Korea should be carried out at the same time.

At the first round of the JNCC meetings, South Korea proposed a draft inspection regime based on its principle of reciprocity and equal ceilings. According to the South's proposal, a total of fifty-six places could be visited on each side per year through regular and special inspections. More than one visit to the same place would be allowed and counted against the total. Among the fifty-six

Figure 19.1 **Differing Positions on Reciprocal Inspections**

	North Korea	South Korea
selection of inspection objects	nuclear facilities ‑‑‑‑‑‑‑‑‑‑‑‑‑‑‑‑‑‑ nuclear facilities military bases ‑‑‑‑‑‑‑‑‑‑‑‑> military bases	
inspection principle	principle of simultaneous dissolution of suspicions	principle of reciprocity and equal ceilings
special inspection	impossible	essential

    _____ North (asymmetrical)

    ---------- South (symmetrical)

places, twenty were military bases, for which only special inspections were allowed. Regular inspections would be performed quarterly for the places that were chosen by the other side and agreed upon between the two sides.

The special inspections proposed by South Korea would be carried out up to twelve times a year on places designated unilaterally by the requesting party. Special inspections were also referred to as "inspections with no sanctuaries." The inspections would be performed with twenty-four hours advance notification, and the inspected party would be denied the right of refusal. Seoul emphasized that these inspections were essential to eliminate mistrust and build mutual confidence. But Pyongyang refused to accept the South's proposal, which, the North argued, violated Article 4 of the denuclearization declaration.

The differing positions of both sides on nuclear inspections are summarized in Figure 19.1.

Reasons for the Temporary Failure

The early impasse over verification in the high-level talks and at the JNCC illustrates that prospects for promoting arms control and verification on the Korean Peninsula do not appear favorable. Three major reasons for the failure of the bilateral inspections negotiations can be identified.

The first hurdle is that virtually no trust exists between the two Koreas. Even though the basic agreement was reached and several committees and commissions were subsequently formed, the implementation of the agreement has been delayed. In May 1993, Pyongyang responded to Seoul's request to put the agreement into practice by proposing an exchange of presidential envoys, which showed the North's lack of interest in implementing the agreement. Trust is something that must be nurtured, especially between two countries scarred by a history of war, massive military counterdeployments, and harsh, threatening rhetoric. Furthermore, on March 19, 1994, the North Korean chief delegate to the special envoy exchange negotiations remarked that, should a war break out, Seoul would become "a sea of flames."[18]

The second stumbling block is North Korea's traditional resistance to openness, which has spawned a passive attitude toward verification. For example, in the nonaggression section of the basic agreement, the two Koreas agreed on five measures, including mutual notification and control of major military movements and exercises. Pyongyang strongly opposed the exchange of observers for such exercises. North Korean resistance to accepting observers implies the North's sensitivities, which have grown with the totalitarian system that has dominated North Korea for more than forty years.

The third obstacle is that the two Koreas lack extensive independent monitoring capabilities. Therefore, verification between the two countries would be fully dependent on on-site inspections (OSIs). However, OSIs are the most intrusive means of verification, and the two Koreas have hardly built enough confidence to initiate such procedures. The United States and the Soviet Union were able to carry out OSIs only after years of confidence-building measures, including hot lines, notifications, and data exchanges. OSIs were the culmination, not the beginning, of the verification process in the East–West context.

Inter-Korean Options to Facilitate Denuclearizing the Korean Peninsula

The Joint Declaration on the Denuclearization of the Korean Peninsula is the first disarmament agreement signed between North and South Korea. The North promised to abandon its illegal nuclear weapons program, and U.S. nuclear weapons would be withdrawn from the South. Although the implementation of the declaration has been delayed, not only the two Koreas but the regional powers as well have fully supported a nuclear weapons–free Korean Peninsula. As talks between the DPRK and the United States continue and their relations improve, the North–South negotiations on inspection regulations are expected to resume soon.

Assuming that a country's ambition to go nuclear results from the complex calculations of its national interests, a network of measures taking political, economic, and security factors into account should be devised in order to deter the country from developing nuclear weapons. That is, multifaceted means for tension reduction, exchanges, and cooperation as well as reciprocal inspection regulations must be adopted. From this perspective, the two Koreas could do more than they have done thus far to achieve true and sustained denuclearization of the peninsula. The following subsections discuss measures that the two Koreas could take.

Efficient Reciprocal Inspections

Raison D'être of Reciprocal Inspections

Inter-Korean dialogue on the reciprocal inspection regime would begin only after the IAEA's ad hoc and routine inspections of North Korean nuclear facilities were on track. With the normalization of the IAEA inspections, the international community's concerns about the DPRK's nuclear program would diminish, as would the urgency of its resolve to counter Pyongyang's attempt to proliferate nuclear weapons. Therefore, the following questions regarding the rationale for the reciprocal inspections could be raised both domestically and internationally.

First, if South Korea persists in approaching the issue of reciprocal inspections as it was discussed in early 1992, it would bring about unnecessary tension and cause serious conflicts in inter-Korean relations.

Second, considering that the North opposes the idea of inspections per se, Seoul's proposal to implement stringent reciprocal inspections would harm inter-Korean relations.

Third, even if the two Koreas agreed on inspection regulations, doubts would arise as to the effectiveness and value of the inspections unless the inspection regime were stricter than the IAEA safeguards regime.

In spite of these doubts, however, reciprocal inspections should be implemented for the following reasons.

First, the two Koreas have legal obligations to implement the inspections according to Article 4 of the denuclearization declaration. Without inspections, it would be impossible to verify whether the two sides are complying with the declarations, which would result in the declaration's becoming a dead letter. It would be difficult to adhere to the declaration without implementing its most important article—assuring compliance of the two parties.

Second, the North Korean nuclear problem is both an international and an inter-Korean issue. Thus, as IAEA inspections are needed from an international perspective, reciprocal inspections are justified from an inter-Korean perspective. In particular, it is important for the two Koreas to maintain the independent nature of the inspections and thereby establish a clear precedent that problems on the Korean Peninsula can be resolved by the Koreans themselves. Successful implementation of the inspections would enable the Korean people keep their self-reliance and avoid unnecessary interference from other countries. In other words, it would have a significant symbolic meaning for Korean sovereignty.

Third, reciprocal inspections are also essential to strengthen bilateral exchanges and cooperation in the field of the peaceful uses of nuclear energy. Without transparency regarding each other's nuclear programs, cooperation in the nuclear industry would hardly be possible. That is, mutual opening of nuclear activities through inspections is necessary not because one side is suspicious of the other's nuclear intentions but because increased transparency is essential to enhance exchanges and cooperation for the peaceful uses of nuclear energy.

Fourth, from a technical standpoint, North–South inspections could compensate for the limitations inherent in the IAEA inspection system. IAEA inspections are allowed only for facilities directly involved with nuclear materials. Uranium mines and refineries are not subject to IAEA inspection either. Such an inspection regime is therefore not suitable for North Korea, which has achieved a complete nuclear fuel cycle. On the other hand, even if two different inspections were performed on the same objects, the results would not be the same. In case of the reciprocal inspections, the inspectors would speak the same language and have the same cultural background and sentiments. Thus, the reciprocal inspections would make it possible to obtain important information that inspectors of other nationalities might fail to notice.

Finally, it cannot be ignored that the U.S. government regards the denuclearization declaration and the reciprocal inspections on the Korean Peninsula as a good model that can be applied in other regions.[19] In view of the obvious limitations of IAEA inspections as revealed in the Iraqi case, the United States acknowledges that inspections between the two Koreas are critical in order to complement the IAEA inspection system.[20] Therefore, it is believed that the United States strongly supports the realization of a strict bilateral inspection mechanism in Korea with a view to using the Korean case as a prototype for establishing similar inspection regimes in other regions. From this perspective, if the two Koreas do not implement the inspections, there might be conflicts in both ROK-U.S. relations and DPRK-U.S. relations. In fact, Washington might exert pressure on the two Koreas to carry out the reciprocal inspections after the IAEA inspection issues are resolved.

Some Suggestions for Reciprocal Inspections

There is no doubt that the reciprocal inspections need to be more effective and stringent than the IAEA inspections. However, the practicability of the inspections should not be ignored. Up until now, the two Koreas have made non-negotiable proposals for unrealistic inspection schemes. It would be wise for each side to facilitate negotiations on the inspection regime by withdrawing unacceptable demands made upon the other side.

To this end, Seoul should cease insisting on special inspections with no sanctuaries. In return, Pyongyang should forgo its attempts to conduct simultaneous inspections of all U.S. military bases in South Korea and abandon its demand for the past history of the presence of U.S. nuclear weapons in the South. The two Koreas should also establish a ground rule that limits inspections to nuclear materials and facilities and, in exceptional cases, military bases. Compared with military bases, it would be easy to agree on the inspection regulations for nuclear materials and facilities because those regulations would be based on scientific and technical facts, thus minimizing room for political maneuver.

In order to complement the IAEA inspections, the scope of reciprocal inspections could be expanded as follows.

First, compared with the IAEA inspectors, who have limited access only to the facilities where nuclear materials are reported to be present, the access of the reciprocal inspectors could be extended to such installations as control rooms, annex buildings, and other sites that the inspectors want to visit.

Second, since North Korea is reported to have significant amounts of natural uranium and to run a uranium refinery, those facilities and yellowcake should also be subject to inspection.

Third, when a reprocessing plant is in operation, IAEA inspectors are normally at the facility full-time. As the so-called radiochemical laboratory is a reprocessing facility, continuous inspection of the plant would be required until Pyongyang completely dismantles the facility.

Bilateral Exchanges and Cooperation

North Korea's reluctance to open its system to the outside world is a major obstacle that hinders the elimination of confrontation on the Korean Peninsula. The North's antiopenness tendencies have been revealed in various inter-Korean negotiating forums and also explain why Pyongyang opposed Seoul's intrusive inspection proposal at the JNCC negotiations.

The history of arms control in Europe demonstrates that a country's willingness to accept intrusive verification measures like OSIs is proportional to the degree of openness and democratization of its regime. In the late 1950s, the United States and the Soviet Union conducted negotiations on a comprehensive test ban treaty (CTBT), and a critical issue in the negotiations was whether OSIs should be conducted. The United States wanted sufficient OSIs allowed, but the USSR hoped to limit OSIs, citing its concern that OSIs could infringe on sovereignty and be used for espionage. The two countries could not agree on the number of OSIs and only agreed on the Partial Test Ban Treaty, which places much less importance on OSIs.[21] The differences in the two sides' positions on OSIs did not narrow until fundamental changes were made by President Gorbachev in the Soviet Union. Gorbachev issued a series of important arms-control proposals that led to changes in the Soviet position on verification in general and OSIs in particular. Such changes made a great contribution to the successful negotiation of the Stockholm Document in 1986.[22] However, even in this negotiation, OSIs were one of the last two stumbling blocks,[23] which illustrates the difficulties in agreeing on OSIs in an arms-control treaty.

Suspicions about North Korea's nuclear weapons development may not be completely eliminated unless Pyongyang undergoes fundamental changes in its system and subsequent changes in its position on verification, as in the case of the Soviet Union. To this end, the regional powers and South Korea are encouraged to adopt a policy of engagement, which would help induce North Korea to join the international community and get accustomed to the norms and rules of international society. A concrete action plan would involve measures to facilitate reducing political tension, increasing economic cooperation, and promoting cultural and social exchanges.

Increasing the Transparency of the Two Koreas' Nuclear Activities

Although ongoing dialogue between the two Koreas has focused on establishing a strict inspection system, it should be noted that inspection is only a first-aid measure to alleviate concerns about Pyongyang's nuclear weapons program. More fundamental steps to enhance nuclear transparency on the Korean Peninsula may need to be taken unilaterally as well as cooperatively.

On the one hand, in view of the fact that the two Koreas attempted to develop nuclear weapons,[24] it is urgent that the North and South take immediate and independent measures to increase the transparency of their nuclear activities in order to eliminate international suspicions. Such unilateral transparency measures, in combination with full cooperation with the IAEA and implementation of the reciprocal inspections, could contribute to enhancing international society's confidence regarding the peaceful intentions of the two Koreas. In this context, South Korea's recent decision to establish the Technology Center for Nuclear Control (TCNC) is a step in the right direction.

Established in March 1994, the TCNC is responsible for making South Korean nuclear activities more transparent and for developing inspection techniques and resources. The TCNC will focus on four major areas for enhancing transparency. In the area of research and development (R&D) on nuclear control policy systems at the state level, the TCNC will conduct studies on laws and regulation systems relevant to (1) domestic inspection, (2) nuclear material accounting, (3) physical protection, and (4) import and export control of internationally controlled materials. To develop a domestic safeguards inspection regime, the TCNC is charged with (1) inspection training and technical support, (2) collection and analysis of technical information, and (3) development of inspection techniques. In the area of nuclear material accounting and measurement, the TCNC will work on (1) program development and management of computer-based accounting, (2) database management of the import and export of internationally controlled materials, and (3) R&D on the nondestructive assay of nuclear materials and its field application. Finally, for R&D on techniques for analyzing environmental samples from inspection activities, the TCNC is responsible for (1) implementation of chemical analysis and verification of samples from inspection activities, (2) trace element analysis of environmental samples for tracking undeclared nuclear activities, and (3) radiological control for inspectors and to ensure their health and physical safety.

On the other hand, bilateral cooperation on the peaceful uses of nuclear energy can be another important measure to increase the transparency of the two Koreas' nuclear activities. It should be pointed out that neither the joint declaration nor the agreement on the formation of the JNCC mentioned any measures for mutual cooperation. It was suggested that Seoul and Pyongyang grant the JNCC the authority to jointly control the two sides' nuclear activities and to implement cooperative measures to exchange nuclear resources and technologies.[25]

Such efforts would provide South Korea with an ongoing opportunity to monitor North Korea's nuclear activities through regular information exchanges and mutual cooperation. Thus, the transparency of North Korean nuclear activities could be enhanced and its intention to develop nuclear weapons deterred. The same logic applies to South Korea as well.

Inter-Korean Arms Control and Reduction

As noted earlier, the joint declaration is the first disarmament agreement between the two Koreas, affirming that they will not possess a category of weapons of mass destruction. To be effective under the circumstances of deeply rooted distrust and tension between the two sides, the declaration should be pursued in conjunction with other military confidence-building measures.

The South, being threatened by the offensively deployed North Korean forces along the demilitarized zone (DMZ), has emphasized structuring its forces defensively. The North, on the other hand, has said little about defensive structuring and has taken a "force reduction first" approach. In order to promote the success of the bilateral arms-control negotiations, the two sides' military strategies should be adjusted in accordance with a strategy of defensive sufficiency. Accordingly, arms-control talks between the two Koreas should be pursued on the basis of the doctrine of nonoffensive defense.[26] With respect to the object of reduction, at least until a later stage of arms reduction, it is suggested that the two Koreas focus on land forces, which are ultimately a means to seize and hold terrain and are thus perceived as more threatening than air and sea powers.

Although the two Koreas agreed to negotiate on various confidence-building measures at the Joint Military Commission (JMC), talks at the JMC just started and are expected to require time-consuming and painful efforts. On the other hand, an agreement concluded multilaterally and opened to other countries for signature such as the Chemical Weapons Convention (CWC) provides the two Koreas with an opportunity for easy cooperation. By January 1, 1994, 154 nations, including South Korea, had signed the convention. Reciprocal action from North Korea is long overdue.

Inter-Korean Open Skies

The Open Skies Treaty was signed on March 24, 1992, by a total of twenty-seven nations, including all the North Atlantic Treaty Organization (NATO) allies, East European members of the former Warsaw Pact, Russia, Ukraine, Belarus, Georgia, and Kazakhstan. Treaty parties will conduct short-notice unarmed observation overflights using aircraft equipped with sensors that have a twenty-four-hour, all-weather capability. All territory can be overflown, even sensitive military sites. The information from all Open Skies flights will be made available to all participants. Thus, cooperative aerial inspections will allow participants to see firsthand what their neighbors are up to, providing at once a confidence-building measure and a tool for use in crisis management, should tensions arise among Open Skies signatories. The objective of Open Skies is to bring greater stability to a region undergoing dramatic political, military, and economic changes.

A similar aerial observation measure on the Korean Peninsula would promote openness and transparency regarding military forces and activities in the region.[27] Open Skies would allow the two Koreas to assess the status of opposing military forces while literally and figuratively maintaining a safe distance. An Open Skies agreement is not as intrusive as inspections on the ground. Cooperative overflights need not interrupt normal patterns of military or civilian life. Indeed, unless they were advised of the flights, citizens on the ground might not even be aware that they were taking place. Since Open Skies requires partial rather than total transparency, it would be readily accepted by North Korea.

If the two Koreas, with no experience in arms control, encounter difficulties in negotiating a new bilateral Open Skies agreement, they could join a ready-made one in Europe. The Open Skies Treaty, six months after it went into effect, is open to any state in the world, if accepted by the Open Skies Consultative Commission—the implementation body of the treaty.[28]

Regional Powers' Options for Supporting the Denuclearization of the Korean Peninsula

The denuclearization of the Korean Peninsula is the first major nonproliferation achievement in Northeast Asia. It must have had a positive influence on international nonproliferation efforts. North and South Korea have assured the world that even the two Koreas, which experienced a bitter war four decades ago and still confront each other with massive military forces, can create a nuclear weapons–free regime. In this respect, the two Koreas deserve high compliments from the community of nations.

In contrast to the two Koreas' efforts, the regional powers' attitudes toward nonproliferation and tension reduction are disappointing. Although the denuclearization of the Korean Peninsula is a bilateral measure between the two Koreas, the neighboring countries in the region should respond positively to the declaration if it is to be effective and successful. The proproliferation and tension-increasing tendencies of the regional powers, particularly China and Japan, have given the Korean people no confidence that their efforts on nonproliferation are fruitful and worthwhile in enhancing peace and security in the region.

The joint declaration is only a starting point for realizing a denuclearized Korean Peninsula. Under the present circumstances, in which the regional powers are expanding their military capabilities, the two Koreas' efforts to delegitimize nuclear weapons would have little influence to curb regional proliferation attempts. Four measures that the regional powers could implement to support the denuclearization of the Korean Peninsula are presented in the following subsections.

Comprehensive Security Assurance

Nuclear weapons states currently provide two kinds of security assurances: positive and negative. Non–nuclear weapons states have asserted that the security assurances must be improved. The Korean Peninsula could be a model case for applying firmer security assurances encompassing both the positive and the negative.

Positive Security Assurance

Just before the signing of the NPT, the United States, the former Soviet Union, and Great Britain each declared to the U.N. Security Council "its intention, as a permanent member of the United Nations Security Council, to seek immediate Security Council action to provide assistance, in accordance with the Charter, to any non–nuclear weapon state party to the treaty on the nonproliferation of nuclear weapons that is a victim of an act of aggression or an object of a threat of aggression in which nuclear weapons are used."[29]

This positive security assurance was adopted by the Security Council as Resolution 255 on June 19, 1968, just before the signing of the NPT. A number of non–nuclear weapons states expressed their views that a positive security assurance is nothing more than what is already contained in the U.N. Charter. Furthermore, the statements made by the three nuclear powers amount to only their intentions and subject to the right of veto in the Security Council.[30]

Negative Security Assurance

Since the first NPT Review Conference in 1975, nuclear have-nots dissatisfied with the inadequacy of the positive security assurance have pressed for a specific negative security assurance that the nuclear weapons states will not use or threaten to use nuclear weapons against them.[31] Up to now, four of the five permanent members of the Security Council (all except China) have made unilateral declarations with conditions, limitations, and exceptions.

At the 1978 U.N. Special Session on Disarmament, the Soviet Union had announced that it would never use nuclear weapons against those states that "renounce the production and acquisition of such weapons and do not have them on their territories."[32] Russia recently made statements indicating that it had backed away from its previous no-first-use pledge. The Russian Defense Ministry confirmed that the Russian military doctrine adopted on November 2, 1993, abandoned the old Soviet pledge renouncing the first use of nuclear weapons, which was made in 1982 by Leonid Brezhnev.[33]

The United States declared that it would not use nuclear weapons against any non–nuclear weapons state that is a party to the NPT or "any comparable internationally binding agreement not to acquire nuclear explosive devices," except in the event of an attack on the United States, its territories or armed forces, or its allies by a non–nuclear weapons state "allied to" or "associated with" a nuclear weapons state in carrying out or sustaining the attack.[34] A similar statement was made by Great Britain.[35]

The position of France was that it would give assurances of nonuse of nuclear weapons, in accordance with arrangements to be negotiated, only to those states that have "constituted among themselves non-nuclear zones."[36] The decade-old negotiations in the Conference on Disarmament have made no progress toward removing the conditions contained in the four nuclear weapons states' negative security assurances.[37]

Only China has extended a nonuse guarantee in unqualified terms. Since 1964, the Chinese government has solemnly declared that at no time and under no circumstances would China be the first to use nuclear weapons. It has also undertaken not to use or threaten to use nuclear weapons against non–nuclear weapons states or nuclear-free zones. China strongly calls for negotiations by all nuclear weapons states aimed at concluding an international convention on unconditional no first use of nuclear weapons as well as nonuse and nonthreat of use of nuclear weapons against non–nuclear weapons states and nuclear-free zones, possibly in conjunction with the negotiation of a CTBT.[38]

U.N. Resolution Providing a Comprehensive Security Assurance
to the Korean Peninsula

In spite of China's firm commitment to a negative security assurance, the Chinese government has never issued a positive security assurance, nor has the French government taken any position on that issue. Now that the two remaining nuclear weapons states have joined the NPT (China in March 1992 and France in August of that year), it is possible to strengthen the positive security assurance. In particular, China's commitment to a positive security assurance would put a pressure on North Korea not to develop and use nuclear weapons. Furthermore, a formula needs to be devised to address the nuclear have-nots' concerns regarding the incompleteness of the negative security assurance.

The Korean Peninsula could be a prototype for such purposes. Probably, China could get the other four nuclear weapons states to support a U.N. Security Council resolution in which they would make the following promises:

- Never to use or threaten to use nuclear weapons on the Korean Peninsula under any circumstances
- To take immediate Security Council actions to provide support and assistance to the two Koreas in case they are threatened or attacked with nuclear weapons by the newly emerging nuclear weapons states

The Question of Chinese Nuclear Policy on the Korean Peninsula

China's sound nuclear policy of unconditional negative security assurance should be appreciated by the community of nations. There is no doubt that the other nuclear weapons states should follow China's lead.

But the Mutual Aid, Cooperation and Friendship Treaty between Beijing and Pyongyang, signed in 1961, raises an important question or an ambiguity with respect to the Chinese nuclear policy. Article 2 of the treaty stipulates that "the two signatory nations guarantee to adopt all necessary measures to oppose any country that might attack either nation" (emphasis added). The question is whether "all necessary measures" includes the use or threat of use of nuclear weapons.

According to Luo Renshi, a Chinese scholar, the friendship treaty was signed in 1961, and China conducted its first nuclear test in 1964. So "all necessary measures" mentioned in the treaty did not consider the use of nuclear bombs.[39] Renshi expressed his personal opinion that the probability of China's using nuclear weapons to defend North Korea could be completely ruled out, especially in the post–Cold War era. But the Chinese government should make a clear-cut, official statement on this issue.

Regional Nuclear Nonproliferation Measures

Regional cooperation on nuclear nonproliferation is an indispensable component of a nuclear-free Korean Peninsula. Nuclear testing should be prohibited in this region, and China should take the initiative on the test ban issue as it did on the issue of security assurance for the non–nuclear weapons states. Up to now, the Chinese position on the CTBT has been that only after the CTBT is concluded and takes effect will China abide by it and stop its nuclear tests.[40] Even before a CTBT is concluded, however, regional test ban negotiations among China, Russia, Japan, and the two Koreas could be launched.

In addition, military activities involving nuclear weapons should be limited, and the number of nuclear weapons deployed in this region should be minimized. Considering the ambiguities regarding the differences between peaceful and military uses of fissile materials, the regional powers' nuclear activities in both the civilian and military fields should be more transparent. Creation of a regional mechanism to control fissile materials should also be seriously considered.

And finally, establishing a regional network of seismic stations to detect and identify nuclear test explosions could be an important confidence-building measure in the region. Such a seismic network could be developed into a regional monitoring agency for verifying compliance with regional and international arms-control treaties in the future.

Promoting the Peaceful Uses of Nuclear Energy

As a means of convincing the two Koreas that their denuclearization efforts are important and valuable, not only for international peace and security but also for their own economic interests, the peaceful uses of nuclear energy on the Korean Peninsula should be promoted by regional states. Considering that the Korean Peninsula does not have an abundance of natural energy resources, it is very important that the two Koreas benefit fully from the peaceful uses of atomic energy.

For that purpose, nuclear exporting countries must provide predictable, long-term assurances regarding the supply of nuclear fuels. The need for such assurances was confirmed in the Final Declaration of the Third Review Conference of the Non-Proliferation Treaty in 1985.[41] The two Koreas should also receive preferential treatment over other nations, not to mention the non-NPT parties, for access to or supply of nuclear material, equipment, and services as well as for the transfer of scientific and technological information on the peaceful uses of nuclear energy. A regional conference on the promotion of cooperation in the peaceful uses of atomic energy could be initiated by countries with advanced nuclear technologies, such as Japan.

Regional Arms-Control and Arms-Reduction Efforts

Regional cooperation on nuclear nonproliferation needs to be complemented by military confidence building. Considering that bilateral relationships are far more developed than multilateral ones in Northeast Asia, bilateral security dialogues should be promoted and lead to the resolution of existing disputes. The two Koreas' signing of a nonaggression agreement and negotiating of confidence-building measures is an important precedent. Similar progress should be made in other bilateral relationships in the region.

Bilateral efforts could be conducted in conjunction with multilateral confidence-building endeavors. An Asian version of multilateral dialogues has been proposed by several nations—for example, President Gorbachev's May 1985 proposal of an "All Asian Forum" and Canada's July 1990 proposal of a "North Pacific Cooperative Security Dialogue."[42] A similar forum in Northeast Asia for the purpose of military confidence building could be created with a smaller number of countries and a more limited zone of application—the eastern region of China, Japan, the two Koreas, and the Far Eastern region of Russia—and could be a stepping-stone for establishing a broader security framework in East Asia.[43]

Notes

1. Wendy Lambourne, "Asia/Pacific Security Backgrounder," *Pacific Research* 5, no. 3 (August 1992): 14.
2. *Joong-ang Daily News,* August 7, 1992.
3. Lambourne, "Asia/Pacific Security Backgrounder," 14.
4. Jonathan Dean and Randall Watson Forsberg, "CFE and Beyond: The Future of Conventional Arms Control," *International Security* 17, no. 1, (summer 1992): 112.
5. Seongwhun Cheon, "Countering Proliferation: South Korea's Strategic Choices," paper presented at the Eleventh Annual Ottawa Verification Symposium on Non-proliferation and Multilateral Verification: The Comprehensive Nuclear Test Ban Treaty (CTBT), March 2–5, 1994, Montebello, Quebec, 1.
6. *Rodong Sinmun,* November 8, 1956.
7. *Rodong Sinmun,* October 11, 1980.
8. This meeting was the first official and public occasion at which the nuclear issue surfaced as a point of contention between North and South Korea.
9. Peter Hayes, *Pacific Powderkeg: American Nuclear Dilemmas in Korea* (Lexington, MA: Lexington Books, 1991), 203–206.
10. During this period, the only South Korean proposal for establishing an NWFZ on the Korean Peninsula was made by the president of the Unification Party, an opposition party, on January 16, 1976.
11. On May 11–16, 1992, Hans Blix, director general of the International Atomic Energy Agency (IAEA), paid an official visit to North Korea. He was quoted as saying that the radiochemical laboratory was 80 percent complete in terms of its construction and 40 percent complete in terms of its facilities and that, once finished, it would indeed conform to the definition of a reprocessing plant. Programme for Promoting Nuclear Non-proliferation, *Newsbrief,* no. 18 (summer 1992): 9.
12. *Hankook Ilbo,* December 17, 1991.
13. FBIS-EAS-91–218, November 12, 1991, 14–15.
14. FBIS-EAS-91–206, October 24, 1991, 7.
15. North Korean Ministry of Foreign Affairs, FBIS-EAS-91–227, November 25, 1991.
  The North Korean ambassador to Vienna also mentioned that although inspections of North Korean nuclear facilities would be done by the IAEA, North Korea and the United States should negotiate and decide detailed objects and methods for inspecting the withdrawal of U.S. forces in South Korea. *Joong-ang Daily News,* December 8, 1991.
  When U.S. Congressman Stephen Solarz visited North Korea, Pyongyang made it clear that it stuck to asymmetrical inspections. *Chosun Ilbo,* December 23, 1991.
16. North Korean Ministry of Foreign Affairs, FBIS-EAS-91–246, December 23, 1991, 11.
17. Keynote speech of the South Korean prime minister at the opening session of the South–North High-Level talks in Seoul, FBIS-EAS-91–238, December 11, 1991, 19–20.
18. *Time,* April 4, 1994, 14.
19. For example, in 1992, Ronald Lehman, then director of the U.S. Arms Control and Disarmament Agency, remarked that "Indeed, we may see experience gained here in Korea which may provide concepts useful elsewhere such as in the Middle East and South Asia. The two Koreas have a long way to go, but there are other regions which have not even taken the steps in the nuclear area already begun by Seoul and Pyongyang. One region where the development of nuclear CBMs [confidence-building measures] is less advanced is South Asia. . . ." Ronald Lehman, "Arms Control and Disarmament on the Korean Peninsula," Four

Nations Arms Control Seminar on the Korean Peninsula, Seoul, June 2, 1992, 24–25.

20. Ronald Lehman stressed the importance of the inspections between the two Koreas to clear international suspicions about North Korea's nuclear program and called for South Korea's patience and persistence in working out an effective reciprocal inspection system. *Korea Herald,* June 3, 1992.

21. In December 1962, then Soviet General Secretary Nikita Khrushchev suggested that he might be willing to accept two or three on-site inspections a year. The United States was unwilling to accept fewer than six. Ivo Daalder, "The Limited Test Ban Treaty," in *Superpower Arms Control: Setting the Record Straight,* ed. Albert Carnesale and Richard Haass (Cambridge, MA: Ballinger Publishing, 1987), 12–13.

22. James Goodby, "The Stockholm Conference: Negotiating a Cooperative Security System for Europe," in *U.S.-Soviet Security Cooperation: Achievements, Failures, Lessons,* ed. A. George, P. Farley, and A. Dallin (New York: Oxford University Press, 1988), 158.

23. The other problem was to decide thresholds of notification and observation. John Borawski, *From the Atlantic to the Urals* (New York: Pergamon–Brassey's International Defense Publishers, 1988), 99.

24. Seongwhun Cheon, "National Security and Stability in East Asia: The Korean Peninsula," in *East Asia and Nuclear Non-proliferation,* ed. Darryl Howlett and John Simpson, papers from the Twelfth PPNN Core Group Meeting, Keidanren Guest House, Shizuoka, Japan, November 28–29, 1992, 38.

25. North and South Korea already indicated the possibility of such cooperation. On September 17, 1991, the South Korean minister of science and technology said that if North Korea accepted the IAEA inspections, the South would be willing to provide the North with atomic technologies and cooperate with the North. Choe U-chin, deputy director of North Korea's Disarmament and Peace Institute and co-chairman of the JNCC, also argued that if North Korea's suspicions were eliminated through IAEA inspections, the two Koreas should cooperate to use nuclear energy for peaceful purposes. *Han-Kyoreh Shinmun,* May 20, 1992.

26. Seongwhun Cheon, "A Theoretical Study on Non-offensive Defense (NOD)," paper (in Korean) presented at the Annual Meeting of the Korean Association of International Studies, Seoul, Korea, December 1993.

27. Amy Smithson and Seongwhun Cheon, "'Open Skies' over the Korean Peninsula: Breaking the Impasse," *Korea and World Affairs* 17, no. 1 (spring 1993): 57–77.

28. By December 15, 1993, twelve out of the twenty-seven signatory nations had deposited their instruments of ratification. The treaty will enter into force after twenty states deposit instruments of ratification and after all signatories with passive quotas more than eight ratify. *Arms Control Reporter* (Cambridge, MA: Institute for Defense and Disarmament Studies,1994), 409.A.1.

29. Lewis Dunn, "Containing Nuclear Proliferation," Adelphi Paper 263 (London: International Institute for Strategic Studies, 1991), 43.

30. Aga Shahi, "Defense, Disarmament, and Collective Security," in *Nonoffensive Defense: A Global Perspective* (New York: UNIDIR, 1990), 184.

31. William Epstein, *The Prevention of Nuclear War: A United Nations Perspective* (Cambridge, MA: Gunn & Hain, 1984), 30.

32. U.N. document A/S-10/PV.5.

33. Serge Schmemann, "Russia Drops Pledge of No First Use of Atom Arms," *New York Times,* November 4, 1993, A8.

34. U.N. document A/S-10/AC.1/30.

35. U.N. document A/S-10/PV.26.

36. U.N. document A/S-10/PV.27.

37. Shahi, "Defense, Disarmament, and Collective Security," 184.

38. "Statement by the Government of the People's Republic of China on the Question

of Nuclear Testing," October 5, 1993.

39. Personal communication with Luo Renshi, senior fellow of the China Institute for International Strategic Studies," January 24, 1994.

40. "Statement by the Government of the People's Republic of China on the Question of Nuclear Testing."

41. United Nations Department for Disarmament Affairs, U.N. document NPT/CONF, III/64/I, Annex I, 1985.

42. Recently, former Japanese Prime Minister Nakasone Yasuhiro insisted on the need for a collective security system in Asia. *Joong-ang Daily News,* September 22, 1992.

43. The United States, which has military forces stationed in the area, would have to participate, even though its territory would not be covered.

20

Engaging the DPRK in a Verifiable Nuclear Weapons–Free Zone: Addressing Nuclear Issues Involving the Korean Peninsula

Dingli Shen

A nuclear weapons–free zone (NWFZ) scheme might serve the purpose of regional institution building of a nuclear nonproliferation regime on the Korean Peninsula. A regional nonproliferation regime should properly address the security concerns of the parties that would be involved in a possible Korean Peninsula NWFZ while seeking from them cooperation regarding intrusive and symmetrical safeguard inspections. It is hoped that powers outside the region would also help the denuclearization process on the peninsula.

Origin of the NWFZ Idea

With the end of the Cold War, tensions in Northeast Asia have generally been greatly reduced, although unfortunately, this has not been the case on the Korean Peninsula. The rivalry between the Democratic People's Republic of Korea (DPRK, referred to hereinafter as North Korea) and the Republic of Korea (ROK, hereinafter referred to as South Korea), a legacy left over from the Cold War, has yet to be resolved. At the moment, the striking confrontation between North Korea and the International Atomic Energy Agency (IAEA), as well as between North Korea and the United States, regarding special inspections of North Korea's suspected nuclear facilities, has again become the focal point of world attention.

The Korean nuclear issue is challenging human wisdom to produce a workable solution to nuclear nonproliferation.

Proposals for breaking the Korean nuclear impasse vary—from economic sanctions to "surgical" military preemptive strikes, to peaceful settlement through talks and dialogue. As modern history has shown, economic sanctions usually do not work.[1] Given the unique political culture of North Korea, this author is doubtful that the North would succumb to pressure at all.[2] Resorting to sanctions would seem to be counterproductive to curtail the spread of nuclear weapons in that part of the world, to say nothing of the undesired effects, such as regional unrest, that sanctions would likely bring about. In my opinion, a plausible approach to solving the problem would be to address North Korea's security concerns carefully and take appropriate measures accordingly.

Admittedly, nonproliferation of weapons of mass destruction has been widely accepted as an international norm. Nevertheless, going nuclear is still a viable option for any country if it deems that its national interest would thus be best guaranteed and if it prefers not to be bound by any international norms. Although the current status and even the purpose of North Korea's nuclear program are still uncertain, an adequate analysis of the North's security environment and considerations, as made by Andrew Mack, would suggest that it is not inconceivable that North Korea might have embarked on a nuclear program with weapons potential.[3]

In this regard, if the North's interest in such a nuclear program is to be discouraged, the best formula would be to work out a security arrangement in which the international nonproliferation regime would be effectively preserved and, at the same time, the North would feel adequately secure. This chapter explores how a nuclear weapons–free zone scheme on the Korean Peninsula could help serve this purpose. It is understood that the interests of the relevant powers—namely, the United States, Russia, China, and Japan—converge in this area. Their contributions to establishing such a zone would be crucial and therefore highly desirable.[4]

Various Regional NWFZs

This section briefly reviews various kinds of nuclear weapons–free zones.[5] The concept of an NWFZ is not a new one. It originated in the 1950s as a form of arms control, calling for a ban on the possession of nuclear weapons in a certain area defined by an NWFZ treaty. Polish Foreign Minister Adam Rapacki proposed this idea as early as 1957.

During the Cold War, the issue of NWFZs was frequently raised and debated at various international arms control forums, but the debates were often clouded by propaganda considerations. The United States, wary that its free access to certain areas might be impeded and hence its national interests undermined, often had a negative view of NWFZ proposals. For instance, there had been serious talks on the creation of an NWFZ in the ASEAN (Association of Southeast Asian Nations) region. However, the United States immediately made it clear that this would be contrary to its national interests and that pursuing this idea would jeopardize U.S. protection for the states concerned. In Europe, proposals for NWFZs at subregional levels—in the northern region, in the Baltic, along the Central Front, and in the Balkans—all failed because of the different alliance strategies of the Cold War.[6]

Now that the strategic landscape has been reshaped, the concept of nuclear weapons–free zones has gained wider support. The government of South Africa has renounced its nuclear weapons program and instead taken a position in support of the creation of an African NWFZ.[7] On May 29, 1991, U.S. President George Bush announced a Middle East arms-control initiative that, among other things, urged that a verifiable ban on the production and acquisition of weapons-usable nuclear materials be implemented by states in that region. The Clinton administration has demonstrated continuing enthusiasm for establishing an NWFZ in the Middle East.[8]

In addition, there has been congressional interest in urging the U.S. government to join the South Pacific Nuclear Free Zone Treaty, as part of the overall American nonproliferation strategy toward the comprehensive test ban treaty (CTBT) and the extension of the Nuclear Non-Proliferation Treaty (NPT).[9] Most recently, the United States proposed a "5 + 2 + 2" multilateral conference on nuclear nonproliferation and regional security with the aim of establishing an NWFZ mechanism in South Asia,[10] an issue highlighted during U.S. Deputy Secretary of State Strobe Talbott's visit to New Delhi and Islamabad in early April 1994.[11]

Currently, two types of nuclear weapons–free zones exist: one for populated areas, such as Latin America and the South Pacific; the other for unpopulated areas, such as the Antarctic, the seabed, and outer space.

Populated Areas

Treaty for the Prohibition of Nuclear Weapons in Latin America (Treaty of Tlatelolco). This treaty, which entered into force on April 22, 1968, prohibits the testing, use, manufacture, production, or acquisition by any means as well as the receipt, storage, installation, deployment, and any form of possession of any nuclear weapons by Latin American countries. The parties permit verification of this commitment by a regional inspection organization known as the Agency for the Prohibition of Nuclear Weapons in Latin America (known by its Spanish acronym, OPANAL). Argentina and Chile have recently ratified the treaty.[12] (Brazil signed the treaty in 1968 but has yet to ratify it. Cuba is the only major state in this region that remains outside the treaty.) Recognizing the provision regarding not stationing nuclear weapons, the United States has signed two protocols to the Treaty of Tlatelolco. China is a party to Additional Protocol II of the treaty.

South Pacific Nuclear Free Zone Treaty (Treaty of Rarotonga). This treaty, which entered into force on December 11, 1986, prohibits the manufacture or acquisition by other means of any nuclear explosive devices, as well as possession or control over such devices by the parties anywhere inside or outside the specifically described zone area. The parties also undertake not to supply nuclear material or equipment, unless subject to IAEA safeguards, and to prevent the stationing as well as the testing of any nuclear explosive device in their territories. Each party remains free to allow visits, as well as transit, by foreign ships and aircraft. China has signed Protocols 2 and 3 to the treaty, whereas the United States has not yet agreed to the protocols to honor their restrictions.

Unpopulated Areas

Antarctic Treaty. This treaty, which entered into force on June 23, 1961, declares the Antarctic an area to be used exclusively for peaceful purposes. It prohibits any measure of a military nature in the Antarctic, such as establishing military bases and fortifications, carrying out military maneuvers, or testing any types of weapons. The treaty also bans any nuclear explosions as well as the disposal of radioactive waste material in Antarctica.

Treaty on the Prohibition of the Emplacement of Nuclear Weapons and Other Weapons of Mass Destruction on the Seabed and the Ocean Floor in the Subsoil Thereof (The Seabed Treaty). This treaty, effective as of May 18, 1972, prohibits implanting or placing on the seabed and the ocean floor and in the subsoil thereof, beyond the outer limit of a 12–mile coastal zone, any nuclear weapons or any types of weapons of mass destruction as well as structures, launching installations, or any other facilities specifically designed for storing, testing, or using such weapons.

Treaty on Principles Governing the Activities of States in the Exploration and Use of Outer Space, Including the Moon and Other Celestial Bodies (Outer Space Treaty). This treaty became effective on January 27, 1967. As its name implies, the Outer Space Treaty prohibits placing into orbit around the Earth any objects carrying nuclear weapons or any other kinds of weapons of mass destruction, the installation of such weapons on celestial bodies, or their stationing in outer space in any other manner. Also forbidden are the establishment of military bases, installations, and fortifications; the testing of any type of weapons; and the conduct of military maneuvers on celestial bodies.

All these existing NWFZs, as well as other NWFZ types of arms-control initiatives, have a common feature: possession and/or even the physical presence of nuclear weapons in the zone area is banned by a nuclear weapons–free zone treaty. Such regional nuclear weapons nonproliferation institutions require states within the zone to pledge at least to forgo developing and possessing nuclear weapons. NWFZ treaties usually require nuclear powers to honor relevant treaty provisions and comply with their respective obligations.

Establishing an NWFZ on the Korean Peninsula

Both North and South Korea have expressed commitment to the peaceful use of nuclear energy.[13] As a signatory to the NPT, a country should unconditionally accept international inspections, including special (or challenge) inspections, of all its nuclear facilities. Fairness aside, this is the obligation a signatory should have understood before acceding to the NPT since such inspection provisions have already been established as part of the NPT/IAEA safeguards regime. However, Pyongyang argues that, at the moment, its case is special as its decision to withdraw from the NPT is being temporarily suspended.

The North's conflict with the IAEA involves the IAEA's request for full inspections of two suspected sites at Yongbyon. One of the two places is reported to be a typical waste site that could be associated with an earlier Soviet-supplied 5 MWt (IRT-DPRK) reactor in Yongbyon. This place is reportedly almost exactly like the waste site near the Soviet-supplied nuclear reactor in Iraq. The other suspected facility is a two-floor building, code-named Building 500 by the U.S. Central Intelligence Agency (CIA), built in 1991–1992, with tanks believed to be in a concealed lower level. IAEA inspectors did visit this building during an earlier inspection and found no evidence of clandestine activities there.[14] When the IAEA was later inclined to drill through the basement of the building, Pyongyang responded by threatening to withdraw from the NPT, three days after the start of the 1993 "Team Spirit" military exercise, on the grounds that inspection of its military facilities would infringe on North Korea's national security.

To strike a balance, a party to the NPT does have the right to withdraw from the treaty if it determines that continuing to abide by the treaty's provisions would be harmful to its national interests. It is obvious that the nonproliferation regime would incur a serious setback if the North did quit. It is therefore evident that keeping the North in the NPT would be of vital importance both to nuclear nonproliferation and to ensuring regional stability in Northeast Asia.

That being the case, a balanced approach to dealing with this thorny problem is to consider a Korean Peninsula nuclear weapons–free zone (KP-NWFZ), which would have at least two features.

First, as a regional approach, the KP-NWFZ would mandate a regional nonproliferation regime based on the willingness of the states in that region. North Korea has repeatedly indicated that it has neither the capability nor the desire to make a nuclear bomb; South Korea has said more categorically that it will forswear any nuclear fuel–cycle program that could lead to a weapon end use.[15] So why should North and South Korea not establish a KP-NWFZ to formalize their positive intentions? Unlike some South Asian states, neither North nor South Korea has linked its non-nuclear proposal to a global nondiscriminatory nonproliferation regime. The current NPT is indeed discriminatory. However, exercising restraint on nuclear capability before the NPT is reformed would make it a lot easier to contain the spread of nuclear weapons at the regional level.

Second, the basic tenet of an NWFZ treaty is that all parties to it must assume the same responsibility not to acquire nuclear weapons. As the Treaties of Tlatelolco and Rarotonga have shown, the NWFZ approach would impose symmetrical obligations on all signatories in the respective region. At this time, the Korean nuclear problem remains focused on the "special inspections." A symmetrical treatment of intrusive verification of nuclear activities in both Koreas, as would be mandated by a KP-NWFZ treaty, might render full inspections more acceptable, provided cooperative measures were taken.

In fact, in the December 1991 "Joint Declaration for a Non-nuclear Korean Peninsula," the two Koreas already pledged themselves to the following:[16]

- Not to test, produce, receive, possess, store, deploy, or use nuclear weapons
- Not to possess facilities for nuclear reprocessing and uranium enrichment
- To use nuclear energy solely for peaceful purposes
- To verify compliance upon the request of one party but agreed to by both
- To ensure implementation through the establishment and regular meeting of a South–North Joint Nuclear Control Commission (JNCC).[16]

Such pledges are solid foundations for establishing an NWFZ on the Korean Peninsula.

Issues Critical to a KP-NWFZ

Successful implementation of a nuclear weapons–free zone must guarantee the security of nations in the region if they forgo the nuclear weapons option. Otherwise, the NWFZ approach would be unattractive to potential participants and would eventually fail.

On the Korean Peninsula, an NWFZ regime must ensure that

- Neither North nor South Korea develops or possesses nuclear weapons
- Out of their own willingness, the two Koreas develop their civilian nuclear programs in a way that is designed to minimize the chances of diversion of nuclear materials to military applications
- All nuclear powers honor the restrictions regarding this zone
- An effective, symmetrical verification regime is put in place

The remainder of this section addresses the following critical issues: defining a relevant NWFZ in Northeast Asia; obtaining a negative nuclear security assurance from the nuclear powers; ensuring the peaceful use of nuclear energy in the zone area; establishing a confidence-building system of safeguards; eliminating the presence of foreign troops and ensuring conventional arms control in the region.

Geographical Limits of the Proposed Zone

The country in question is North Korea, which is situated on the Korean Peninsula, or in a larger geographical sense, in Northeast Asia. Normally, Northeast

Asia is considered to be comprised of Far Eastern Russia, northeastern China, Japan, the Koreas, and Mongolia. Russia and China are the two nuclear states in the region. The United States once stationed naval and tactical nuclear weapons abroad, including in Japan and South Korea, but has now declared that such weapons have been withdrawn.

What size would the NWFZ in this region be? Should it include the whole of Northeast Asia? This depends upon the geopolitical situation of this region. Apparently, Russia—and perhaps China, too—would not be interested in establishing an NWFZ where their territories would be involved.

If a Northeast Asia nuclear weapons–free zone (NEAN-WFZ) is to cover Russia, Russia's sea exit of nuclear force to the Pacific would be likely blocked. It is understood that Russia's Pacific fleet, whose home ports are on the Kamchatka Peninsula and at Far East coastal bases near Vladivostok and around the Sea of Okhotsk, includes nuclear-powered ballistic missile submarines (SSBNs). It is hard to imagine that Russia, a nuclear power, would impose a nuclear-free zone on its own territory and territorial waters. With respect to China, there has been no credible information in the public domain regarding the basing of its nuclear weapons. Thus, it is impossible to ascertain whether nuclear weapons have been based in northeastern China. Needless to say, a regional non-nuclear sanctuary would ideally include China, an acknowledged nuclear power.

Even though it seems unlikely that Russia and China would endorse an NEA-NWFZ involving themselves, the governments of the two countries have supported a nuclear-free zone on the Korean Peninsula proper.

Japan has long had a non–nuclear weapons provision in its constitution. Although there have been pronuclear sentiments in Japan, the nuclearization of Japan is out of the question in the foreseeable future. What does concern the world community is Japan's technical capability to go nuclear in a crash program. Japan's excessive accumulation of plutonium also upsets the world at large. It would be beneficial if Japan were to join the two Koreas in a regional NWFZ arrangement. But Japanese politicians might not be interested in being treated the same as the Koreans, especially if the nuclear powers of the region did not participate in the NWFZ. In order not to complicate the urgent task of denuclearizing the Korean Peninsula, one could conceive of an NWFZ established just on the peninsula. Japan might not be involved at the outset. Meanwhile, if the two Koreas pledged in the NWFZ treaty not to enrich uranium or reprocess plutonium, Japan should consider giving up its plutonium-recycling program.

The final Northeast Asian country, Mongolia, is neither a contributor to the Korean nuclear problem nor a critical factor in the context of the Korean Peninsula.

Obtaining a Negative Security Assurance from the Nuclear Powers

The nuclear powers should provide a negative security assurance to the proposed KP-NWFZ. It seems clear that Russia and China are ready to provide a negative security assurance to this region. In fact, China is inviting other nuclear powers to sign a global "no-first-use" agreement.[17] Also, it would do no harm for Britain and France to follow suit.

For many years, the United States stationed nuclear weapons in South Korea. But in recent years, the United States is believed to have withdrawn its tactical nuclear weapons in light of the changing security environment. The fact that the United States has promised North Korea, through a joint statement on June 11, 1993, that it will agree in principle to provide assurances against the threat and use of force, including nuclear weapons, is a welcome development.[18] It is a sign that the United States is departing from its current conditional no-first-use policy.

However, the United States is still providing South Korea with a nuclear umbrella. Thus, the United States has adopted contradictory policies: while providing a negative security assurance to North Korea, it provides a positive security assurance to South Korea at the same time, according to the 1954 U.S.-Korean Mutual Defense Treaty. In a legal sense, the United States cannot do this. It can adhere to one of these policies, but not on both. Of course, it would be very constructive for the United States to withdraw its nuclear protection from South Korea in the post–Cold War era. It seems that North Korea doesn't have any nuclear support on its side. Furthermore, South Korea and the United States have adequate conventional means to handle a crisis on the Korean Peninsula, even a nuclear crisis.

Ensuring the Peaceful Use of Nuclear Energy in the Zone

To realize a KP-NWFZ, both North and South Korea should turn their nuclear programs to peaceful uses. Since both sides have expressed the intention not to retain uranium enrichment and plutonium-reprocessing capabilities, they have promised to go beyond the normal requirements against nuclear proliferation. This is certainly welcome. One should be aware, however, that some nationalist elements in South Korea advocate reversing the course set by Roh Tae Woo. And it is hard to accept that the Yongbyon "radiochemistry" laboratory is not a reprocessing facility and could be exempted from inspection. Furthermore, providing North Korea with the means to produce less nuclear waste from its nuclear power generation would be helpful. Providing an LWR (light-water reactor) is probably an alternative.[19]

Establishing a Confidence-building Safeguards System

North Korea may not have acquired kilogram quantities of plutonium, but its lack of cooperation in accepting inspections does raise suspicions about its nuclear ambitions. It is expected that the international community would insist on intrusive inspections of the North's nuclear program, particularly to investigate the DPRK's plutonium-reprocessing history. It could be painful for Oriental countries to accept intrusive inspections. Nevertheless, it is an important step in becoming a respected member of an established world order, even though the order itself needs to be improved. Thus, an appropriately cooperative attitude is highly desirable. In order for North Korea to be more cooperative in accepting inspections, the North would probably insist that similar intrusive inspections be imposed on South Korea's nuclear facilities. An NWFZ scheme would provide a means by which intrusive and symmetrical safeguards could be applied equally to both Koreas.

Removing Foreign Troops and Ensuring Conventional Arms Control

Finally, let me address an important factor that remains outside the nuclear realm—that is, the annual U.S.–South Korean annual "Team Spirit" exercises. To be sure, North Korea should unconditionally accept inspections as long as it is still a signatory to the NPT. And the NPT does not recognize any connection between one party's acceptance of nuclear safeguards and another party's military exercises with a nuclear power. However, the Korean nuclear issue is far more complicated than this simple reasoning. North Korea demands that such exercises be stopped since the North feels insecure about having a rival allied with a nuclear power that demonstrates its support through military exercises. In my opinion, the United States could take a significant step toward helping the denuclearization of North Korea partly by permanently canceling the "Team Spirit" exercises. To demonstrate U.S. goodwill, the United States should not condition its cancellation of such exercises on North Korea's acceptance of nuclear inspections.

In turn, the positive U.S. initiative could evoke a positive response from North Korea.

Besides, there is no longer a need to keep U.S. troops in South Korea. Obviously, no foreign troops have been stationed in North Korea. As mentioned earlier, no nuclear power seems ready to unfold a nuclear umbrella over North Korea. Given the fact that South Korea's population is twice that of the North and the South's economy is more than ten times greater, Seoul is predicted to match the force level of the North within this decade. So there is indeed no need for Americans to defend South Korea. It would be quite logical at this time to let American troops go home.[20] This could only serve to remove any remaining reasons for North Korea to stay on the margins of the NPT.

It is understood that conventional arms reduction should be undertaken simultaneously with the denuclearization process on the Korean Peninsula. A DPRK Army of more than 1.1 million troops vis-à-vis an ROK Army of 0.6 million plus provides no sense of security to either side but simply depletes a large portion of their national resources. Conventional arms control and transparency building deserve due attention.

Conclusion

Given a Korean Peninsula receiving negative security assurances from all nuclear powers, the U.S. Army's withdrawal from South Korea, a permanent cancellation of the "Team Spirit" exercises, and the removal of the nuclear umbrella over South Korea, the prospects for applying an intrusive and symmetrical safeguards regime to both North and South Korea would be greatly enhanced. In this way, North as well as South Korea could be integrated into a verifiable regional NWFZ scheme. The world community at large should facilitate the process of denuclearizing the Korean Peninsula by establishing an NWFZ in this area.

Notes

1. Kimberly Ann Elliot pointed out that, of 115 cases of economic sanctions imposed since World War I, only 23 percent have been successful in achieving "major goals." See "Will Sanctions Work against North Korea?" NAPSN Working Paper 24, December 17, 1993, 7–9.

2. As John Curtis Perry has put it, the "DPRK will change only in its own way." See "Dateline North Korea: A Communist Holdout," *Foreign Policy*, no. 80 (fall 1990): 172.

3. Andrew Mack, "The Nuclear Crisis on the Korean Peninsula," *Asian Survey* 33, no. 4 (April 1993): 339–359; Andrew Mack, "North Korea and the Bomb," *Foreign Policy*, no. 83 (summer 1991): 87–104. For the nuclear threat against North Korea, see also Bruce Cumings, "Spring Thaw for Korea's Cold War?" *Bulletin of the Atomic Scientists* (April 1992): 14–23; Bruce Cumings, "Who's Intimidating Whom?" in "Ending the Cold War: Cuba, North Korea, and Vietnam," *Defense Monitor* 23, no. 1 (1994): 5.

4. There is extensive literature on the interrelations between the Koreas and the United States, Russia, and Japan. For Chinese analyses in English on Sino-Korean relations, see Jia Hao and Zhuang Qubing, "China's Policy toward the Korean Peninsula," *Asian Survey* 32, 12 (December 1992): 1137–1156; Hao Yufan, "China and the Korean Peninsula: A Chinese View," *Asian Survey* 27, no. 8 (August 1987): 862–884; Hong Li, "The Sino–South Korean Normalization: A Triangular Explanation," *Asian Survey* 33, no. 11 (November 1993): 1083–1094.

5. Zachary S. Davis and Warren H. Donnelly, "A Nuclear Weapons–Free Zone in the Middle East: Background and Issues," CRS Issue Brief, Library of Congress (order code: IB92041), updated October 1, 1993. *SIPRI Yearbook 1993: World Armaments and Disarmament* (Stockholm/New York: SIPRI/Oxford University Press [OUP], 1993), 759–762.

6. *SIPRI Yearbook 1990: World Armaments and Disarmament* (Stockholm/New York: SIPRI/OUP, 1990), 578. At the Fourth Review Conference of the Treaty on the Non-Proliferation of Nuclear Weapons (NPT), Indonesia and Malaysia again strongly endorsed the proposal for an NWFZ in the ASEAN region. See *SIPRI Yearbook 1991: World Armaments and Disarmament* (Stockholm/New York: SIPRI/OUP, 1991), 565.

7. *SIPRI Yearbook 1992: World Armaments and Disarmament* (Stockholm/New York: SIPRI/OUP, 1992), 99.

8. Davis and Donnelly, "Nuclear Weapons–Free Zone in the Middle East."

9. Zachary S. Davis and Warren H. Donnelly, "The South Pacific Nuclear Free Zone Treaty [The Treaty of Rarotonga]," CRS Report for Congress, Library of Congress, 93–610–ENR, June 25, 1993.

10. The proposed "5 + 2 + 2" nine-nation conference would involve the five perma-

nent members of the U.N. Security Council, together with Germany and Japan, and India and Pakistan.

11. K.K. Katyal, "India Not for Nuclear Talks Proposed by U.S.," *Hindu,* April 2, 1994, 1; "U.S. Keen on Stronger Ties," *Hindu,* April 7, 1994, 1; P.S. Suryanarayana, "Pak. Cool to U.S. Plans," *Hindu,* April 6, 1994, 13; " 'Broad Accord' with Pak: Talbott," *Hindu,* April 10, 1994, 1.

During Talbott's visit, the United States proposed the objective of "first capping, then reducing and eventually eliminating weapons of mass destruction and ballistic missiles from South Asia." The United States is believed to have urged New Delhi and Islamabad to give up their nuclear weapons option, cut off production of unsafeguarded fissile materials, and place future civilian nuclear materials production and nuclear facilities under an international safeguards regime.

12. U.S. Department of State, Bureau of Public Affairs, *Dispatch* 5, no. 5 (January 31, 1994): 47.

13. North and South Korea announced a "Joint Declaration for a Non-nuclear Korean Peninsula" in Panmunjom on December 13, 1991. The two sides pledged not to test, produce, receive, possess, store, deploy, or use nuclear weapons and not to possess facilities for nuclear reprocessing and uranium enrichment. On November 8, 1991, South Korean President Roh Tae Woo announced that the South would not manufacture, retain, stockpile, equip itself with, or use nuclear weapons. He also pledged to accept full-scope international safeguard inspections of the South's nuclear facilities and materials. See Agence France Press, November 8, 1991; Xu Baokang, "A Sound Basis for Nuclear-Free Korea," *Beijing Review,* December 16–22, 1991, 10–11.

14. Satellite photos taken during the construction of Building 500 showed what looked like a heavily shielded nuclear waste storage site in the basement. See "North Korea at the Crossroads: Nuclear Renegade or Regional Partner?" *Arms Control Today,* 23, no. 4 (May 1993): 3–14 (transcript of a press conference featuring Spurgeon Keeny, David Albright, and Michael Mazarr): 4; *Arms Control Reporter* (IDDS) (June 1993), section 457.E, 2.

15. See note 13. Most recently, North Korean President Kim Il Sung said on April 16, 1994, that he had no plans to develop nuclear weapons and wanted peace. Associated Press, April 17, 1994.

16. Michael Krepon, Dominique M. McCoy, and Matthew C.J. Rudolph, eds., *A Handbook of Confidence-Building for Regional Security,* Handbook no. 1 (Washington, DC: Henry L. Stimson Center, September 1993), 30.

17. Xinhua News Agency, March 24, 1994.

18. "Joint Statement of the Democratic People's Republic of Korea and the United States of America," New York, June 11, 1993.

19. Within the Northeast Asia Peace and Security Network, there have already been some analyses on supplying LWRs to the DPRK. See Peter Hayes, "Light Water Reactor Technology Transfer to North Korea: Does It Make Sense?" Working Paper 21, September 1993; Salomon Levy, "Supply of Light Water Reactors to Pyongyang: Technical Issues and Their Possible Resolution," Working Paper 22, December 1993; Victor Gilinsky and William Manning, "A U.S.-Type Light Water Reactor for North Korea? The Legal Implications," Working Paper 23, December 1993.

20. In July 1977, General Bernard Rogers, chief of staff of the U.S. Army (1976–1979), quoted a South Korean colonel as saying, "We will hate to see our friends go, but if we are going to grow up, and, we are going to walk alone, you have to take this [step of withdrawing]. I think the time has come." See "Mission Accomplished in Korea: Bringing U.S. Troops Home," *Defense Monitor* 19, no. 2 (1990): 7.

21

Conclusion: Moving Beyond a Nuclear Weapons–Free Korea toward Sustainable Energy Development in Northeast Asia

Peter Hayes and Young Whan Kihl

In this concluding chapter, we return to an earlier argument in the introductory chapter—that two sets of questions now confront the various actors concerned about the Korean peninsula and regional security issues related to peace and development. These are (1) "sustainable" energy development and (2) nuclear disarmament via both horizontal and vertical nonproliferation. Furthermore, the Agreed Framework between the United States and the Democratic People's Republic of Korea (DPRK), in resolving North Korean nuclear issues through dialogue and diplomacy, is one thing that the international community may consider positive. How to implement the terms of this agreed framework without fail, however, is a separate issue that challenges both North Korea and the United States and its allies. The Korean Peninsula Energy Development Organization (KEDO) was established to carry out provisions of the Agreed Framework, and a separate agreement was signed between the KEDO and the DPRK in December 1995 to supply North Korea with two light-water reactors (LWRs) by the year 2003, as stipulated in the Agreed Framework.

Now that the charter of the KEDO (see appendix B) is being implemented, we can move ahead in a competitive, nonconfrontational fashion to resolve the most important issues between the DPRK and the international community. In the short term, the most pressing issue is to broaden the relationship between the

DPRK and the international community as embodied in the Korean Peninsula Energy Development Organization by provision of nuclear technology and fuel oil to other, non-nuclear energy development in the DPRK. This step is necessary to increase the probability of North Korea's remaining non-nuclear and, along with it, South Korea (the Republic of Korea, or ROK), Japan, and Taiwan. In the medium term, the urgent imperative is to expand the nuclear nonproliferation regime in Northeast Asia to encompass all three nuclear weapons states present in the region. Specifically, we argue that the non-nuclear states should exert pressure on the nuclear weapons states to commit, in principle, to the goal of totally eliminating nuclear weapons and, short of its realization, to arms-control measures covering nuclear weapons in the region. Each of these regional peace and security issues will be examined, in detail, in terms of (1) sustainable energy development and (2) nuclear disarmament and the dismantlement of nuclear weapons in Northeast Asia.

Sustainable Energy Development and Environmental Security in Northeast Asia

As noted in earlier chapters, Northeast Asia faces an emerging dilemma regarding how to supply sufficient energy to develop without degrading the environment, which sustains human life. In the coming decade, rapid economic growth will drive a huge increase in energy demand. However, the primary projected strategies to meet the demand—expansion of (dirty) coal and/or nuclear power—are deeply problematic on both environmental and security grounds.

The primary problem with (dirty) coal is a large and insupportable increase in greenhouse gas emissions plus acid rain–causing sulfur emissions, both within and across borders. Acid rain has widespread impacts on terrestrial and ocean ecosystems, as well as on human health. On the security side, tensions have already erupted between China and Japan and South Korea over cross-border sulfur emissions from coal-fired plants in northern and southeastern China. Ocean and marine degradation caused by oil transport is another likely source of regional conflict. Thus, a first and necessary ingredient of any sustainable energy strategy is to make coal fuel cycles cleaner, especially in China and the two Koreas, and to minimize and better manage the maritime oil trade.[1]

The profound problems posed by coal have prompted some analysts to promote nuclear power as an environmentally cleaner and more secure alternative. Nuclear power, however, is also plagued with environmental problems, including the production of radioactive waste, routine emissions, and the possibility of a catastrophic accident. The security problems posed by nuclear power are even more acute—especially Japan's promotion of the plutonium economy and the example this sets for other states.[2]

A third alternative is to switch fuels—especially to gas—and to minimize waste in both the production, distribution, and consumption of energy. A strategy that combines cleaner coal technologies to control sulfur emissions with fuel switching *and* improvements in end-use energy efficiency in all sectors may be optimal. This alternative is preferable on economic, environmental, *and* security grounds. Because capital will be a constraining factor in energy technology choice and investment paths, it is crucial that the relative costs of different strategies be assessed rigorously.

Critical questions for ongoing research include the following, and seeking answers to these and related questions must continue, so as to enhance the quality of life and environmental security in Northeast Asia:

- *Baseline assessment:* What is the existing status of acid rain in Northeast Asia according to modeling activity and monitoring of actual deposition? Do these two sources of information provide a sufficiently robust foundation for developing response policies? How do atmospheric transport of precursor emissions and deposition rates across national boundaries compare with the experience in other heavily studied regions such as North America and Europe?

- *Energy and acid rain projections:* What are the projected levels of acid rain and related environmental and economic damages, given trends in energy use and energy conversion and emission-control technologies in the region? In particular, can critical loads be determined for vulnerable ecosystems such as forests and cropping cultures for deposition levels at a resolution level that is capable of guiding siting, land use, and investment allocation decisions in each country in the region?

- *Technological alternatives:* What are the current and appropriate technological alternatives for reducing energy emissions, and what are their associated costs and externalities?

- *Regional cooperation strategies:* What regional strategies can be identified and implemented to mitigate acid rain in terms of technology transfer, financial assistance, technical assistance and training, institutional reforms, energy pricing and regulatory reforms, institutional and human resource development, and utility demand-side management programs? What would be the best vehicle and format for a joint initiative in this regard?

- *Policy tools:* What policy tools are available to achieve an integrated assessment of alternative strategies to reduce acid rain to an acceptable level? Relatedly, what does prior experience with regional conventions and agreements to control long-range air pollution suggest for dealing with acid rain in Northeast Asia? There are important precedents for monitoring and verifying international environmental agreements, at the regional level in Europe and globally in the ozone-depletion convention. This experience provides some guidelines for how binding regional environmental agreements in Northeast Asia, including those that might concern acid rain, could be monitored, verified, and enforced.

- *Innovative energy financing and the trade–environment interface:* What approaches might be adopted to overcome financial and trade-related barriers to sustainable energy development in the region? Is there room to implement common regional energy standards and to explore innovative financing mechanisms for the transfer and dissemination of environmentally sound energy technologies? Such approaches include BOT (build-own-transfer) and BOO (build-own-operate) power plants; transnational twinning of energy organizations, especially utilities; creation of energy efficiency service companies (financed out of energy savings); partnerships between private nongovernmental organizations and public agencies (especially utilities) to establish demand-side management and energy efficiency programs; and joint implementation.[3]

    It is critically important to address both the urgent need for front-end investment capital for the construction and operation of transferred plants and equipment and know-why (the research, development, design, demonstration, and deployment of technology). Financing should extend to techniques of incremental learning involved in fine-tuning existing plants and equipment and in managing the organizational changes that foster such learning.[4] The very notion of technology transfer therefore needs to be recast and the meaning of the concept expanded and deepened.

- *Capacity building:* In addition to building capacity to deal with the cross-sectoral, complex issues of sustainable development at the national level, *regional* programs for environmental cooperation also entail developing *regional* capacities in the medium and long term. Nowhere is this more true than in the energy sector, in terms of regulated operation of private energy and financial markets, environmental monitoring, and technology adoption and diffusion.

- *Global dimensions:* Some global issues may inter-relate with regional acid rain issues in ways that cannot be ignored. Climate change, for example, may redistribute regional atmospheric circulation and precipitation patterns, thereby affecting concerns such as transfrontier pollution, ecosystem management, and desertification at a regional level and requiring a regional response.

- *Costs and financing:* The issue of who will pay for the costs of controlling sulfur emissions is crucial. Donors need to recognize that resources must be provided to build requisite national and regional capacities to participate effectively in regional environmental agreements. Donors must also incorporate environmental conditionalities into development financing and develop their own internal capacities to identify benefits associated with regional environmental cooperation.

- *Nongovernmental organizations and public awareness:* Without active participation by citizens—including scientists, academics, and businesspeople, as well as religious, civic, and environmental groups—many environmental policies are doomed to failure. Regional efforts are no less subject to this imperative than local, national, or global activities. It is therefore crucial to involve nongovernmental organizations in regional deliberations and activities in Northeast Asia at the outset rather than as an afterthought. Comparison and contrast of the North American and European experiences in this regard may provide insights as to how best to design consultative processes in the diverse political cultures of Northeast Asia.

- *Energy and military security:* One proposed solution to the (dirty) coal/acid rain dilemma is to promote nuclear power and the plutonium economy.[5] But is this realistic given capital markets?

Regional Peace through Nuclear Disarmament

The issue of how best to eliminate nuclear weapons in Northeast Asia is dominated by the residual or modernizing nuclear forces of the three existing nuclear-armed states, as was explained in previous chapters by Ralph Cossa, Dunbar Lockwood, and Gerald Segal. Thus, the nuclear states are primarily concerned with elimination in a global, not a regional, context. Yet the process of elimination at the global level will reflect on vital interests of each of the three powers in this region, and regional states can influence the global agenda of the three nuclear weapons states. Japan is in a particularly influential position in this regard as its long-standing national policy has favored the eventual total abolition of nuclear weapons. It is clearly in Japan's interest for the United States and Russia to implement a stage-by-stage reduction of nuclear weapons to the point at which China can no longer avoid controlling and disarming its own nuclear forces as part of three-way (or five-way if France and the United Kingdom join) global nuclear arms elimination talks. Rather than simply react to U.S. moves to eliminate nuclear weapons at the global level—to which the recent Stimson Center report is a precursor—it would be prudent and productive if regional states generated their own vision of a non-nuclear future built on conventional rather than nuclear forces.[6]

Relatedly, it is unrealistic to expect the two Koreas and Japan to accept forever a second-class status relative to the great powers that surround them or relative to each other given their past enmities. Thus, a discriminatory nonproliferation regime is not a durable framework for ensuring that the four non-nuclear states of Northeast Asia (the two Koreas, Japan, and Taiwan) remain non-nuclear in the long run. There is no shortcut to a non-nuclear Northeast Asia. But equally, there is no alternative to the elimination of nuclear weapons in the long run.

The burning question, therefore, is what interim, transitional steps can the nuclear weapons states take to ease the security dilemmas of regional non-nuclear states, and what proposals can the non-nuclear states make either unilaterally or jointly to expedite the process of eliminating nuclear weapons on a global basis?[7] For scholars, some of the tasks entailed by this political agenda are evident already. Promotion of interactive dialogue and negotiation between nuclear weapons–states and non-weapons states, such as between the United States and the DPRK, must be encouraged with a view to arriving at compromise on difficult and contentious issues. Seven specific measures broadly reflecting historical lessons can be identified.

- *Historical lessons:* What revisions to the various axioms and myths developed to rationalize the Cold War balance of terror are in order now that U.S. and Russian archives are opening to scholarly investigations? Do nuclear weapons stabilize this currently anarchic region that lacks even nascent forums for discussing regional security dilemmas, let alone institutionalized means for resolving them? What credible scenarios exist for the actual first use of nuclear weapons between the nuclear weapons states or against a non-nuclear state? Do past rationales lend themselves to explaining nuclear escalation in these future nuclear war scenarios in the region?
- *Pace and sequence:* What are the crucial milestones in a global and regional nuclear build-down by the nuclear weapons states, and do these have specific time lines or chronological sequences to which the states must adhere in order for the process of elimination to unfold? How would taking such steps affect regional security relationships? Are concepts such as "minimum deterrence" and "stable deterrence during the transition" useful and meaningful rationales for ever-dwindling stockpiles of increasingly obsolete nuclear weapons? Would the transition to elimination entail extending more rather than less nuclear deterrence to friends and allies to counter possible horizontal proliferation? What would be the end point for total elimination of nuclear weapons? Would a trial period be necessary during which the nuclear weapons states could retain a right to reactivate their nuclear forces?[8] Is the main factor deterring breakout simply the prospect that nuclear-capable states could reactivate their nuclear arsenals in short order? What should and would the international community do in response to an actual or threatened breakout after elimination has been achieved? Would strategic defenses facilitate or obstruct the process of totally eliminating nuclear weapons in the region, and what would be the regional security impacts of deploying such systems?
- *Costs and externalities:* What are the direct and indirect costs of nuclear weapons stockpiles, delivery systems, and infrastructure (including environmental costs), both globally and regionally? And how do these compare with the costs of conventional forces that might be needed to substitute for the military functions ostensibly fulfilled by nuclear weapons if tensions do not subside in proportion to nuclear arms reductions? Which nuclear missions should be eliminated first, and what aspects of the security of non-nuclear states would be affected in the course of such adjustments in the posture of the nuclear weapons states?

- *Confidence building:* What can regional non-nuclear states do to assist in mutual learning by the nuclear weapons states in ways that facilitate the elimination process? Can non-nuclear states create mechanisms at a regional level that provide for increased transparency (with respect, for example, to nuclear fuel cycle facilities or military bases) and that would eventually extend to the nuclear weapons states?

- *Monitoring and verification:* What measures related to monitoring and verification will be needed to achieve the virtual or actual elimination of nuclear weapons? Is it easier in terms of monitoring and verification to move quickly to zero or to move gradually to ever smaller numbers?

- *Legal aspects:* Should elimination be enshrined in regional laws such as a regional nuclear-free zone between the non-nuclear states with protocols for nuclear weapons states or in a global treaty pursuant to the fulfillment of the obligations of nuclear weapons states under Article 6 of the Nuclear Non-Proliferation Treaty? Might the latter—which will seek comprehensive, unambiguous, and global commitments—be incompatible with cultural values and orientations in the non-nuclear states of the region, which often emphasize partial measures, studied ambiguity, and regional arrangements?

- *Nuclear hegemony versus conventional community:* The willingness of the United States to participate in a multilateral security community regime based on conventional forces rather than a hegemonic alliance system built around nuclear weapons is a crucial issue for non-nuclear and nuclear weapons states alike. To date, the U.S. propensity has been to reach for conventional weapons but to keep nuclear arms in a back pocket "in reserve" for first use. Such "counterproliferation" combines the worst of both worlds—an unwillingness to forgo the coercive power implicit in nuclear weapons combined with a reluctance to undertake the full-blown revision of conventional force postures and alliance relationships entailed by the elimination of nuclear weapons.[9] For its part, China is proceeding full speed ahead with the modernization of its nuclear forces while Russia clings to its strategic forces in spite of its dire domestic political and economic problems. Waiting for the United States, Russia, or China to abandon its nuclear pretensions will needlessly prolong the urgent task of eliminating nuclear weapons. Non-nuclear states owe it to themselves and their neighbors to identify the pressure points on the nuclear weapons states to elevate this issue on their list of priorities.

Of course, a gradual but actual elimination of nuclear weapons would be the result of a world in which their threatened or actual use would become less relevant and less probable, and therefore, their final elimination less urgent. As Ronald Lehman II put it trenchantly, a world that eliminated nuclear weapons "could not be a world in which totalitarian regimes with advanced nuclear capability could exist."[10] The major reason to push urgently for the total elimination of nuclear weapons is not so much the risk that these weapons might be used between nuclear weapons states, once force levels fall to tens or hundreds of deliverable warheads. By the time that the world achieves that state, much more important political, economic, and environmental issues will crowd the stage.

No, the reason that it is terribly urgent to push for the rapid and total elimination of nuclear weapons is to stem the proliferation of new nuclear weapons states and the outbreak of new[11] Cold Wars on a regional or even global scale that might match or even exceed that between the United States and the former Soviet Union. This is the main lesson from the Korean example since 1991.

Epilogue

As of early 1996, the DPRK is off the front pages of U.S. newspapers. Among nonproliferation analysts, attention has shifted from the Korean Peninsula to the Indian-Pakistani nuclear standoff and the negotiation of the Comprehensive Test Ban Treaty in the face of Indian opposition and Chinese intransigence. In the U.S. government, the issue has been downgraded from "crisis management" at the White House and National Security Council and devolved to "operational" levels in the bowels of the State Department.[12] As long as the DPRK keeps its nuclear freeze intact, American officials appear content to move ahead slowly—or as fast as the DPRK permits—with incremental steps envisaged under the Agreed Framework. Apart from the tortuous efforts required to implement the agreement to transfer light-water reactors and fuel oil to the DPRK, discussions have commenced concerning return of the remains of U.S. soldiers missing in action during the Korean War, establishment of liaison offices, and so forth. Discussions concerning North Korea's bringing its missile exports into compliance with the Missile Technology Control Regime and other "hard" issues such as redeployment and reduction of conventional forces have barely begun.

The major exception to the "minimalist" rule on the U.S. side has been its willingness to provide $2 million of food aid to the DPRK in the aftermath of the tremendous floods that hit in July–August 1995. In response to the United Nations World Food Program (WFP) appeals for emergency food assistance to North Korea, the United States pledged an additional $6 million, while its allies Japan and South Korea pledged $6 million and $3 million, respectively. This move—which was justified on humanitarian grounds already established as U.S. policy prior to the Agreed Framework—was motivated primarily by a desire to prevent starvation-induced instability from threatening the North Korean regime, combined with an awareness in Washington that this gesture would strengthen the hand of proponents of the Agreed Framework in Pyongyang.

Meanwhile, the DPRK seems to be trapped in a stop–start stasis. Some North Korean delegations will appear unexpectedly at international events, whereas other delegations cancel on short notice. Some economic technocrats appear to have been given marching orders to attack foreign investment regardless of politics or ideology, but the domestic infrastructure and requisite regulatory and financial environments to support this policy are almost totally absent. Remarkably, the DPRK regime has allowed apparently contradictory policy currents to swirl to the surface, most notably in February 1996 when a foreign affairs spokesman referred to the military as opposing food aid in the course of explaining why the DPRK would no longer accept such contributions. North Korea announced, in late February 1996, that it would no longer follow the rules of the 1953 armistice signed at the end of the Korean War. It proposed, in its place, a tentative agreement with the United States, until a permanent peace agreement could be concluded, and a joint DPRK–U.S. military body to replace the Military Armistice Commission. This unilateral act was followed by North Korea's provocative move, deliberately violating the armistice, of sending scores of armed troops into the joint security area at Panmunjom from April 5 to April 7.

Thus, in both Washington and Pyongyang, the mood seems to be gloomy in 1996 rather than upbeat. U.S. policy is more or less on hold until after the November 1996 presidential elections. DPRK policy seems to be immobilized by uncertainty surrounding Kim Jong Il's succession to the paramount political posts in the DPRK polity, fear of the domestic impacts of opening up the DPRK's economy and society to external influences, and indecisiveness about engaging the United States at official and unofficial levels.

To these formidable constraints must be added the ROK's inability to fashion and implement a consistent *nordpolitik.* The political turmoil associated with the arrest in early 1996 of two past South Korean generals-turned-presidents charged with treason and corruption has made it impossible for the ROK to engage the DPRK—even if the latter desired such a dialogue. Given these limitations— reinforced by China's preference for the status quo in Korea, Russia's absorbing introspection, and Japan's wrenching political reforms and contradictory coalition governments—the time appears inauspicious for bold, visionary changes in policies toward Korean security or the reunification of the Korean Peninsula.

Yet the authors of this volume have documented a radical shift in U.S. policy from unilateral and bilateral militant containment dependent primarily on the exercise of military power to bilateral and multilateral cooperative engagement of one of the United States' major Cold War and post–Cold War adversaries. Admittedly, the changes achieved to date by this shift in emphasis have been limited, albeit significant. Although military capabilities buttressed diplomatic efforts in the arduous U.S.-DPRK negotiations since 1992—and may have proved decisive in making North Korean leaders blink at critical junctures— diplomacy as embodied in the Agreed Framework has achieved U.S. goals at far lower cost than might have been the case if the two sides had exchanged military blows over the nuclear issue. In 1992, it was inconceivable to most American analysts that the DPRK might seek to resolve the major issues that separate Pyongyang and Washington. Yet in early 1996, DPRK diplomats were testing how fast and far U.S. policy makers were willing to go toward diplomatic normalization in spite of the retarding effect of the U.S. presidential election.

Undoubtedly, the Clinton administration wants primarily to keep the DPRK off the front pages, thereby depriving the Republicans of another stick with which to bludgeon the Democrats. For this reason, the DPRK has some unexpended leverage to move forward in its relationship with the United States as its price for not misbehaving before the U.S. presidential election. Indeed, insofar as Cuba's shooting down of unarmed civilian aircraft in February 1996 allows Clinton and his Republican opponents to appear tough, Fidel Castro has given Kim Jong Il a political opening for further U.S.-DPRK reciprocal moves, albeit of a limited kind.

U.S. president Bill Clinton and ROK president Kim Young Sam, during their Cheju Island summit on April 15, unveiled a new peace initiative toward North Korea that called for four-party talks with South Korea, North Korea, the United States, and China. This meeting would seek to establish a permanent peace in Korea in an attempt to defuse the tensions that resulted from the North Korean demands for changing the existing armistice regime. Pyongyang has taken a wait-and-see policy stance, and his response to the summit proposal has been lukewarm and noncommittal.

Finally, the DPRK has exhibited a remarkable resilience in playing the games not only of nuclear diplomacy but also of survival strategy. Even in the face of the collapse of communism, a failing economy, and severe food shortages, North Korea has managed to survive and even thrive. The Kim Jong Il regime has successfully extracted concessions, one after another, from the United States and its allies. If the DPRK's negotiations on the October 1994 Agreed Framework with the United States is any indication, Pyongyang emerged as the victor by playing the nuclear "ambiguity" card with skill and tact.

The outcome of the United States–North Korea nuclear deal making, however, is neither obvious nor self-evident. The Agreed Framework, "while hardly perfect, represents a reasonable compromise on the nuclear issue in Korea" and, as such, is "qualified victory" to both sides of the controversy.[11] Yet the Agreed Framework may fall apart unless both sides implement the terms of the agreement. Thus, the verdict of the ongoing diplomatic process between Pyongyang and Washington will not be known until the year 2003 or 2004, when the construction and transfer of two LWRs by KEDO to North Korea is complete. The prospect of peace and security in Northeast Asia is uncertain, however, because "bargaining power in the negotiation process is not the same as bargaining power in the implementation process." The jury is still out deliberating "who won or who lost." Hopefully, in moving from here (1994–1996) to there (2003–2004), both parties will be declared the winners rather than the losers.

Notes

1. L. Zarsky and P. Hayes, "Environmental Cooperation and Sustainable Development in Northeast Asia" (paper presented at the Sixth U.S.-Korea Academic Symposium:

Economic and Regional Cooperation in Northeast Asia, University of Chicago, Korea Economic Institute, and Korea Institute of Economic Policy (Chicago, Illinois, September 6–8, 1995).

2. See E. Skolnifoff, T. Suzuki, and K. Oye, "International Responses to Japanese Plutonium Programs," working paper MIT E38-648, Center for International Studies, Cambridge, MA, August 1995.

3. See D. Beg, "Privatization Initiatives in Developing Countries with Particular Reference to the Power Sector," and P. Saint-Andrew, "Cooperation as a Vehicle for Technology Transfer," in *Energy Technology Cooperation for Sustainable Economic Development*, ed. J. Gray et al. (Lanham, MD: University Press of America, 1993); M. Hoskote, "Independent Power Projects (IPPS)," in *Energy Themes* (Washington, DC: World Bank, May 1995); A. Churchill and R. Saunders, "Financing of the Energy Sector in Developing Countries" (Washington, DC: World Bank Industry and Energy Department, April 1989); Tadashi Aoyagi, "Financing a Sustainable Energy Future for Developing Countries," Mitsubishi Research Institute (paper presented at the Presidio Energy Workshop, U.S.–Japan Perspectives on Sustainable Energy Future, January 19, 1995).

4. See M. Bell, *Continuing Industrialization, Climate Change and International Technology Transfer* (Sussex, UK: Science Policy Research Unit, Sussex University, December 1990), 75–80.

5. See, for example, Ryukichi Imai, "The Long Shadow of Nuclear Weapons," policy paper 114E, International Institute for Global Peace, Tokyo, July 1993, 12.

6. See *An Evolving U.S. Nuclear Posture: Second Report of the Steering Committee, Project Eliminating Weapons of Mass Destruction* (Washington, DC: Stimson Center, 1996).

7. See R. Cowen Karp, ed., *Security Without Nuclear Weapons: Different Perspectives on Non-nuclear Security* (New York: Oxford University Press, 1992).

8. A question posed by R. Lehman II, "Deterrence, Denuclearization, and Proliferation: Alternative Visions of the Next Fifty Years," in *Bridging the Nonproliferation Divide: The United States and India,* ed. F. Frankel, Center for the Advanced Study of India, University of Pennsylvania (Lanham, MD: University Press of America, 1995), 44.

9. See K. Kristensen and J. Handler, *Changing Targets: Nuclear Doctrine from the Cold War to the Third World* (Washington, DC: Greenpeace International, March 1, 1995).

10. R. Lehman II, "Nuclear Deterrence and Disarmament after the Cold War," in *Old Issues and New Strategies for Arms Control and Verification,* ed. J. Brown (Amsterdam: VU University Press, 1995), 358.

11. Michael J. Mazarr, *North Korea and the Bomb: A Case Study in Nonproliferation* (New York: St. Martin's Press, 1994), 240.

Text of the 1994
Geneva Agreed Framework

Agreed Framework between the United States of America and
the Democratic People's Republic of Korea
Geneva, October 21, 1994

Delegations of the Governments of the United States of America (U.S.) and the Democratic People's Republic of Korea (DPRK) held talks in Geneva from September 23 to October 17, 1994, to negotiate an overall resolution of the nuclear issue on the Korean Peninsula.

Both sides reaffirmed the importance of attaining the objectives contained in the August 12, 1994 Agreed Statement between the U.S. and the DPRK and upholding the principles of the June 11, 1993 Joint Statement of the U.S. and the DPRK to achieve peace and security on a nuclear-free Korean peninsula. The U.S. and the DPRK decided to take the following actions for the resolution of the nuclear issue:

I. Both sides will cooperate to replace the DPRK's graphite-moderated reactors and related facilities with light-water reactor (LWR) power plants.

1) In accordance with the October 20, 1994 letter of assurance from the U.S. President, the U.S. will undertake to make arrangements for the provision to the DPRK of a LWR project with a total generating capacity of approximately 2,000 MW(e) by a target date of 2003.

—The U.S. will organize under its leadership an international consortium to finance and supply the LWR project to be provided to the DPRK. The U.S., representing the international consortium, will serve as the principal point of contact with the DPRK for the LWR project.

—The U.S., representing the consortium, will make best efforts to secure the conclusion of a supply contract with the DPRK within six months of the date of this Document for the provision of the LWR project. Contract talks will begin as soon as possible after the date of this Document.

—As necessary, the U.S. and the DPRK will conclude a bilateral agreement for cooperation in the field of peaceful uses of nuclear energy.

2) In accordance with the October 20, 1994 letter of assurance from the U.S. President, the U.S., representing the consortium, will make arrangements to offset the energy forgone due to the freeze of the DPRK's graphite-moderated reactors and related facilities, pending completion of the first LWR unit.

—Alternative energy will be provided in the form of heavy oil for heating and electricity production.

—Deliveries of heavy oil will begin within three months of the date of this Document and will reach a rate of 500,000 tons annually, in accordance with an agreed schedule of deliveries.

3) Upon receipt of U.S. assurances for the provision of LWR's and for arrangements for interim energy alternatives, the DPRK will freeze its graphite-moderated reactors and related facilities and will eventually dismantle these reactors and related facilities.

—The freeze on the DPRK's graphite-moderated reactors and related facilities will be fully implemented within one month of the date of this Document. During this one-month period, and throughout the freeze, the International Atomic Energy Agency (IAEA) will be allowed to monitor this freeze, and the DPRK will provide full cooperation to the IAEA for this purpose.

—Dismantlement of the DPRK's graphite-moderated reactors and related facilities will be completed when the LWR project is completed.

—The U.S. and DPRK will cooperate in finding a method to store safely the spent fuel from the 5 MW(e) experimental reactor during the construction of the LWR project, and to dispose of the fuel in a safe manner that does not involve reprocessing in the DPRK.

4) As soon as possible after the date of this document, U.S. and DPRK experts will hold two sets of expert talks.

—At one set of talks, experts will discuss issues related to alternative energy and the replacement of the graphite-moderated reactor program with the LWR project.

—At the other set of talks, experts will discuss specific arrangements for spent fuel storage and ultimate disposition.

II. The two sides will move toward full normalization of political and economic relations.

1) Within three months of the date of this Document, both sides will reduce barriers to trade and investment, including restrictions on telecommunications services and financial transactions.
2) Each side will open a liaison office in the other's capital following resolution of consular and other technical issues through expert level discussions.
3) As progress is made on issues of concern to each side, the U.S. and DPRK will upgrade bilateral relations to the Ambassadorial level.

III. Both sides will work together for peace and security on a nuclear-free Korean peninsula.

1) The U.S. will provide formal assurances to the DPRK, against the threat or use of nuclear weapons by the U.S.
2) The DPRK will consistently take steps to implement the North–South Joint Declaration on the Denuclearization of the Korean peninsula.
3) The DPRK will engage in North–South dialogue, as this Agreed Framework will help create an atmosphere that promotes such dialogue.

IV. Both sides will work together to strengthen the international nuclear nonproliferation regime.

1) The DPRK will remain a party to the Treaty on the Non-Proliferation of Nuclear Weapons (NPT) and will allow implementation of its safeguards agreement under the Treaty.
2) Upon conclusion of the supply contract for the provision of the LWR project, ad hoc and routine inspections will resume under the DPRK's safeguards agreement with the IAEA with respect to the facilities not subject to the freeze. Pending conclusion of the supply contract, inspections required by the IAEA for the continuity of safeguards will continue at the facilities not subject to the freeze.
3) When a significant portion of the LWR project is completed, but before delivery of key nuclear components, the DPRK will come into full compliance with its safeguards agreement with the IAEA (INFCIRC/403), including taking all steps that may be deemed necessary by the IAEA, following consultations with the Agency with regard to verifying the accuracy and completeness of the DPRK's initial report on all nuclear material in the DPRK.

Kang Sok Ju—Head of the Delegation for the Democratic People's Republic of Korea, First Vice-Minister of Foreign Affairs of the Democratic People's Republic of Korea

Robert L. Gallucci—Head of the Delegation of United States of America, Ambassador at Large of the United States of America

Appendix:

The following are the talking points used by U.S. officials to explain the text up until the time it was released.

US–DPRK Talks: Press Themes

—After sixteen months of negotiations, the United States and North Korea have reached an agreement that ends the recent threat of nuclear proliferation in Northeast Asia and provides the basis for more normal relations between North Korea and the rest of the world.

—This agreement serves the interests of our allies, South Korea and Japan, as well as the United States. It will bring greater security to this dangerous part of the world and contribute to our efforts to end nuclear proliferation globally. Here are its principal features:

—First, it will bring the DPRK into full compliance with its Non-proliferation obligations under the Non-Proliferation Treaty (NPT). The DPRK affirms its NPT member status, commits to complying with its IAEA safeguards agreement, and states willingness to implement the South–North Denuclearization Declaration.

—Second, it terminates the existing DPRK nuclear program. Activity at the DPRK's nuclear facilities (5 megawatt (MW) reactor, reprocessing facility, and 50 and 200 MW reactors now under construction) will remain frozen, under the supervision of IAEA inspectors. When light water reactors are nearing completion, North Korea will dismantle those facilities.

—Third, it ensures safe disposition of the spent fuel now in North Korea. The DPRK will forgo reprocessing, and instead will safely store and eventually ship the spent fuel out the country.

—Fourth, it addresses the question of the past. The DPRK will accept special inspections or other steps deemed necessary by the IAEA before it receives any nuclear components for a light water reactor.

—Lastly, this agreement will draw North Korea out of its dangerous isolation. It will help integrate Pyongyang into the economic and political mainstream of East Asia.

—Our part of the bargain is straightforward. We will lead an international consortium which will oversee construction of two 1000 MW light water reactors of proliferation resistant design in the DPRK over the next decade. Funding will chiefly come from South Korea; Japan will also make a major contribution.

—We and the DPRK will establish liaison offices in each other's capitals—something that will help us oversee the implementation of this agreement and open a channel to deal with other issues that concern us.

—We plan to reduce economic and financial restrictions selectively on US citizens' dealings with the DPRK, in close consultation with the Congress.

—We will provide a "negative security assurance." It would pledge us not to use nuclear weapons against North Korea as long as it remains a member in good standing of the NPT regime. (We have provided similar assurances to other signatories of the NPT).

—To compensate the DPRK for loss of energy production from further operation of its 5 MW reactor and from abandoning 50 and 200 MW reactors under construction, the consortium will provide the North 500,000 tons of heavy fuel oil annually for use in a specific power plant (50,000 tons in the first three months, and 150,000 tons in the first year of the agreement).

—This agreement attains all our goals, including the North's commitment to pursue South–North dialogue, without which there can be no permanent resolution of questions of peace and security on the Korean Peninsula.

—We consulted our allies, Japan and South Korea, at every stage of this arduous negotiation, including frequent conversations between the President and President Kim Young Sam. Korea and Japan's strong support has been essential to the success of the talks with North Korea. They are fully on board, and doubtless will have more to say themselves.

—Secretary Perry will visit South Korea and Japan on October 20–22.

Annex: President Bill Clinton's Letter to Kim Jong Il

THE WHITE HOUSE
WASHINGTON

October 20, 1994

Excellency:

I wish to confirm to you that I will use the full powers of my office to facilitate arrangements for the financing and construction of a light-water nuclear power reactor project with the DPRK, and the funding and implementation of interim energy alternatives for the Democratic People's Republic of Korea pending completion of the first reactor unit of this light-water reactor project. In addition, in the event that this reactor project is not completed for reasons beyond the control of the DPRK, I will use the full powers of my office to provide, to the extent necessary, such a project from the United States, subject to approval of the U.S. Congress. Similarly, in the event that the interim energy alternatives are not provided for reasons beyond the control of the DPRK, I will use the full powers of my office to provide, to the extent necessary, such interim energy alternatives from the United States, subject to the approval of the U.S. Congress.

I will follow this course of action so long as the DPRK continues to implement the policies described in the Agreed Framework Between the United States of America and the Democratic People's Republic of Korea.

Sincerely,

Signed
Bill Clinton

His Excellency Kim Jong Il
Supreme Leader of the Democratic People's Republic of Korea
Pyongyang

Appendix B

Charter of the KEDO (Korean Peninsula Energy Development Organization)

The Government of the Republic of Korea, the Government of Japan, and the Government of the United States of America;

Affirming the objective of an overall resolution of the North Korean nuclear issue, as referred to in the Agreed Framework Between the United States of America and the Democratic People's Republic of Korea, signed in Geneva on October 21, 1994 (hereinafter referred to as "the Agreed Framework");

Recognizing the critical importance of the nonproliferation and other steps that must be taken by North Korea, as described in the Agreed Framework, as a condition of implementation of the Agreed Framework;

Bearing in mind the paramount importance of maintaining peace and security on the Korean Peninsula;

Wishing to cooperate in taking the steps necessary to implement the Agreed Framework, consistent with the Charter of the United Nations, the Treaty on the Non-Proliferation of Nuclear Weapons, and the Statute of the International Atomic Energy Agency; and

Convinced of the need to establish an organization, as contemplated in the Agreed Framework, to coordinate cooperation among interested parties and to facilitate the financing and execution of projects needed to implement the Agreed Framework;

Have agreed as follows:

Article I

The Korean Peninsula Energy Development Organization (hereinafter referred to as "KEDO" or the "Organization") is established upon the terms and conditions hereinafter set forth.

Article II

- (a) The purposes of the Organization shall be to:
  - (1) provide for the financing and supply of a light-water reactor (hereinafter referred to as "LWR") project in North Korea (hereinafter referred to as "the DPRK") consisting of two reactors of the Korean standard nuclear plant model with a capacity of approximately 1,000 MW(e) [megawatts electric] each, pursuant to a supply agreement to be concluded between the Organization and the DPRK;
  - (2) provide for the supply of interim energy alternatives in lieu of the energy from the DPRK's graphite-moderated reactors pending construction of the first light-water reactor unit; and
  - (3) provide for the implementation of any other measures deemed necessary to accomplish the foregoing or otherwise to carry out the objectives of the Agreed Framework.
- (b) The Organization shall fulfill its purposes with a view toward ensuring the full implementation by the DPRK of its undertakings as described in the Agreed Framework.

Article III

In carrying out these purposes, the Organization may do any of the following:

(a) Evaluate and administer projects designed to further the purposes of the Organization;

(b) Receive funds from members of the Organization or other states or entities for financing projects designed to further the purposes of the Organization, manage and disburse such funds, and retain for Organization purposes any interest that accumulates on such funds;

(c) Receive in-kind contributions from members of the Organization or other states or entities for projects designed to further the purposes of the Organization;

(d) Receive funds or other compensation from the DPRK in payment for the LWR project and other goods and services provided by the Organization;

(e) Cooperate and enter into agreements, contracts, or other arrangements with appropriate financial institutions, as may be agreed upon, for the handling of funds received by the Organization or designated for projects of the Organization;

(f) Acquire any property, facilities, equipment, or goods necessary for achieving the purposes of the Organization;

(g) Conclude or enter into agreements, contracts, or other arrangements, including loan agreements, with states, international organizations, or other appropriate entities, as may be necessary for achieving the purposes and exercising the functions of the Organization;

(h) Coordinate with and assist states, local authorities and other public entities, national and international institutions, and private parties in carrying out activities that further the purposes of the Organization, including activities promoting nuclear safety;

(i) Dispose of any receipts, funds, accounts, or other assets of the Organization and distribute the proceeds in accordance with the financial obligations of the Organization, with any remaining assets or proceeds therefrom to be distributed in an equitable manner according to the contributions of each member of the Organization, as may be determined by the Organization; and

(j) Exercise such other powers as shall be necessary in furtherance of its purposes and functions, consistent with this Agreement.

Article IV

(a) Activities undertaken by the Organization shall be carried out consistent with the Charter of the United Nations, the Treaty on the Non-Proliferation of Nuclear Weapons, and the Statue of the International Atomic Energy Agency.

(b) Activities undertaken by the Organization shall be subject to the DPRK's compliance with the terms of all agreements between the DPRK and KEDO and to the DPRK acting in a manner consistent with the Agreed Framework. In the event that these conditions are not satisfied, the Organization may take appropriate steps.

(c) The Organization shall obtain formal assurances from the DPRK that nuclear materials, equipment, or technology transferred to the DPRK in connection with projects undertaken by the Organization shall be used exclusively for such projects, only for peaceful purposes, and in a manner that ensures the safe use of nuclear energy.

Article V

(a) The original members of the Organization shall be the Republic of Korea, Japan, and the United States of America (hereinafter referred to as the "original Members").

(b) Additional states that support the purposes of the Organization and offer assistance, such as providing funds, goods, or services to the Organization, may, with the approval of the Executive Board, also become members of the Organization (hereinafter jointly with the original Members referred to as "Members") in accordance with the procedures in Article XIV(b).

Article VI

(a) The authority to carry out the functions of the Organization shall be vested in the Executive Board.

(b) The Executive Board shall consist of one representative of each of the original Members.

(c) The Executive Board shall select a Chair from among the representatives serving on the Executive Board for a term of two years.

(d) The Executive Board shall meet whenever necessary at the request of the Chair of the Executive Board, the Executive Director, or any representative serving on the Executive Board, in accordance with rules of procedure it shall adopt.

(e) Decisions of the Executive Board shall be made by a consensus of the representatives of all of the original Members.

(f) The Executive Board may approve such rules and regulations as may be necessary or appropriate to achieve the purposes of the Organization.

(g) The Executive Board may take any necessary action on any matter relating to the functions of the Organization.

Article VII

(a) The General Conference shall consist of representatives of all the Members.

(b) The General Conference shall be held annually to consider the annual report, as referred to in Article XII.

(c) Extraordinary meetings of the General Conference shall be held at the direction of the Executive Board to discuss matters submitted by the Executive Board.

(d) The General Conference may submit a report containing recommendations to the Executive Board for its consideration.

Article VIII

(a) The staff of the Organization shall be headed by an Executive Director. The Executive Director shall be appointed by the Executive Board as soon as possible after this Agreement enters into force.

(b) The Executive Director shall be the chief administrative officer of the Organization and shall be under the authority and subject to the control of the Executive Board. The Executive Director shall exercise all the powers delegated to him or her by the Executive Board and shall be responsible for conducting the ordinary business of the Organization, including the organization and direction of a headquarters and a staff, the preparation of annual budgets, the procurement of financing, and the approval, execution and administration of contracts to achieve the purposes of the Organization. The Executive Director may delegate such powers to other officers or staff members as he or she deems appropriate. The Executive Director shall perform his or her duties in accordance with all rules and regulations approved by the Executive Board.

(c) The Executive Director shall be assisted by two Deputy Executive Directors. The two Deputy Executive Directors shall be appointed by the Executive Board.

(d) The Executive Director and the Deputy Executive Directors shall be appointed for terms of two years and may be reappointed. They shall be nationals of the original Members. The terms of employment, including salaries, of these officers shall be determined by the Executive Board. The Executive Director and the Deputy Executive Directors may be removed prior to the expiration of their terms by a decision of the Executive Board.

(e) The Executive Director shall have the authority to approve projects, execute contracts, and enter into other financial obligations on behalf of the Organization within the guidelines adopted by the Executive Board and the limits of the approved budget, provided that the Executive Director shall obtain the prior approval of the Executive Board for projects, contracts, or financial obligations that exceed a specified value, which shall be determined by the Executive Board based on the need for effective and efficient operation of the Organization.

(f) The Executive Director shall establish staff positions and terms of employment, including salaries, subject to the approval of the Executive Board. The Executive Director shall appoint qualified personnel to such staff positions and dismiss personnel as necessary, in accordance with rules and regulations to be approved by the Executive Board. The Executive Director shall seek to appoint a staff in which the nationals of the original Members are fairly represented, paying due regard to the importance of securing the highest standards of integrity, efficiency, and technical competence.

(g) The Executive Director shall report to the Executive Board and the General Conference on the activities and finances of the Organization. The Executive Director shall promptly bring to the notice of the Executive Board any matter that may require Executive Board action.

(h) The Executive Director, with the advice of the Deputy Executive Directors, shall prepare rules and regulations consistent with this Agreement and the purposes of the Organization. The rules and regulations shall be submitted to the Executive Board for its approval prior to implementation.

(i) In the performance of their duties, the Executive Director and the staff shall not seek or receive instructions from any government or from any other authority external to the Organization. They shall refrain from any action that might reflect on their position as international officials responsible only to the Organization. Each Member undertakes to respect the exclusively international character of the responsibilities of the Executive Director and the staff and not to seek to influence them in the discharge of their responsibilities.

Article IX

(a) The Executive Board shall establish Advisory Committees to provide advice to the Executive Director and the Executive Board, as appropriate, on specific projects being carried out by the Organization or proposed to be carried out by the Organization. Advisory Committees shall be established for the light-water reactor project, the project for the provision of the interim energy alternatives, and such other projects as the Executive Board may determine.

(b) Each Advisory Committee shall include representatives of the original Members and other Members that support the project for which the Advisory Committee was established.

(c) The Advisory Committees shall meet at such times as they may determine.

(d) The Executive Director shall keep the Advisory Committees fully informed of matters pertinent to their respective projects, and the Executive Board and Executive Director shall give due consideration to the recommendations of the Advisory Committees.

Article X

(a) The budget for each fiscal year shall be prepared by the Executive Director and shall be approved by the Executive Board. The Organization's fiscal year shall be from January 1 to December 31.

(b) Each Member may make voluntary contributions to the Organization by providing or making available such funds as it deems appropriate. Such contributions may be made directly to the Organization or by paying the Organization's contractors. Contributions shall be made by cash deposit, escrow, letter of credit, promissory note, or by such other legal means and in such currency as may be agreed between the Organization and the contributor.

(c) The Organization may seek contributions from such other public or private sources as it deems appropriate.

(d) The Organization shall establish an account or accounts to receive funds from Members or other sources, including independent accounts for those funds to be reserved, for specific projects and the administration of the Organization. Interest or dividends accruing on such accounts shall be reinvested for activities of the Organization. Excess funds shall be distributed as set forth in Article III(i).

Article XI

(a) Members may make available to the Organization or its contractors goods, services, equipment, and facilities that may be of assistance in achieving the purposes of the Organization.

(b) The Organization may accept from such other public or private sources as it deems appropriate any goods, services, equipment, and facilities that may be of assistance in achieving the purposes of the Organization.

(c) The Executive Director shall be responsible for valuing in-kind contributions to the Organization, whether direct or indirect. Members shall cooperate with the Executive Director in the valuation process, including by providing regular reports of in-kind contributions and access to records necessary to verify the value of such contributions.

(d) In the event of a dispute concerning the value of an in-kind contribution, the Executive Board shall review the matter and render a decision.

Article XII

The Executive Director shall submit to the Executive Board for its approval an annual report on the activities of the Organization, which shall include a description of the status of the LWR project and other projects, a comparison of planned activities to completed activities, and an audited statement of the Organization's accounts. Upon the approval of the Executive Board, the Executive Director shall distribute the annual report to the Members. The Executive Director shall submit to the Executive Board such other reports as may be required by the Executive Board.

Article XIII

(a) To carry out its purposes and functions, the Organization shall possess legal capacity and, in particular, the capacity to: (1) contract; (2) lease or rent real property; (3) acquire and dispose of personal property; and (4) institute legal proceedings. Members may accord the Organization such legal capacity in accordance with their respective laws and regulations where necessary for the Organization to carry out its purposes and functions.

(b) No Member shall be liable, by reason of its status or participation as a Member, for acts, omissions, or obligations of the Organization.

(c) Information provided to the Organization by a Member shall be used exclusively for the purposes of the Organization and shall not be publicly disclosed without the express consent of that Member.

(d) Implementation of this Agreement in the Members' territories shall be in accordance with the laws and regulations, including budgetary appropriations, of such Members.

Article XIV

(a) This Agreement shall enter into force upon signature by the original Members.

(b) States approved by the Executive Board for membership in accordance with Article V(b) may become Members by submitting an instrument of acceptance of this Agreement to the Executive Director, which shall become effective on the date of receipt by the Executive Director.

(c) This Agreement may be amended by written agreement of the original Members.

(d) This Agreement may be terminated or suspended by written agreement of the original Members.

Article XV

A Member may withdraw from this Agreement at any time by giving written notice of withdrawal to the Executive Director. The withdrawal shall become effective ninety days after receipt of the notice of withdrawal by the Executive Director.

DONE at New York, this ninth day of March, 1995, in three copies in the English language.

For the Government of the Republic of Korea:

For the Government of Japan:

For the Government of the United States of America:

Joint U.S.–DPRK Press Statement, Kuala Lumpur, June 13, 1995

The delegations of the United States of America (U.S.) and the Democratic People's Republic of Korea (DPRK) held talks in Kuala Lumpur from May 19 to June 12, 1995, with respect to implementation of the DPRK–U.S. Agreed Framework of October 21, 1994.

Both sides reaffirmed their political commitments to implement the U.S.–DPRK Agreed Framework, and with particular regard to facilitating the light water reactor (LWR) project as called for in the Agreed Framework, decided as follows:

I. The U.S. reaffirms that the letter of assurance from the U.S. President dated October 20, 1994 concerning the provision of the LWR project and interim energy alternatives continues in effect.

The Korean Peninsula Energy Development Organization (KEDO), under U.S. leadership, will finance and supply the LWR project in the DPRK as called for in the Agreed Framework. As specified in the Agreed Framework, the U.S. will serve as the principal point of contact with the DPRK for the LWR project. In this regard, U.S. citizens will lead delegations and teams of KEDO as required to fulfill this role.

II. The LWR project will consist of two pressurized light water reactors with two coolant loops and a generating capacity of approximately 1,000MW(E) [megawatts electric] each. The reactor model, selected by KEDO, will be the advanced version of U.S.-origin design and technology currently under production.

III. The Commission for External Economic Relations, representing the DPRK Government, and KEDO will conclude a supply agreement at the earliest possible date for the provision of the LWR project on a turnkey basis. On the basis of this statement, the DPRK will meet with KEDO as soon as possible to negotiate the outstanding issues of the LWR supply agreement.

KEDO will conduct a site survey to identify the requirements for construction and operation of the LWR project. The costs of this site survey and site preparation will be included in the scope of supply for the project.

KEDO will select a prime contractor to carry out the project. A U.S. firm will serve as program coordinator to assist KEDO in supervising overall implementation of the LWR project; KEDO will select the program coordinator. A DPRK firm will enter into implementing arrangements as necessary to facilitate the LWR project.

IV. In addition to the LWR project, the two sides decided to take the following steps towards implementation of the Agreed Framework.

Experts from the two sides will meet in the DPRK as soon as possible in June to agree on a schedule and cooperative measures for phased delivery of heavy fuel oil in accordance with the Agreed Framework. KEDO will begin immediately to make arrangements for an initial delivery of heavy fuel oil, subject to conclusion of the above agreement.

The DPRK–U.S. Record of Meeting of January 20, 1995, on safe storage of spent fuel will be expeditiously implemented. In this regard, a U.S. team of experts will visit the DPRK as soon as possible in June to begin implementation.

Appendix D

Agreement on Supply of a Light-Water Reactor Project to the Democratic People's Republic of Korea Between the Korean Peninsula Energy Development Organization and the Government of the Democratic People's Republic of Korea

The Korean Peninsula Energy Development Organization (hereinafter referred to as "KEDO") and the Government of the Democratic People's Republic of Korea (the Democratic People's Republic of Korea is hereafter referred to as the "DPRK"),

Recognizing that KEDO is an international organization to finance and supply a light-water reactor project (hereinafter referred to as the "LWR project") to the DPRK as specified in the Agreed Framework between the United States of America and the Democratic People's Republic of Korea of October 21, 1994 (hereinafter referred to as the "U.S.-DPRK Agreed Framework"),

Recognizing that the U.S.-DPRK Agreed Framework and the June 13, 1995, U.S.-DPRK Joint Press Statement specify that the U.S. will serve as the principal point of contact with the DPRK for the LWR project, and

Reaffirming that the DPRK shall perform its obligations under the relevant provisions of the U.S.-DPRK Agreed Framework and shall accept the LWR project as specified in the June 13, 1995, U.S.-DPRK Joint Press Statement.

Have agreed as follows:

Article I: Scope of Supply

1. KEDO shall provide the LWR project, consisting of two pressurized light-water reactor (LWR) units with two coolant loops and a generating capacity of approximately 1,000 MW(e) each, to the DPRK on a turnkey basis. The reactor model, selected by KEDO, will be the advanced version of U.S.-origin design and technology currently under production.

2. KEDO shall be responsible for the scope of supply for the LWR project, specified in Annex 1 to the Agreement. The DPRK shall be responsible for other tasks and items necessary for the LWR project, specified in Annex 2 to the Agreement.

3. The LWR project shall conform to a set of codes and standards equivalent to those of the IAEA and the U.S. and applied to the reactor model referred to in paragraph 1 of this Article. The set of codes and standards shall apply to the design, manufacture, construction, testing, commissioning, and operation and maintenance of the LWR plants, including safety, physical protection, environmental protection, and storage and disposal of radioactive waste.

Article II: Terms of Repayment

1. KEDO shall finance the cost of the tasks and items specified in Annex 1 to the Agreement to be repaid by the DPRK on a long-term, interest-free basis.

2. The amount to be repaid by the DPRK will be jointly determined by KEDO and the DPRK based on examination by each side of the technical description of the LWR project specified in the commercial supply contract for the LWR project, the fair and reasonable market value of the LWR project, and the contract price payable by KEDO to its contractors and subcontractors under the commercial supply contracts for the tasks and items specified in Annex 1 to the Agreement. With respect to the tasks and items specified in Annex 1 to the Agreement, the KEDO shall not be responsible for any additional costs, other than those that result from actions by the KEDO or from its failure to take actions for which it is responsible, in which case the repayment amount shall be increased by an amount jointly determined by KEDO and the DPRK, based on actual added cost to the LWR project payable by KEDO.

3. The DPRK shall repay KEDO for each LWR plant in equal, semiannual installments, free of interest, over a 20–year term after completion of each LWR plant, including a three-year grace period beginning upon completion of that LWR plant. The DPRK may pay KEDO in cash, cash equivalents, or through the transfer of goods. In the event that the DPRK pays cash equivalents or goods

(such payment is hereinafter referred to as "in-kind payment"), the value of such in-kind payment shall be determined jointly by KEDO and the DPRK, based on an agreed formula for determining fair and reasonable market price.

4. Details concerning the amount and terms of repayment shall be specified in a separate protocol between KEDO and the DPRK pursuant to the Agreement.

Article III: Delivery Schedule

1. KEDO shall develop a delivery schedule for the LWR project aimed at achieving a completion date of 2003. The schedule of relevant steps to be performed by the DPRK under the U.S.-DPRK Agreed Framework, as specified in Annex 3 to the Agreement, shall be integrated with the delivery schedule for the LWR project with the aim of achieving the performance of such steps by 2003 and the smooth implementation of the LWR project. As specified in the U.S.-DPRK Agreed Framework, the provision of the LWR project and the performance of the steps specified in Annex 3 to the Agreement are mutually conditional.

2. For purposes of the Agreement, "completion" of an LWR plant means completion of performance tests that is satisfactory in accordance with the set of codes and standards specified in Article I(3). Upon completion of each plant, the DPRK shall issue to KEDO a take-over certificate for each respective plant.

3. Details concerning the delivery schedule for the delivery of the LWR project and the performance of the steps specified in Annex 3 to the Agreement, including mutually agreed procedures for any necessary changes and completion of a significant portion of the LWR project as specified in Annex 4 to the Agreement, shall be specified in a separate protocol between KEDO and the DPRK pursuant to the Agreement.

Article IV: Implementing Arrangements

1. The DPRK may designate a DPRK firm as its agent and authorize the firm to enter into implementing arrangements as necessary to facilitate the LWR project.

2. KEDO shall select a prime contractor to carry out the LWR project and shall conclude a commercial supply contract with this prime contractor. A U.S. firm will serve as program coordinator to assist KEDO in supervising overall implementation of the LWR project, and KEDO will select the program coordinator.

3. KEDO and the DPRK shall facilitate practical arrangements that both sides deem necessary, including efficient contacts and cooperation among the participants in the LWR project, to ensure the expeditious and smooth implementation of the LWR project.

4. Written communications required for the implementation of the Agreement may be executed in the English or Korean languages. Existing documents and data may be used or transmitted in their original languages.

5. KEDO, its contractors and subcontractors shall be permitted to operate offices at the project site and other directly related locations such as the nearby port or airport as shall be agreed between KEDO and the DPRK, as the progress of the LWR project may require.

6. The DPRK shall recognize KEDO's independent juridical status and shall accord KEDO and its staff such privileges and immunities in the territory of the DPRK as necessary to carry out the functions entrusted to KEDO. KEDO's juridical status and privileges ... shall be specified in a separate protocol between KEDO and the DPRK pursuant to the Agreement.

7. The DPRK shall take steps to protect the safety of all personnel sent to the DPRK by KEDO, its contractors and subcontractors and their respective property. Appropriate consular protection in conformity with established international practice shall be allowed for all such personnel. Necessary consular arrangements shall be specified in a separate protocol between KEDO and the DPRK pursuant to the Agreement.

8. KEDO shall take steps to ensure that all personnel sent to the DPRK by KEDO, its contractors and subcontractors shall undertake to respect the relevant laws of the DPRK, as shall be agreed between KEDO and the DPRK, and to conduct themselves at all times in a decent and professional manner.

9. The DPRK shall not interfere with the repatriation, in accordance with customs clearance procedures, by KEDO, its contractors and subcontractors of construction equipment and remaining materials from the LWR project.

10. The DPRK shall seek recovery solely from the property and assets of KEDO for the satisfaction of any claims arising under the Agreement or from any of the acts and omissions, liabilities, or obligations of KEDO, its contractors and subcontractors in direct connection with the Agreement, protocols and contracts pursuant to the Agreement.

Article V: Site Selection and Study

1. KEDO shall conduct a study of the preferred Kumho area near Sinpo City, South Hamgyong Province to ensure that the site satisfied appropriate site selection criteria as shall be agreed between KEDO and the DPRK and to identify the requirements for construction and operation of the LWR plants, including infrastructure improvements.

2. To facilitate this study, the DPRK shall cooperate and provide KEDO with access to the relevant available information, including the results of the studies that were performed previously at this site. In the event that such data is not sufficient, KEDO shall make arrangements to obtain additional information or to conduct the necessary site studies.

3. Details concerning site access and the use of the site shall be specified in a separate protocol between KEDO and the DPRK pursuant to the Agreement.

Article VI: Quality Assurance and Warranties

1. KEDO shall be responsible for design and implementation of a quality assurance program in accordance with the set of codes and standards specified in Article I(3). The quality assurance program shall include appropriate procedures for design, materials, manufacture and assembly of equipment and components, and quality of construction.

2. KEDO shall provide the DPRK with appropriate documentation on the quality assurance program, and the DPRK shall have the right to participate in the implementation of the quality assurance program, which will include appropriate inspections, tests, commissioning, and review by the DPRK of the results thereof.

3. KEDO shall guarantee that the generating capacity of each LWR plant at the time of completion, as defined in Article III(2), will be approximately 1,000 MW(e). KEDO shall guarantee that the major components provided by relevant contractors and subcontractors will be new and free from defects in design, workmanship, and material for a period of two years after completion, but in no event longer than five years after the date of shipment of such major components. The LWR fuel for the initial loading for each LWR plant shall be guaranteed in accordance with standard nuclear industry practice. KEDO shall guarantee that the civil construction work for the LWR project will be free of defects in design, workmanship, and material for a period of two years after completion.

4. Details concerning the provisions of this Article and the content and procedures for issuance and receipt of warranties shall be specified in a separate protocol between KEDO and the DPRK pursuant to the Agreement.

Article VII: Training

1. KEDO shall design and implement a comprehensive training program in accordance with standard nuclear industry practice for the DPRK's operation and maintenance of the LWR plants. Such training shall be held at mutually agreeable locations as soon as practicable. The DPRK shall be responsible for providing a sufficient number of qualified candidates for this program.

2. Details concerning the training program shall be specified in a separate protocol between KEDO and the DPRK pursuant to the Agreement.

Article VIII: Opration and Maintenance

1. KEDO shall assist the DPRK to obtain LWR fuel, other than that provided pursuant to Annex 1 to the Agreement, through commercial contracts with a DPRK preferred supplier for the useful life of the LWR plants.

2. KEDO shall assist the DPRK to obtain spare and wear parts, consumables,

special tools, and technical services for the operation and maintenance of the LWR plants, other than those provided pursuant to Annex 1 to the Agreement, through commercial contracts with a DPRK-preferred supplier for the useful life of the LWR plants.

3. KEDO and the DPRK shall operate to ensure the safe storage and disposition of the spent fuel from the LWR plants. If requested by KEDO, the DPRK shall relinquish any ownership rights over the LWR spent fuel and agree to the transfer of the spent fuel out of its territory as soon as technically possible after the fuel is discharged, through appropriate commercial contracts.

4. Necessary arrangements for the transfer of LWR spent fuel out of the DPRK shall be specified in a separate protocol between KEDO and the DPRK pursuant to the Agreement.

Article IX: Services

1. The DPRK shall process for approval all applications necessary for completion of the LWR project expeditiously and free of charge. These approvals shall include all permits issued by the DPRK nuclear regulatory authority, customs clearance, entry and other permits, licenses, site access rights, and site take-over agreements. In the event that any such approval is delayed beyond the normally required time or denied, the DPRK shall notify KEDO promptly of the reasons thereof, and the schedule and cost for the LWR project may be adjusted as appropriate.

2. KEDO, its contractors and subcontractors, and their respective personnel shall be exempt from DPRK taxes, duties, charges and fees as shall be agreed between KEDO and the DPRK, and expropriation in connection with the LWR project.

3. All personnel sent to the DPRK by KEDO, its contractors and subcontractors shall be allowed unimpeded access to the project site and to appropriate and efficient transportation routes, including air and sea links, to and from the project site as designated by the DPRK and agreed between KEDO and the DPRK. Additional routes will be considered as the progress of the LWR project may require.

4. The DPRK shall, to the extent possible, make available at a fair price port services, transportation, labor, potable water, food, off-site lodging and offices, communications, fuel, electrical power, materials, medical services, currency exchanges and other financial services, and other amenities necessary for living and working by personnel sent to the DPRK by KEDO, its contractors and subcontractors.

5. KEDO, its contractors and subcontractors, and their respective personnel shall be allowed unimpeded use of available means of communications in the DPRK. In addition, KEDO, its contractors and subcontractors shall be permitted by the DPRK to establish secure and independent means of communications for

their offices, based on a timely and case-by-case review of equipment requests and in accordance with relevant telecommunications regulations of the DPRK.

6. Details concerning the above-referenced services shall be specified, as appropriate, in one or more separate protocols between KEDO and the DPRK pursuant to the Agreement.

Article X: Nuclear Safety and Regulation

1. KEDO shall be responsible for assuring that design, manufacture, construction, testing, and commissioning of the LWR plants are in compliance with nuclear safety and regulatory codes and standards specified in Article I(3).

2. The DPRK shall issue a site take-over certificate to KEDO upon completion of the site survey. A construction permit shall be issued by the DPRK nuclear regulatory authority to KEDO, prior to the power block excavation, based on its review of the preliminary safety analysis report and the site studies on its determination of whether the LWR project complies with the nuclear safety and regulatory codes and standards specified in Article I(3). A commissioning permit shall be issued by the DPRK nuclear regulatory authority to KEDO prior to initial fuel loading, based on its review of the final safety analysis report, which includes the as-built design of the LWR plant, and results of non-nuclear commissioning tests. KEDO shall provide the results of nuclear commissioning tests and operator training records to the DPRK in support of its issuance of an operating permit to the operator. KEDO shall provide the DPRK, in a timely manner, with the safety analysis reports, necessary information including that on the codes and standards, and such other documents as KEDO deems necessary in order to make the required determination. The DPRK shall ensure that these permits will be issued in a timely manner not to impede the project schedule.

3. The DPRK shall be responsible for the safe operation and maintenance of the LWR plants, appropriate physical protection, environmental protection, and, consistent with Article VIII(3) the safe storage and disposal of radioactive waste, including spent fuel, in conformity with the set of codes and standards specified in Article I(3). In this regard, the DPRK shall assure that appropriate nuclear regulatory standards and procedures are in place to ensure the safe operation and maintenance of the LWR plants.

4. Prior to the shipment of any fuel assemblies to the DPRK, the DPRK shall observe the provisions set forth in the Convention on Nuclear Safety (done at Vienna, September 20, 1994), the Convention on Early Notification of a Nuclear Accident (adopted at Vienna, September 26, 1986), the Convention on Assistance in the Case of a Nuclear Accident or Radiological Emergency (adopted at Vienna, September 26, 1986), and the Convention on the Physical Protection of Nuclear Material (opened for signature at Vienna and New York, March 3, 1980).

5. After the completion of the LWR plants, KEDO and the DPRK shall conduct safety reviews to ensure the safe operation and maintenance of the LWR plants. In this regard, the DPRK shall provide necessary assistance to enable such reviews to be conducted as expeditiously as possible and shall give due consideration to the results of such reviews. Details concerning the schedule and procedures for conducting the safety reviews shall be specified in a separate protocol between KEDO and the DPRK pursuant to the Agreement.

6. In the event of a nuclear emergency or accident, the DPRK shall permit immediate access to the site and information by personnel sent by KEDO, its contractors and subcontractors to determine the extent of safety concerns and to provide safety assistance.

Article XI: Nuclear Liability

1. The DPRK shall ensure that a legal and financial mechanism is available for meeting claims brought within the DPRK for damages in the event of a nuclear incident (as defined in the Vienna Convention on Civil Liability for Nuclear Damage, done at Vienna, May 21, 1963) in connection with the LWR plants. The legal mechanism shall include the channeling of liability in the event of a nuclear incident to the operator on the basis of absolute liability. The DPRK shall ensure that the operator is able to satisfy such liabilities.

2. Prior to the shipment of any fuel assemblies to the DPRK, the DPRK shall enter into an indemnity agreement with KEDO, and shall secure nuclear liability insurance or other financial security to protect KEDO, its contractors and sub-contractors, and their respective personnel in connection with any third party claims in any court or forum arising from activities undertaken pursuant to the Agreement in the event of nuclear damage or loss occurring inside or outside the territory of the DPRK as a result of a nuclear incident in connection with the LWR plants. Details concerning the indemnity agreement and insurance or other financial security shall be specified in a separate protocol between KEDO and the DPRK pursuant to the Agreement.

3. The DPRK shall bring no claims against KEDO, its contractors and subcontractors, and their respective personnel arising out of any nuclear damage or loss.

4. This Article shall not be construed as acknowledging the jurisdiction of any court or forum or as waiving any immunity of either side.

5. The domestic legal system of the DPRK may provide that, if the operator proves that the nuclear damage resulted wholly or partly either from the gross negligence of the person suffering the damage or from an act or omission of such person done with intent to cause damage, the operator may be relieved wholly or partly from his obligation to pay compensation in respect of the damage suffered by such person. The operator shall have a right of recourse only if the damage caused by a nuclear incident results from an act or omission done with intent to cause damage, against the individual acting or omitting to act with such intent.

For purposes of this paragraph, the terms "person" and "individual" shall have the same meaning as in the Vienna Convention on Civil Lability for Nuclear Damage (done at Vienna, May 21, 1963).

Article XII: Intellectual Property

1. In the course of performing its obligations under the Agreement, each side may receive, directly or indirectly, information relating to the intellectual property of the other side. All such information and any materials or documents containing such information (collectively, the "Intellectual Property") are proprietary and confidential to such other side, whether or not protected by patent or copyright law. Each side agrees to protect the confidentiality of the other side's Intellectual Property and to use it only for the purposes of the LWR project as provided for in the Agreement and in accordance with international norms, including practices established by the Paris Convention on the Protection of Industrial Property Rights.

2. Except as otherwise agreed between the two sides, neither side shall replicate, copy, or otherwise reproduce any of the equipment or technology of the other side provided in connection with the LWR project.

Article XIII: Assurances

1. The DPRK shall use the reactors, technology, and nuclear material (as defined in accordance with international practice) transferred pursuant to the Agreement, as well as any nuclear material used therein or produced through the use of such items, exclusively for peaceful, non-explosive purposes.

2. The DPRK shall ensure that the reactors, technology, and nuclear material transferred pursuant to the Agreement, as well as any nuclear mate rial used therein or produced through the use of such items, are used properly and exclusively for the purposes of the LWR project.

3. The DPRK shall provide effective physical protection in accordance with international standards with respect to the reactors and nuclear material transferred pursuant to the Agreement, as well as any nuclear material used therein or produced through the use of such items for the useful life of such reactors and nuclear material.

4. The DPRK shall apply IAEA safeguards to the reactors and nuclear material transferred pursuant to the Agreement, as well as any nuclear material used therein or produced through the use of such items, for the useful life of such reactors and nuclear material.

5. The DPRK shall at no time reprocess or increase the enrichment level of any nuclear material transferred pursuant to the Agreement, or any nuclear material used in or produced through the use of any reactor or nuclear material transferred in the LWR project.

6. The DPRK shall not transfer any nuclear equipment or technology or

nuclear material transferred pursuant to the Agreement, or any nuclear material used therein or produced through the use of such items outside the territory of the DPRK unless otherwise agreed between KEDO and the DPRK, except as provided for in Article VIII(3).

7. The above-referenced assurances may be supplemented by DPRK assurances, through appropriate arrangements, to KEDO members that provide to the DPRK any components controlled under the Export Trigger List of the Nuclear Suppliers Group for the LWR project, if and when such KEDO member or members and the DPRK deem it necessary.

Article XIV: Force Majeure

Either side's performance shall be considered excusably delayed if such delay is due to one or more events that are internationally accepted to constitute force majeure. Each such evem is herein referred to as an event of "Force Majeure." The side whose performance is delayed by an event of Force Majeure shall provide notice of such delay to the other side promptly after such event has occurred and shall use such efforts as are reasonable in the circumstances to mitigate such delay and the effect thereof on such side's performance. The two sides shall then consult with each other promptly and in good faith to determine whether alternative performance and the adjustment of the schedule and cost of the LWR project are necessary.

Article XV: Dispute Resolution

1. Any disputes arising out of the interpretation or implementation of the Agreement shall be settled through consultations between KEDO and the DPRK, in conformity with the principles of international law. KEDO and the DPRK shall organize a coordinating committee composed of three people from each side to help settle disputes that may arise in the process of implementing the Agreement.

2. Any dispute that cannot be resolved in this manner shall, at the request of either side and with the consent of the other side, be submitted to an arbitral tribunal composed as follows: KEDO and the DPRK shall each designate one arbitrator, and the two arbitrators so designated shall elect a third, who shall be the Chairman. If, within thirty days of the mutual agreement for arbitration, either KEDO or the DPRK has not designated an arbitrator, either KEDO or the DPRK may request the President of the International Court of Justice to appoint an arbitrator. The same procedure shall apply if, within thirty days of the designation or appointment of the second arbitrator, the third arbitrator has not been elected. A majority of the members of the arbitral tribunal shall constitute a quorum, and all decisions shall require the concurrence of two arbitrators. The arbitral procedure shall be fixed by the tribunal. The decisions of the tribunal shall be binding on KEDO and the DPRK. Each side shall bear the cost of its

own arbitrator and its representation in the arbitral proceedings. The cost of the Chairman in discharging his duties and the remaining costs of the arbitral tribunal shall be borne equally by both sides.

Article XVI: Actions in the Event of Noncompliance

1. KEDO and the DPRK shall perform their respective obligations in good faith to achieve the basic objectives of the Agreement.

2. In the event that either side fails to take its respective steps specified in the Agreement, the other side shall have the right to require the immediate payment of any amounts due and financial losses in connection with the LWR project.

3. In the event of late payment or nonpayment by either side with respect to financial obligations to the other side incurred in implementing the Agreement, the other side shall have the right to assess and apply penalties against that side. Details concerning the assessment and application of such penalties shall be specified in a separate protocol between KEDO and the DPRK pursuant to the Agreement.

Article XVII: Amendments

1. The Agreement may be amended by written agreement between the two sides.

2. Any amendment shall enter into force on the date of its signature.

Article XVIII: Entry into Force

1. The Agreement shall constitute an international agreement between KEDO and the DPRK, and shall be binding on both sides under international law.

2. The Agreement shall enter into force on the date of its signature.

3. The Annexes to the Agreement shall be an integral part of the Agreement.

4. The Protocols pursuant to the Agreement shall enter into force on the date of their respective signature.

IN WITNESS WHEREOF, the undersigned, being duly authorized, have signed the Agreement.

DONE at New York City on this 15th day of December, 1995, in duplicate in the English language.

For the Korean Peninsula Energy Development Organization

For the Government of the Democratic People's Republic of Korea

Annex 1

The scope of supply of the LWR plants referenced in Article 1 of the Agreement for which KEDO shall be responsible shall consist of the following tasks and items.

1. Site survey

2. Site preparation, which shall consist of the clearing and leveling of the site and provision of electricity necessary for construction at the site, and water services at the site necessary for completion of the LWR plants.

3. Preconstruction infrastructure that KEDO deems is integral to and exclusively for use in the construction of the LWR plants, which shall consist of roads within the site boundary, access roads from the site to off-site roads, barge docking facilities and a road from there to the site, a waterway and water catchment facilities including weir, and housing and related facilities for KEDO, its contractors, and subcontractors.

4. Technical documents necessary for the operation and maintenance of the LWR plants, including the construction schedule.

5. Power plant systems, facilities, buildings, structures, equipment, and auxiliary facilities, including laboratory and measurement equipment and cold machine shop, that KEDO deems necessary for the two LWR plants.

6. A low and medium radioactive waste storage-building with a ten-year storage capacity for the two LWR plants.

7. All tests required up to take-over.

8. The inventory of spare parts, wear parts, consumables, and special tools as KEDO deems necessary for a two-year period of plant operation, in accordance with standard nuclear industry practice.

9. Nuclear fuel for the initial loading of each LWR, including such fuel rods as may be necessary to preserve safety for initial operation.

10. A comprehensive training program for the operation and maintenance of the LWR plants implemented by KEDO and its contractors in accordance with standard nuclear industry practice, including provision of a full-scope simulator.

11. Technical support services as KEDO deems necessary for operation and maintenance of the first LWR plant for one year after completion of that LWR plant, in accordance with standard nuclear industry practice.

12. Overall project management.

Annex 2

The tasks and items referenced in Article 1(2) of the Agreement for which the DPRK shall be responsible shall consist of the following:

1. Securing the site (land and manne) for the LWR project, including relocation of population, existing structures and facilities.

2. Provision of/access to information and documents necessary for implementation of the LWR project available in the DPRK.

3. Stable supply of electricity for commissioning of the two LWR plants as available in the DPRK.

4. Access to existing harbor, rail, and airport facilities designated by the DPRK and agreed between KEDO and the DPRK in the vicinity of the site for the transportation of materials and equipment necessary for the LWR project.

5. Securing aggregate and quarry site.

6. Communication lines to the LWR project site, to the extent possible, pursuant to Article IX of the Agreement.

7. Qualified operators trained by KEDO to participate in the commissioning.

Annex 3

The relevant steps to be performed by the DPRK in connection with the supply of the LWR project under the U.S.-DPRK Agreed Framework, as referenced in Article III(1) of the Agreement, consist of the following:

1. The DPRK will remain a party to the Treaty on the Non-Proliferation of Nuclear Weapons and will allow implementation of its safeguards agreement under the Treaty, as specified in the U.S.-DPRK Agreed Framework.

2. The DPRK will continue the freeze on its graphite-moderated reactors and related facilities and provide full cooperation to the IAEA in its monitoring of the freeze.

3. The DPRK will refrain from the construction of new graphite-moderated reactors and related facilities.

4. In the event that U.S. firms will be providing any key nuclear components, the DPRK and the U.S. will conclude a bilateral agreement for peaceful nuclear cooperation prior to the delivery of such components. Such agreement will not be implemented until a significant portion of the LWR project is completed, as specified in Annex 4 to the Agreement. For purposes of the Agreement, "key nuclear components" are the components controlled under the Export Trigger List of the Nuclear Suppliers Group.

5. The DPRK will continue cooperation on safe storage and ultimate disposition of spent fuel from the 5MW(e) experimental reactor.

6. Upon the signing of the Agreement, the DPRK will permit resumption of ad hoc and routine inspections under the DPRK's safeguards agreement with the IAEA with respect to facilities not subject to the freeze.

7. When a significant portion of the LWR project is completed, but before delivery of key nuclear components, the DPRK will come into full compliance with its IAEA safeguards agreement, including taking all steps that may be deemed necessary by the IAEA.

8. When the first LWR plant is completed, the DPRK will begin dismantlement of its frozen graphite-moderated reactors and related facilities, and will

complete such dismantlement when the second LWR plant is completed.

9. When delivery of the key nuclear components for the first LWR plant begins, the transfer from the DPRK of spent fuel from the 5 MW(e) experimental reactor for ultimate disposition will begin and will be completed when the first LWR plant is completed.

Annex 4

A significant portion of the LWR project, referenced in Article III(3) of the Agreement, means the following. A further elaboration of the definition will be specified in the separate protocol referenced in Article III(3).

1. Conclusion of the contract for the LWR project.

2. Completion of site preparation, excavation, and completion of facilities necessary to support construction of the LWR project.

3. Completion of initial plant design for the selected site.

4. Specification and fabrication of major reactor components for the first LWR unit as provided for in project plans and schedules.

5. Delivery of essential non-nuclear components for the first LWR unit, including turbines and generators, according to project plans and schedules.

6. Construction of the turbine buildings and other auxiliary buildings for the first LWR unit, to the stage provided for in project plans and schedules.

7. Construction of the reactor building and containment structure for the first LWR unit to the point suitable for the introduction of components of the Nuclear Steam Supply System.

8. Civil construction and fabrication and delivery of components for the second LWR unit according to project plans and schedules.

A Chronology of the
Nuclear Controversy, 1993–95

Background: In 1965 North Korea installs a small nuclear reactor obtained
from the Soviet Union in Yongbyon; North Korea joins IAEA in
September 1974; North Korea signs the NPT in Moscow on December 12, 1985, in exchange for Soviet promise to transfer advanced nuclear reactors to DPRK; North Korea signs IAEA
Safeguards Accord, on January 30, 1992, after a delay of more
than six years; IAEA Director General Hans Blix visits North
Korea (May 1992); IAEA on-site inspections conducted from
June to December 1992.

1993

January   IAEA inspection reveals anomalies in North Korea's claims regarding plutonium extraction.

February   IAEA requests "special inspections" of two undeclared sites containing nuclear wastes to resolve issue of plutonium extraction.

March   North Korea denies IAEA examination of waste sites and announces it is giving the required 90–day notice for withdrawal
from the Nuclear Non-Proliferation Treaty (NPT) (March 12).

     U.S. and ROK resume Team Spirit annual military exercise.

June   First "High-Level" U.S.-DPRK Meeting. USG prepared to discuss any security Issues.

            DPRK agrees to "suspend" withdrawal from NPT.

            USG sets following premises for continuation of USG-DPRK high-level negotiations:

            1. The DPRK does not leave the NPT;
            2. There is no more reprocessing of spent fuel while the talks go on;
            3. The DPRK does not refuel the 5mw reactor without IAEA supervision;
            4. There is progress in North-South Korean discussions; and
            5. The U.S.-DPRK talks make progress.

July   Second Round of U.S.-DPRK talks.

            USG offers to help shift North Korean nuclear power program from graphite moderated reactors to light-water reactors (LWR). DPRK agrees to continue "continuity of safeguards" inspections by IAEA, and to discuss with IAEA the requested "special inspections." North Korea agrees to engage in discussions with the ROKG.

August   IAEA able to conduct only partial and unsatisfactory continuity of safeguards inspection.

            DPRK refuses to meet with ROKG to discuss promised exchange of envoys.

            USG concludes there is therefore no basis on which to proceed with the third round bilateral dialogue in September as originally planned.

December   In response to perceived North Korean wishes, USG agrees to enlarge the next high-level bilateral discussion and agree to a "broad and thorough" discussion of economic and political issues as well as the security issues which had been the subject of discussions thus far. If the DPRK thus wished to place additional matters on the table, the USG indicated that it would also expect to put additional concerns into the discussions.

1994

January   Since December, IAEA and DPRK in discussion on parameters for an effective "continuity of safeguards" inspection (to assure that no further reprocessing had taken place since the original IAEA inspection in 1992).

February   IAEA and DPRK agree on inspection arrangements.

USG and ROK make announcements that if inspection completed satisfactorily, and North-South exchange of envoys proceeds as promised, then:

1. U.S.-ROK "Team Spirit" military exercise would be suspended; and
2. Third round of high-level U.S.-DPRK talks would be held to address political and economic as well as security issues in a "broad and thorough" manner.

March   IAEA inspection is incomplete. DPRK refuses to allow two critical tests which had been fully agreed in the advance negotiations. IAEA declares it cannot assure "continuity of safeguards."

North Korea refuses to meet with ROKG to arrange exchange of envoys.

Consequently, Third Round U.S.-DPRK meeting not held; and suspension of Team Spirit exercise lifted.

March 31   UN Security Council President issues unanimously approved statement calling on DPRK to permit full safeguards inspection. China is active in statement negotiation.

April   ROKG announces that it will no longer hold out for a prior exchange of North-South envoys before third round U.S.-DPRK talks are held. This leaves satisfactory continuity of safeguards inspection by IAEA as only remaining condition for 3rd-round of talks.

DPRK announces that it will refuel the Yongbyon 5mw reactor in May.

IAEA and DPRK commence discussions to work out modalities for IAEA supervision of refueling. USG officials confirm that unsupervised refueling would result in breaking off efforts to negotiate with DPRK.

May   DPRK refuses to allow IAEA to take samples of fuel rods. IAEA announces it cannot reach agreement on satisfactory arrangements to supervise refueling.

IAEA team returns to Korea and is allowed to complete inspection procedures interrupted in March, but North Korea begins refueling 5 MW reactor without supervision and IAEA monitoring proposals are rejected.

United States, Japan and the ROK begin working for UN sanctions against North Korea. North Korea announces it will withdraw from the IAEA.

June   Former U.S. President Jimmy Carter visits North Korea and extracts pledge for "good faith" negotiations and summit meeting with South Korean President Kim Young-Sam. Deal includes concept of freeze in North Korean nuclear program in return for freeze in U.S. push for sanctions and resumption of more normal relations.

July   U.S.-North Korean high-level negotiations resume in Geneva. North Korean President Kim Il-Sung dies of heart attack on July 8. North says summit meeting with the South is off.

August   U. S.-North Korean negotiators in Geneva outline potential agreement envisaging provision of light-water reactor technology to North Korea and more normal U.S.-DPRK relations in return for freezing and ultimate dismantling of the DPRK nuclear program, full compliance with the IAEA, and resumption of dialogue with South Korea.

October   On October 21, U.S. and North Korean negotiators reach overall framework agreement for freezing and eventually dismantling the North Korean nuclear program, return of the DPRK to full IAEA safeguards, U.S.-led consortium provision of light-water power reactors and interim alternative energy (heavy fuel oil) to North Korea, resumption of the North-South dialogue, and establishment of liaison offices between U. S. and DPRK. Hailed by President Clinton, Japan, ROK and China. Implementation projected over five or more years.

November   IAEA confirms construction halted on DPRK 50 MW and 200 MW reactors. 5MW reactor not being refueled. Fuel rods under scrutiny.

1995

January   United States delivers first 50,000 tons of oil to North Korea
              under agreement. North Korea lifts restrictions on imports from
              U.S. U.S. slightly eases sanctions against economic activity with
              North Korea.

March   Korean Peninsula Energy Development Organization (KEDO)
              formed in New York City by 20 nations, with the United States,
              the Republic of Korea and Japan in the lead.

April   DPRK asserts it will not accept South Korean light-water reac-
              tors, and U.S.-DPRK officials' meeting in Berlin ends in stale-
              mate.

May   North Korea ends its cooperation with the Neutral Nations Super-
              visory Commission (Korean War armistice) and expels Czech and
              Polish commission members.

              U.S.-DPRK meeting convened in Kuala Lumpur in late May to
              seek to resolve LWR issue.

June 13   United States and DPRK conclude agreement in Kuala Lumpur
              on provision of light-water reactors (LWRs) through KEDO, with
              a U.S. firm to serve as program coordinator; arrangements for
              safe storage of downloaded fuel rods will begin immediately.

              KEDO selects the Korean standard nuclear plant model and des-
              ignates Korea nuclear reactors Ulchin 3 and 4 as reference mod-
              els; KEDO further selects the Korea Electric Power Company
              (KEPCO) as prime contractor; Directs preparations for site survey
              and for next shipment of heavy fuel oil to DPRK, subject to
              conclusion of U.S.-DPRK agreement on measures to monitor
              usage and concurrent with steps to ensure safe storage of spent
              nuclear fuel.

December 15   KEDO and DPRK sign "Agreement on Supply of a LWR Project
              to the DPRK" with four separate annexes.

Select Bibliography

1. The North Korean Nuclear Controversy

Bermudez, Joseph, "North Korea's Nuclear Programme," *Jane's Intelligence Review* (September 1991): 404–411.

Berry, Jr., William E., "Nuclear Proliferation on the Korean Peninsula: The Clinton Administration's Response," Occasional Paper #3, U.S. Air Force Academy Institute of National Security Studies, 1995.

Dingman, Roger, "Atomic Diplomacy During the Korean War," *International Security*, Vol. 13, No. 3 (Winter 1988–1989): 60–86.

Kihl, Young Whan, "Confrontation or Compromise on the Korean Peninsula? The North Korean Nuclear Issue," *The Korean Journal of Defense Analysis*, Vol. 6, No. 2 (Winter 1994): 101–129.

Kihl, Young Whan, Chung In Moon, and David I. Steinberg, eds., *Rethinking the Korean Peninsula: Arms Control, Nuclear Issues and Economic Reformation.* Washington, D.C.: Georgetown University Asian Studies Center, and Osaka, Japan: International Society for Korean Studies, 1993.

Koh, Byung Chul, "Confrontation and Cooperation on the Korean Peninsula: The Politics of Nuclear Nonproliferation," *The Korean Journal of Defense Analysis*, Vol. 6, No. 2 (Winter 1994): 85–100.

Mazarr, Michael J., *North Korea and the Bomb: A Case Study in Nonproliferation*, New York: St. Martin's Press, 1995.

Mack, Andrew, "North Korea and the Bomb," *Foreign Policy*, No. 83 (Summer 1991): 87–104.

———, "The Nuclear Crisis on the Korean Peninsula," *Asian Survey*, Vol. 33, No. 4 (April 1993): 339–59.

North Korea's Nuclear Program: Challenge and Opportunity. A Report of the North Korea Working Group of the United States Institute of Peace. Washington, D.C.: USIP, February 1994.

The North Korean Nuclear Challenge: The Post-Kim Il Sung Phase Begins. Special Report. Washington, D.C.: USIP, October 1994.

Oh, Kongdan, and Ralph C. Hassig, "North Korea's Nuclear Program." In *Korea and the World: Beyond the Cold War*, ed. Young Whan Kihl. Boulder, CO: Westview Press, 1994, pp. 233–252.

Park, Moon Young, "Lure North Korea," *Foreign Policy*, No. 97 (Winter 1994):

Song, Young Sun, "The Korean Nuclear Issue," *Korea and World Affairs*, Vol. 15, No. 3 (Fall 1991):

Wilborn, Thomas L., *Strategic Implications of the U.S.-DPRK Framework Agreement.* Carlisle, PA: U.S. Army War College Strategic Studies Institute, 1995.

2. Security Environment: Global and Regional

Clausen, Peter A., *Nonproliferation and the National Interest: America's Response to the Spread of Nuclear Weapons.* New York: HarperCollins, 1993.

Flournoy, Michele A., ed., *Nuclear Weapons after the Cold War: Guidelines for U.S. Policy.* New York: HarperCollins, 1993.

Hayes, Peter, *Pacific Powderkeg: American Nuclear Dilemmas in Korea.* Lexington: Lexington Books, 1991.

Kihl, Young Whan, ed., *Korea and the World: Beyond the Cold War.* Boulder, CO: Westview Press, 1994.

Korea to the Year 2000: Implications for Australia. Report by the Australian National Korean Studies Centre. Canberra, Australia: East Asian Analytical Unit, Department of Foreign Affairs and Trade, 1992.

Lee, Manwoo, and Richard Mansbach, eds., *The Changing Order in Northeast Asia and the Korean Peninsula.* Seoul: The Institute for Far Eastern Studies, Kyungnam University, 1993.

Mazarr, Michael Jr., John Q. Blodgett, Cha Young-Koo, and William J. Taylor, Jr., eds., *Korea 1991: The Road to Peace.* Boulder, CO: Westview, 1991.

Nuclear Proliferation: Confronting the New Challenges. Report of Independent Task Force. New York: Council on Foreign Relations, 1995.

Nye, Joseph S., Jr., *Nuclear Ethics.* New York: The Free Press, 1986.

Pollack, Jonathan D., and Young Koo Cha, *A New Alliance for the Next Century: The Future of U.S.-Korean Security Cooperation.* Santa Monica, CA: Rand, 1995.

Spector, Leonard, *Nuclear Ambitions: The Spread of Nuclear Weapons, 1989–1990.* Bounder, CO: Westview Press, 1990.

Taylor, Jr., William J., Cha Young-Koo, and John Q. Blodgett, eds., *The Korean Peninsula: Prospects for Arms Reduction Under Global Detente.* Boulder, CO: Westview Press, 1990.

U.S. Department of Defense, *A Strategic Framework for the Asian-Pacific Rim: Looking Toward the 21st Century.* Washington, D.C.: U.S. Government Printing Office, 1990, 1992.

U.S. Department of Defense, *United States Security Strategy for the East Asia-Pacific Region.* Washington, D.C. DOD Office of International Security Affairs, February 1995.

3. Environment and Energy Issues

Hayes, Peter, *Cooperation on Energy Sector Issues with the DPRK.* Berkeley, CA: Nautilus Institute, October 29, 1993.

Hayes, Peter, *Should the United States Supply Light-Water Reactors to Pyongyang?* Berkeley, CA: Nautilus Institute, October 29, 1993.

Lang, S., Y.J. Huang, and M. Levine, *Energy Conservation Standards for Space Heating in Chinese Urban Residential Buildings.* Energy Analysis Program, Energy and Environmental Division. Berkeley, CA: Lawrence Berkeley Laboratory, 1992.

Levine, M., and L. Xueyi, *Energy Conservation Programs in the People's Republic of*

China: LBL-29211. Applied Science Division. Berkeley, CA: Lawrence Berkeley Laboratory and Beijing: Energy Research Institute, People's Republic of China, 1990.

Levine, M., F. Liu, and J. Sinton (1992), "China's Energy System: Historical Evolution, Current Issues, and Prospects," *Annual Review of Energy Environment* Vol. 17 (1992): 405–435.

Liu, F., W.B. Davis, and M.D. Levine, *An Overview of Energy Supply and Demand in China: LBL-32275 UC-350.* Energy Analysis Program, Energy and Environment Division. Berkeley, CA: Lawrence Berkeley Laboratory, 1992.

Liu, Z. P., J. E. Sinton, F. Q. Yang, M. D. Levine, and M. K. Ting, *Industrial Sector Energy Conservation Programs in the People's Republic of China during the Seventh Five-Year Plan (1986–1990): LBL-36395.* Berkeley, CA: Lawrence Berkeley Laboratory and Beijing: Energy Research Institute, Peoples Republic of China, 1994.

Martinot, E., *Technology Transfer and Cooperation for Sustainable Energy Development in Russia: Prospects and Case Studies of Energy Efficiency and Renewable Energy.* Energy and Resources Group. Berkeley, CA: University of California (Summary of a Ph.D. Dissertation, 1994).

"Let Us Further Strengthen the Struggle to Conserve Power," Pyongyang: Nodong Sinmun (21 January, 1995, page 3) (the Nodong Sinmun is the official organ of North Korea's Workers Party).

Plutonium: Deadly Gold of the Nuclear Age. Cambridge, MA: International Physicians Press, 1992.

Reddy, A., *Barriers to Improvements in Energy Efficiency: LBL-31439.* Berkeley, CA: Lawrence Berkeley Laboratory, 1991.

Sathaye, J., "Economics of Improving Efficiency of China's Electricity Supply and Use: Are Efficiency Investments Cost-effective?" Unpublished paper, 1992

Sathaye, J., R. Friedmann, S. Meyers, O. de Buen, A. Gadgil, E. Vargas, and R. Saucedo, "Economic Analysis of Ilumex: A Project to Promote Energy-Efficient Residential Lighting in Mexico," *Energy Policy* (February, 1994), pp. 163–171.

Schipper, L., and E. Martinot, *Energy Efficiency in Former Soviet Republics: Opportunities for East and West: LBL-33929.* Energy Analysis Program, Energy and Environment Division. Berkeley, CA: Lawrence Berkeley Laboratory, 1993. Prepared for U.S. Department of Energy.

Sinton, J., "Physical Intensity of Selected Industrial Products." Unpublished paper. Berkeley, CA: Lawrence Berkeley Laboratory, 1995.

Von Hippel, D., and P. Hayes. *The Prospects for Energy Efficiency Improvements in the Democratic People's Republic of Korea: Evaluating and Exploring the Options.* Berkeley, CA: Nautilus Institute, 1995.

Von Hippel, D., and R. Verzola, *Indicative Study of the Potential Economic and Environmental Impacts of Demand-Side Management in the Philippines.* Berkeley, CA: Nautilus Institute, 1994.

Wang, Q. Y., and J. E. Sinton, *China's Energy Conservation Policies and Their Implementation, 1980 to the Present, and Beyond.* Berkeley, CA: Lawrence Berkeley Laboratory and Beijing: China Energy Research Society, People's Republic of China, 1995.

Williams, R.H., and Larson, E.D., "Advanced Gasification-Based Biomass Power Generation," in *Renewable Energy: Sources for Fuels and Electricity,* ed. T.B. Johansson, H. Kelly, A.K.N. Reddy, and R.H. Williams. Washington, DC: Island Press, 1993.

Yande, D., *An Analysis of the Potential in Investment-Cum-Energy Conservation in Chemical Industry in China.* Energy Research Institute. Beijing: The State Planning Commission, The People's Republic of China, 1993.

4. Korean Politics and Economics: North and South

Cotton, James, ed., *Politics and Policy in the New Korean State: From Roh Tae-Woo to Kim Young-Sam.* New York: St. Martin's Press, 1995.

Eberstadt, Nicholas, *Korea Approaches Reunification.* Armonk, NY: M.E. Sharpe, 1995.

Eberstadt, Nicholas, and Judith Bannister, *The Population of North Korea.* Berkeley: University of California Institute of East Asian Studies, 1992.

Foster-Carter, Aidan, *Korea's Coming Reunification: Another East Asian Superpower?* London: The Economist Intelligence Unit, 1992.

Hwang, Eui-Gak. *The Korean Economies.* Oxford: Clarendon Press, 1993.

Koo, Hagen, ed., *State and Society in Contemporary Korea.* Ithaca, NY: Cornell University Press, 1993.

Noland, Marcus, "The North Korean Economy." In *Economic and Regional Cooperation in Northeast Asia.* Joint U.S.-Korea Academic Studies, Vol. 6 (1996), Washington, D.C.: Korea Economic Institute of America, 1995, pp. 127–178.

Pollack, Jonathan D. and Young Koo Cha, eds., *A New Alliance for the Next Century: The Future of U.S.-Korean Security Cooperation.* Santa Monica, CA: Rand, 1995.

Stueck, William, *The Korean War: An International History.* Princeton: Princeton University Press, 1995.

The Editors and Contributors

Young Whan Kihl is Professor of Political Science at Iowa State University, where he teaches international politics, foreign policy, and comparative Asian politics. His most recent books include *Korea and the World: Beyond the Cold War* (1994), and *Rethinking the Korean Peninsula: Arms Control, Nuclear Issues and Economic Reformation* (co-editor, 1993). He has been on the editorial board of the *Journal of Asian Studies*, and serves as book review editor on Korea.

Peter Hayes is Co-Director, Nautilus Institute, Berkeley; email: *phayes@nautilus.org*. He graduated in History and History and Philosophy of Science and Technology from University of Melbourne. He has a doctorate from the Energy and Resources Group at University of California at Berkeley. Professionally active as an environment and energy consultant in developing countries (working for UNEP, Asian Development Bank, and the World Bank, Canadian International Development Research Council, U.S. Agency for International Development, UN Development Programme), he also writes widely about security and environmental affairs in the Asian-Pacific region. He was first executive-director of the Environment Liaison Centre in Nairobi, Kenya in 1974–76

Seongwhun Cheon is Fellow, Policy Studies Division of the Research Institute for National Unification, Seoul; email: *psr519@chollian.dacom.co.kr*

Ralph Cossa is Executive Director of Pacific Forum CSIS, Honolulu; email: *pacforum@lava.net*

Kimberly Anne Elliott is Research Associate, Institute for International Economics, Washington DC; email: *kelliott@iie.com*

John Endicott is Director, Center for International Strategy, Technology, and Policy at the Georgia Institute of Technology, Atlanta; email: *john.endicott@inta.gatech.edu*

Janice Heppell is Research Associate, Nautilus Institute, Hamburg; email: *104216.1140@compuserve.com*

David Von Hippel is Research Associate, Nautilus Institute, Portland; email: *dvonhip@igc.apc.org*

Salamon Levy is with Levy and Associates, San Jose; email: *slevy@netcom.com*

Dunbar Lockwood is Assistant Director, U.S. Arms Control and Disarmament Agency, Washington DC; email: *dunbarl@aol.com*

Alexandre Mansourov is a member of the Political Science Department, Columbia University, New York; email: *am139@columbia.edu*

Stephen Noerper is Research Associate, Nautilus Institute, Honolulu; email: *noerpers@ewc.hawaii.edu*

Gerald Segal is Senior Research Fellow, International Institute for Strategic Studies, London; email: *gerry@segal.org*

Dingli Shen is Director, Program on Arms Control and Regional Security Studies at the Center for American Studies, Fudan University, Shanghai; email: *dlshen@pucc.princeton.edu*

Scott Snyder is Program Officer, Research and Studies Program, U.S. Institute of Peace, Washington DC; email: *snydersa@aol.com*

Leonard Spector is with the Carnegie Endowment for International Peace, Washington DC; email: *71263.107@compuserve.com*

Mark Valencia is at the East West Center, Honolulu; email; *valencim@ewc.hawaii.edu*

Lyuba Zarsky is Co-Director, Nautilus Institute, Berkeley; email: *lzarsky@nautilus.org*

Index

The Nautilus Institute

The Nautilus Institute is a policy-oriented research and education organization that promotes international cooperation for security and ecologically sustainable development. Programs embrace both global and regional issues, with a focus on Asia-Pacific. Nautilus Institute produces reports, organizes seminars, and provides educational materials and training services for policymakers, media, researchers, and community groups.

Core staff are based in Berkeley and Washington, with associates in Tokyo, Seoul, Shanghai, and Moscow. Research draws from many disciplines, including environmental economics, natural sciences, energy and resource planning, and international relations.

Nautilus Institute is a non-profit organization funded primarily by grants and contributions. The Institute can be contacted at:

1831 2nd St.
Berkeley, CA 94710
USA
ph 1 510 204 9296
fax 1 510 204 9298
e.mail: nautilus@nautilus.org
www: http://www.nautilus.org

When we sang out "We Shall Not Be Moved" in Montgomery and Selma, we were committed to our unshakeable unity against segregation and violence. This important book continues in that struggle—suggesting ways in which we need to do better, and actions we must take against war and continued racism today. If the human race is still here in 2112, the War Resisters League will be one of the reasons why!

    —Pete Seeger, folk singer

In this age and in this climate of political posturing and posing, this book's investigation of the moral issues of our time is so needed. I commend Meyer's, Martínez's, and Carter's insights, their intelligence, and their courage.

    —Dr. Maya Angelou

We Have Not Been Moved recounts so many aspects of our work for civil and human rights, evoking the songs, stories, and struggles that strengthened both our communities and our moral scaffolding as a nation. Matt Meyer, Elizabeth "Betita" Martínez, and Mandy Carter provide new generations with much-needed context and connection to our historic struggles, so that we may forge stronger communities and a more resilient movement for the twenty-first century.

    —Ruby Dee, actress, playwright, and activist

For some it may not be easy to see how racism and militarism, two of Dr. King's Giant Triplets, are joined at the hip, but this book connects the dots very well. Now, in the twenty-first century, this collection of writing punctuates his challenge to us with a bold exclamation point!

    —Oskar Castro, executive director of Military Families Speak; senior program analyst for the American Friends Service Committee

Years ago, I joined with thousands of like-minded people to help bring about peace to the people of Vieques, Puerto Rico. Two thirds of their island was occupied by the U.S. Navy, which used it for military exercises, including bombing with live ammunition near civilian homes and work places. Then, I called that both immoral and abusive. More recently, I have been arrested twice for civil disobedience as I continue to bring attention to the plight of hundreds of thousands of immigrants and American citizens whose families are being divided by an unjust and broken called for by Dr. Martin Luther King Jr.—this nation must live up to the true meaning of our creed and achieve in deed what we have long aspired to in our lofty documents and rhetoric. This means rejecting militarism and racism in all forms. True peace and security can only come from true democracy and justice. While it is nearly impossible to agree, or to disagree, with the totality of this or any other book, I applaud the ways in which *We Have Not Been Moved* helps us sharpen our understanding of these moral and social imperatives. This book is in the best tradition of civil and human rights movements and a welcome addition to the literature on these crucial issues.

—Congressman Luis V. Gutiérrez, (D-IL)

In an era of rampant militarism, growing anti-Islamic sentiment, and racist violence, the essays in *We Have Not Been Moved* provide us with urgently needed analytical frameworks and on-the-ground strategies for challenging structural injustice. The wide range of voices in this collection, spanning generations and social movements, remind us of the interconnectedness of our struggles against racism, militarism, violence, and injustice, and collectively urge us to build a unified, principled movement to resist intensified empire.

—Angela Y. Davis, author, activist, and professor emerita, History of Consciousness, UC–Santa Cruz

With extraordinary clarity and courage, *We Have Not Been Moved* marches up to the elephant in the room, looks it in the eye, and gives it a mighty shove toward the door. This book firmly and clearly addresses the contradictions which have kept us from building a united movement for peace, justice, and freedom across racial and cultural lines. No book has ever been more badly needed by all who yearn and struggle for a more just and peaceful world.

—Rev. Dr. C. Nozomi Ikuta, chair, Interfaith Prisoners of Conscience Project

We Have Not Been Moved brings together a most powerful collection of essays that bear witness to the violence people are capable of inflicting on each other. This book directly confronts U.S. imperialism, and the racism and voracious materialism that undergird it. By boldly naming and immersing us in histories of injustice, the authors challenge us to embrace humanity and work for peace.

—Christine Sleeter, professor emerita, California State University, Monterey Bay; president, National Association for Multicultural Education

What is to be Undone. An often scathing, sometimes inspiring, and never comforting look at the tangled history of anti-racist activism in the United States, where the enemy is often encountered in our own ranks—and hearts. An essential guide for those willing to risk understanding as well as action.

—Terry Bisson, Hugo and Nebula award-winning science-fiction author

We Have Not Been Moved reminds us of our best struggles at a time when we desperately need their inspiration and analysis to keep moving against massive criminality of a sort we could not have imagined just a few decades ago. We need this book because we need the experience and analysis of our true heroes, those no longer taught in our schools and openly defied and defiled in our popular culture. We look to the new generations for new ideas, but those ideas must be rooted in the continuity of those who came before. I am particularly proud to recommend this important collection.

—Margaret Randall, author of *To Change the World: My Years in Cuba* and *As If the Empty Chair/Como Si La Silla Vacia*

One of the biggest stumbling blocks to building a successful movement against war has been our inability to cross racial and cultural lines, bridging the divides created and maintained by the powers that be. Since the 1960s, there have been some hopeful signs—in grassroots groups and in educational efforts—but the road forward is still long and difficult. The contributors to *We Have Not Been Moved*, with extraordinary scope and vision, have given us an indispensable tool to fight oppression, resist war and injustice, and create powerful new coalitions for lasting social change. This volume should be required reading—alongside Howard Zinn's *A People's History of the United States*—in every sociology and political science class.

—Connie Hogarth, lifelong peace and justice activist and inspiration for Manhattanville College's Connie Hogarth Center for Social Action; co-founder and former executive director of the Westchester People's Action Coalition

This historic book and monumental collection of many of the prophetic giants of our time could not appear at a more propitious moment. We are at a fundamental crossroad in the history of America—America as imperial power and America as democratic experiment. Elizabeth "Betita" Martínez, Matt Meyer, and Mandy Carter have given us this prophetic intervention to keep alive the grand legacy of Martin Luther King Jr. These three legendary freedom fighters bring together the best of the peace movement and the best of the anti-racist movement in our time. And Martin Luther King Jr. smiles from his grave—a precious gesture that acknowledges that his true work and witness have not been forgotten in the age of Obama.

—Cornel West, philosopher, author, and civil rights activist

Finally! I've been waiting a long time for a collection that seriously addresses the interconnected histories of racism and militarism in the United States. As a white woman who is committed to educating my own people, I can now say "go read this, please!" In this twenty-first century, I believe we have a critical mass of progressive peoples that could challenge the beast of our empire, but we, white folks, have yet to learn how to work together cross-racially. Between the covers of this book, Betita, Matt and Mandy have given us needed histories, so we don't continue to repeat the past. From the 1950s, movement elders (Barbara Deming, Dave Dellinger, Robert Franklin Williams and Dorothy Day) dialogue about violent and nonviolent change strategies. Their voices are next to writings of contemporary organizers like Andrea Smith, Ruth Gilmore, and Kenyon Farrow in critical counterpoint. I am most challenged by multiracial and cross-class anthologies that offer writings by organizers, academics and poets. This is it. Readers, dig in and let's finally build the revolutionary movement that will change us forever.

 —Lisa Albrecht, activist, writer, educator, founder of the University of
  Minnesota's Social Justice Program; coeditor of *Sing, Whisper, Shout, Pray!*
  Feminist Visions for a Just World; Leadership Team, Let's Build a U.S. for
  All of Us: No Room for Racism

The rich and still-evolving tradition of revolutionary pacifism, effectively sampled in these thoughtful and penetrating essays, offers the best hope we have for overcoming threats that are imminent and grim, and for moving on to create a society that is more just and free. These outstanding contributions should be carefully pondered, and taken to heart as a call for action.

 —Noam Chomsky, Institute Professor of Linguistics at the Massachusetts
  Institute of Technology; philosopher, cognitive scientist, activist, and
  most-cited living author

We Have Not Been Moved provides an essential window on a critical conversation: the quest to heal the wounds of racism as we strive to make peace grounded in justice. The often wildly diverse ideas and perspectives gathered in this collection offer the fuel we need to make difference our greatest strength, to spark a revolution that can bring us together past all the interconnected forms of violence. Taken as whole, this book provides a challenging but illuminating map to journey across boundaries of difference, and, in the process, to radically remake our world.

 —Mark Andersen, cofounder of Positive Force DC and codirector of We
  Are Family